CW01662572

THE MAMMOTH BOOK OF

EROTIC PHOTOGRAPHY

VOLUME 4

EDITED BY MAXIM JAKUBOWSKI

ROBINSON

RUNNING PRESS
PHILADELPHIA • LONDON

Constable & Robinson Ltd
55–56 Russell Square
London WC1B 4HP
www.constablerobinson.com

First published in the UK by
Robinson, an imprint of
Constable & Robinson Ltd, 2013

A copy of the British Library Cataloguing in Publication Data is available from the British Library

UK ISBN: 978-1-78033-999-3
(paperback)
UK ISBN: 978-1-47210-000-9
(ebook)

First published in the United States in 2013 by Running Press Book Publishers, a Member of the Perseus Books Group

Books published by Running Press are available at special discounts for bulk purchases in the United States by corporations, institutions, and other organizations. For more information, please contact the Special Markets Department at the Perseus Books Group, 2300 Chestnut Street, Suite 200, Philadelphia, PA 19103, or call (800) 810-4145, ext. 5000, or e-mail special.markets@perseusbooks.com

US ISBN: 978-0-7624-4944-6
US Library of Congress Control
Number: 2009943392

9 8 7 6 5 4 3 2 1
Digit on the right indicates the number of this printing

Running Press Book Publishers,
2300 Chestnut Street,
Philadelphia, PA 19103-4371

Visit us on the web!
www.runningpress.com

Printed and bound in Italy

Design and layout by
Andrew Barron/Thextension

INTRODUCTION

Some beauties are dazzling, inspirational muses that stir creativity as well as the senses. This collection of the finest contemporary erotic photography is devoted to such muses.

In the previous three Mammoth volumes of erotic photography wonderful photographers from all over the world have have renewed my appreciation of beauty with their depictions of the female form. As a writer of literary erotica, I know how hard it is to keep finding new ways to evoke sensuality and pleasure, and can only profess admiration for these amazing photographers who manage to do so time and again.

I asked all the photographers to go back to the sources of their inspiration and to select their favourite models. It is these muses who provide the focus for each portfolio in this collection. For a handful of photographers who specialise in self-portraits, muse and artist are one and the same.

Many of the photographers are women, offering an intimate, often strikingly different view of the female body. I am confident that all will dazzle you as they explore variations on a seemingly inexhaustible theme.

I am grateful to many of the photographers for generously recommending fellow artists, but I am particularly indebted to the delightful April-Lea Hutchinson from Canada, who first appeared in this series as a model in several portfolios in *The Mammoth Book of New Erotic Photography*. She has since graduated and appears in this collection as a wonderfully talented photographer in her own right (although she appears as a model, too, in another portfolio). I owe her heartfelt thanks for her generosity in recommending photographers and providing their contact details.

Maxim Jakubowski

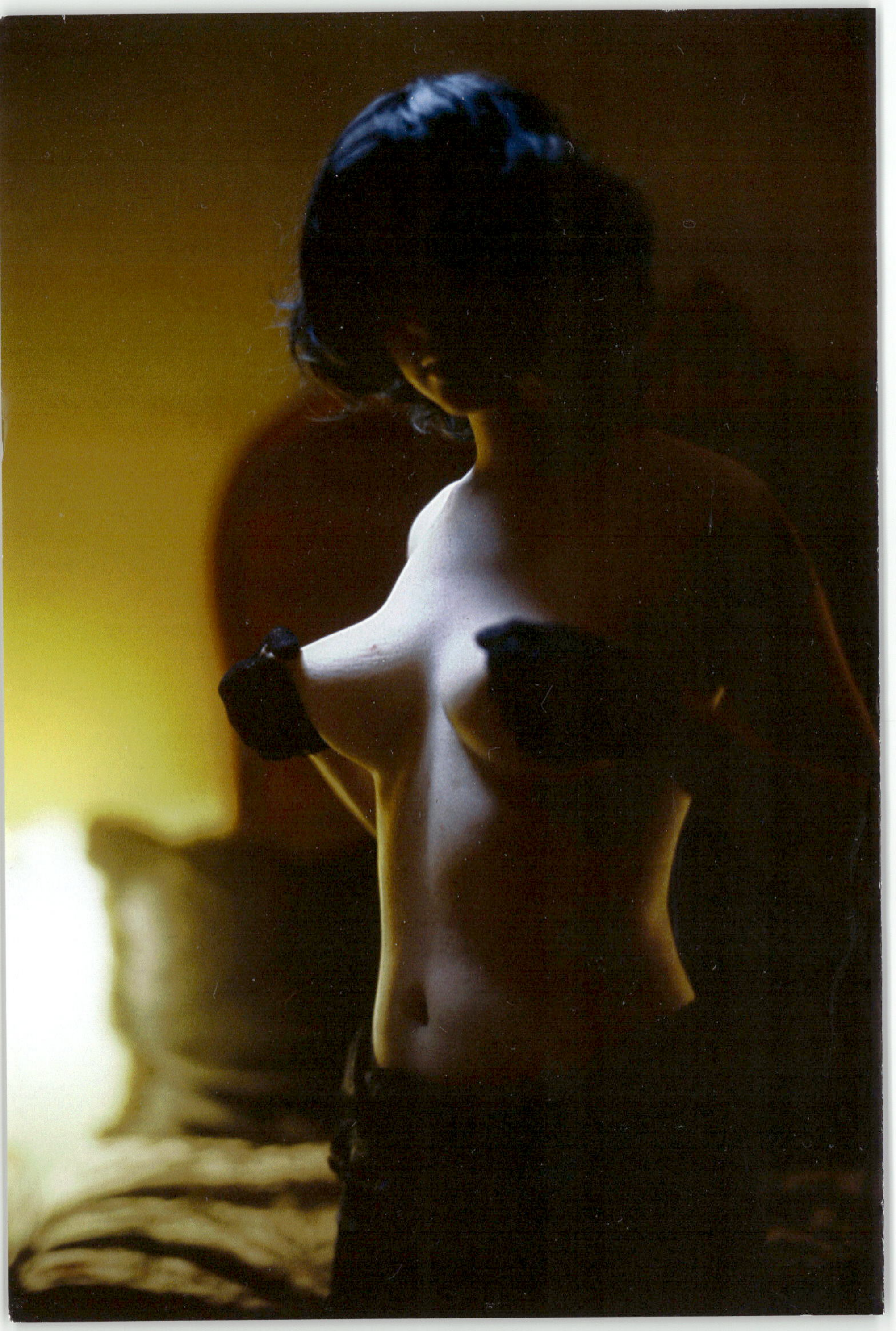

NATHAN APPEL

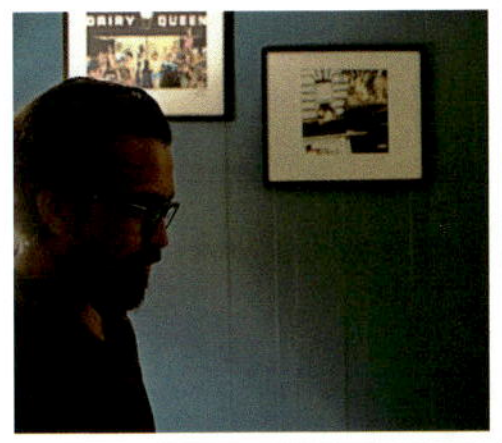

"My main influence is a girl I loved years ago. I was very green and she educated me in style, music, erotic literature, movies and food. My photographs represent my longings and fears. Often the model's face is in shadow or turned away, anonymous. The model is less a muse than a catalyst for a scene from my inner dialogue. Just as my life is raw and awkward, my photographs are sometimes blurred, sometimes nonsensical.

"I met Itzi in 2010 at San Francisco's Phoenix Hotel, at 10 a.m. on a December morning. I had to check out at 11 so had an hour to get my picture. Since then I have photographed her only a few times. I am always prepared to drive a thousand miles for a single photograph."

www.latenightfeelings.com/flngsblog

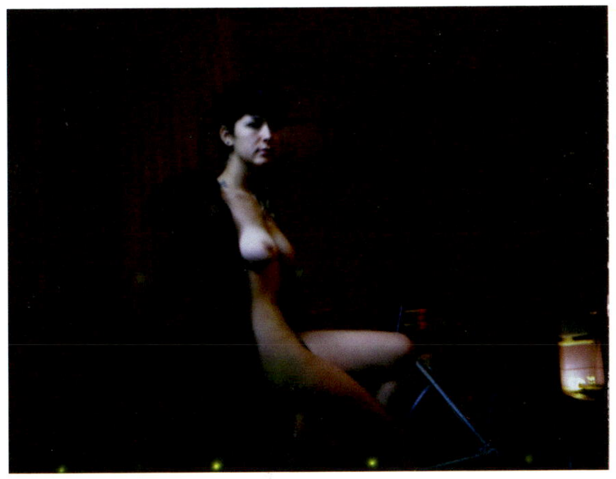

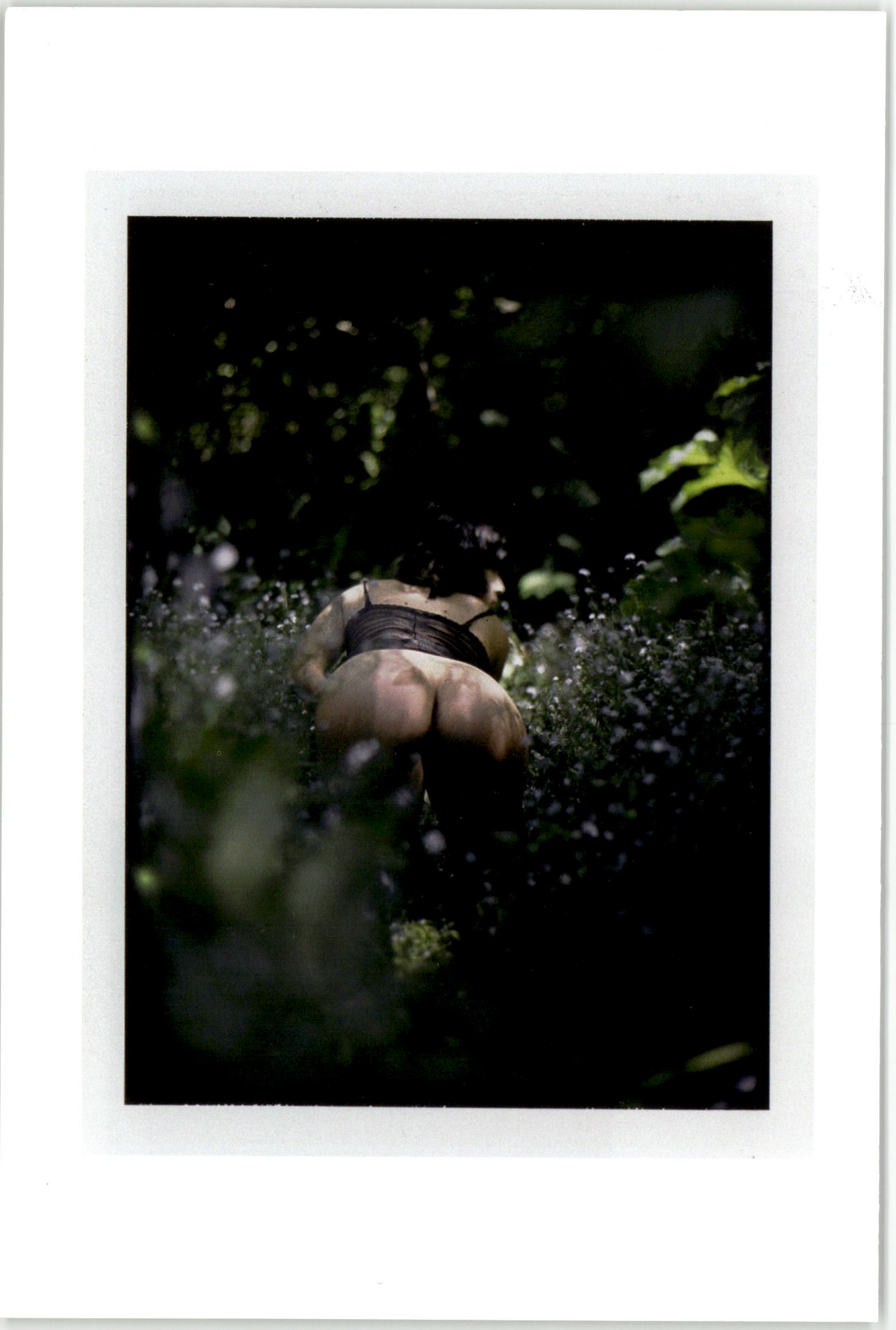

007 NATHAN APPEL

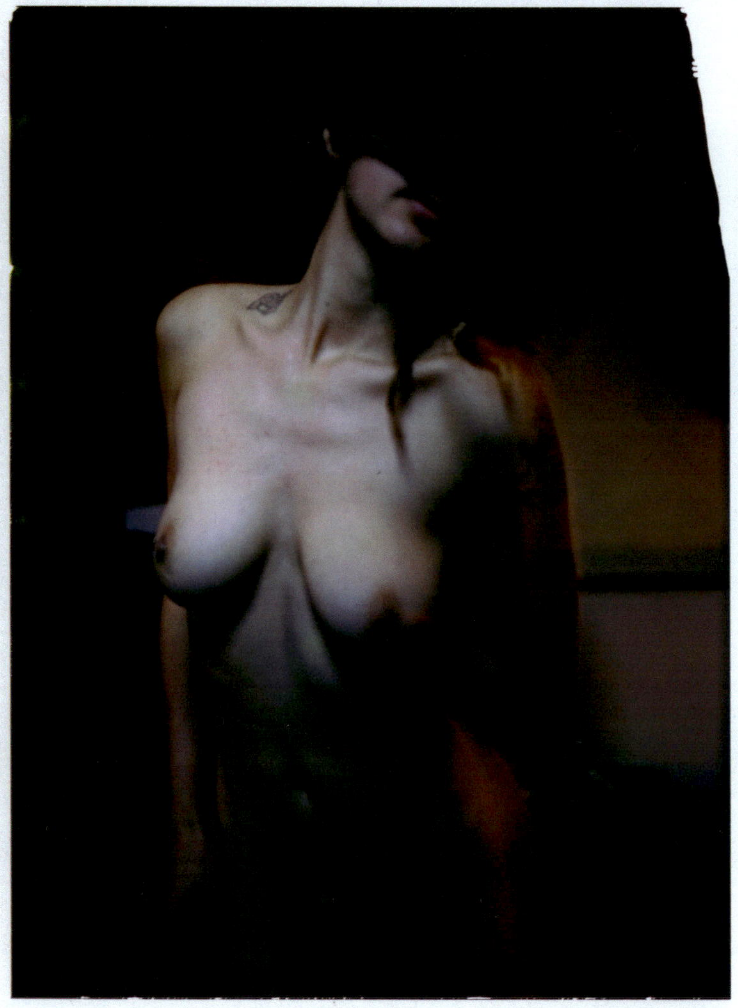

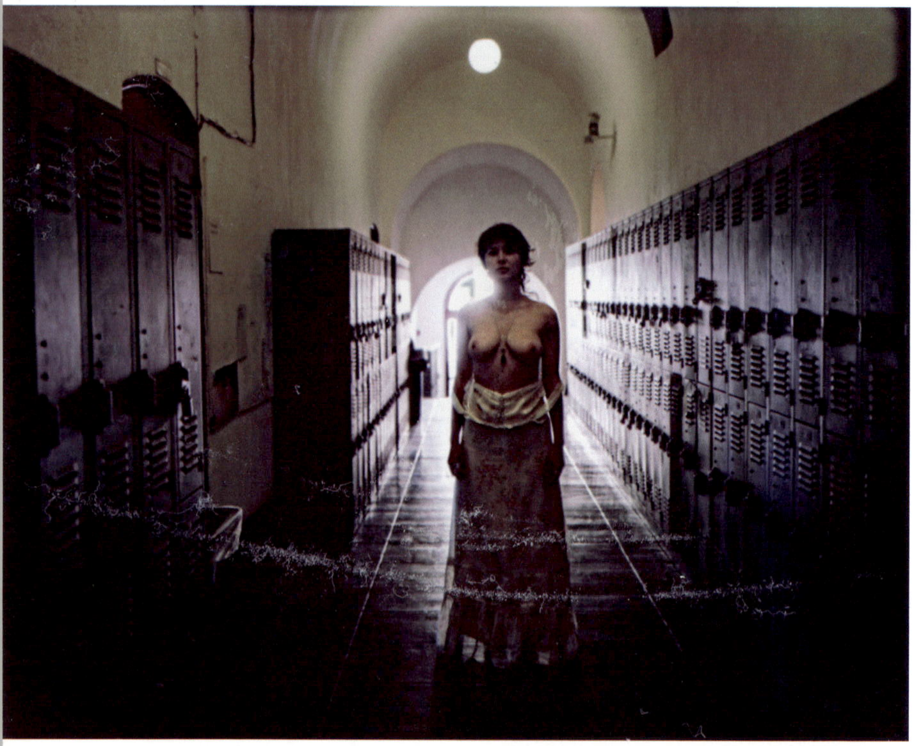

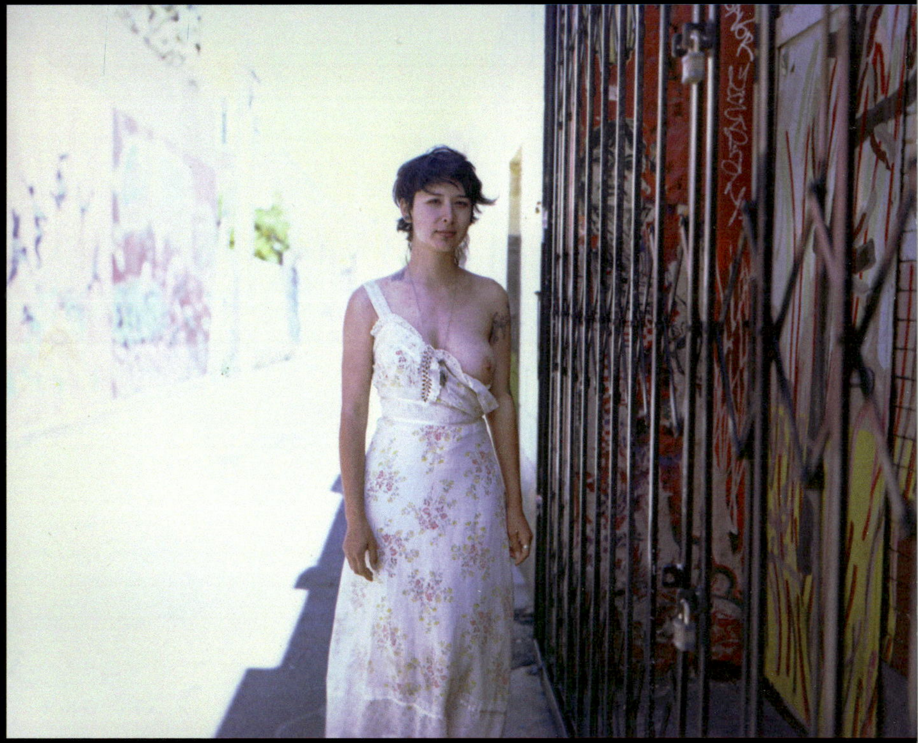

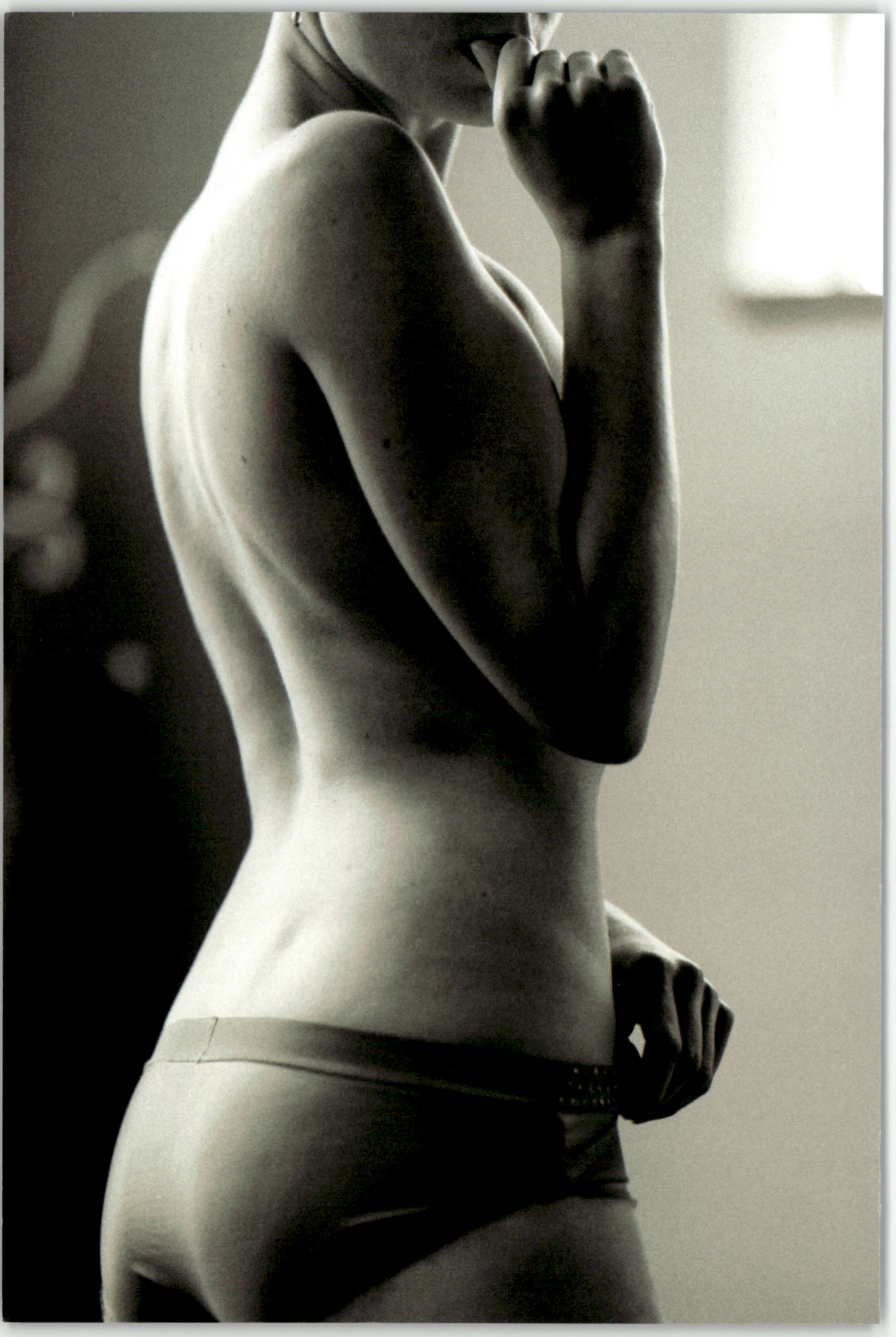

KARL BAXTER

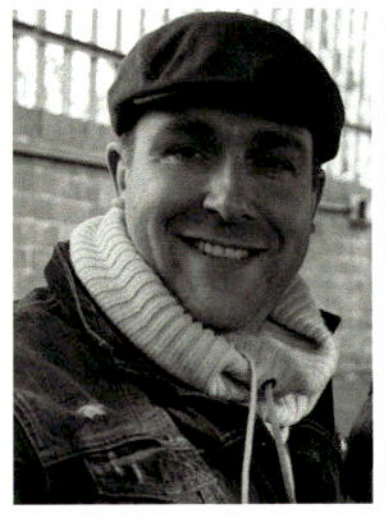

"I was born in 1974 and first became interested in photography when my parents bought me an SLR to document my work as a tattooist. In my early twenties I started a design agency with a friend; this entailed some photography and my interest and skills grew. As my work's creative aspects were lost in the day-to-day demands of running a business, I began to photograph people as a quick release – a creative outlet with absolutely no agenda. I work from a converted corn mill on the West Midlands/Worcestershire border.

"I chose Mina for this project because she is an actress as well as a model – she is fearless, and can show any emotion. She can be funny, sexy, romantic and dirty in a single pose."

www.karlbaxter.co.uk

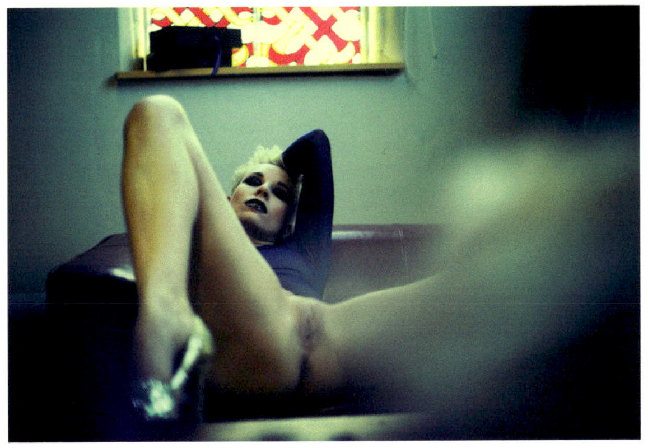

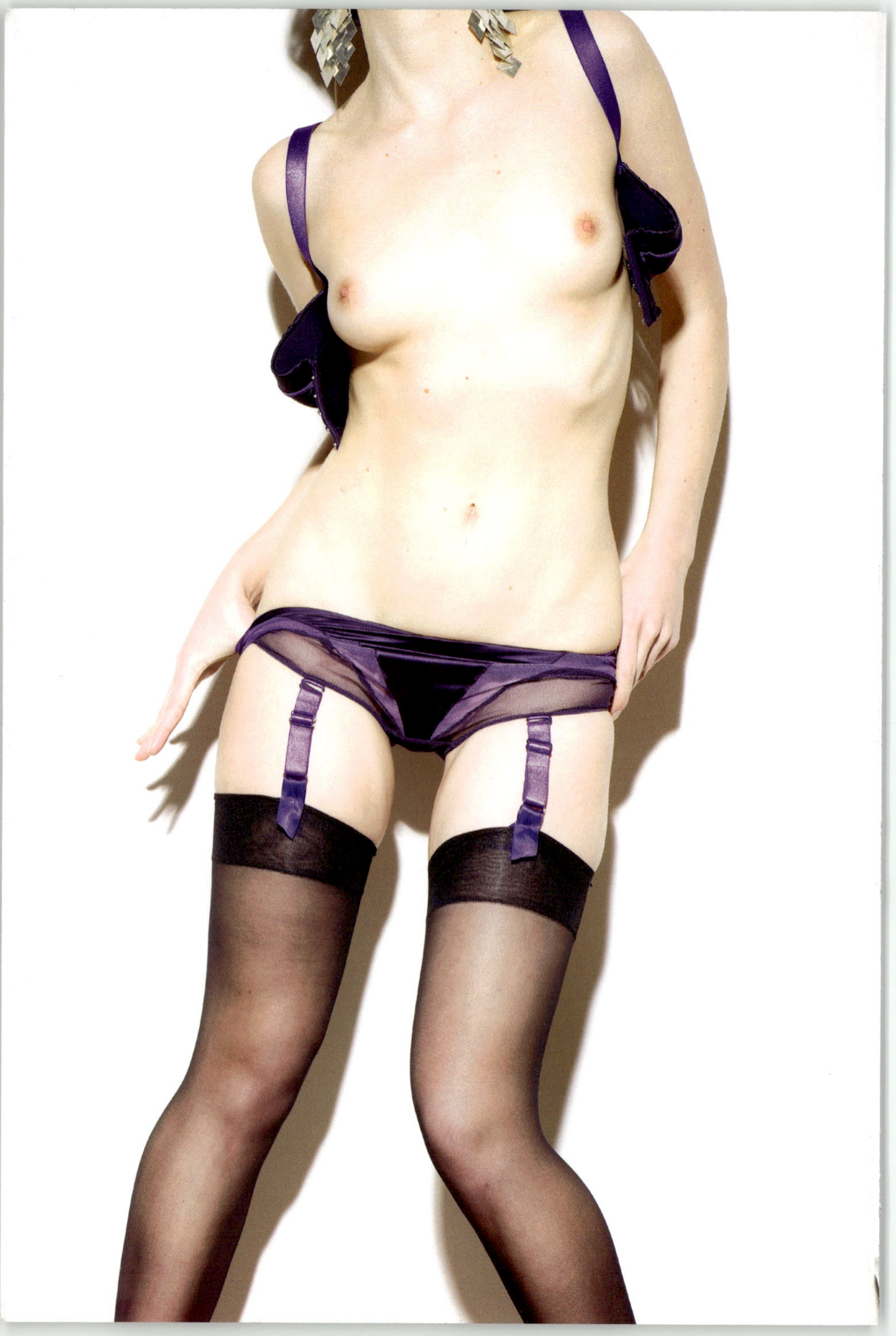

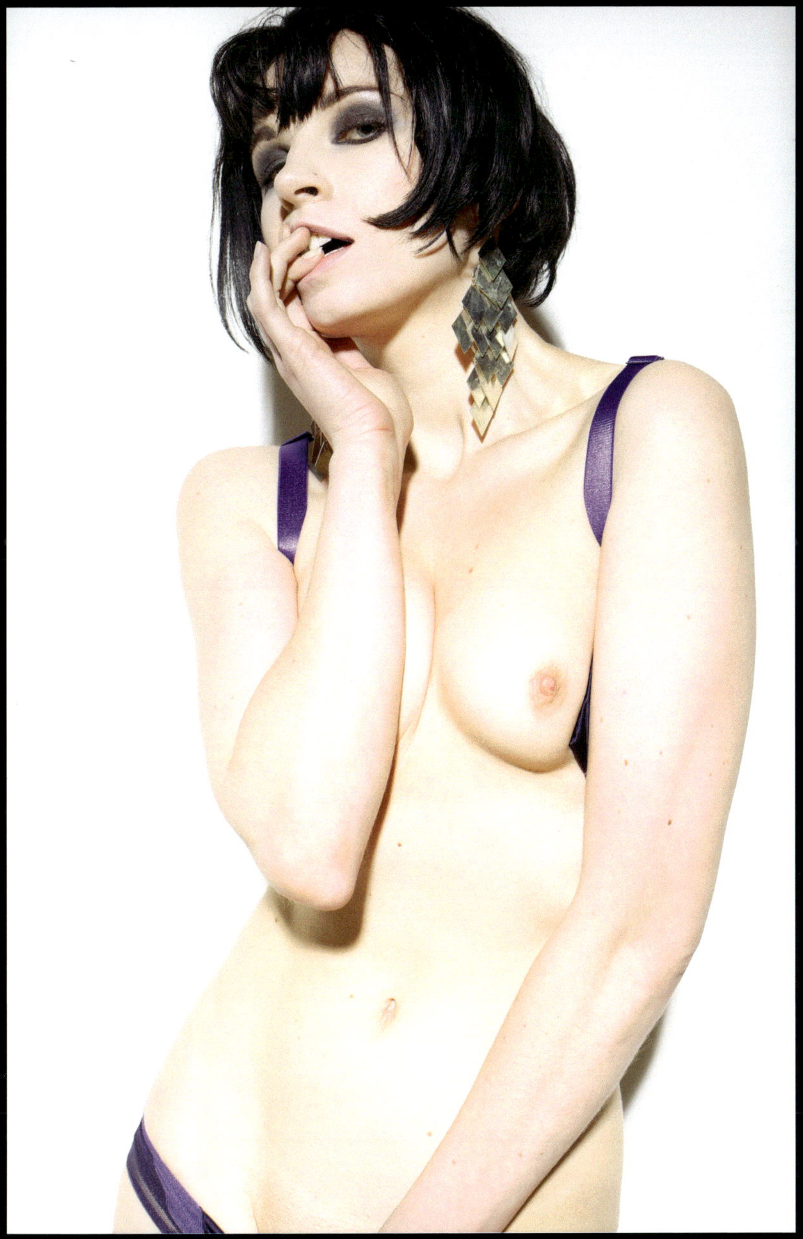

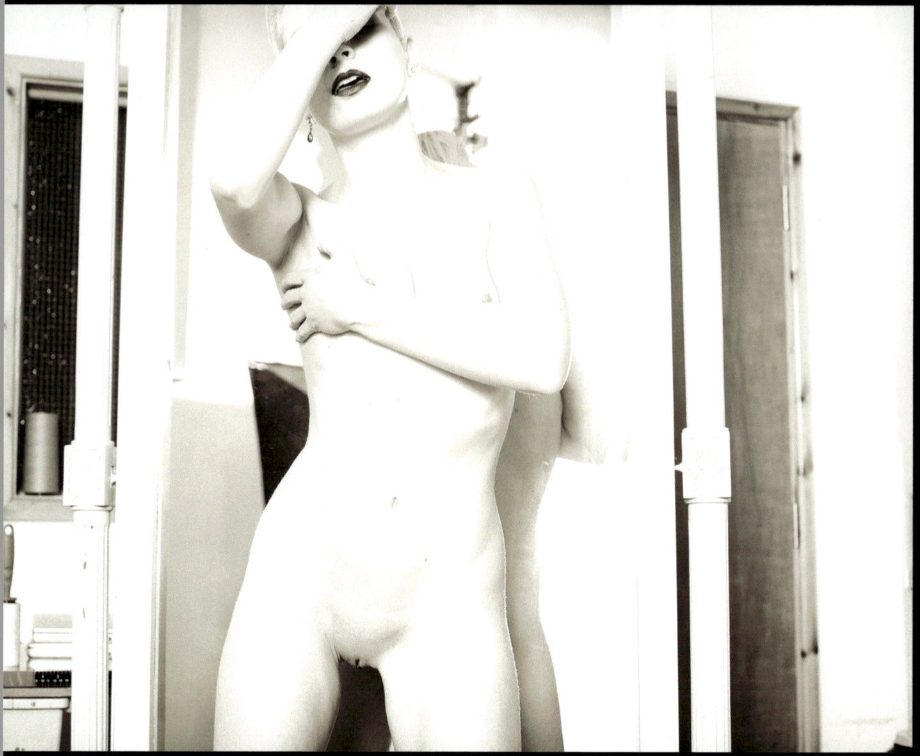

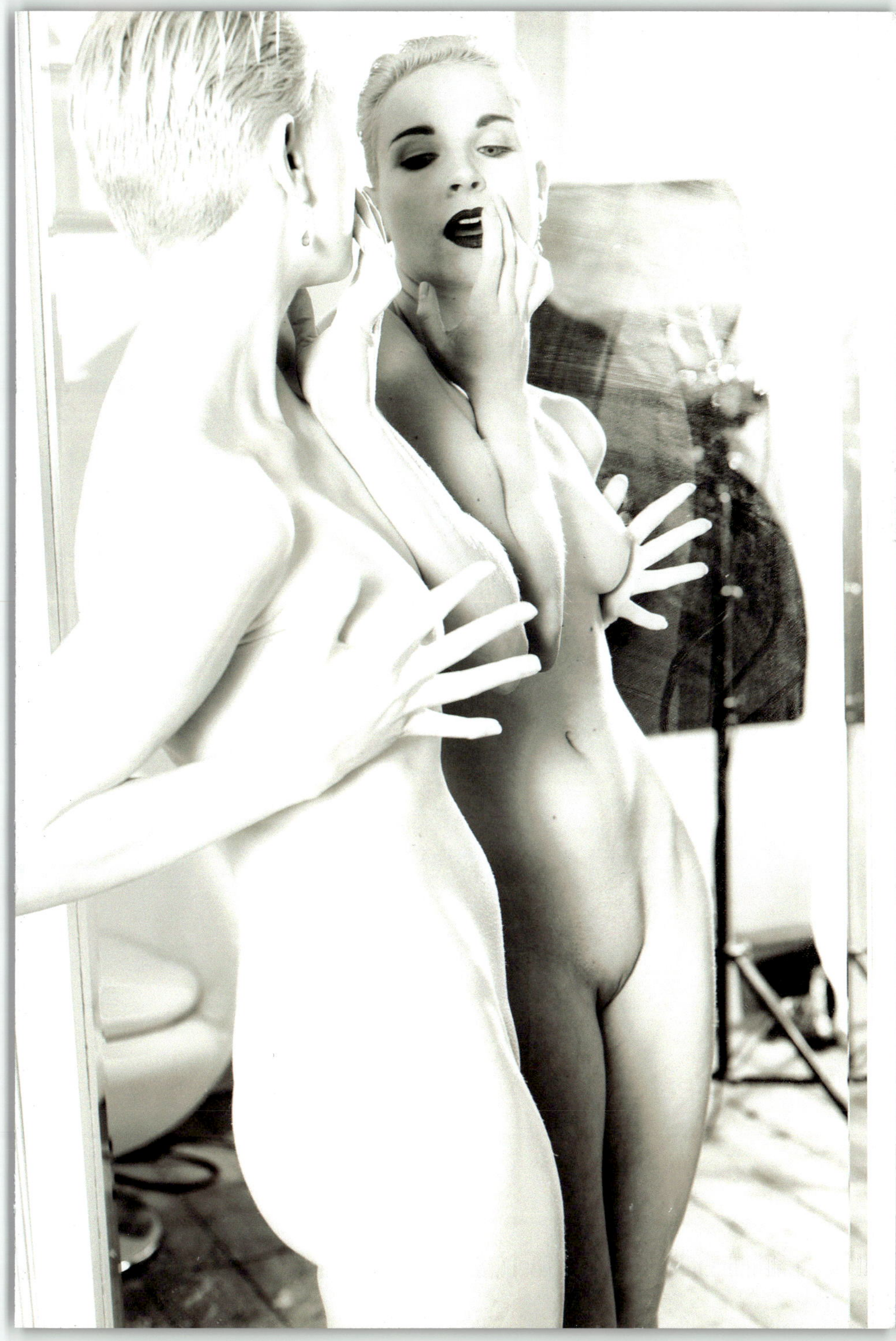

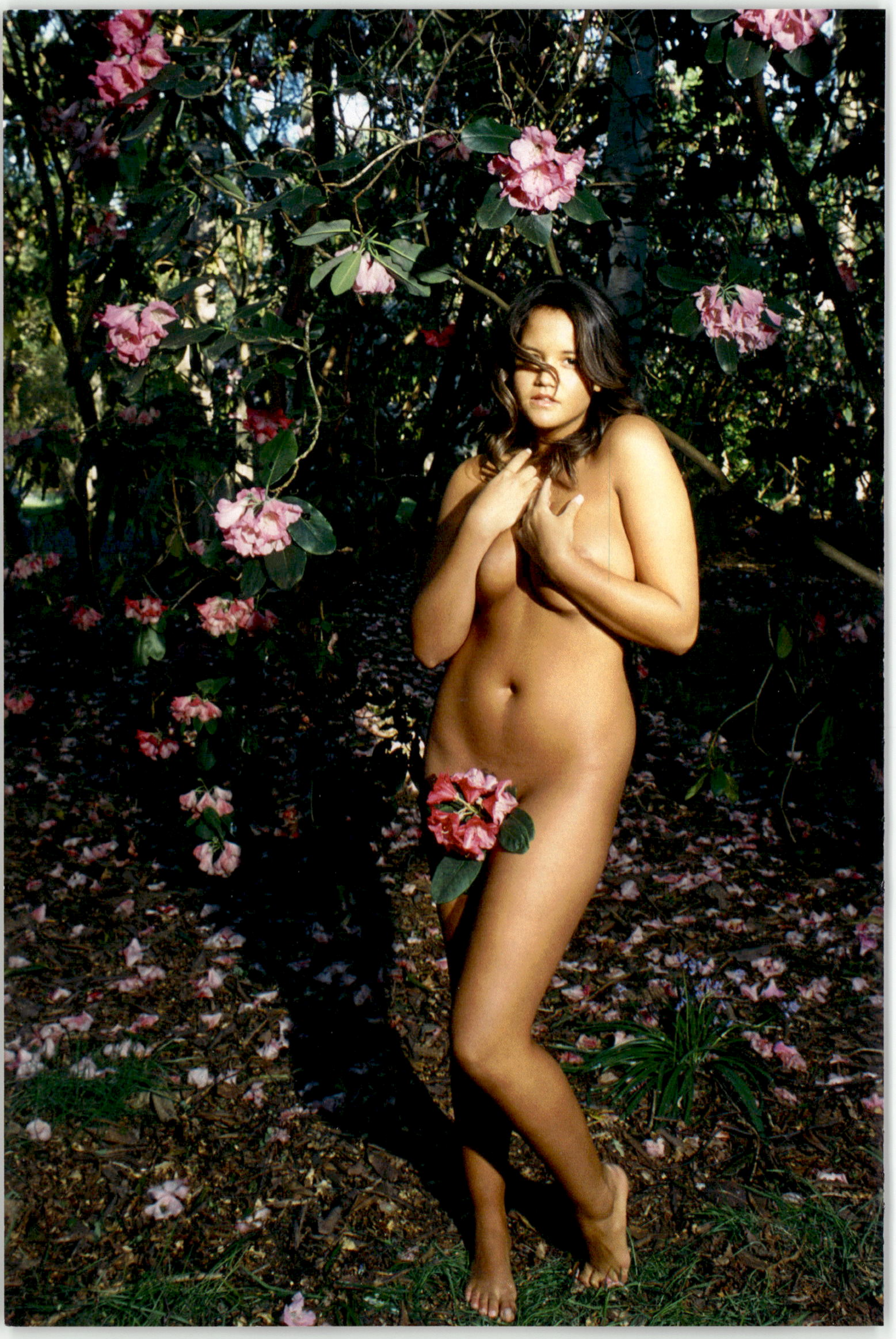

ALVA BERNADINE

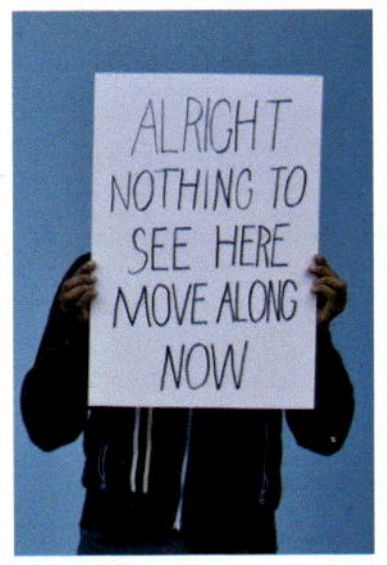

Based in London, Alva Bernadine is self-taught, never having trained as an assistant. He has worked for *Vogue*, *GQ* and *Elle* magazines and *The Sunday Times*. In 1987 he won the Vogue/Sotheby's Cecil Beaton Award for a series of photographs of shoes called "The Fetish", and in 2001 won Erotic Photographer of the Year for his book *Bernadinism*.

"I take the theatricality of surrealism, the elegance of classical haute couture photography, the narrative of reportage and the refinements of advertising photography and mix them all into a 'Bernadinian cocktail' – a radical photographic synthesis."

www.bernadinism.com

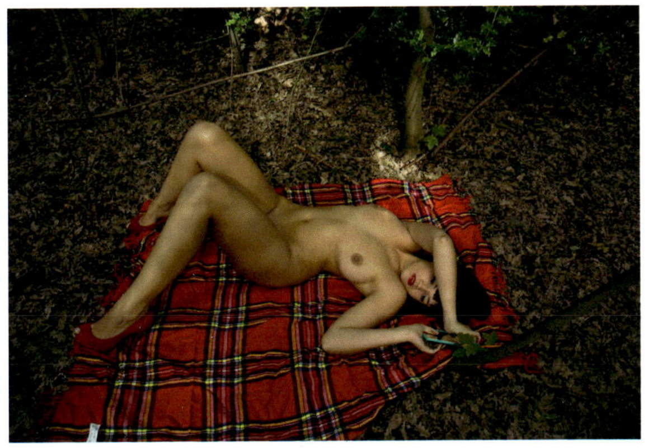

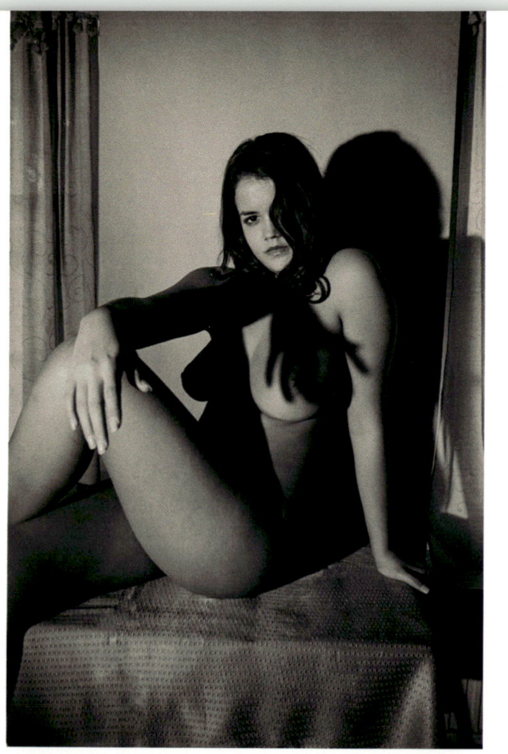

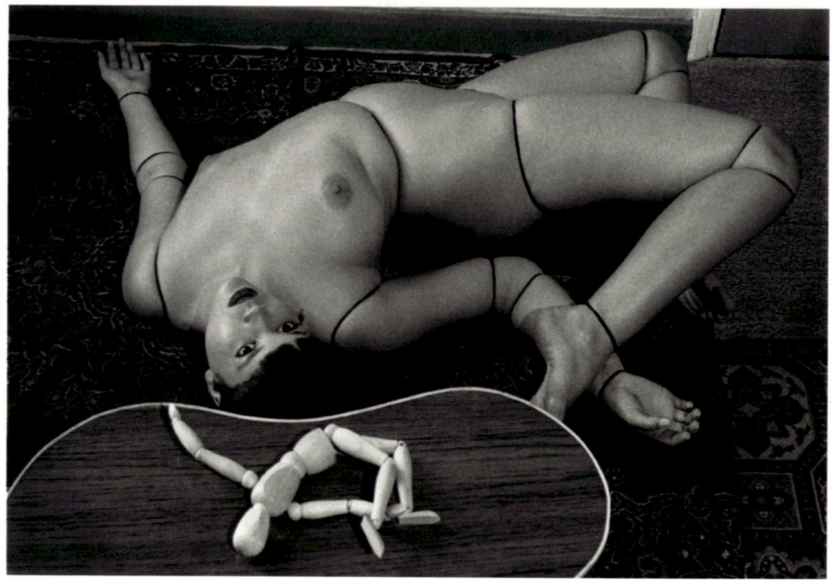

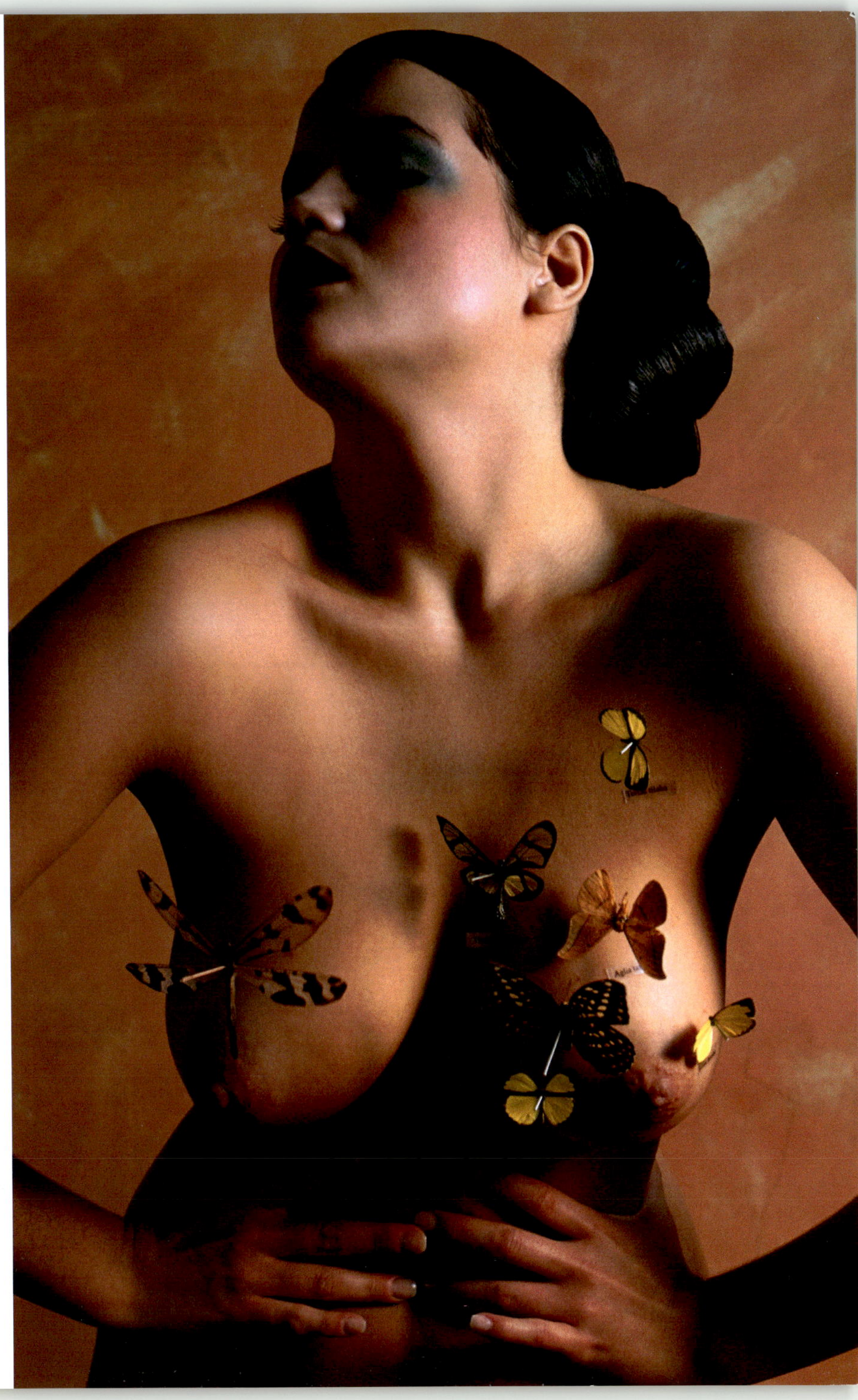

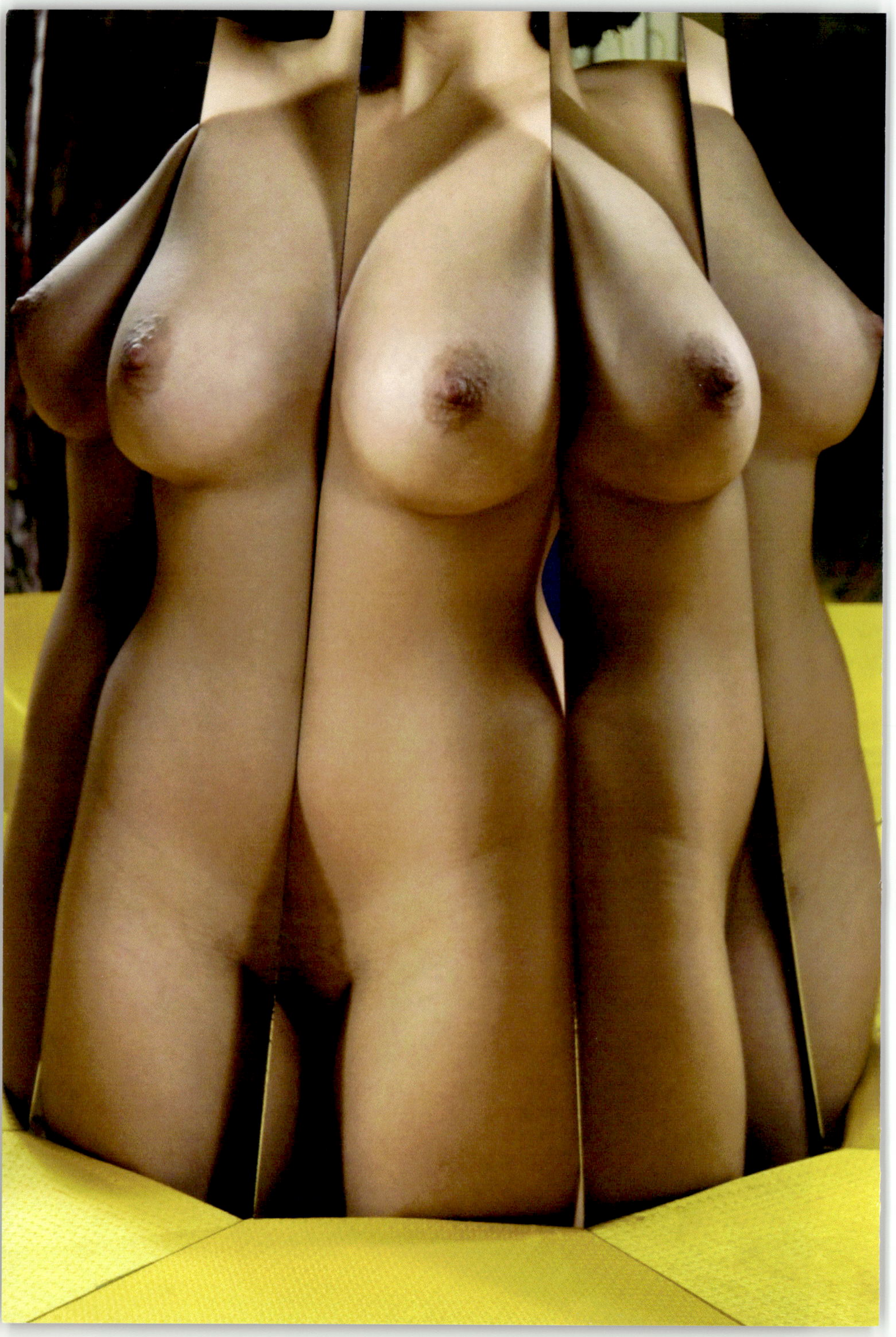

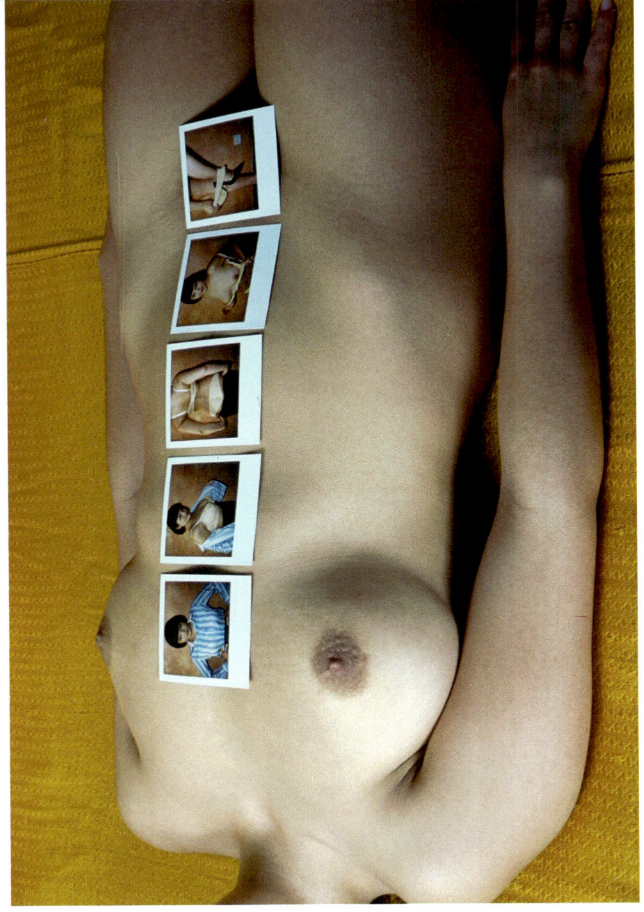

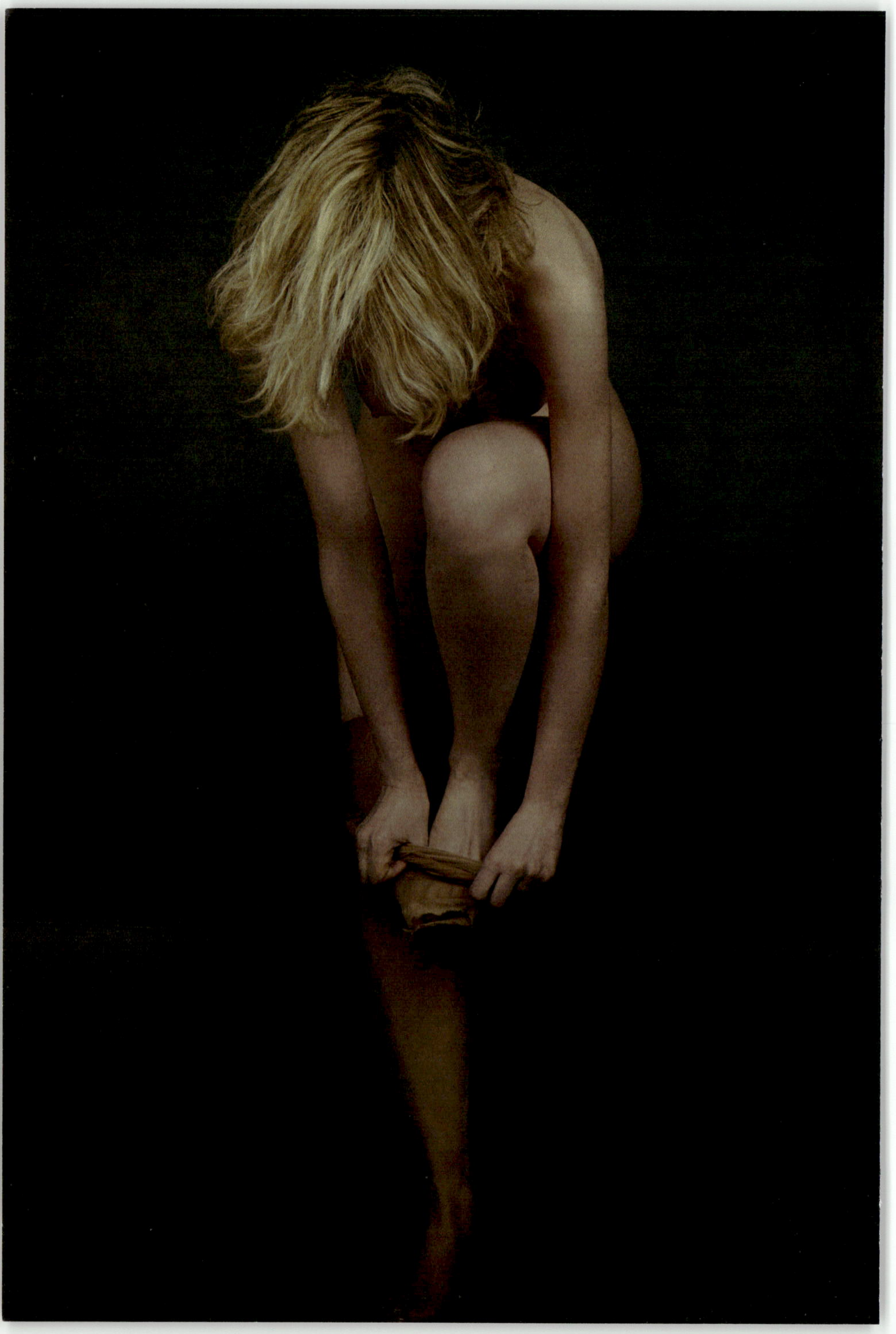

STÉPHANE BIENFAIT

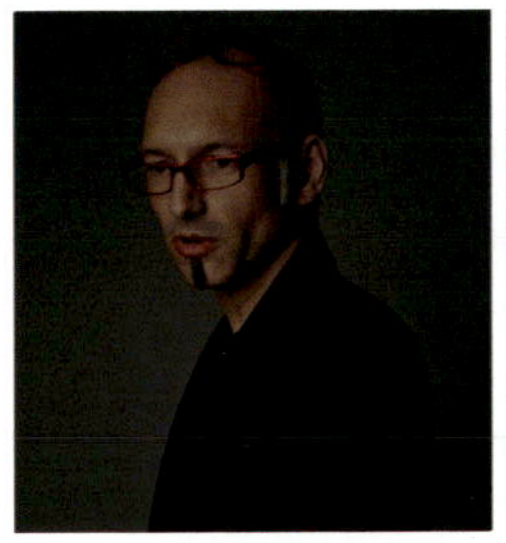

Stéphane Bienfait is a French photographer. His muse is Esa, a model from the Accademia delle Belle Arti in Florence and the Ecole Nationale Supérieure des Beaux-Arts in Paris who has previously worked with Eugenio Miccini, Vanessa Beecroft and Peter Suschitzky. Their work together is highly collaborative, like dancing in space.

www.stephanebienfait.fr

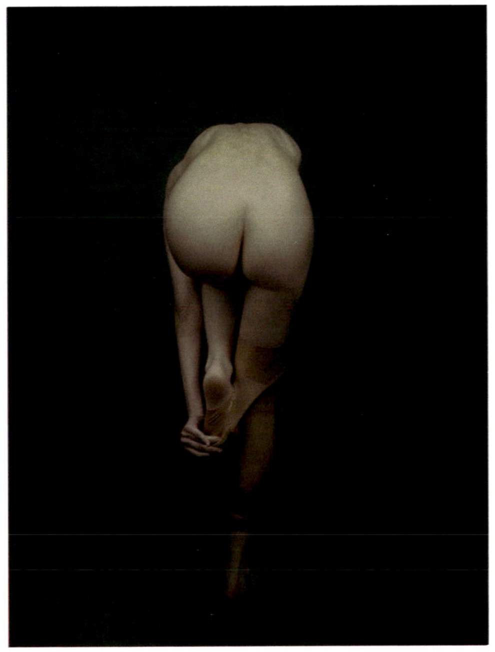

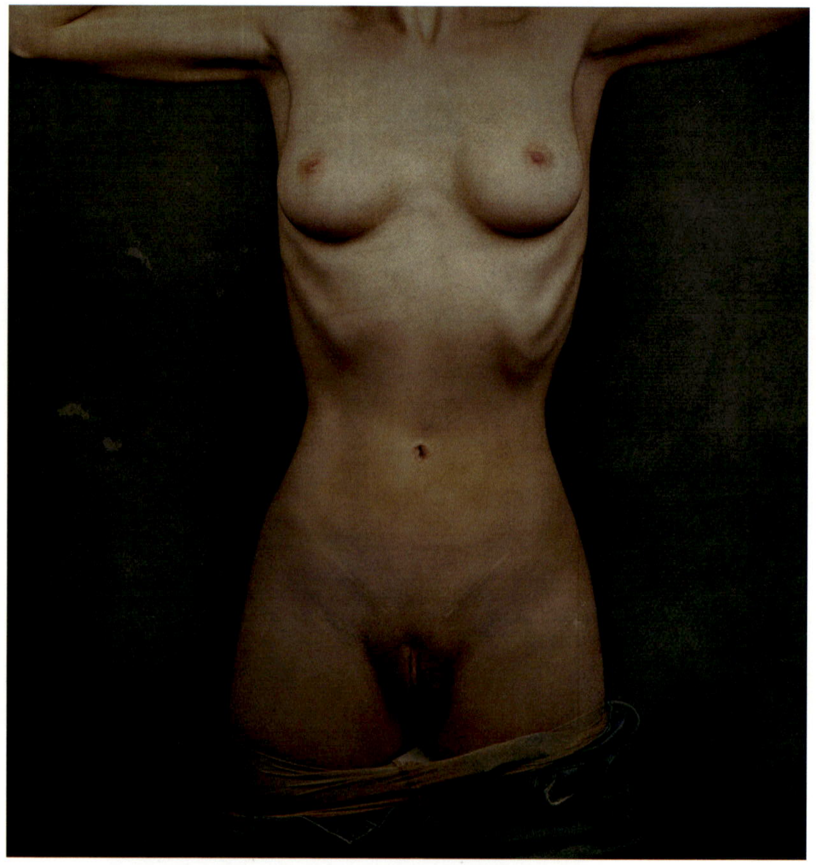

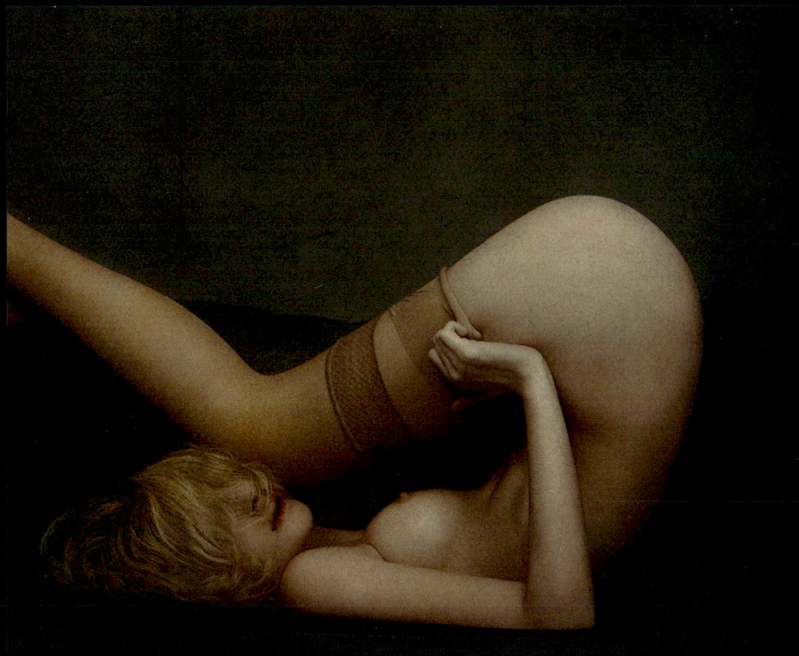

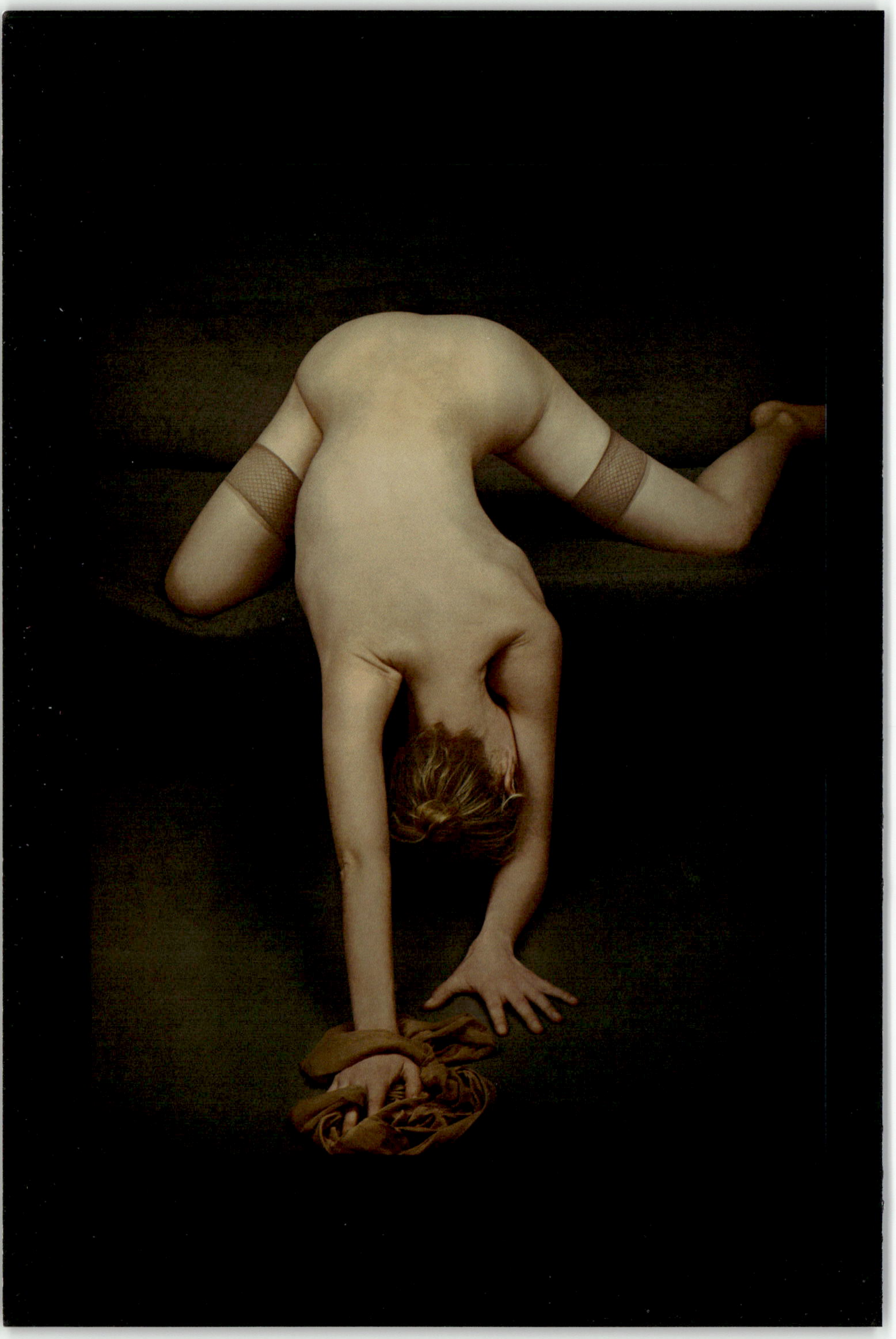

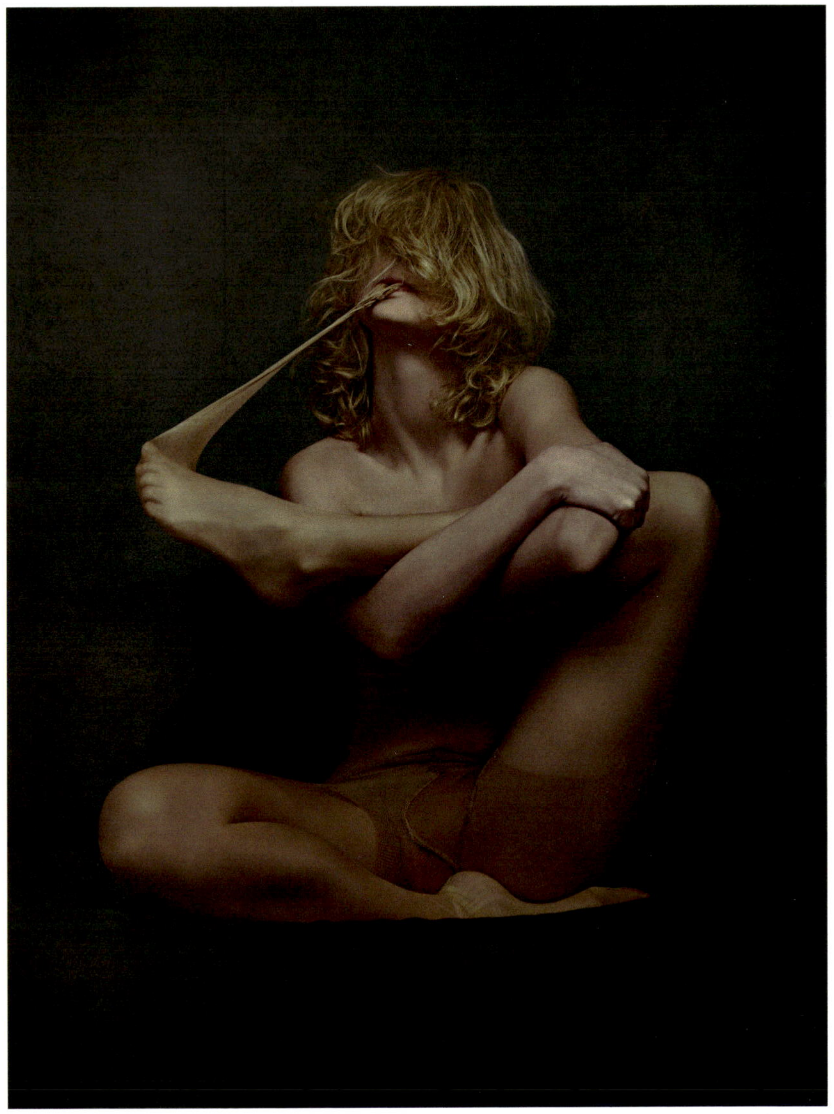

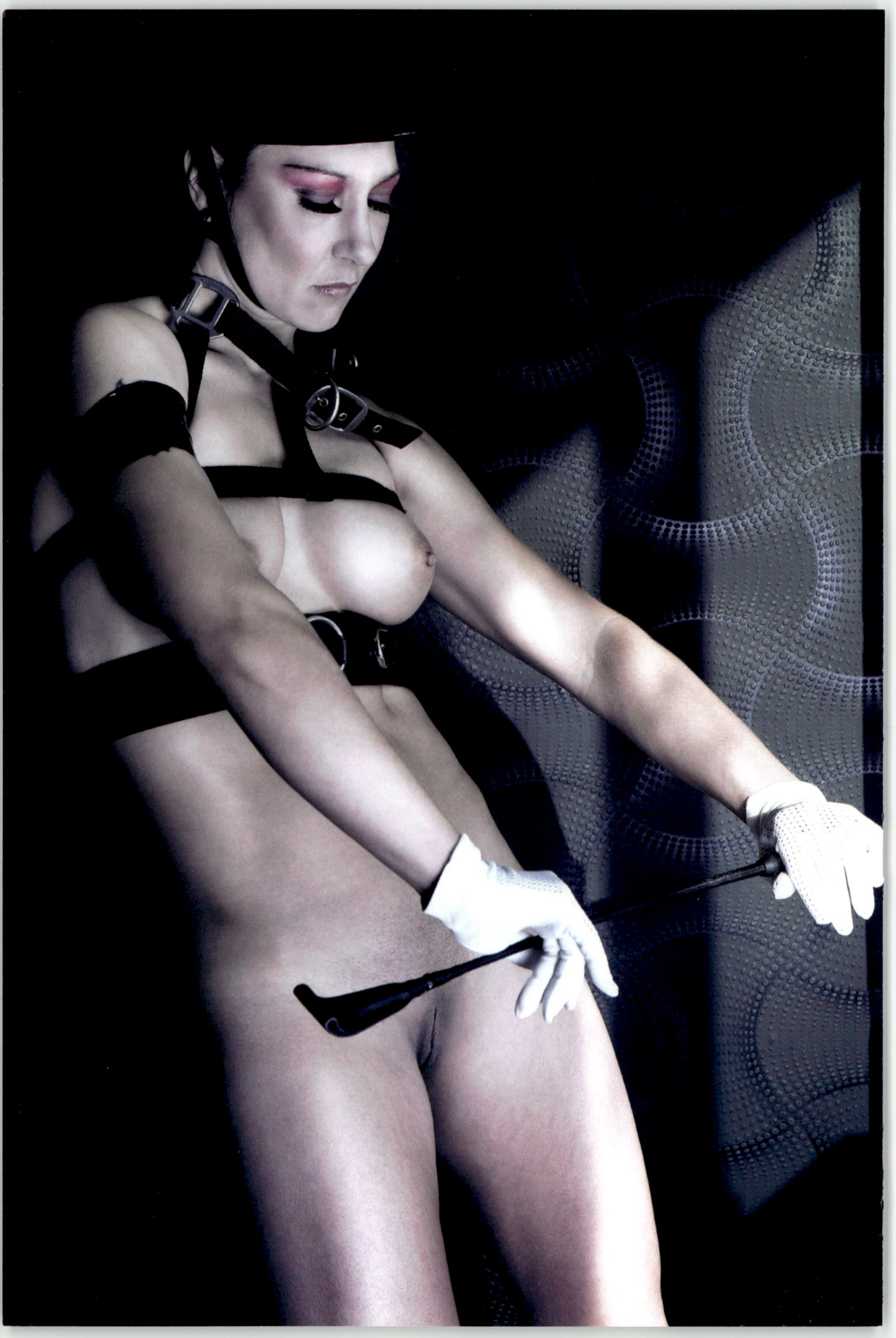

JENNY BOOT

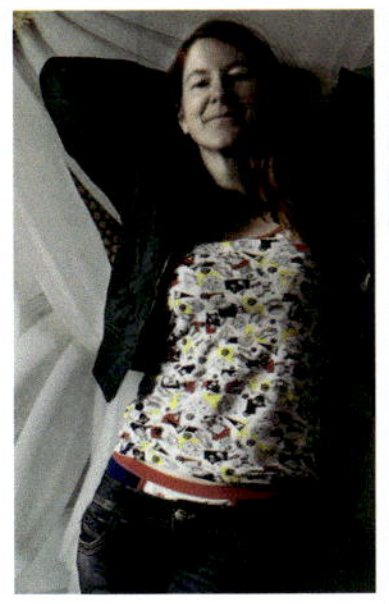

"In my works I search for the limits of my values, then attempt to overcome them. I am curious what the process of creation will bring, once I have freed myself from others' opinions. My work may be raw, cruel or even filthy, but I always strive to present it in a clean, fashionable and aesthetic way. My work has an 'in your face' attitude and leaves little to the imagination. I want to get as intimate as possible, to see the soul, the naked truth, the bare skin, the essence of the personality I'm working with."

Jenny chose Mieke as a model because she is very thankful to her. She learned so much from Mieke's willingness and courage to do the things she had in mind.

www.jennyboot.nl

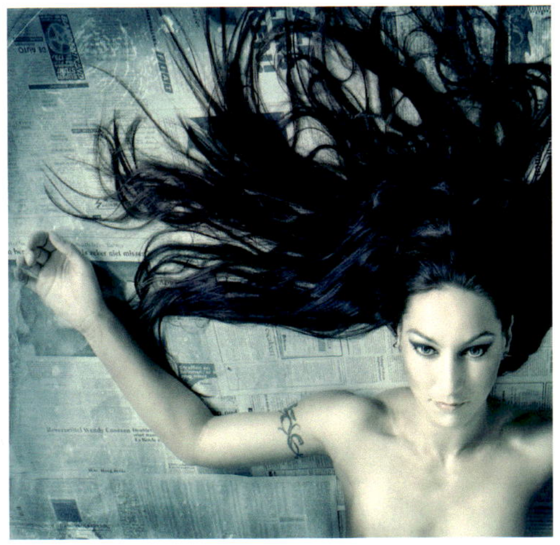

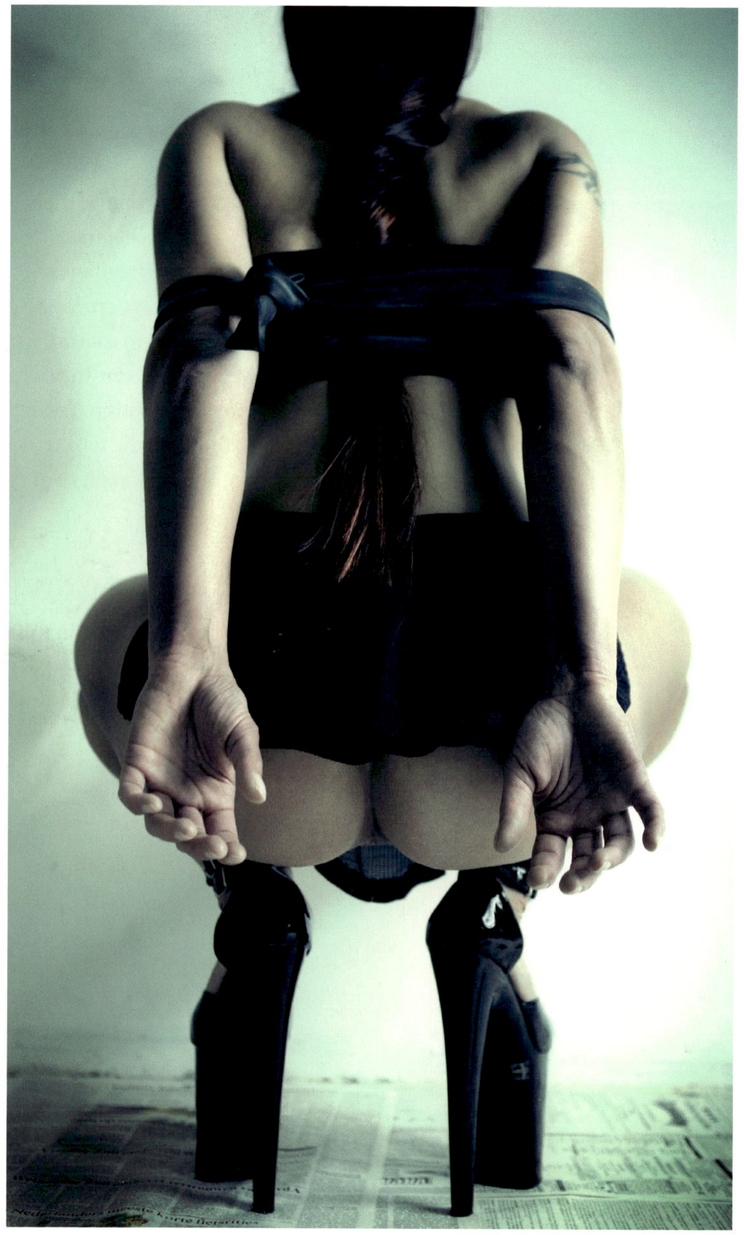

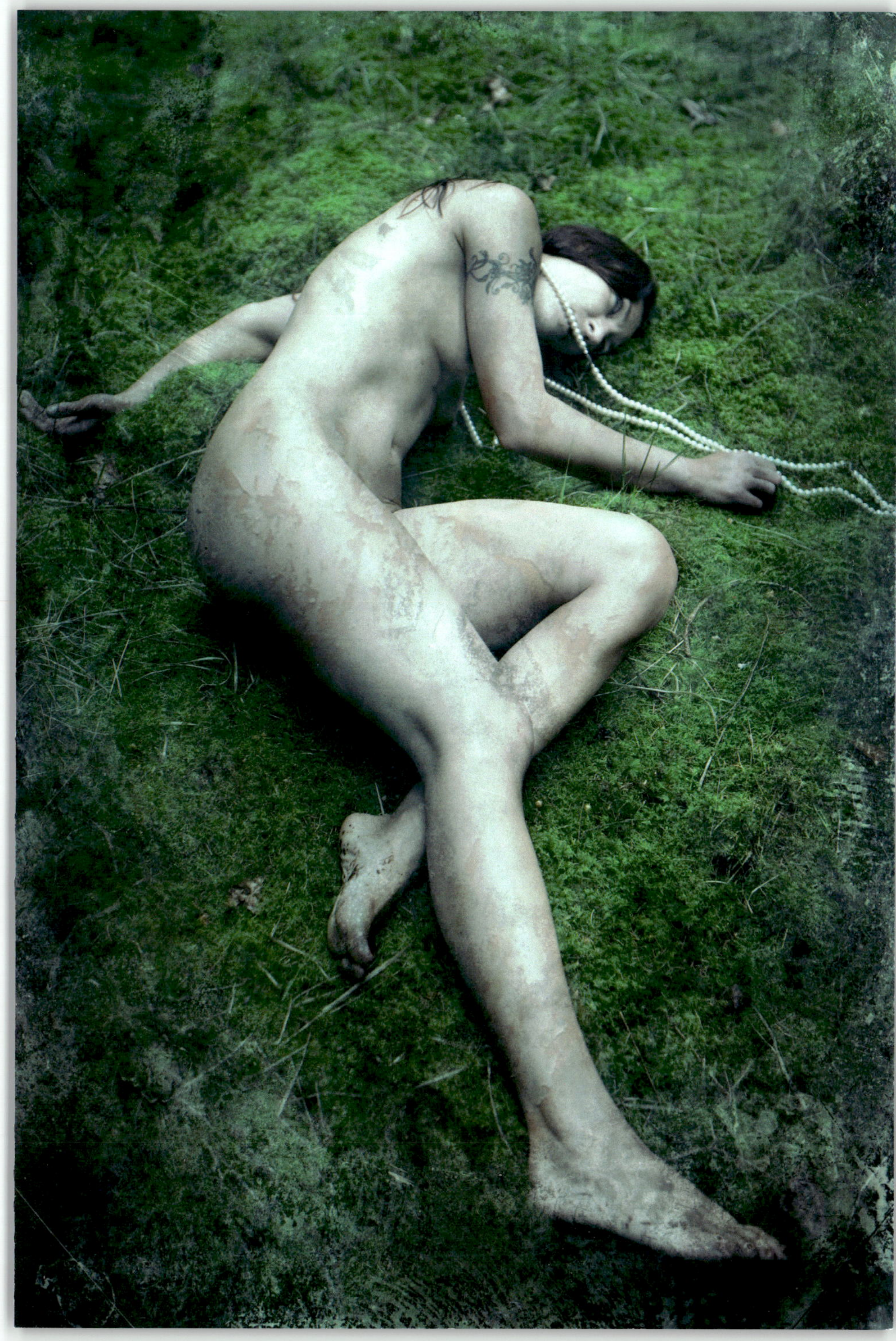

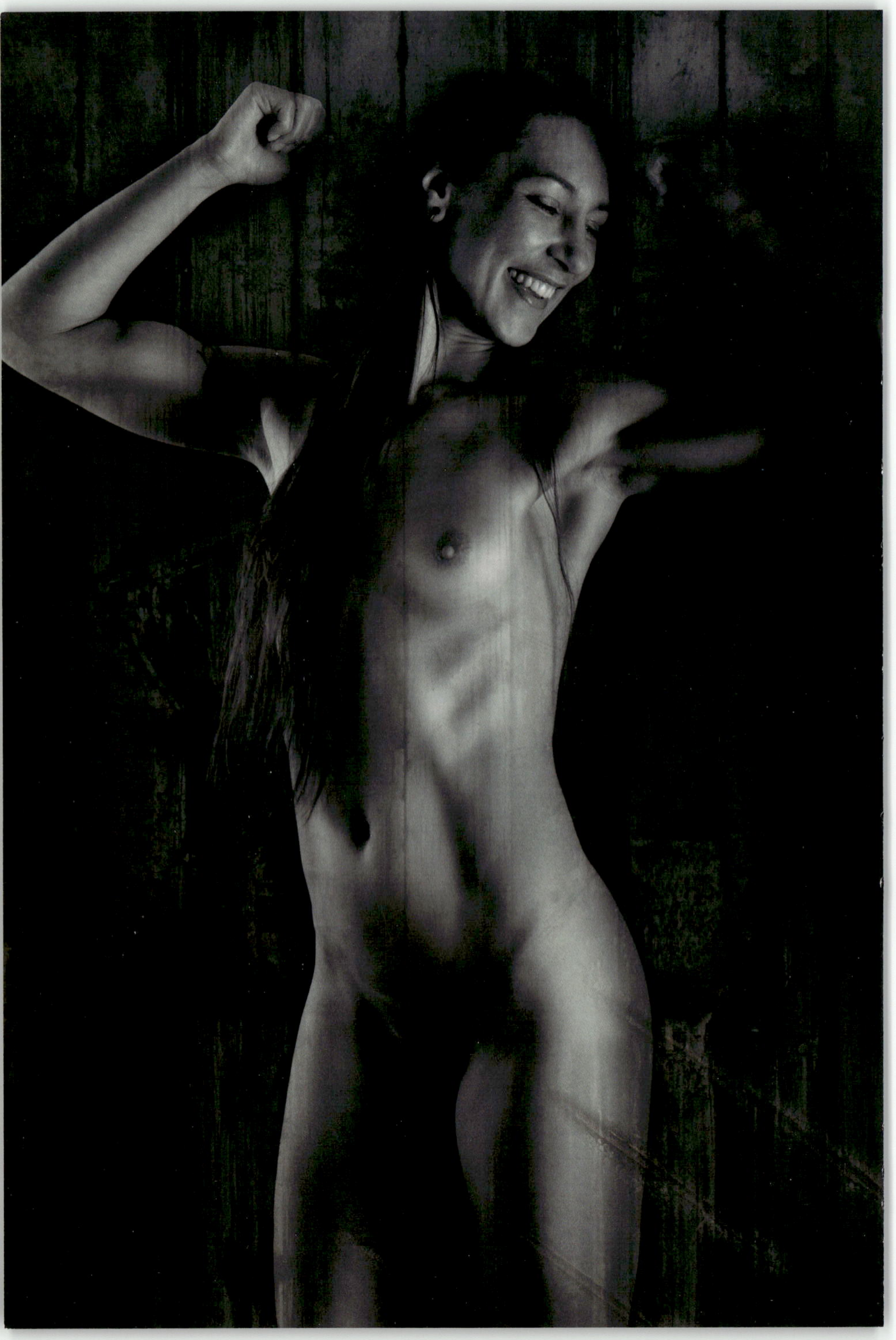

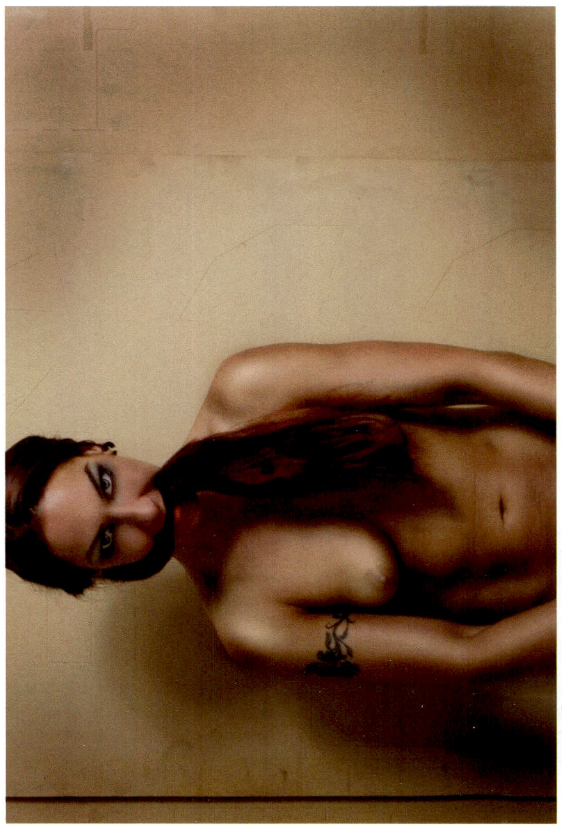

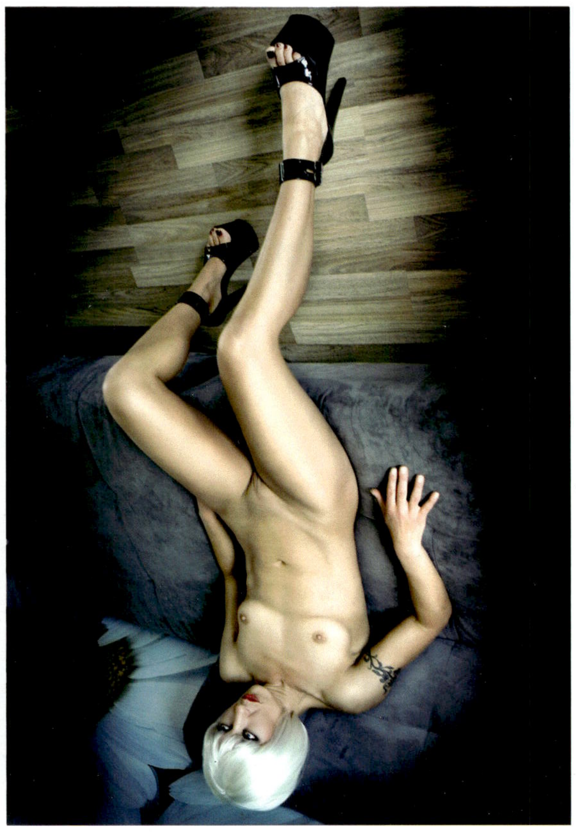

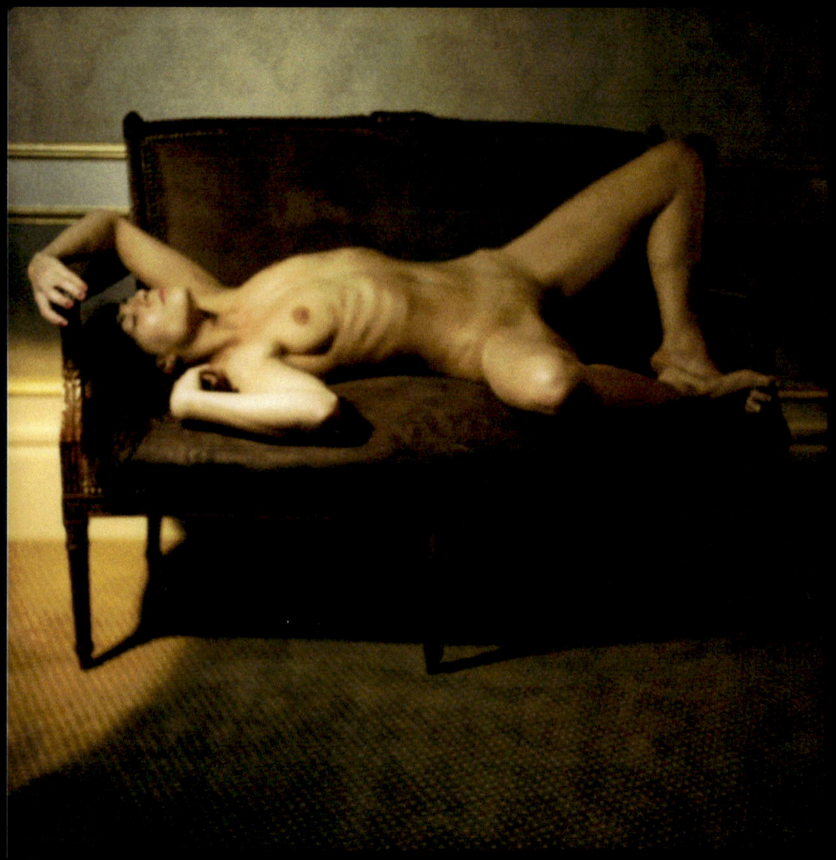

PHILIPPE BOURGOIN

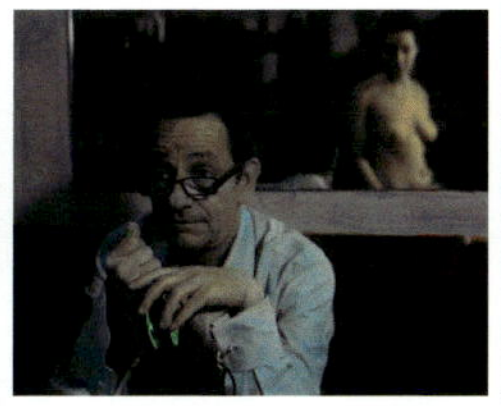

Originally a writer, Philippe Bourgoin later went to New York University Film School to study directing. Although he enjoyed cinematography and camera classes, writing remained his first love. On returning to his native France he had a major record hit, wrote lyrics and produced and published music. He has also written a few short stories. Photography has always been close to his heart, but it has been his full-time passion only since 2006. He met Margot close to the end of her modelling career, while she was completing a Master's degree in psychology. She became a friend and they worked together on many occasions. Margot opened up a world of creation for Philippe, thanks to her patience, willingness, and creative personality.

www.philippe-bourgoin.book.fr
www.flickr.com/people/philippebourgoin

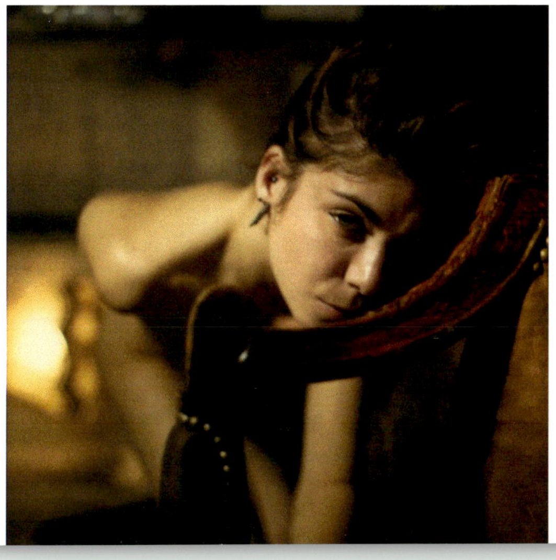

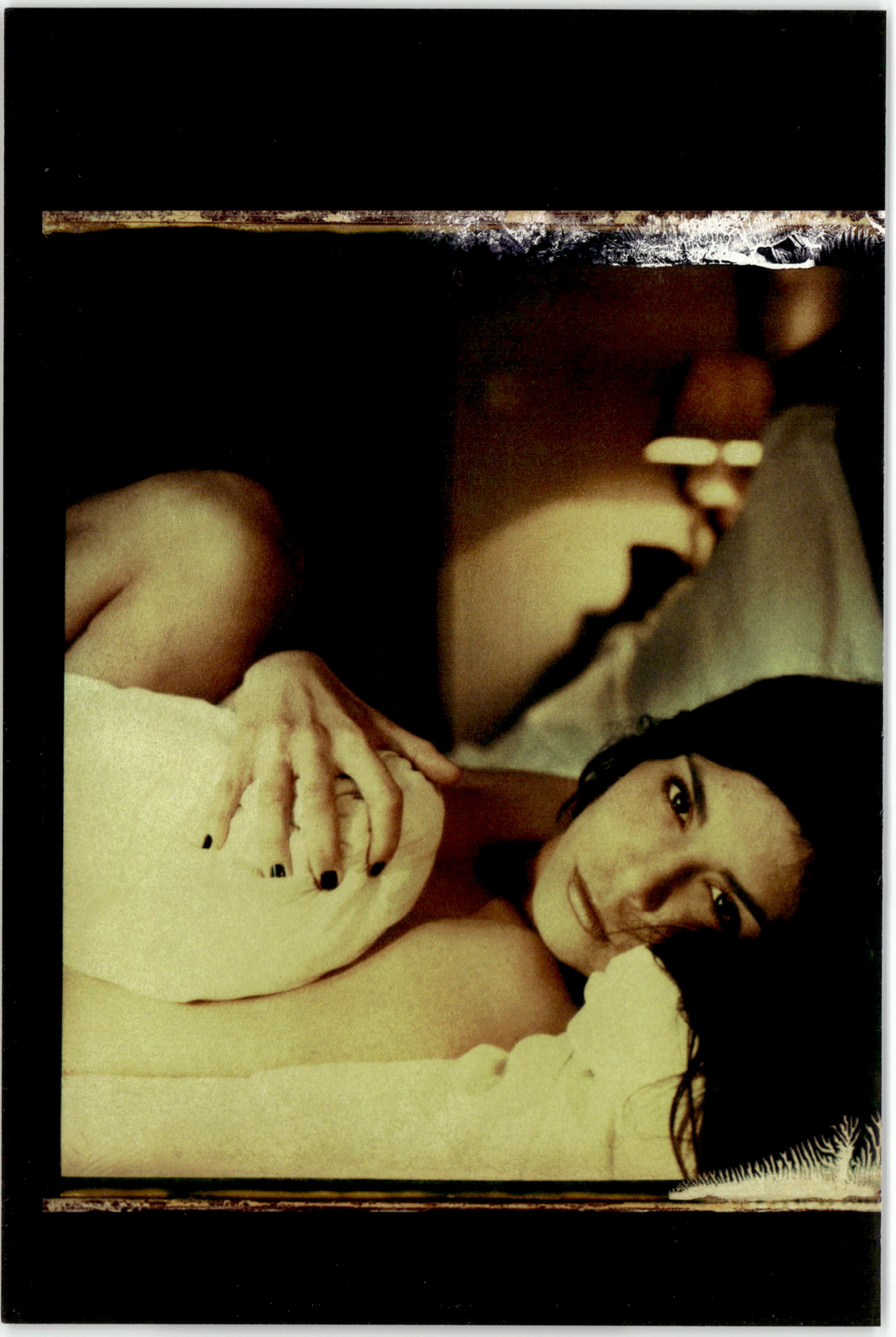

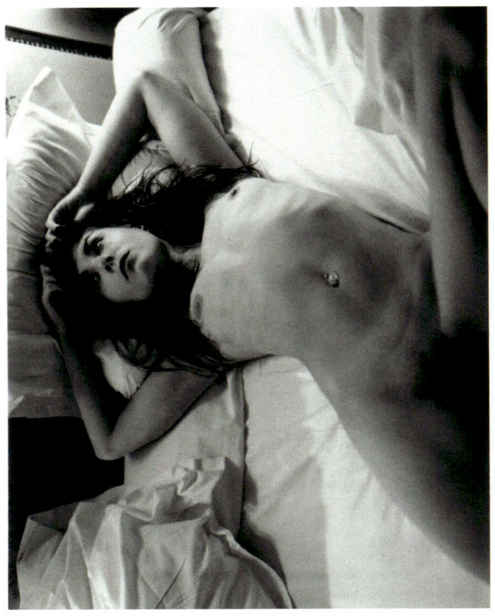

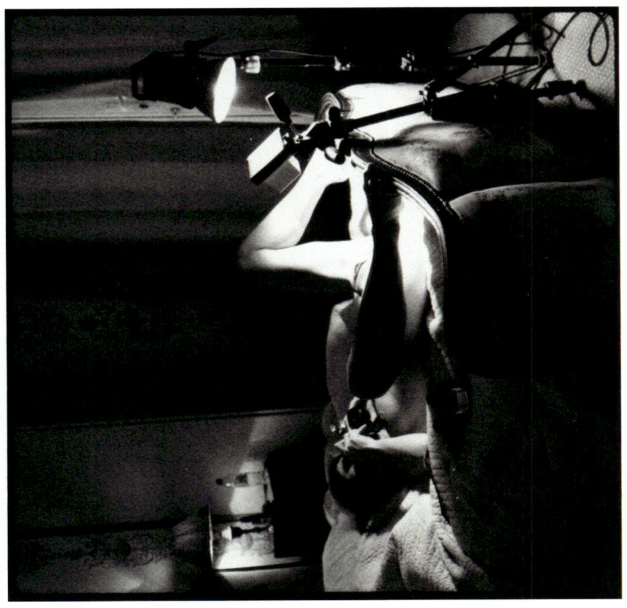

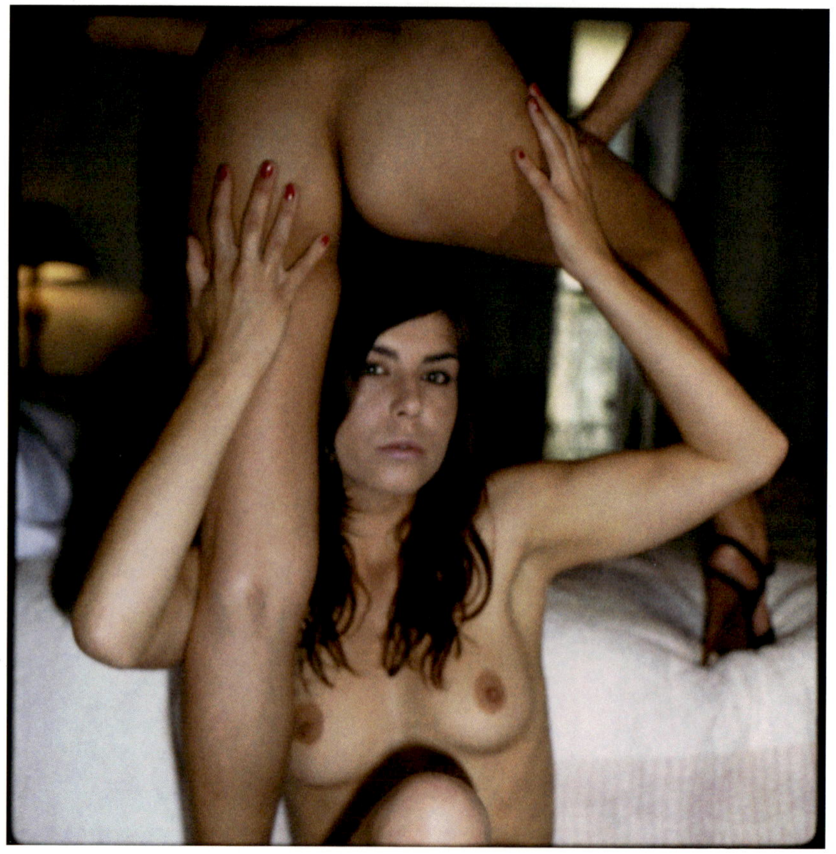

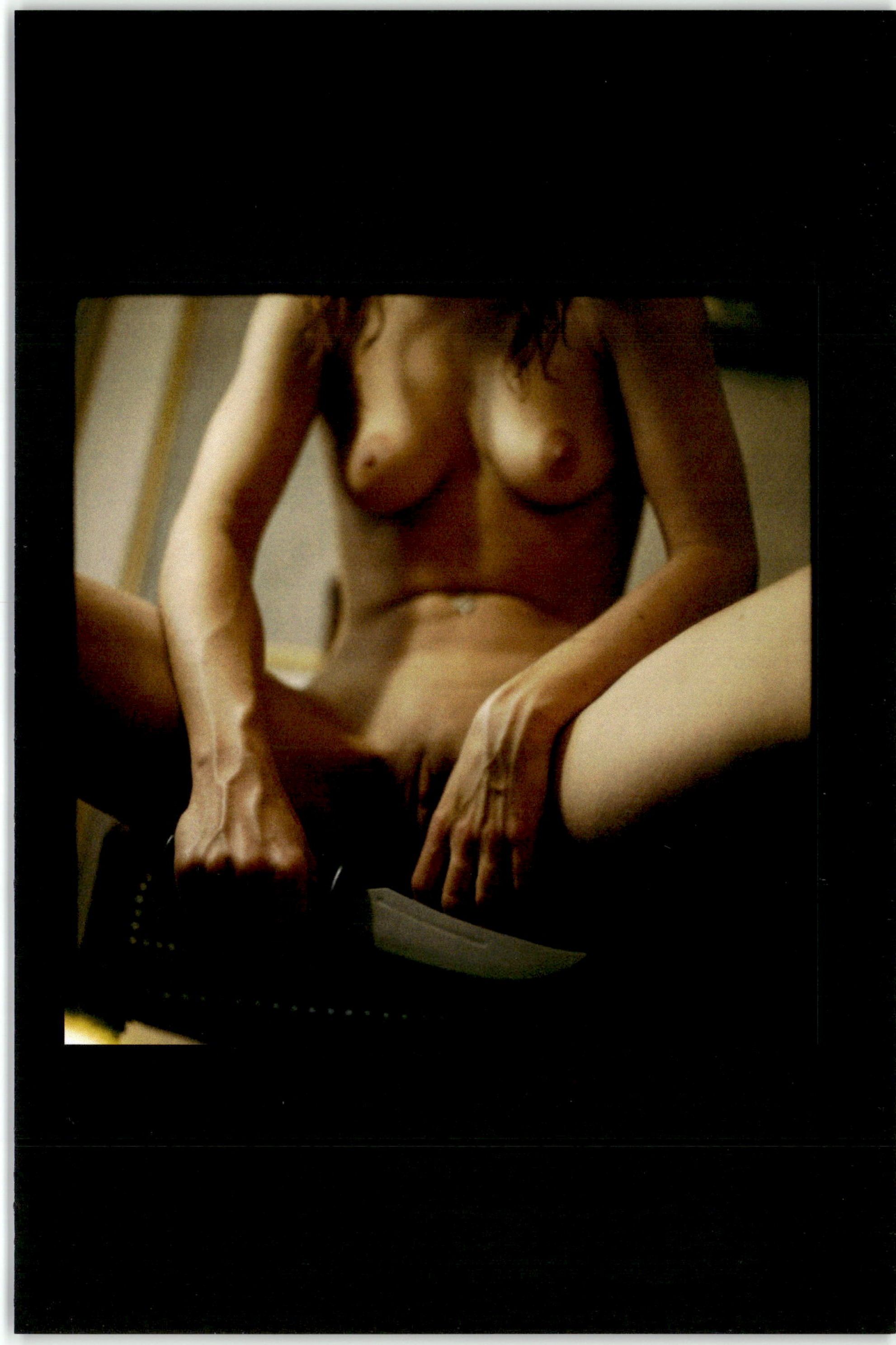

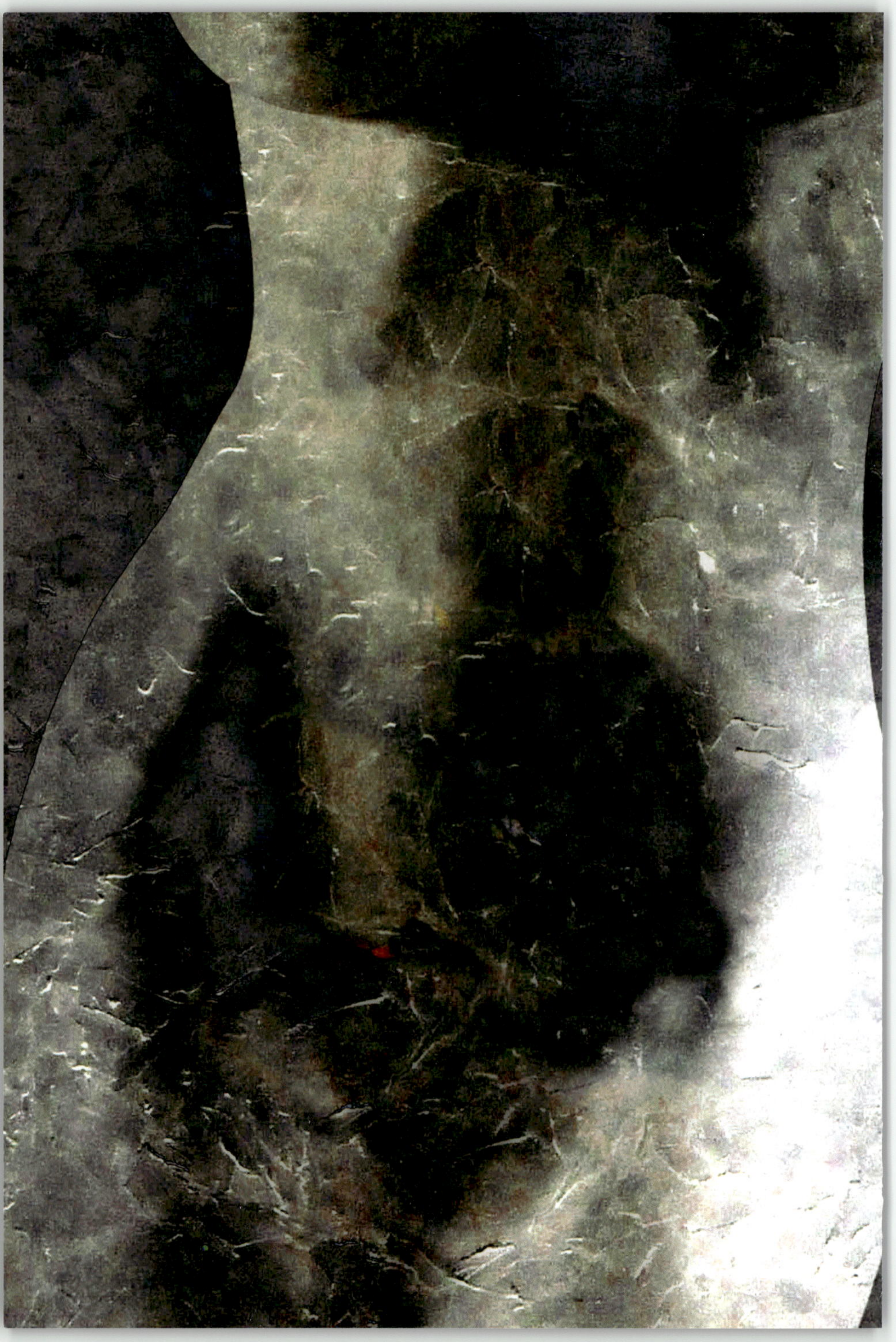

FAUSTO BROZZI

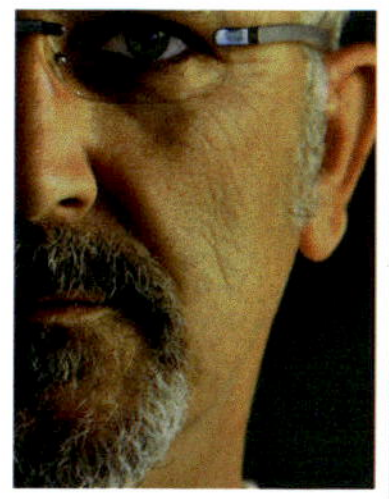

Fausto Brozzi is an Italian photographer, based near Parma, whose erotic and nude photography sometimes evokes the romantic English painters in the way he melds the physical and nature. He often plays with the images and their texture in post-production and his work.

Fausto has been exhibited in many prestigious venues. He has also curated many shows and exhibitions in Venice featuring his work and that of other worldwide artists. His quest for Aphrodite continues.

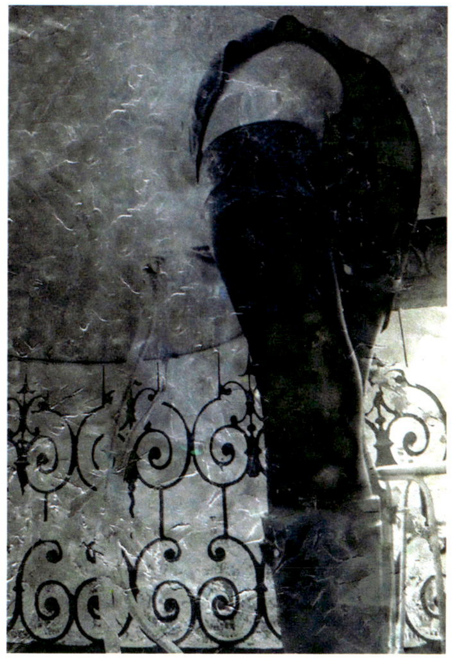

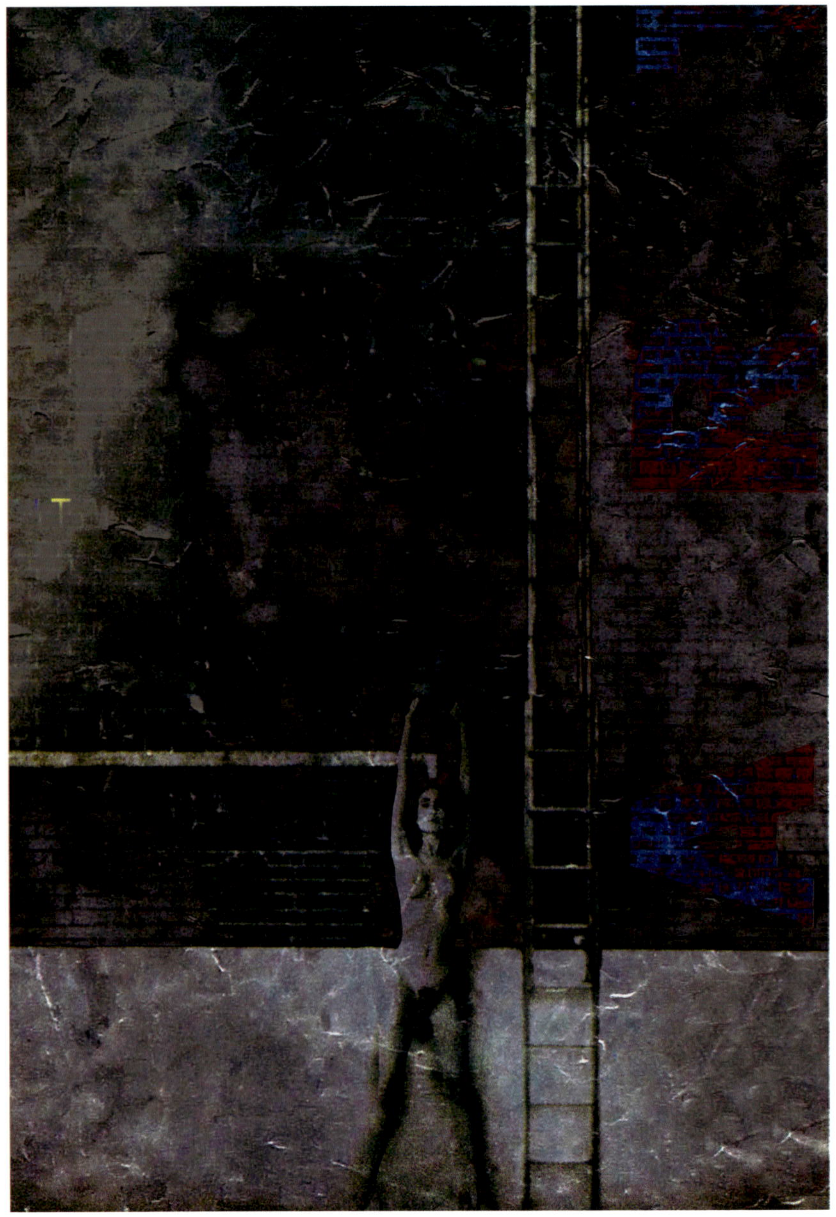

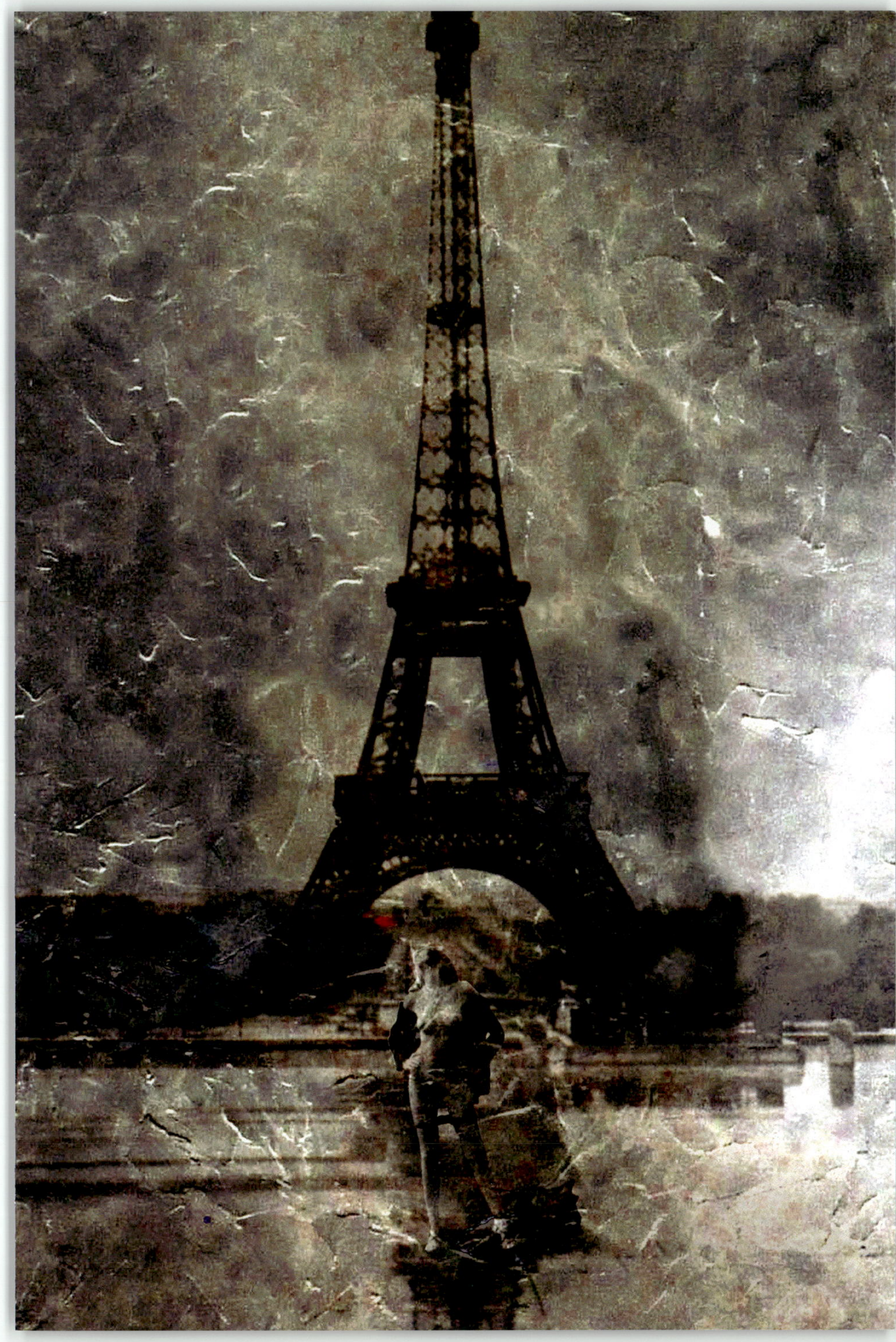

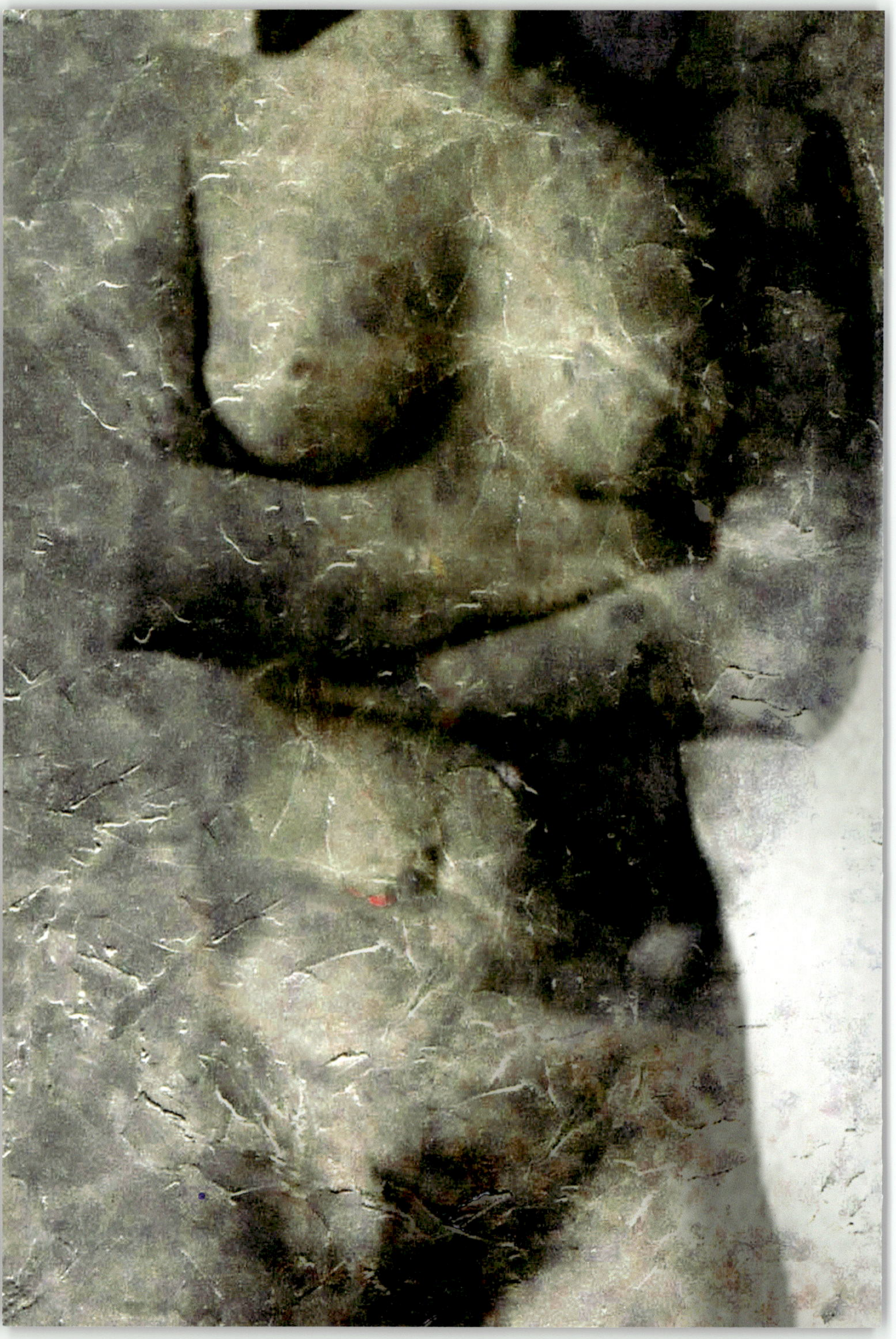

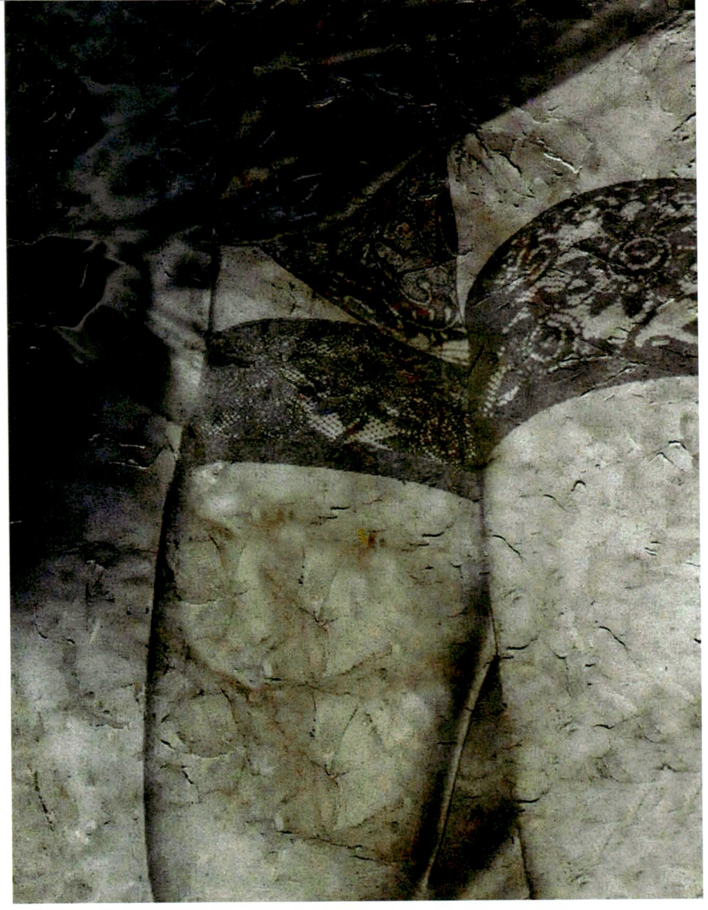

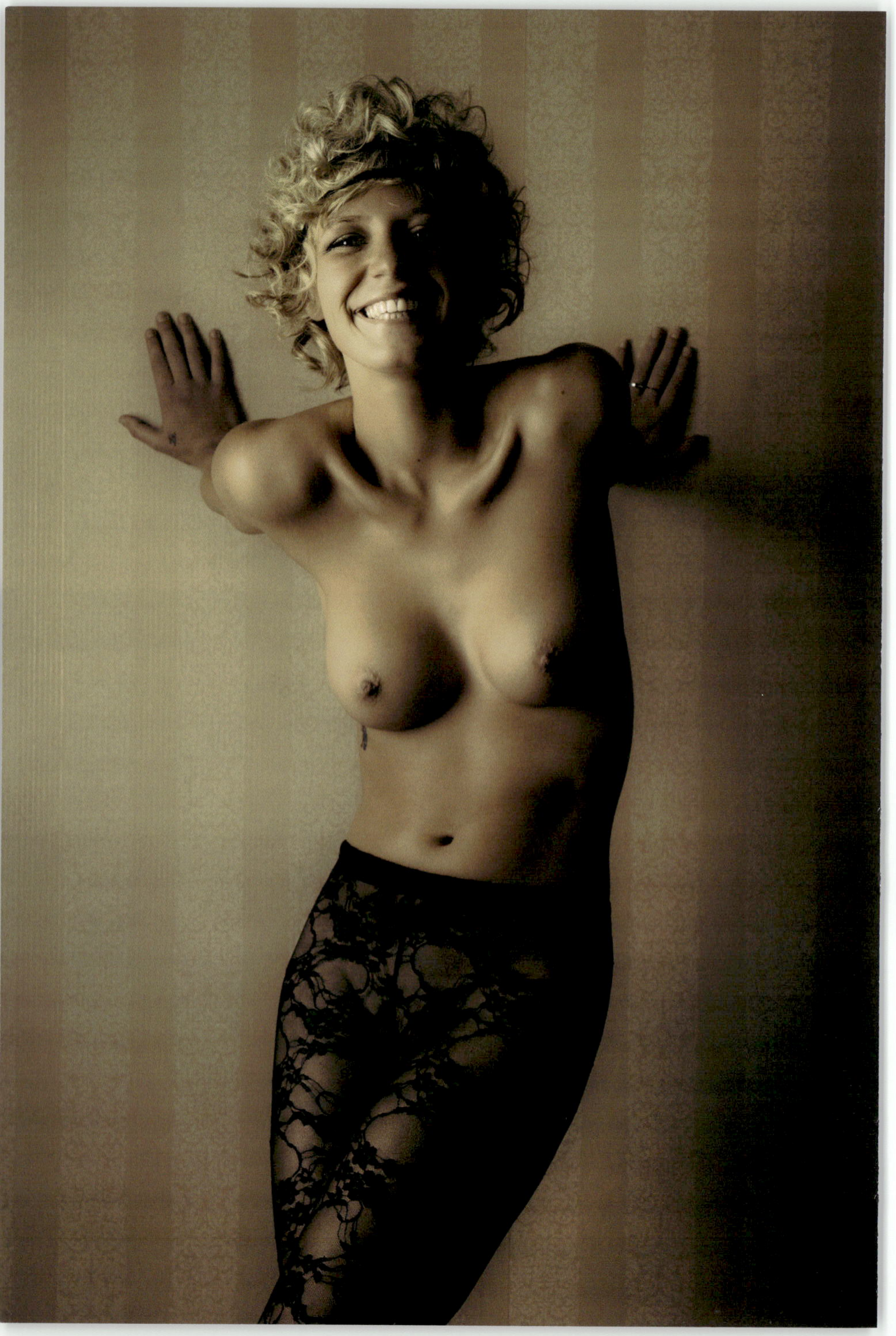

KEVIN CANADA

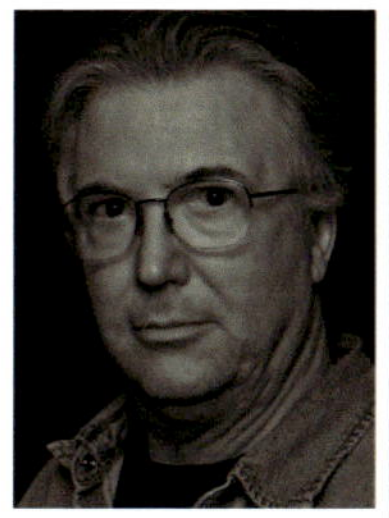

Born in western Canada in 1958, Kevin Canada found his calling early in life, starting street photography at the age of fifteen. For thirty-five years he has shot hundreds of models and won numerous awards in competitions. His photography has been published in many magazines and websites around the world. The images here are taken from a series due to be published in a forthcoming limited edition book *K-Raw: 100 images of 1 model*, which represents twenty-five shoots with the same model over one year.

"I was drawn to this model because of her versatility – her ability to project a range of emotions from innocent to playful, from sophisticated to sinful. At the heart of this project was capturing the many faces of K-Raw that add up to a portrait of an erotic and beautiful woman."

www.kevincanada.com

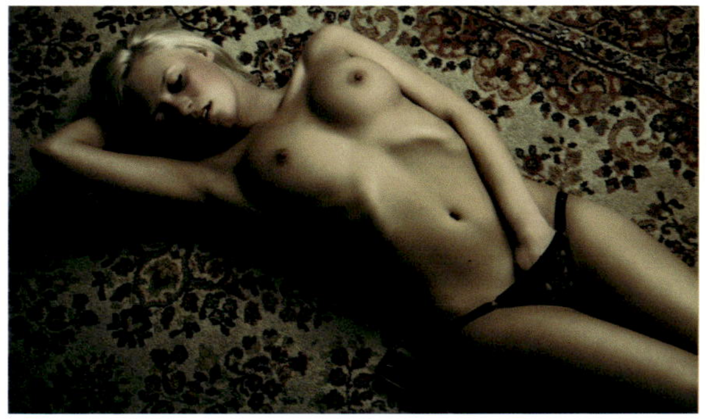

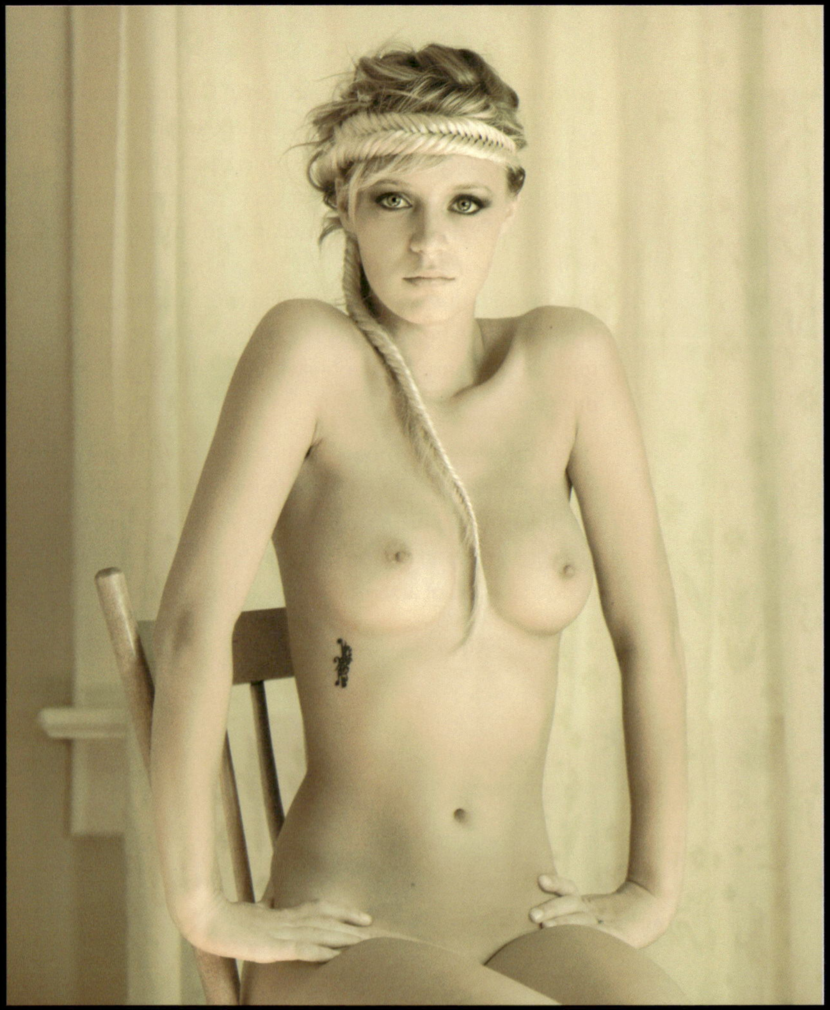

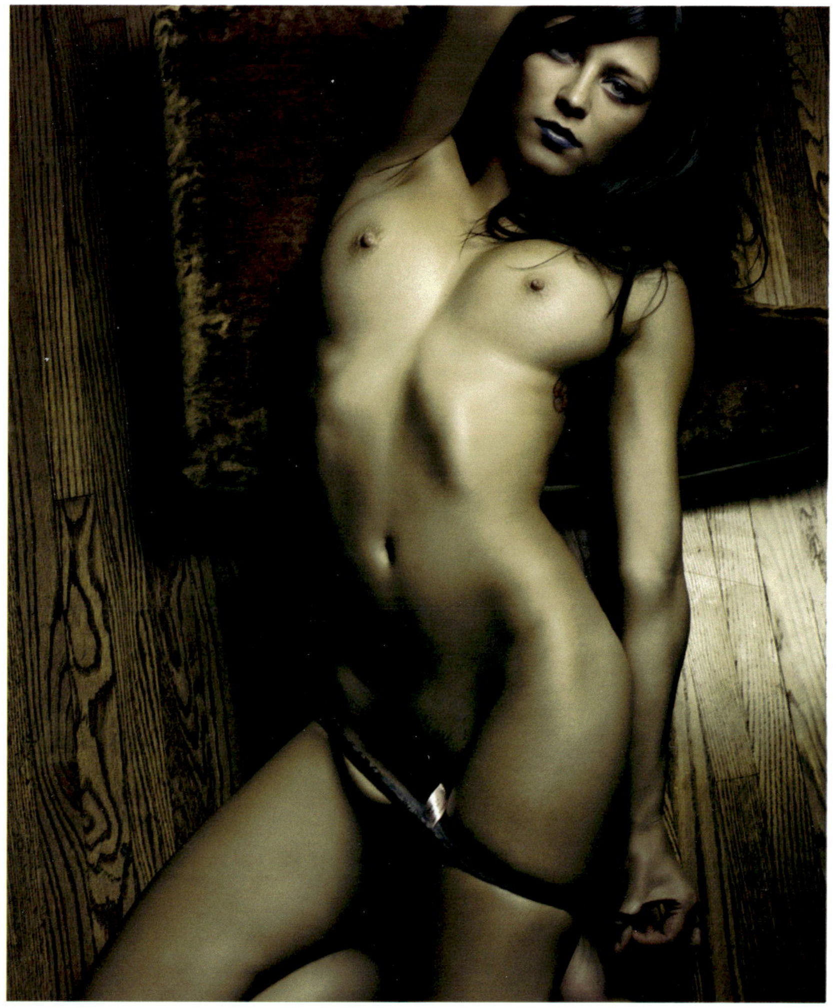

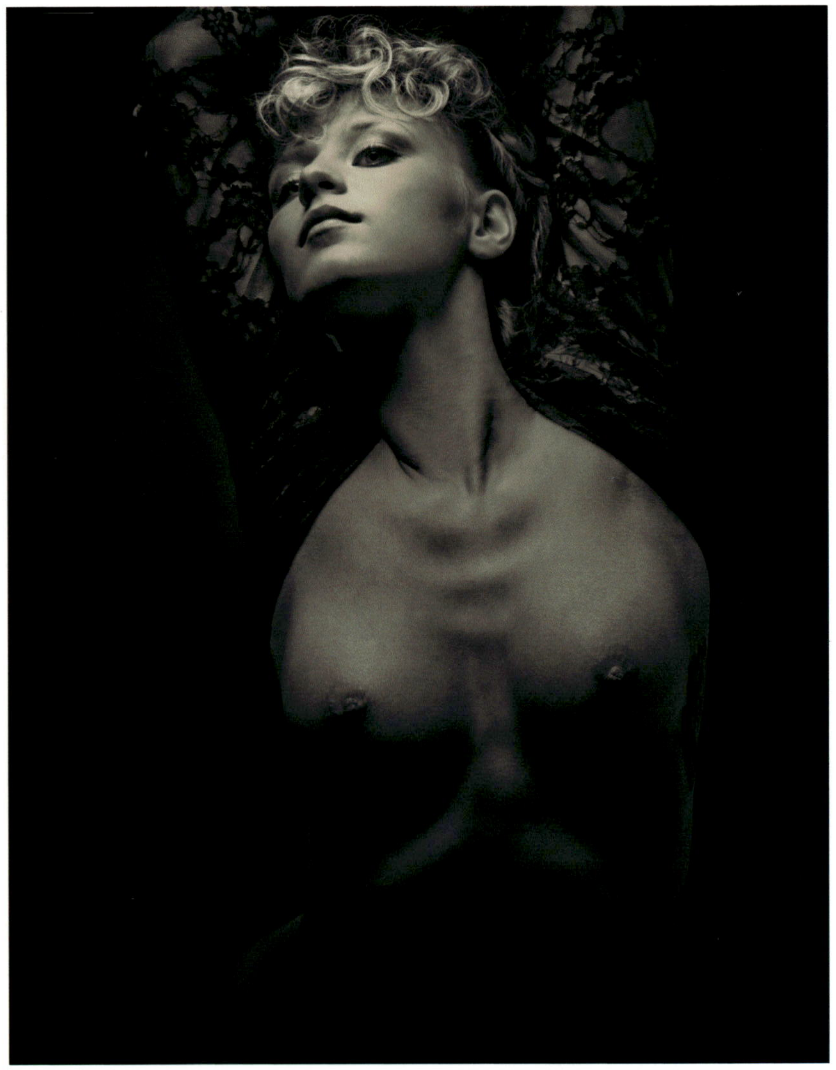

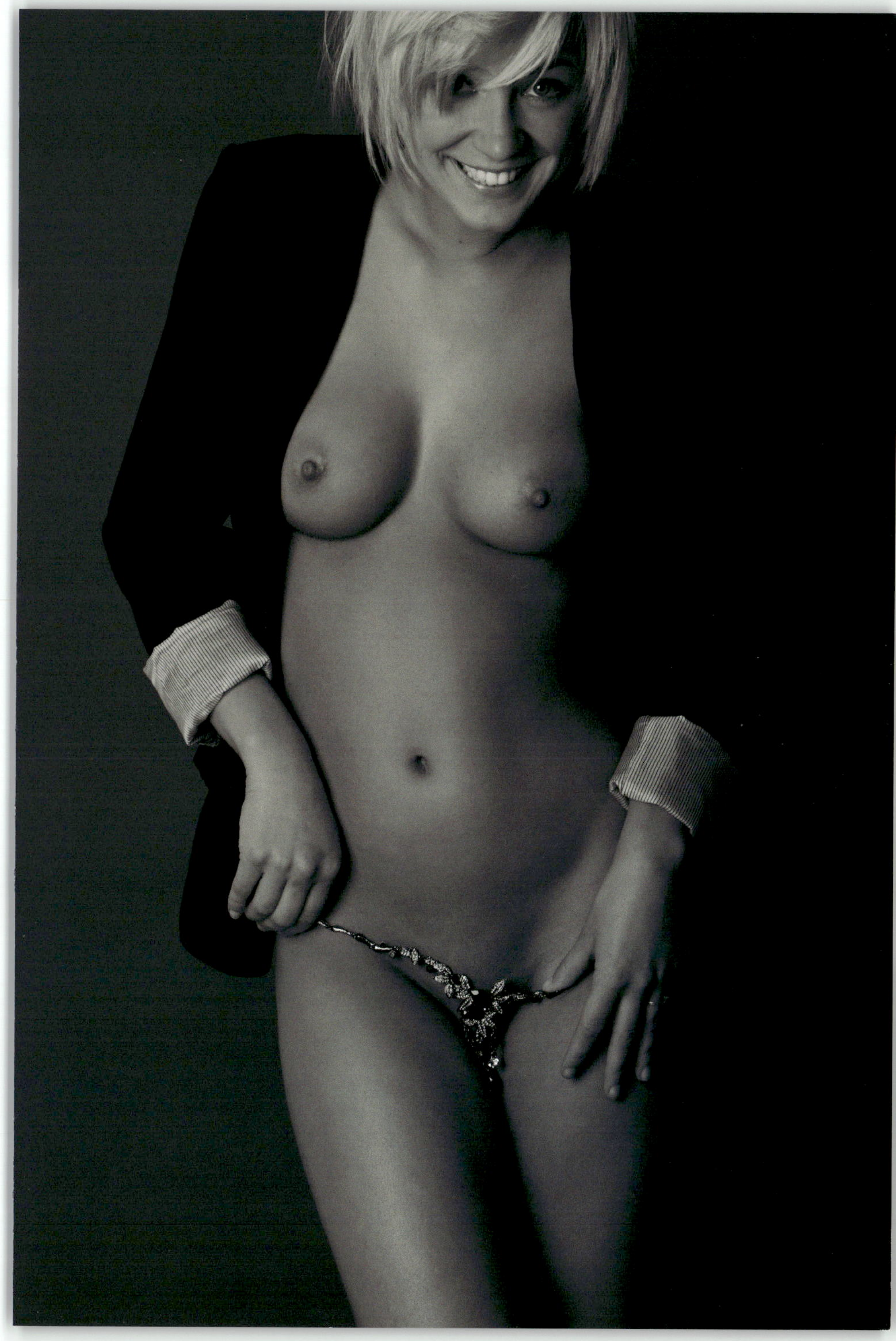

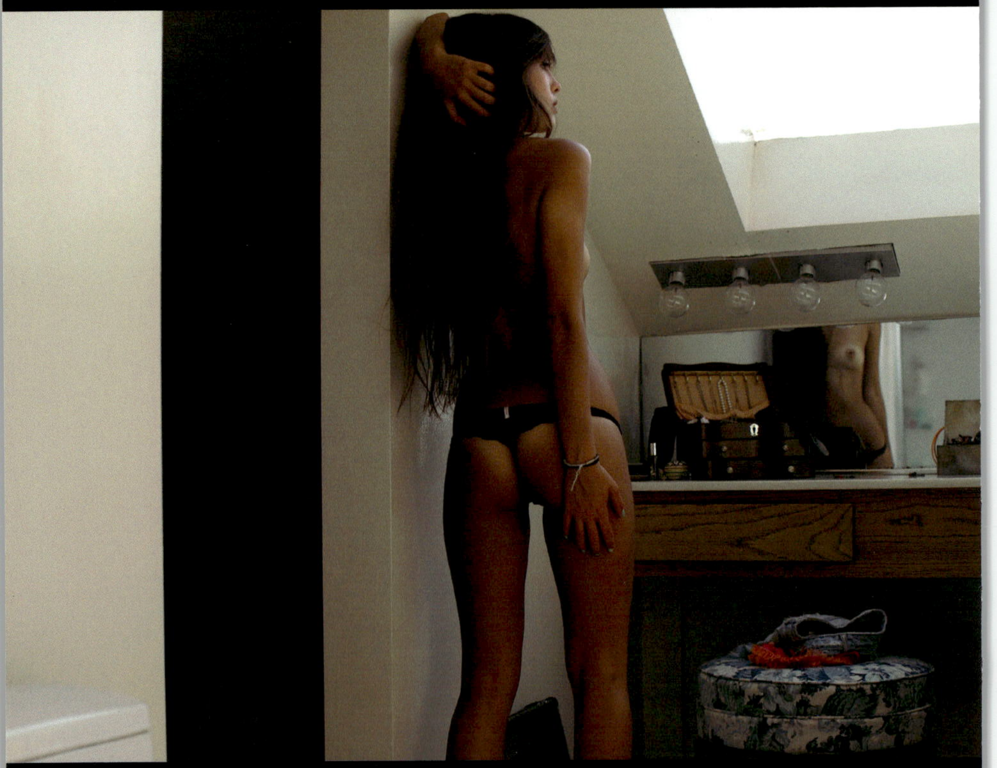

JAY CINISTA

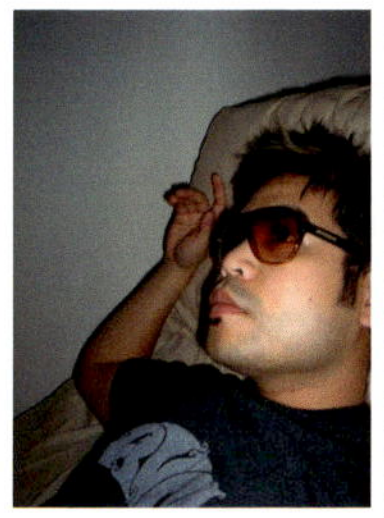

Originally from Los Angeles, Jay Cinista now lives in Las Vegas. His photography is bipolar in direction: from shooting feminine, colourful looks he has flipped to crazed, gritty concepts. Put him in a room full of liquor, a camera and a model... The results are vicious!

www.jaycinista.blogspot.com

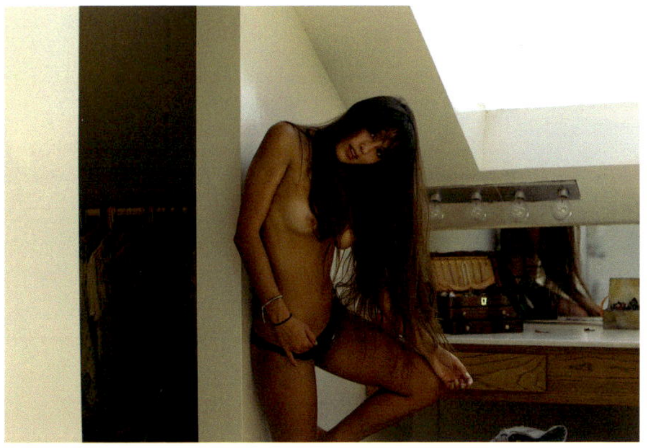

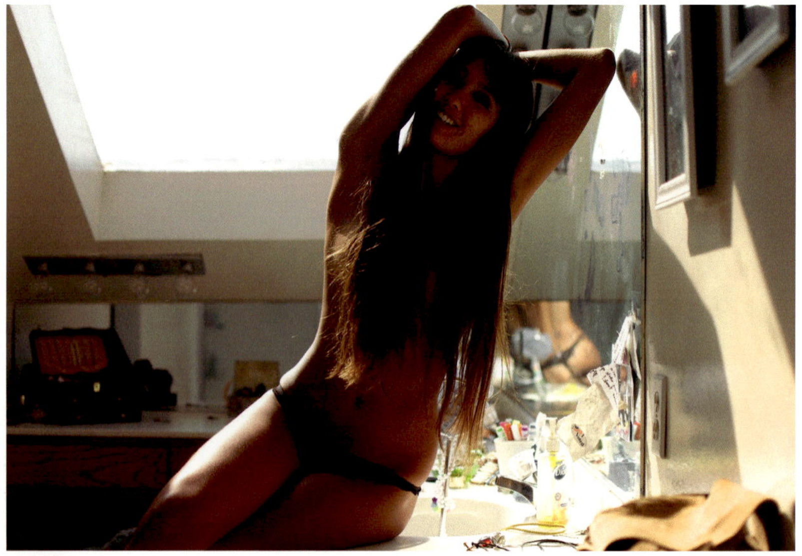
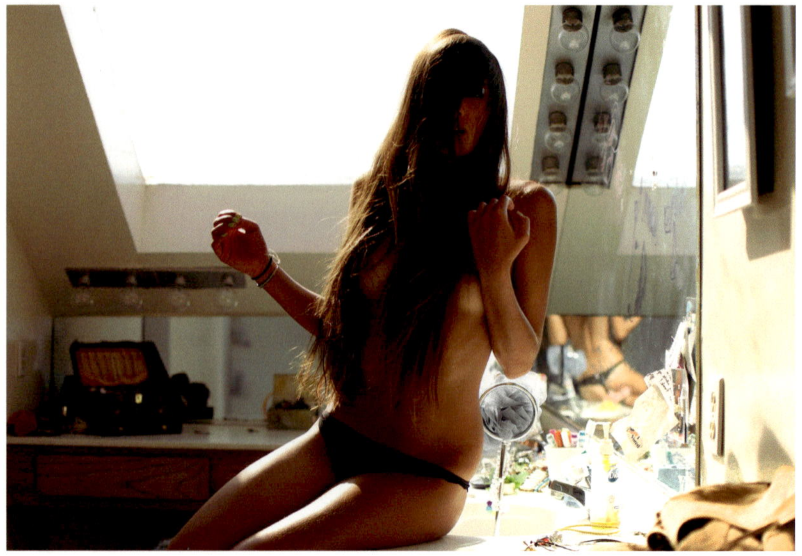

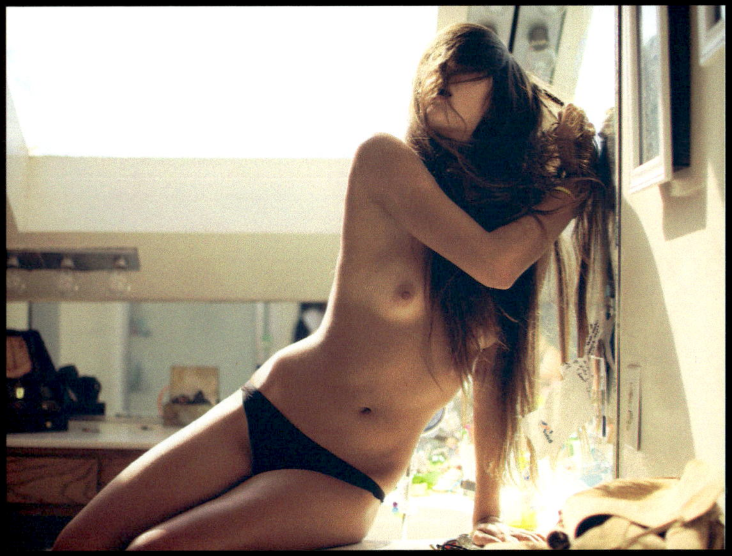

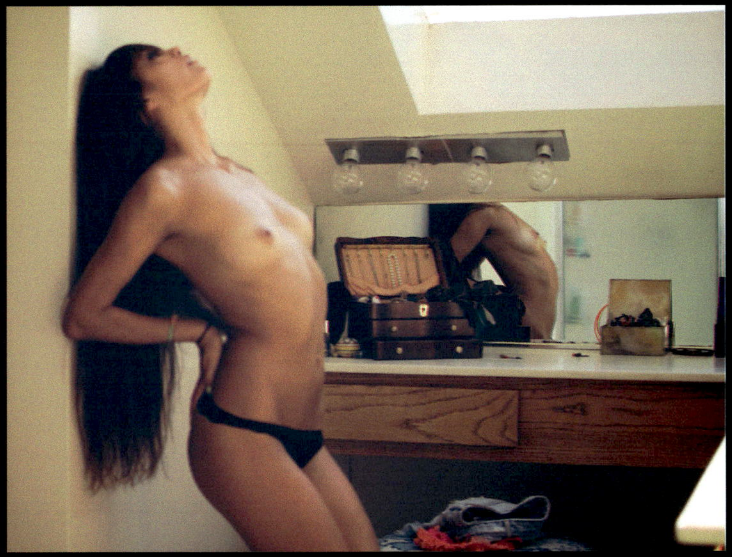

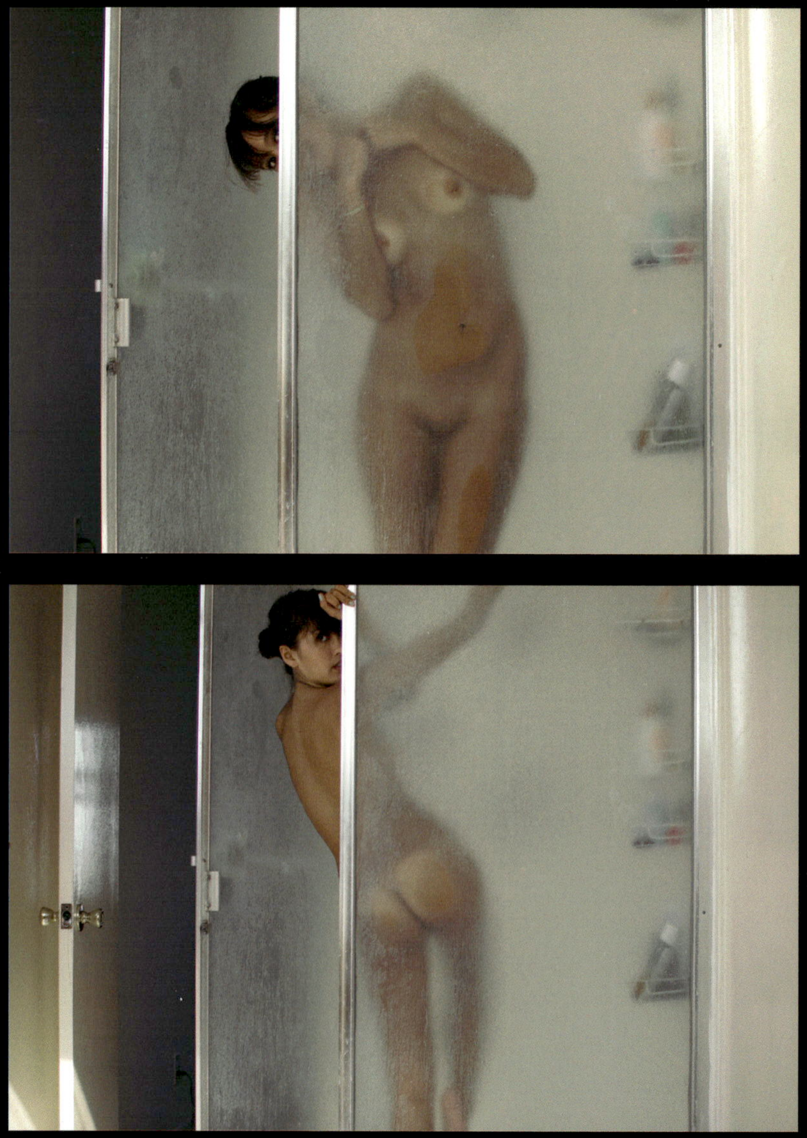

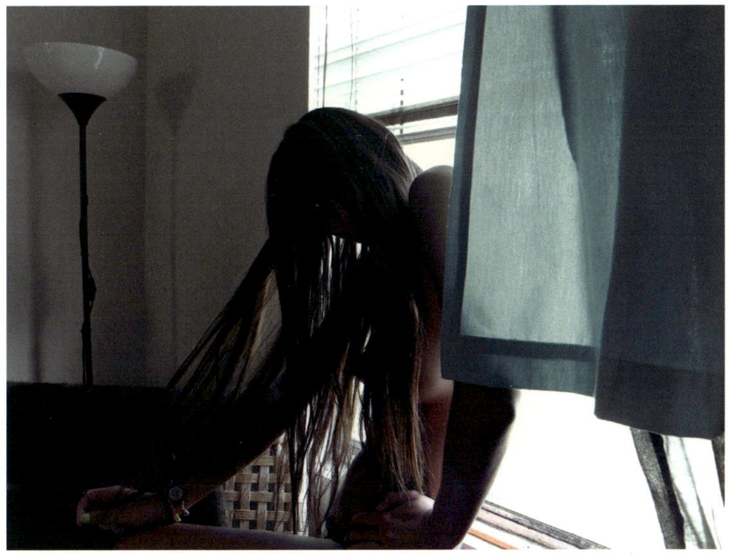

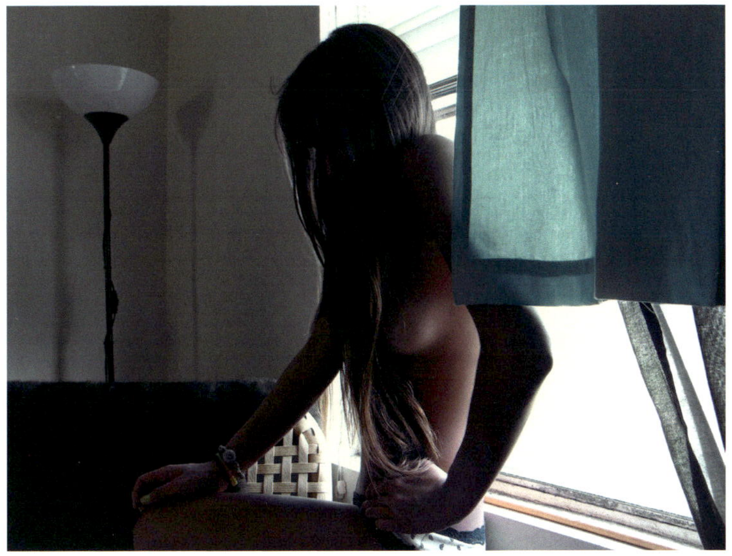

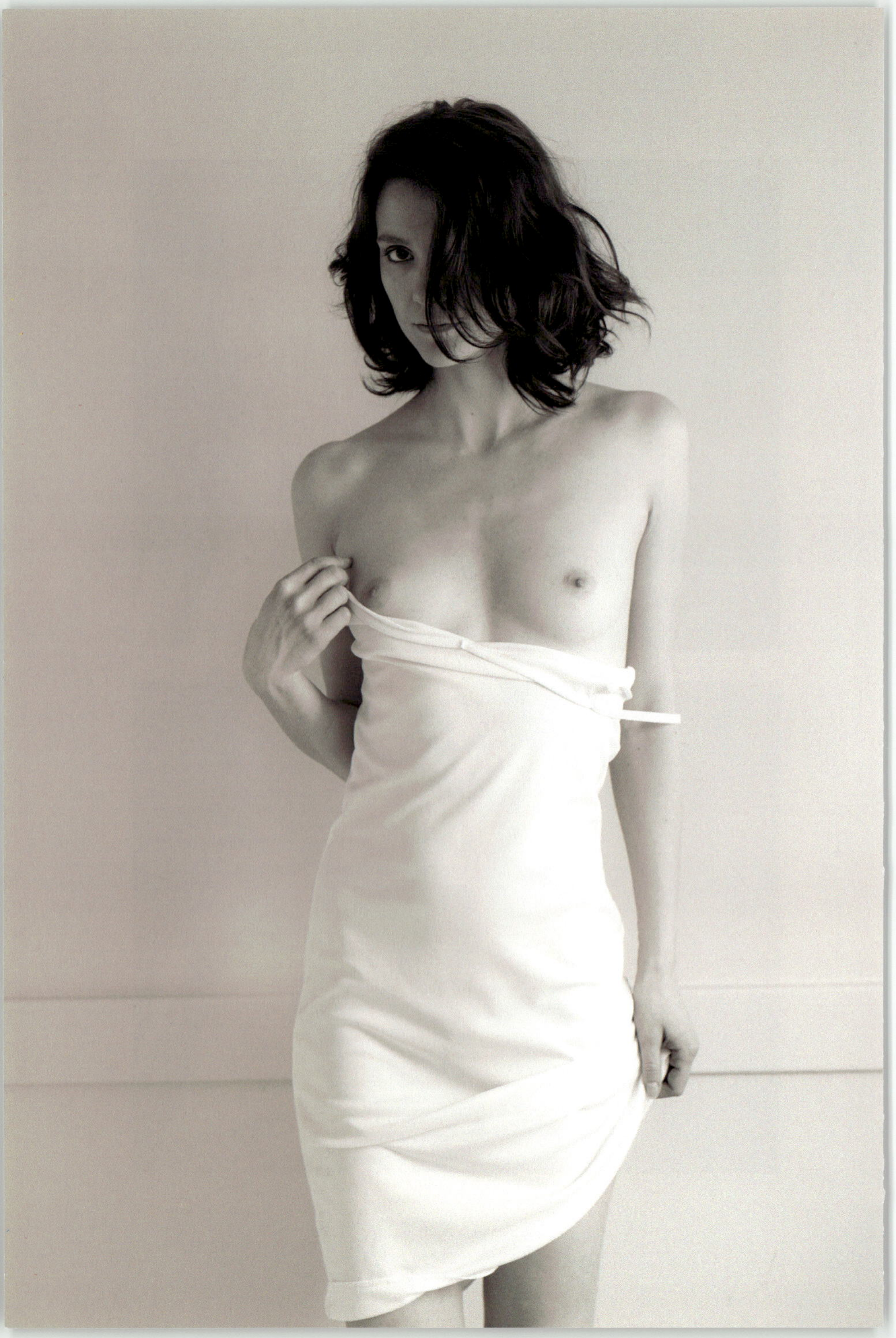

MICHAEL CORDIEZ

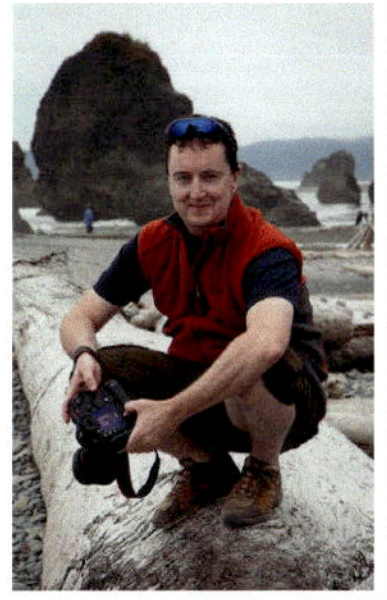

Born in Belgium in 1970, Michael Cordiez now lives in Vancouver. Although he has had a lifelong love of photographs of the nude, he has only recently begun to realize this passion. For this book he has explored the more sensual and erotic aspects of photography. Michael's work is soft, beautiful, honest and natural, and he strives to find the connection between viewer and subject. In his more sensual shots he looks for the intimate and the self-assured, which he captures with a slightly voyeuristic yet sensitive eye.

Michael first worked with Nujen in 2011 and the connection was instantaneous. Since then they have collaborated almost two dozen times and he cherishes her versatility, openness and trust. "We don't fear failing together when we are creating."

www.cordiez.com

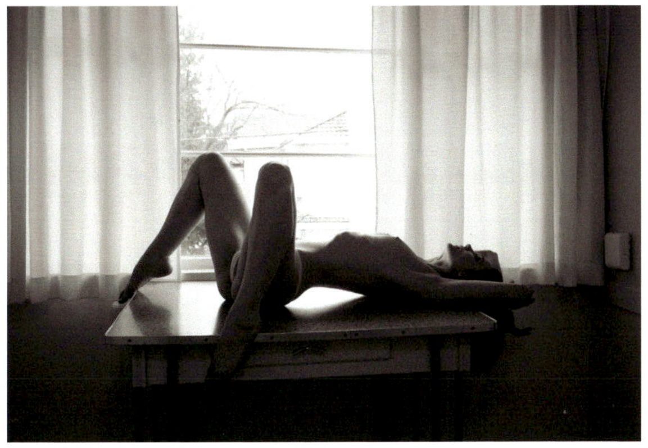

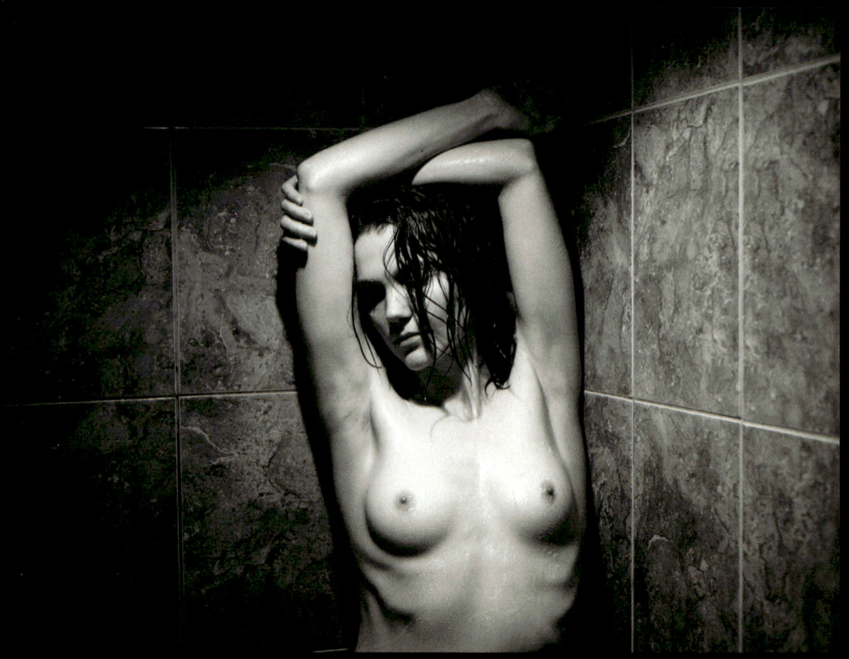

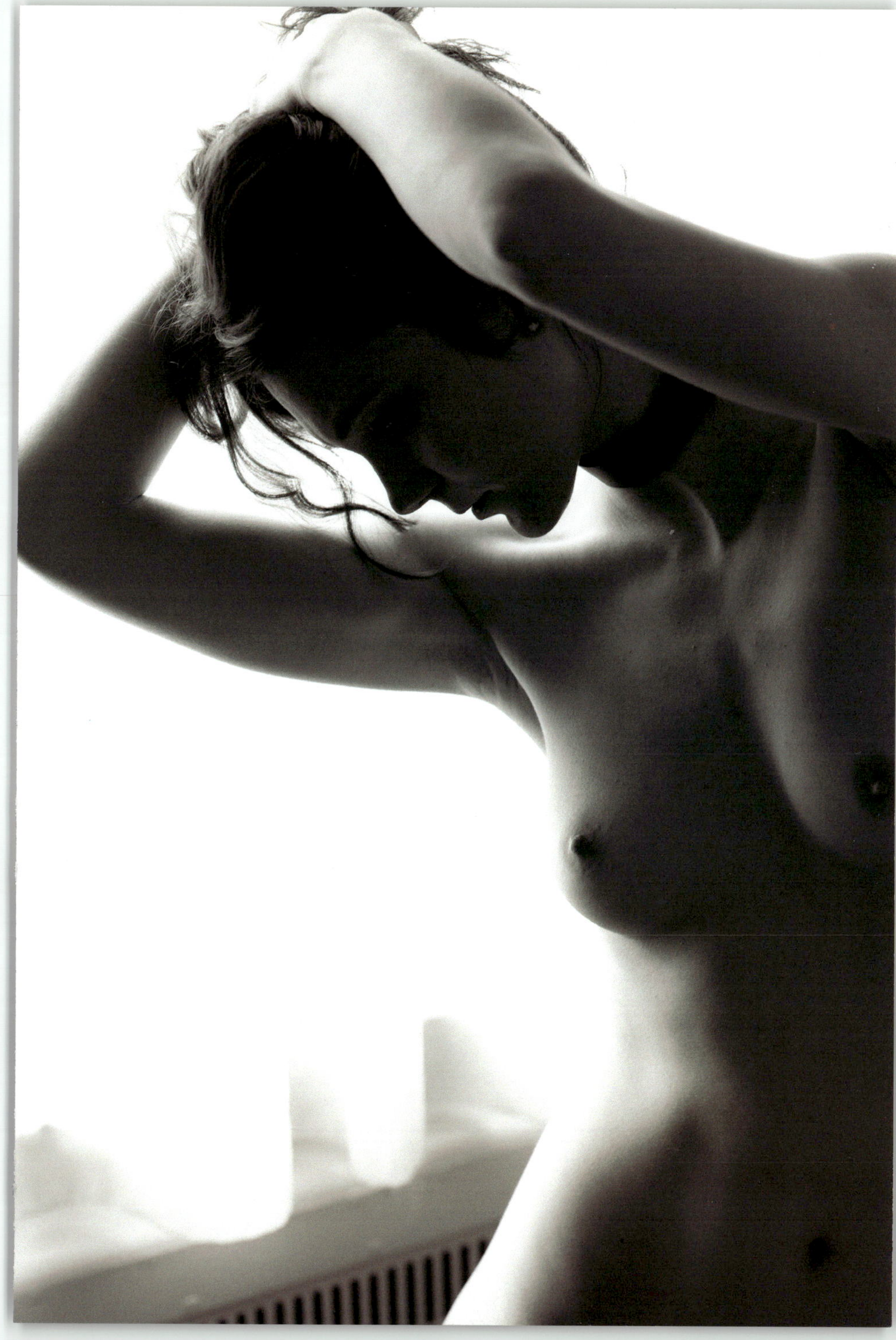

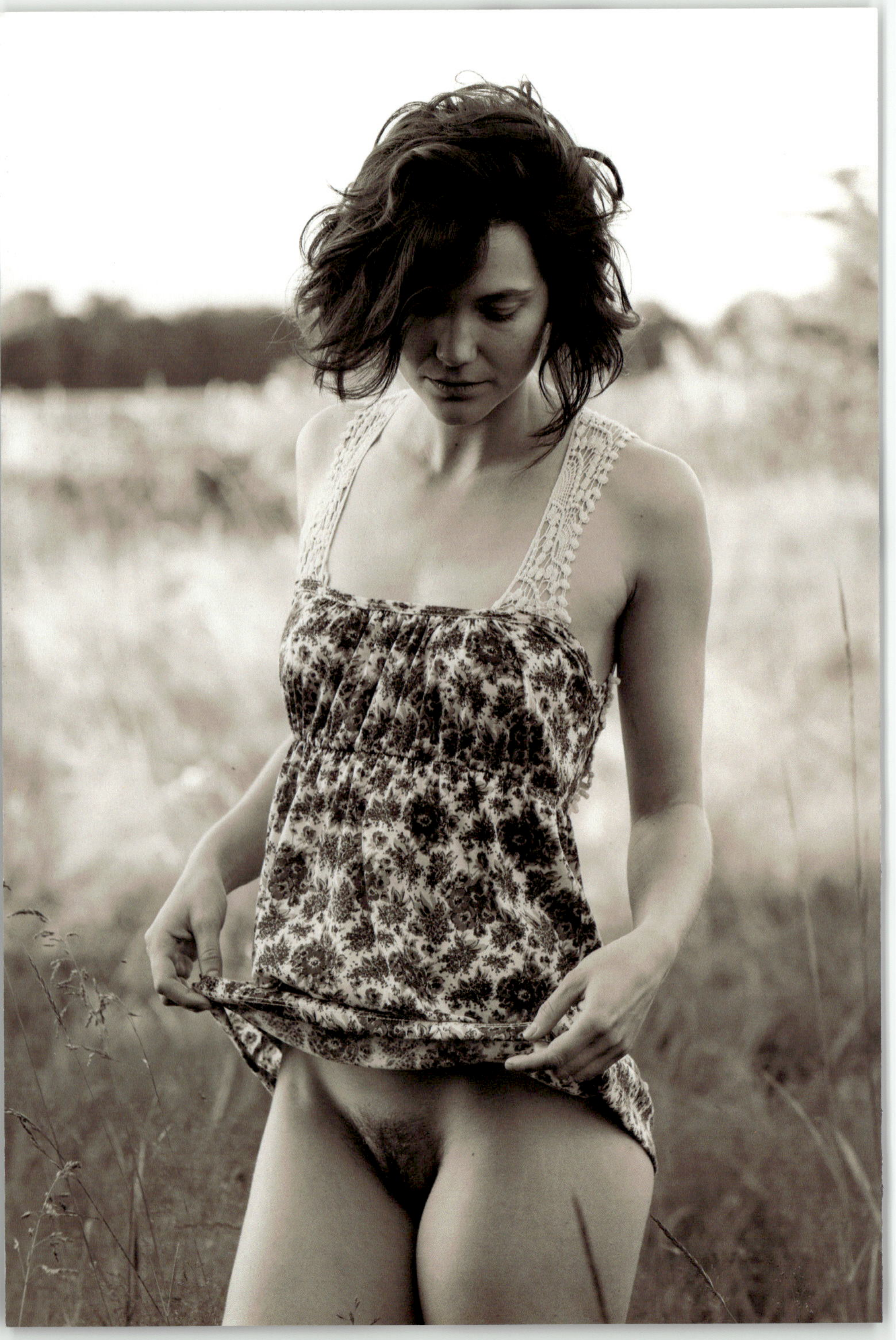

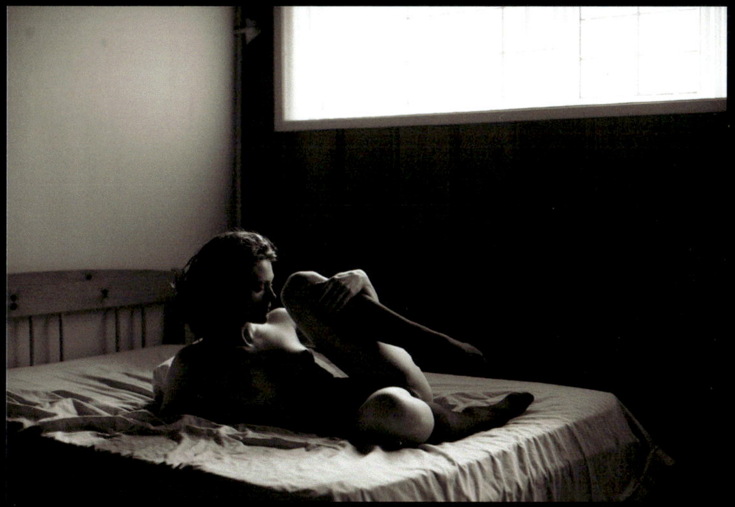

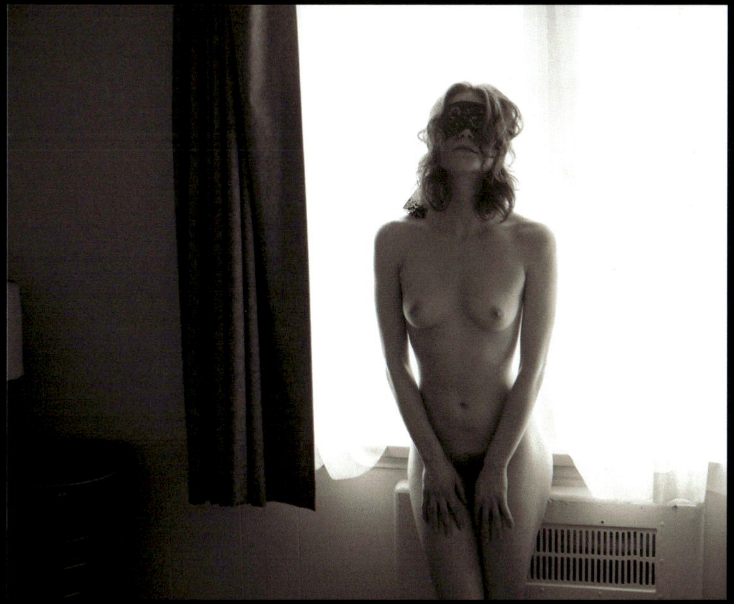

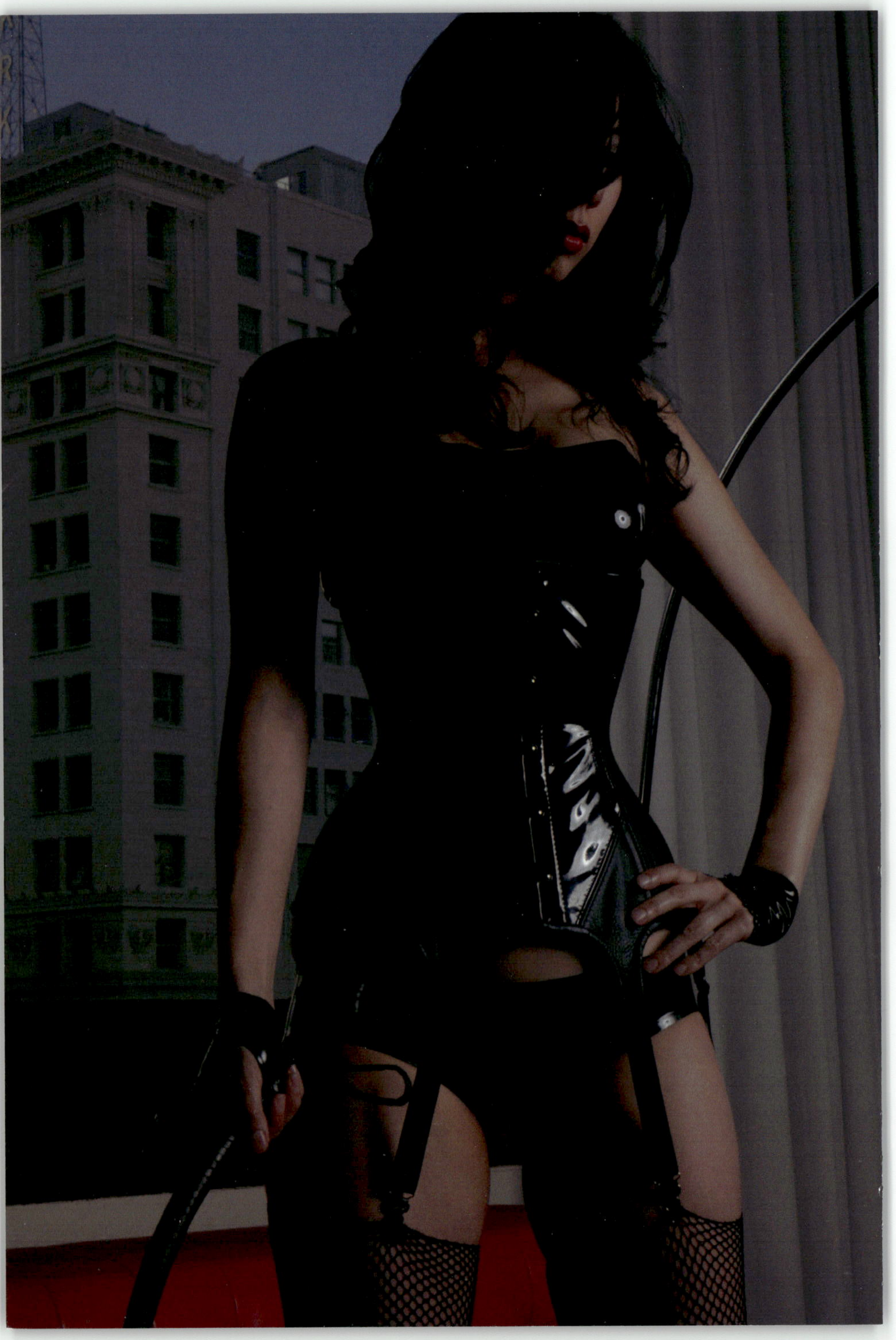

TOMMY CUELLAR

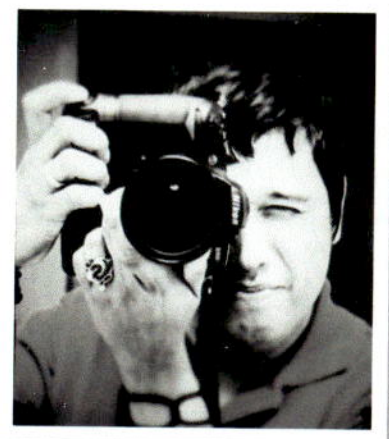

Los Angeles-based Tommy Cuellar began photography at an early age. Later, while teaching English in Japan, he shot street fashion and documented the underground goth and fetish scene. He credits Araki Nobuyoshi and Daido Moriyama with inspiring his photographic style.

Tommy's work has appeared in *The Mammoth Book of New Erotic Photography*, *Domination Directory International* magazine, *Japanzine* and other books and magazines around the world. He specializes in shooting website gallery and advertisement photos for sex workers who wish to maintain anonymity. Most of his work is shooting professional dominatrices in their dungeons, often during live BDSM sessions.

Here Tommy showcases Keva I. Lee. She personifies his ideal of beauty in the context of BDSM, bringing together the hardness of domination and the softness of sensuality.

www.modelmayhem.com/tommycuellar

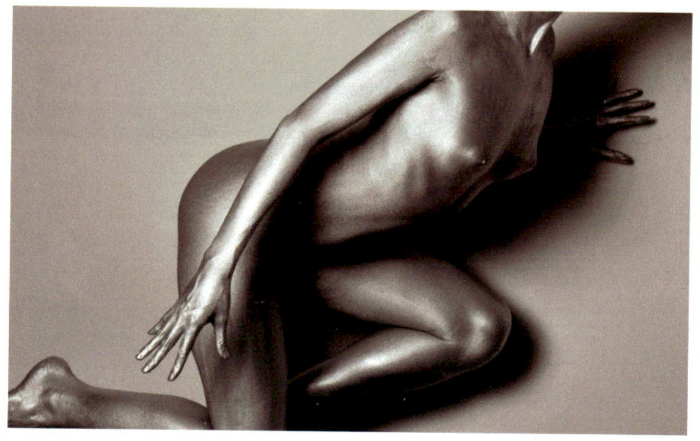

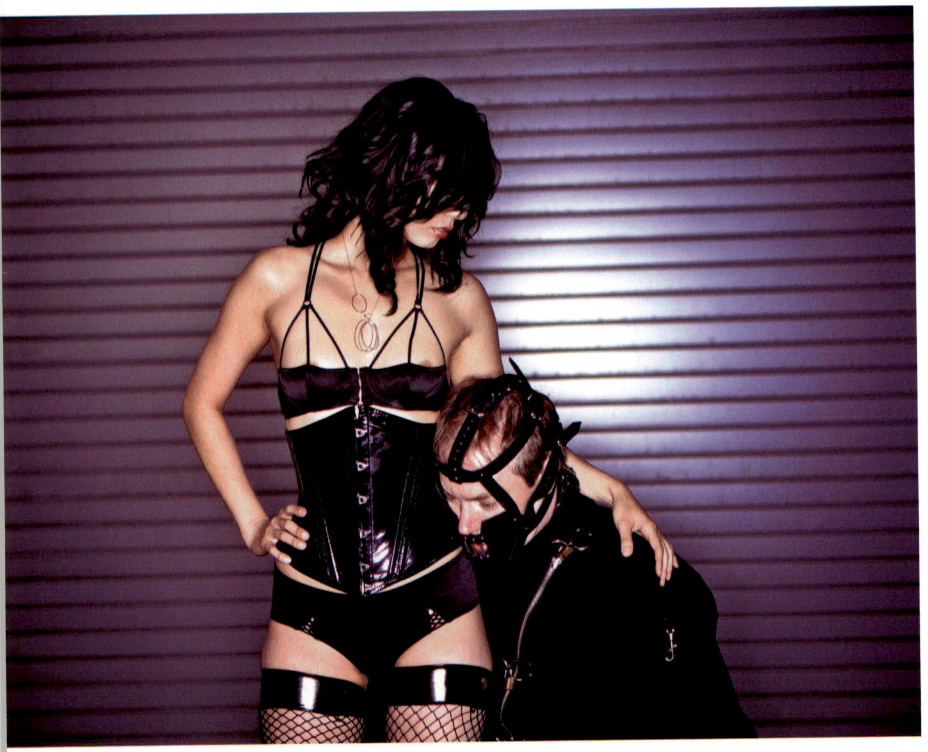

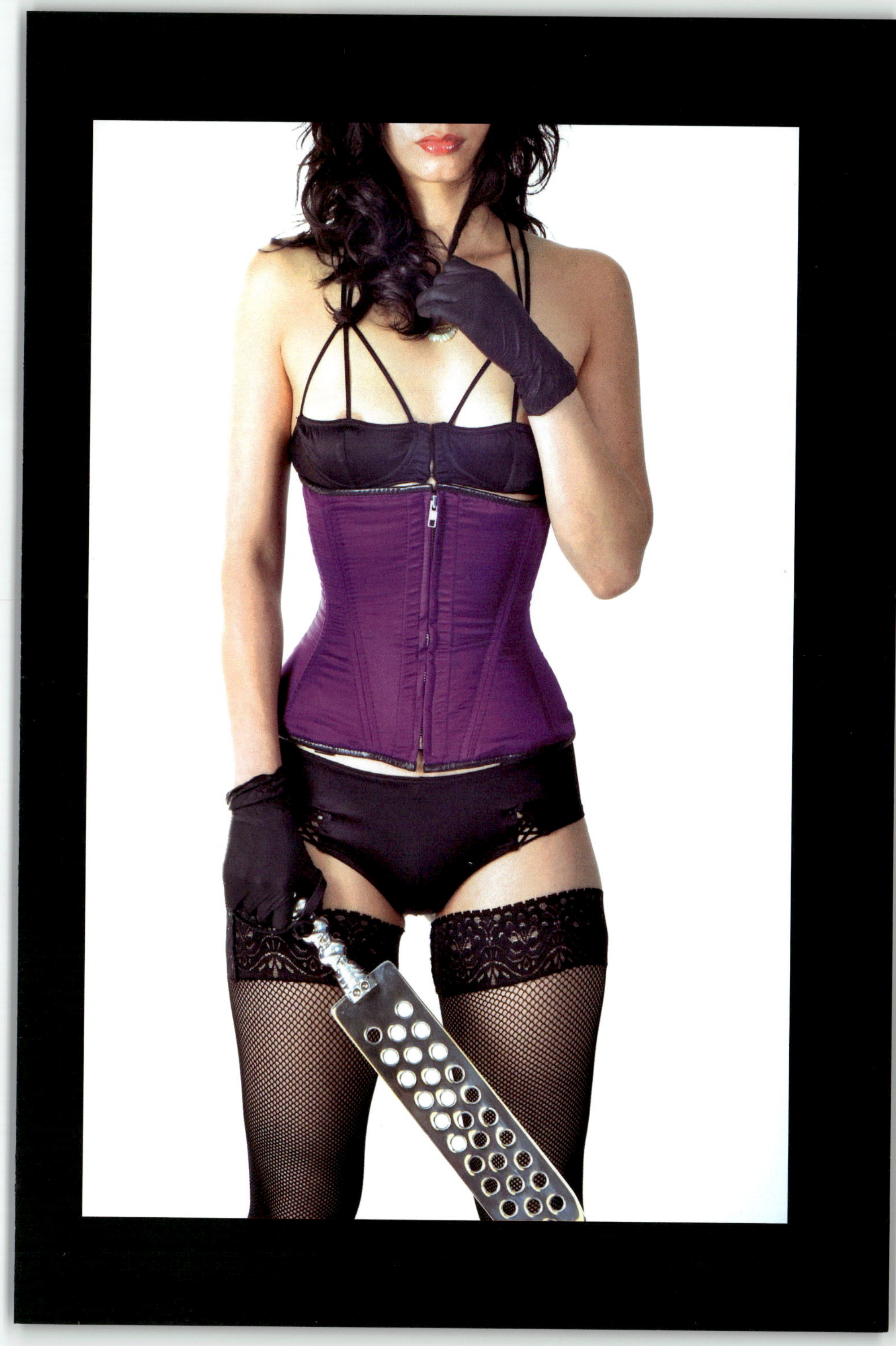

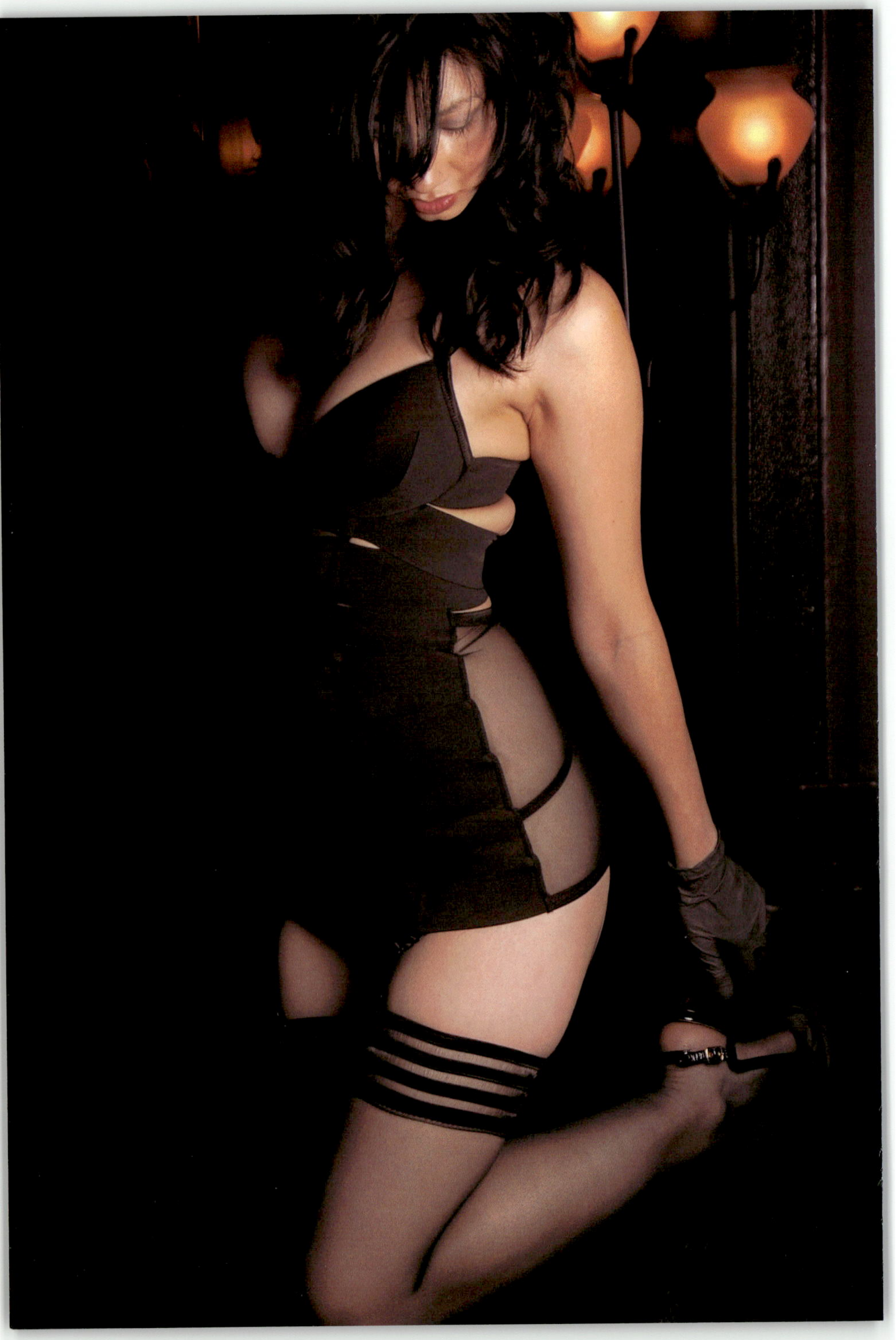

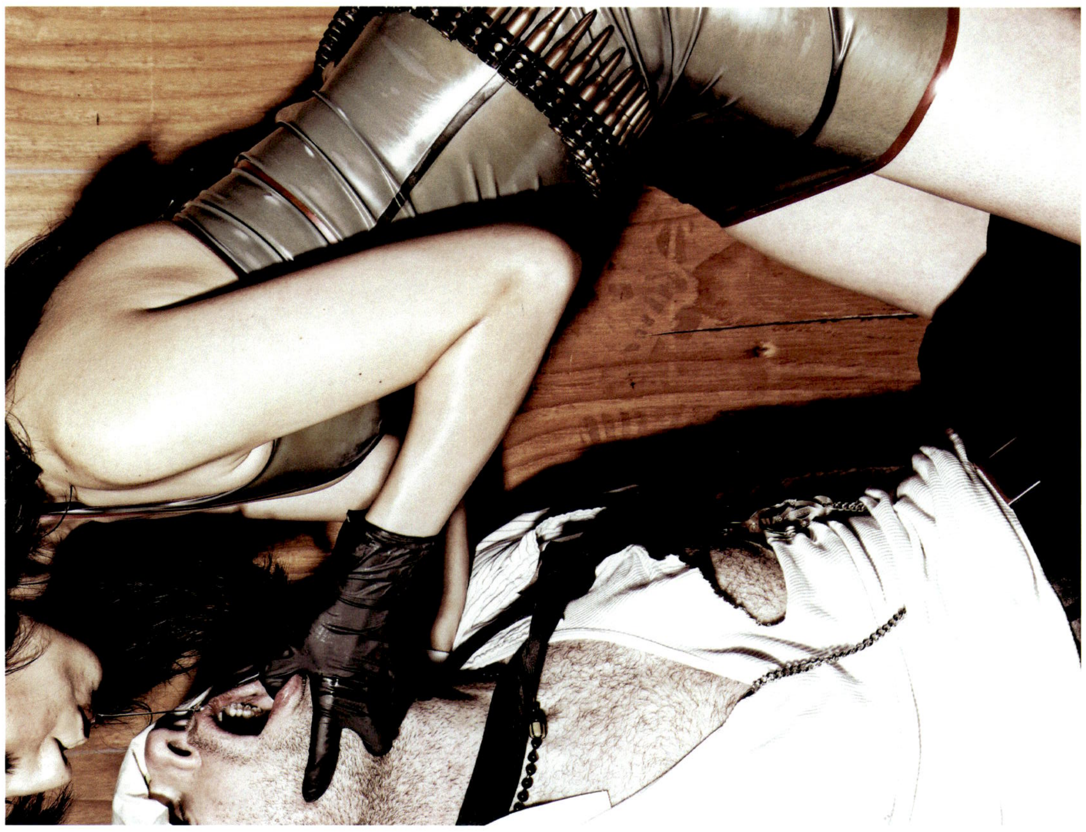

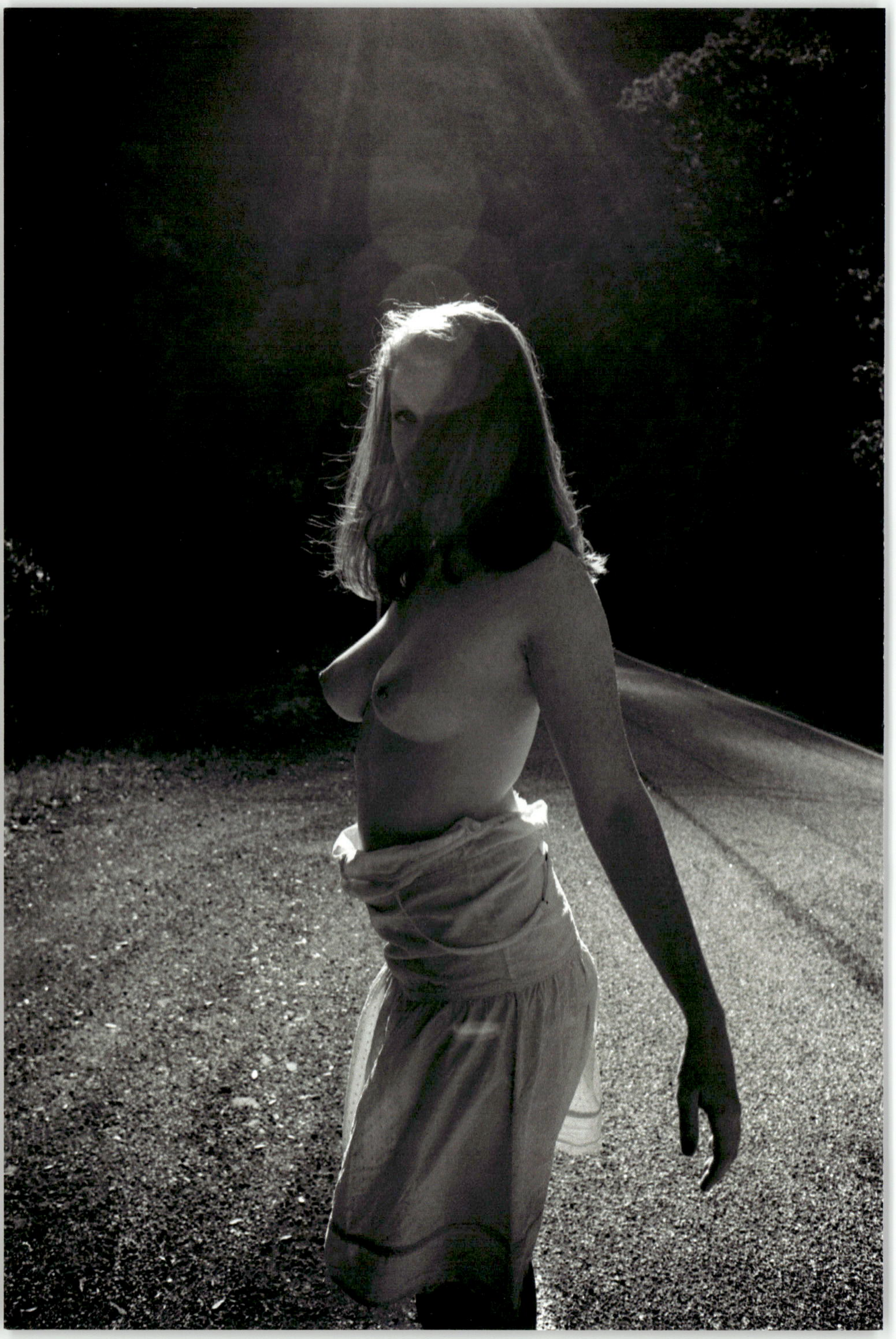

JAMES DENNIS

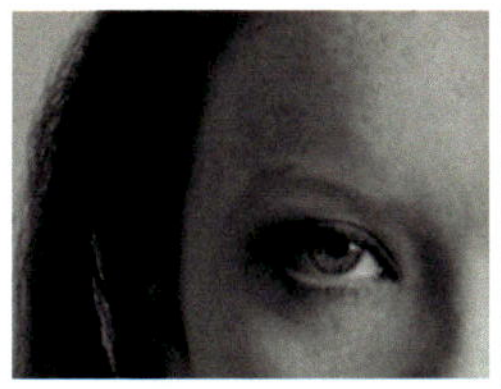

Born in Jamaica in 1964, James Dennis lives in the San Francisco Bay area. He started photography in his teens but took a long break to pursue a career as a musician and software engineer. Music required too much time, however, and he returned to photography when his love of it was rekindled by the digital camera revolution.

James concentrates on portraiture, erotica and artistic photography. He is inspired by many of today's great photographers as well as the personalities and inner beauty he finds in his models. He seeks a sensuality that maintains an innocence however graphic the image. He now shoots most of his work on film and favours B&W for capturing his experiences of the world as moments of shadow, light, love and beauty.

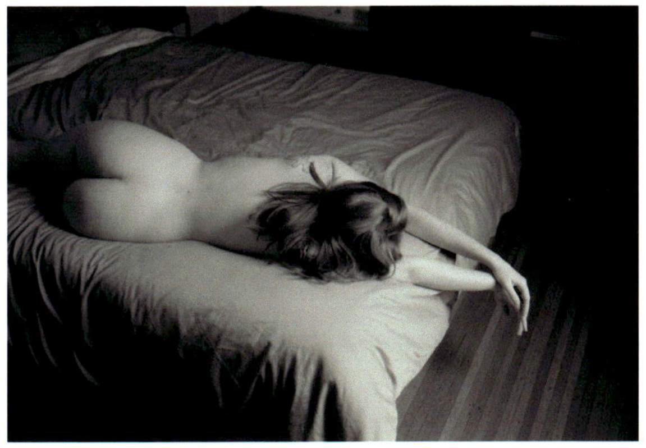

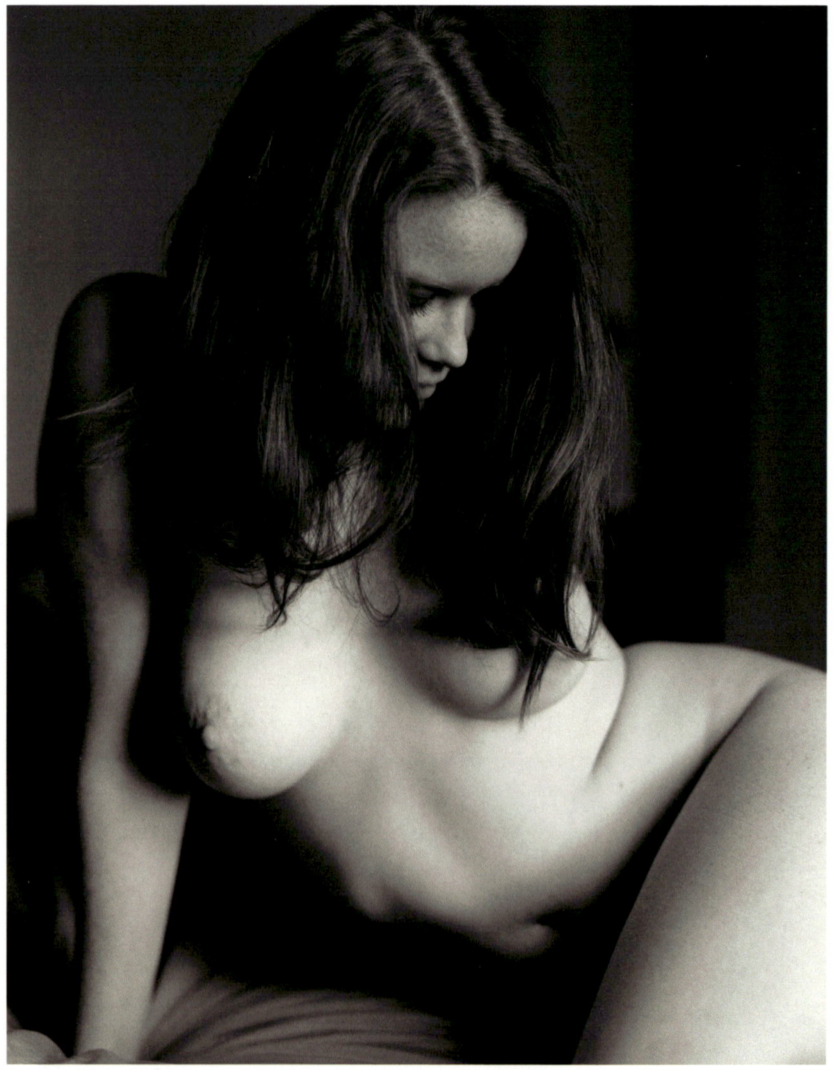

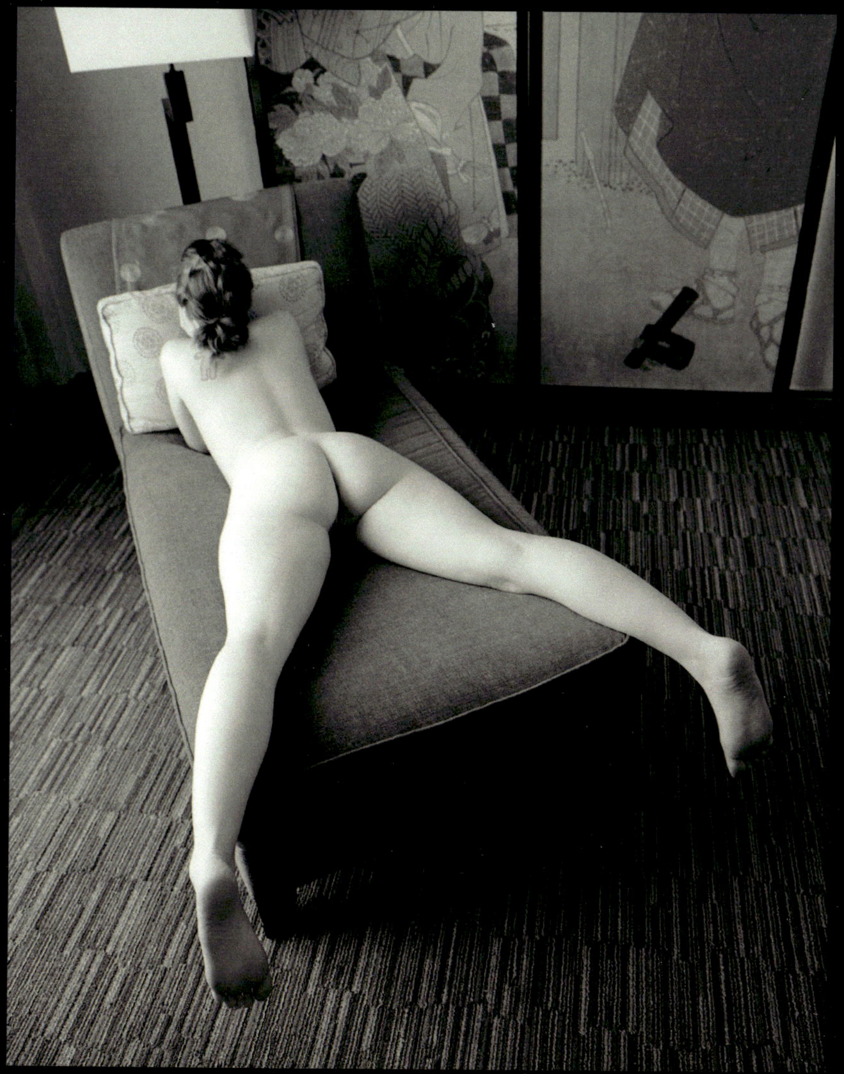

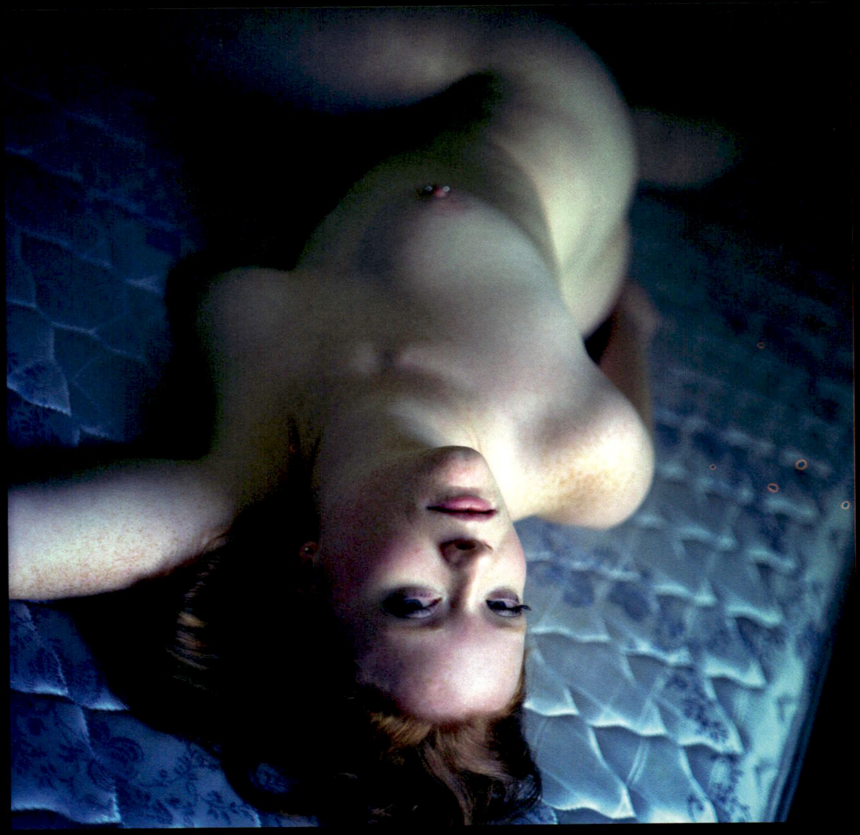

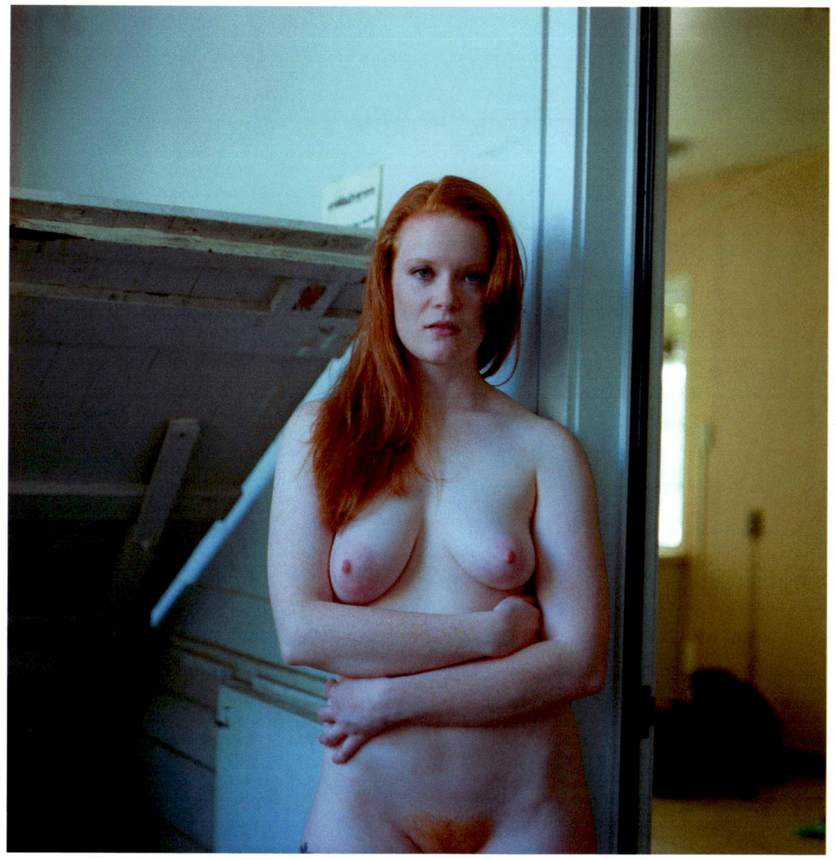

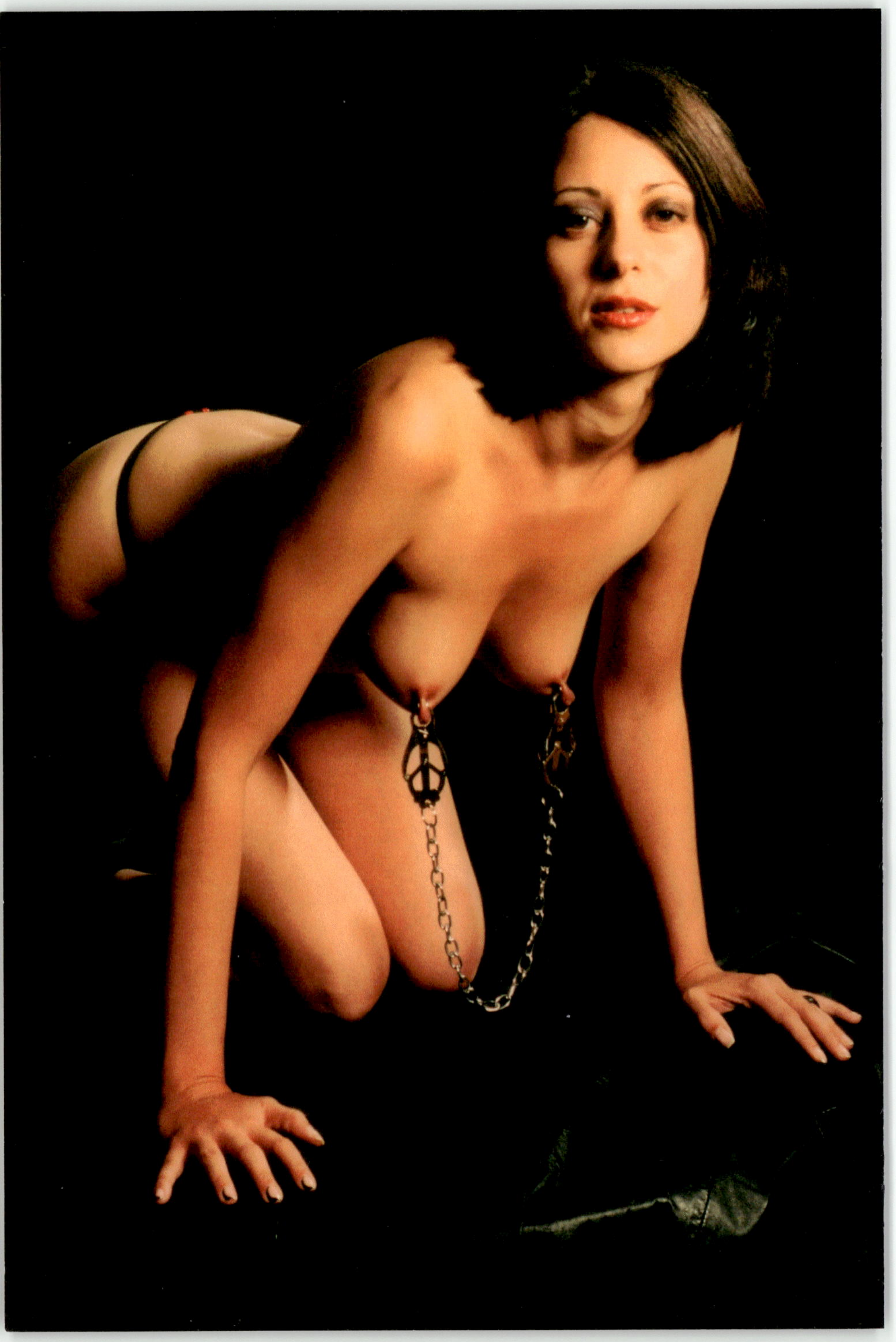

STEVE DT

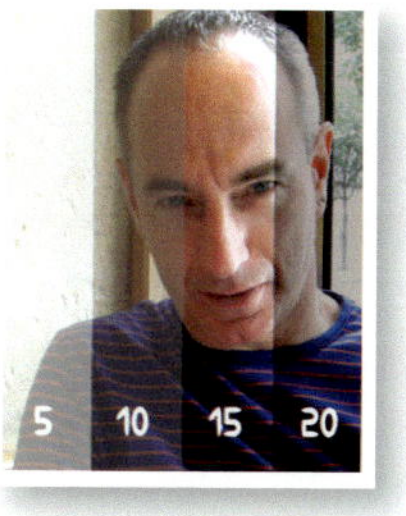

Steve DT is a former music photographer for *Melody Maker* and *Vinyl*. His interests in erotic photography began with exposure to Man Ray, Brassaï and Helmut Newton. His photography embraces portraiture, glamour and fetish. He prefers to shoot themed projects, for example 'Call Me', about escort cards in London's telephone boxes.

Steve's work has been exhibited in the UK, Germany and the USA, and has appeared in magazines and books. His first book, *Personals: Desires in Print* (sdtfoto.com, 2008), coupled his images with genuine personal adult adverts. Steve has worked with his latest muse, Noemi, many times in recent years. For him it was fascination at first sight: her beauty, vibrancy, charm and her being Spanish. And Noemi enjoys the challenge whether the photography explores beauty, the unorthodox or fetish.

www.sdtfoto.com

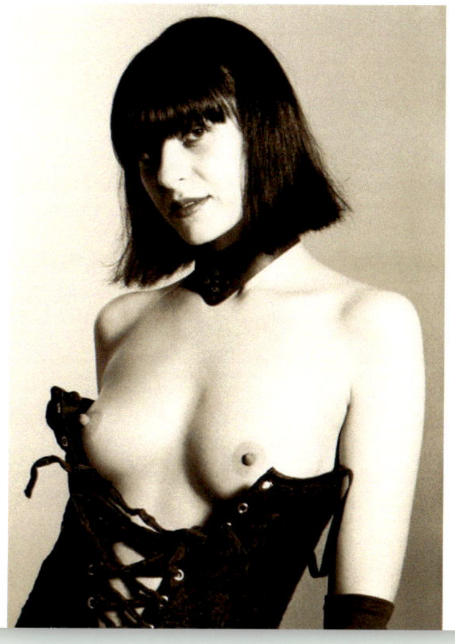

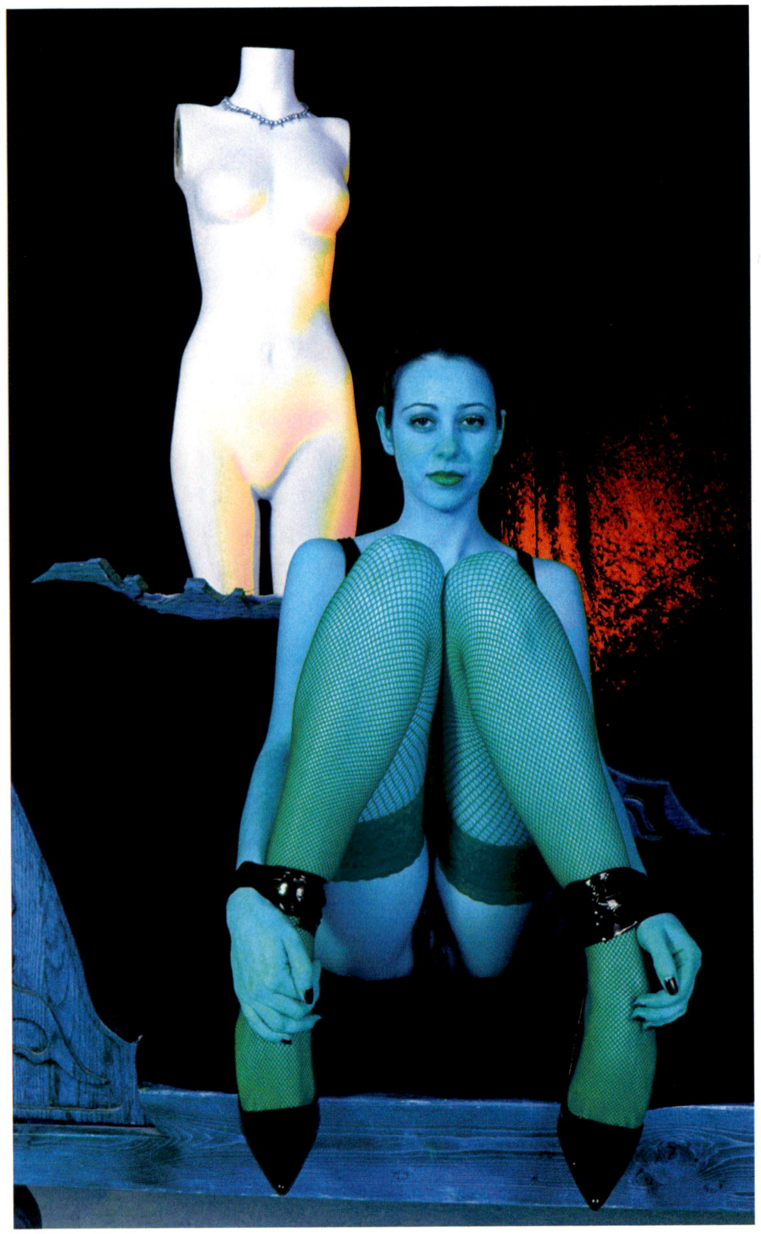

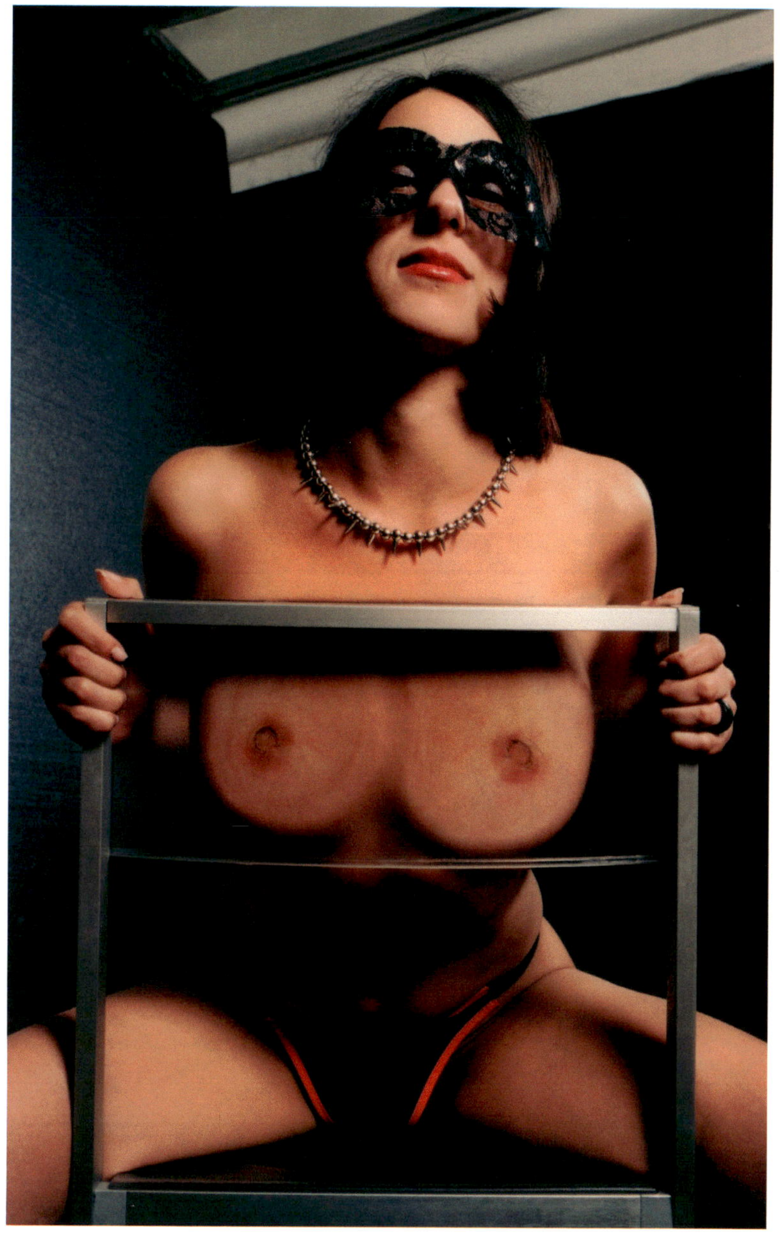

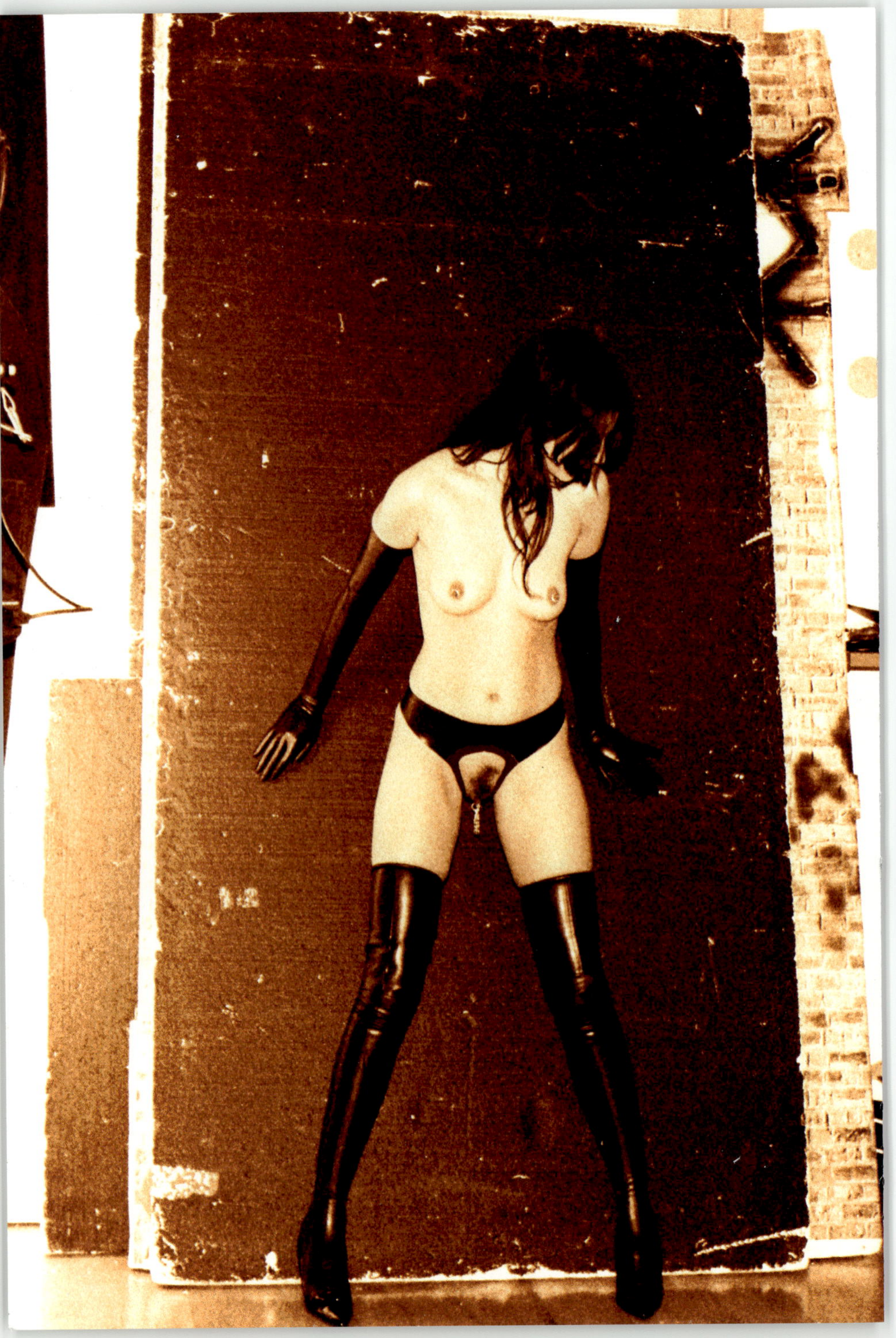

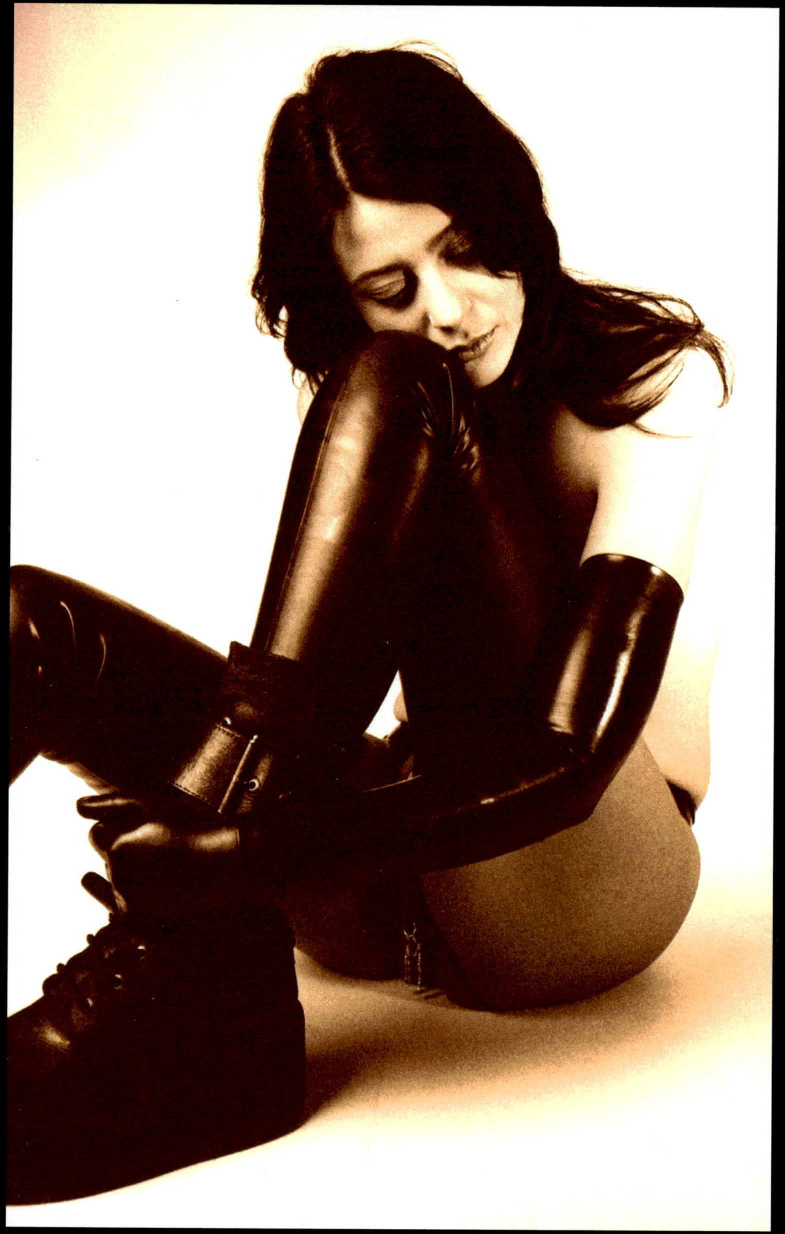

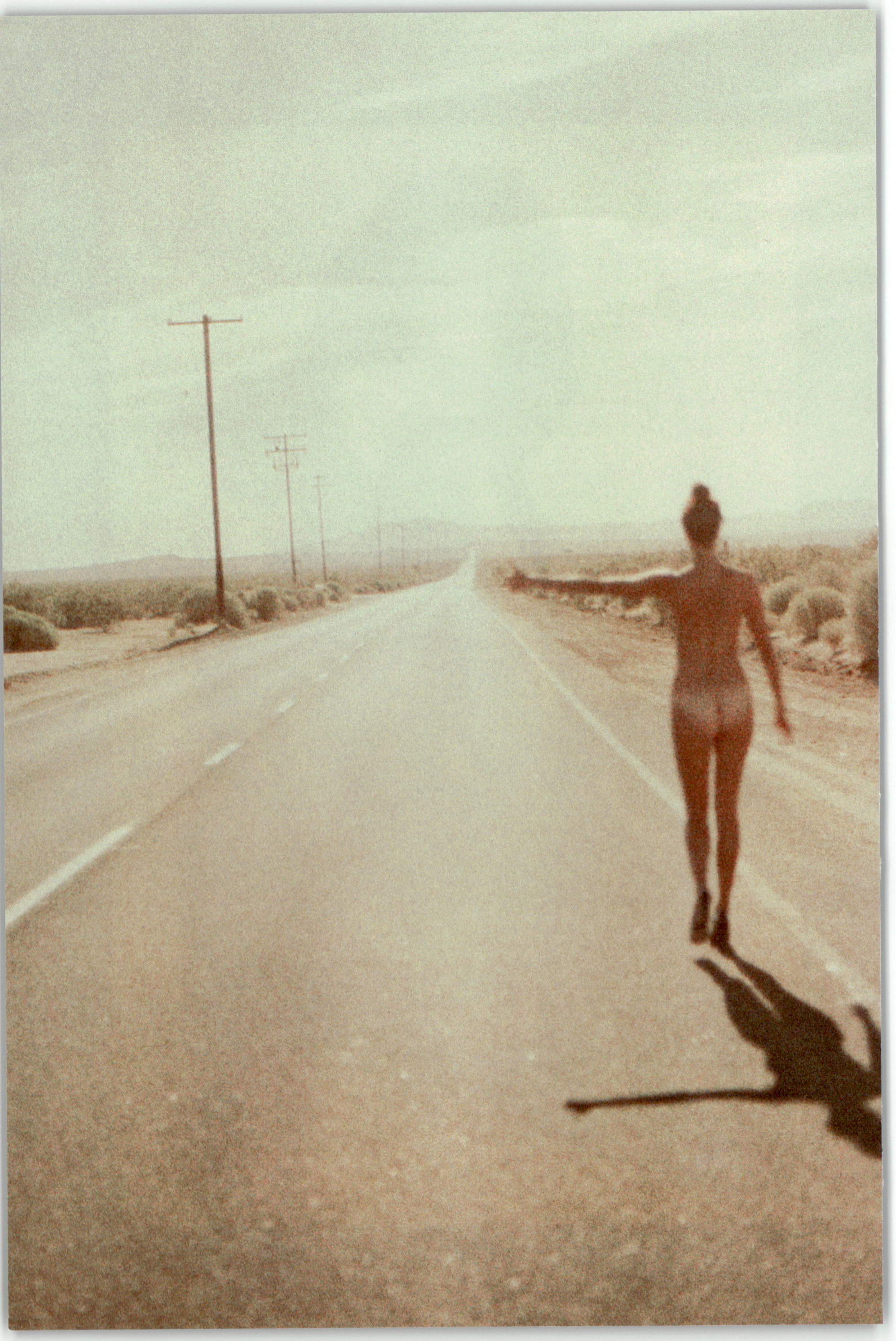

MEGAN K. EAGLES

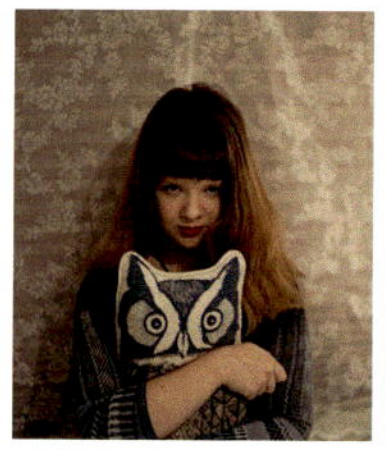

London-based Megan K. Eagles is a self-taught photographer. Her model is her best friend and muse, glamour model Seren Gibson. Seren has been on the covers of magazines including *Maxim*, *FHM* and *Front*. Both long for a time when Photoshop didn't exist, tits were real and bushes were big. They share a love for the all-natural seventies Playmate and want to bring her back to the modern day with their artistic collaboration.

www.mkeagles.co.uk

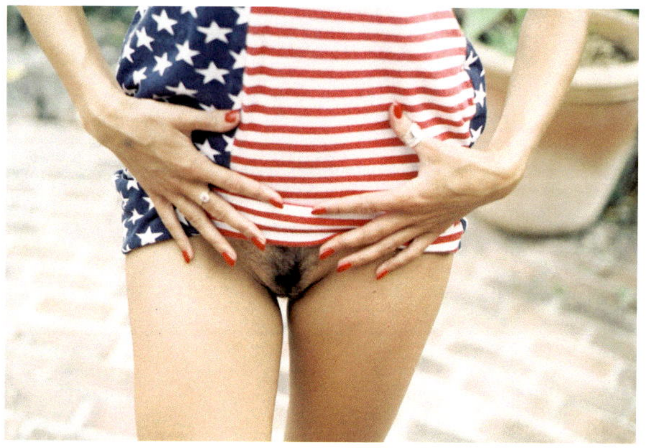

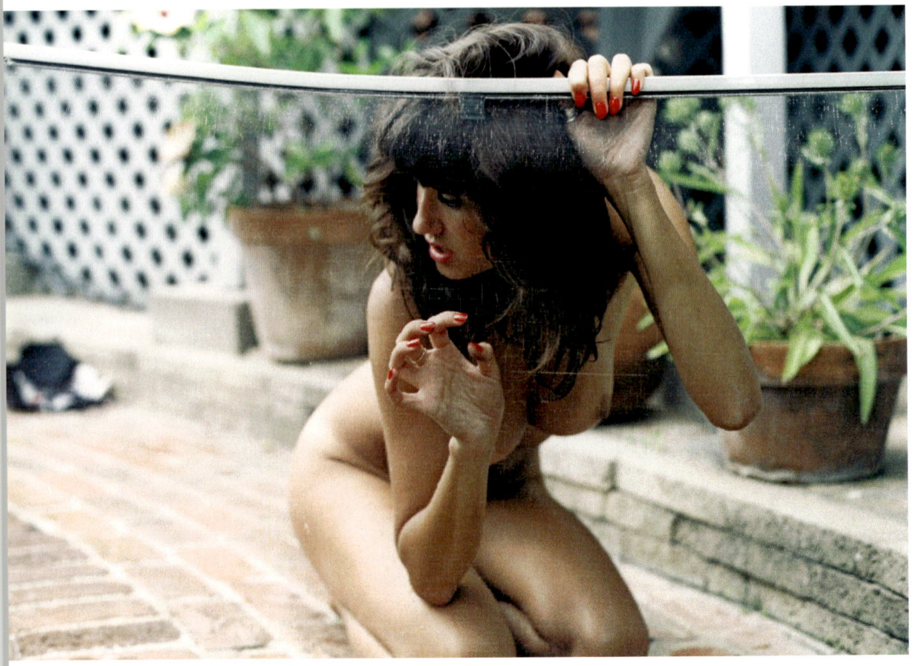

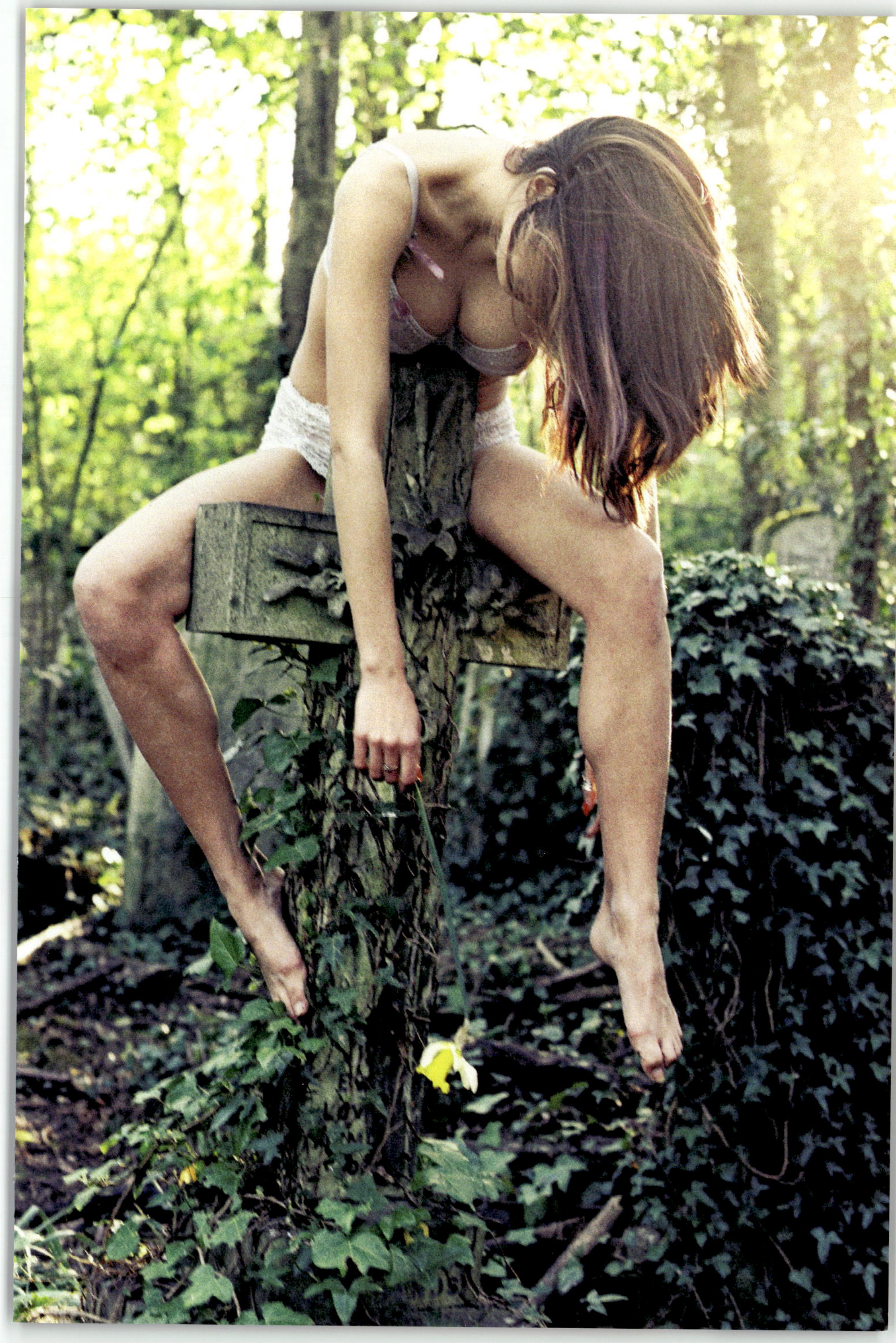

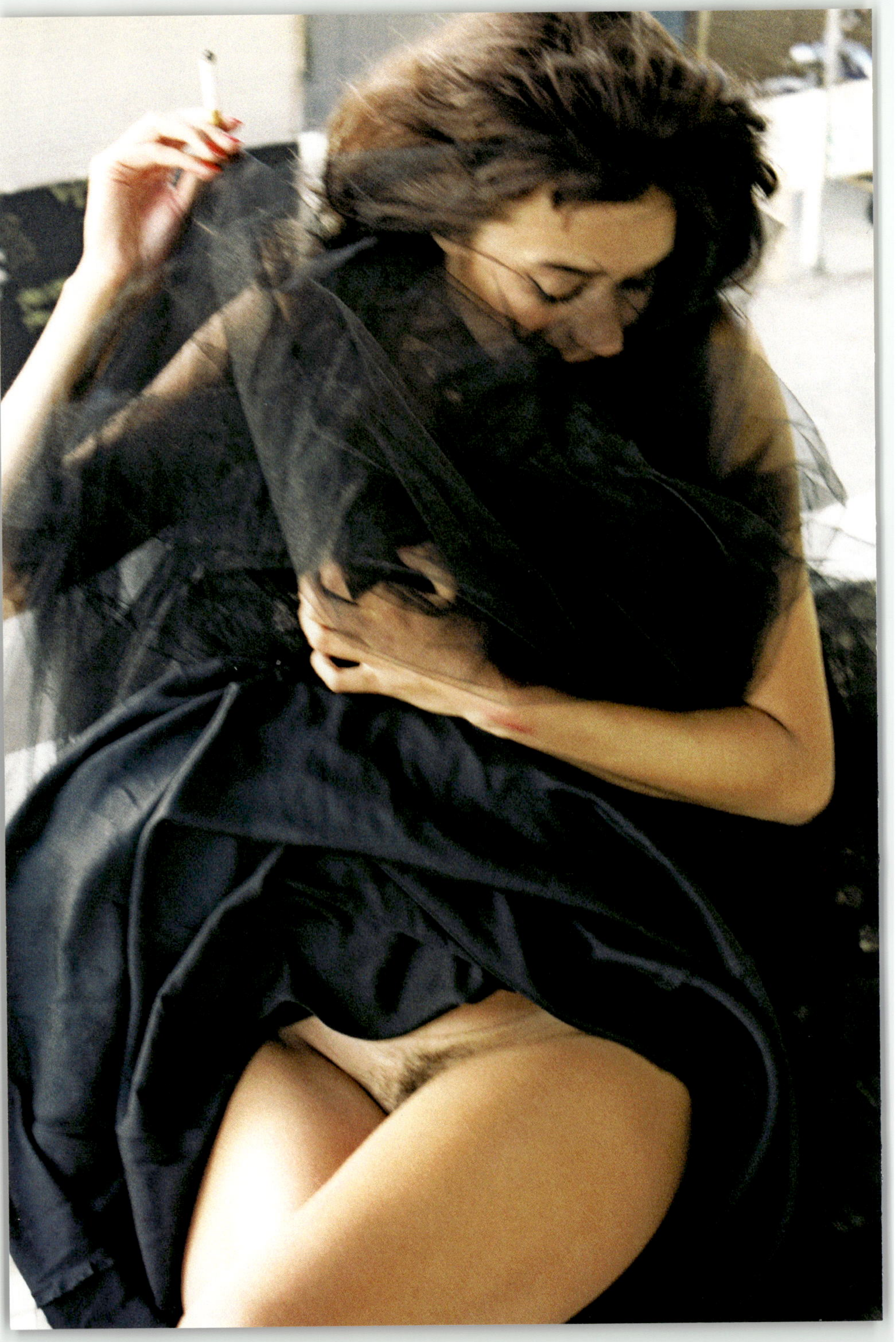

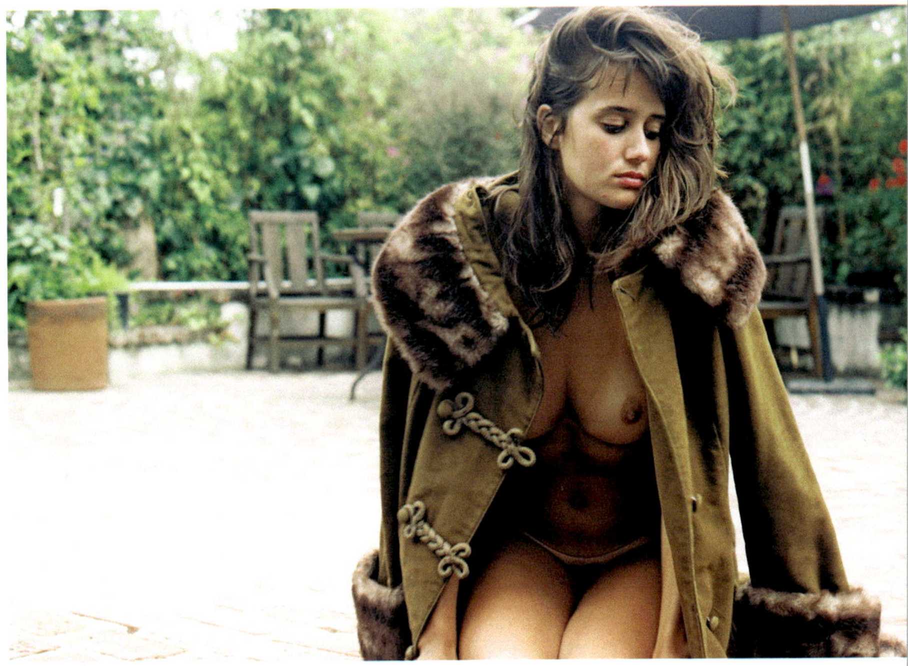

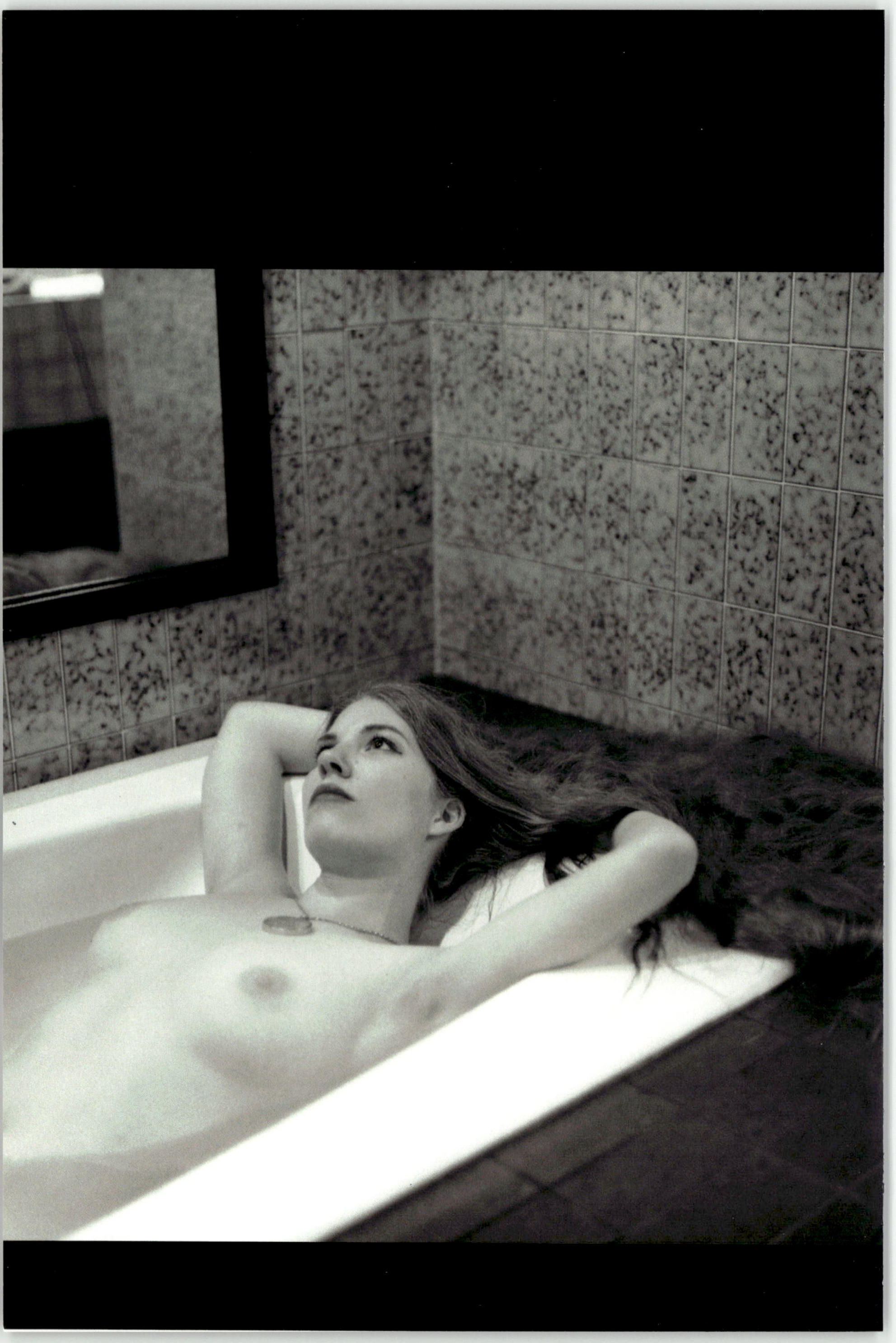

ERIN THE ARTIST

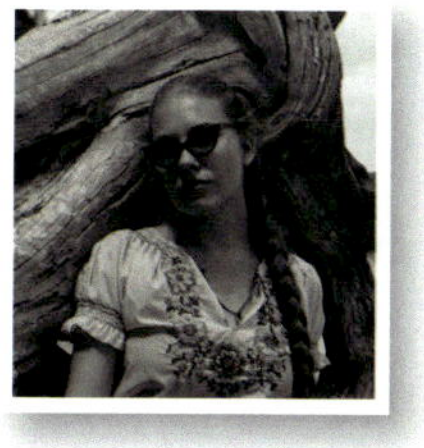

Erin is a freelance artist and photographer who lives in the San Francisco Bay area. She specializes in film and analogue processes. She is an avid self-portraitist who works with vintage themes and showcases her exceptionally long hair in thematic editorial photographs. Her work revolves around emotions and humour and displays her knack for discovering interesting period vignettes.

www.psychedelicpandaparty.tumblr.com

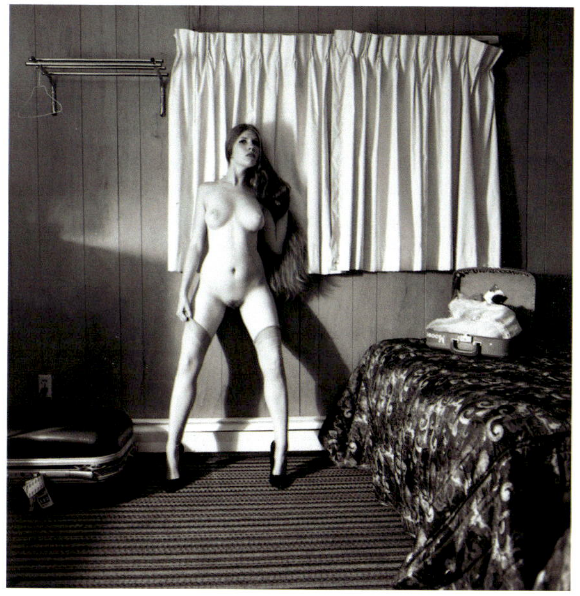

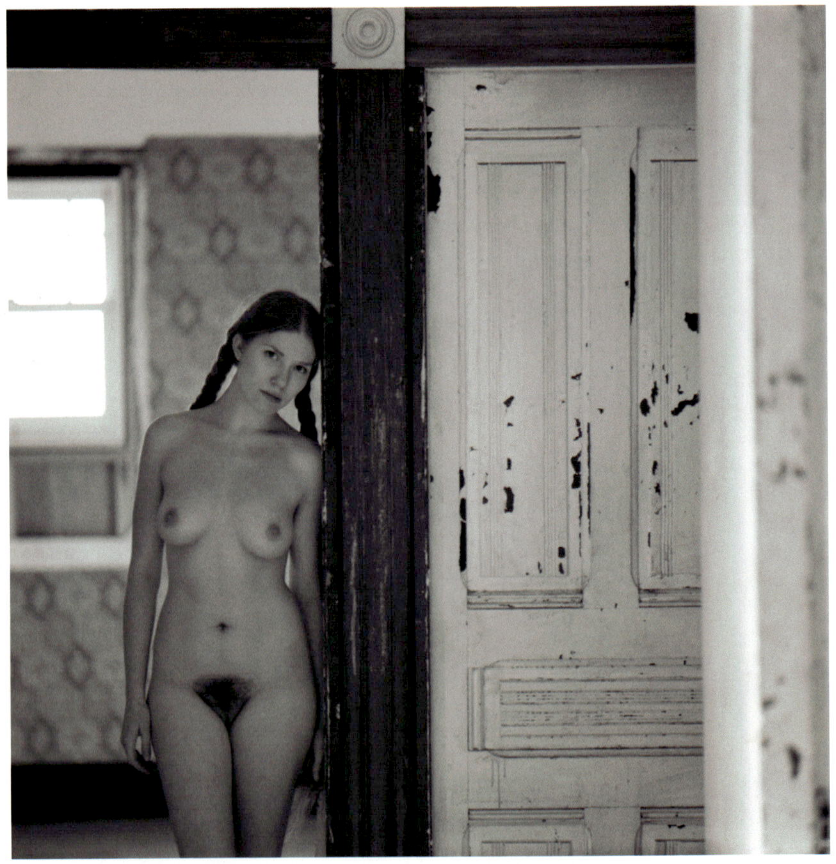

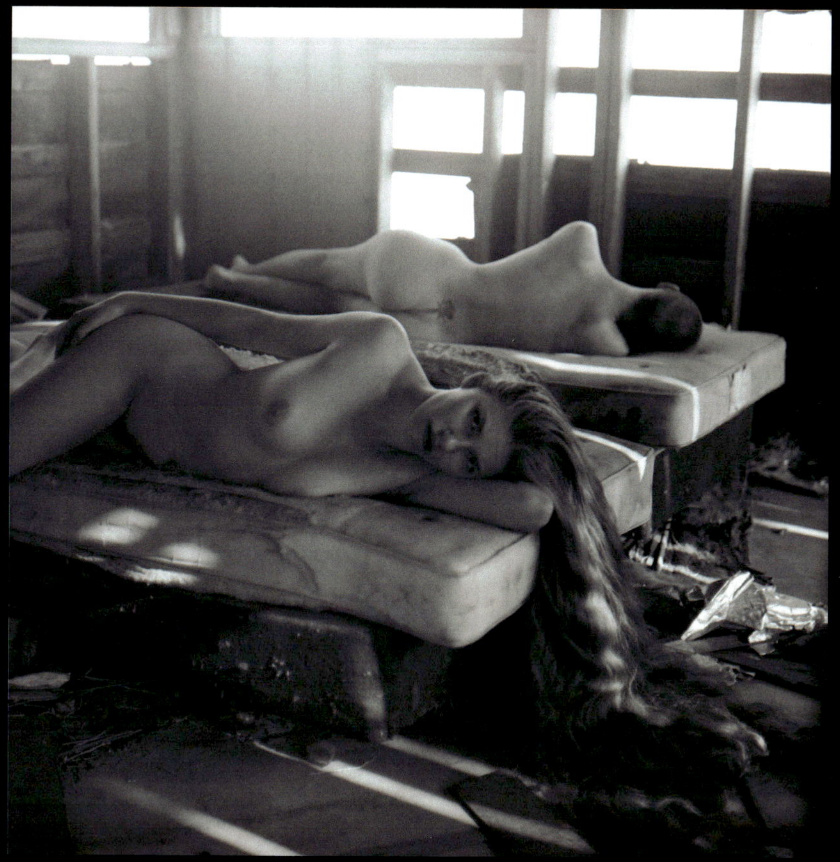

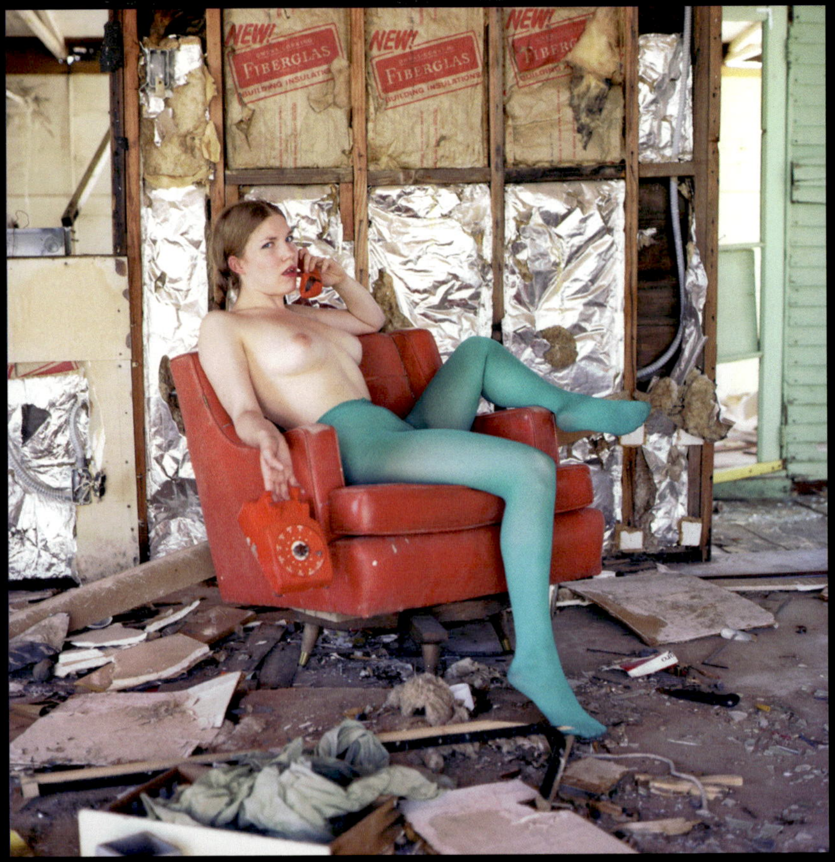
NEW!
FIBERGLAS
NEW!
FIBERGLAS
NEW!
FIBERGLAS

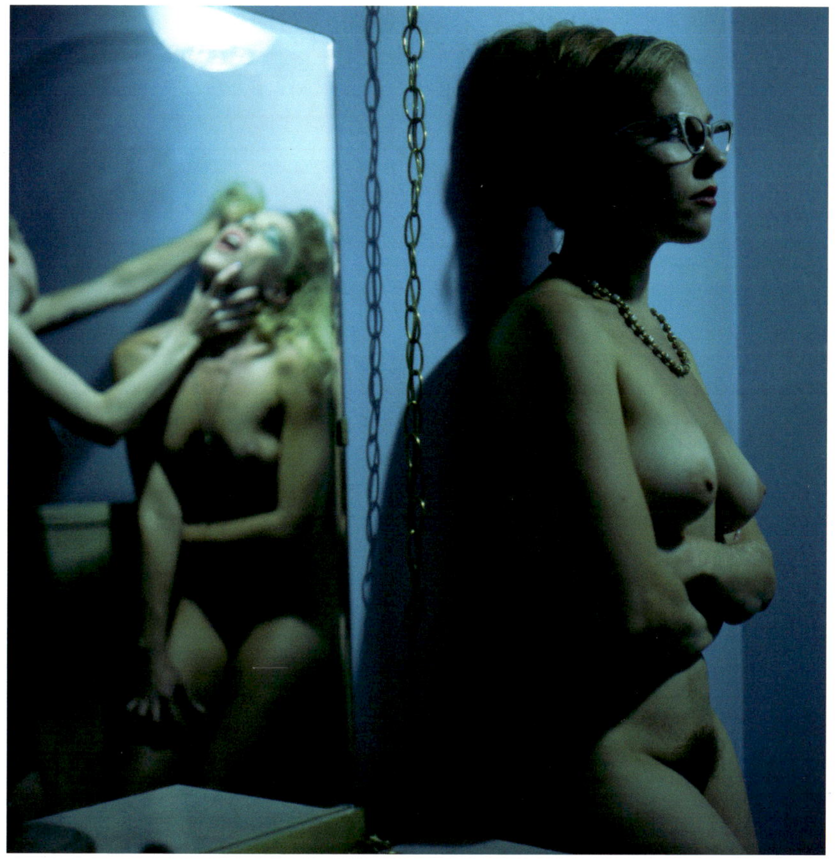

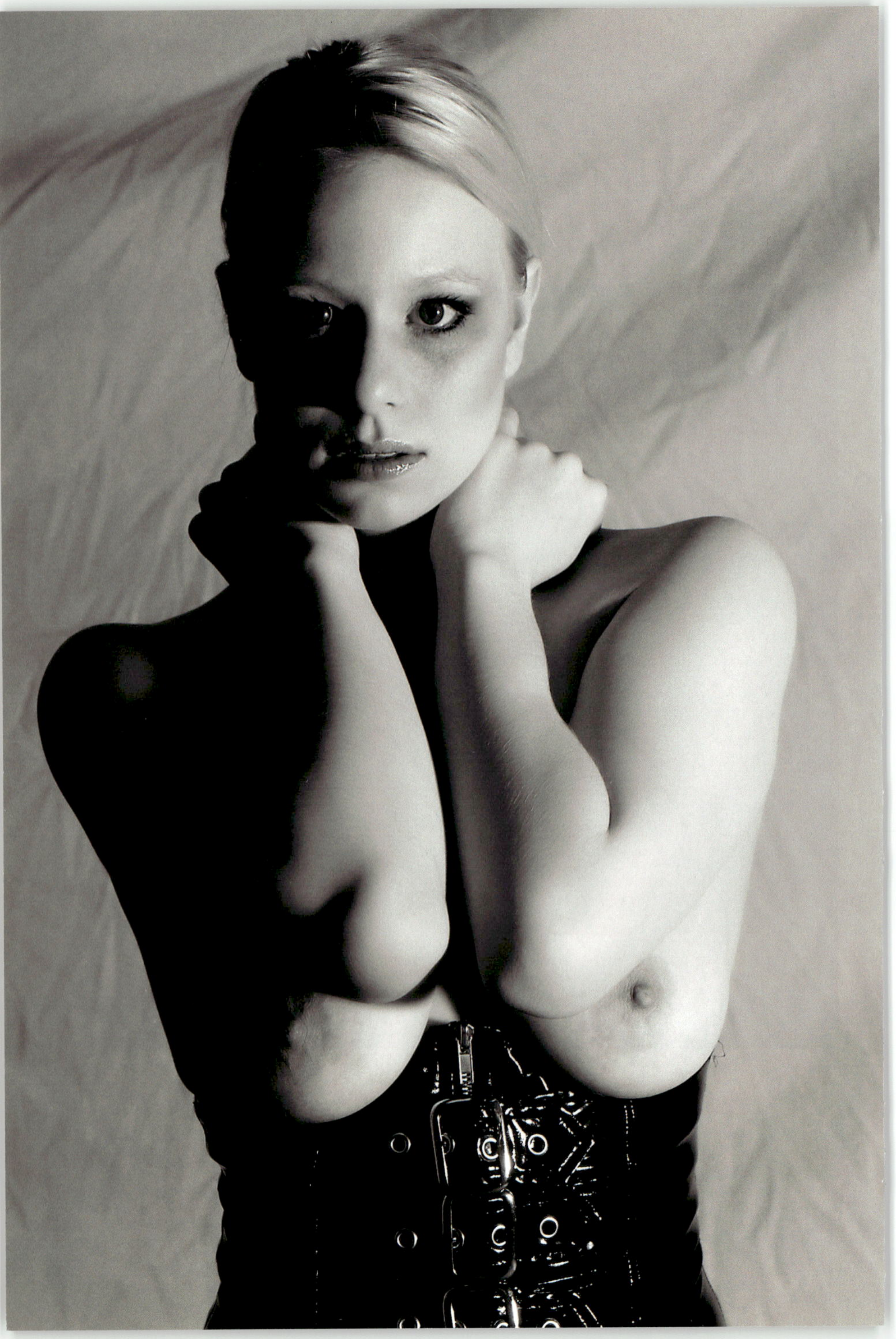

STAN ETHERIDGE

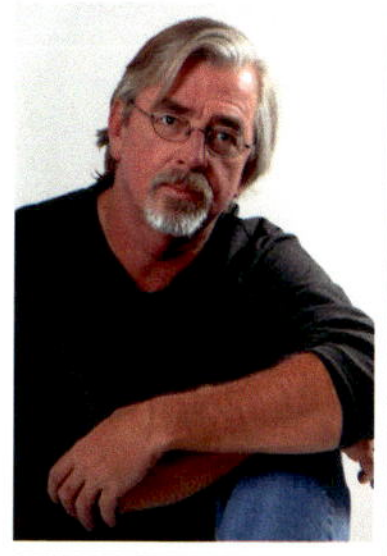

An artist and designer for nearly thirty years, Stan Etheridge lives in the New Orleans area. He studied Fine Art at the University of Mississippi and Architecture at Louisiana State University. In 2004 Stan began exploring photography as an art medium and has enjoyed great success. His style combines meticulous attention to detail with unique and creative lighting techniques. Focusing primarily on portraiture and fine-art figure images, he pursues freedom of expression with an emphasis on the sensual. His photographs have been displayed in art galleries, publications and on several websites.

Stan has chosen Sicilia Ricci as his model, because of her natural body, extensive experience and delightful sense of humour. The images are from three shoots for competitions and have been shown in several galleries and magazines.

www.sdestudio.com

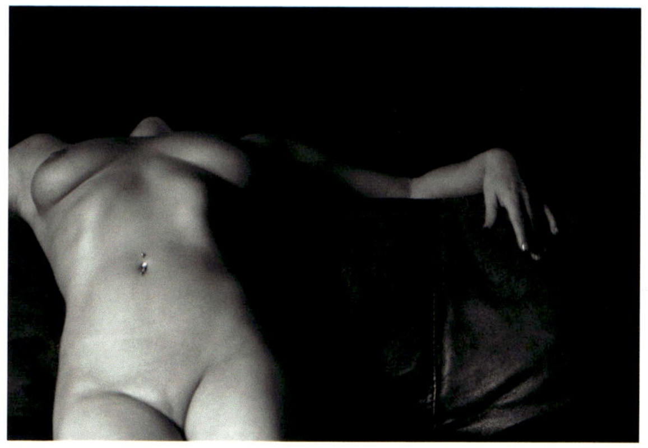

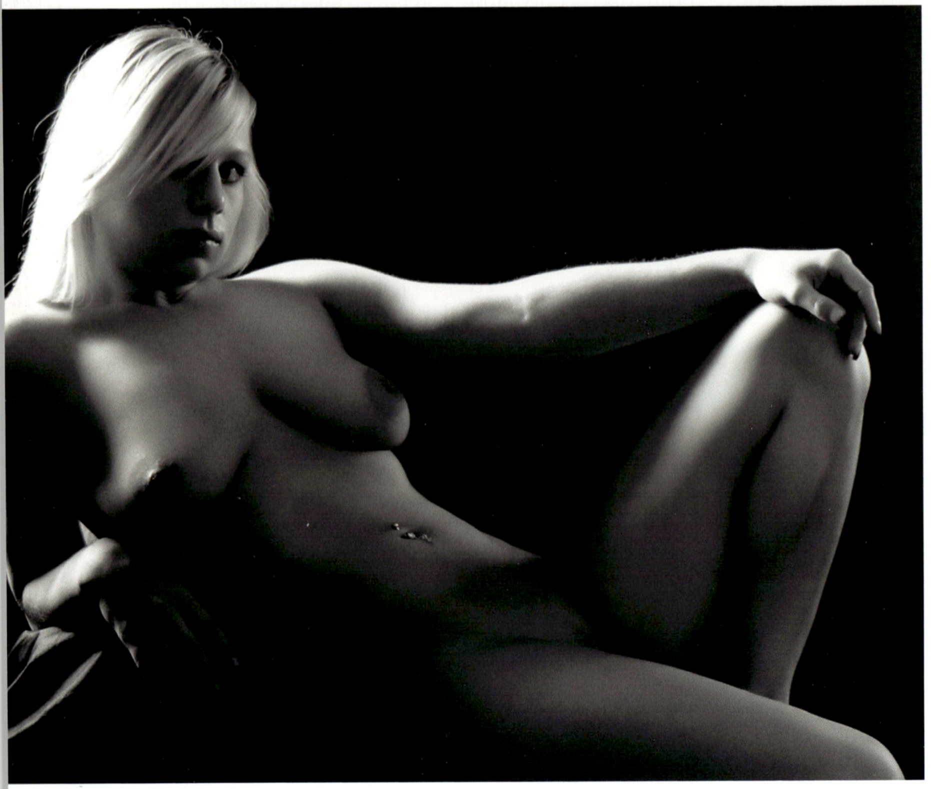

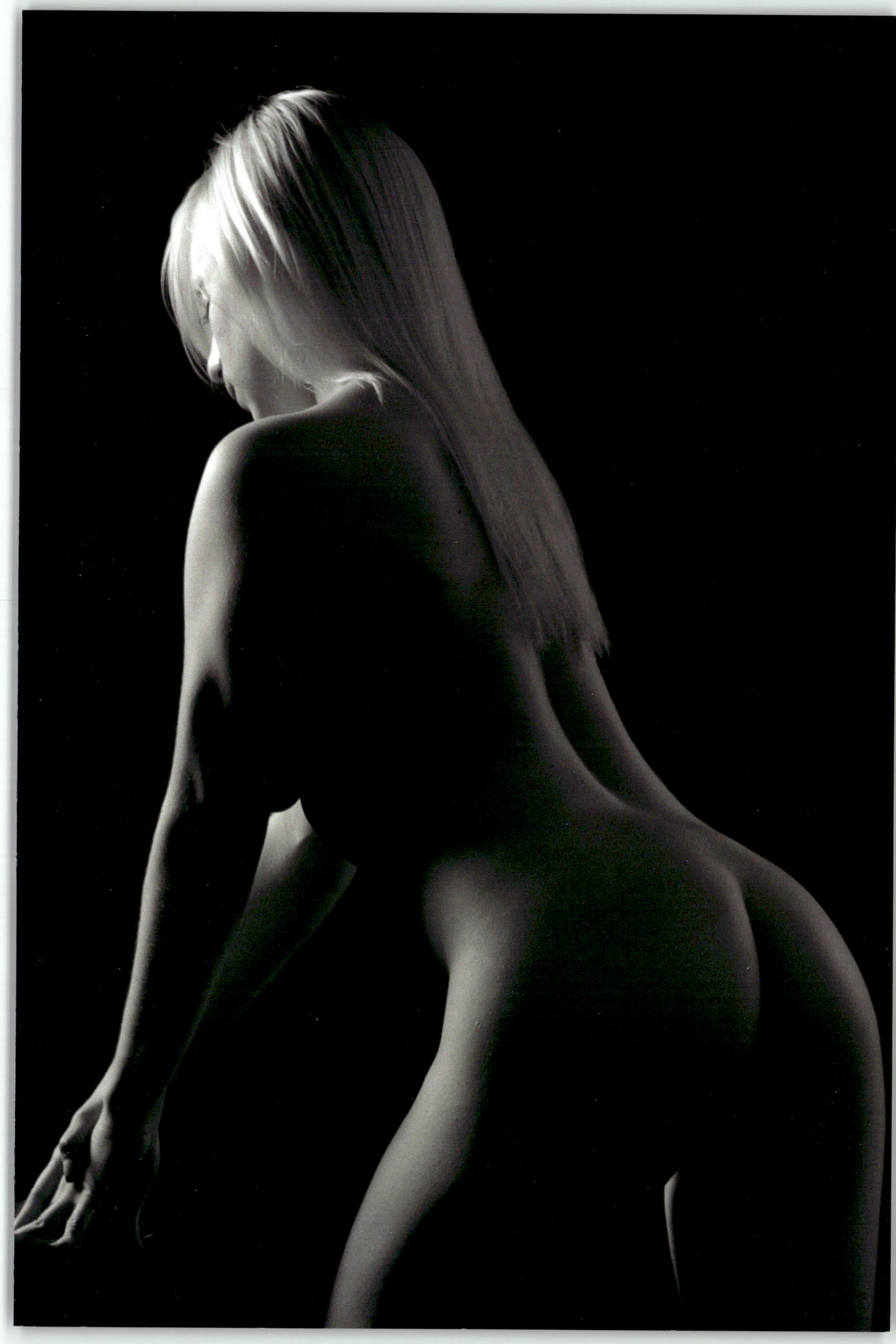

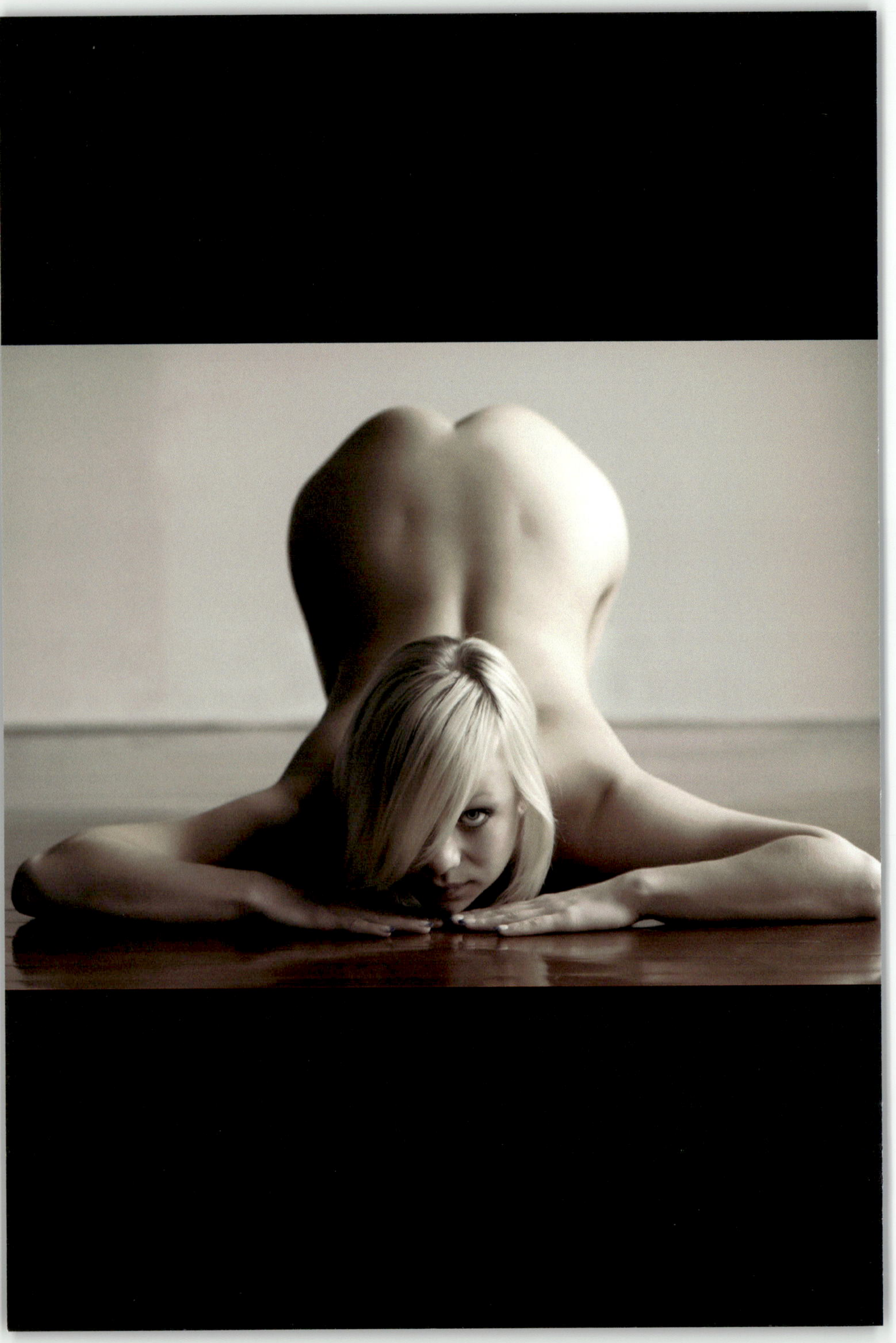

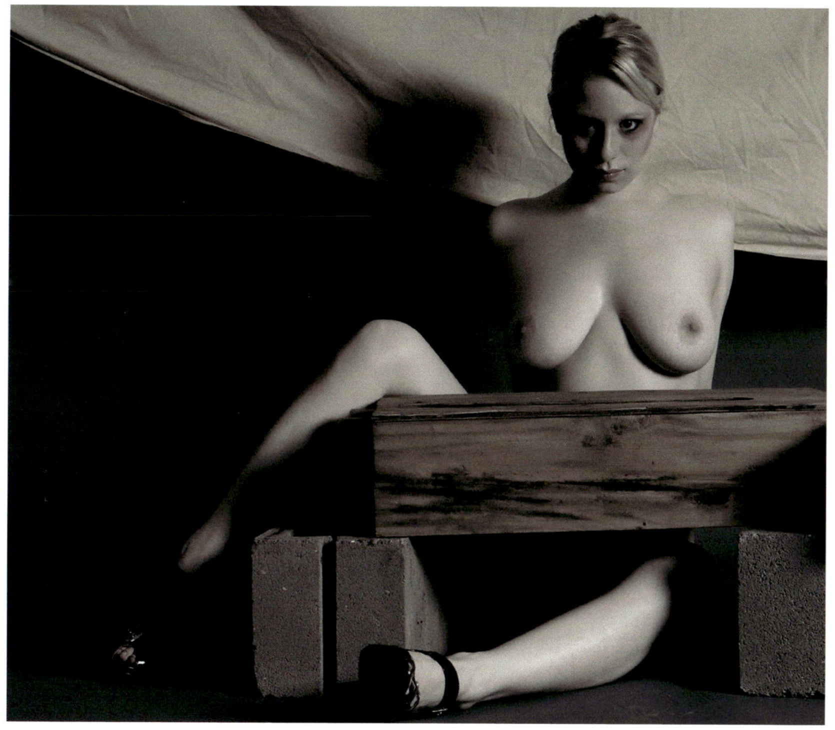

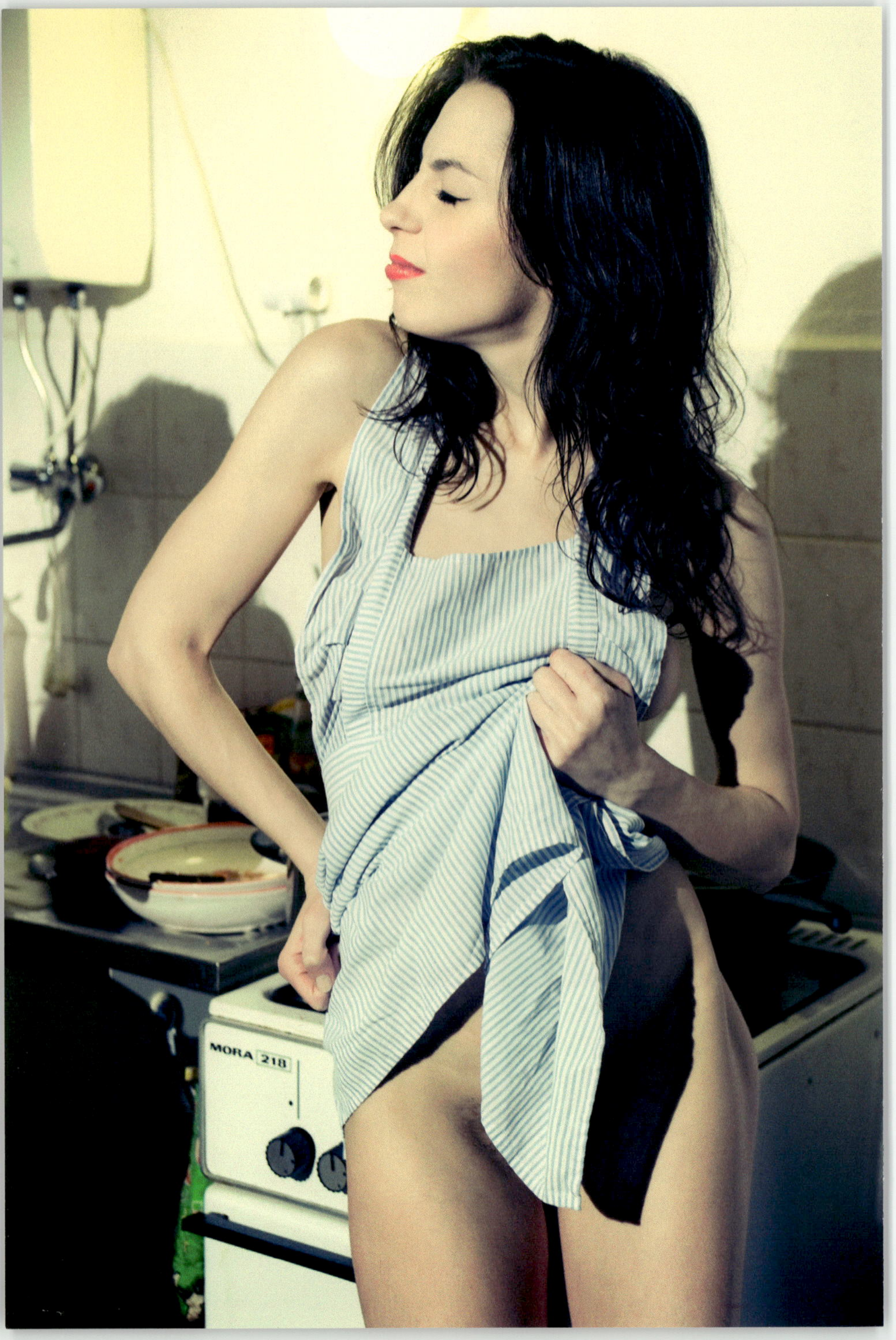
MORA 218

LUDMILA FOBLOVA

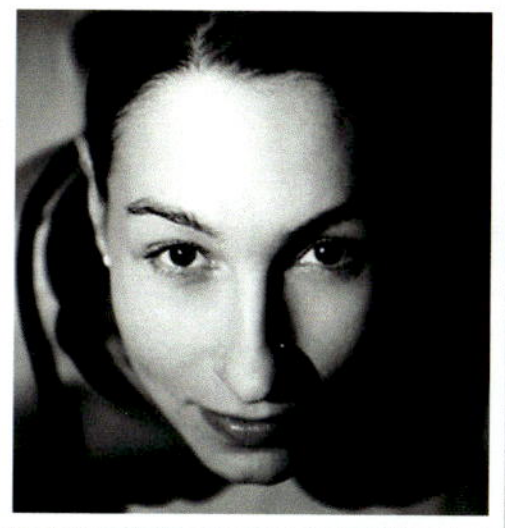

"My photos don't arise spontaneously. Rather than capture randomly ongoing situations, I carefully prepare most of my pictures. Classic nude art photography says nothing to me: I prefer various props and pretended action. I shoot only with models that I know well, so I know what I can expect from them.

"For this book I have chosen a beautiful Russian model, Viktoria aka Vikencia, who is also my close friend and is based in Prague. My ideas are often crazy and she is crazy enough to believe me and realize these things with me. It is always great fun to work together, or rather to play together."

www.ludmilafoblova.com

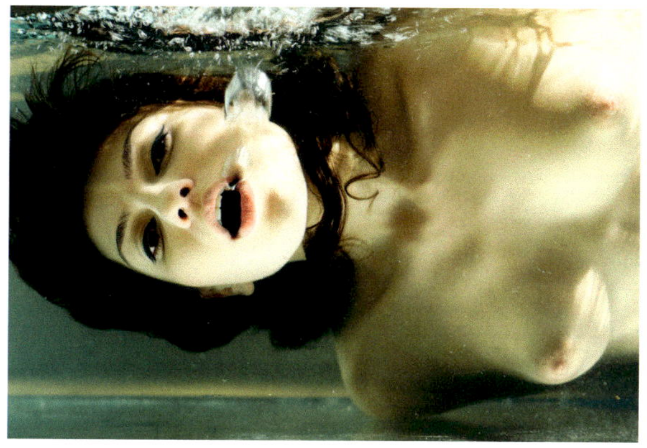

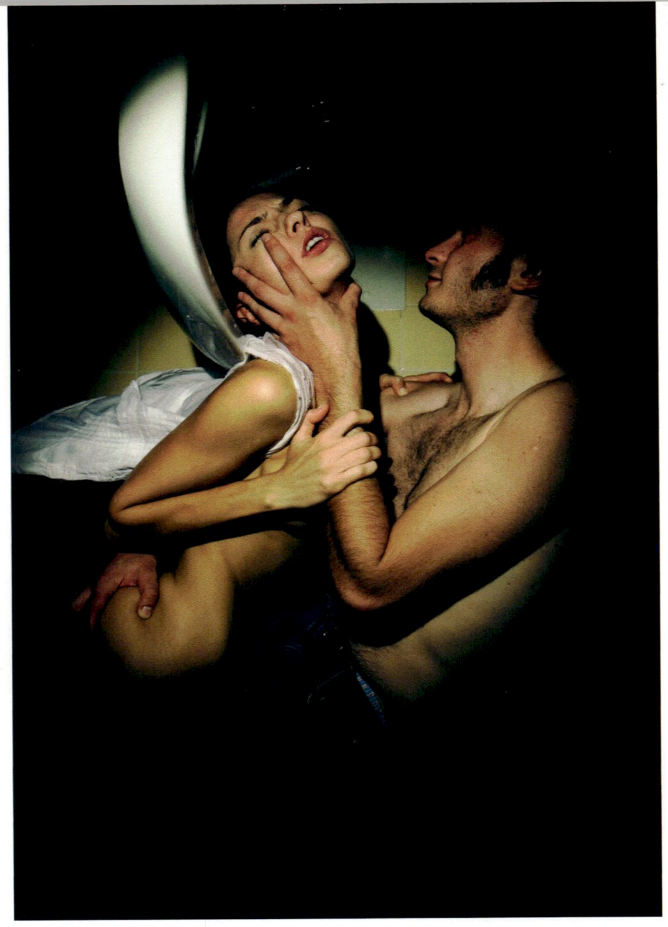

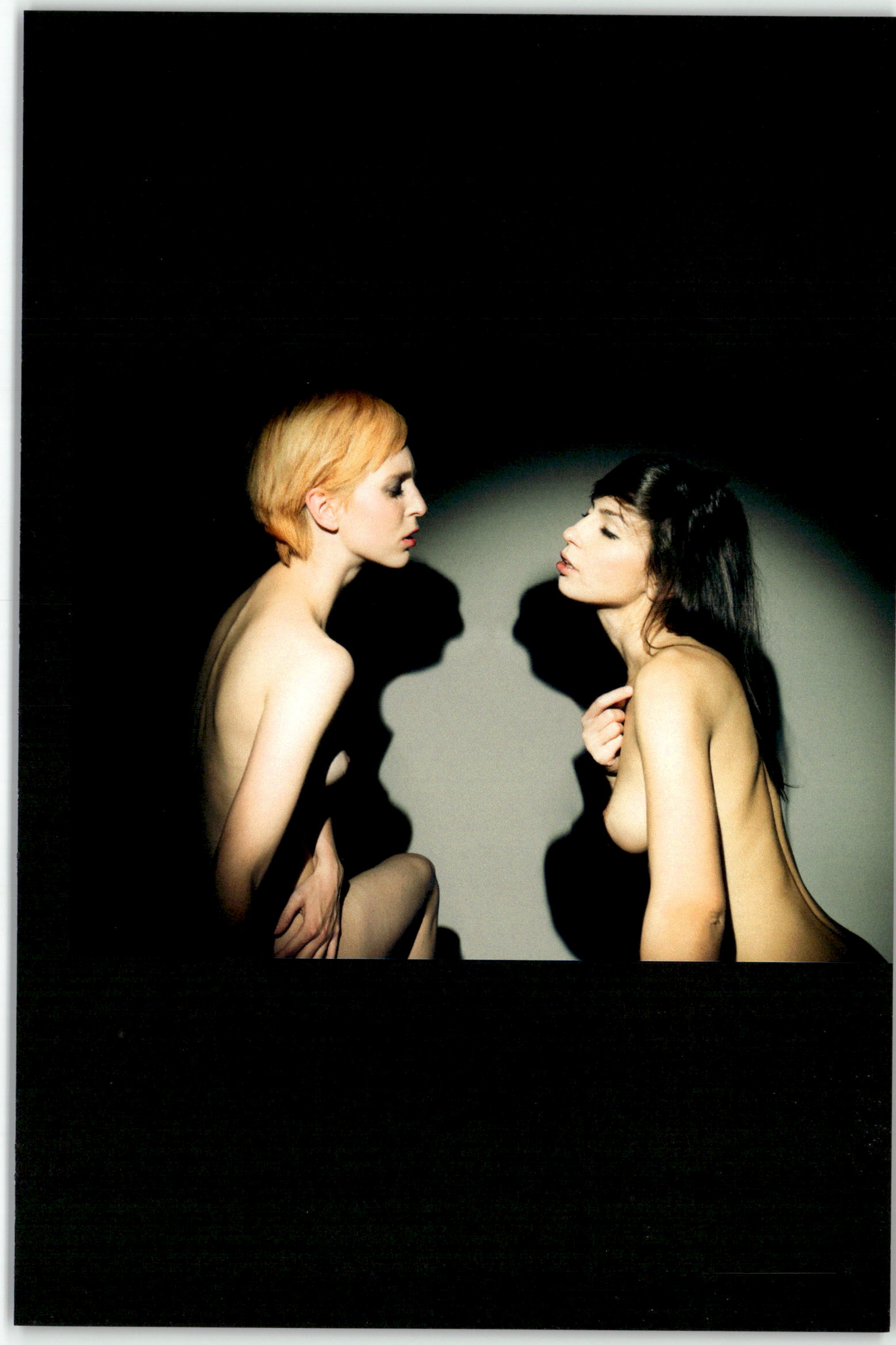

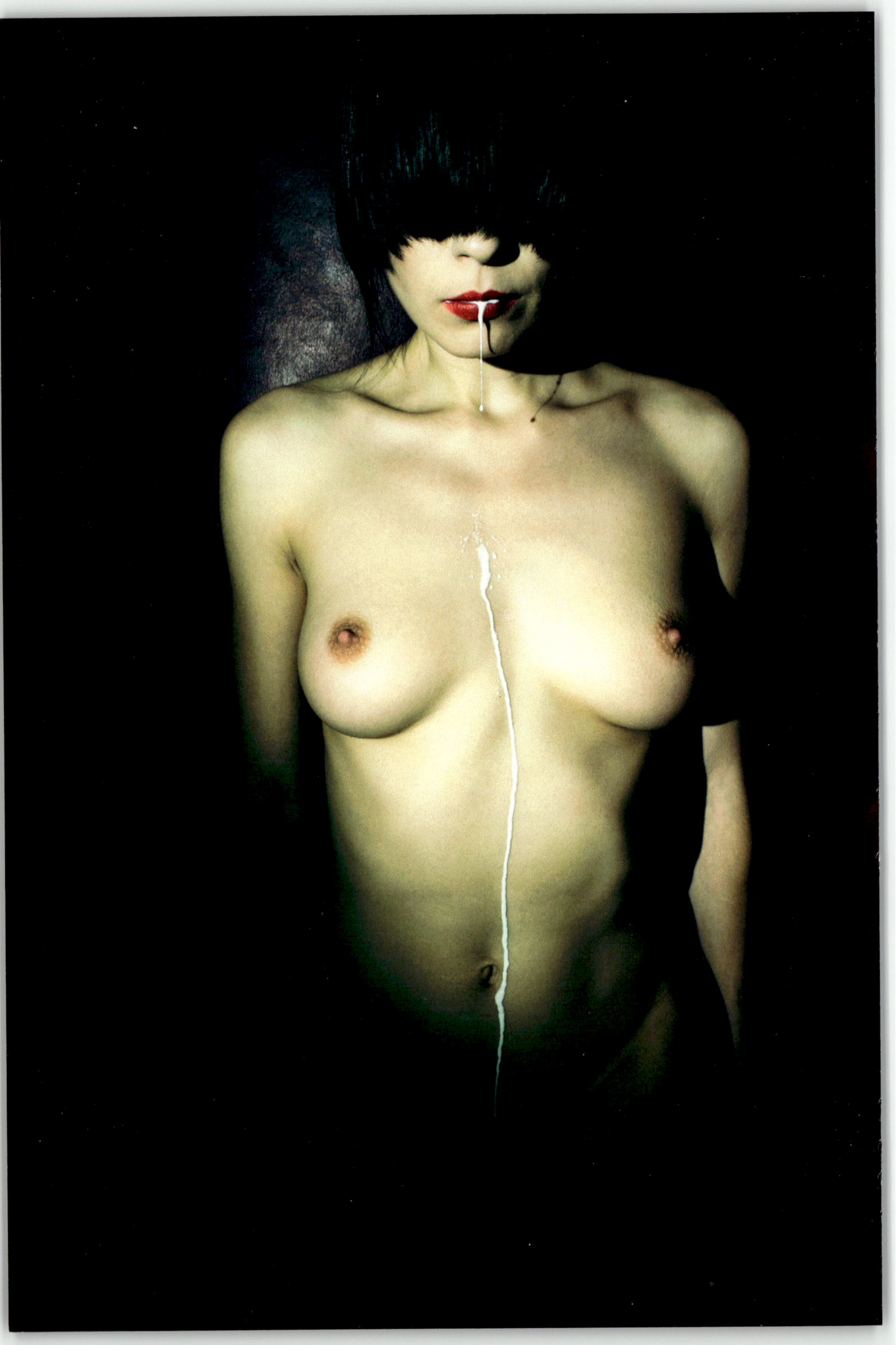

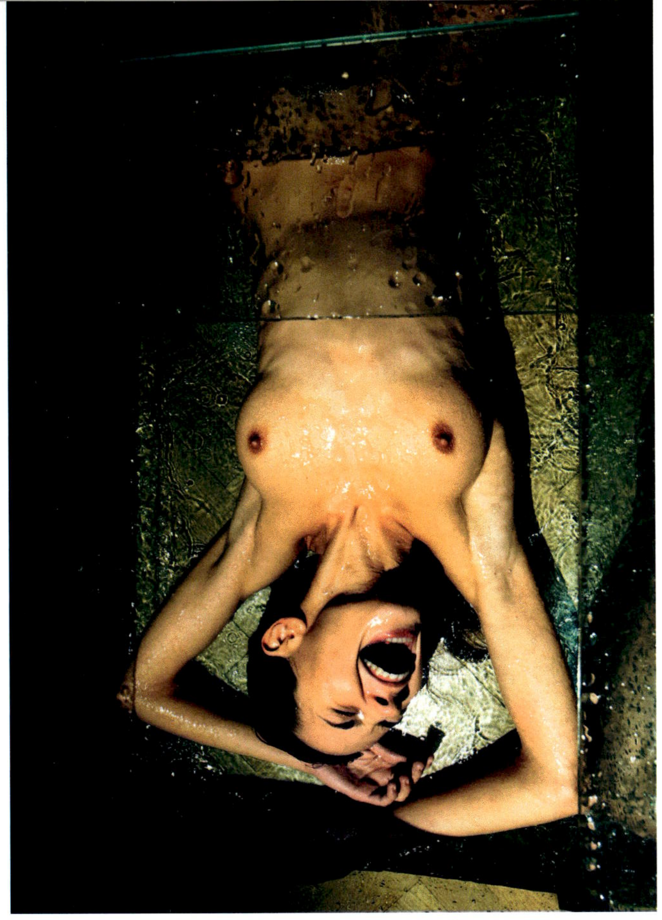

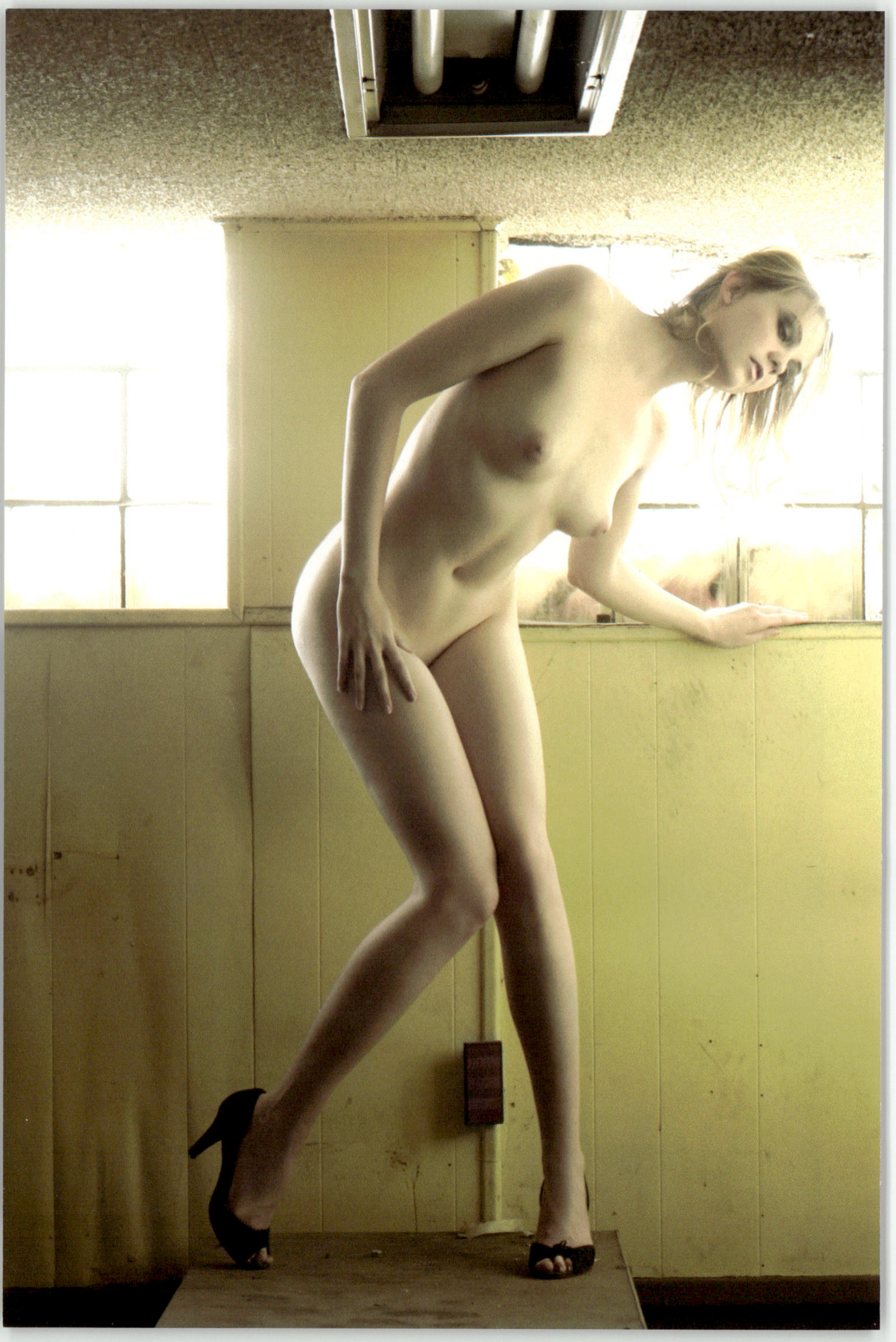

DREW FRITSCHEL

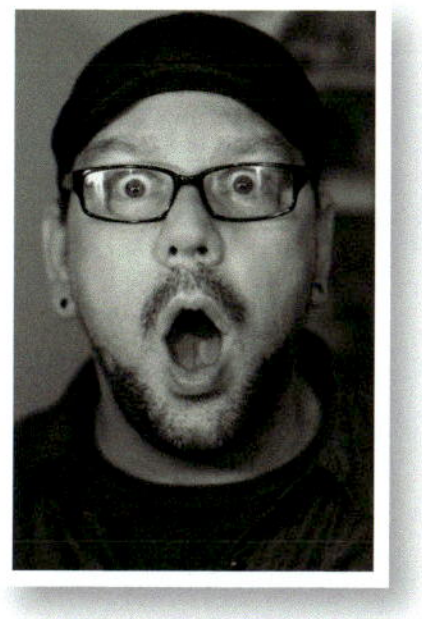

"I am a self-taught photographer who loves skin and curves. The human body has always intrigued me. All bodies are almost alike genetically, yet no two are the same. With every image I take, I want to provoke a thought, an emotion, a feeling.

"I chose Brittney for this book because she is a natural beauty who can fit into any environment. She has the ability to make any location and space beautiful. Brittney is comfortable in her skin and it shows every time the camera is on her. Outside or in the studio, she can turn on the muse switch and go. Some things work without words and are just felt."

www.bluesparrowphoto.com

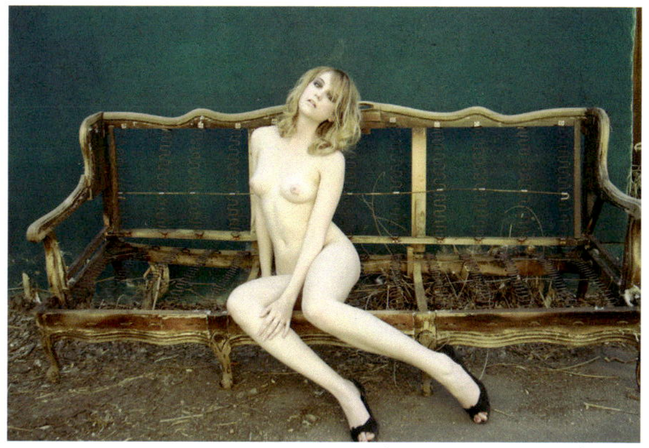

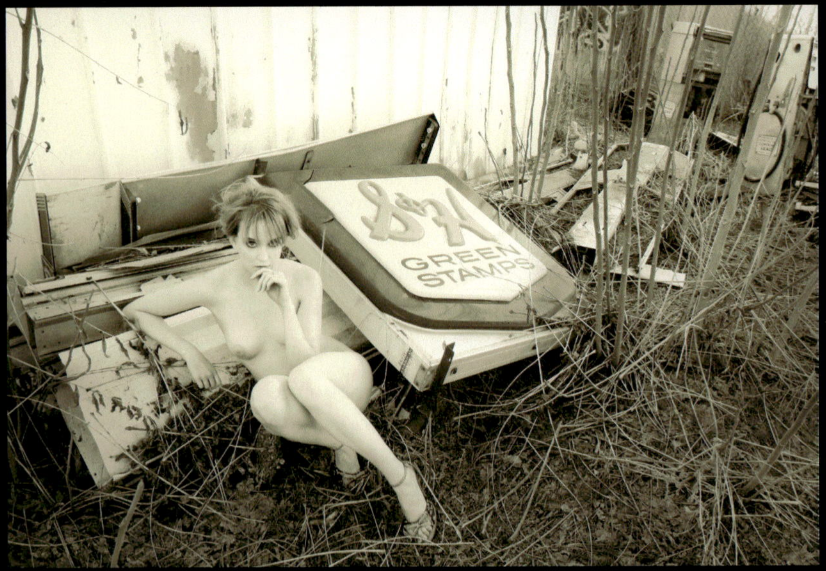
GREEN
STAMPS

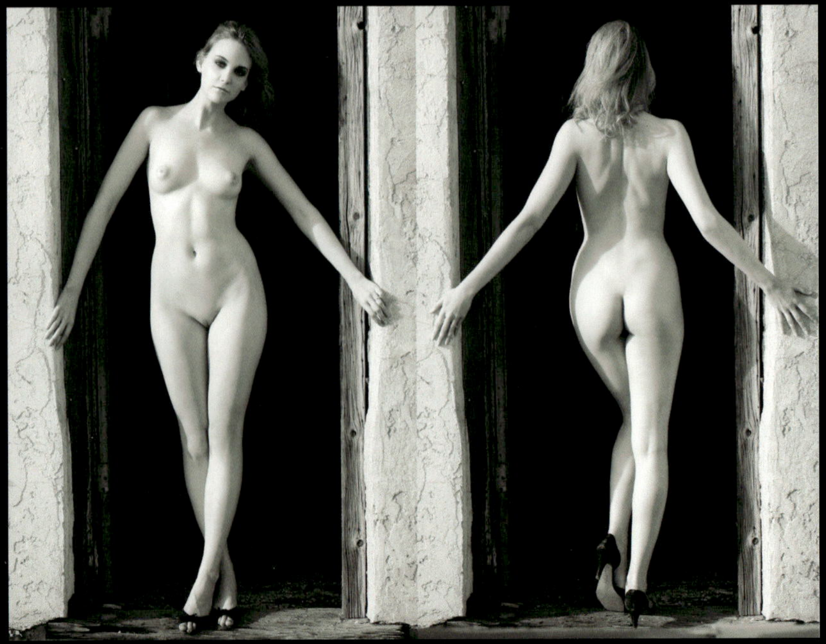

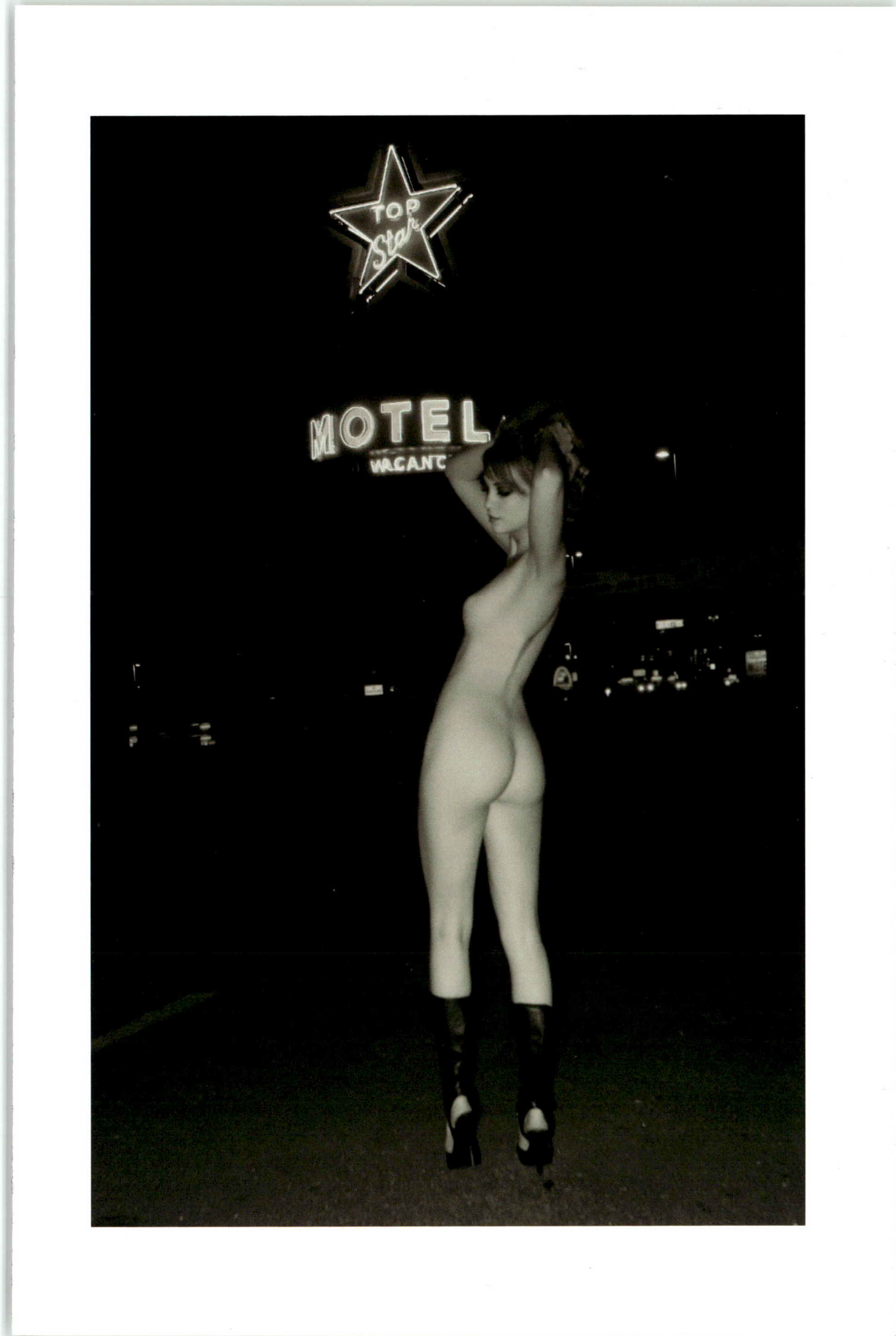
TOP
Star
MOTEL

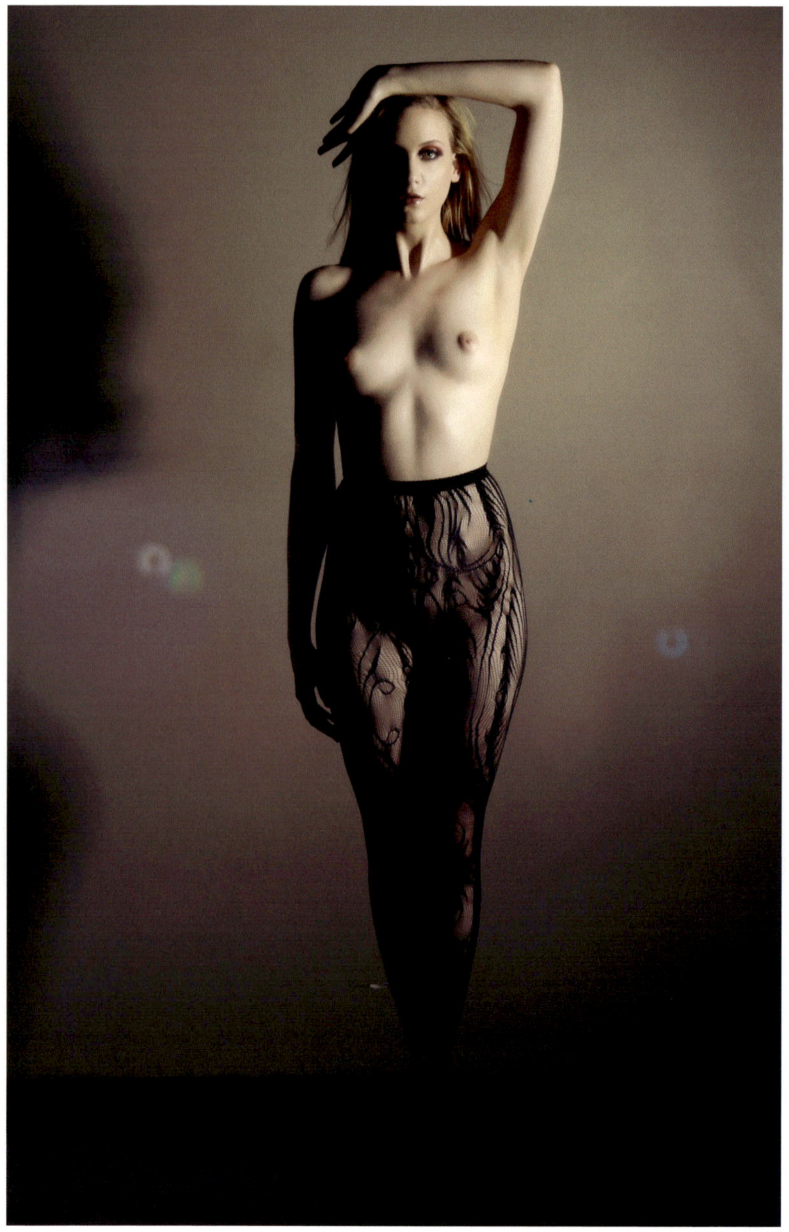

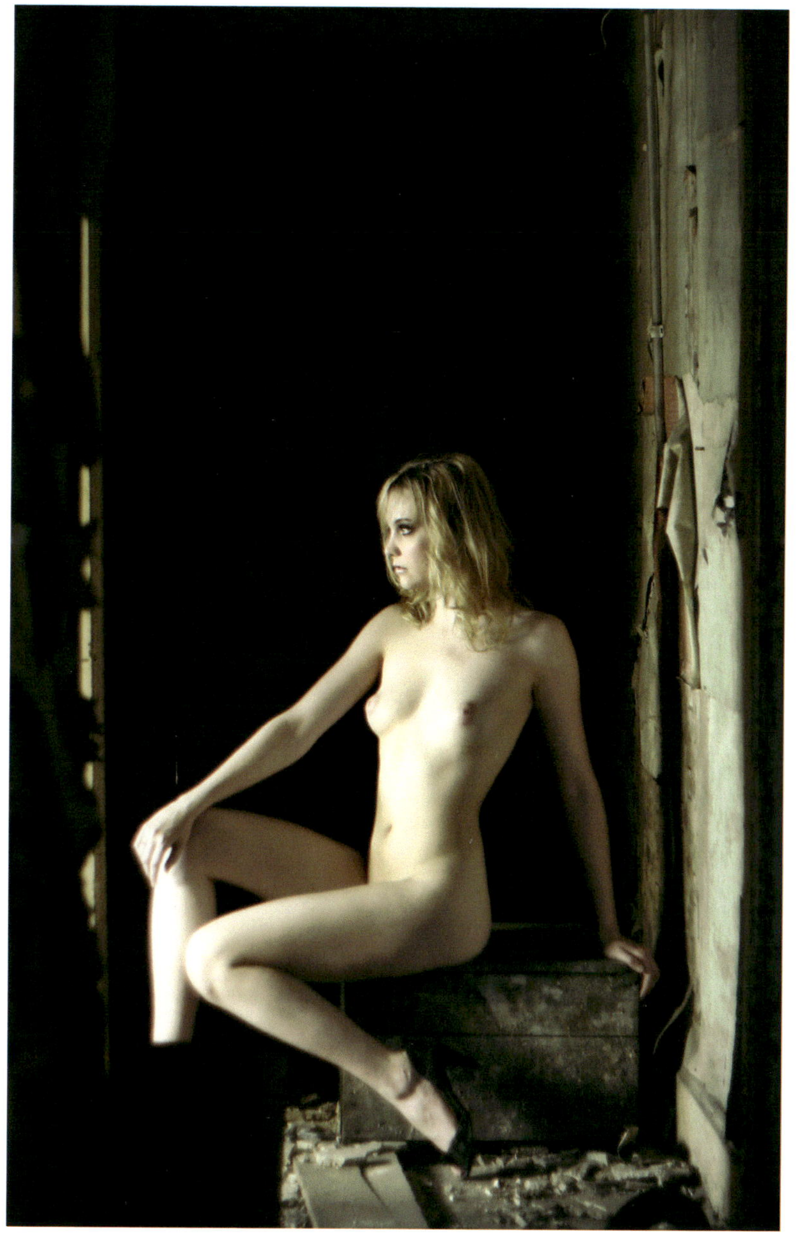

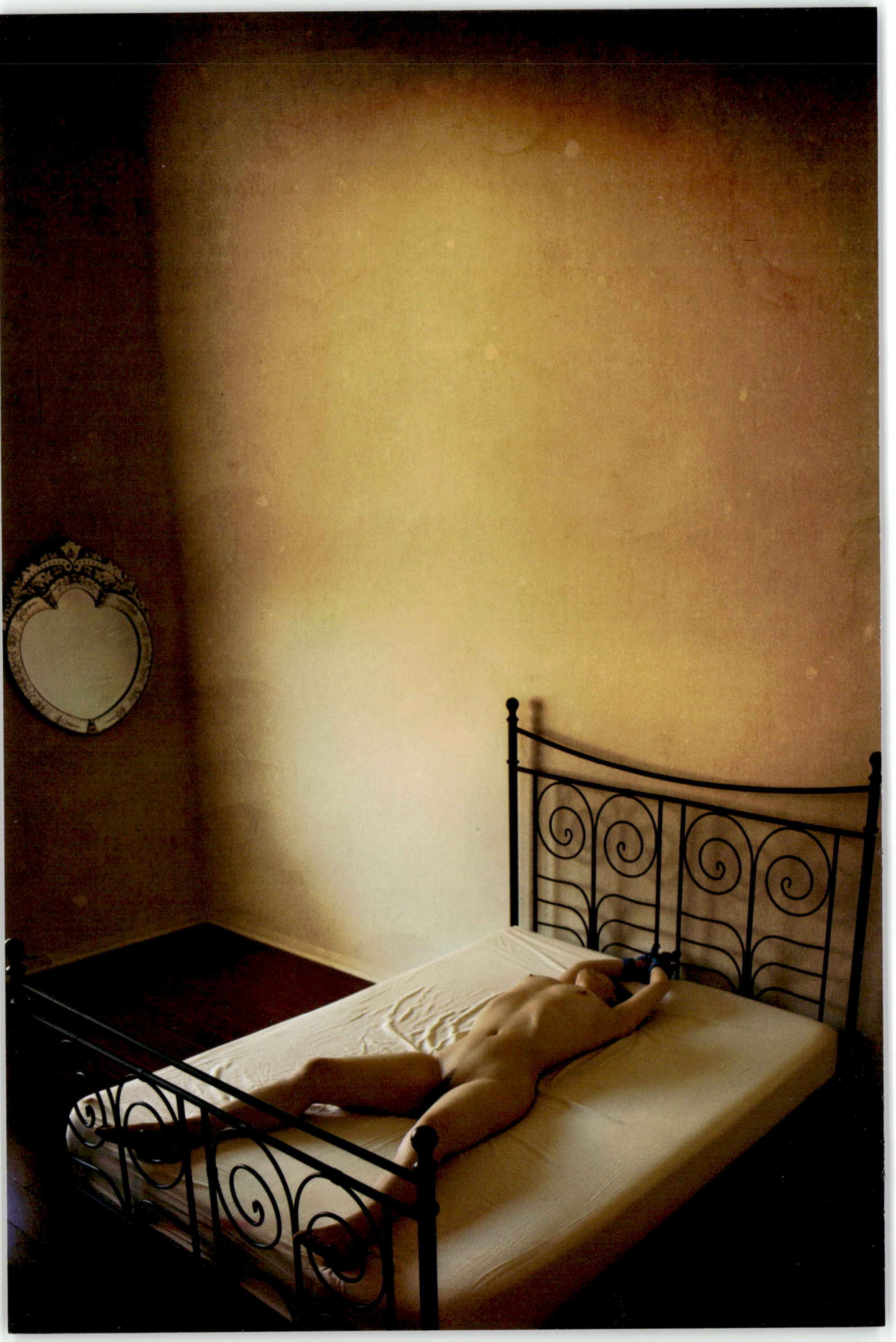

PERRY GALLAGHER

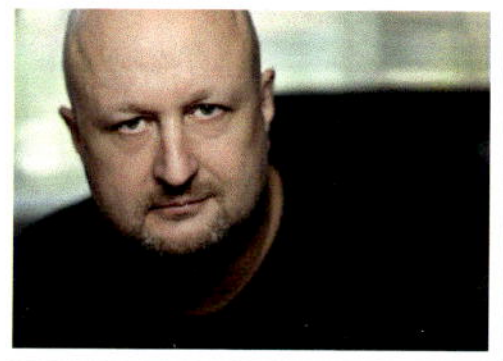

"'Photograph what turns you on,' photojournalist Bernard Mendoza told me. The passion of photographing in this way goes beyond what you simply like, or find beautiful or sexy. It moves you deeply, lifting your work to another level as you evoke that emotion for the viewer. Photographing what turns you on also exposes your vulnerability, allowing the magic between you and your subject to touch your core. My intent is to create images of intimacy that are moving and reflect who I am. Mostly using available light, from either a window or a bedside lamp, I have developed a unique style.

"I chose Mia as my model, because she turns me on deeply. She is also one of the most beautiful people I know and has a very generous soul."

www.perrygallagher.com

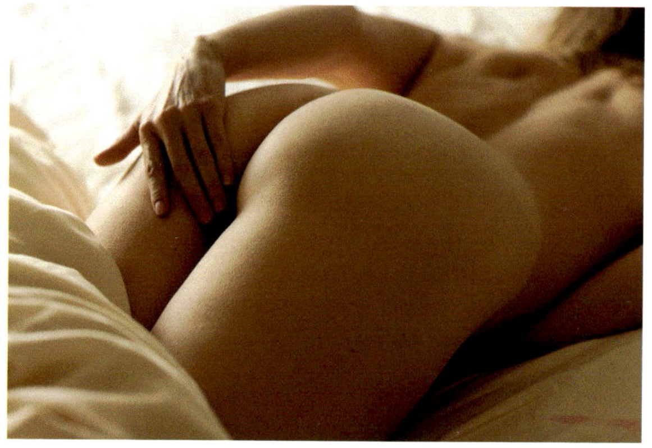

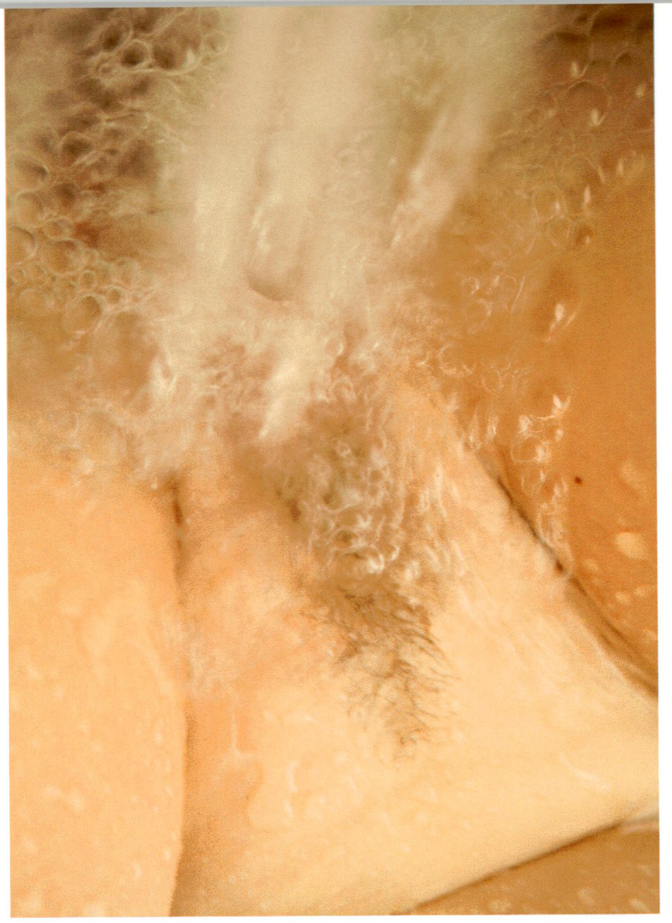

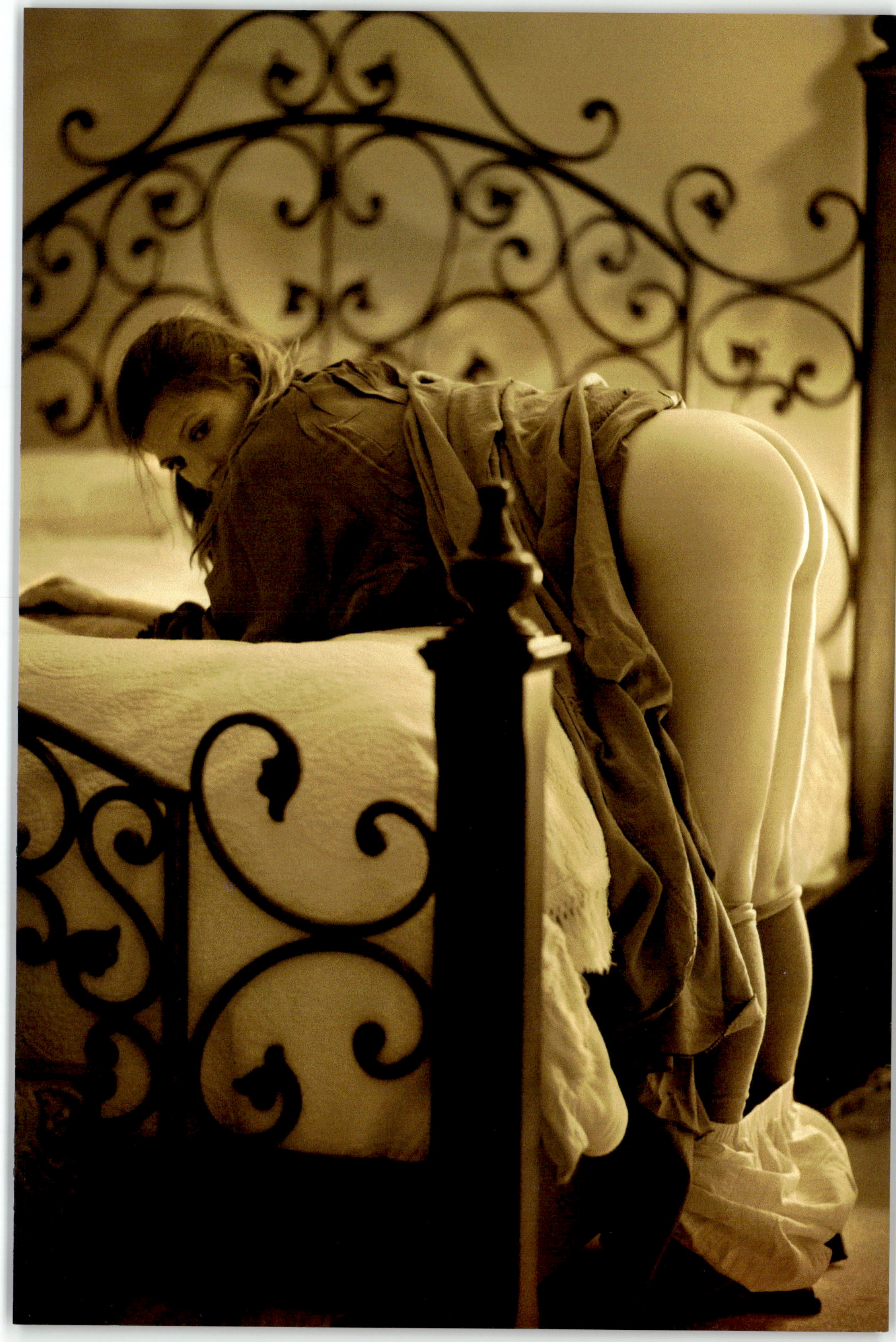

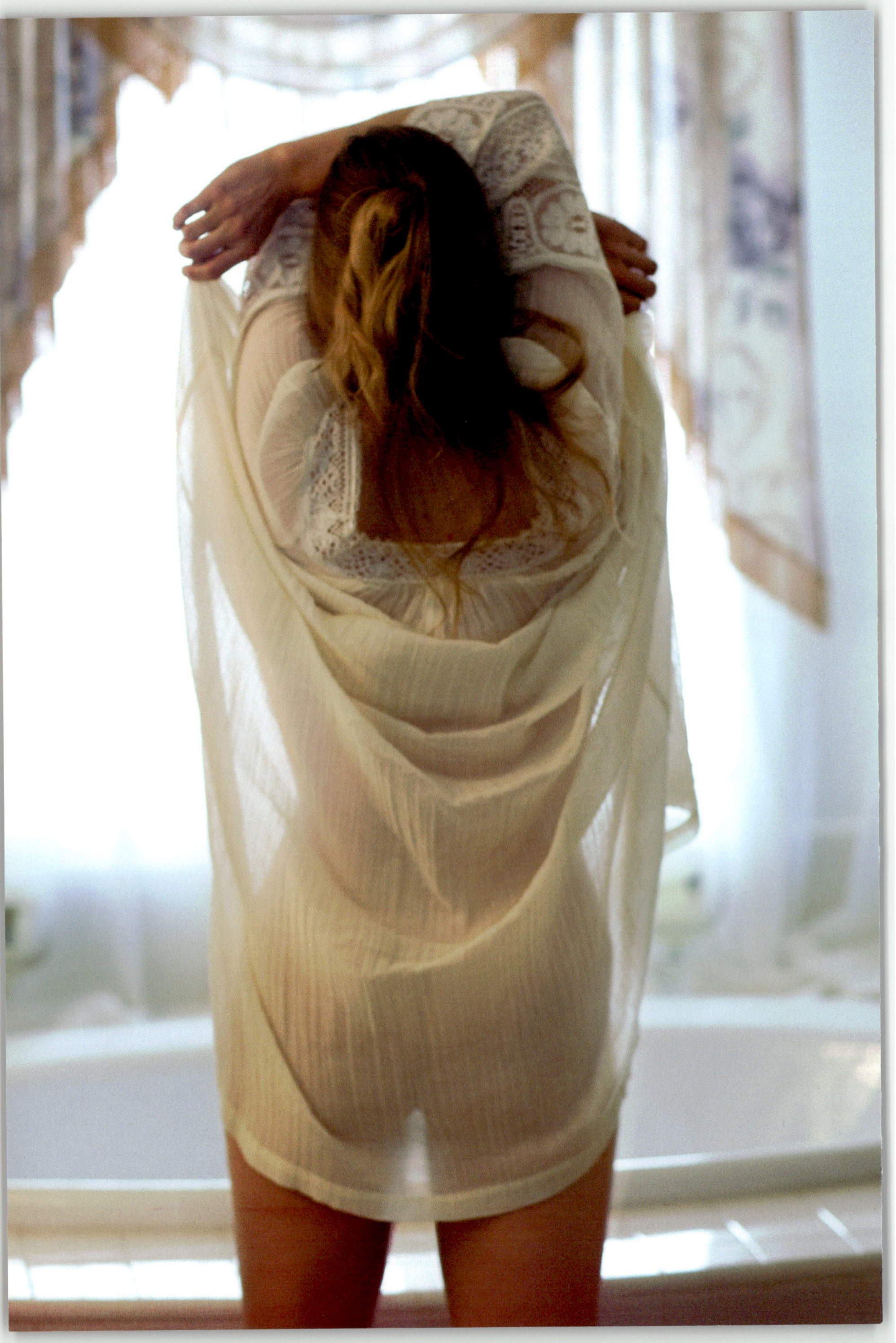

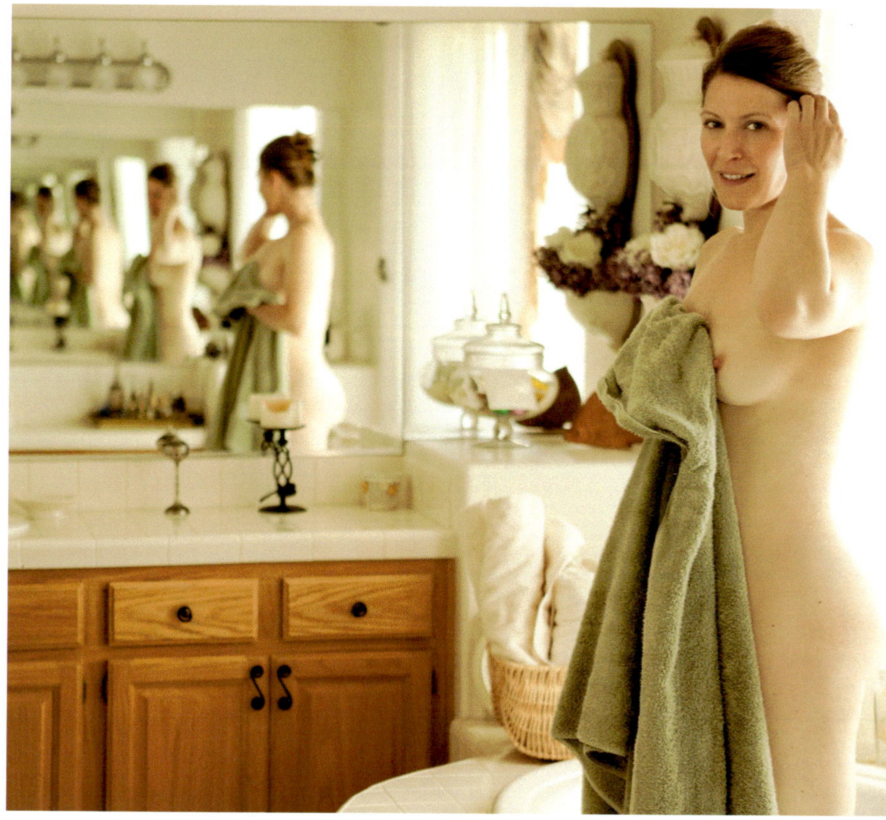

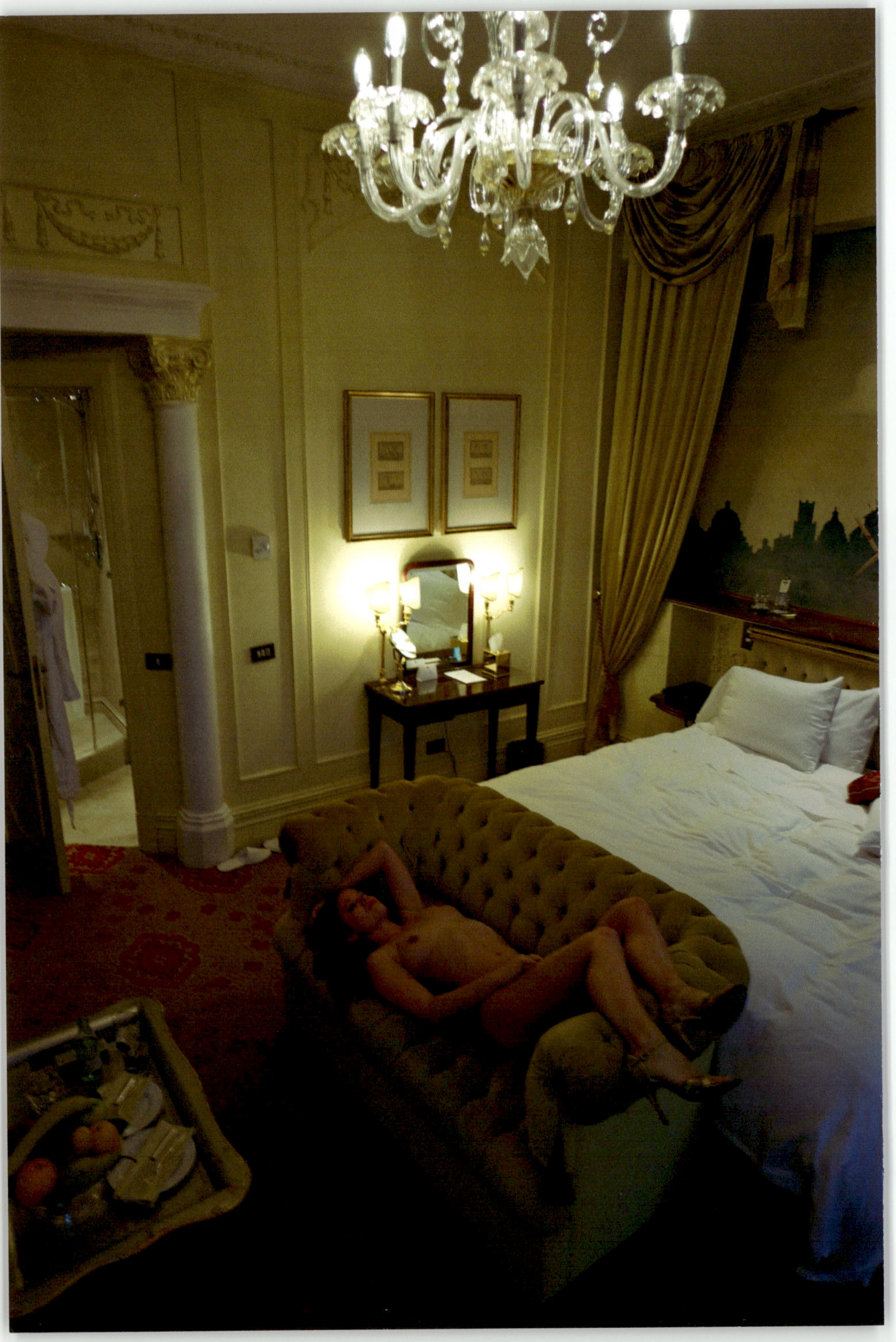

RAVNISH GANDHI

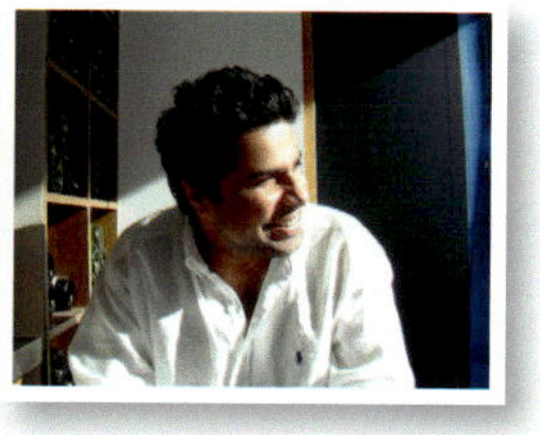

"I have been shooting images on any camera I could find since I was eighteen. By nature I am impulsive and photography serves me as the best creative medium. I usually try to shoot with no plan and instead concentrate more on the model in front of me. My photography is something I do to keep myself happy and grounded, and it is something in me that must be expressed.

"Any photography that involves a model is a collaboration. Thank you, Cody, for being my subject."

www.ravnishgandhi.com

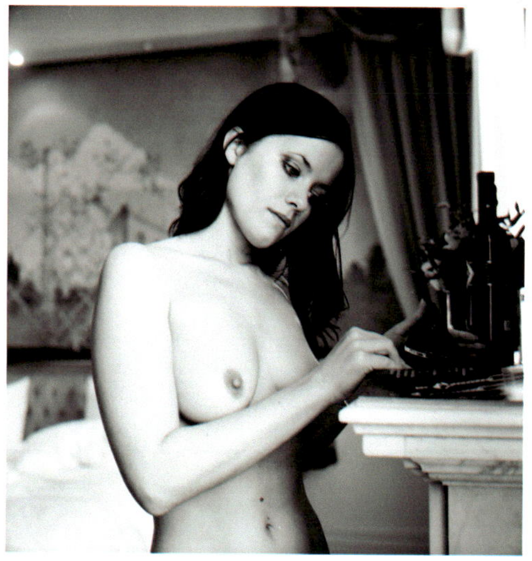

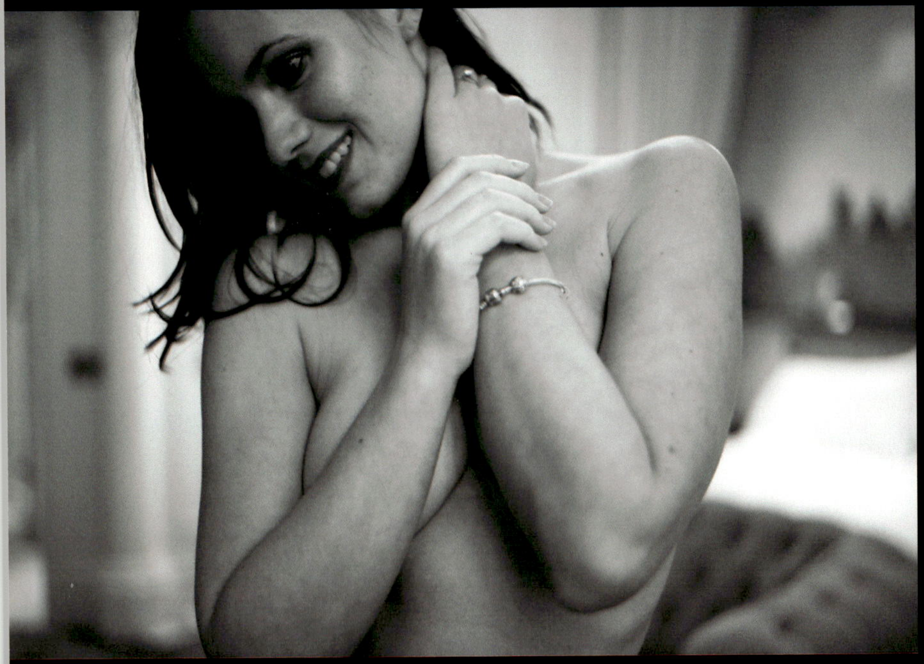

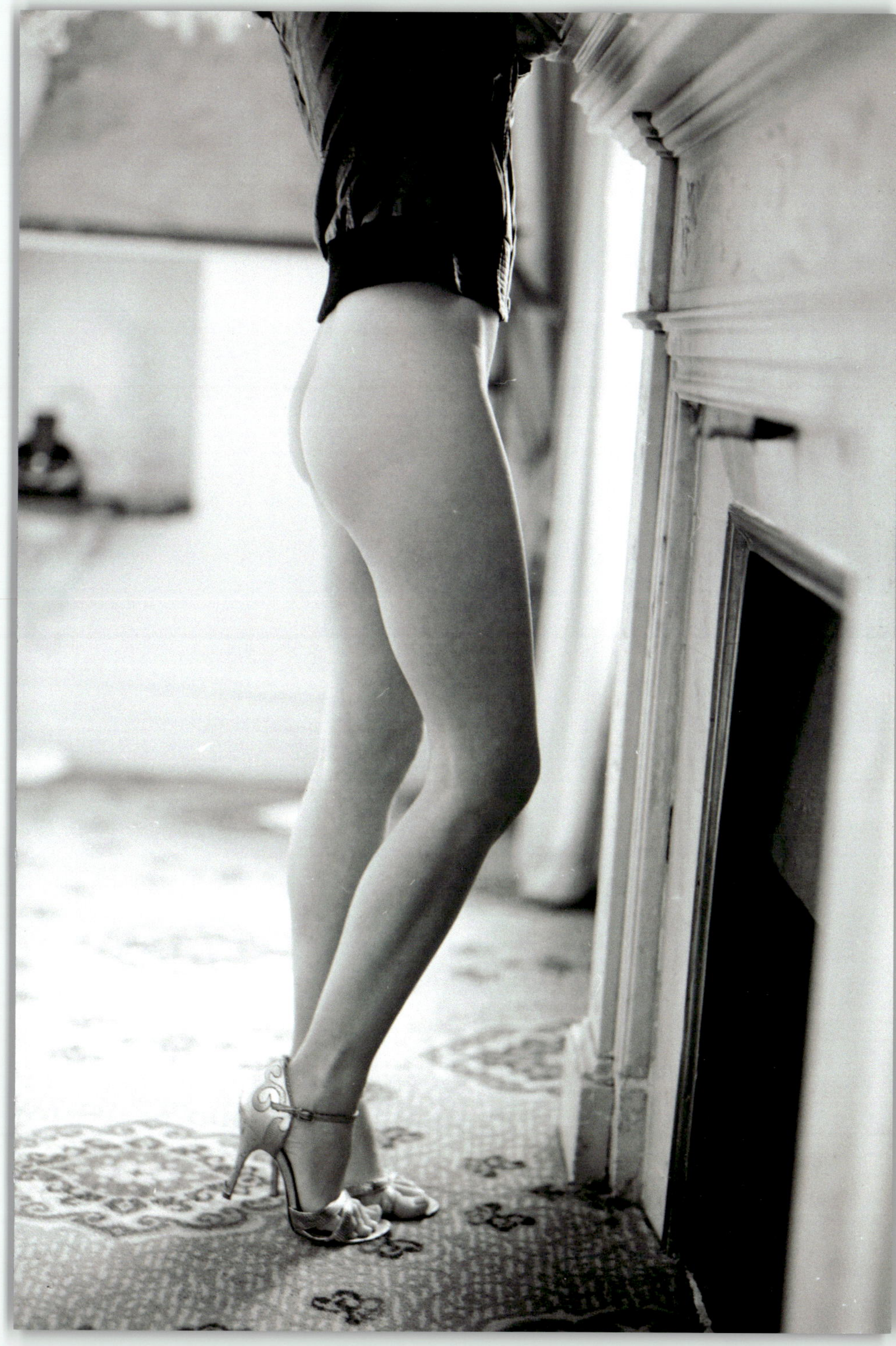

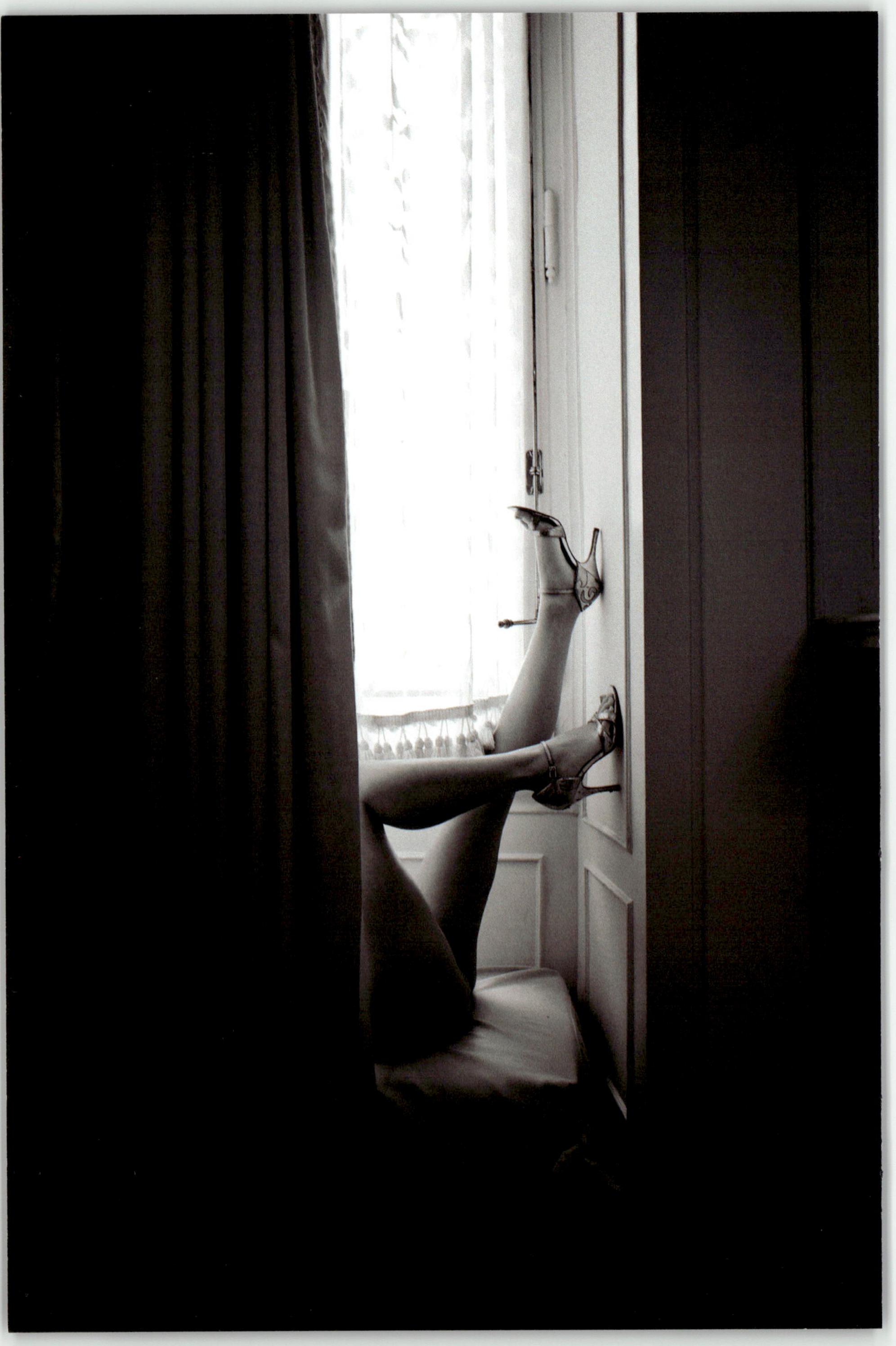

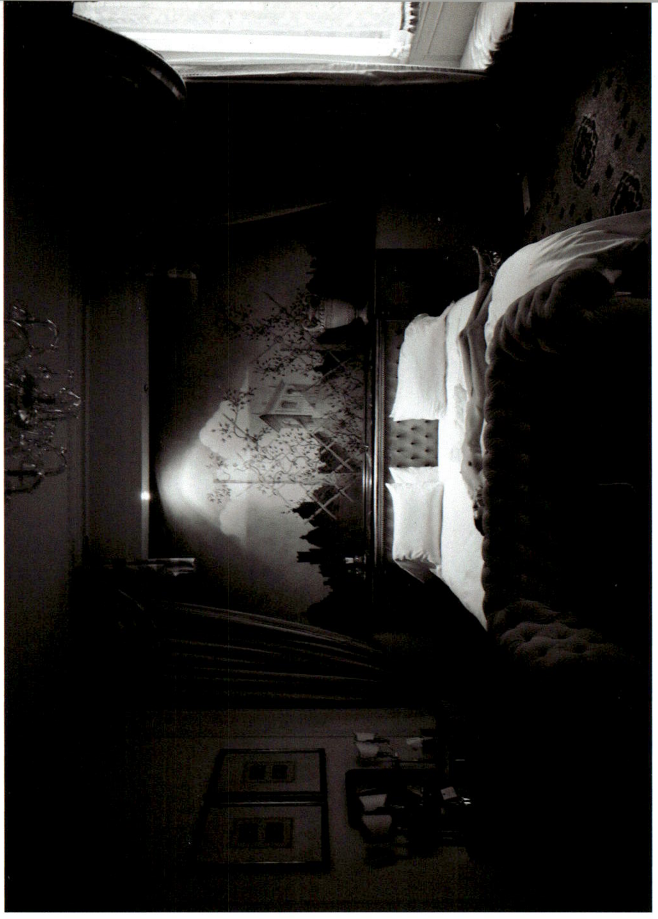

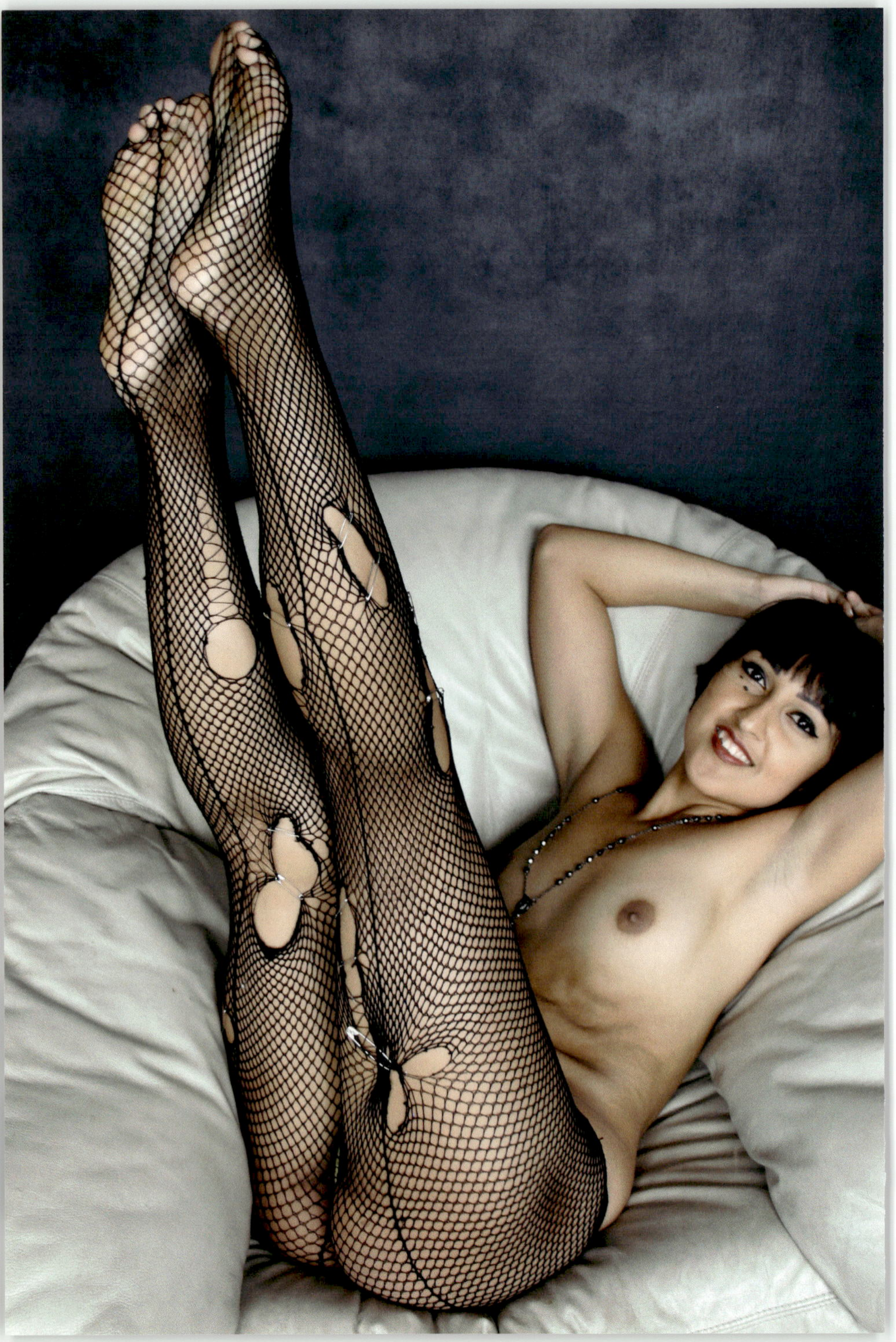

CHARLES GATEWOOD

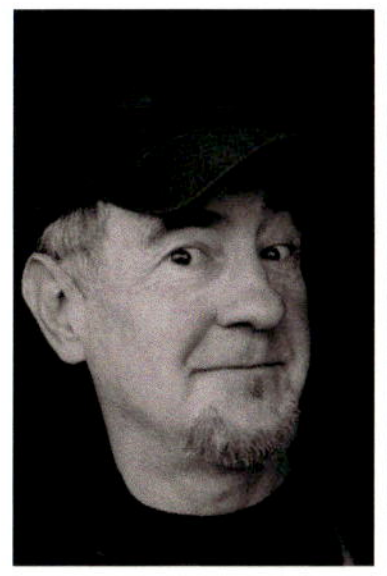

Charles Gatewood has been called "the family photographer of America's sexual underground" and has documented alternative culture for almost fifty years. His books include *Sidetripping* (with William S. Burroughs), *Pushing Ink* (with Spider Webb), *Hellfire*, *Primitives*, *The Body and Beyond*, *Badlands*, *True Blood*, *Messy Girls*, *Photography for Perverts*, *A Complete Unknown* and *Burroughs 23*. He has received numerous awards and has been the subject of two documentary films. Gatewood lives in San Francisco, where his underground adventures continue.

"I chose nineteen-year-old Mari for this book because of her exotic good looks and natural modelling ability. What a beauty!"

www.charlesgatewood.com

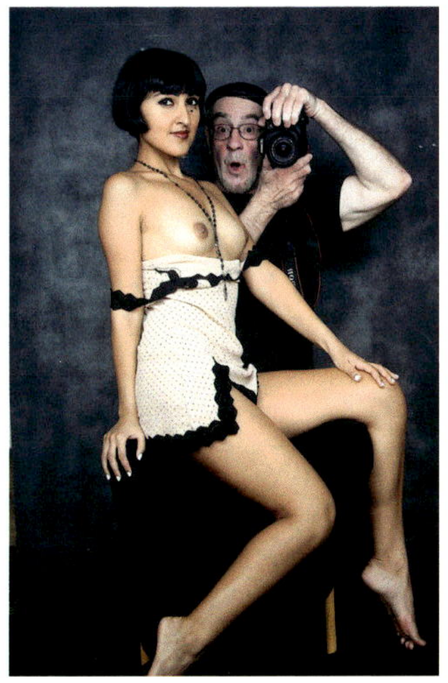

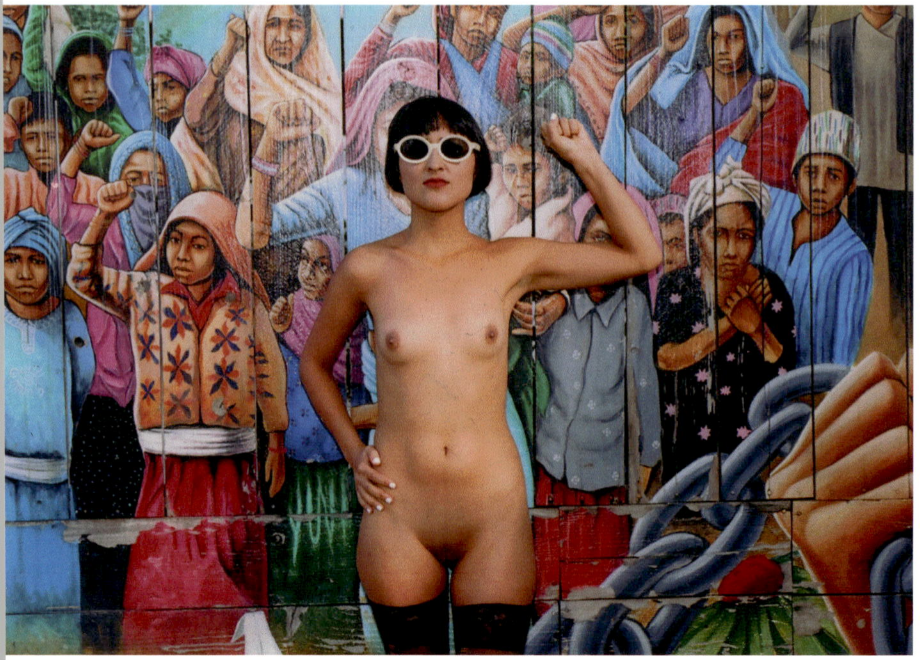

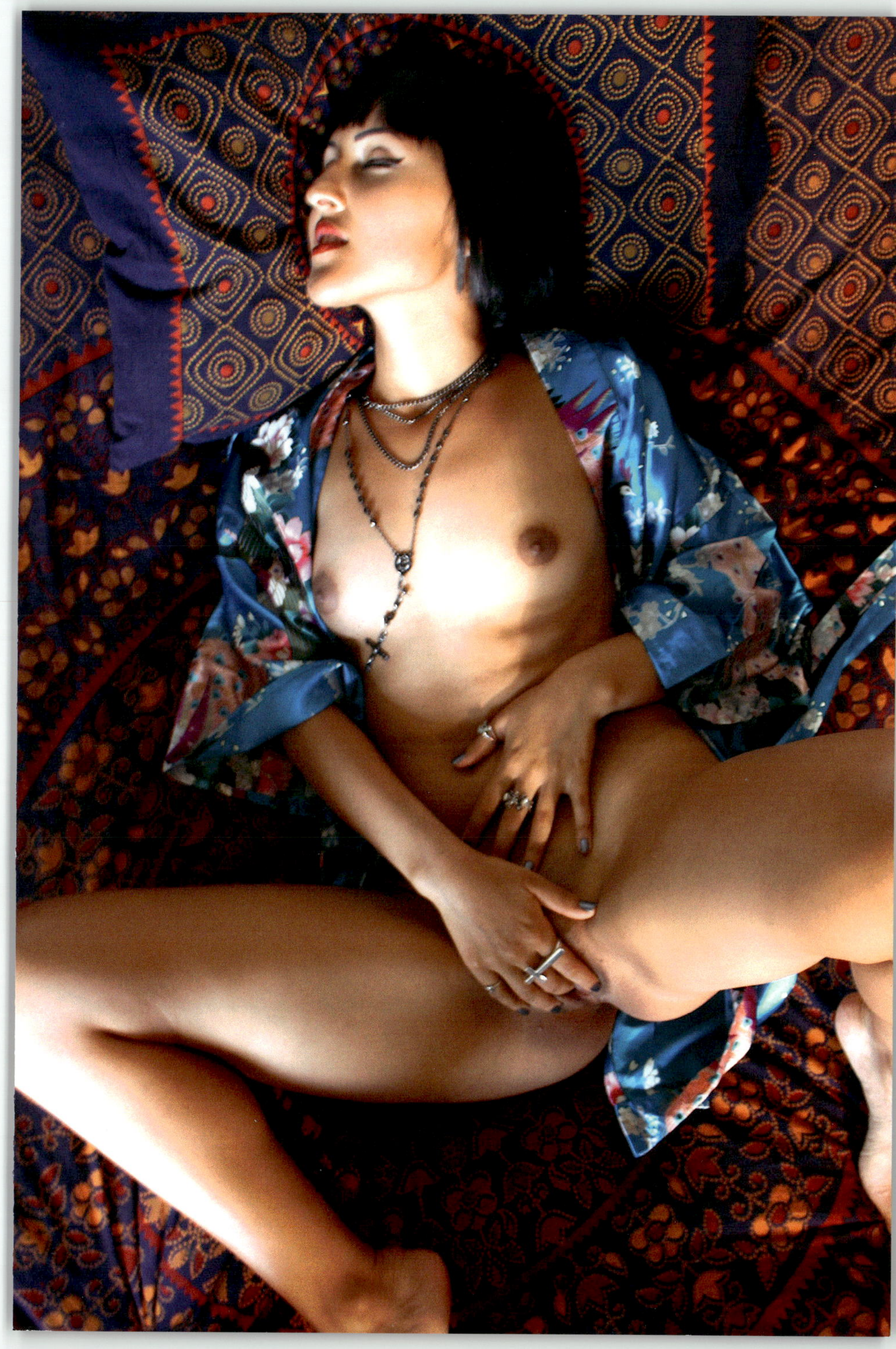

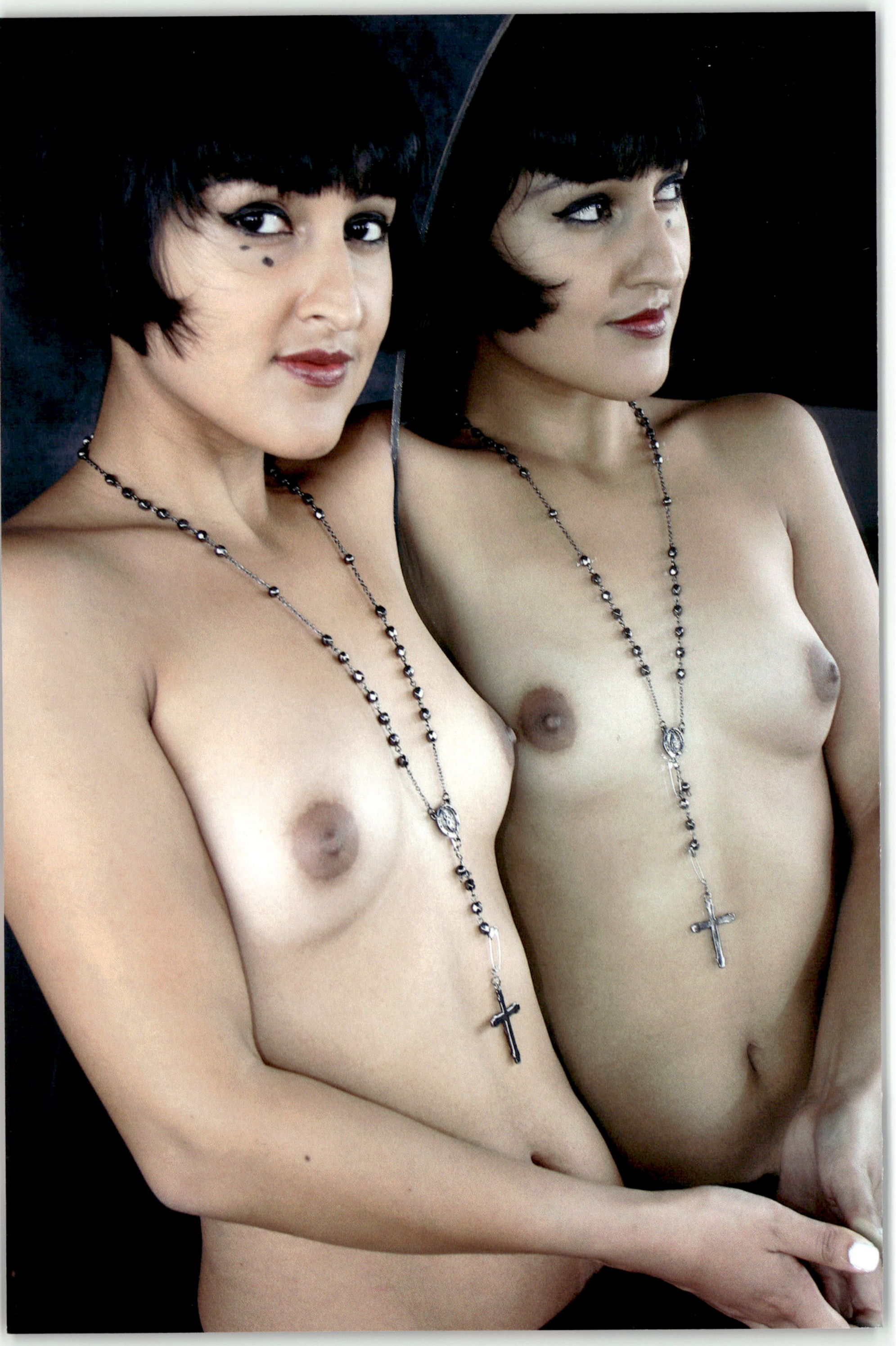

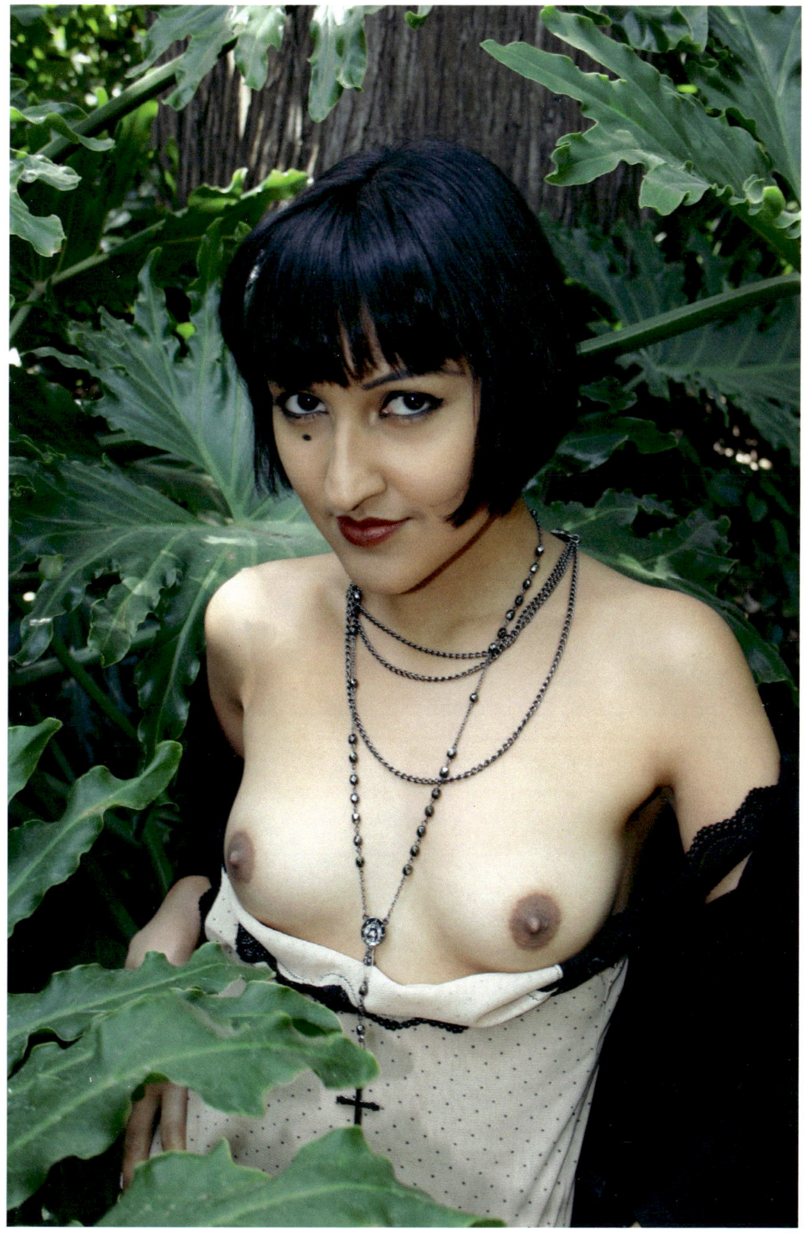

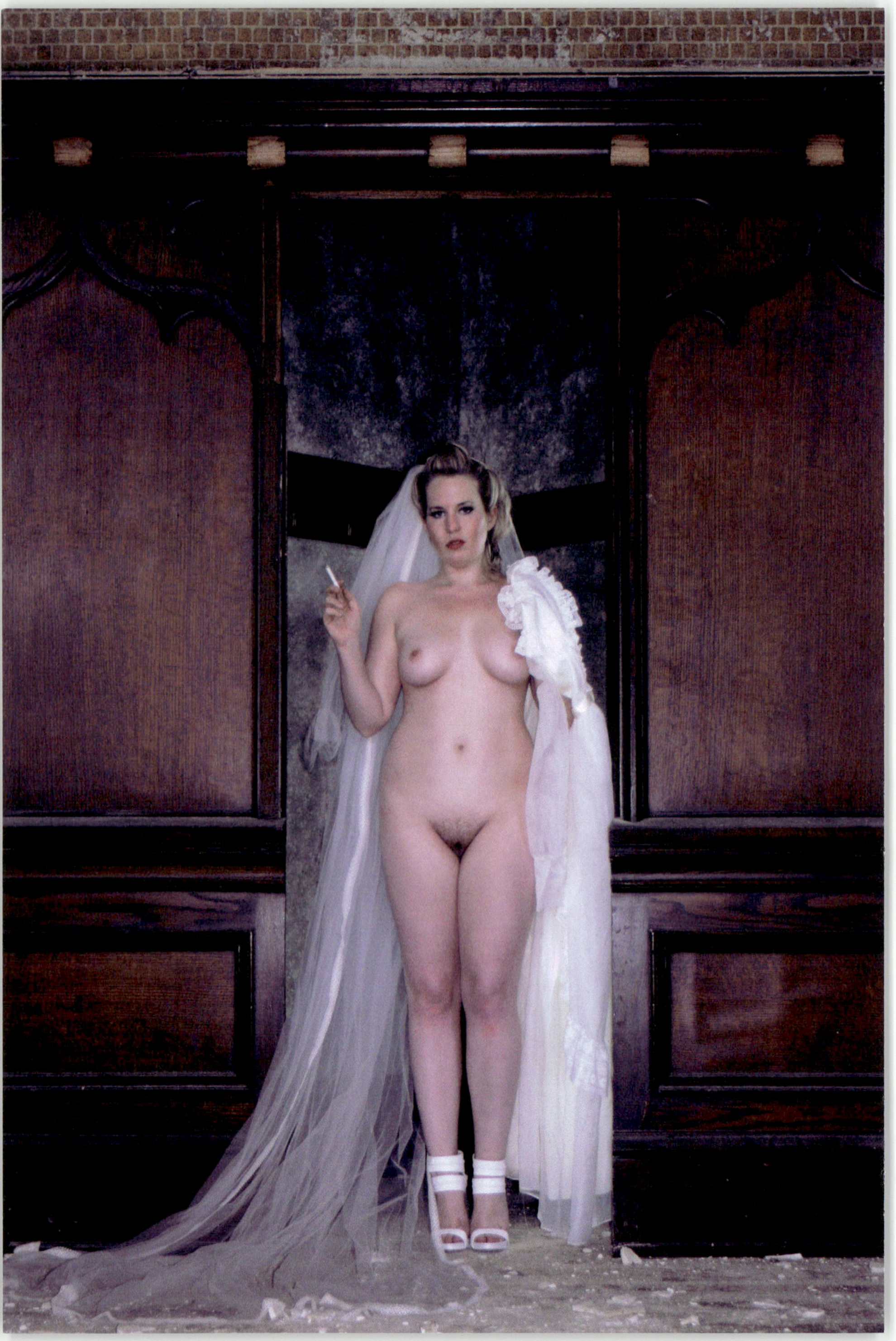

LISOLETTE GILCREST

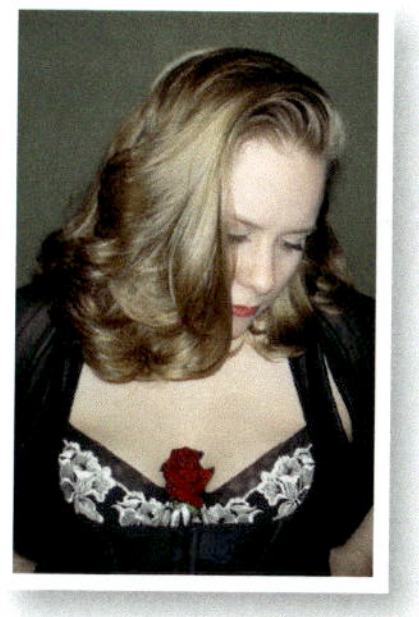

Lisolette Gilcrest made her debut at "The Dirty Show" in Detroit in 2006 with two pieces featuring model, muse and best friend Kathryn Stark. Her photography has been shown in over fifty erotic art exhibitions in the USA and internationally. It is also showcased in *Visions of Eros: A Midwest Perspective* (2011) and in *Expeditions* (Streetwise Art Publishing, 2009), as well as the UK's *Filament* magazine.

"I have always felt safe in going to Kathryn and saying, 'Here's my idea… I have no idea whether it'll work, but I want to try it…' and we've always had a blast doing so. Because we are best friends and feel so free to try (and sometimes fail at) different concepts, we have produced some of the most memorable images."

www.lisolette.com

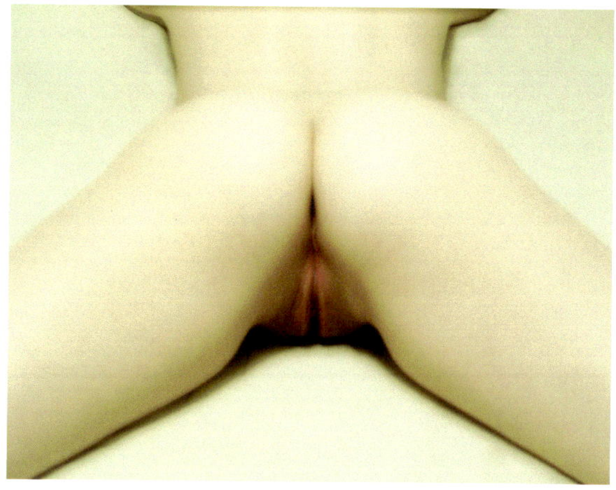

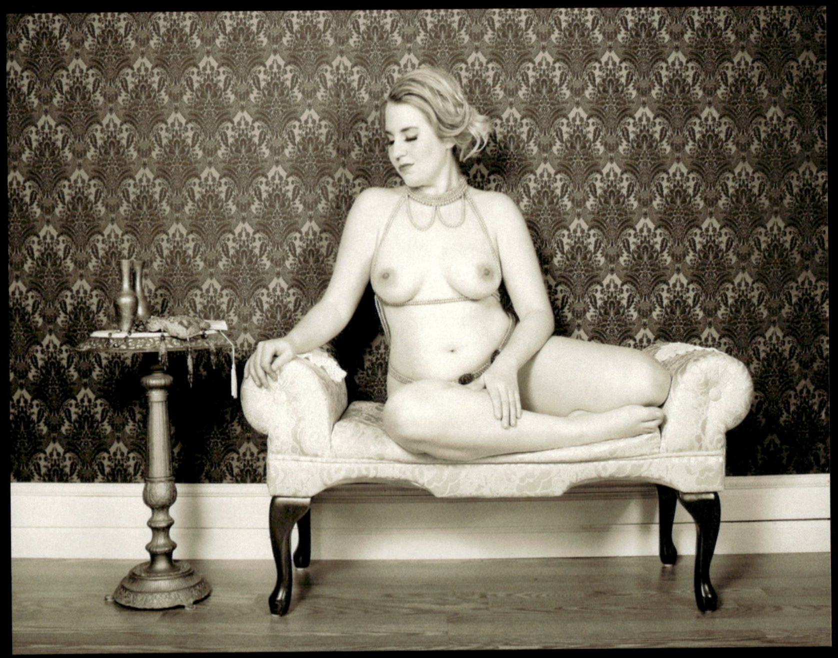

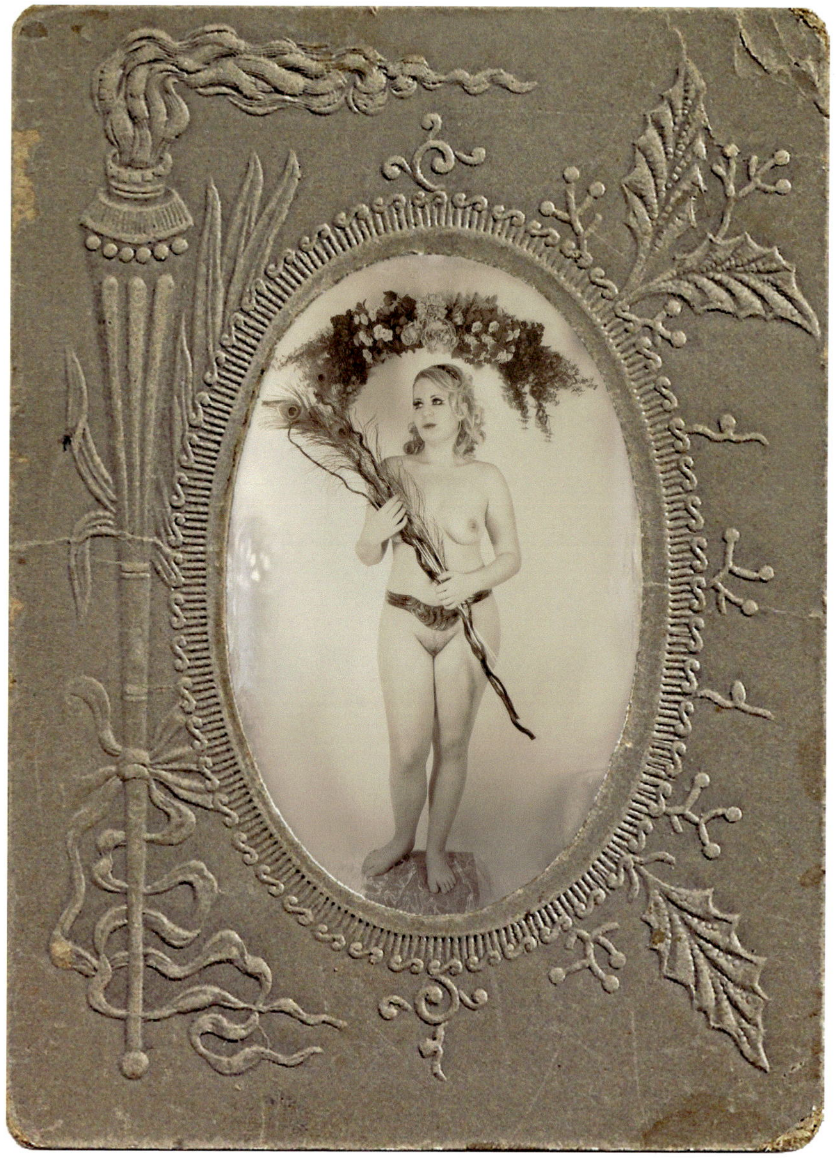

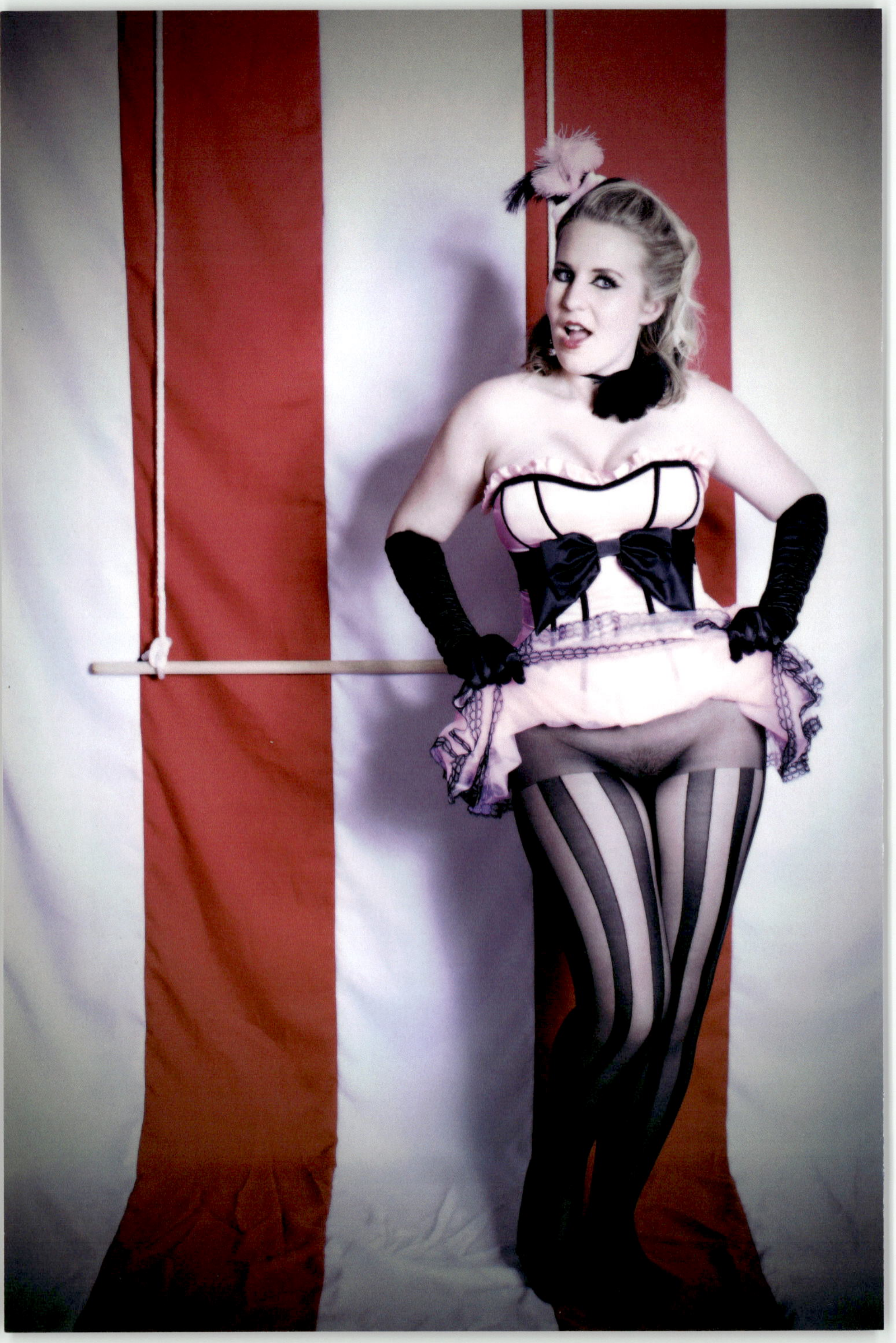

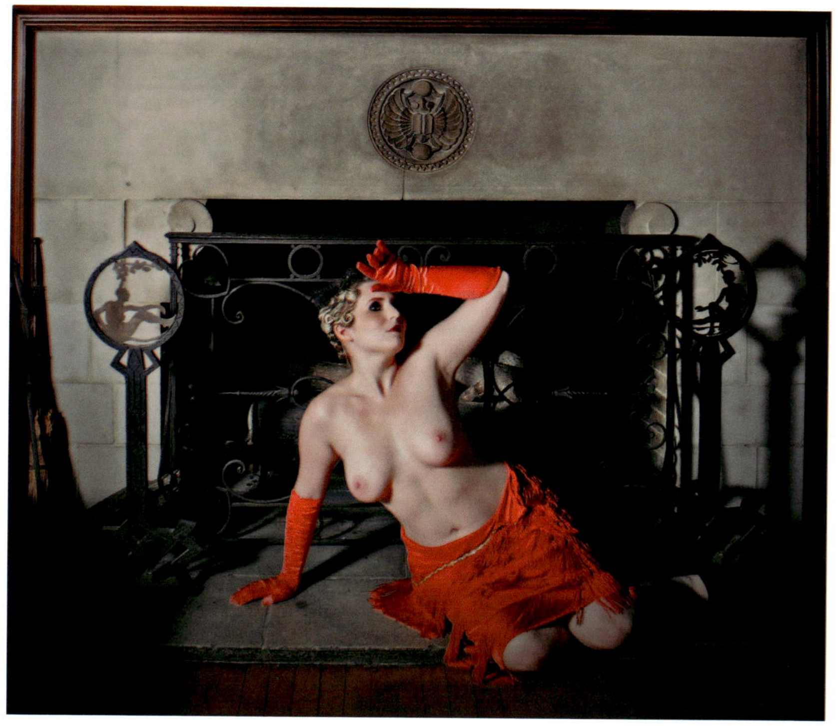

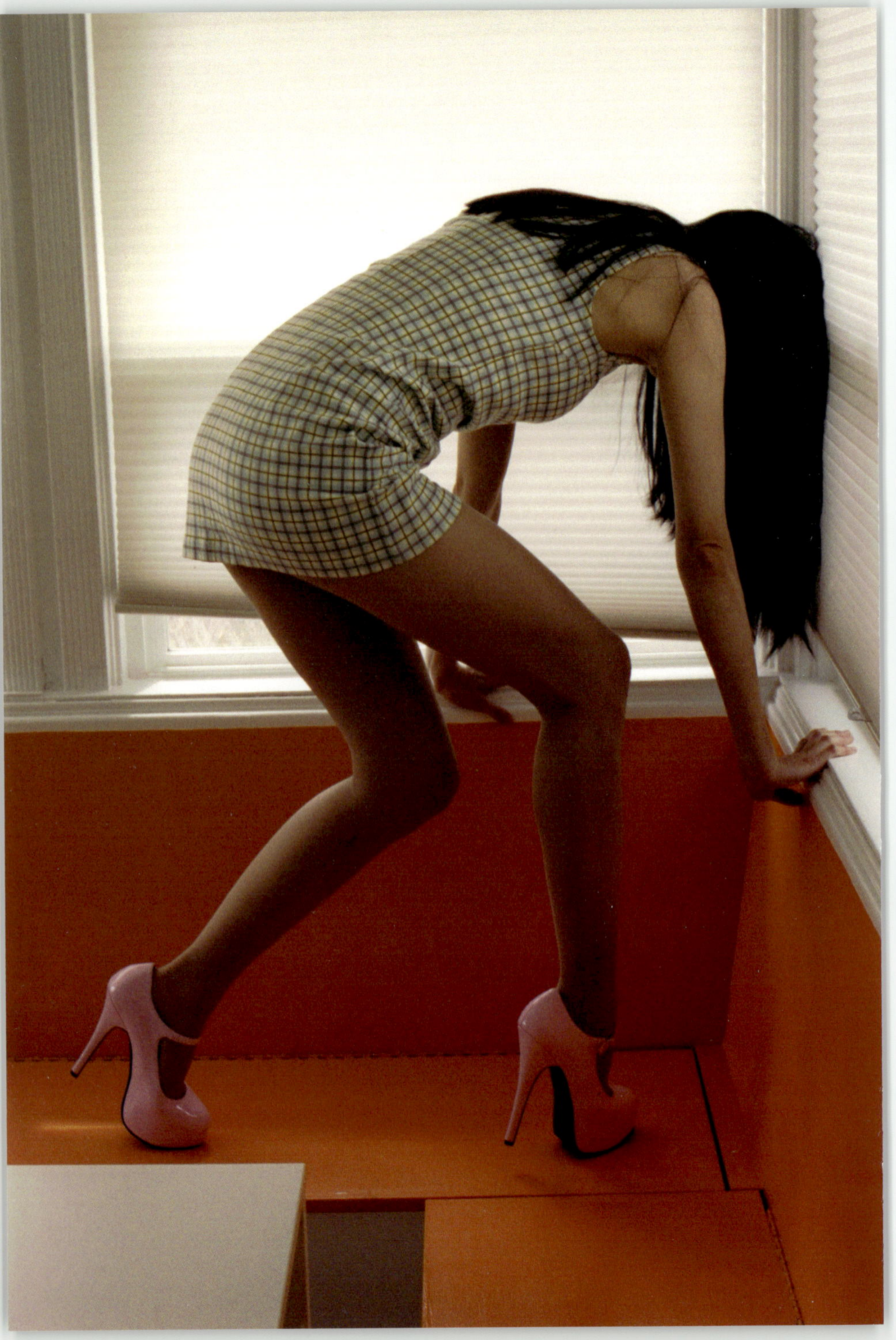

STEVE DIET GOEDDE

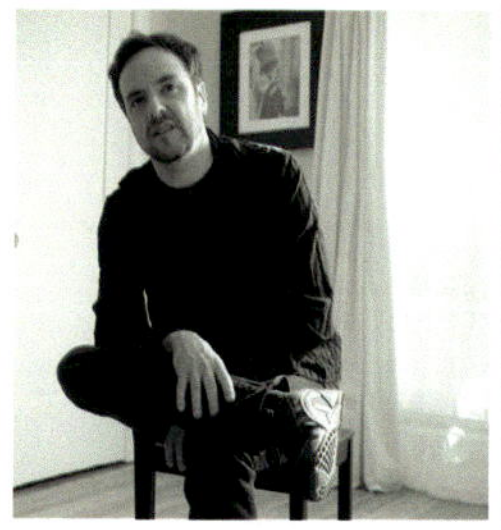

"I met Yee in April of 2011, and we've been a couple ever since. Yee is my favourite kind of model – a non-model who just happens to photograph extremely well.
So much erotica is manufactured for the camera and doesn't have a sense of realness between the model and photographer. Being able to work with Yee in this manner is a fulfilment of this quest to capture legitimate moments of desire."

www.stevedietgoedde.com

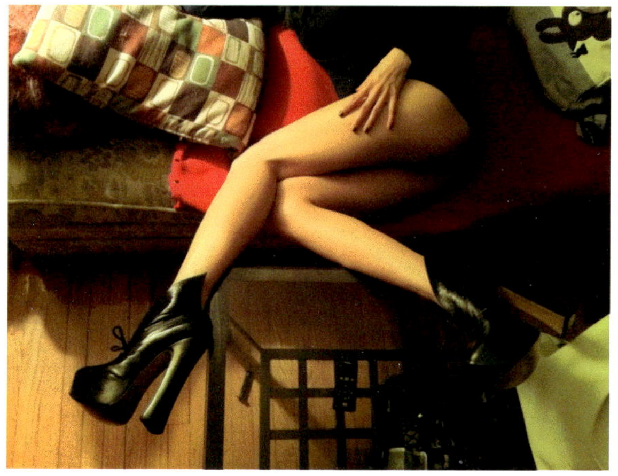

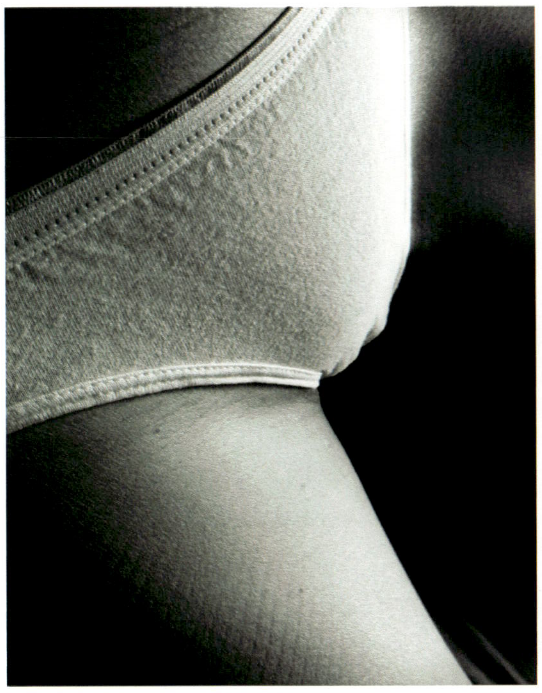

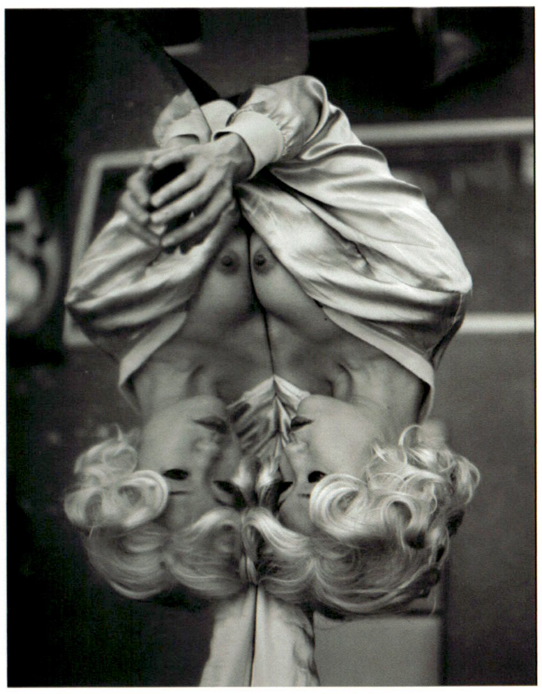

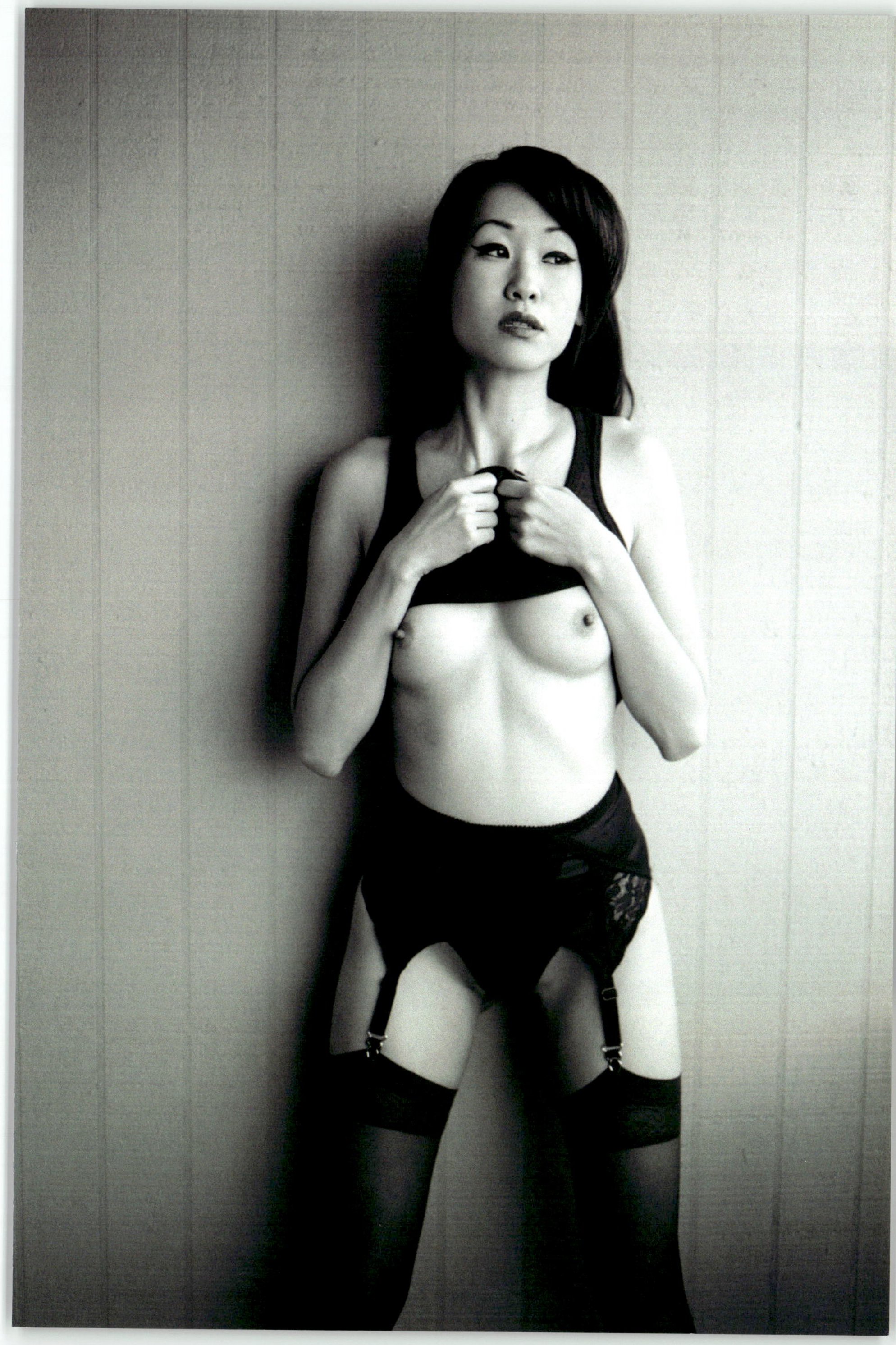

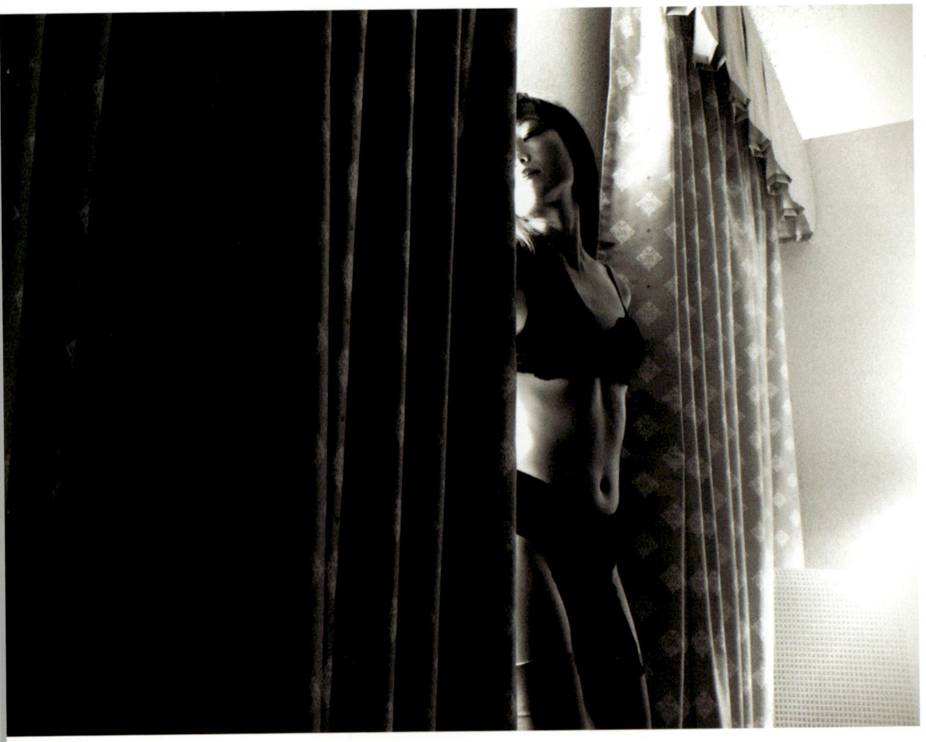

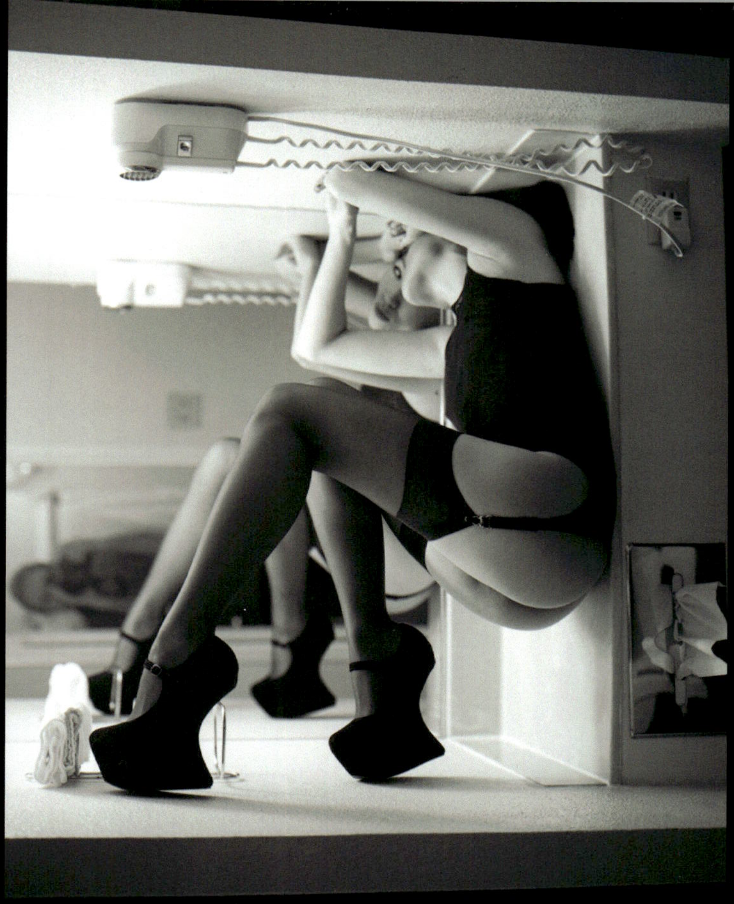

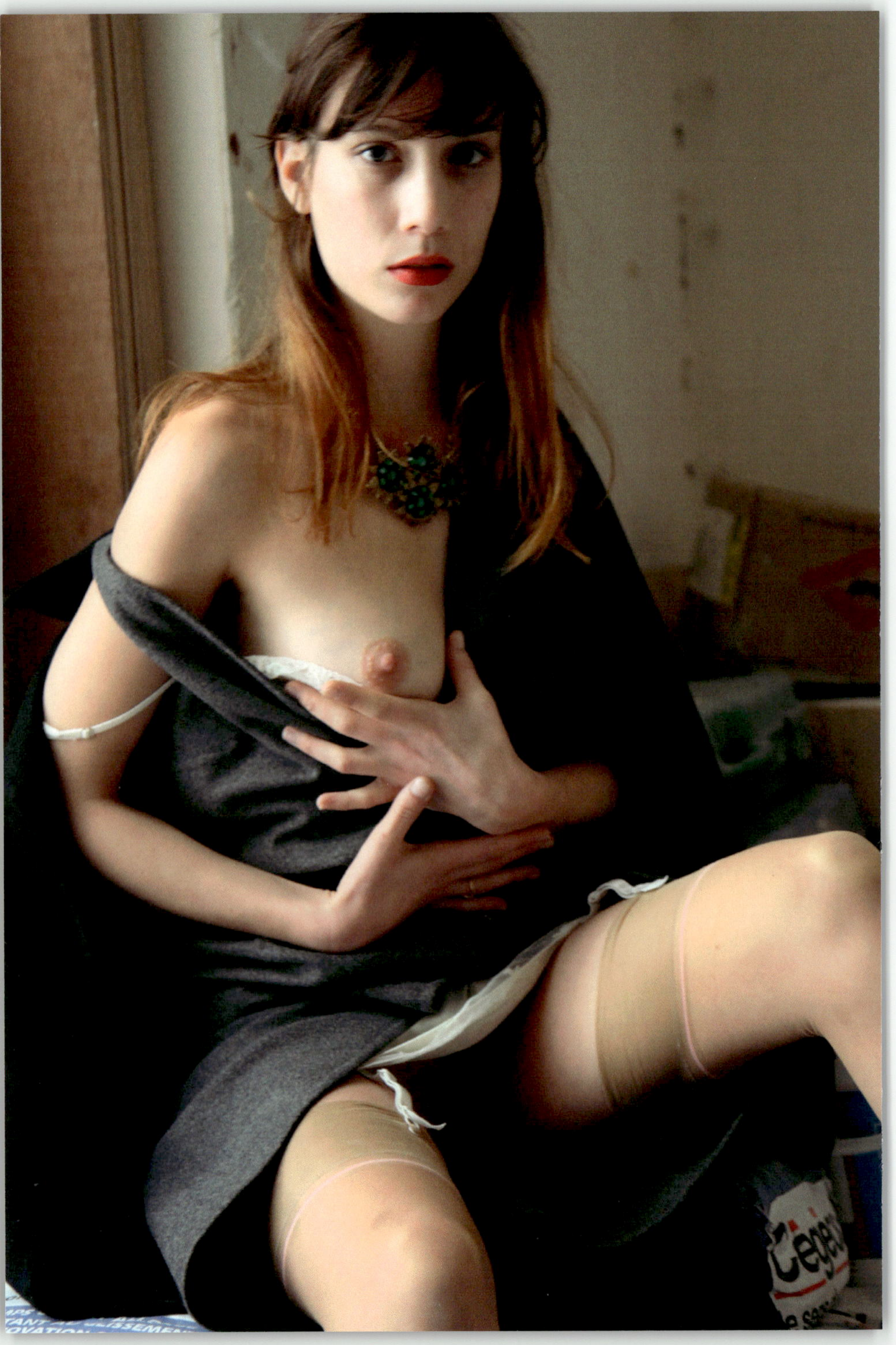

SAM GUELIMI

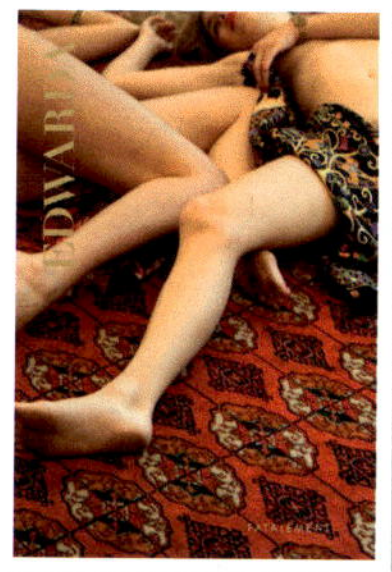

Paris-based French photographer Sam Guelimi runs the fine-art erotic magazine *EDWARDA*, which features many of her photos. Through this highly personal platform she enjoys displaying the shapes of her desire. Writers as well as other photographers join her there for a playful dialogue in which words and images cross-pollinate.

"I choose Eva as her facial features fascinate me. They harbour promises while still holding many things back, which I find so highly ambiguous. She offers me an infinity of possibilities, all well beyond the realm of good and evil."

www.edwarda.fr

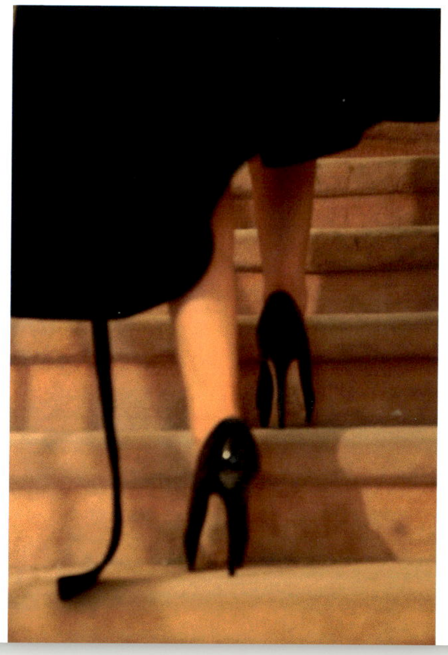

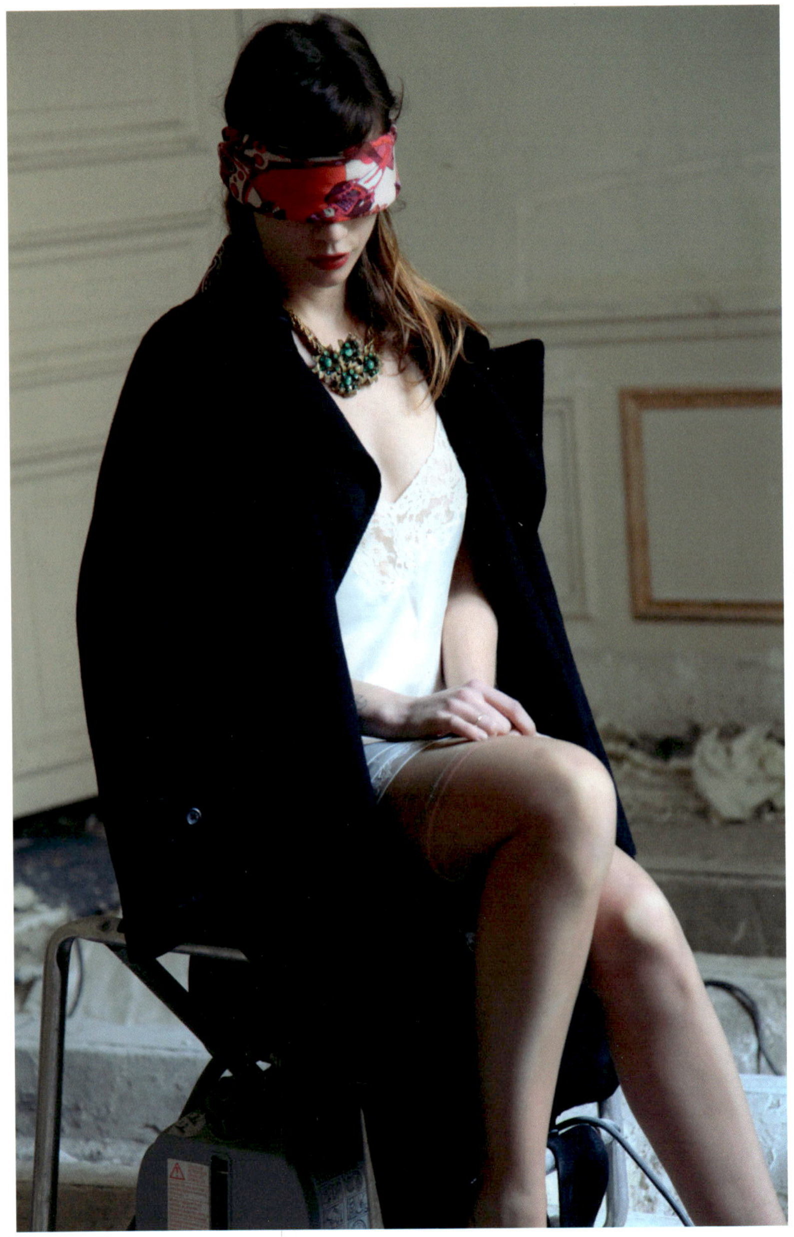

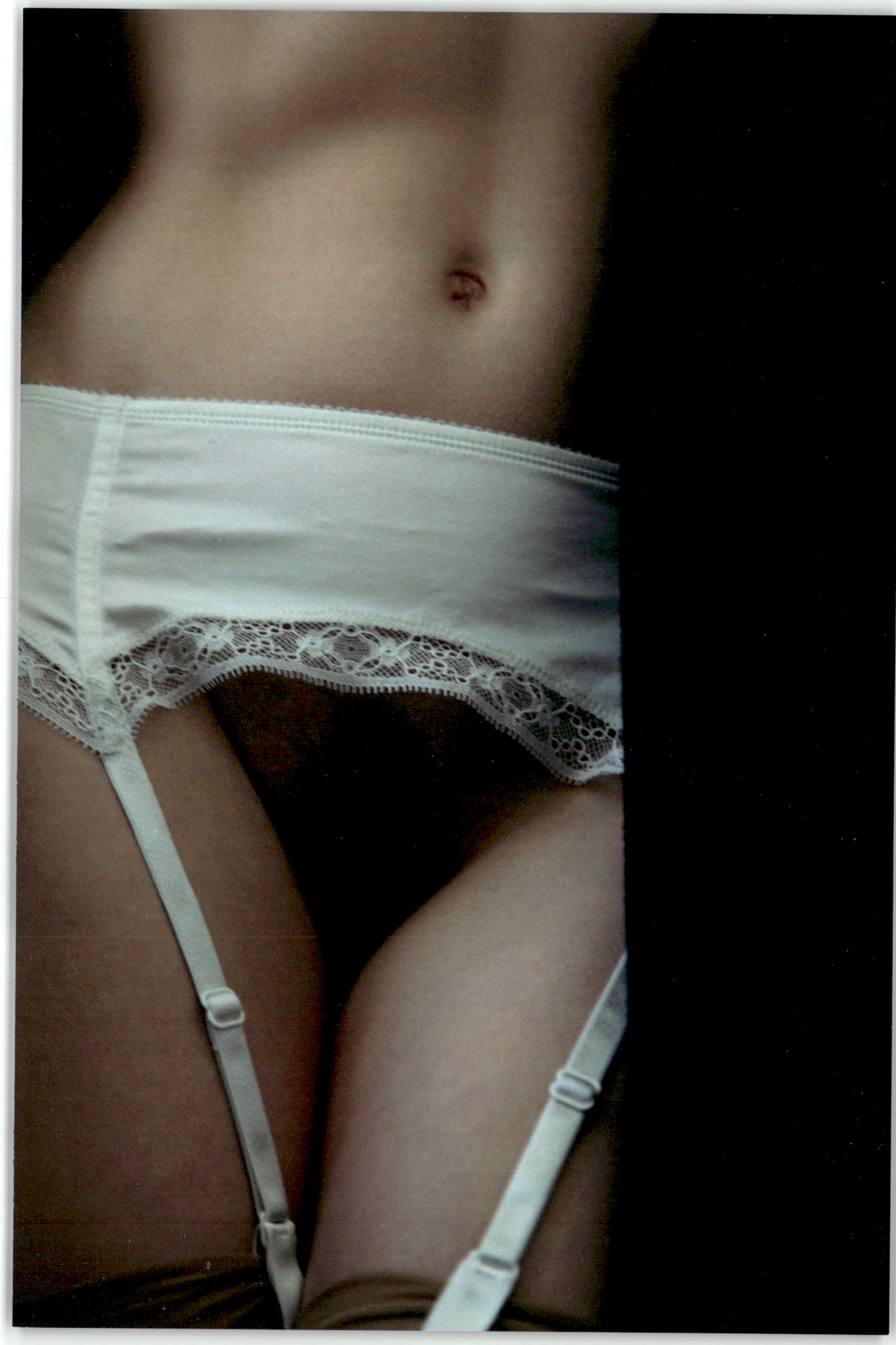

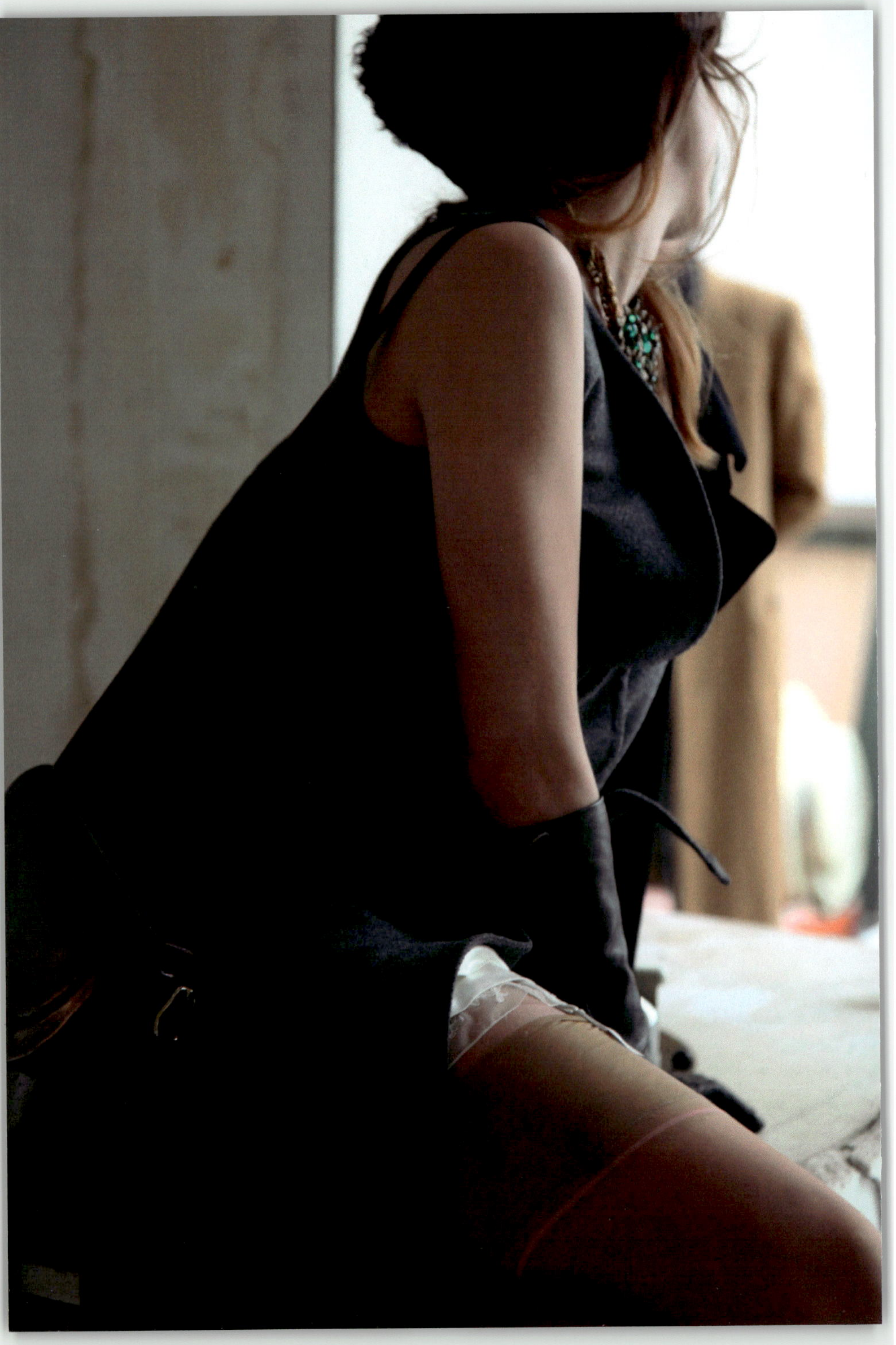

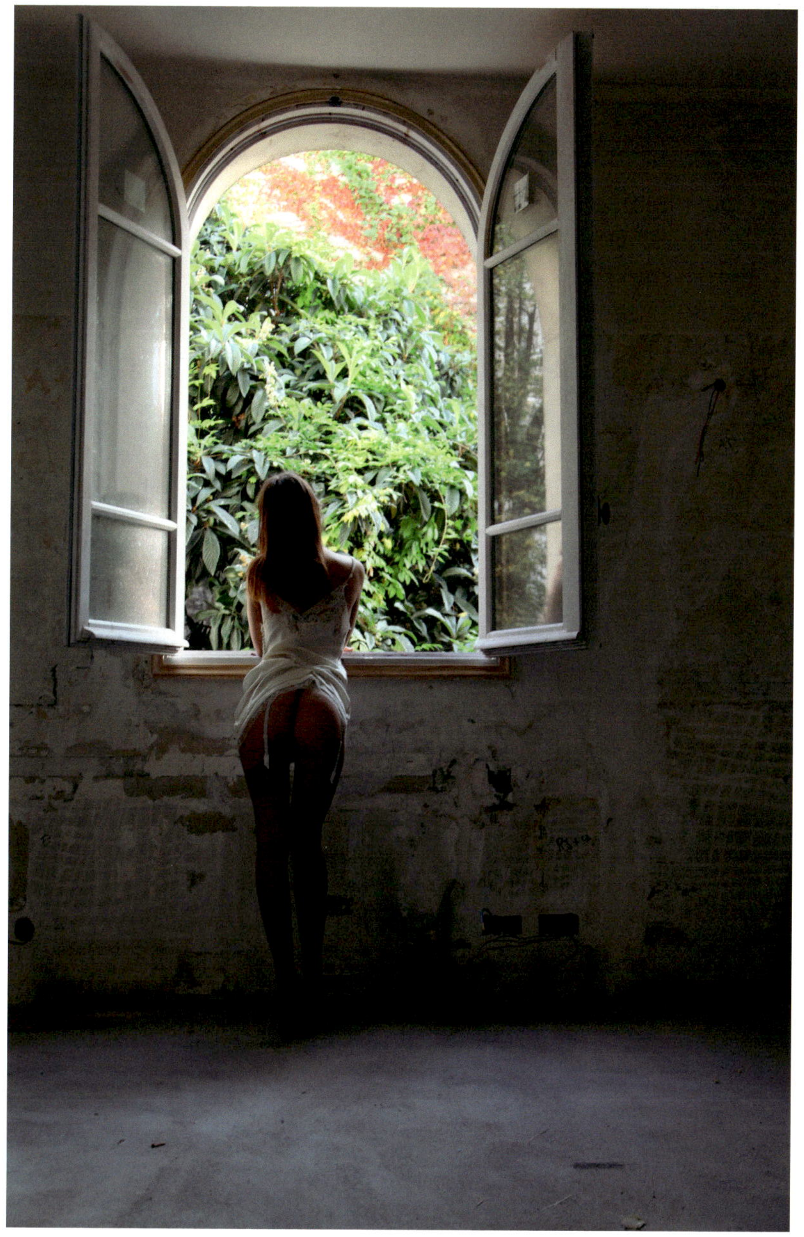

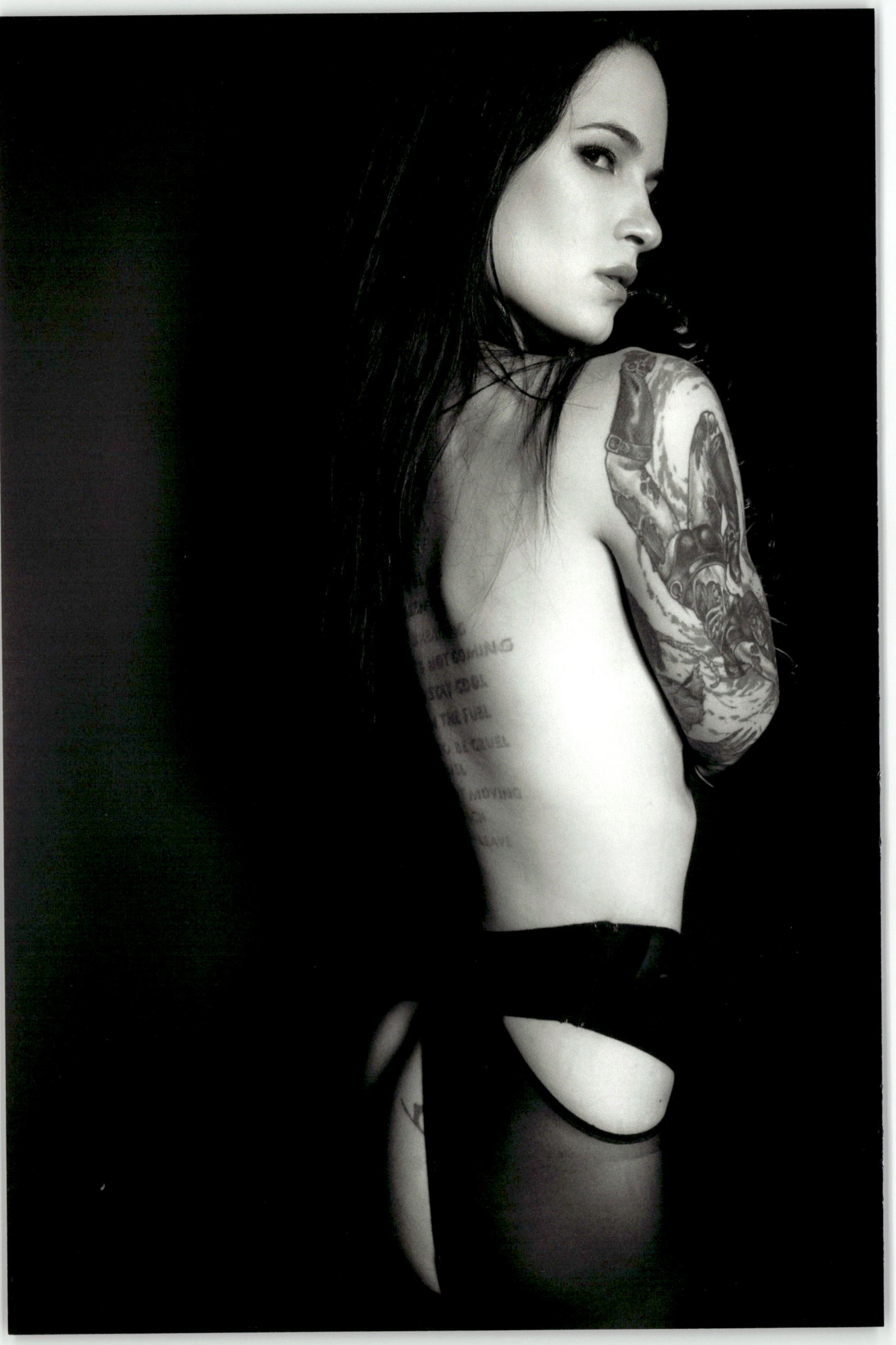

ALEJANDRA GUERRERO

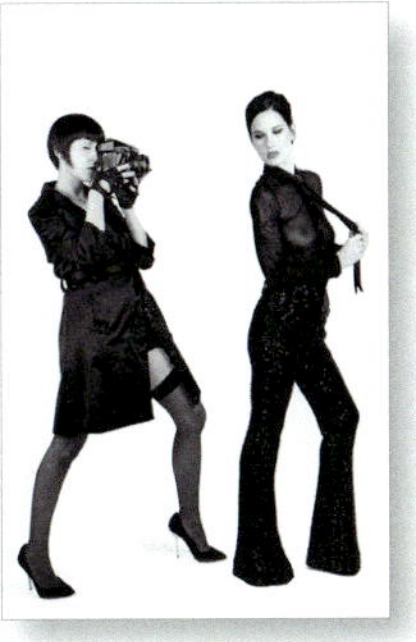

“My work is both behind the camera, as mostly an erotic photographer, and in front, shooting provocative self-portraits. In the first, there are the fantasies and alter egos I depict through the models. In this way I express power, seduction, beauty, sexuality, fetishism, feminism and erotic fictions.

“My self-portraits are more direct expressions of who I am and how I feel in the context of my personal life, in time and space, and of my identity as a woman, but in the context of reality.

“I met Olivia Black on a friend’s recommendation. I didn’t know what to expect the first time we shot, but I was really impressed with the results. As we developed a close friendship our shoots came to reflect what she inspired in me.”

www.alt-er-ego.com

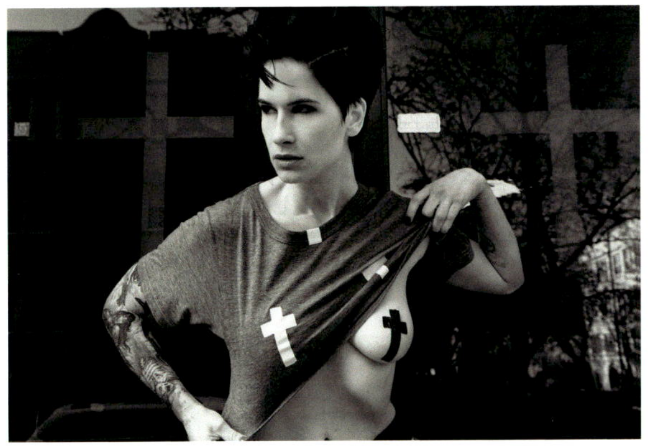

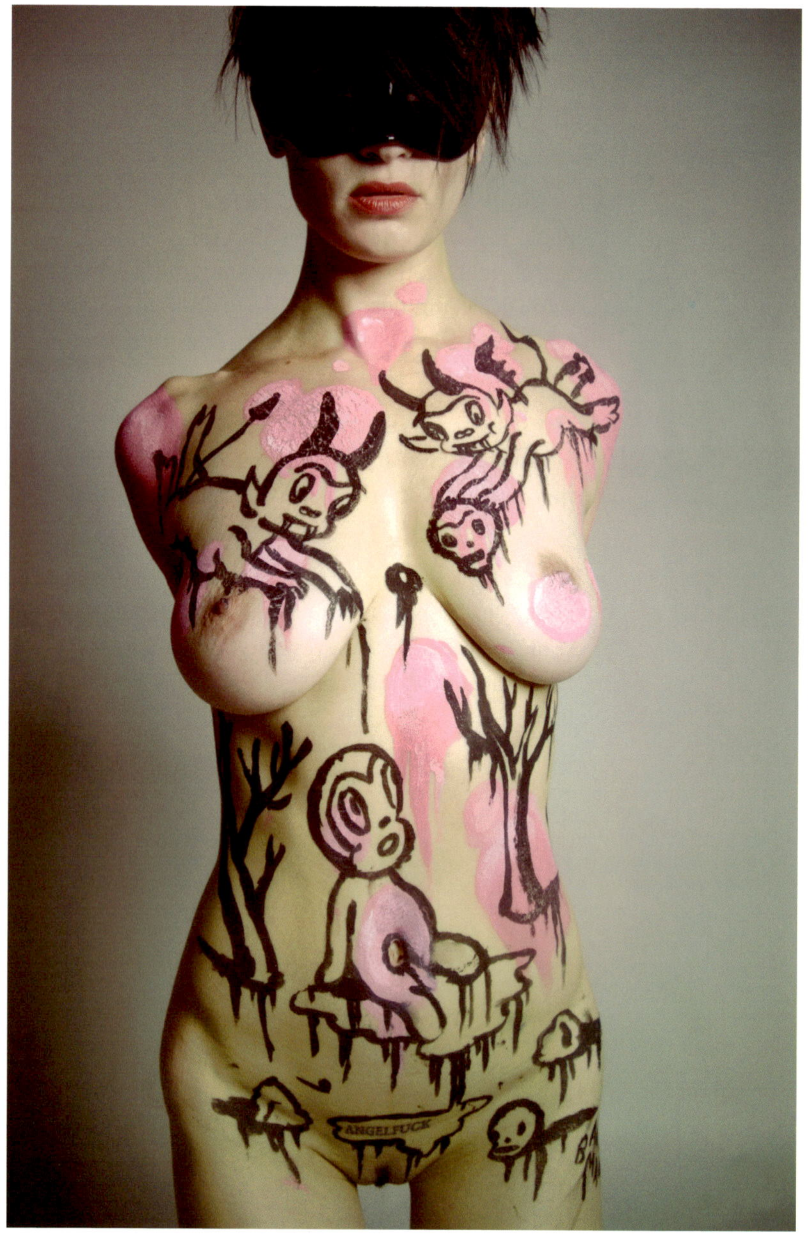

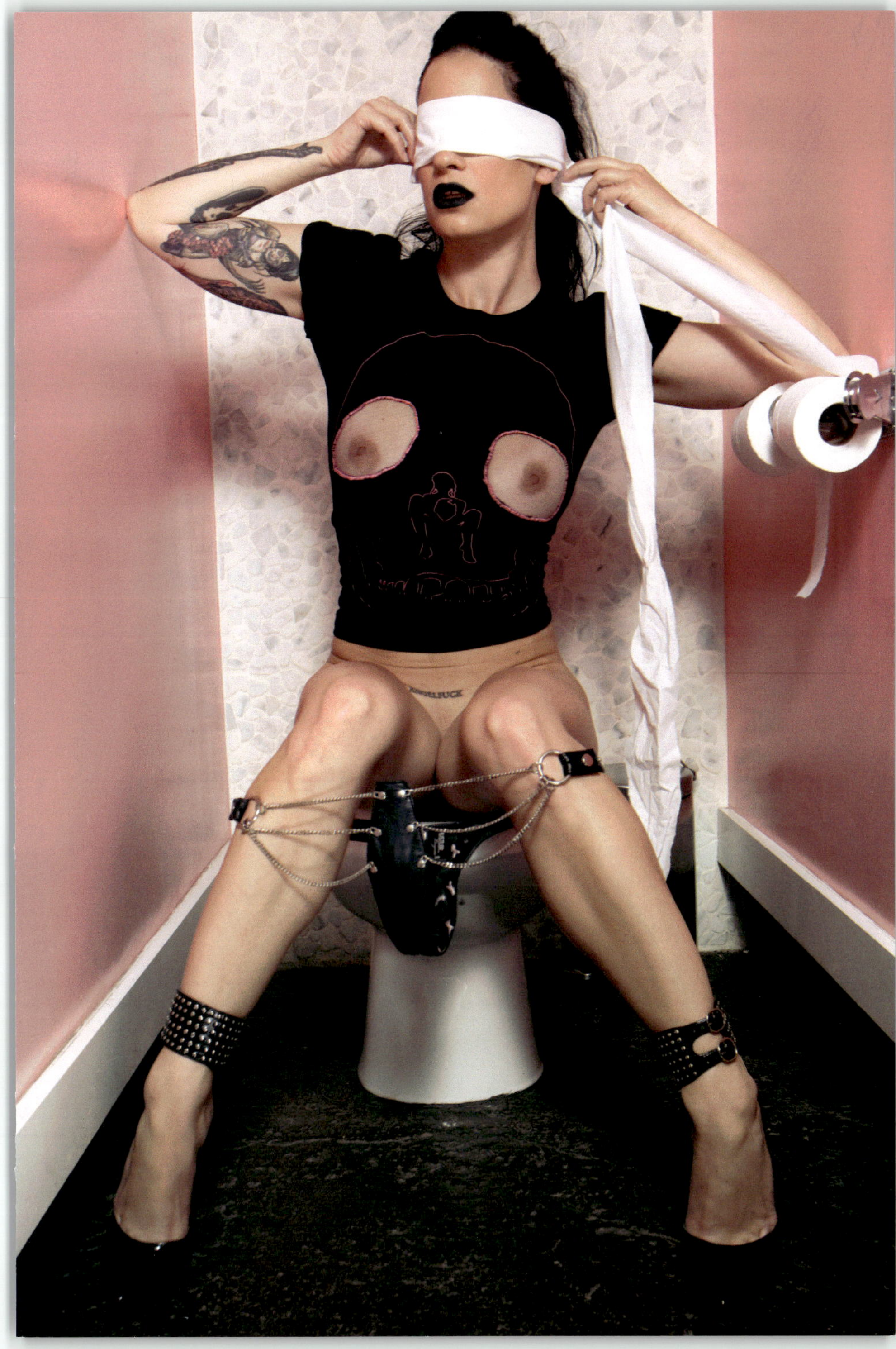

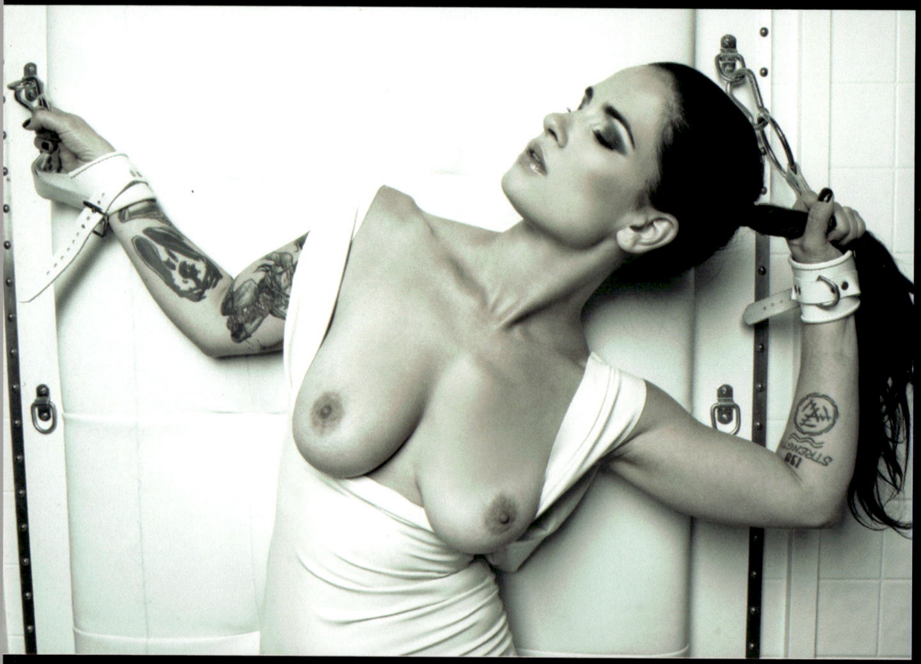

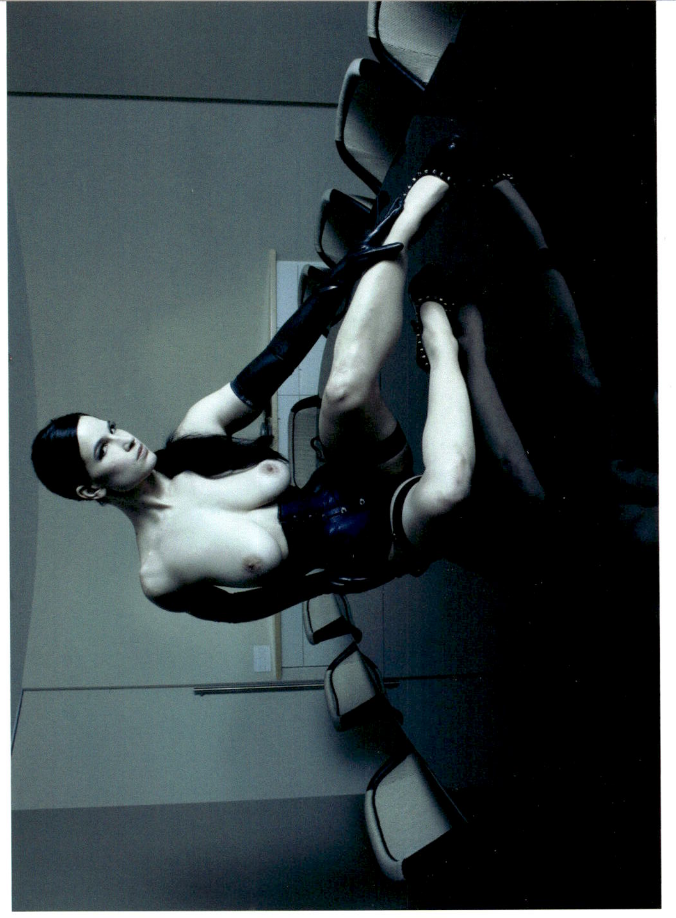

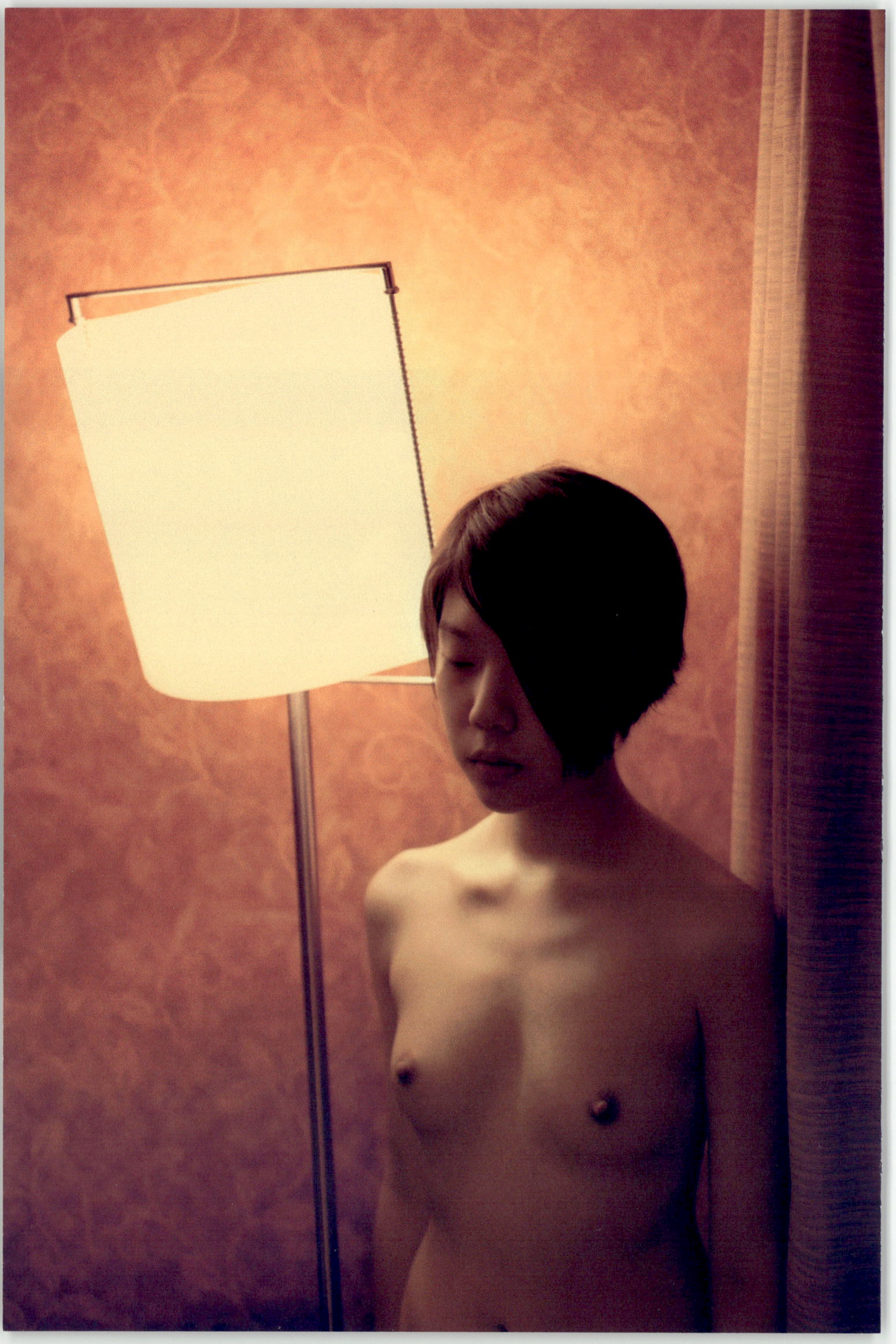

AKIF HAKAN

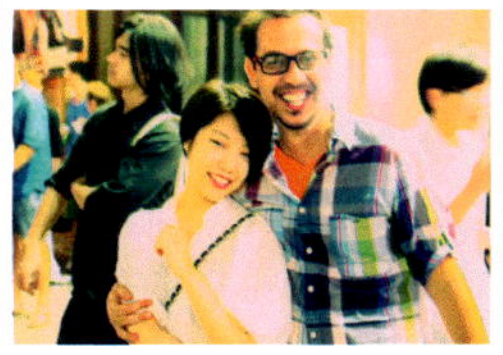

An American of Turkish origin, Akif Hakan experiments with new photographic techniques and styles. He blends current trends in the visual arts with his own creativity, which is influenced by many great movies, especially from the Far East. In most of his images his goal is to give the viewer a story and create a mood. His images are very cinematic, often with unusual colour combinations, and strive to go beyond established styles and widen the boundaries of photographic expression.

“I met TingTing through a photographer friend in Hong Kong. She is very open-minded, a dream subject as I don’t like to have any rules binding me when I work. She loves being a part of the process as well. She helps me create and inspires me.”

www.hakanphotography.com

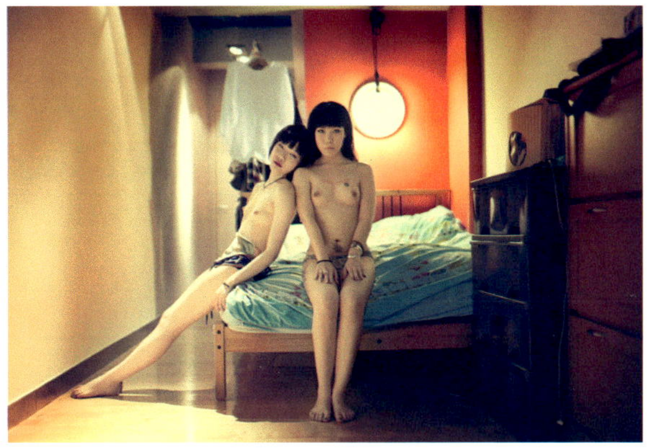

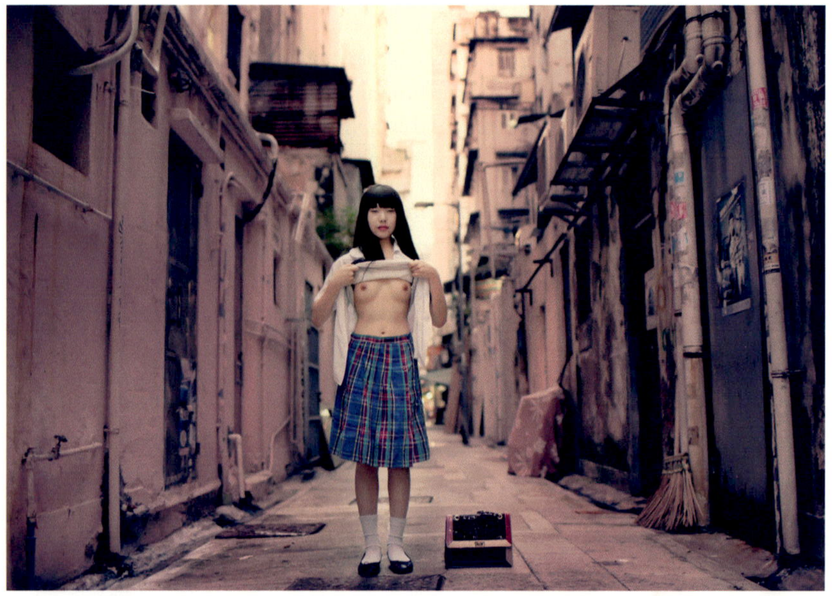

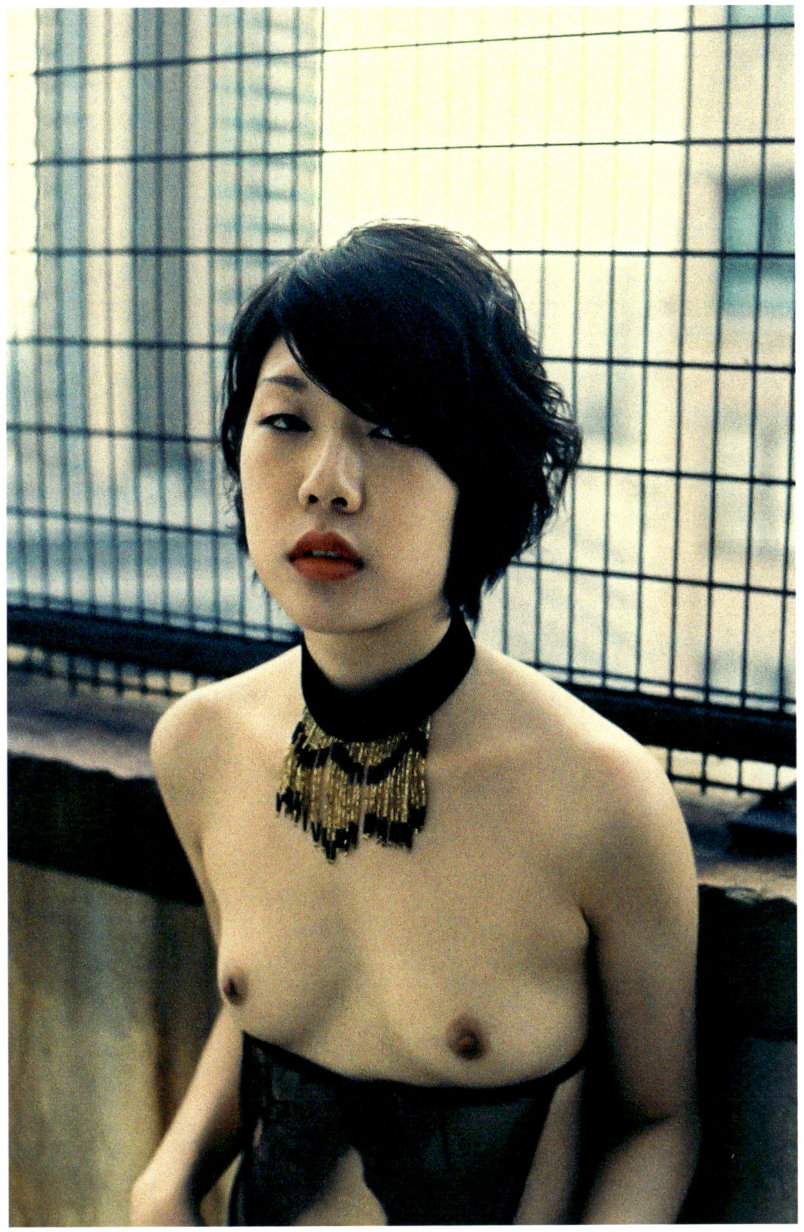

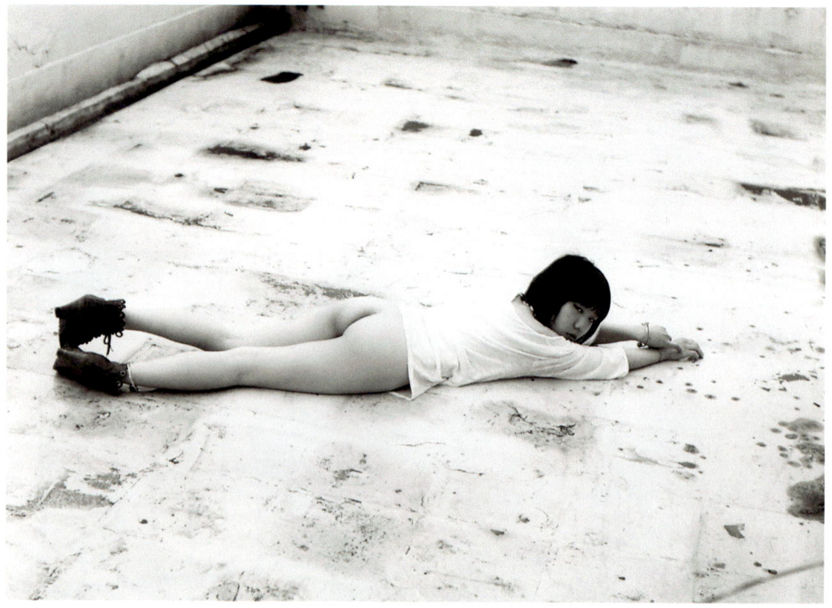

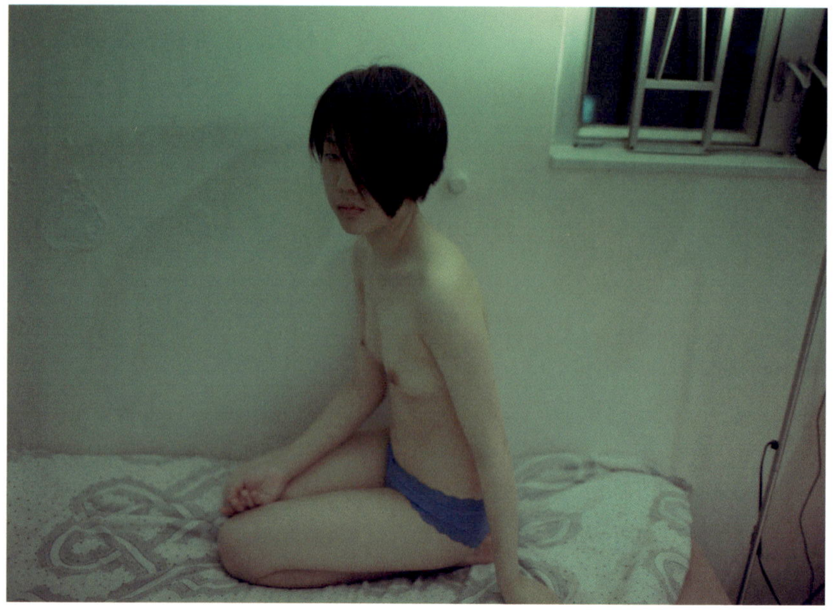

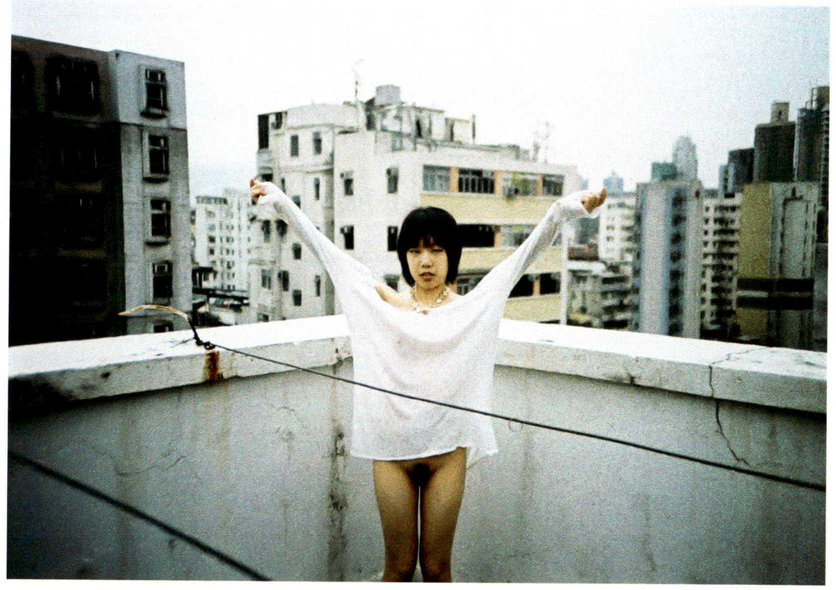

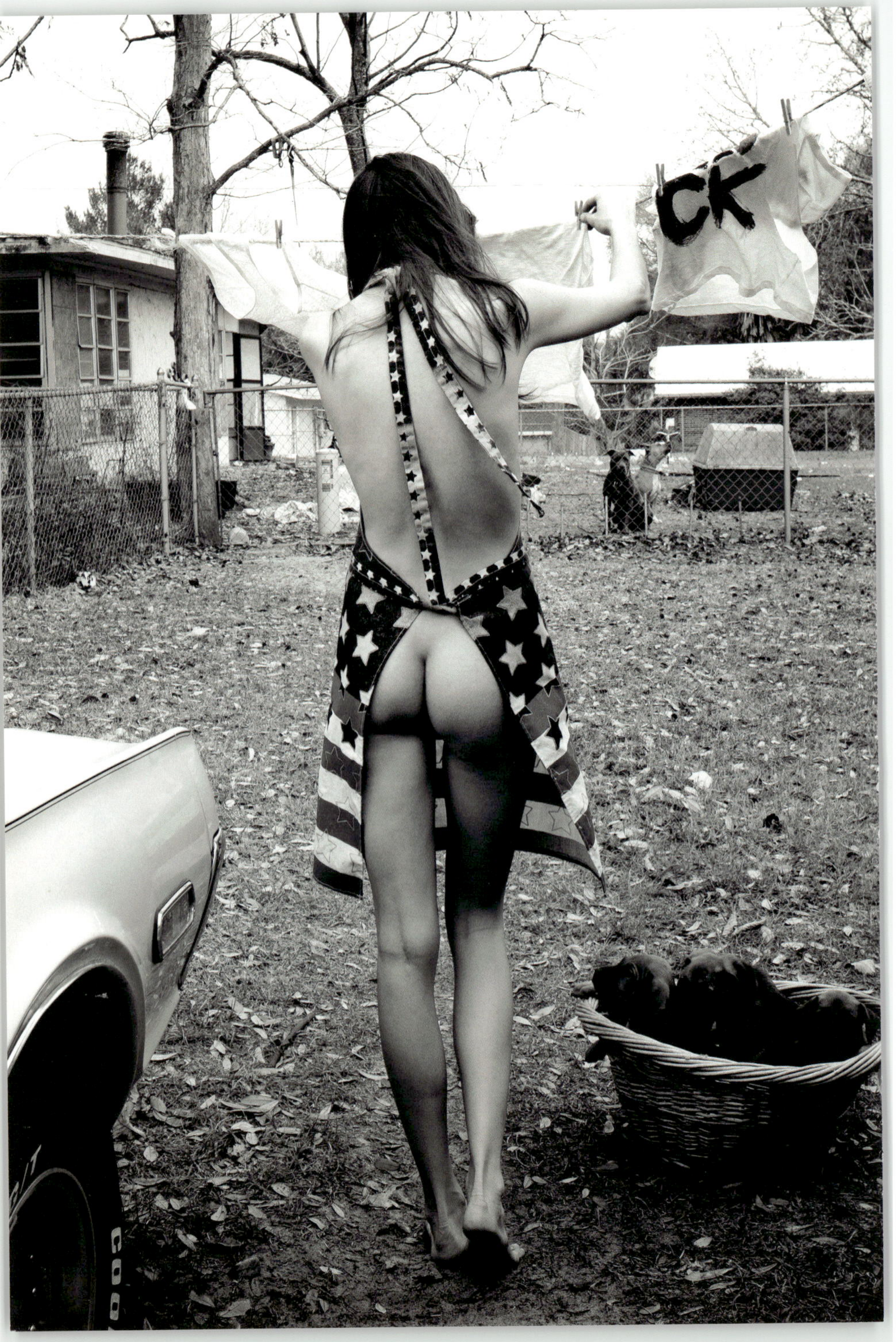
CK

FOX HARVARD

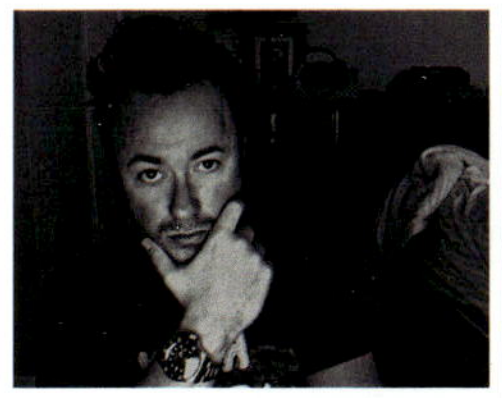

"I'm thirty-seven and essentially a self-taught photographer. I studied Studio Art and Visual Art at the University of South Florida in the late 1990s but photography was not my focus at the time. I grew up with painting as my primary creative outlet and since most of my work was mixed-media I felt the need to shoot my own images for inclusion in those pieces. Since that medium comprised the majority of my work, I've only been actually shooting for about three years now. After dropping out of college I directed a small non-profit gallery in central Florida for a few years, using the upstairs rooms as a studio. However, most of my current work is location- rather than studio-based, and I prefer it that way."

www.foxharvard.pixu.com

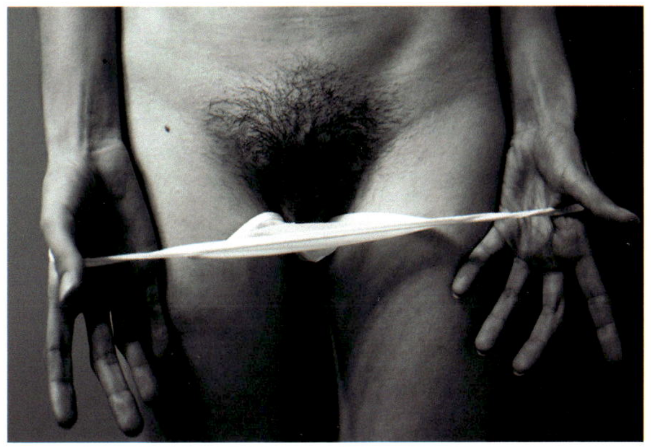

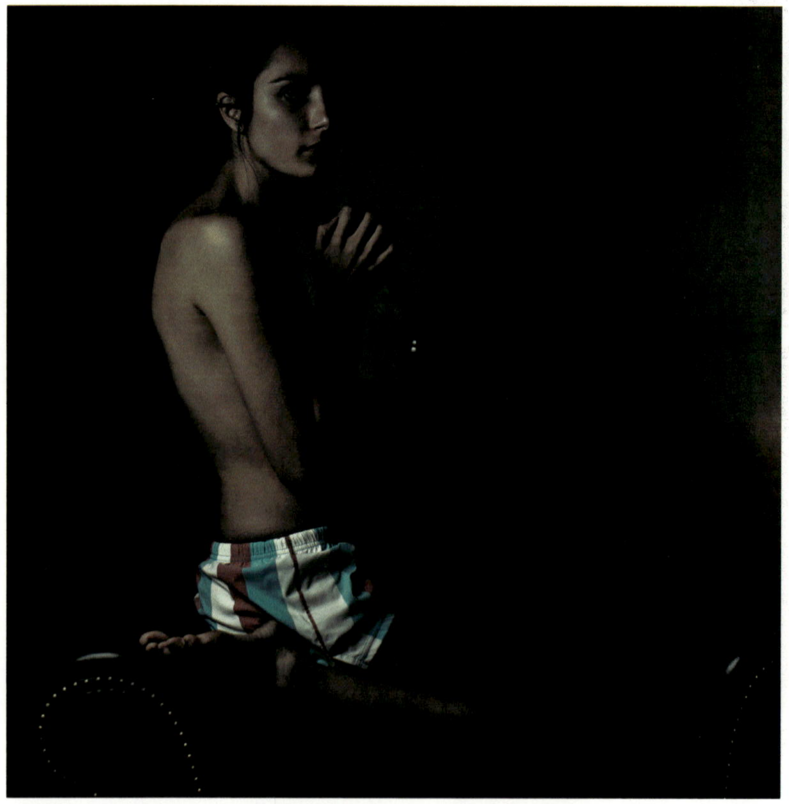

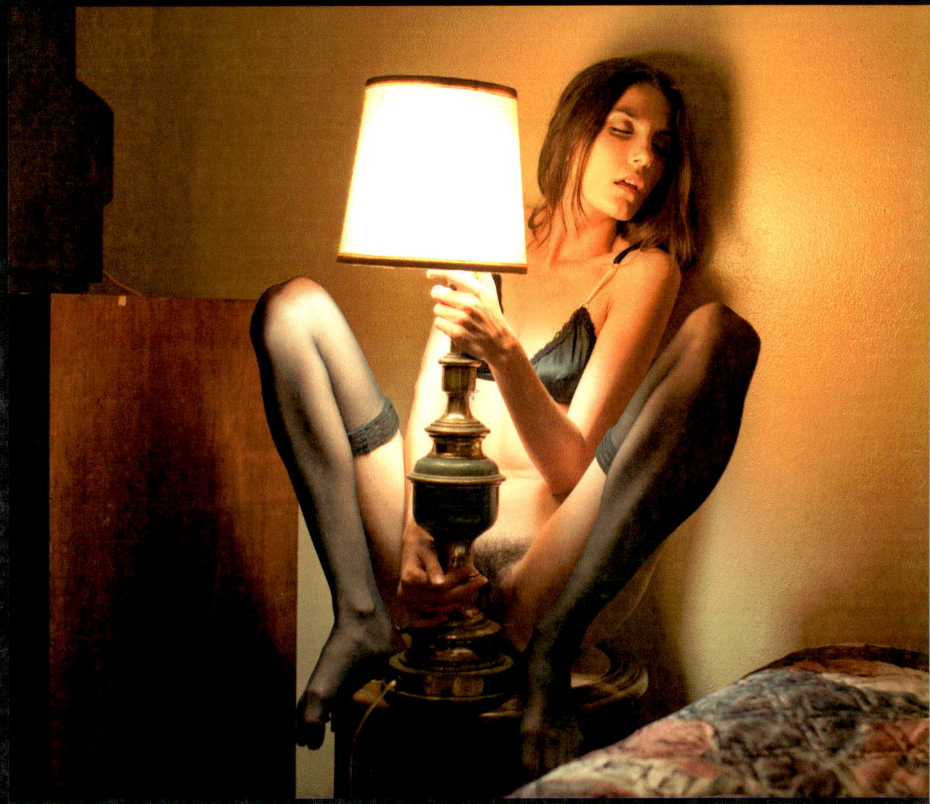

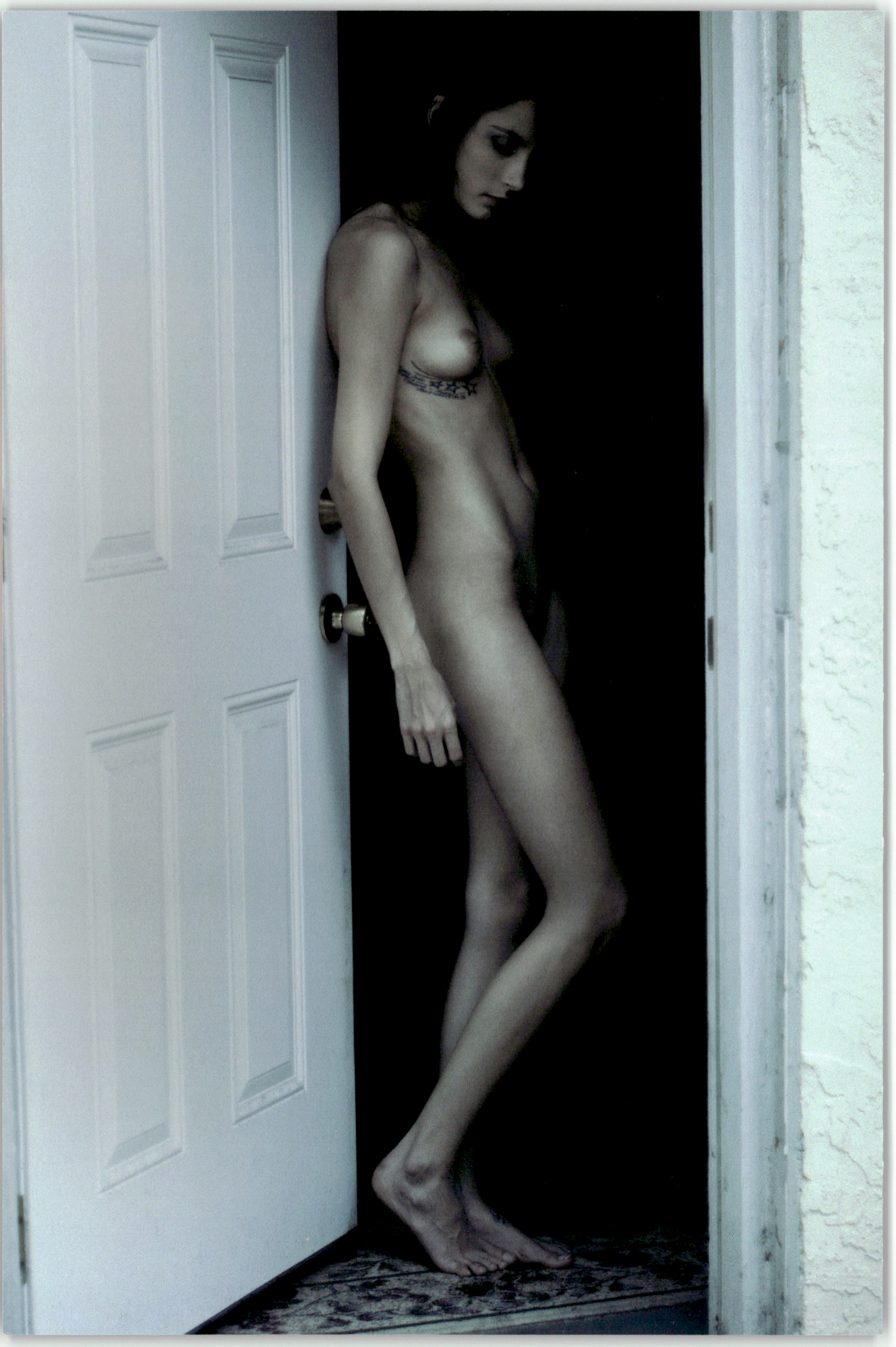

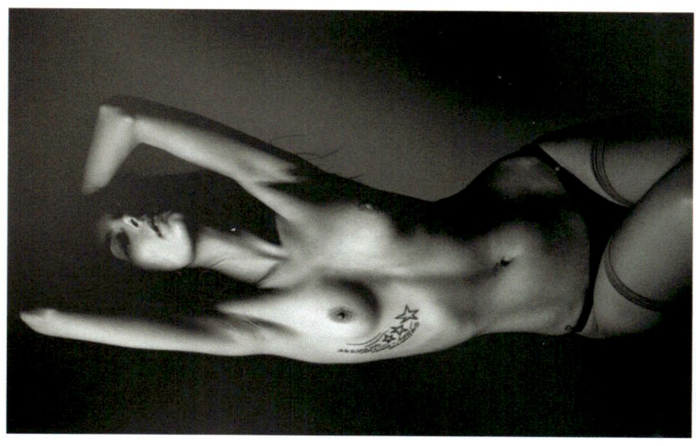

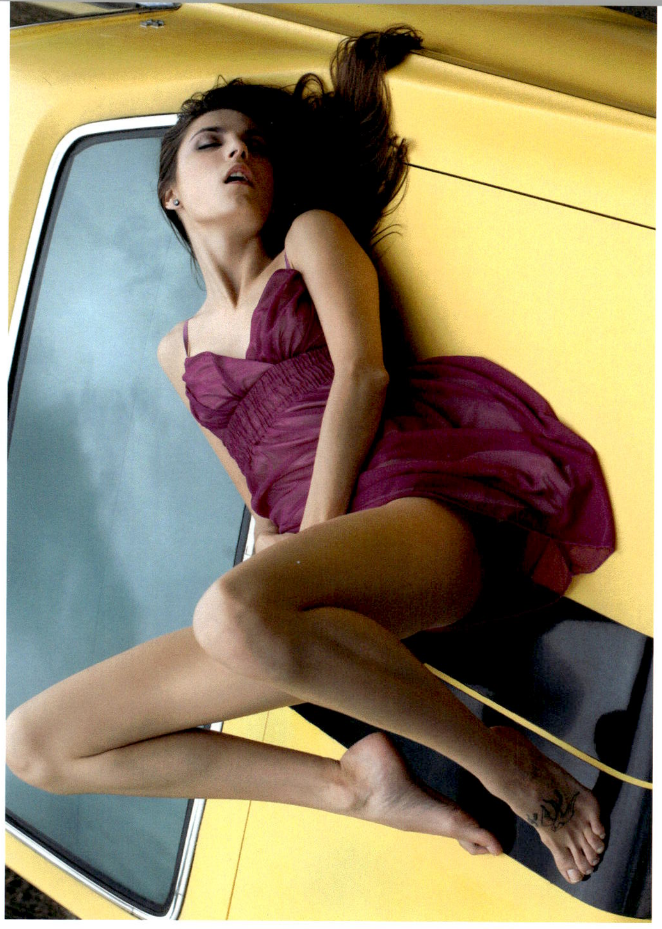

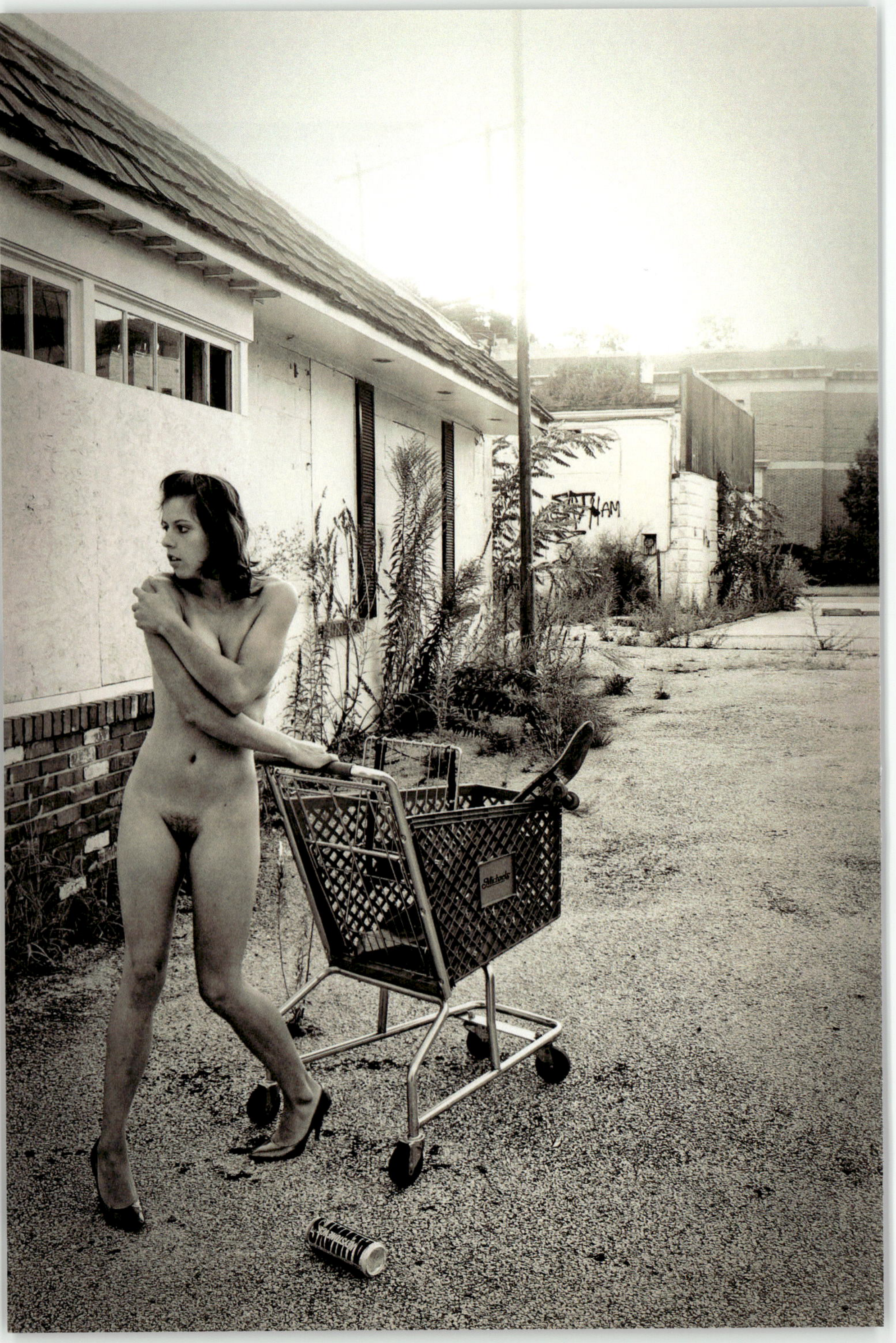

DAVID HILTON

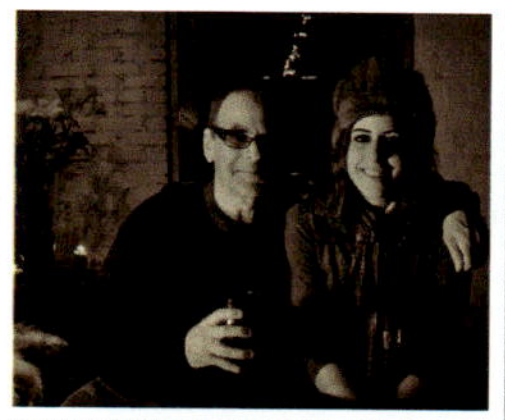

David Hilton has been pursuing his ever-evolving craft for several decades and has exhibited in numerous galleries and been published internationally. Working primarily in fine-art and erotic nudes, he focuses on capturing "who" the subject is. The challenge is to define a look that is at once a pure image of the subject and a unique internal view of singular external beauty.

Stripping away the pretence of most "artistic" images, David's use of light and lines allows each viewer to reach their own conclusion about the relationship of subject and camera. There are elements of the classic as well as unexpected erotic overtones, enticing viewers to experience "the moment".

For this set David chose Katlyn Lacoste, a creative and graceful subject, and an artist herself as both photographer and painter.

www.davidhilton.tumblr.com

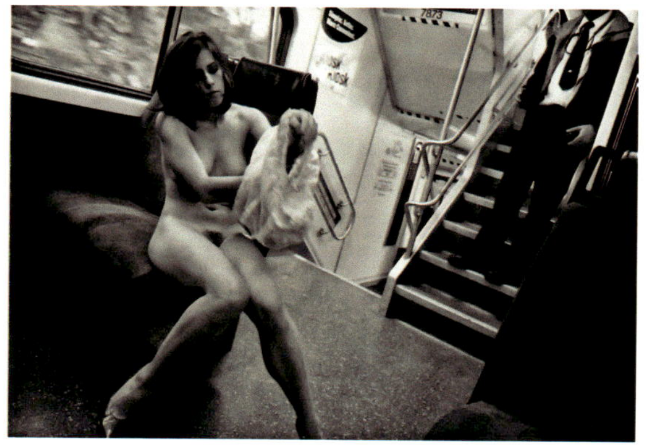

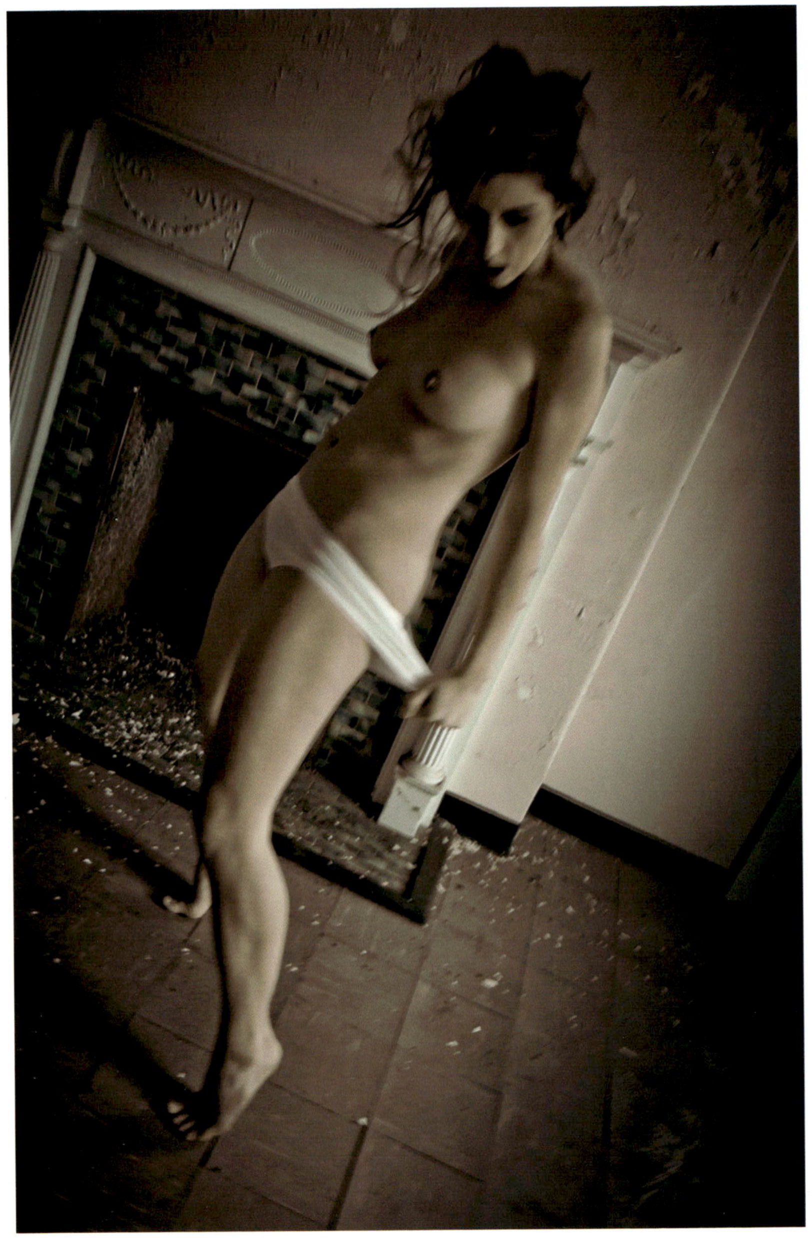

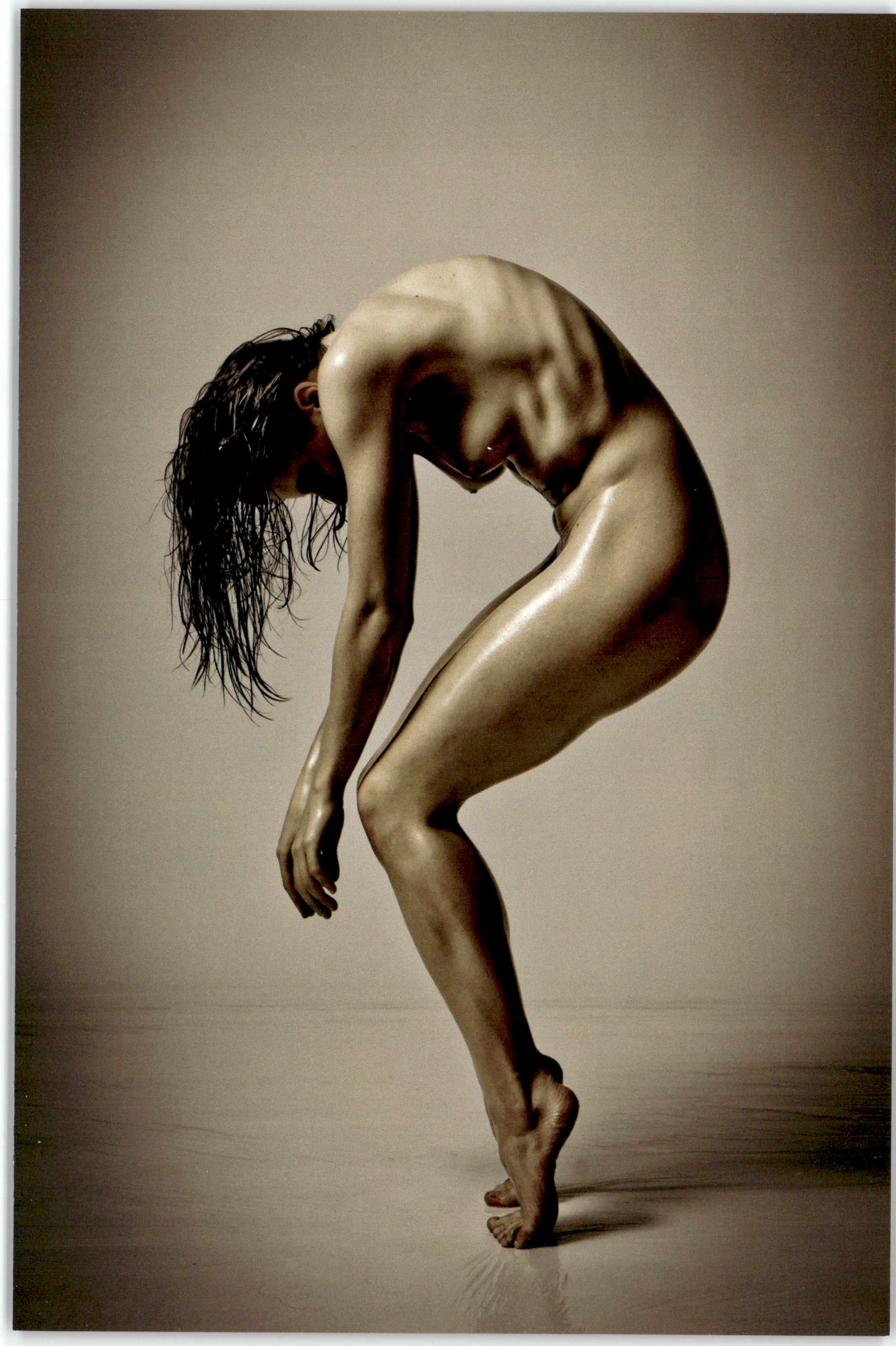

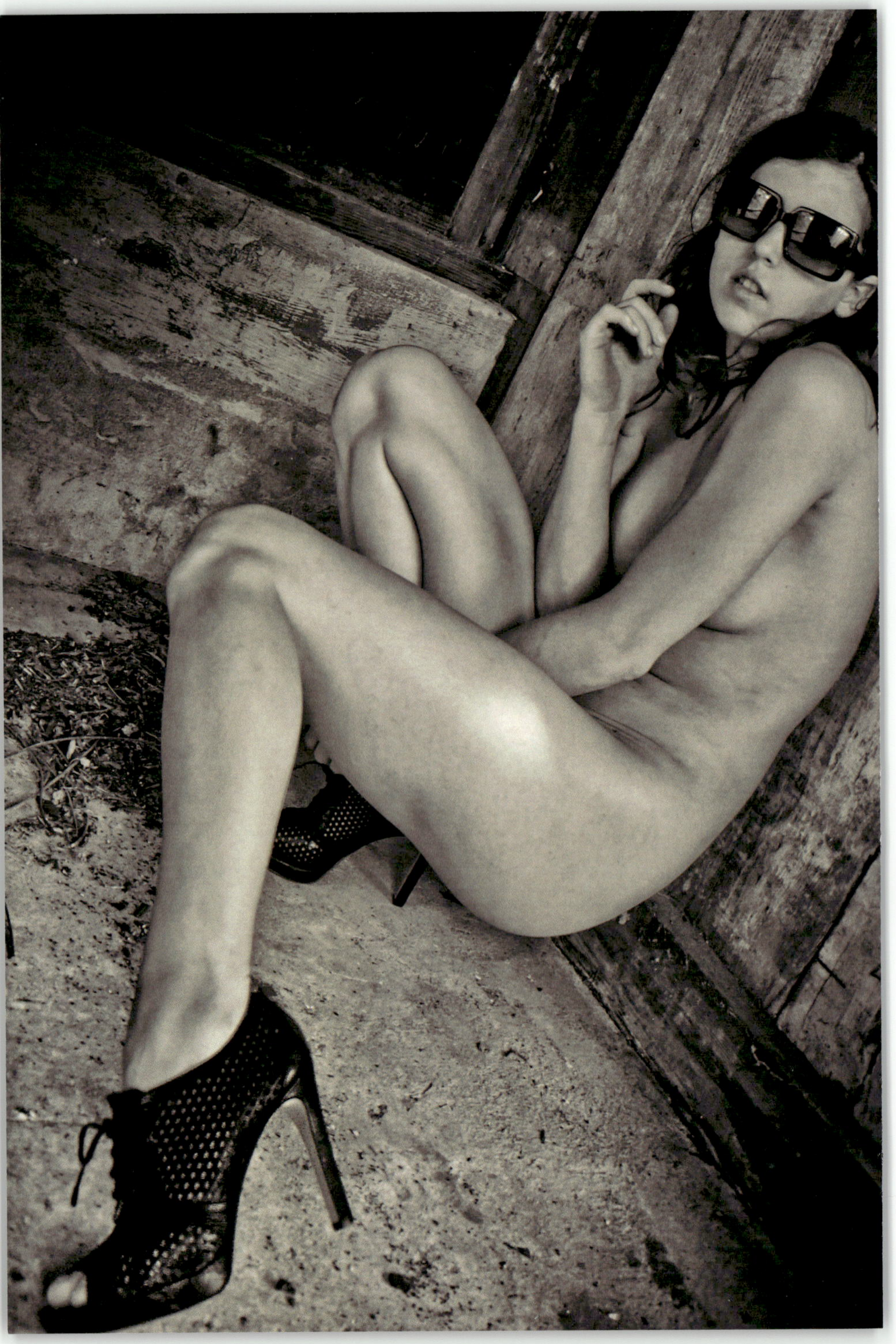

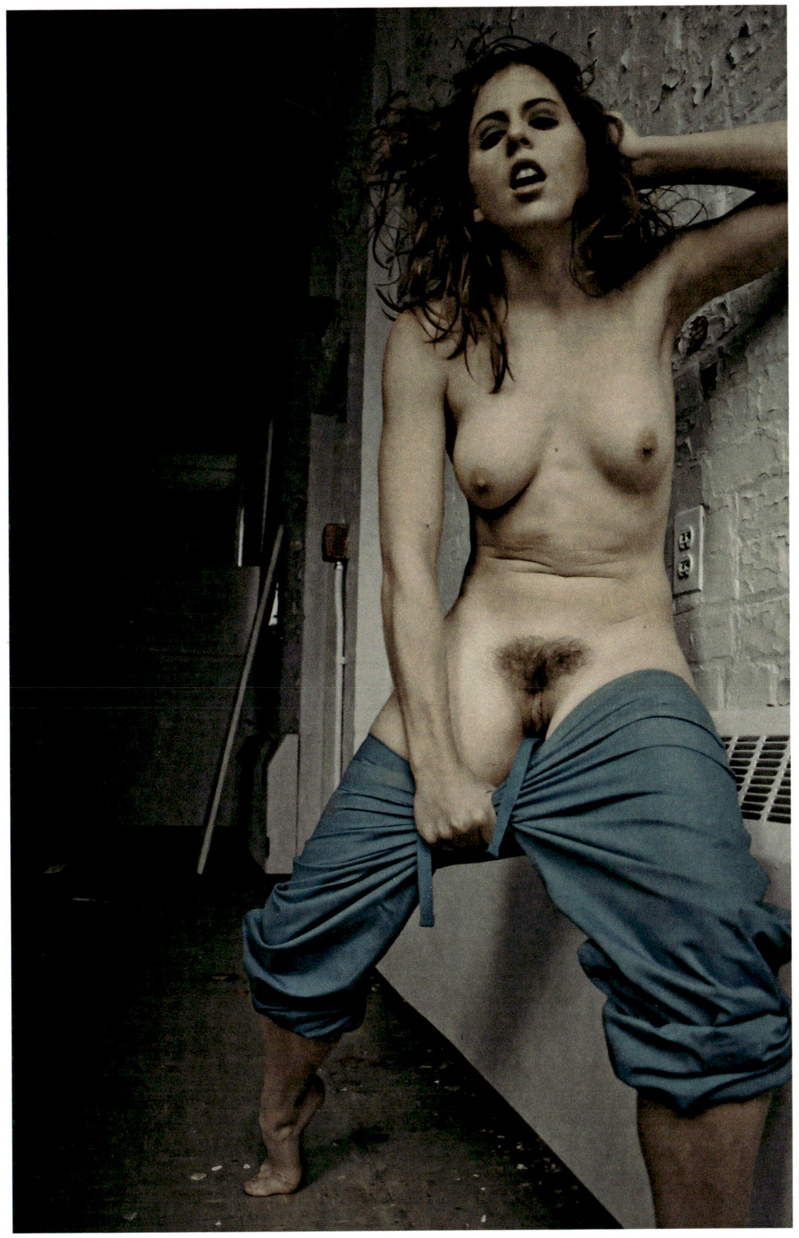

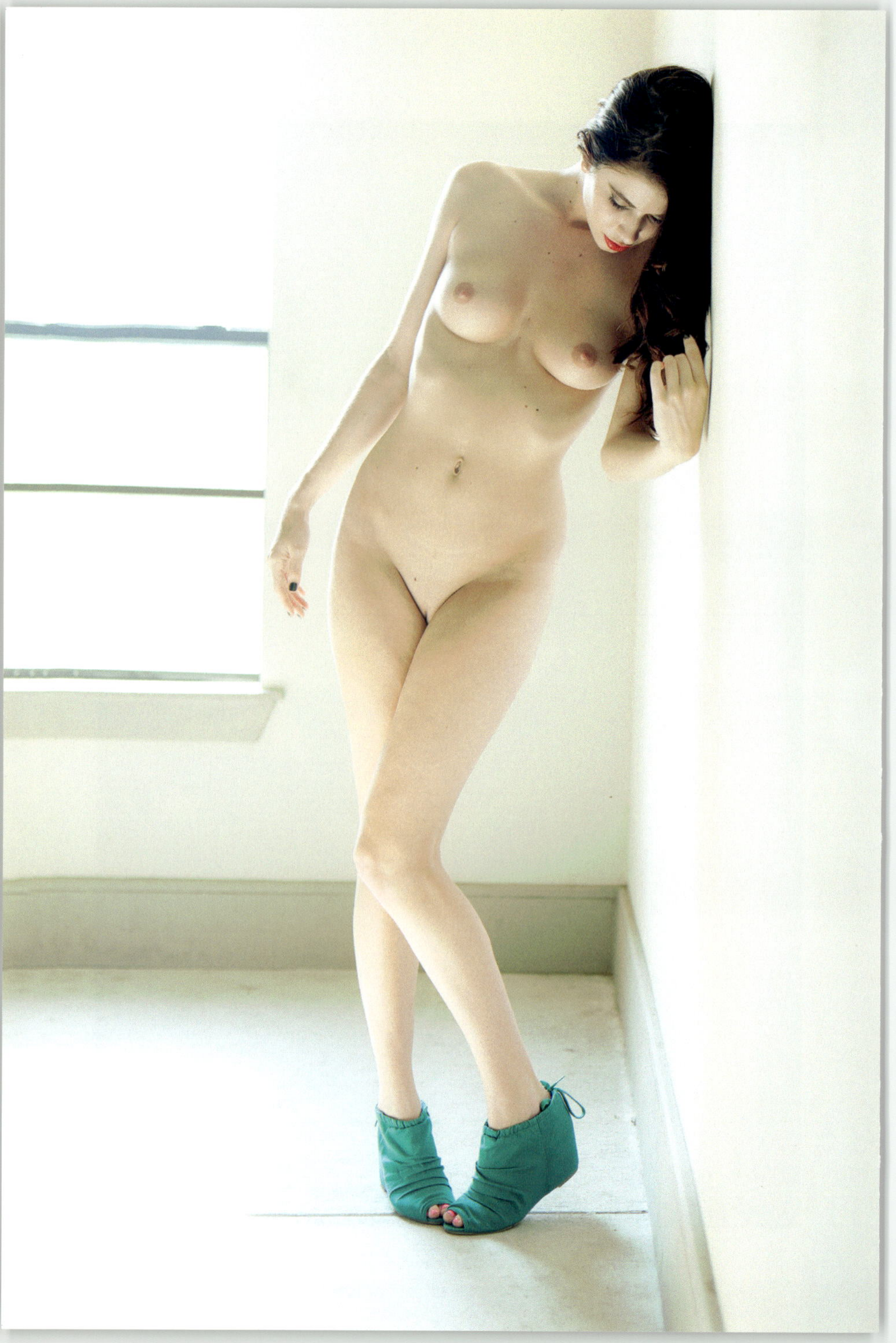

JULIAN HUMPHRIES

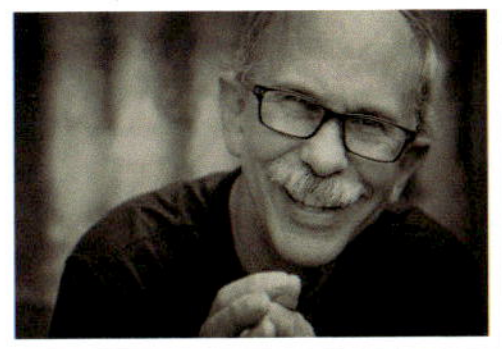

"I was attracted to photography at an early age and most of my pictures were of landscapes and nature, but when I bought my first DSLR I started shooting people, including models. Soon I realized that this passion was deep-seated and I became a full-time professional photographer. I use both analogue and digital cameras, and have a particular fondness for Polaroids. My photographs are mostly portraits that hopefully capture something real and personal, a moment where the subject shows an unguarded aspect of their personality. I would say my work is both honest and timeless.

"The subject of my series, Lucy Secord, is beautiful and talented. We "connected" on a level that meant I had to do nothing more than make subtle suggestions about mood or pose. Lucy rocks!

www.julianhumphries.com

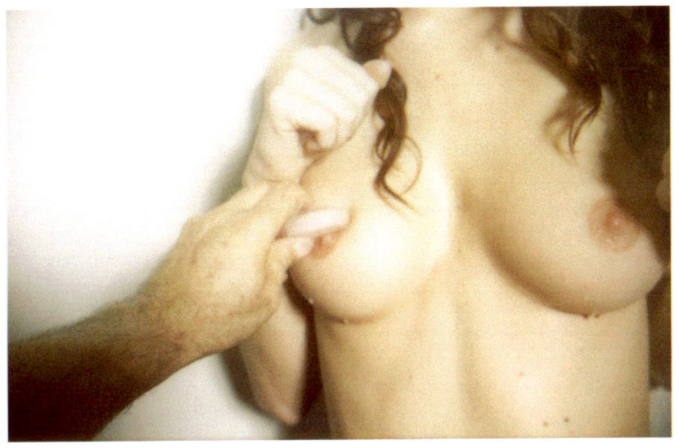

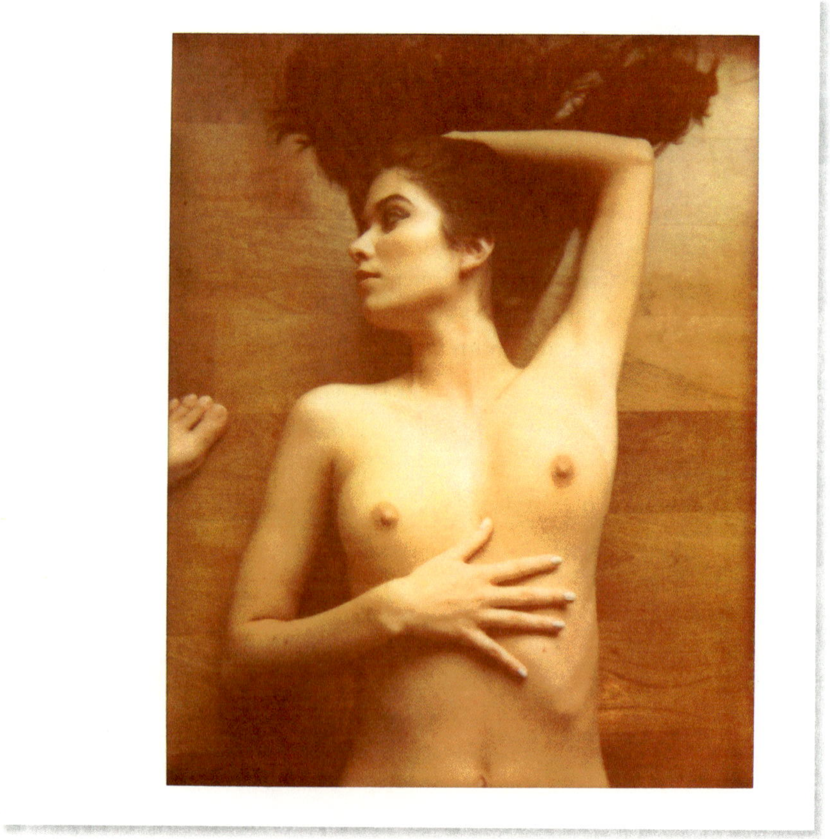

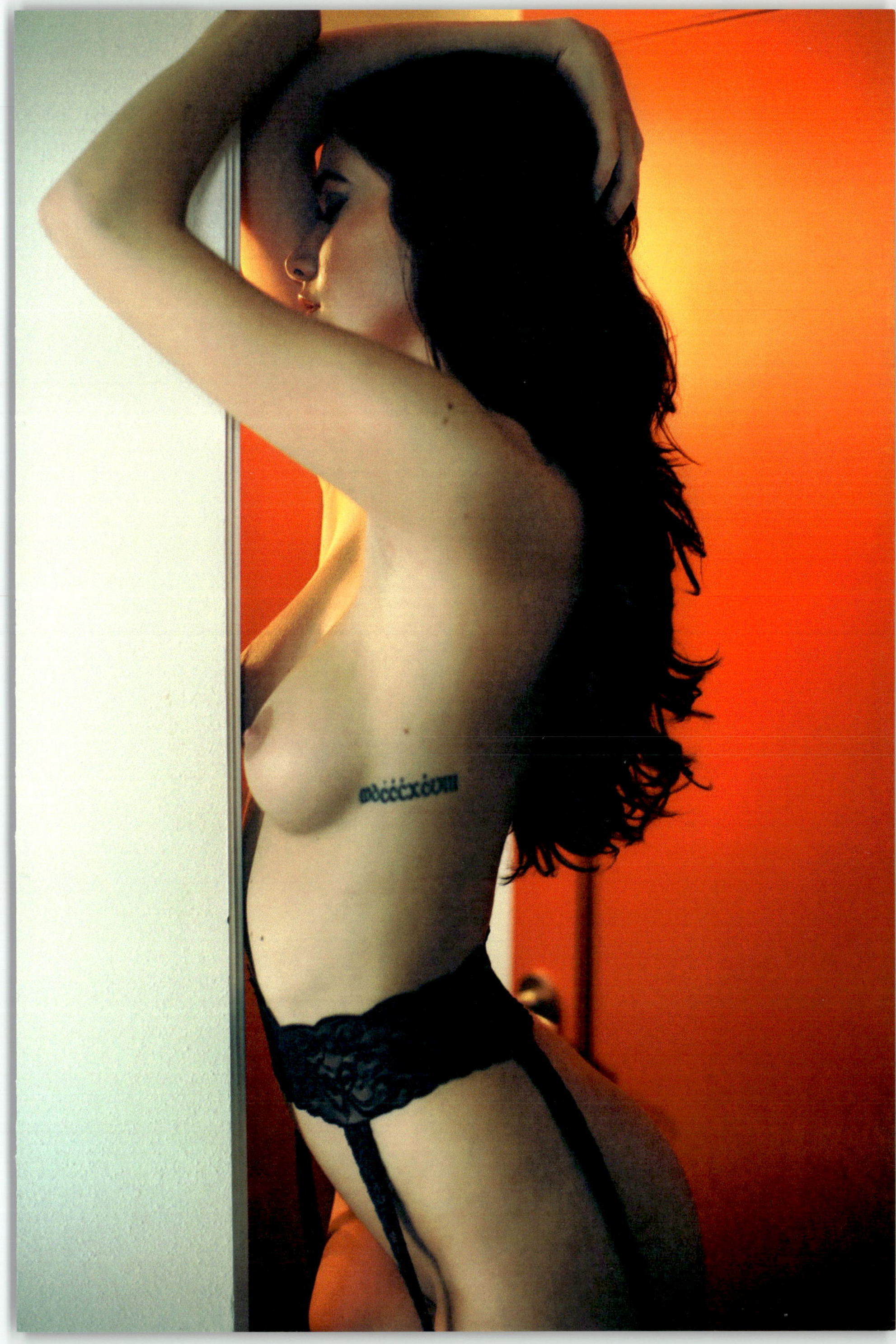

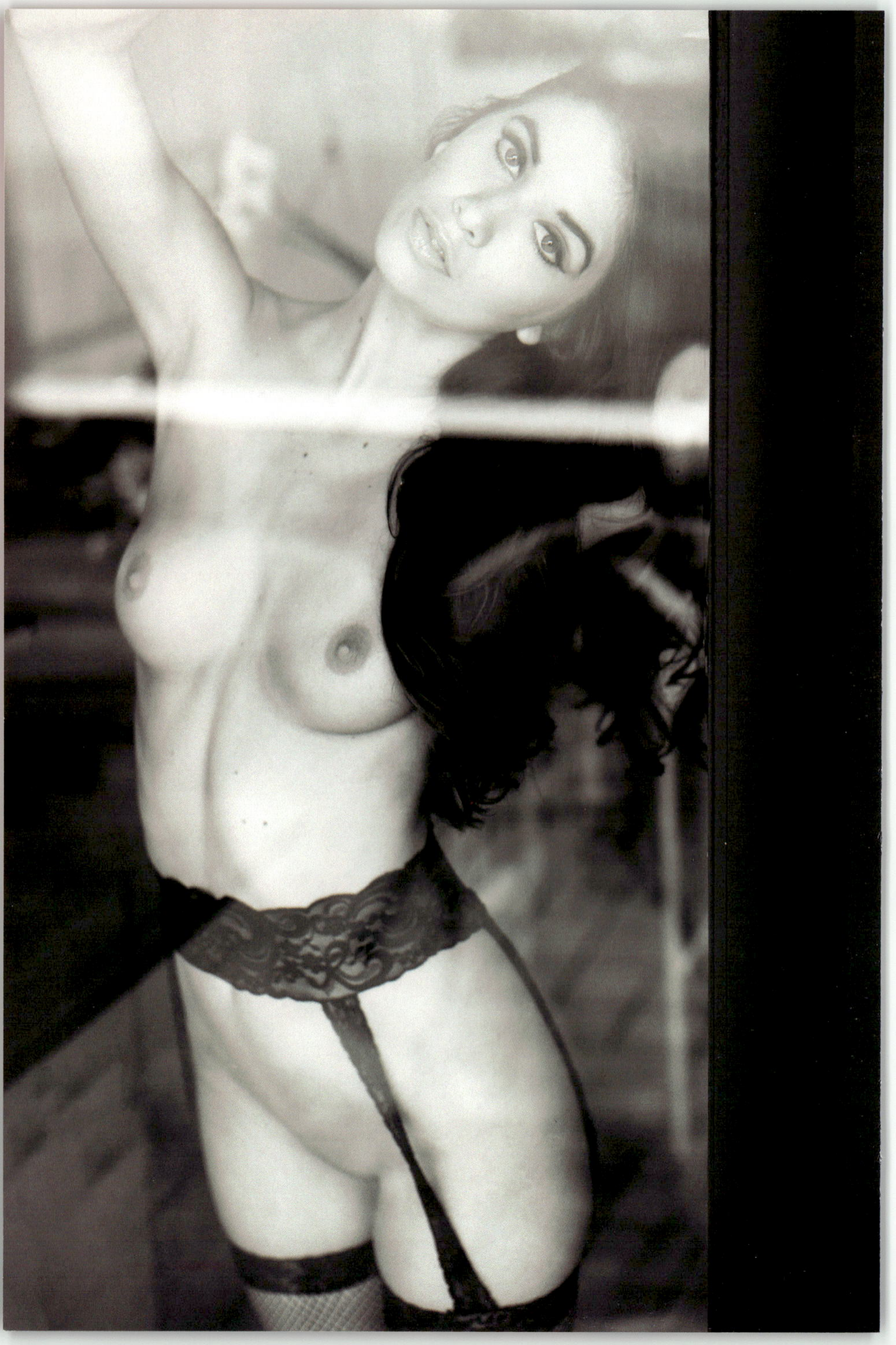

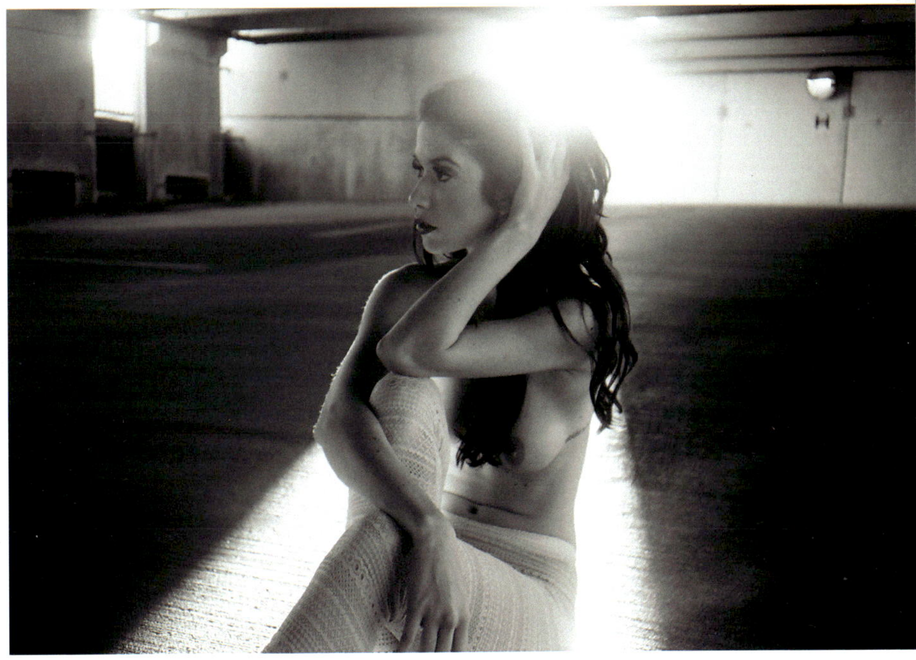

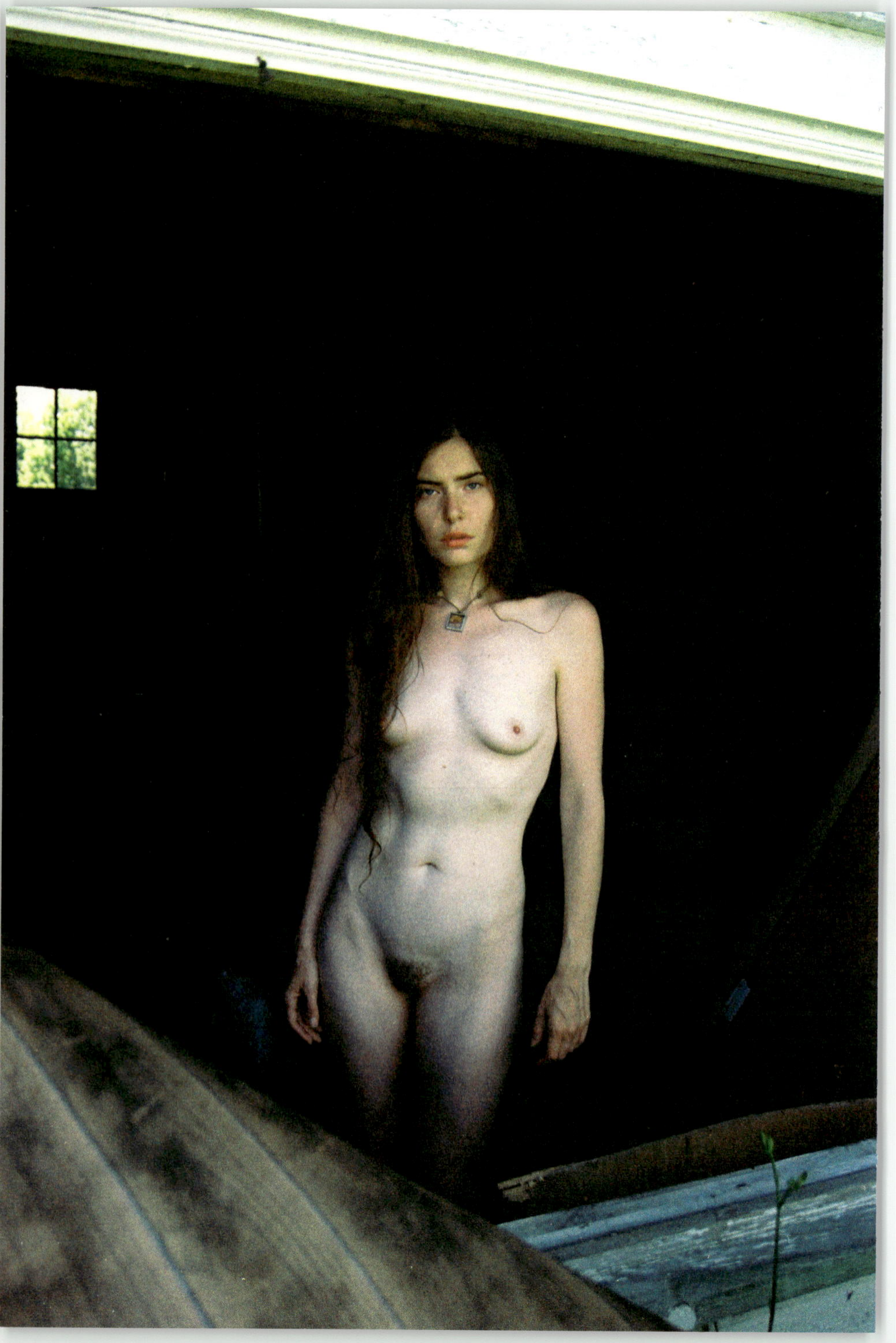

APRIL-LEA HUTCHINSON

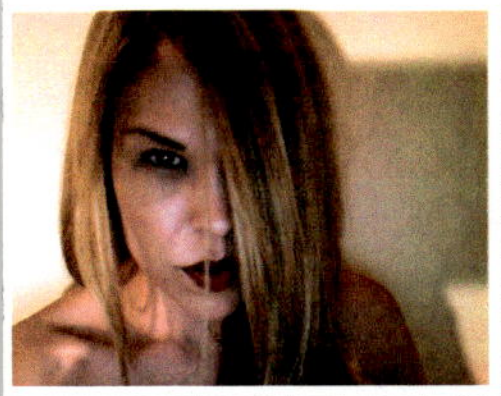

April-Lea Hutchinson is from Toronto. She has a fondness for film and a deep desire to photograph people as people, breaking from expected norms of beauty. Her empathetic relationship with the model infuses her images with comfortable intimacy and perhaps a touch of nostalgia.

The model she chose for this book is one with whom she has a huge emotional connection. They were already friends when they started taking intimate photos together. April loves Celeste's timidity and her vulnerable yet strong look. "The day I met Celeste and shot with her, I knew there was something special about her. Celeste is special and the photographs to me are a diary of my times with her, as a model and just hanging out as a friend. Carefree yet very intimate."

www.soamused.tumblr.com

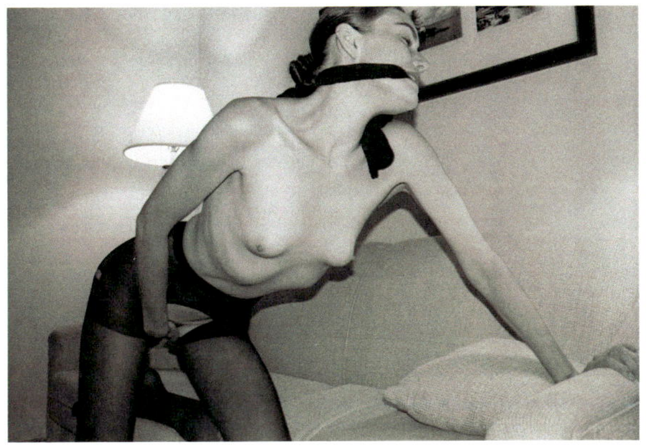

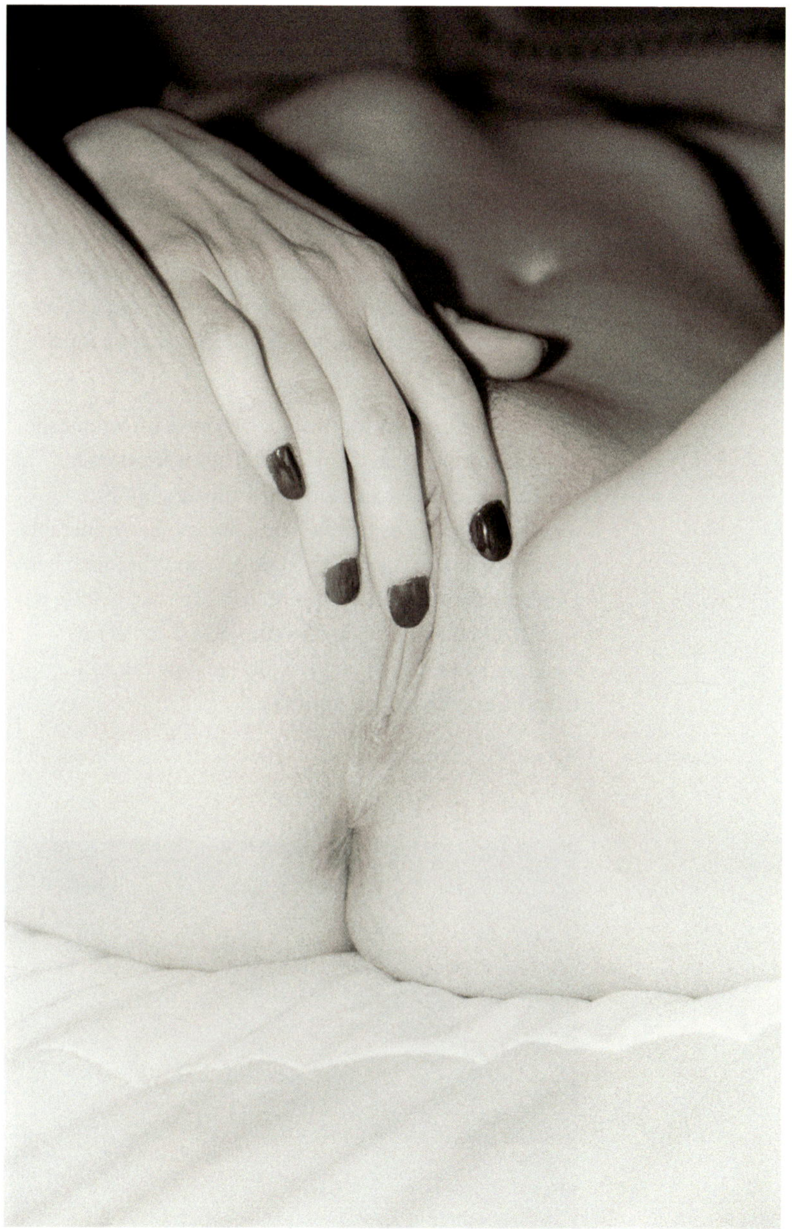

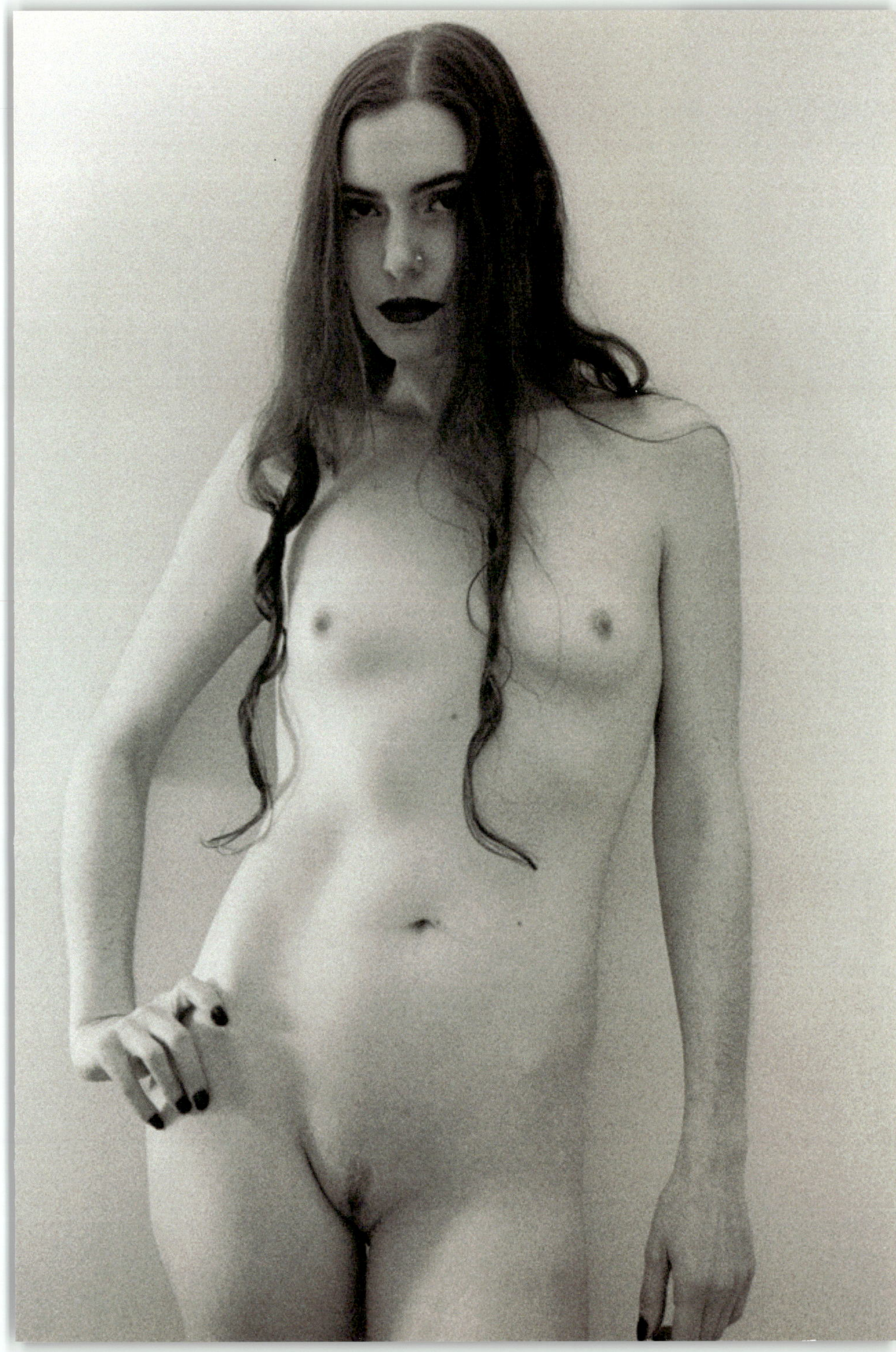

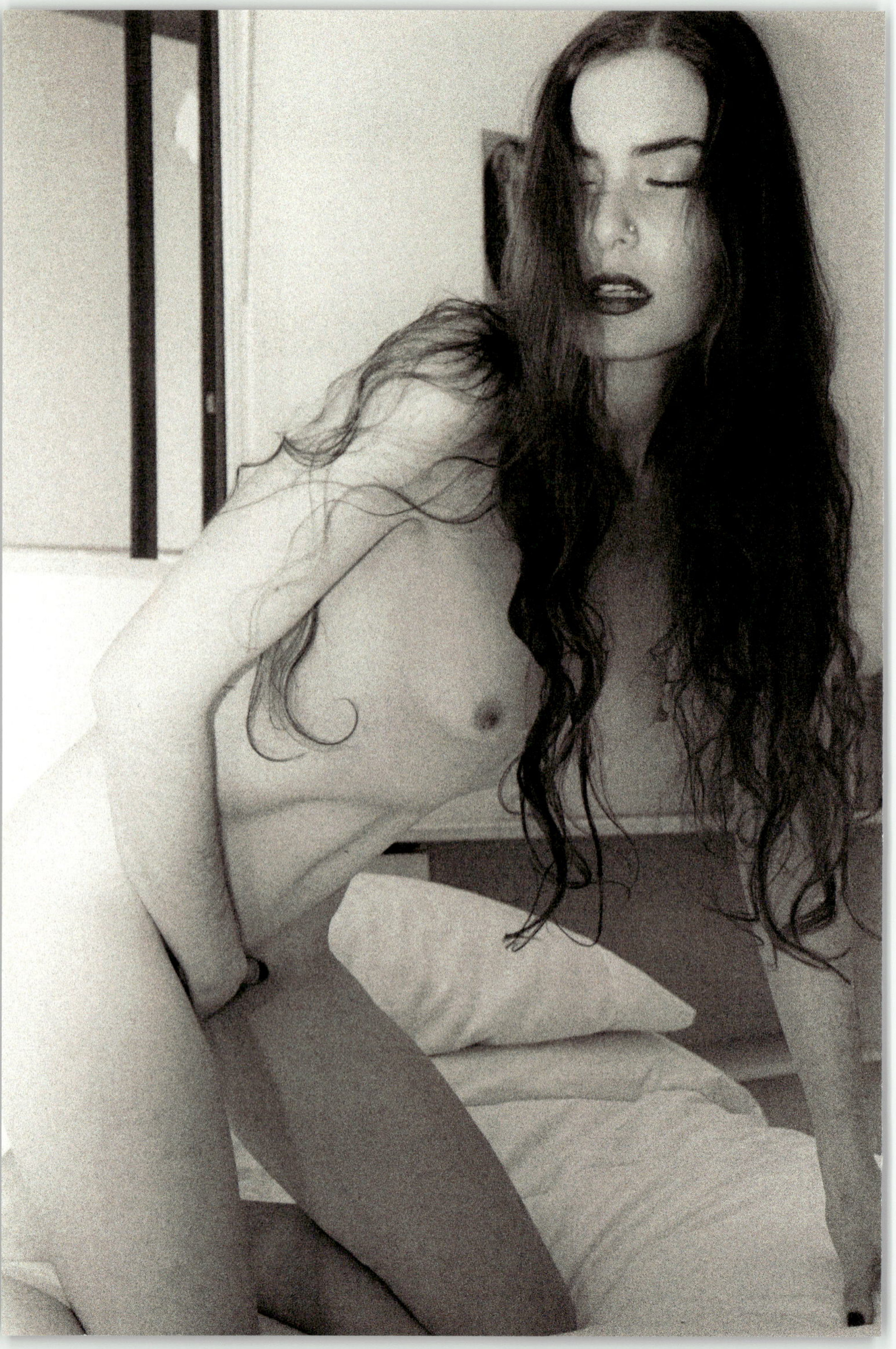

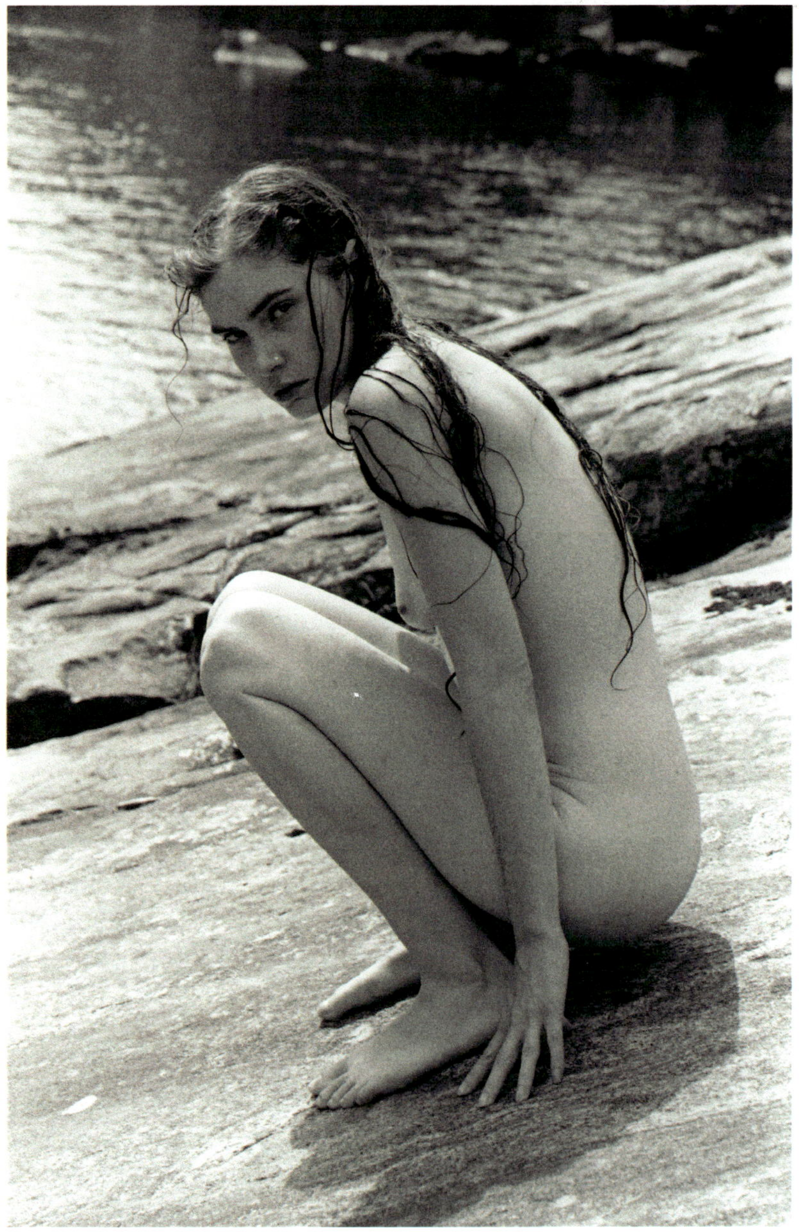

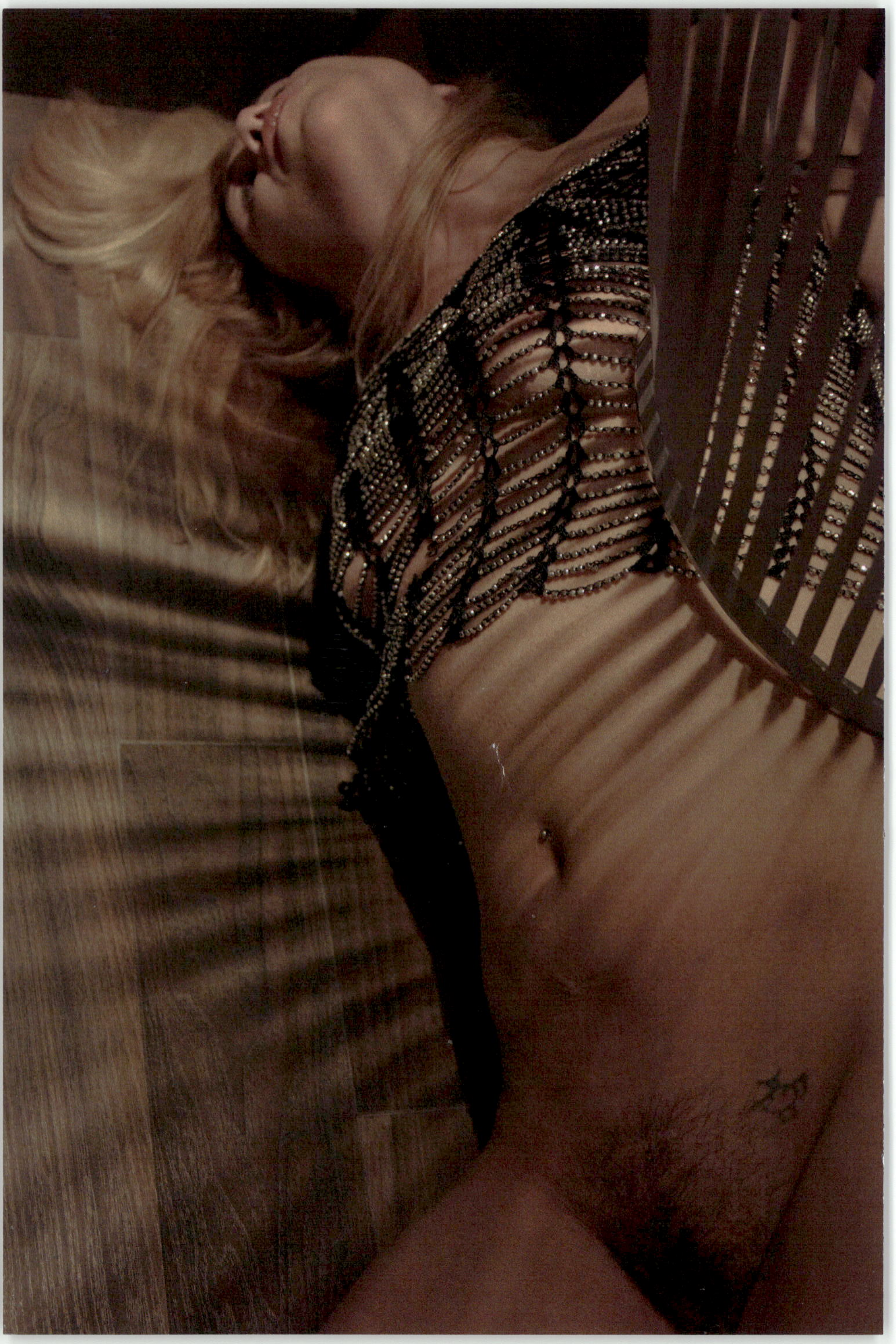

I. K. R. F.

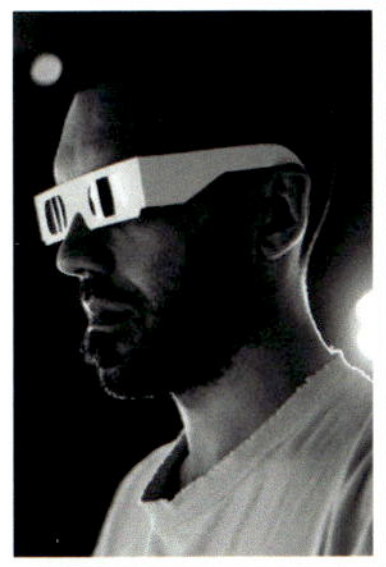

I. K. R. F. has worked in feature films and TV for ten years. After creating his own post-production company in Paris he supervised visual effects on two feature films, worked on VFX and main-title design of many films, TV series, advertising and music videos. He is also a director and art director and a photographer. After recently moving to Canada he is working on a feature film.

I. K. R. F.'s photos with April-Lea Hutchinson are part of a long series of shoots in various places and moods. Over the past year they have shot many photos together, with lots of creativity and a truly collaborative approach to finding ideas, locations and situations. An obsession with creating stunning and unique work drives all their shoots.

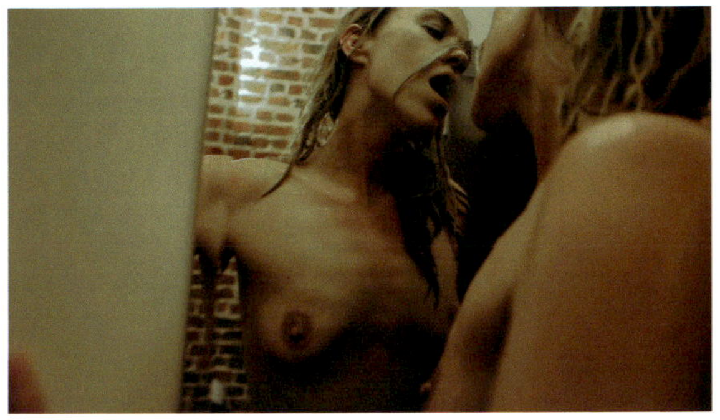

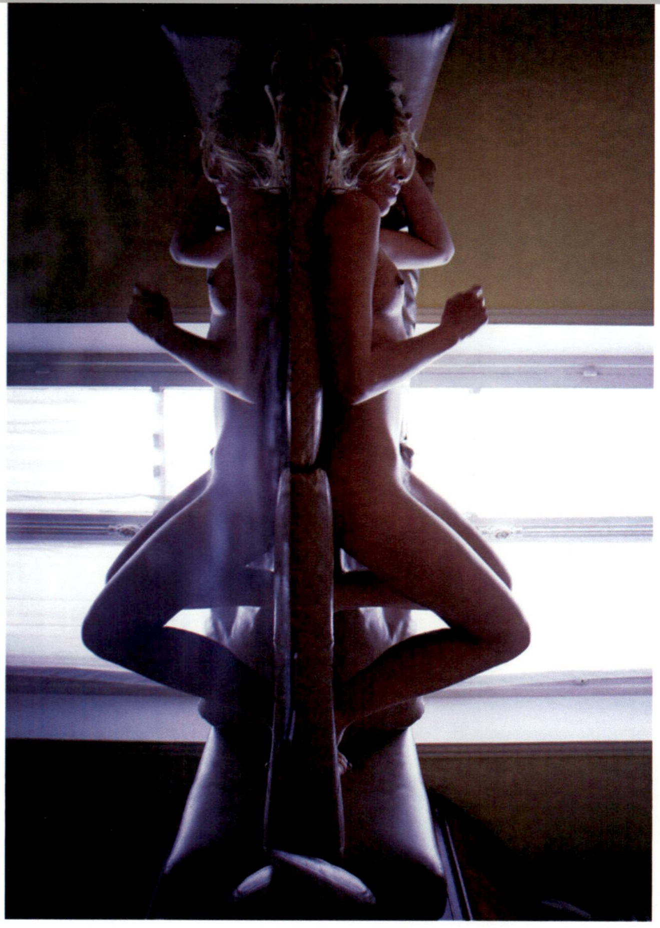

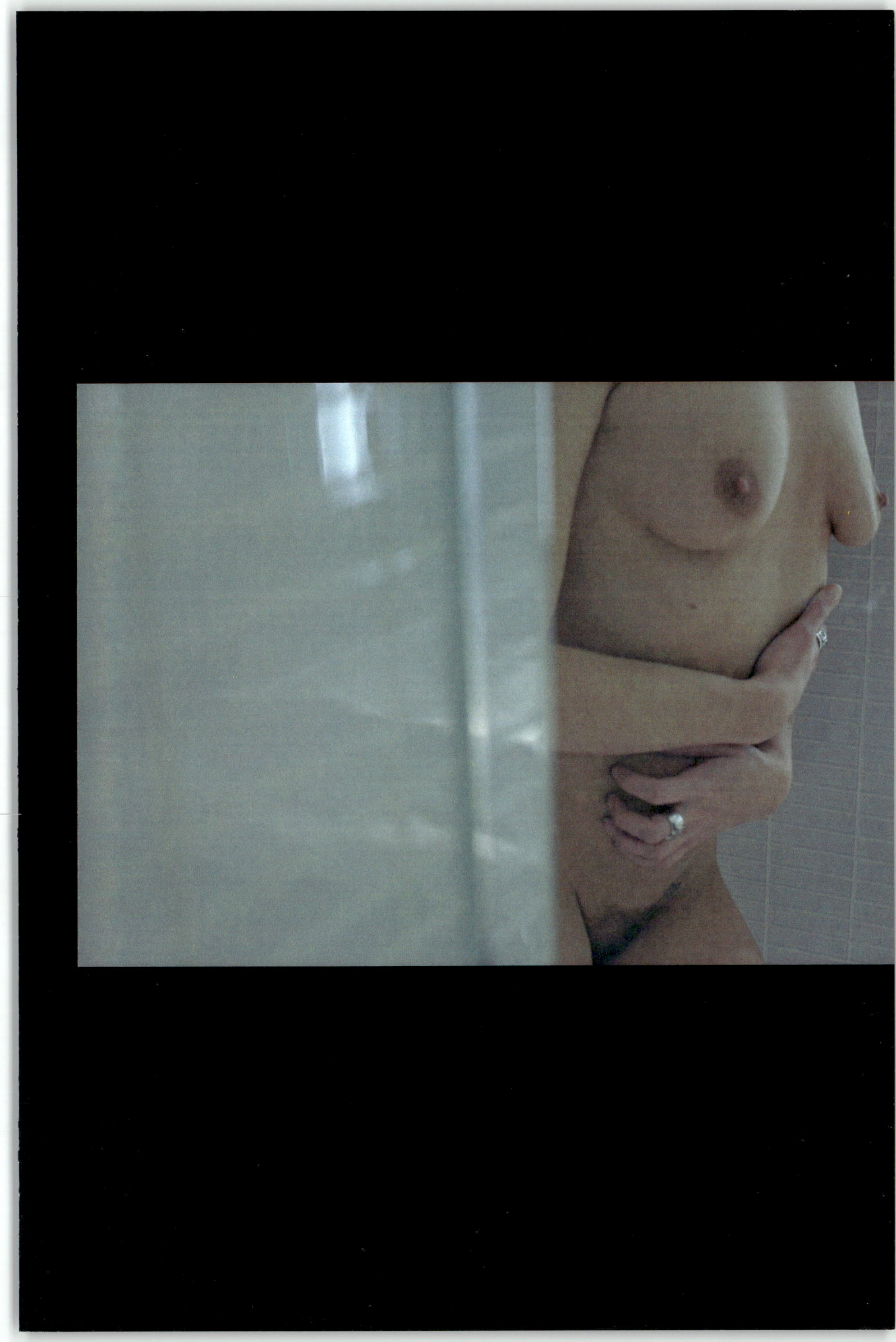

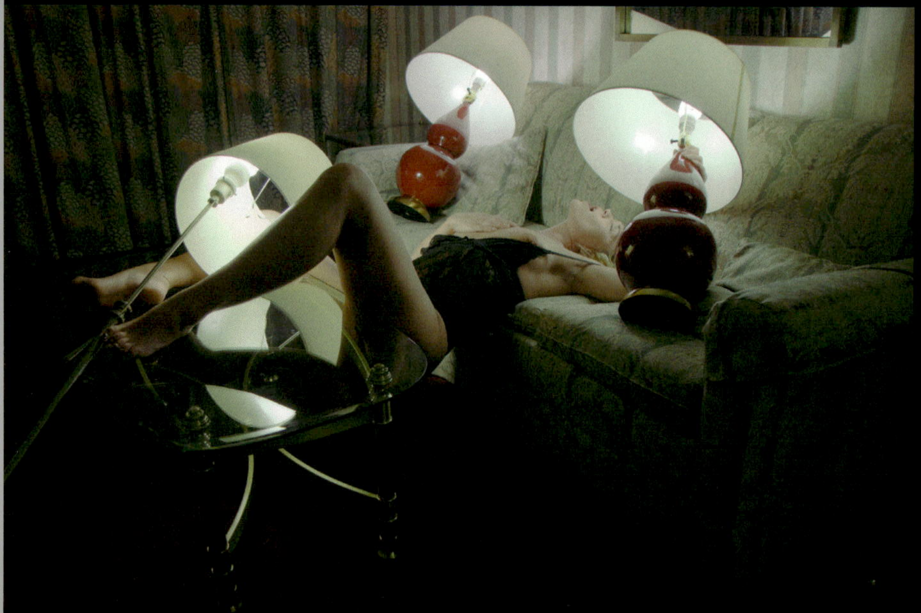

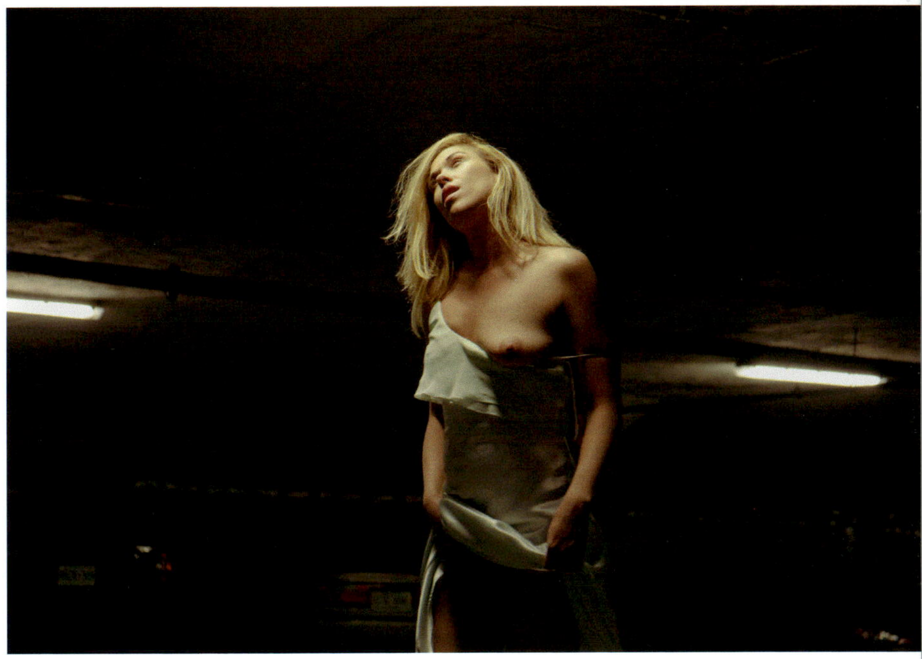

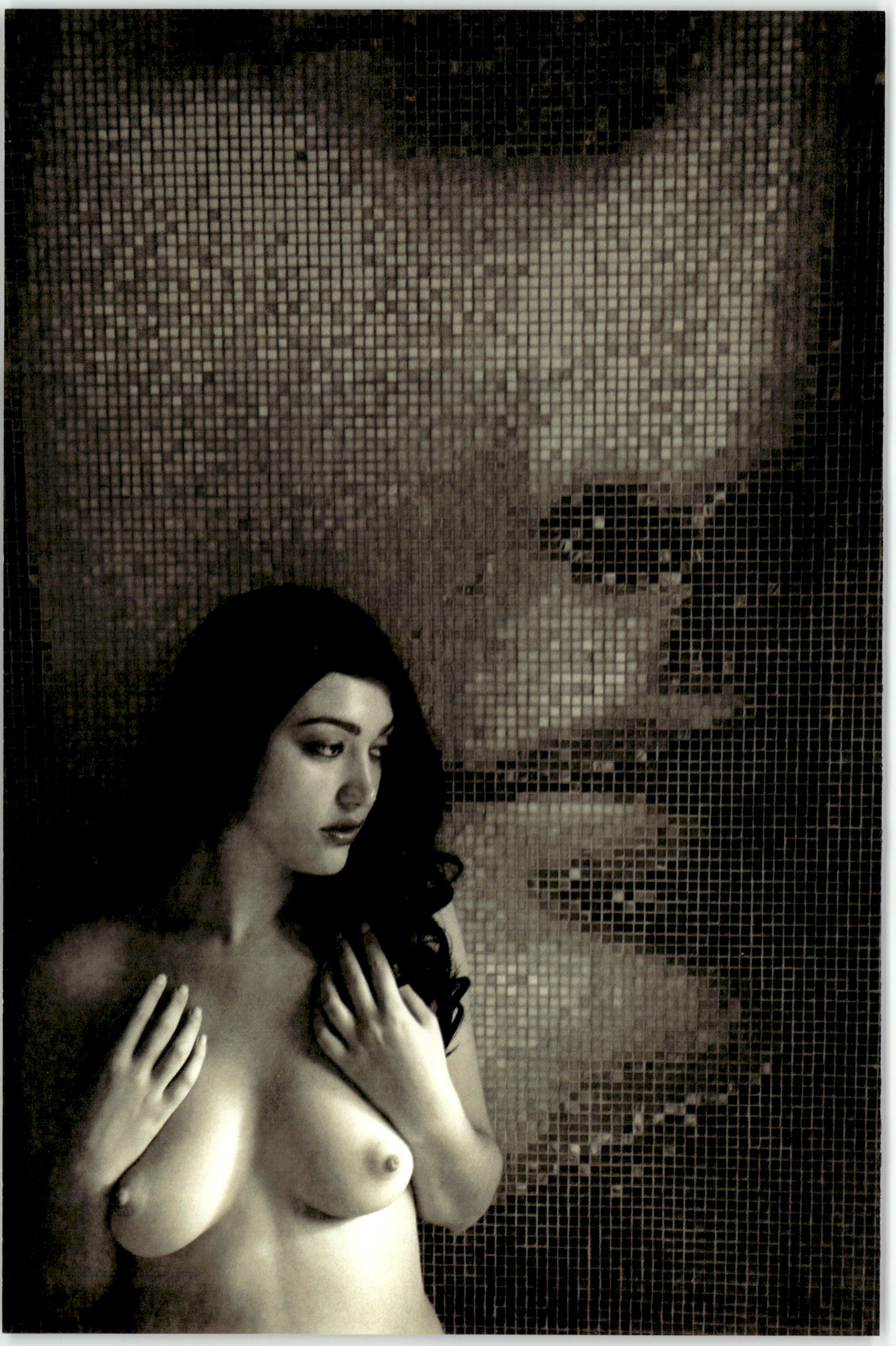

RENÉE JACOBS

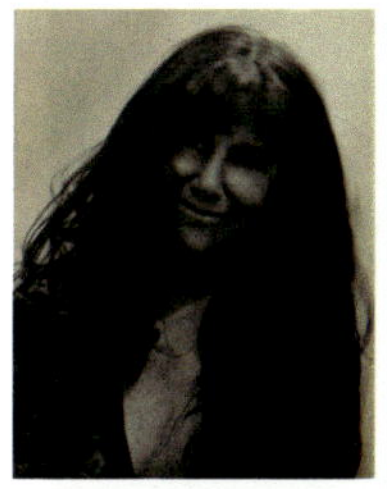

Jock Sturges writes that Renée Jacobs' pictures "have a combination of intensity and honesty that I don't often encounter. These images aren't a symptom of her thinking; they're a symptom of her life… She's making the pictures because she want to keep [the models] fixed in her head and heart for all time. Her models tell her to tell the truth about them. And she does. The 'truth' is of course half hers, a half that is rich in admiration and affection … a singular example of what can be achieved in the photographic medium when the passion behind the camera is far greater than photography itself."

Renée Jacobs has received awards and been published in many books and magazines. Her book of Paris nudes will be published in 2013.

www.reneejacobs.com

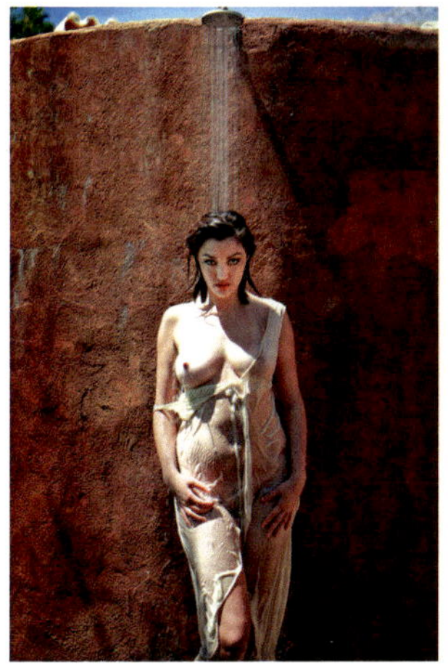

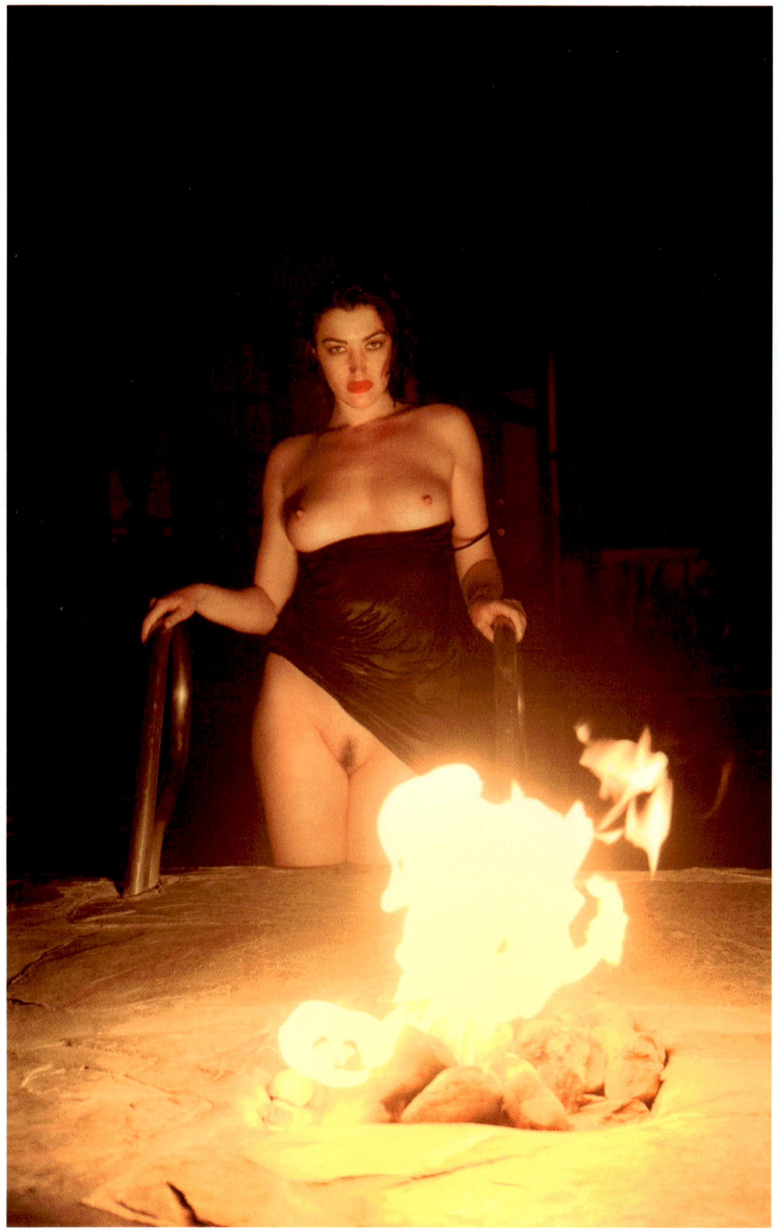

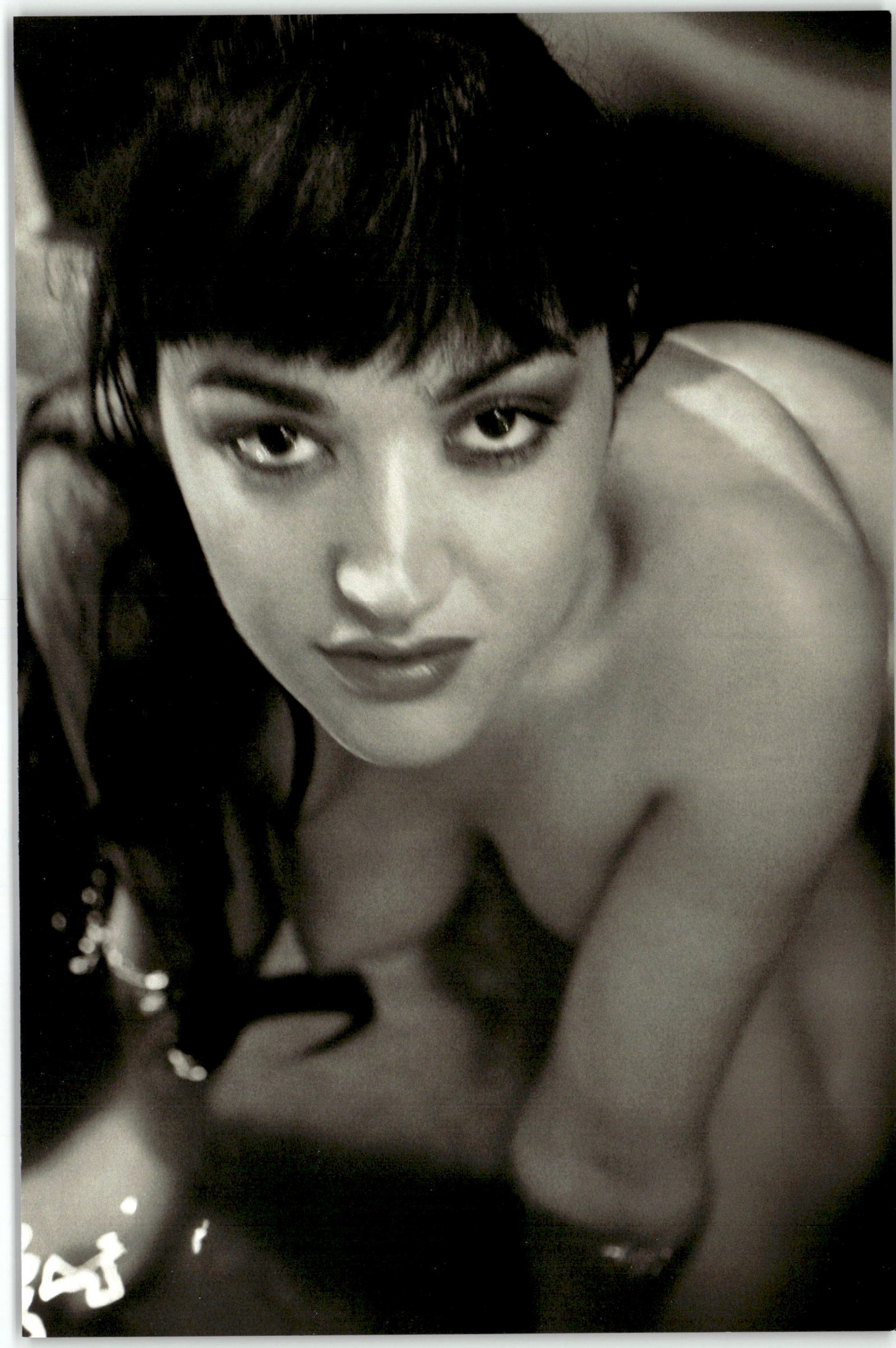

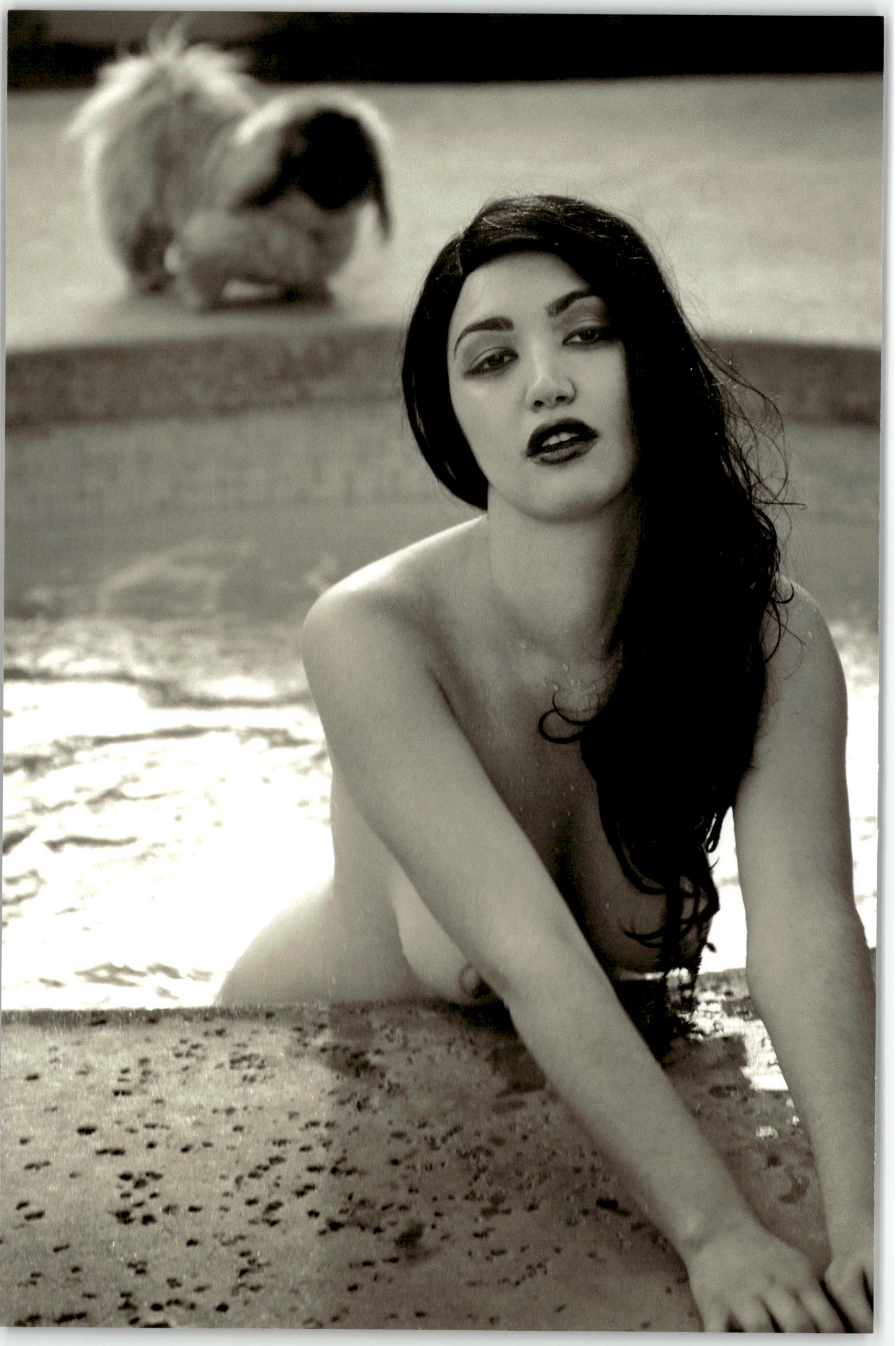

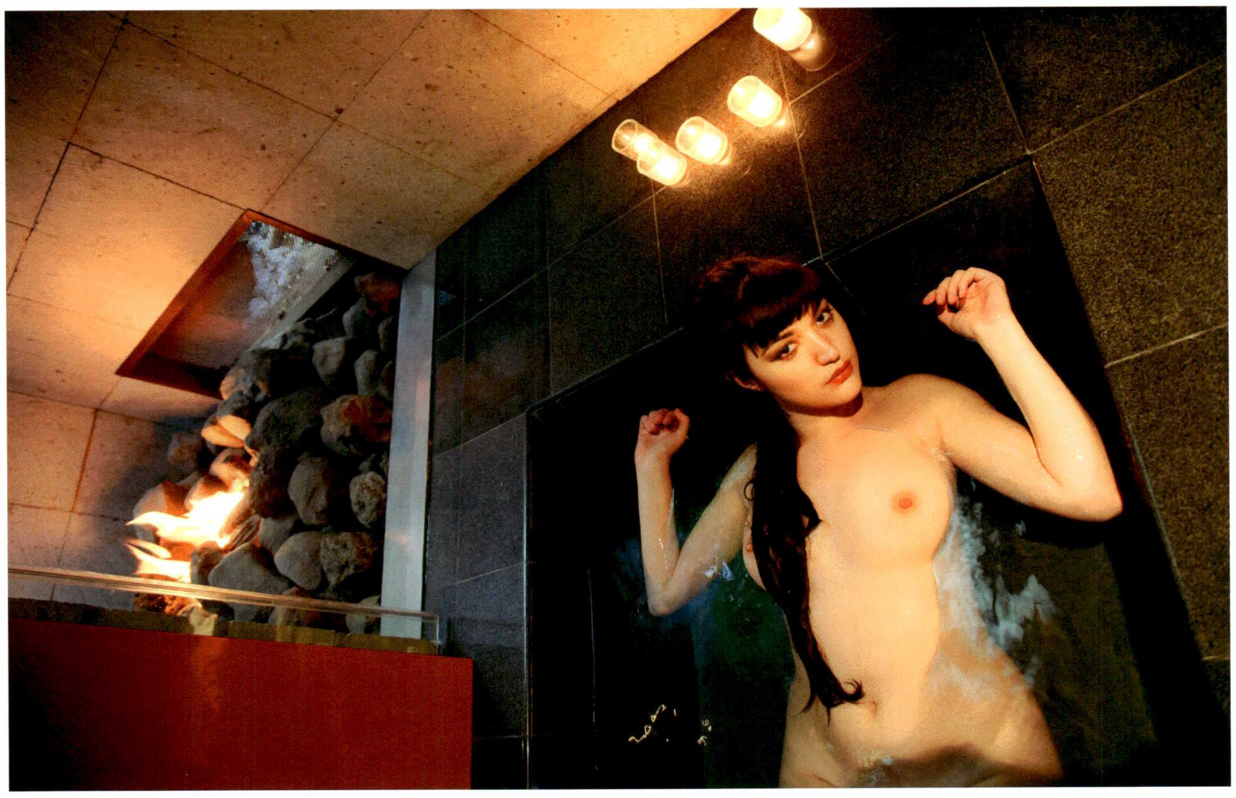

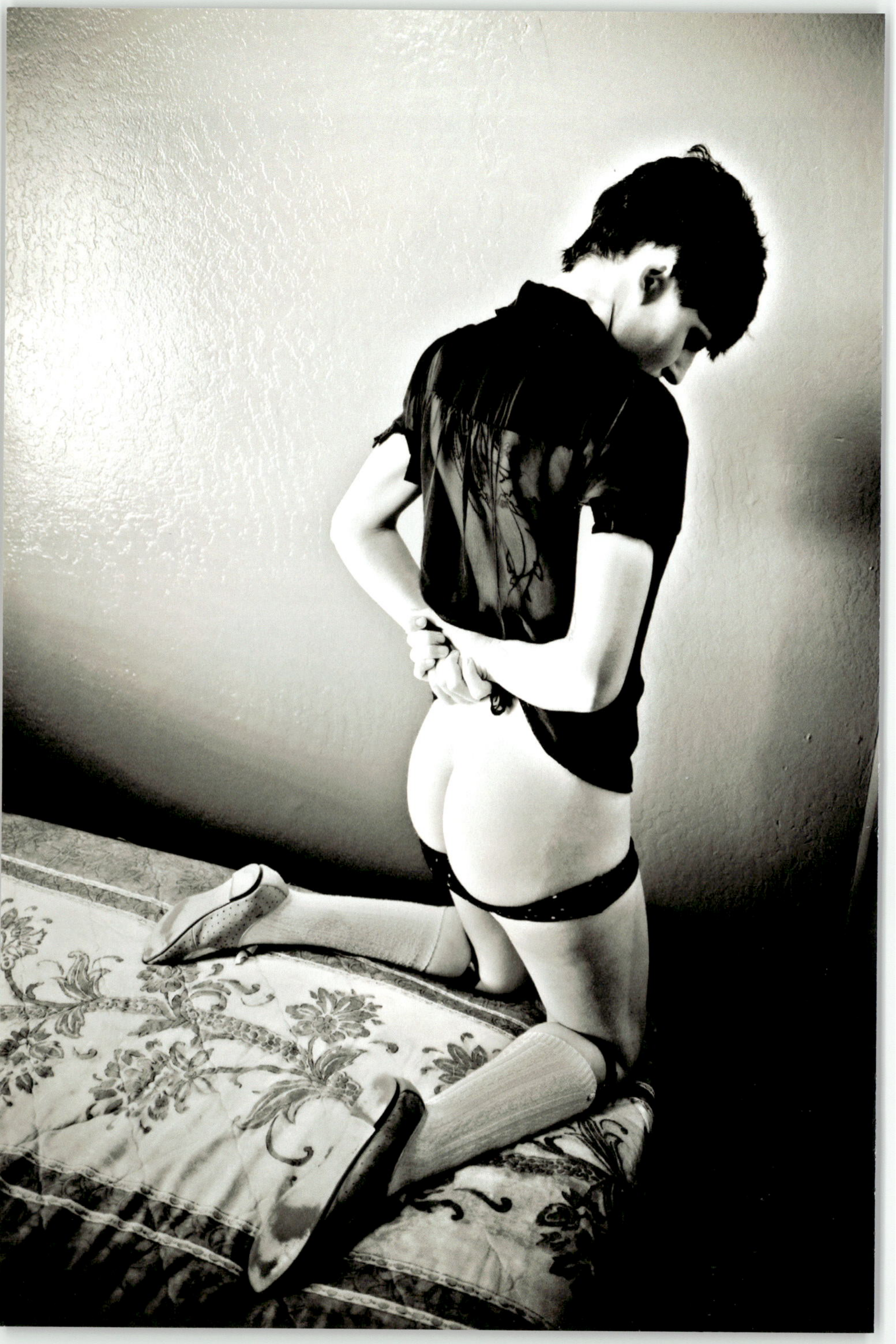

RICHARD KADREY

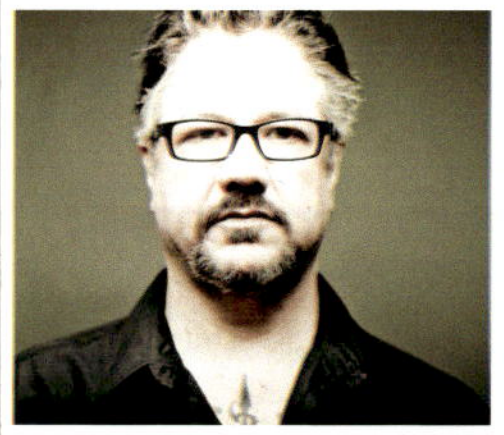

Richard Kadrey has been doing digital and film photography as Kaos Beauty Klinik for over ten years. He's also the author of the *New York Times* bestselling Sandman Slim supernatural thrillers. His latest book in the series is *Devil Said Bang*.

"Vivian de Milo and I always work well together. She's smart, beautiful, playful, soulful, and always brings a million ideas of her own to a shoot. She's also a great make-up artist and can change her look from femme sweet to boyish in just a few minutes. She is and always will be one of my favourite collaborators."

www.richardkadrey.com

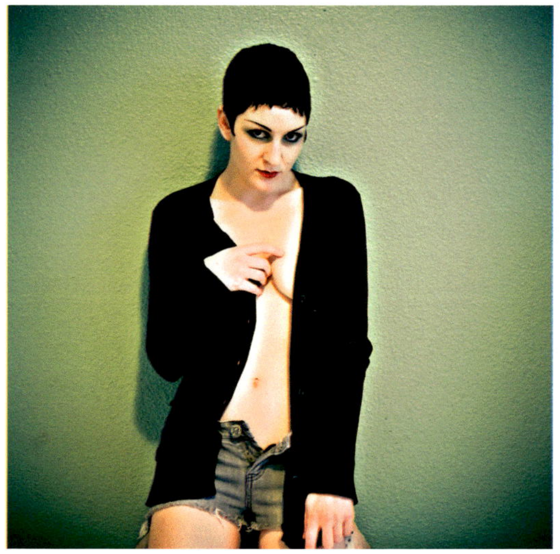

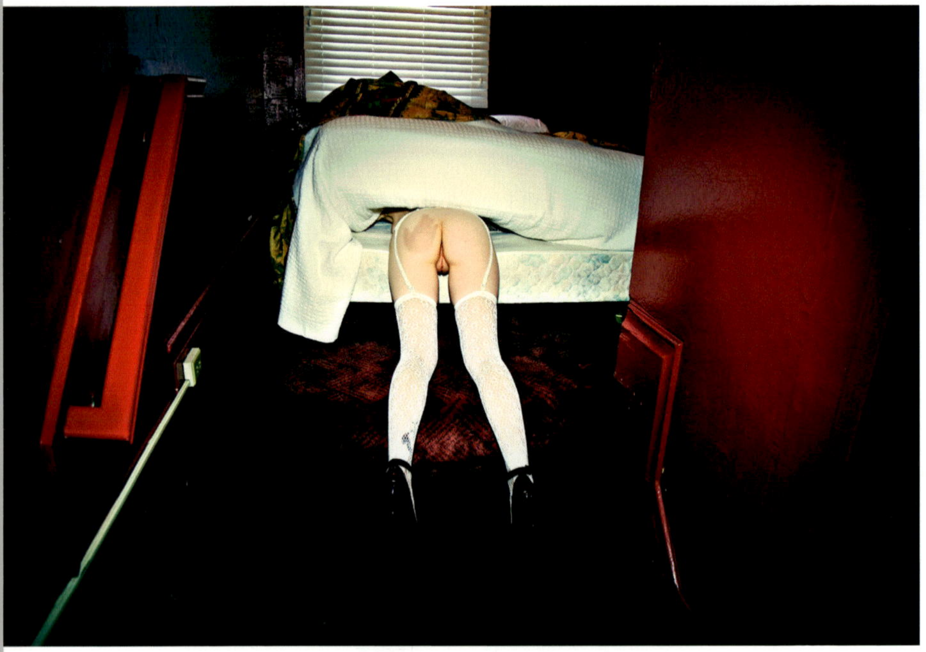

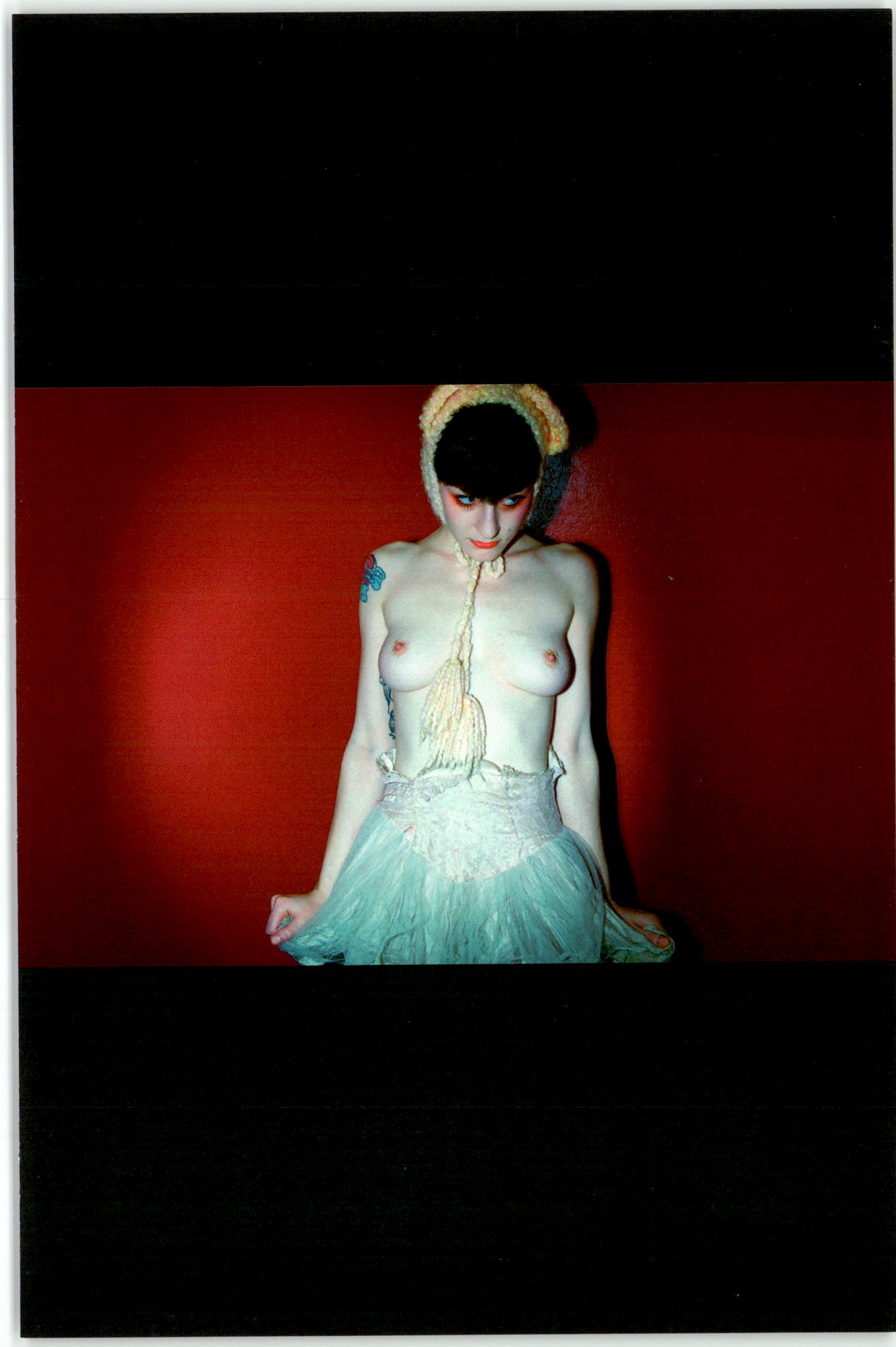

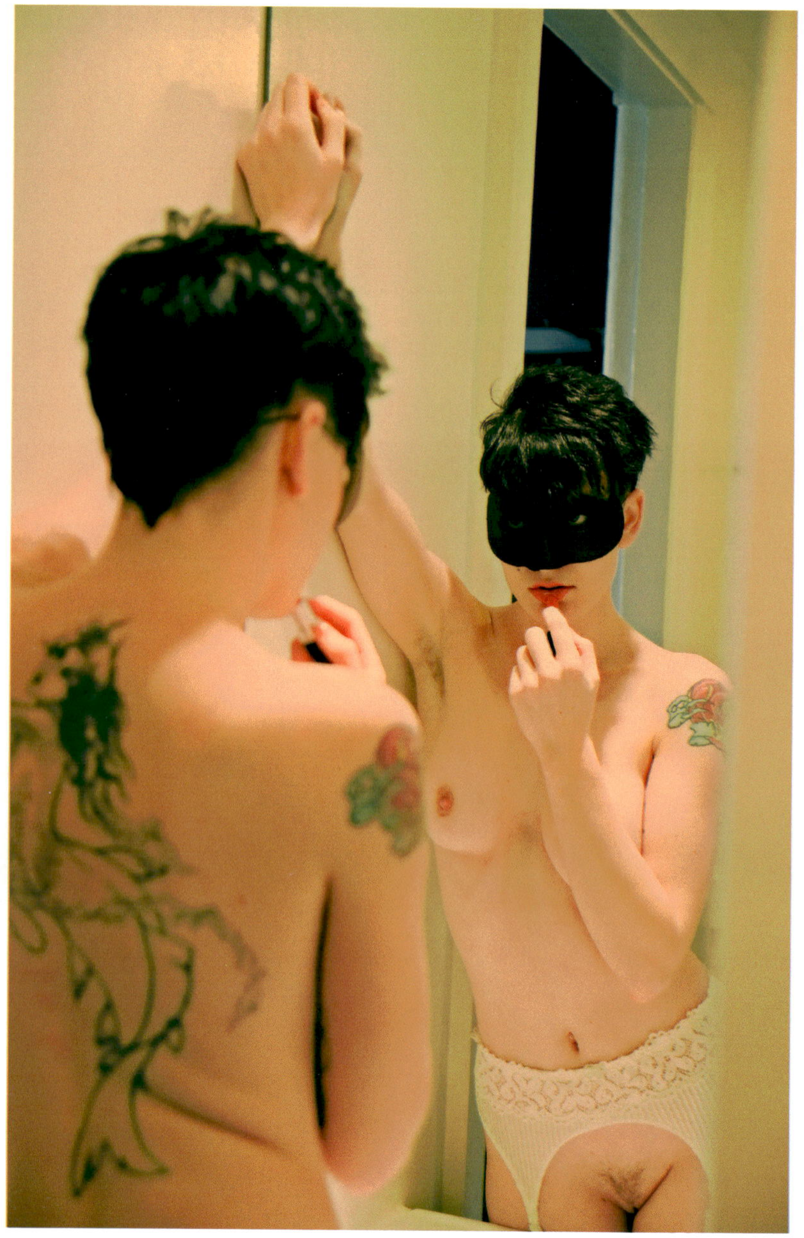

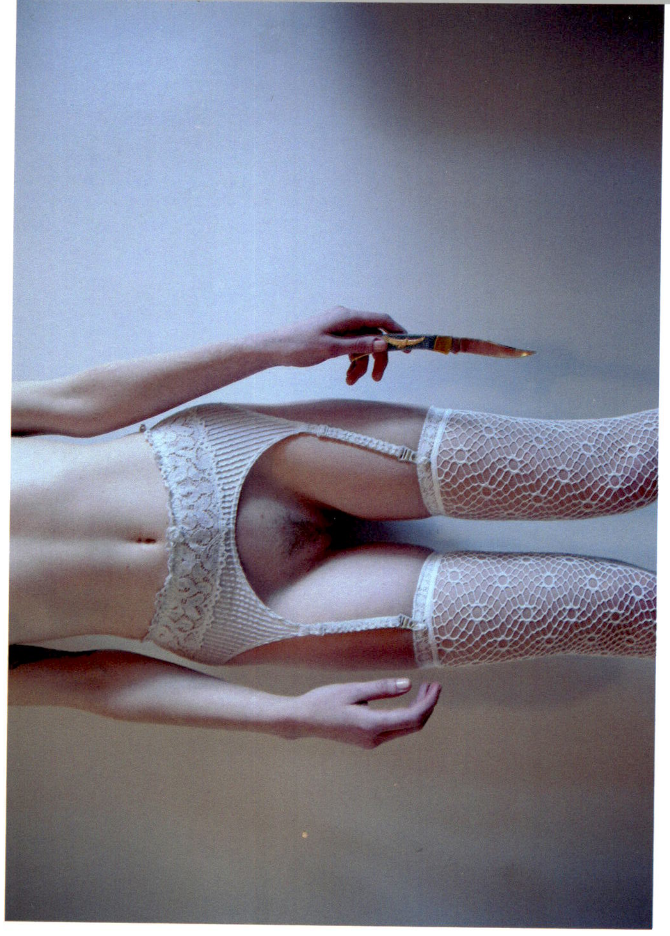

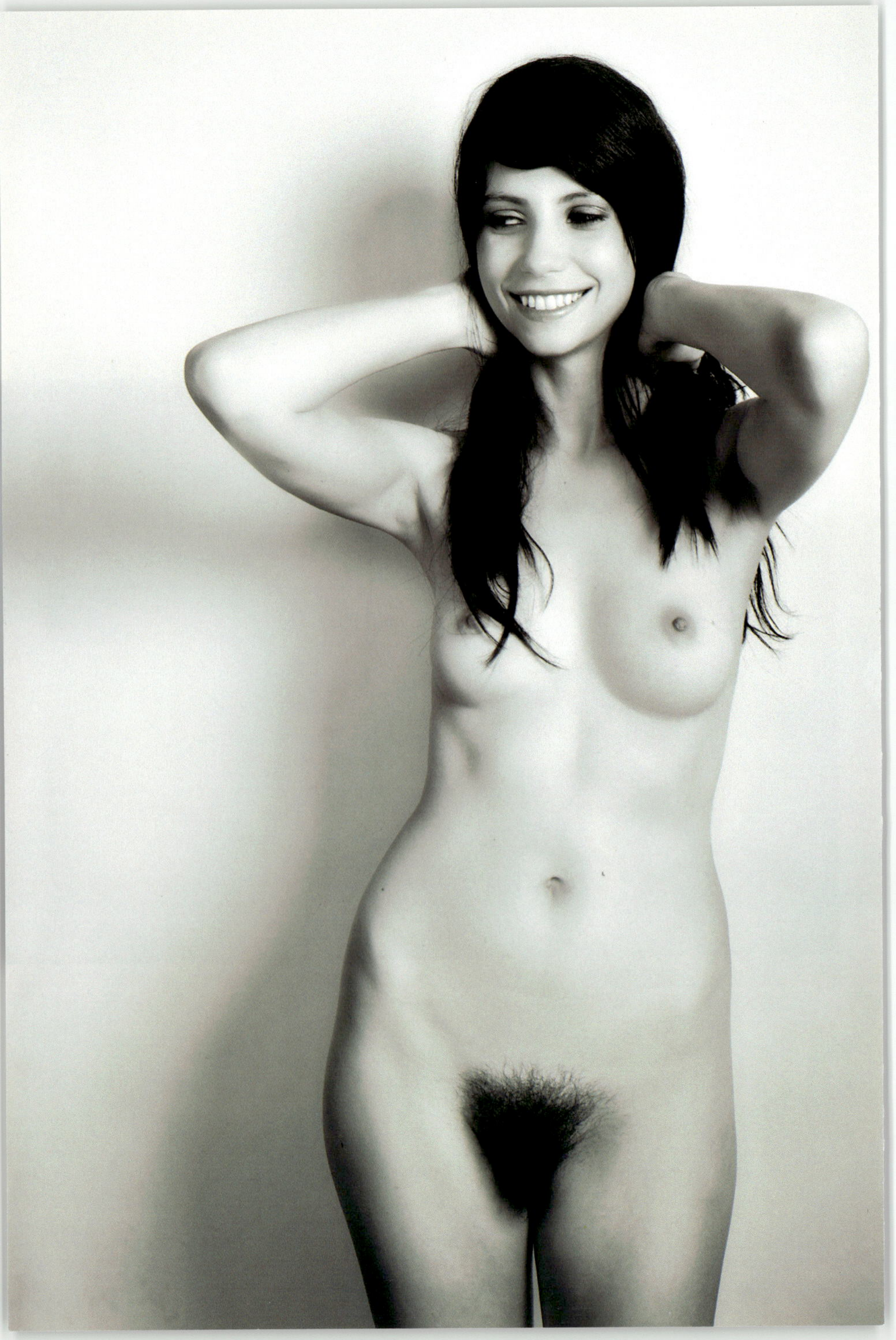

A. J. KAHN

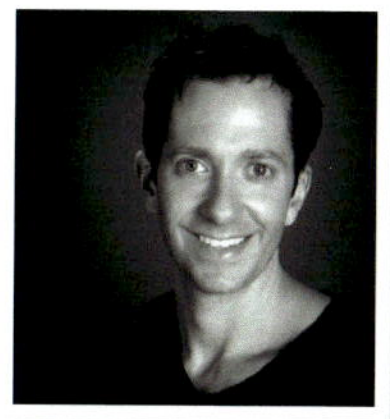

A. J. Kahn has created images of the human form, primarily the nude, for over twenty years. His style is classic with a contemporary inclination.

"From simple appreciation of pure aesthetics to unveiling layers of an individual's soul, few subjects in photography offer such diversity as the nude. I seek the essence of what is beautiful in each subject. One must get beyond what is easily seen and recognized, and discover a subject's profound sense of self, both physically and spiritually.

"I chose model Trishii because she embodies all that is feminine. Beyond her physical beauty, she seems to possess qualities that connect with the viewer in a subtle, yet sensual way. Combine that with an underlying air of mystery, and she represents what it is to be a woman."

www.ajkahn.com

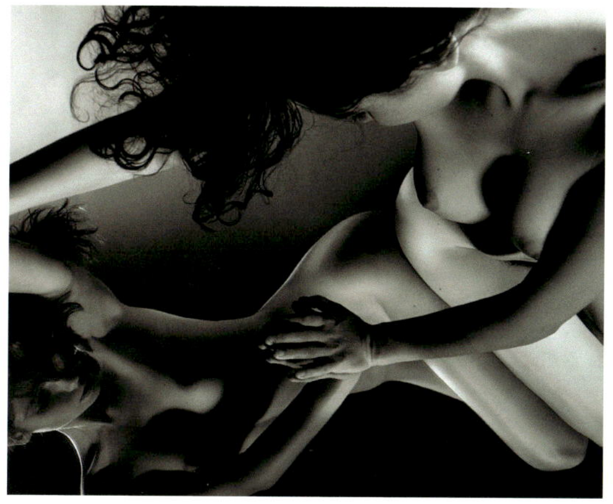

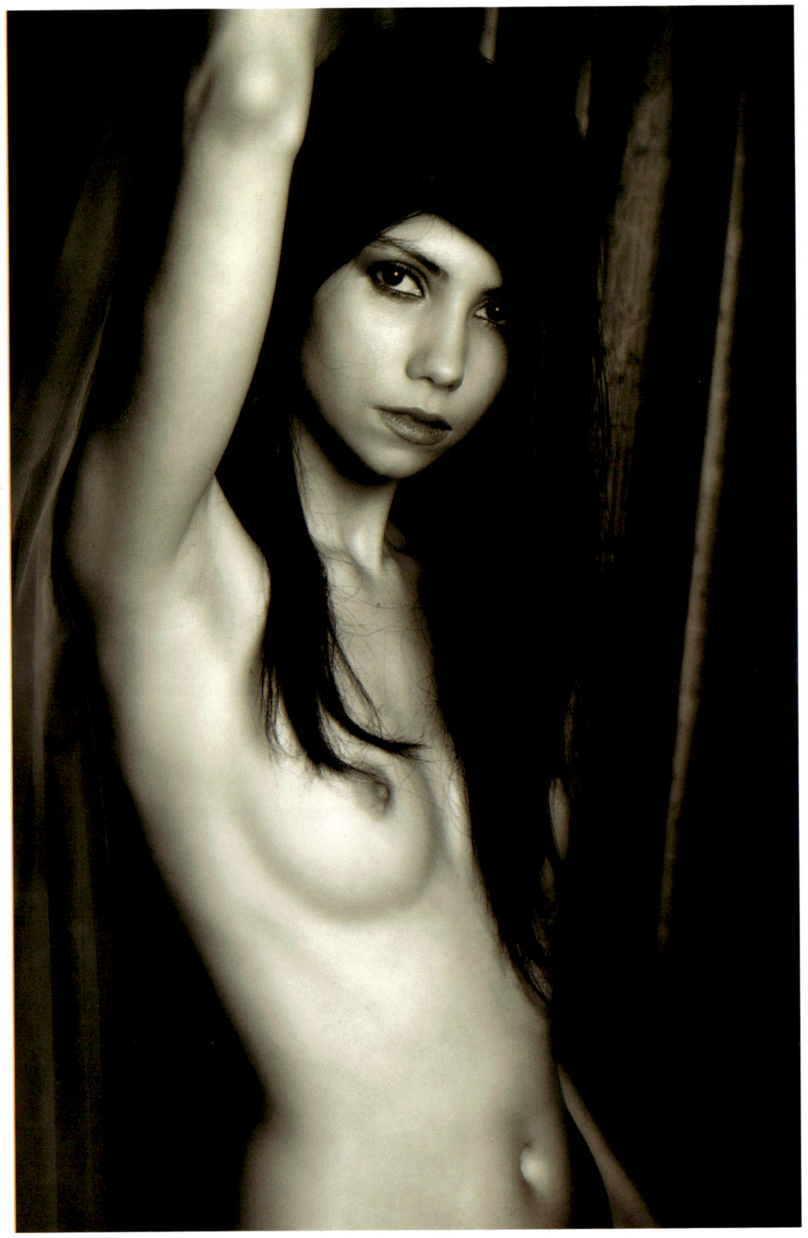

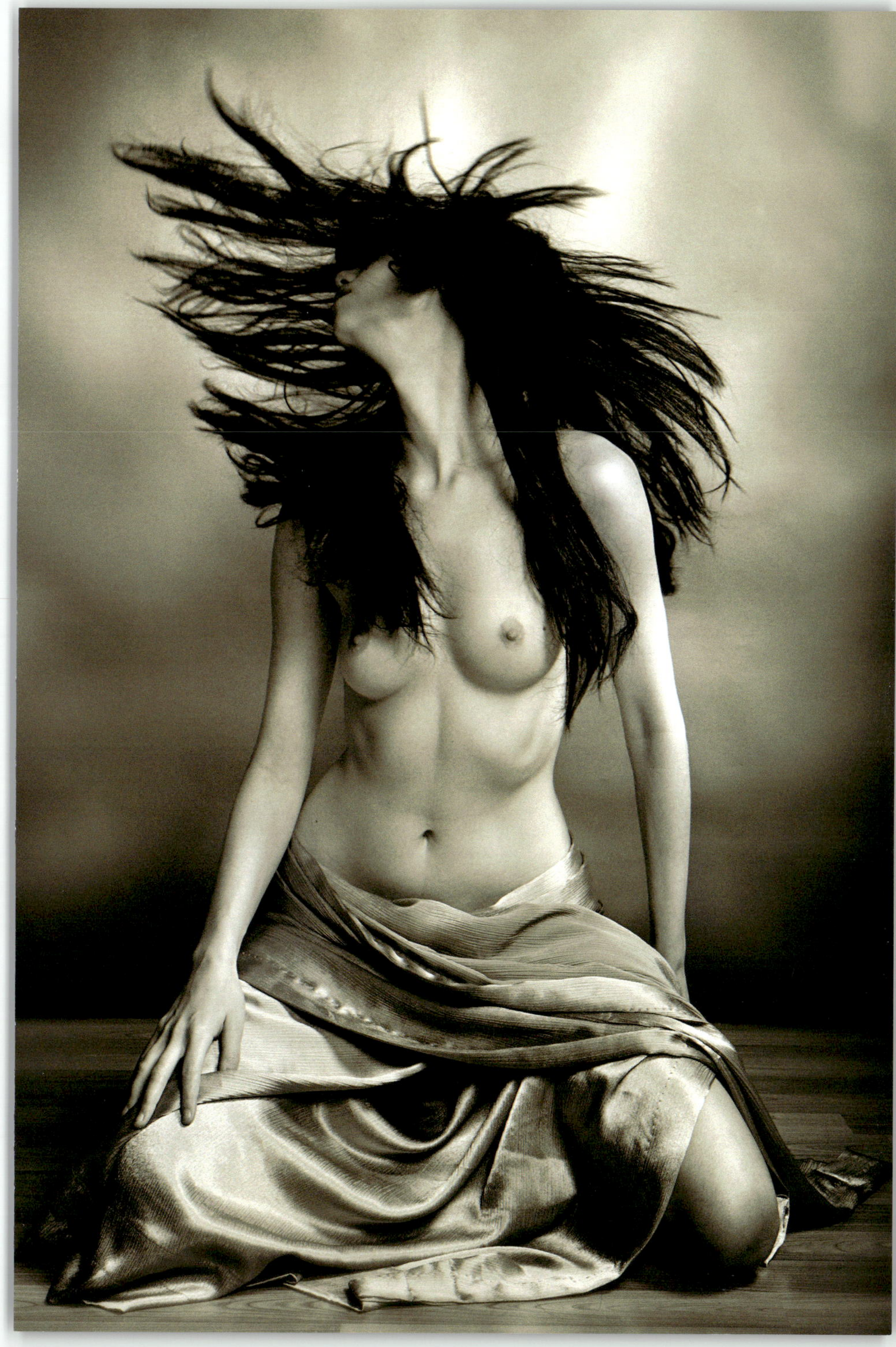

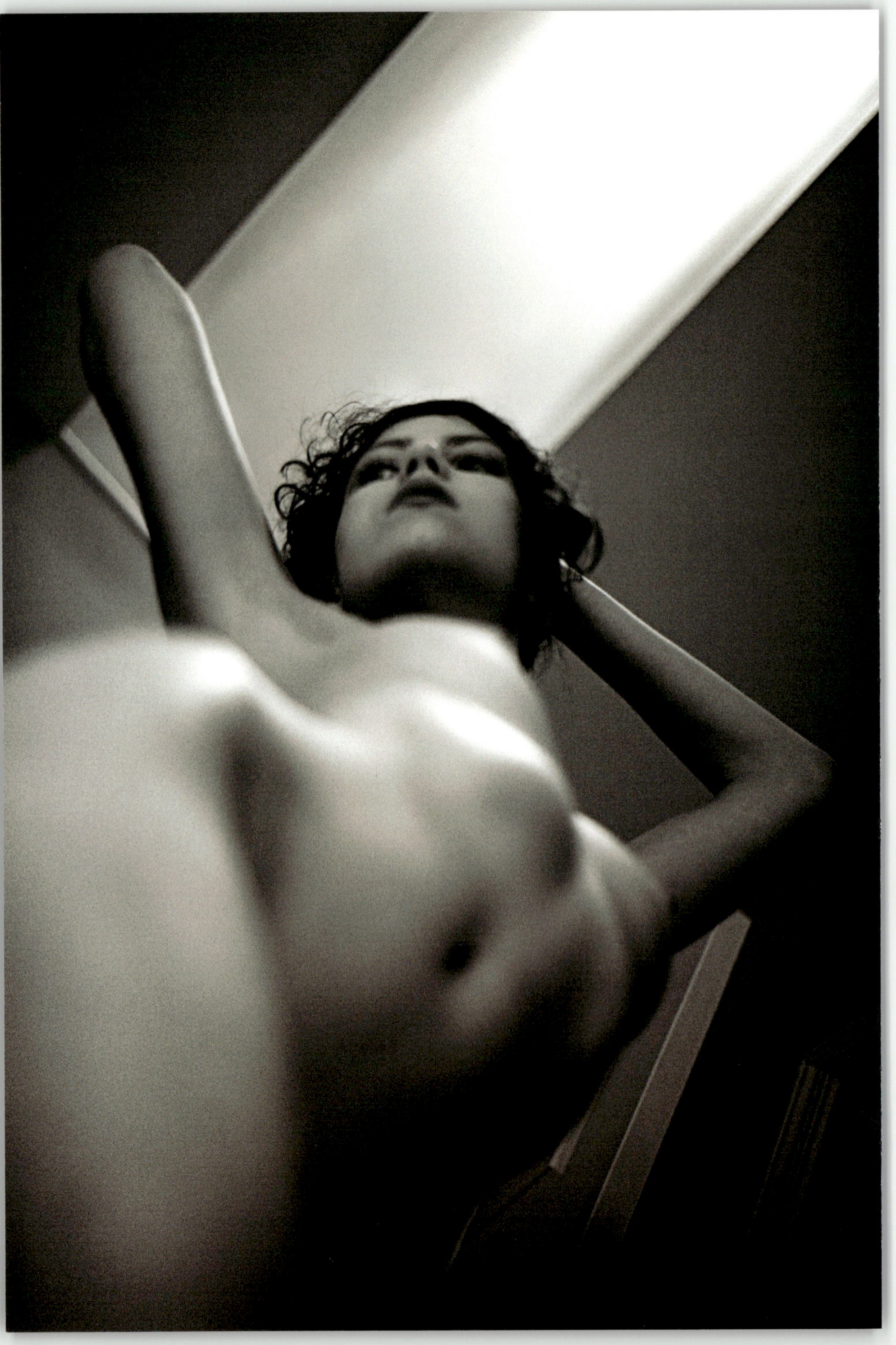

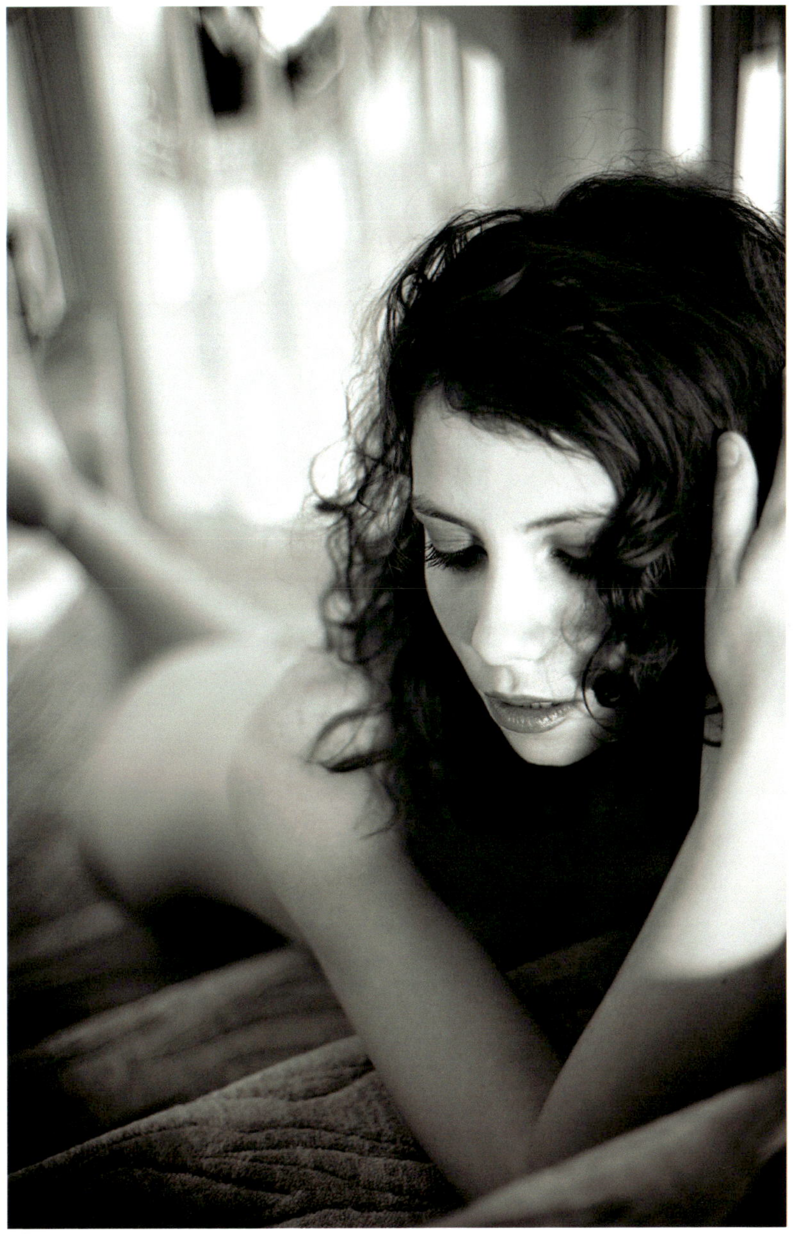

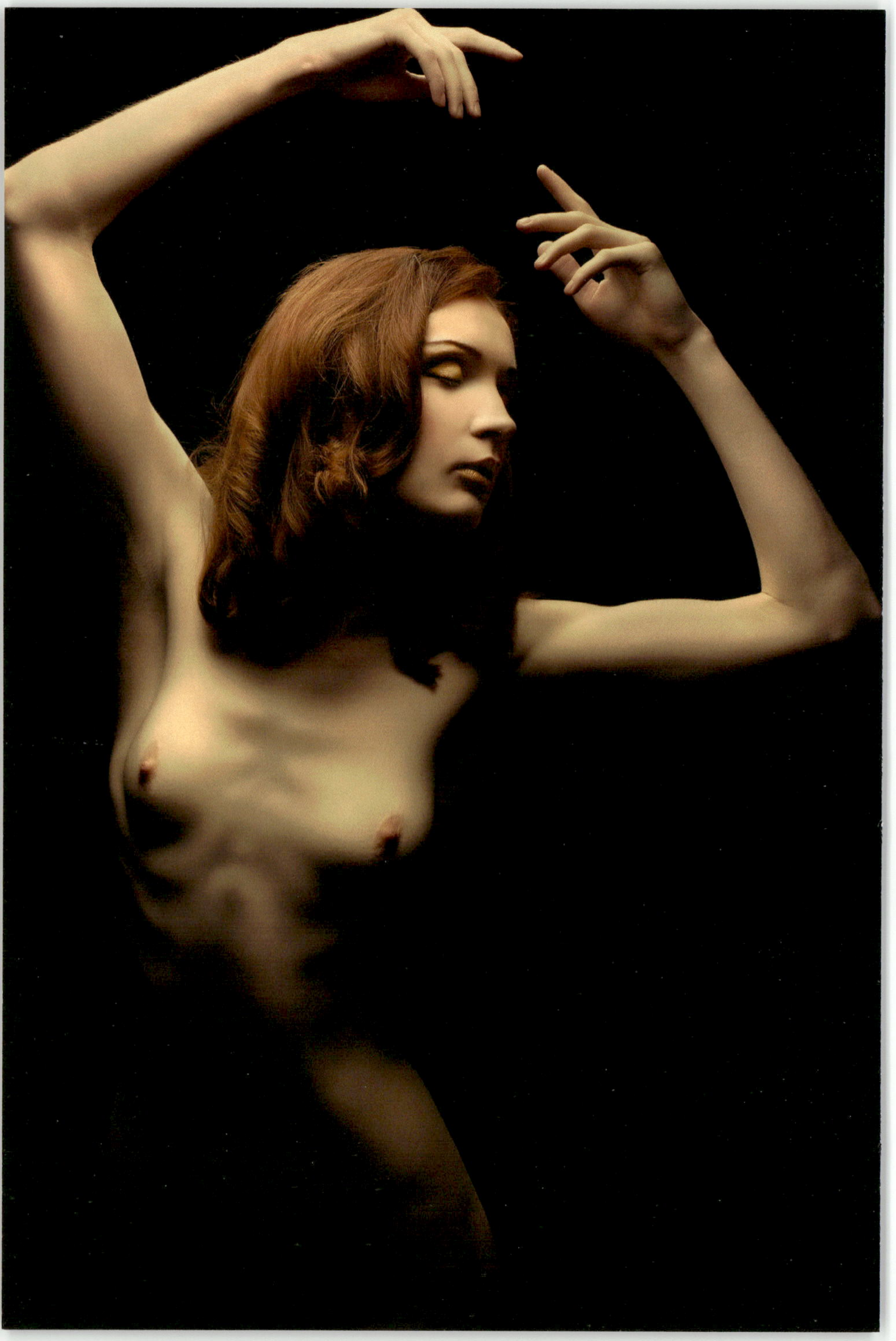

SERGEY KAMINSKY

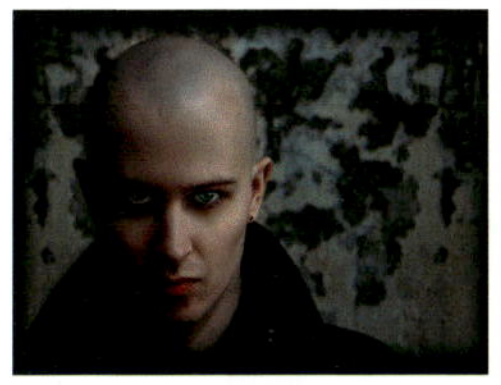

Sergey Kaminsky was born, grew up and currently lives in Moscow. He does nude photography not only because it is his favourite genre, but also because he thinks that it's the most difficult one. Most often he attempts to create a mood in his photos, though sometimes he just tries to show the beauty of the girl he shoots. But every time he manages to portray the soul through the naked body, confirming at the same time that the body is beautiful.

Christina, the model Sergey chose to feature here, is a gorgeous woman with a Nordic look – a natural blonde with blue eyes – who looks equally good in any character and regardless of the genre of photography.

www.vakial.deviantart.com
www.kaminsky.photosight.ru

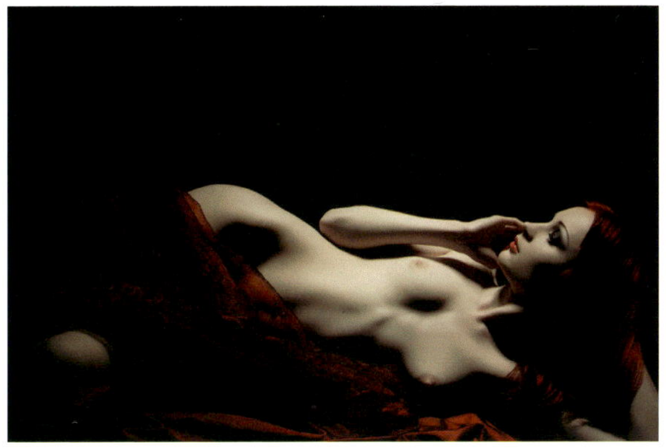

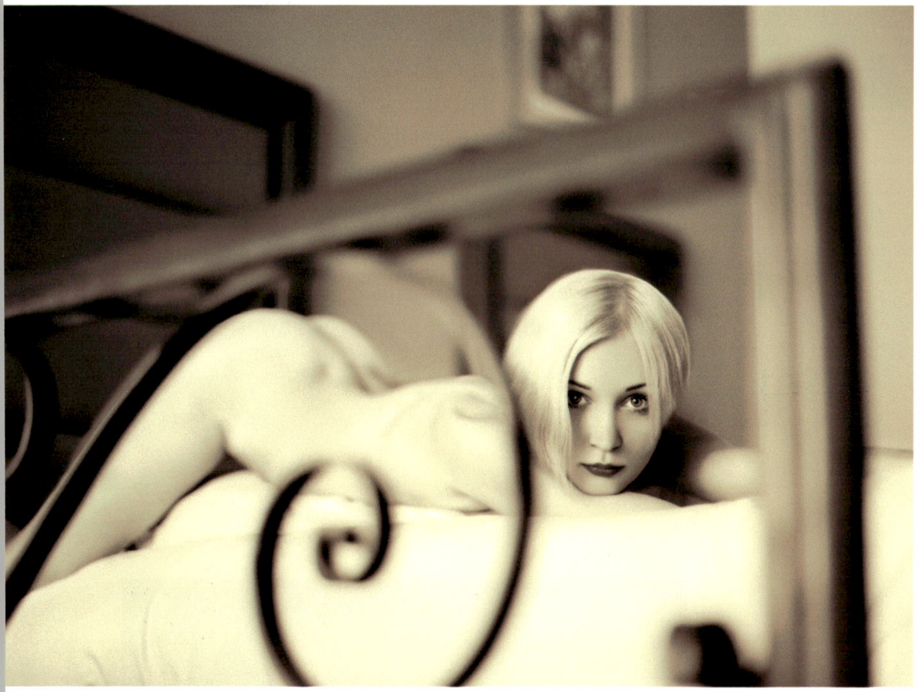

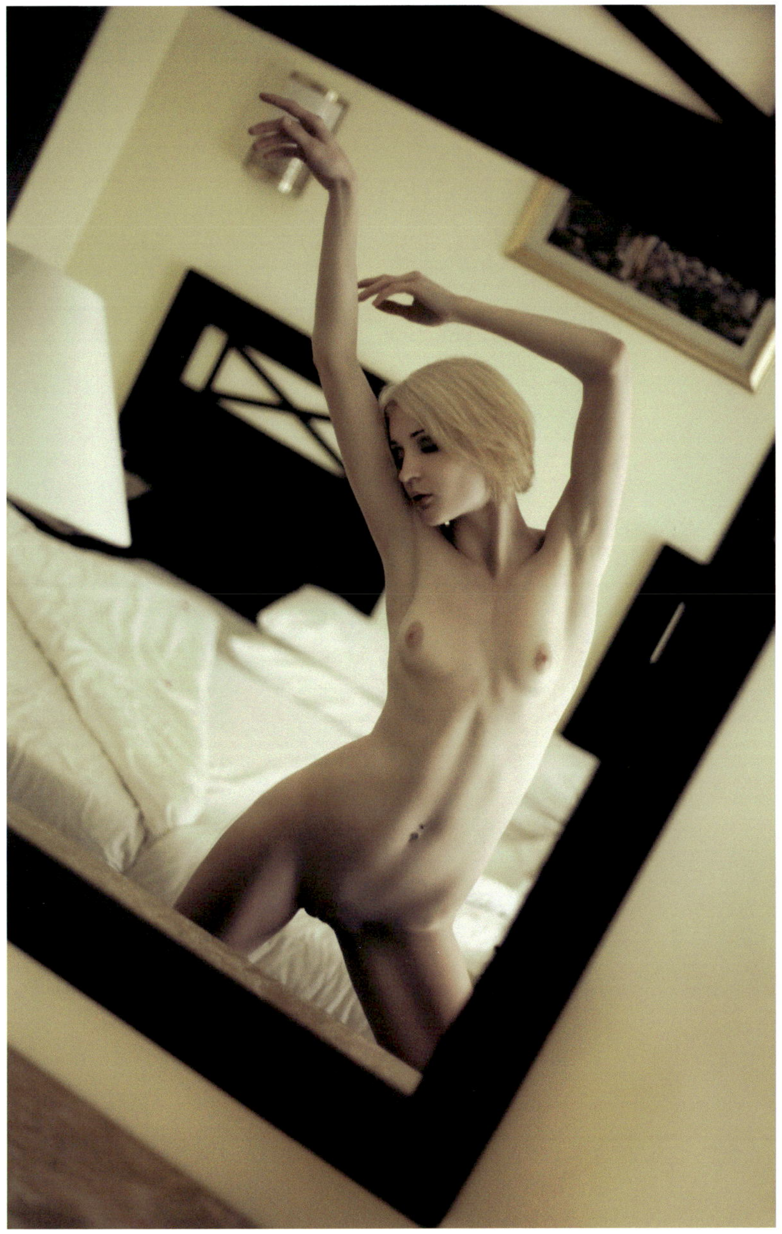

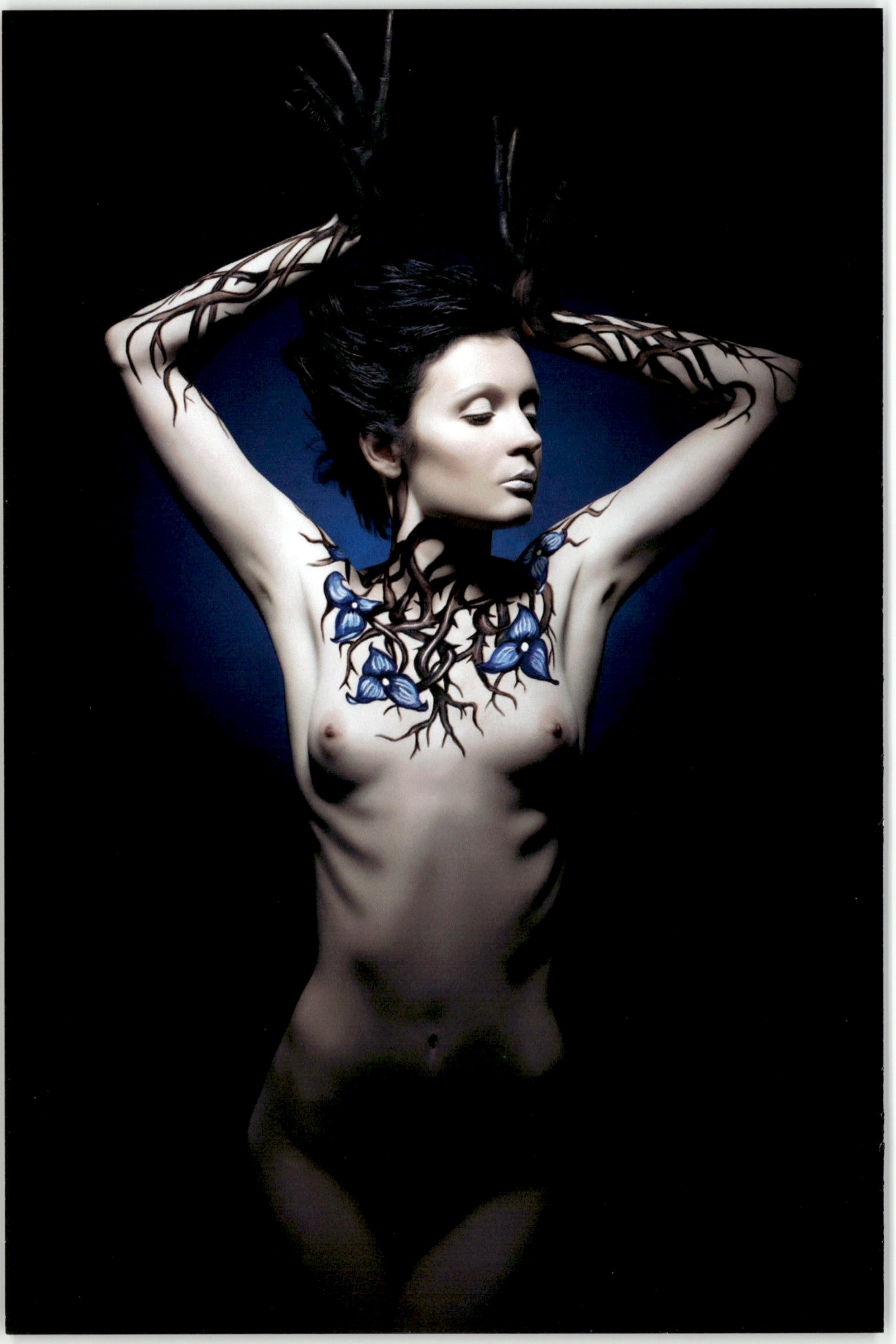

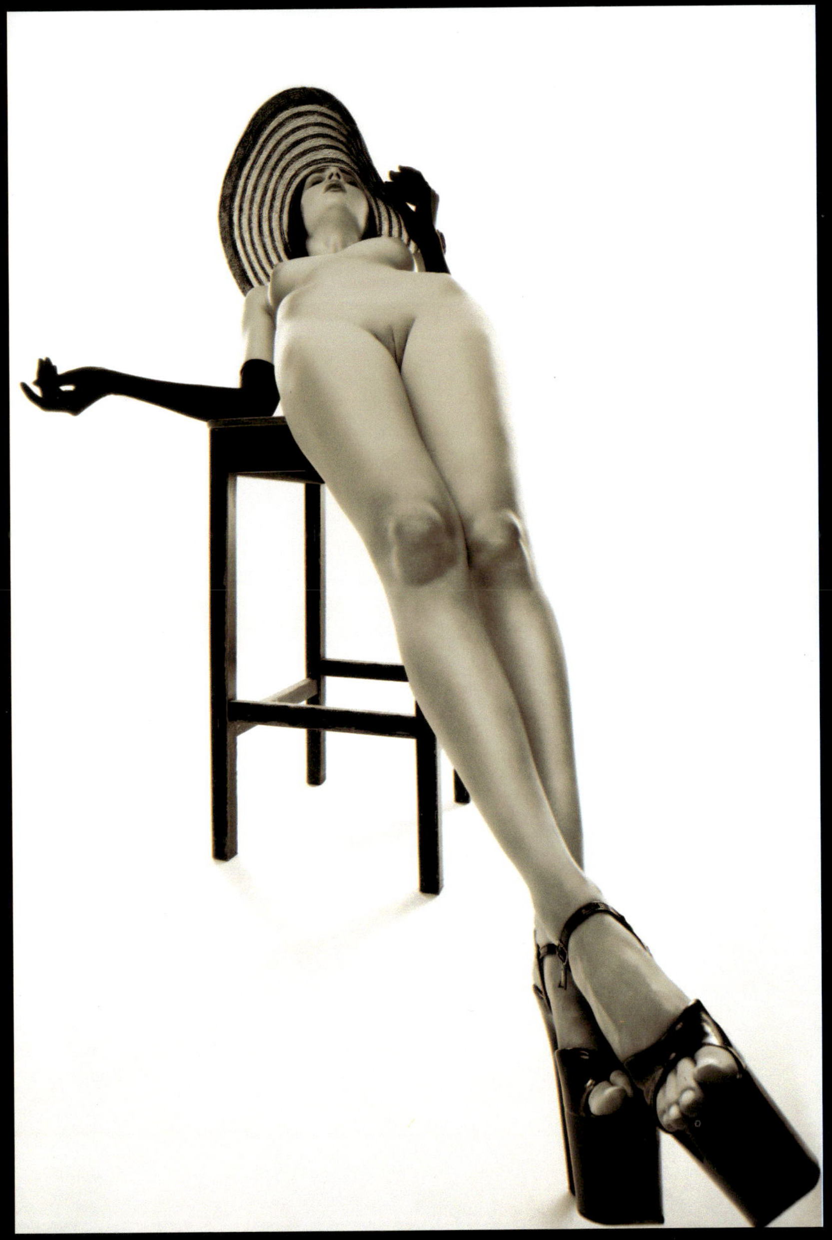

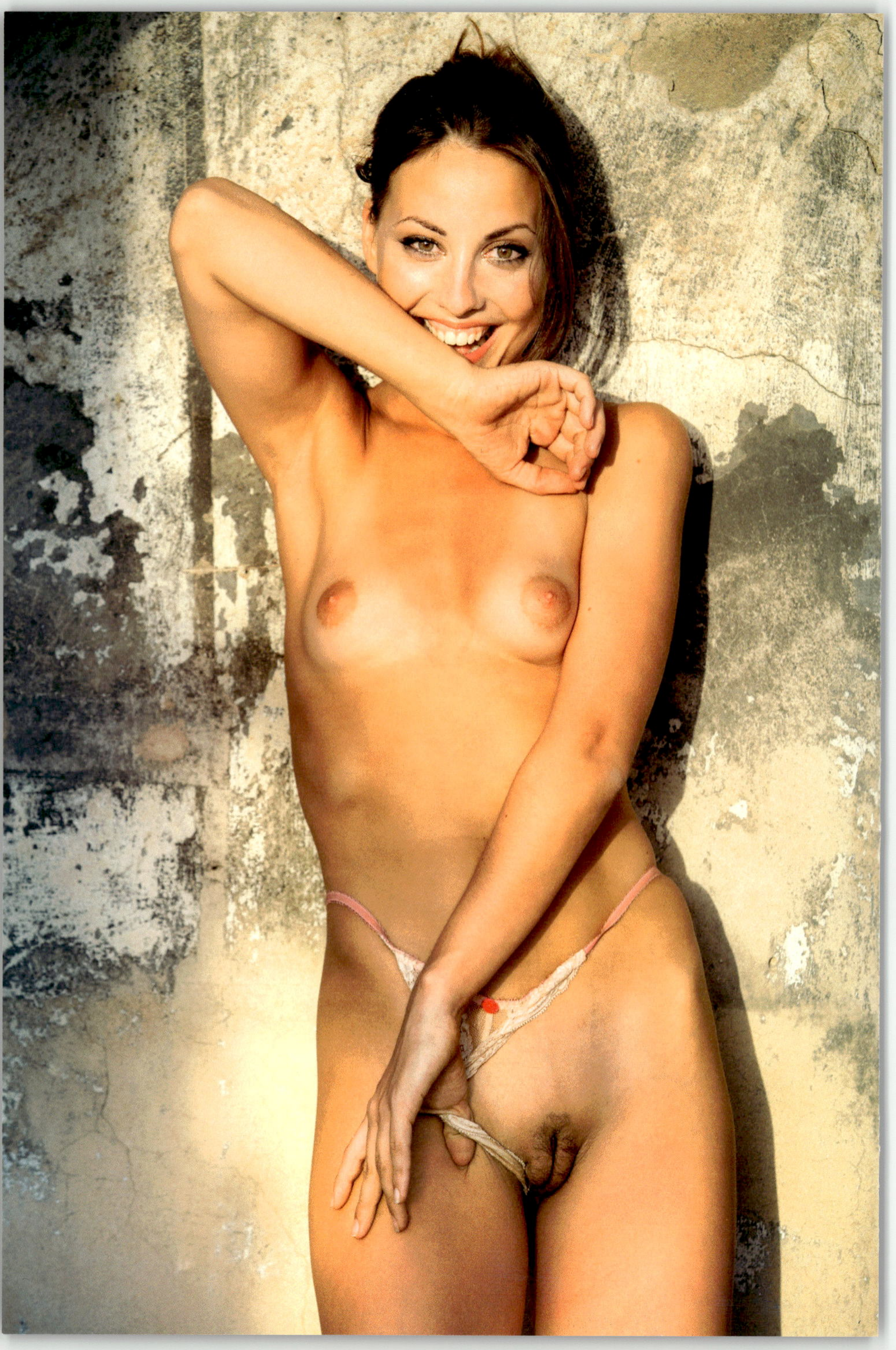

THOMAS KARSTEN

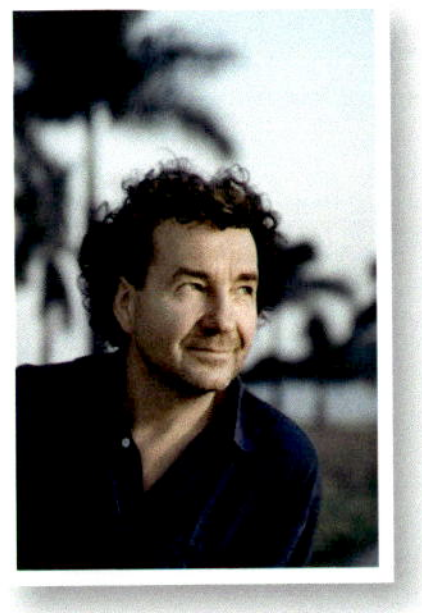

Thomas Karsten was born in 1958 in Eisenach, grew up in Leipzig and since 1982 has lived near Munich. After exploring other artistic fields he became a photographer at twenty-one. Since 1983 he has worked for journals and magazines including *Stern*, *Art*, *Nerve* (New York) and *Capital*. His first solo publication won the Kodak-Fotobuchpreis in 1988, and since then he has published sixteen major books of nudes.

Bianca was a twenty-one-year-old student in Berlin and already a fan of Thomas's work when they first met. Over a period of months they worked intensively, conceiving wild, joyful pictures, outside and inside, in Majorca, Berlin and elsewhere, on the street, in bed, alone and with other women. The images vibrate with pleasure, produce heat and reflect a natural form of desire.

www.thomaskarsten.com

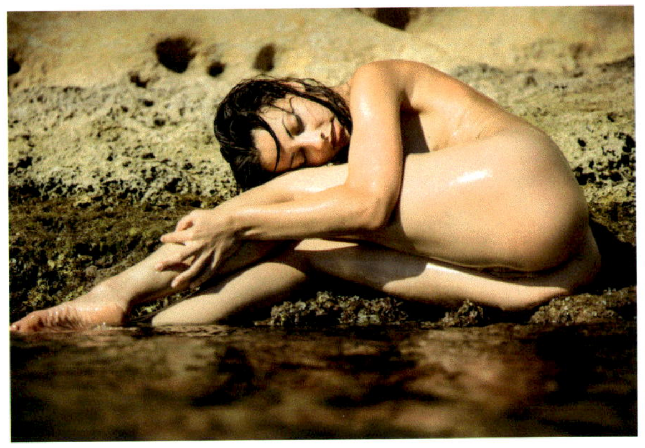

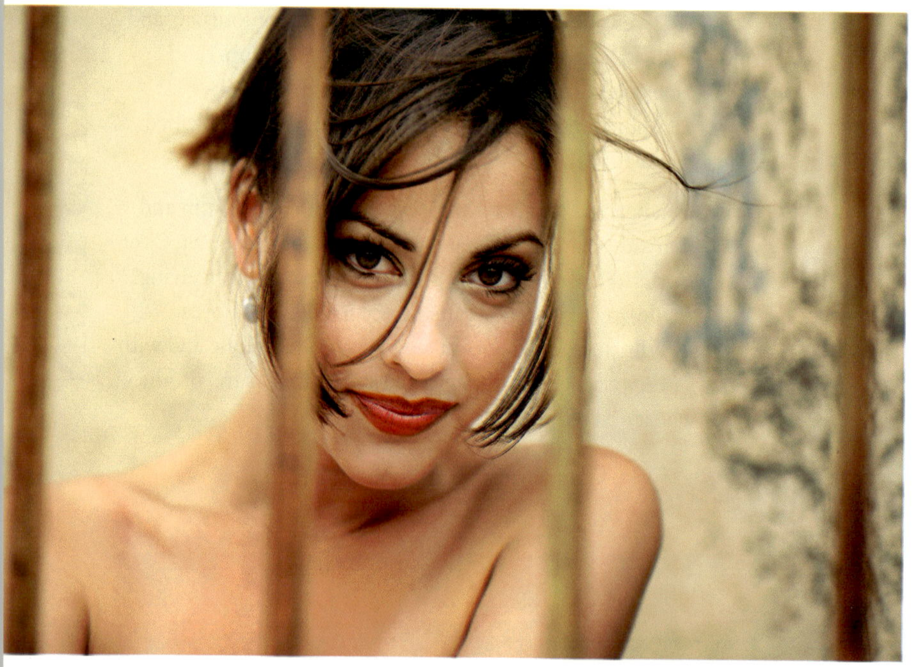

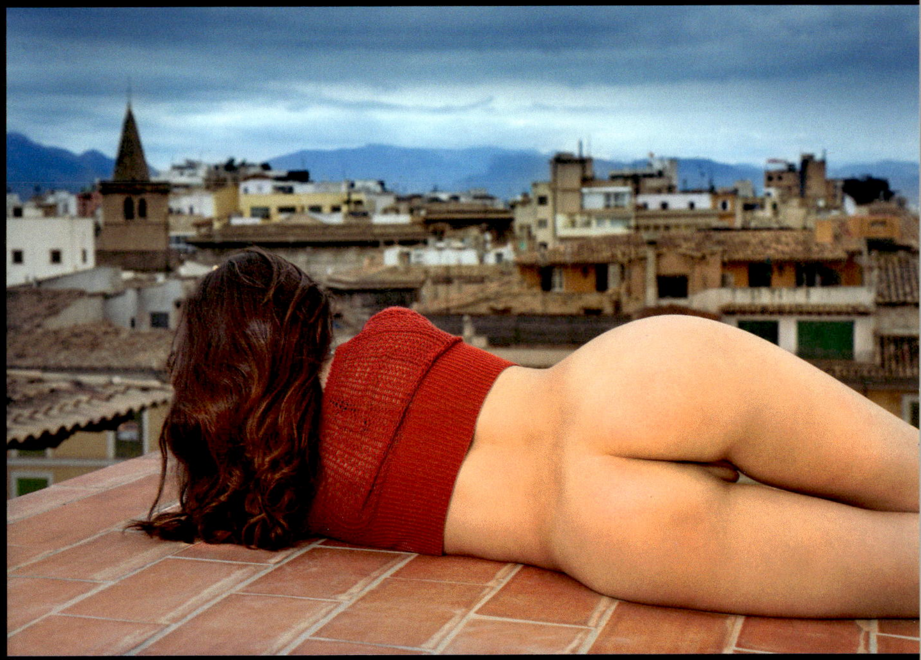

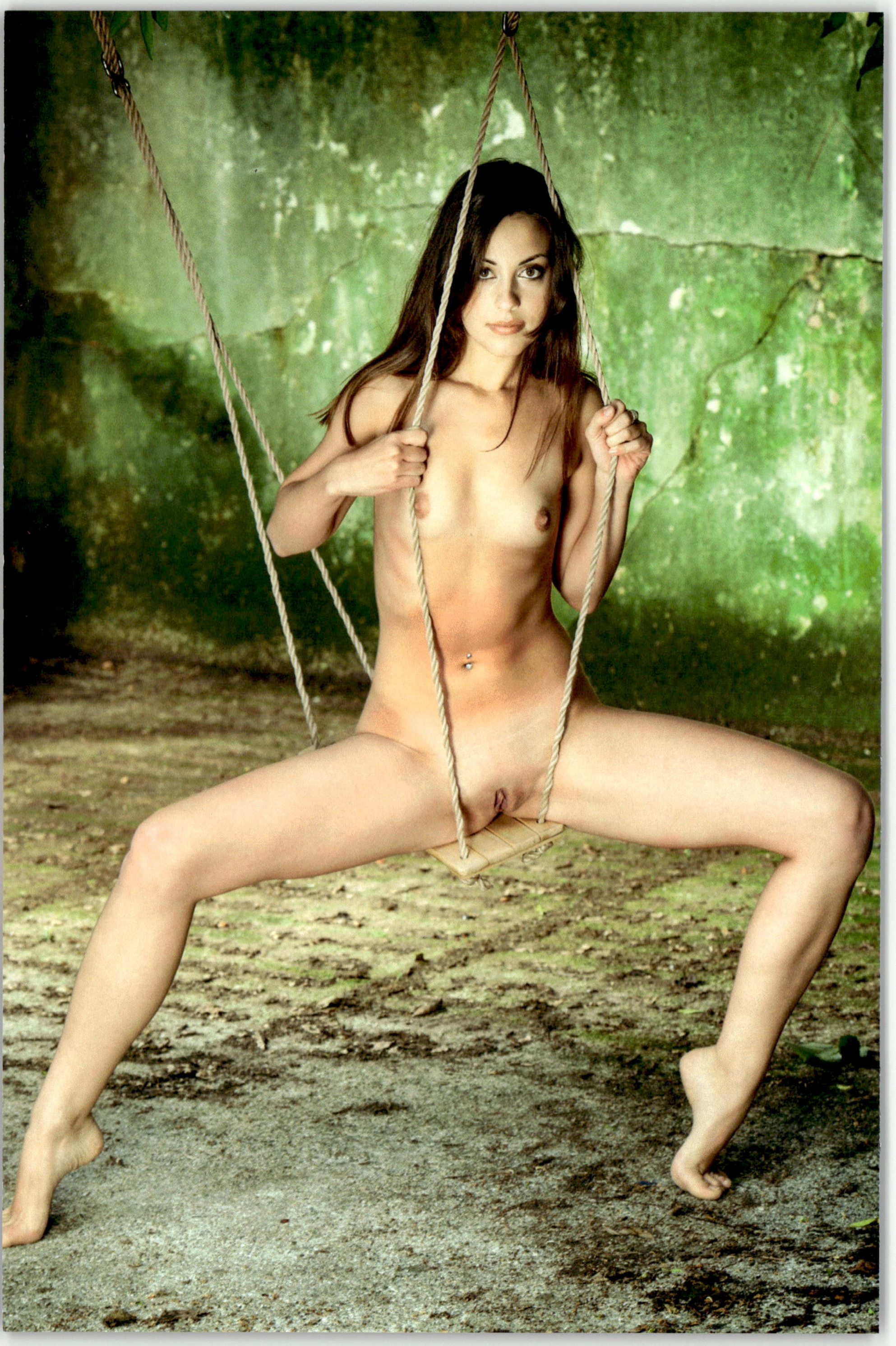

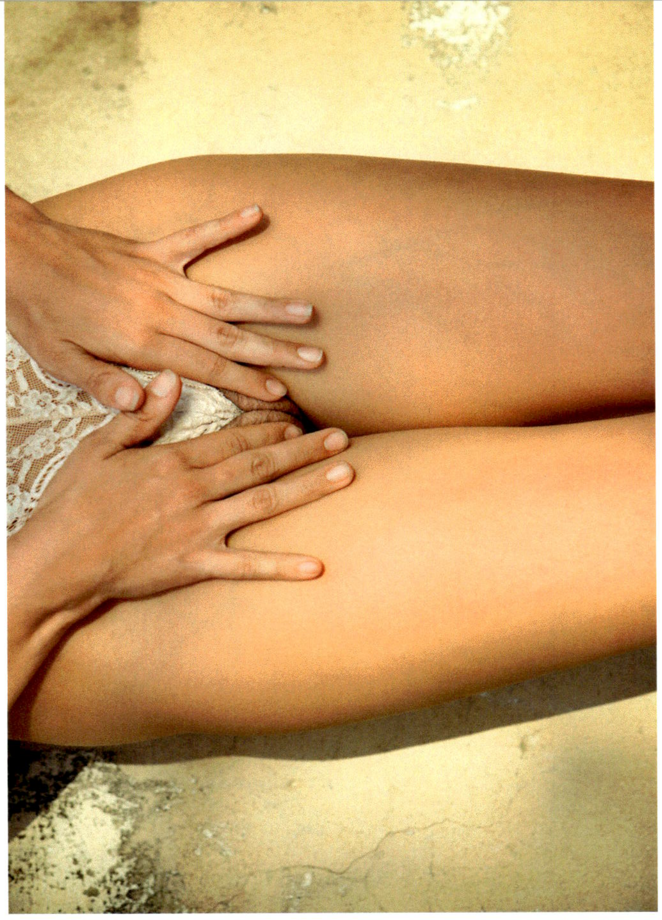

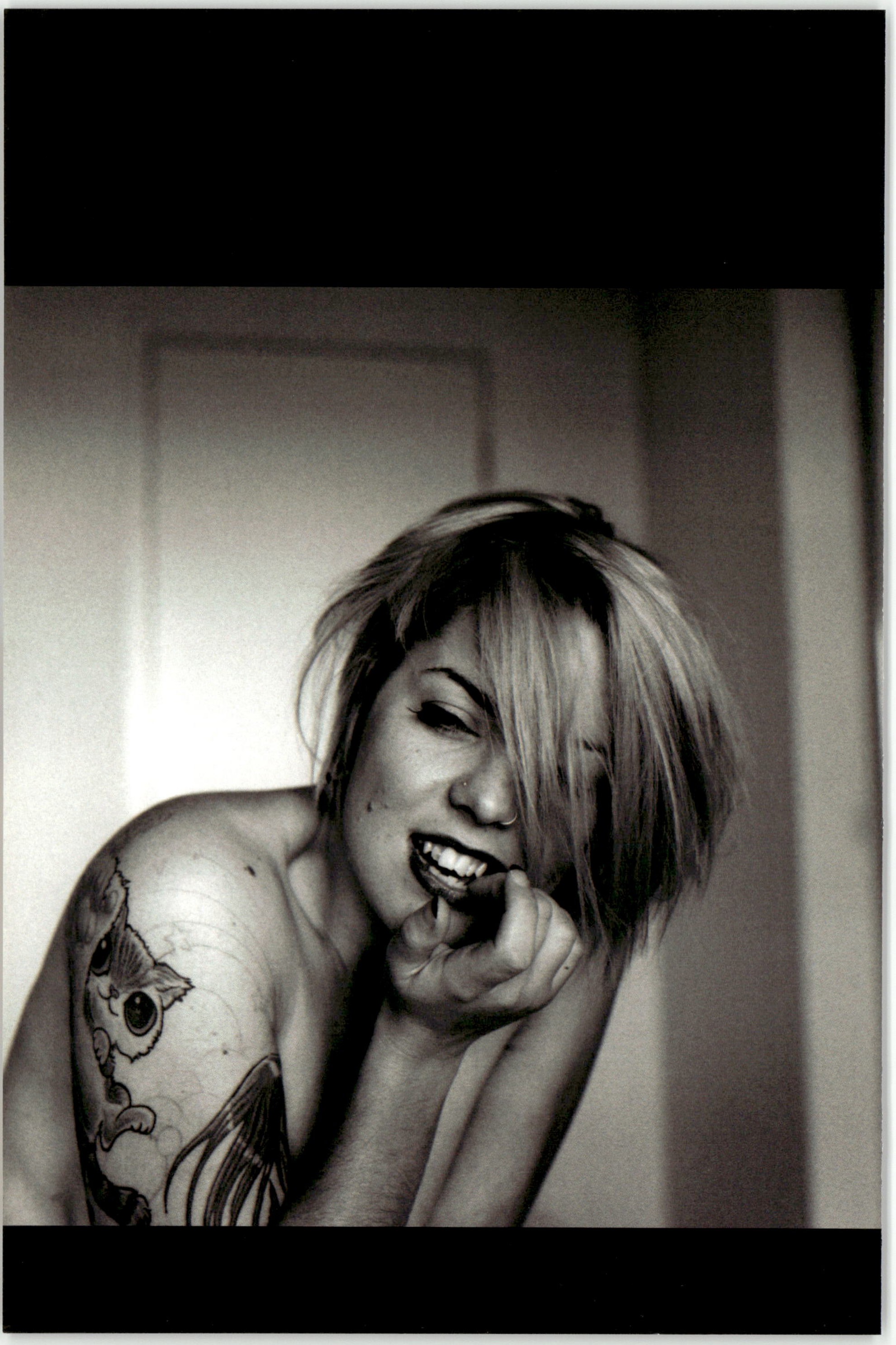

DANIEL KLAAS

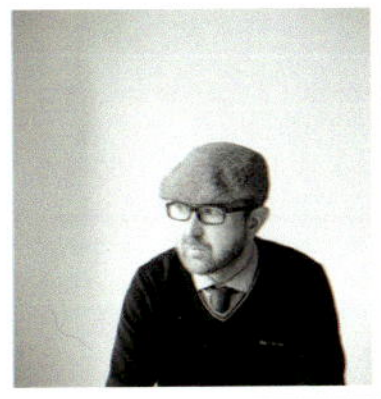

Daniel Klaas is a portrait and fashion photographer based in Melbourne, Australia. After learning and applying his art while living in Innsbruck, Austria, for three years, he returned home to continue his photographic work, predominantly shooting with old film cameras and Polaroids. He mainly uses natural light in his quest to create soft and intimate portraits.

"I chose my model 'Mad-Dame' as we have worked together on a number of occasions and therefore had gotten quite comfortable collaborating. We seem to understand what we are both looking for in our work, and can combine these aspects effectively."

www.danielklaas.com

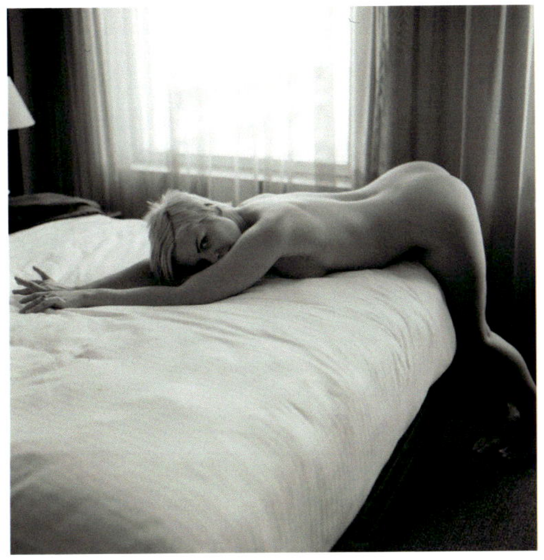

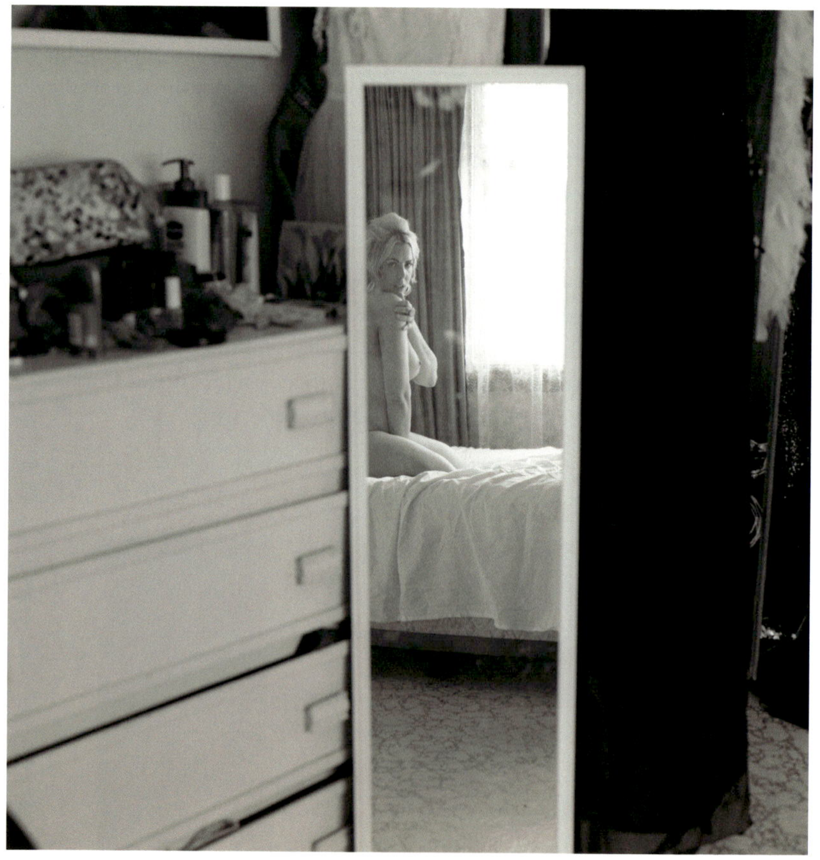

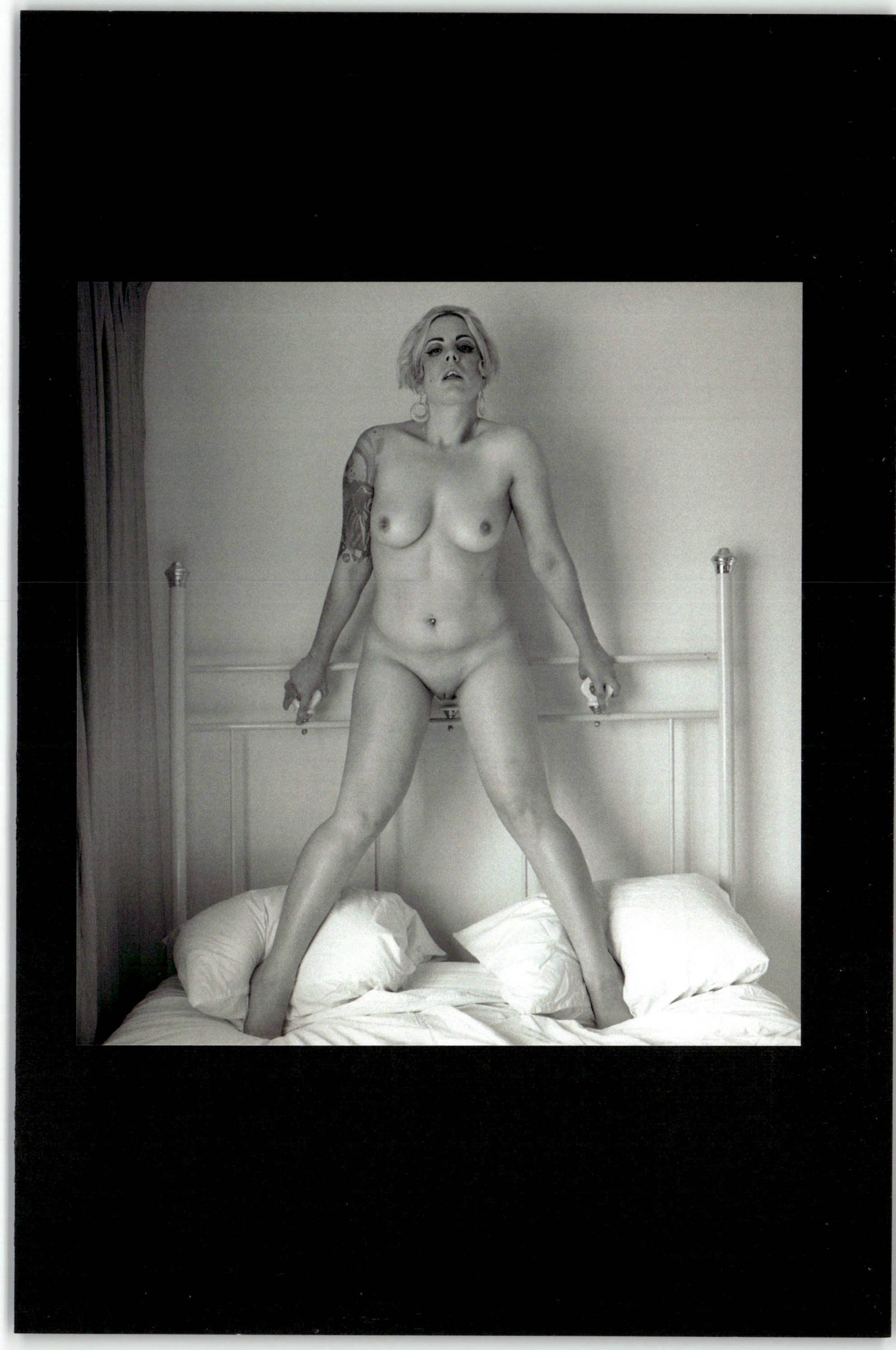

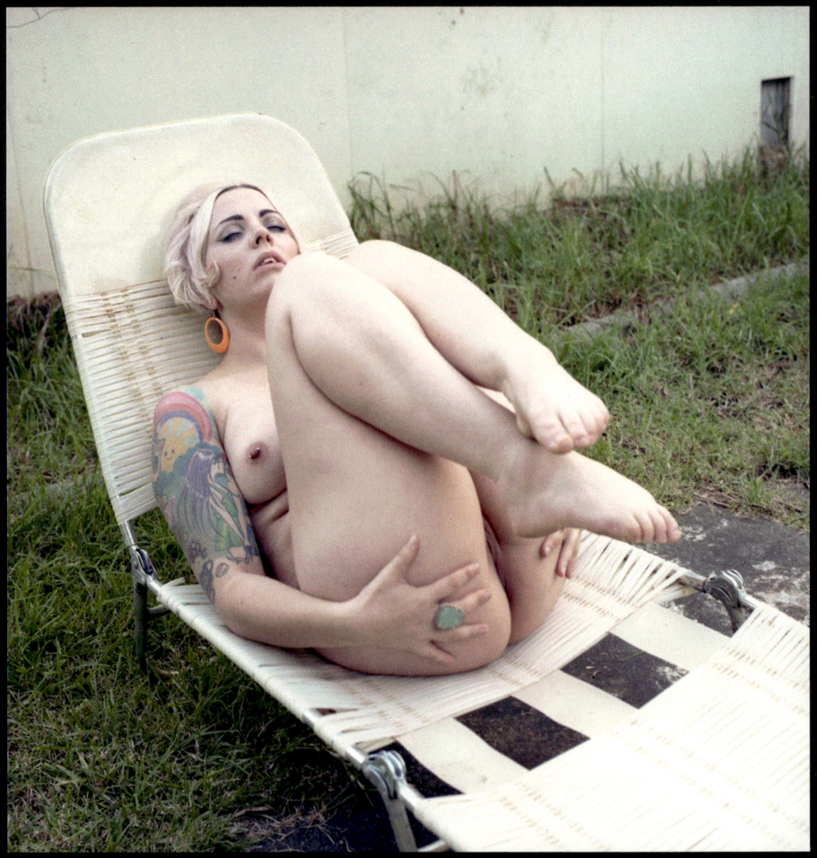

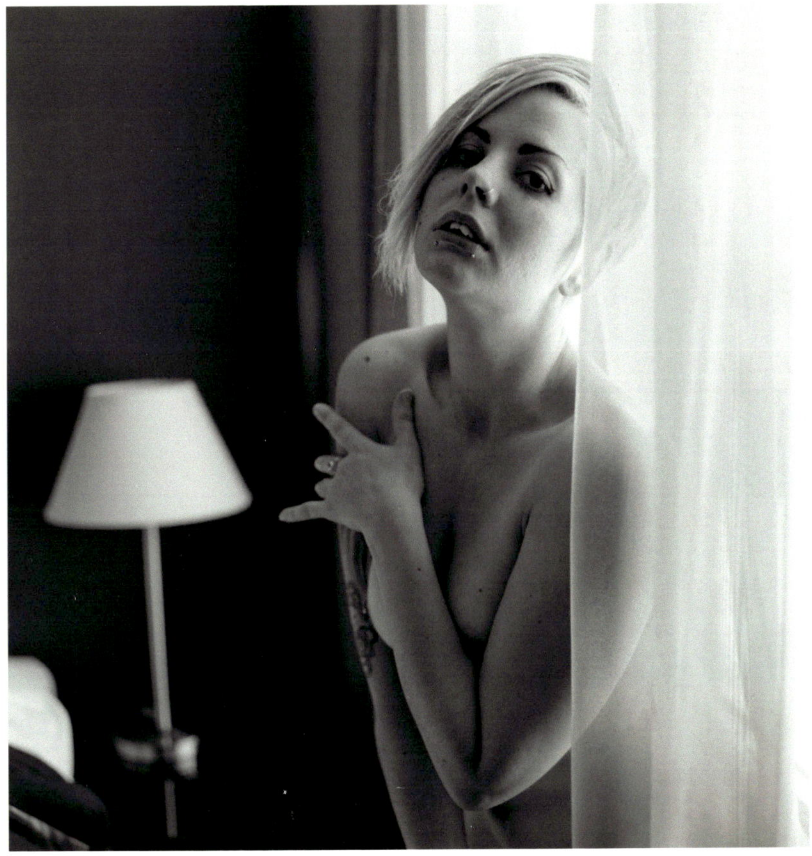

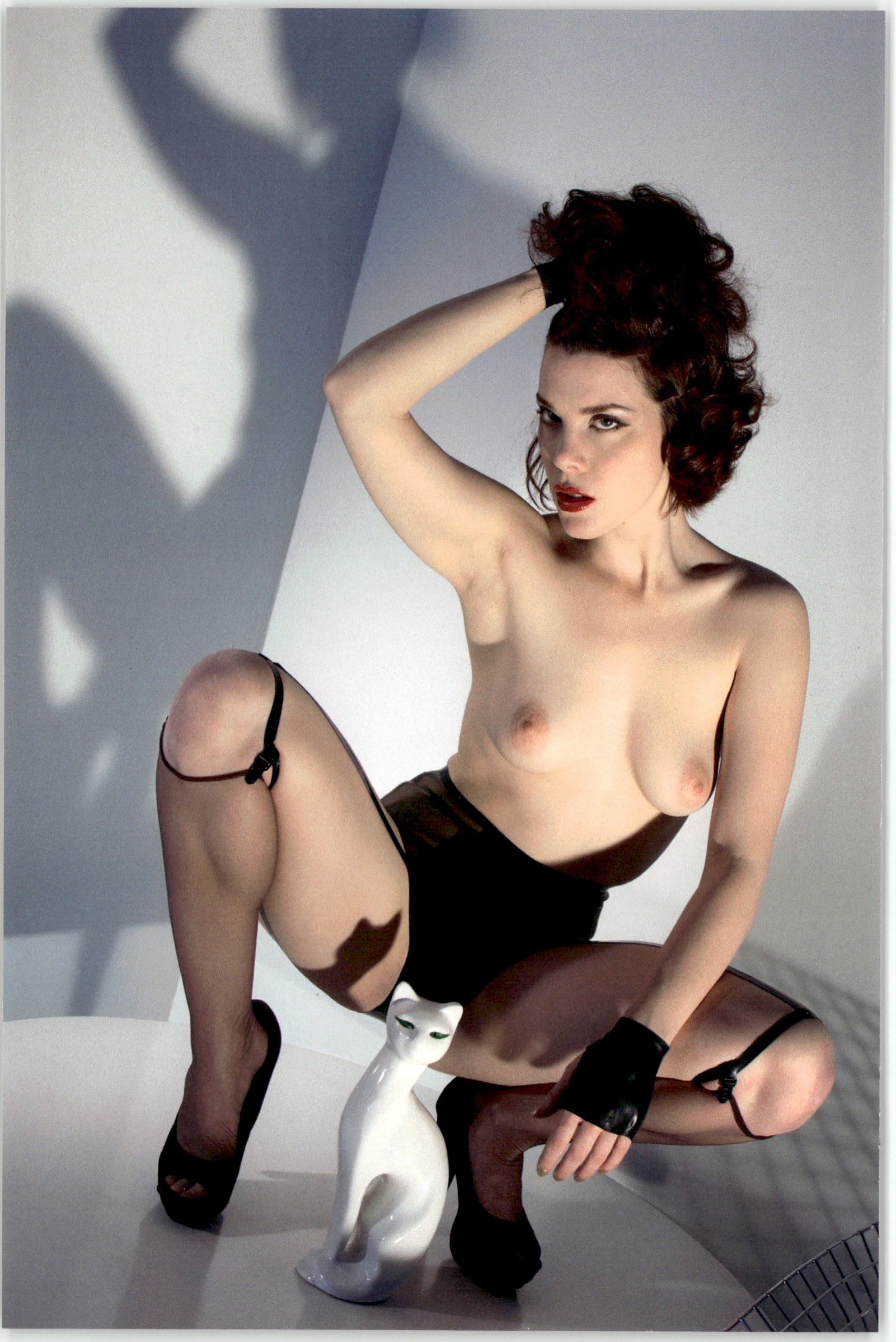

CHAS RAY KRIDER

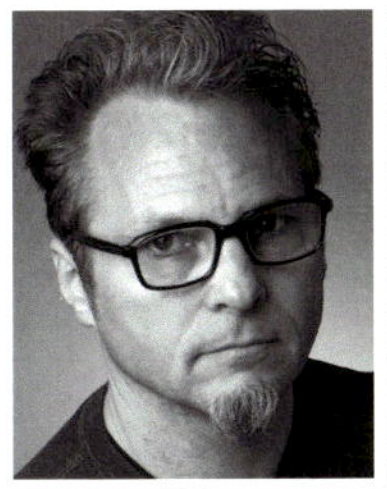

Chas Ray Krider's photographs are part of a tradition of erotic art that employs exaggeration, mystery and the guilty pleasures of voyeurism. His photographs are about the forms employed in narrative-based erotic art. Chas Ray's work is widely exhibited and published, including in two solo books, *Motel Fetish* (Taschen, 2002 and 2012) and *Do Not Disturb* (La Musardine, 2007).

www.motelfetish.com
chasray@motelfetish.com
www.chasraykrider.wordpress.com

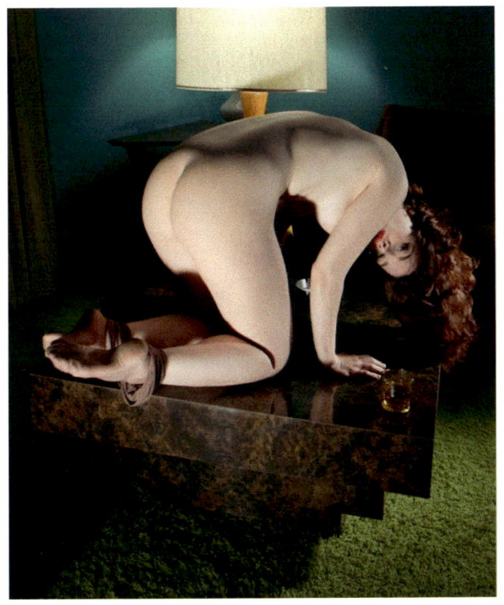

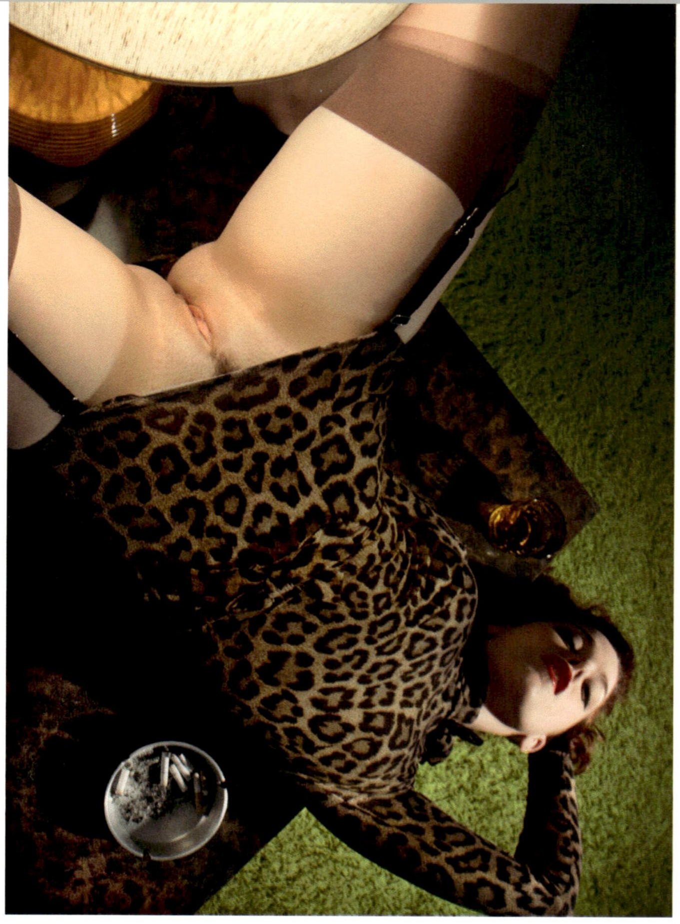

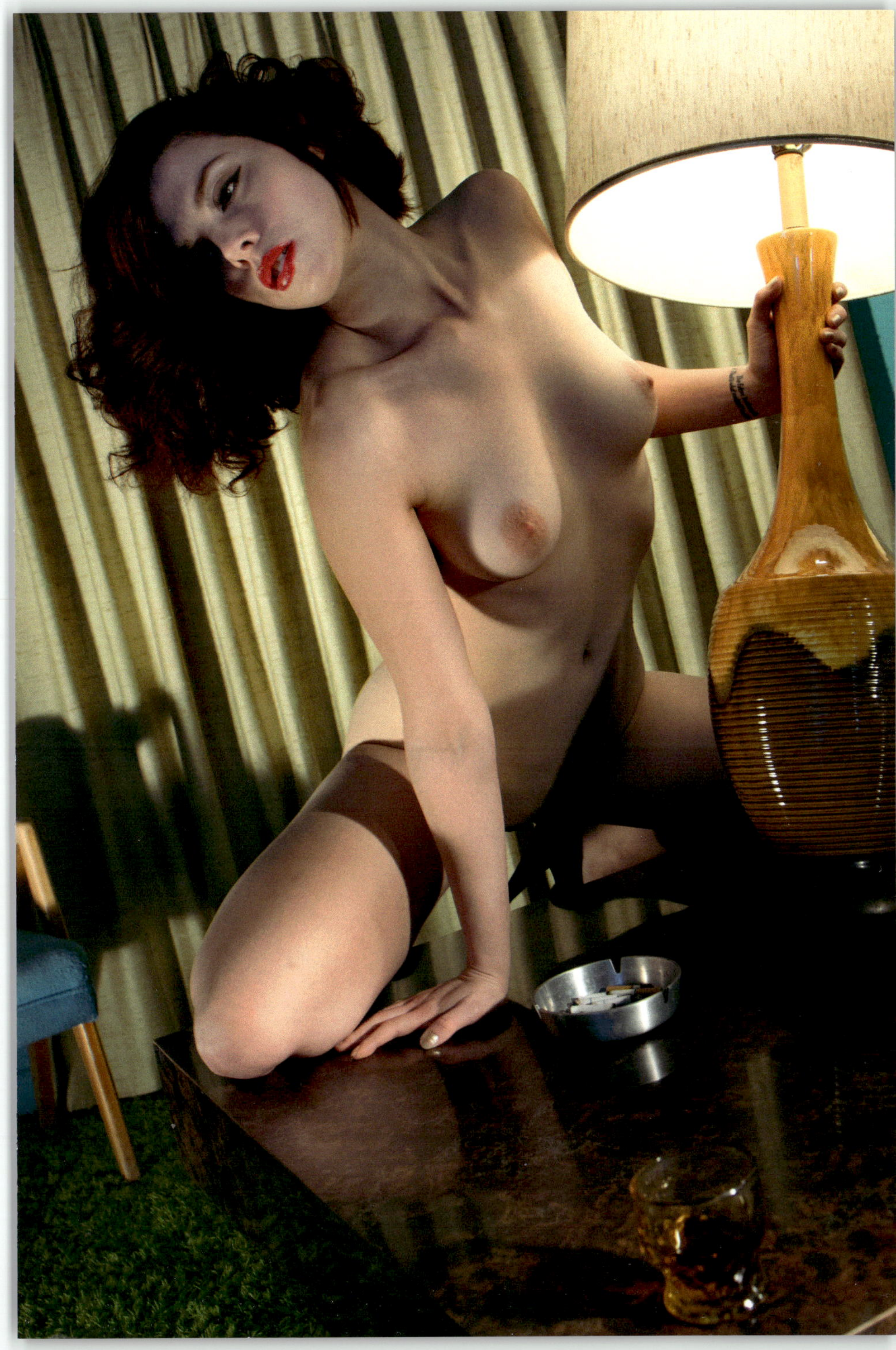

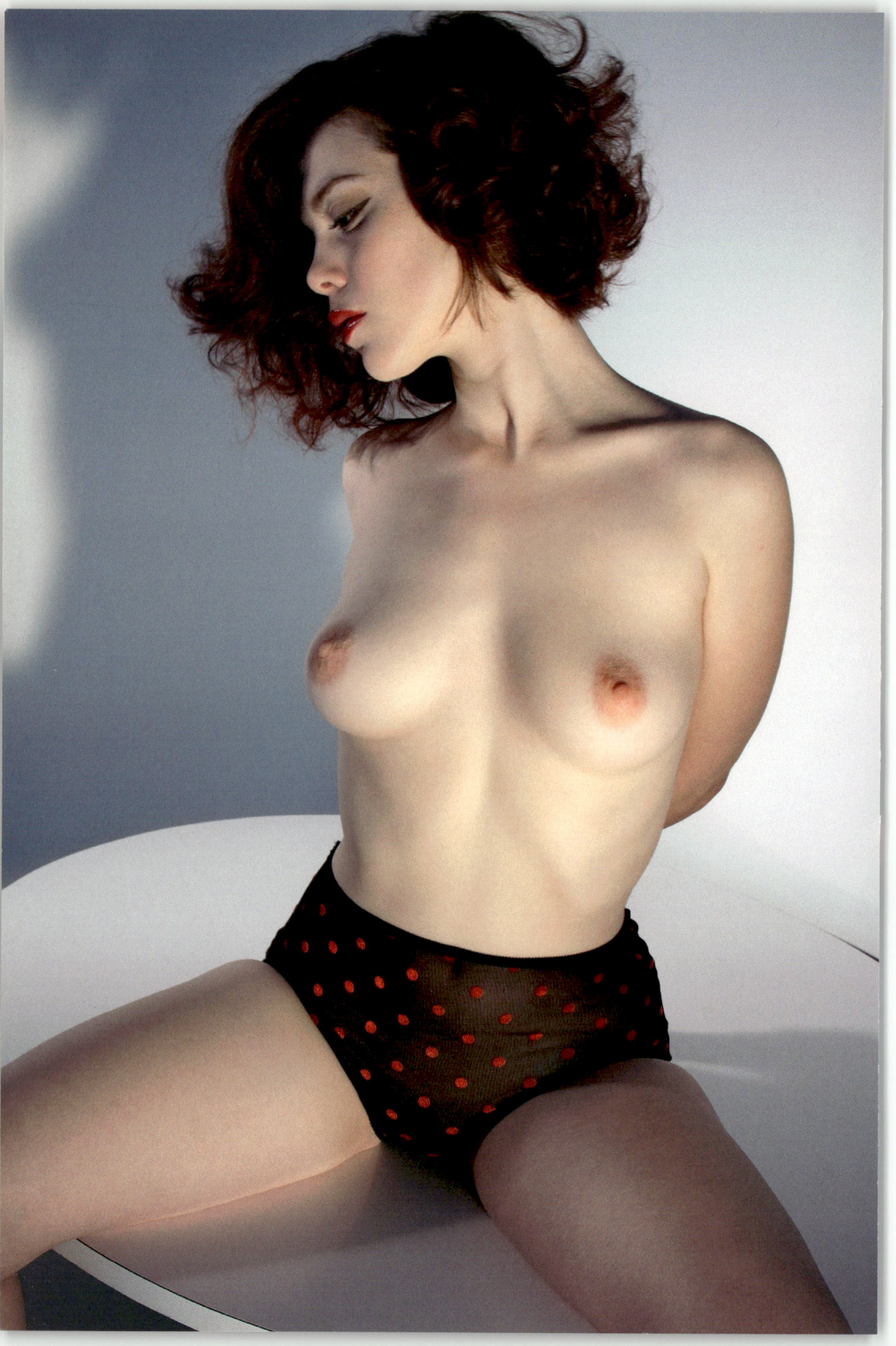

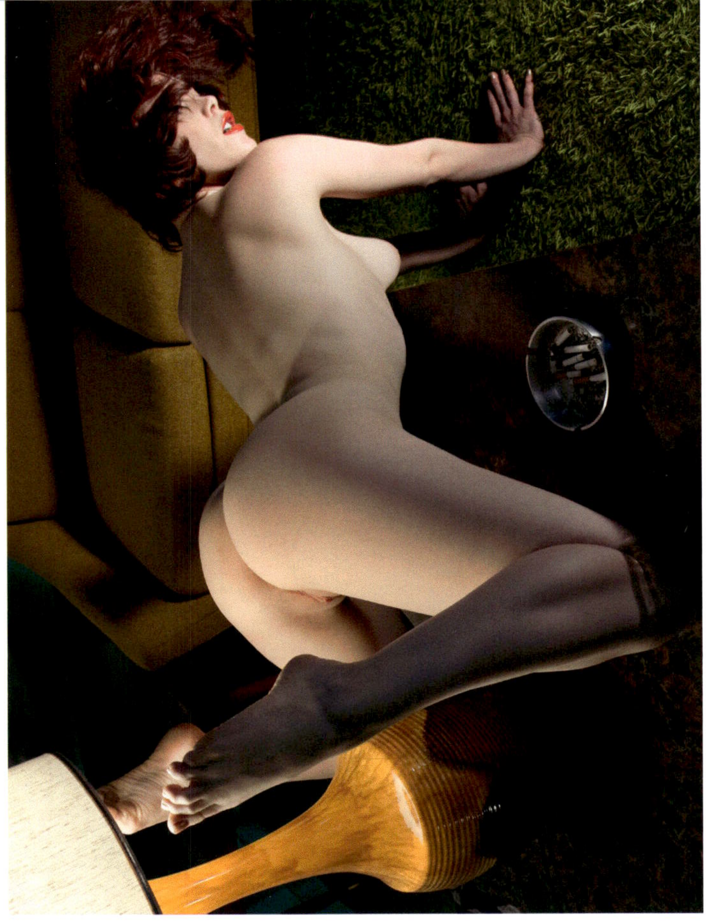

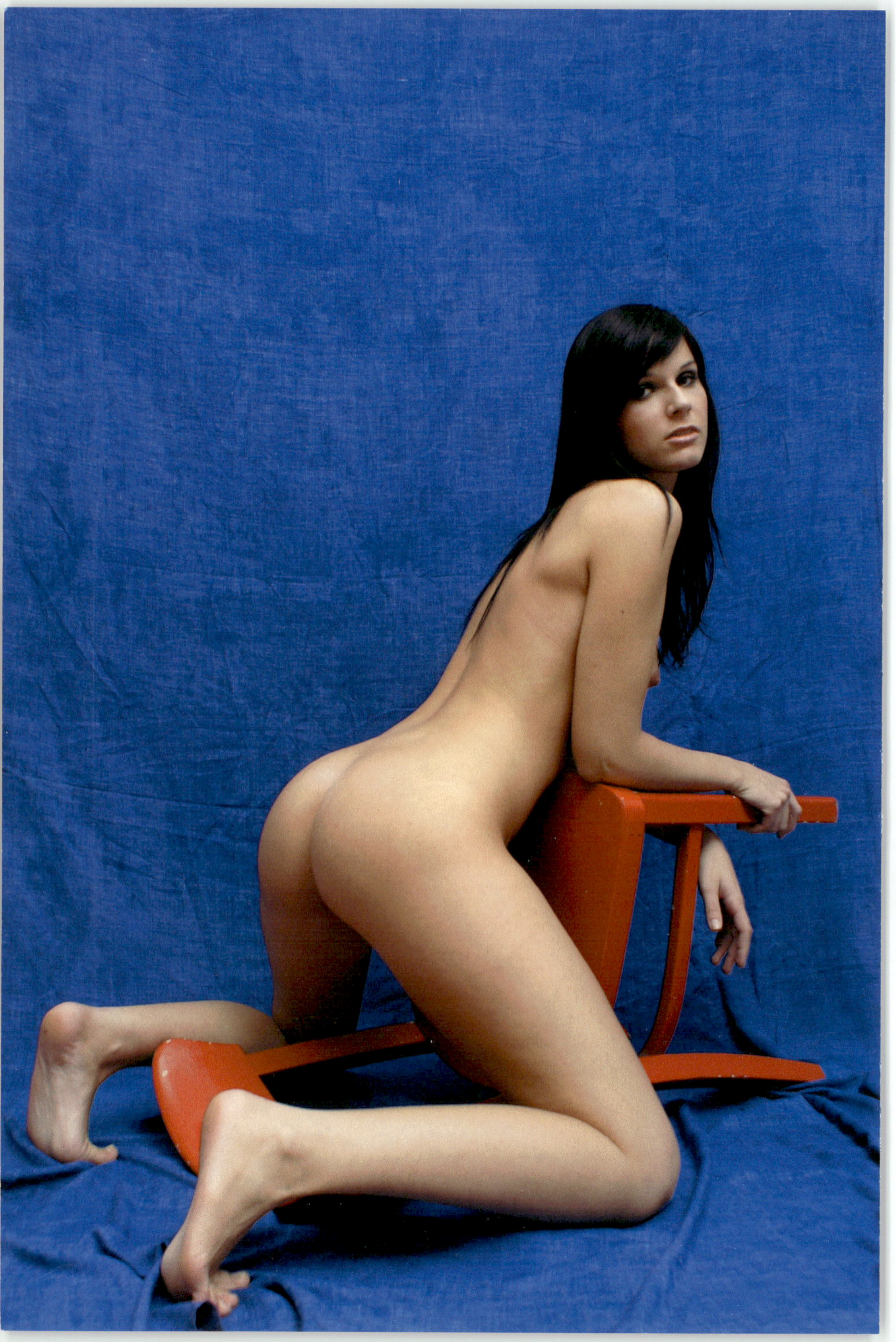

BORIS S. KURYLO

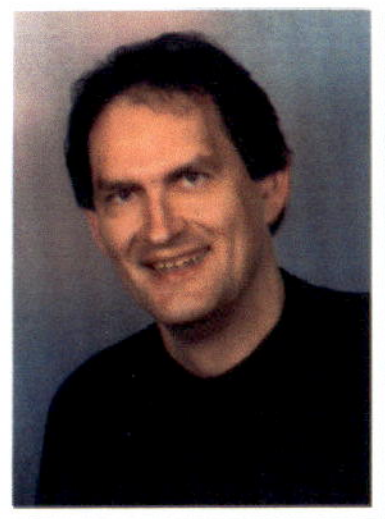

Boris S. Kurylo was born in 1960 in Hünfeld, West Germany. Even as a very young boy, "a photographer" is what he wanted to be. But first he took a course in computer studies for business. He then systematically developed his love of photography, specializing in portraiture and nudes. In the mid-1990s he learned about digital image processing and was able to combine his knowledge of computers with his skill as a photographer. His work has been shown in several exhibitions and published in a number of successful books.

www.kurylo.de

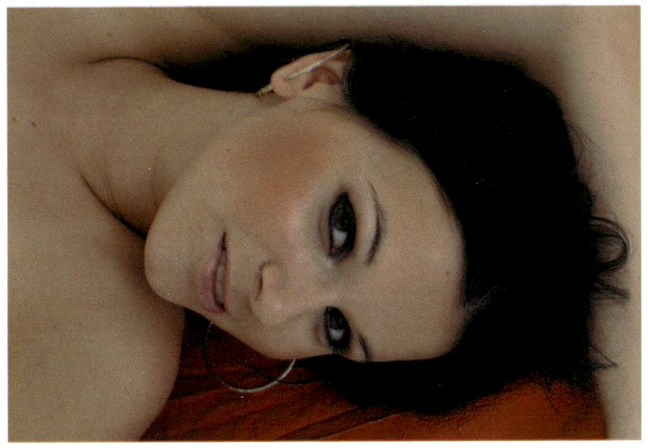

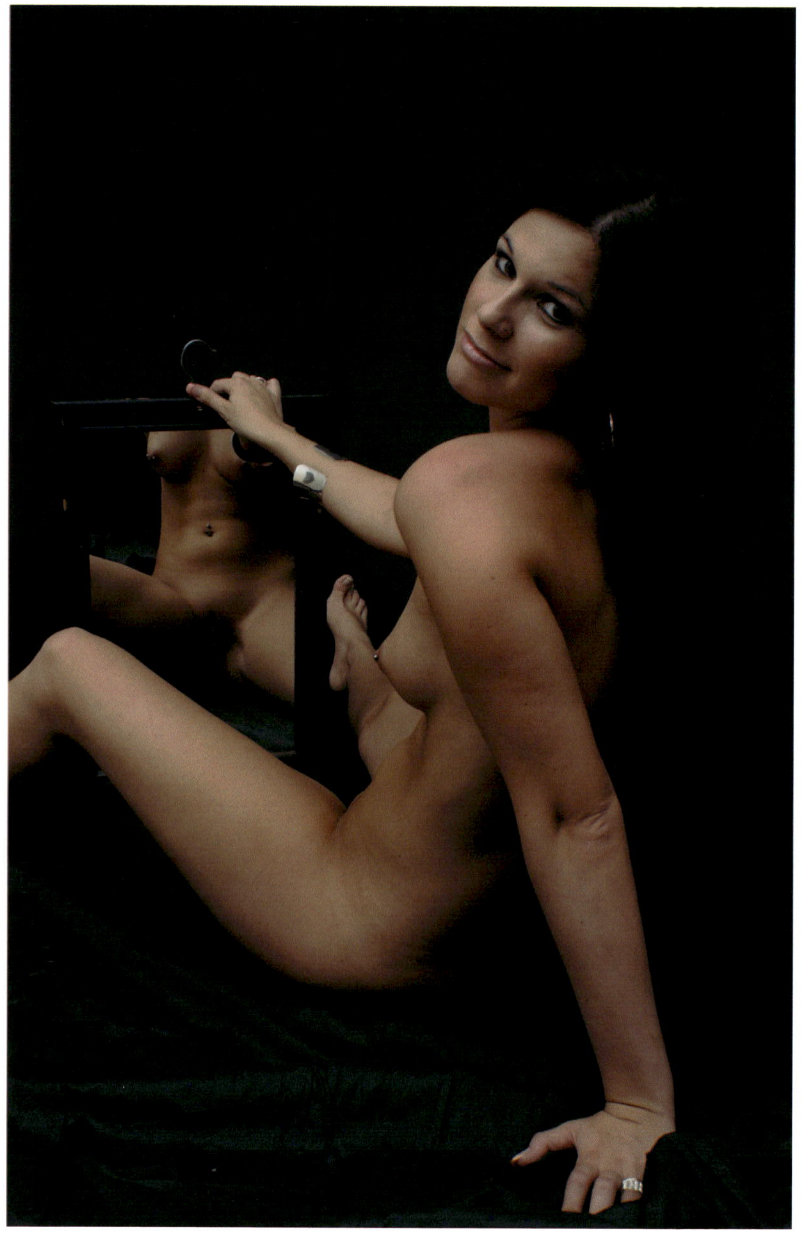

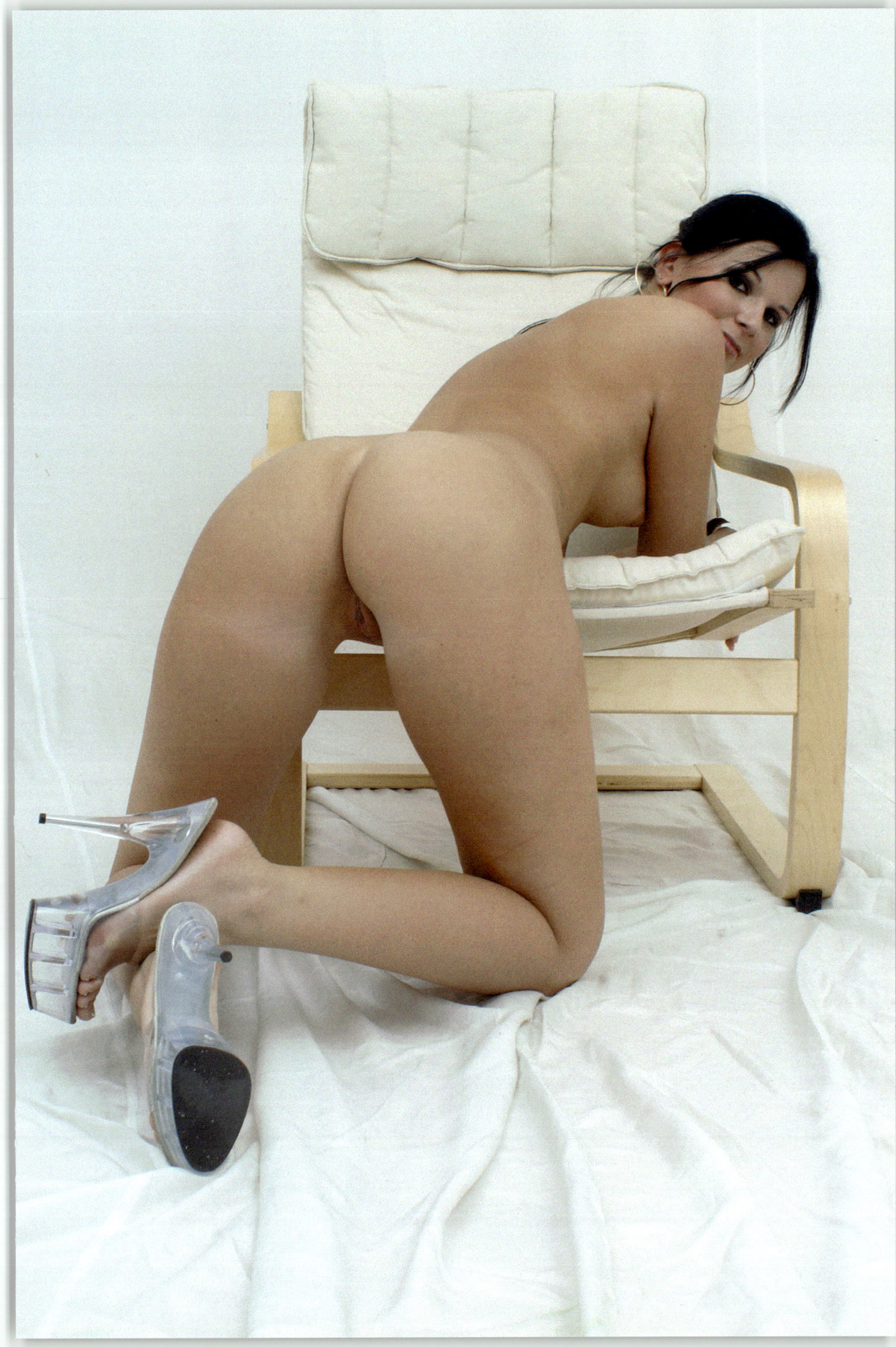

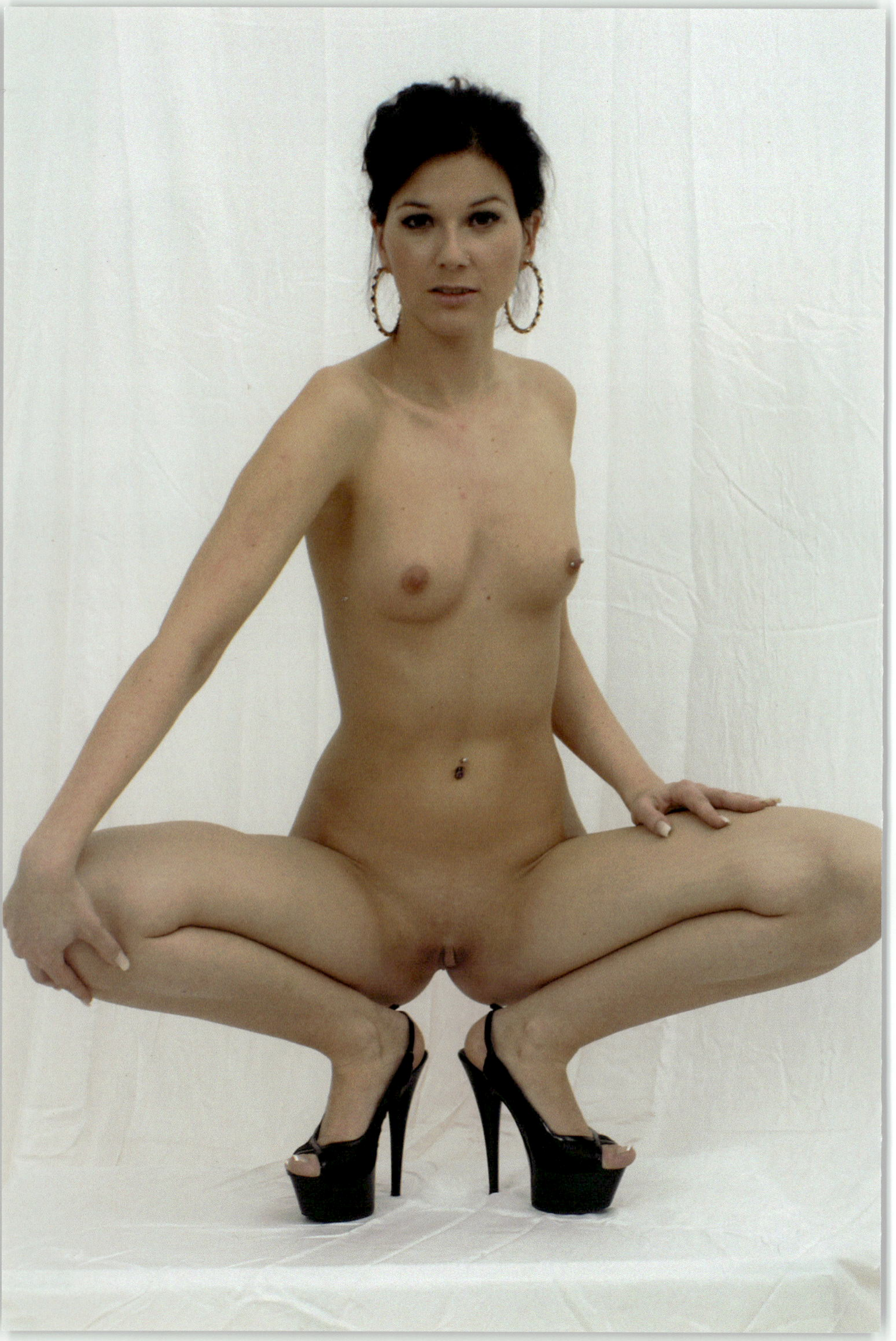

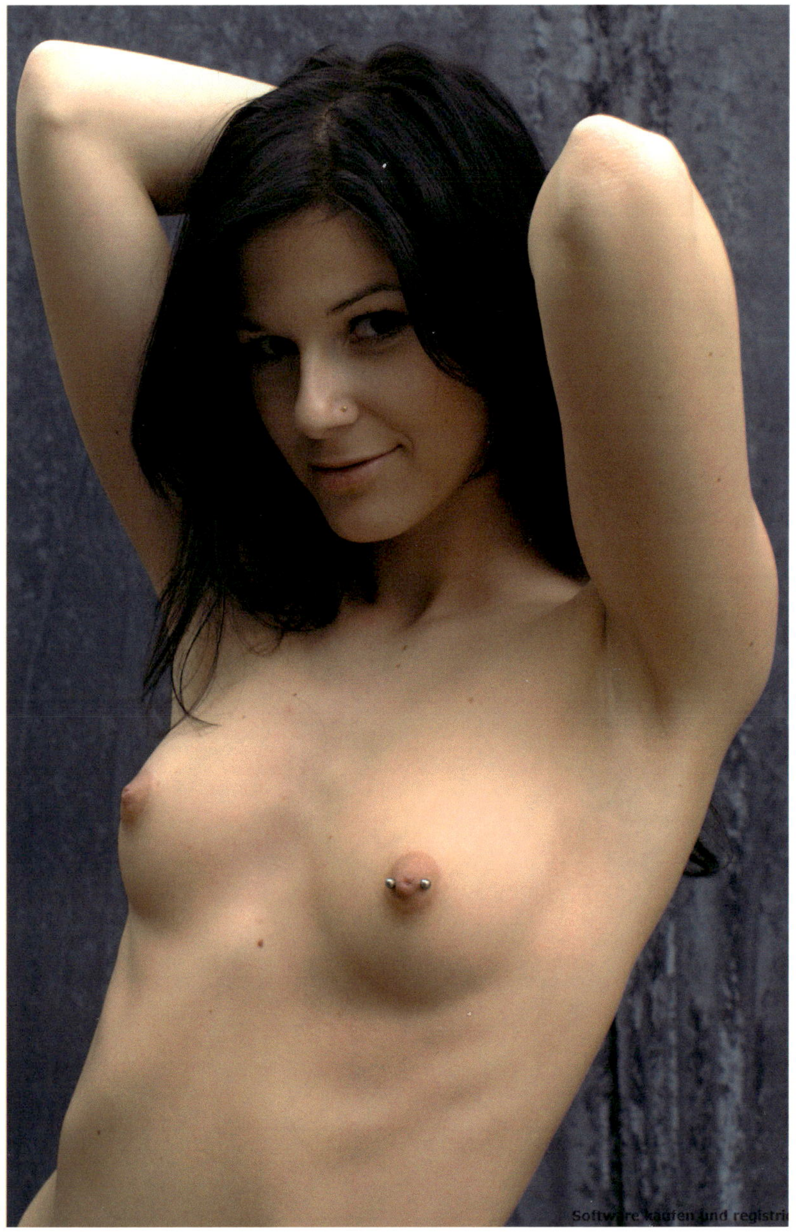

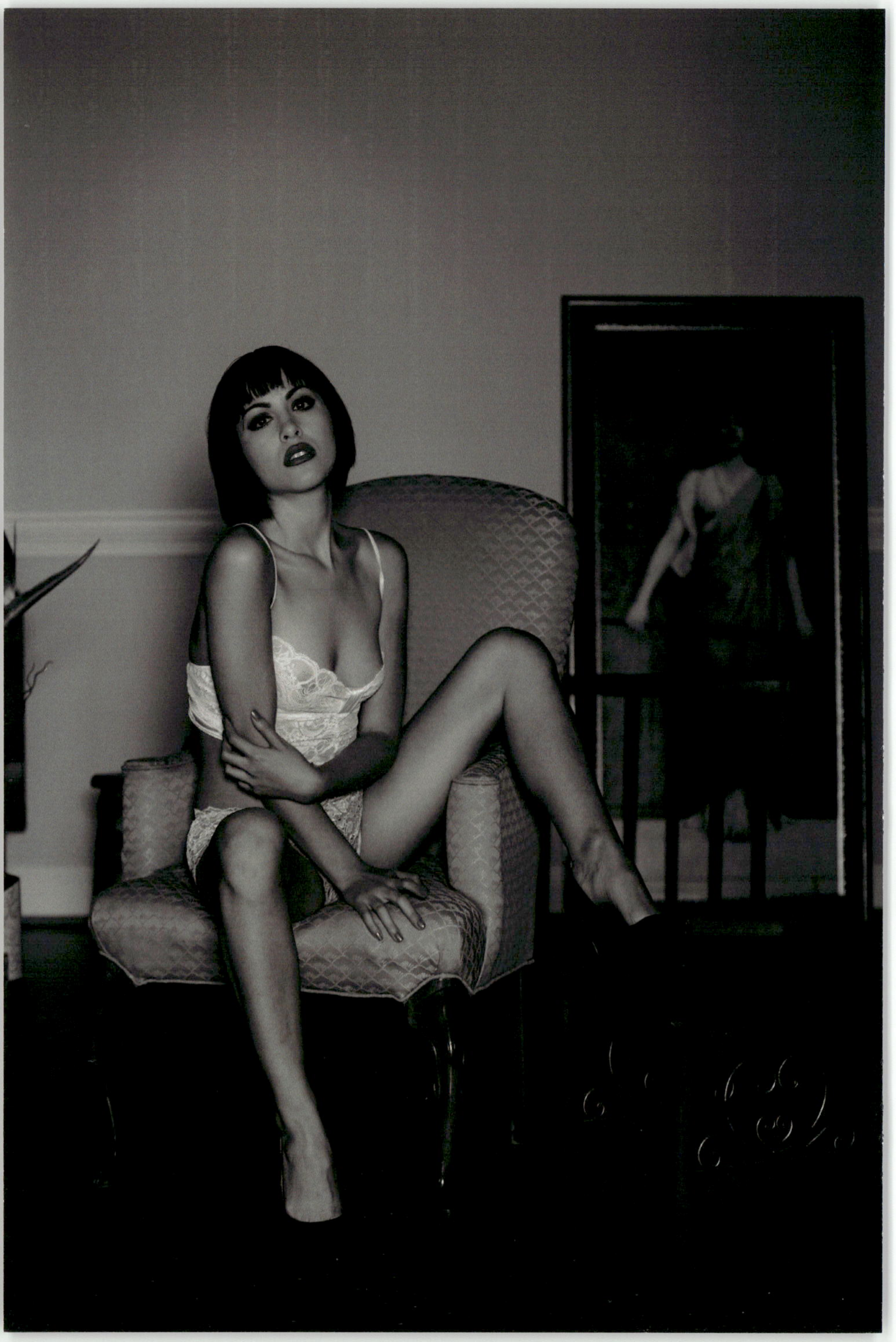

MIKE LAWSON

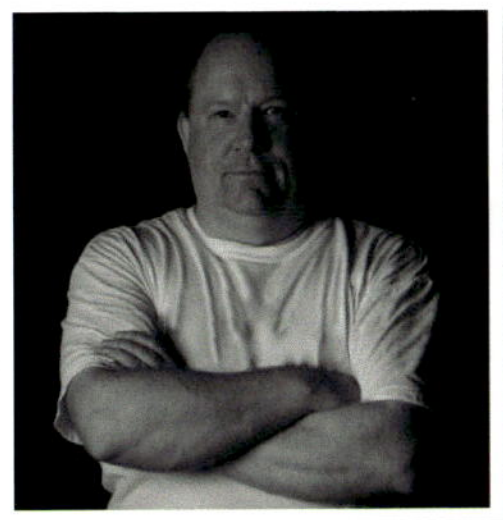

American photographer Mike Lawson lives in the Washington, DC, area and pursues his photography as more of a creative outlet than a profession. He describes his photographic style as "technically unsound" and believes that every shoot is an opportunity to experiment in some way. While he dabbles in the rare landscape or architectural photo, he is most at home with people.

Here Mike shares a small portion of his work with Lächeln, a model familiar from multiple projects. Together they have filled the pressing photographic void between polka-dot bikinis and futuristic space females with superpowers, and the alluring, seductive Irene Adler type.

www.lostforwordsphotography.com

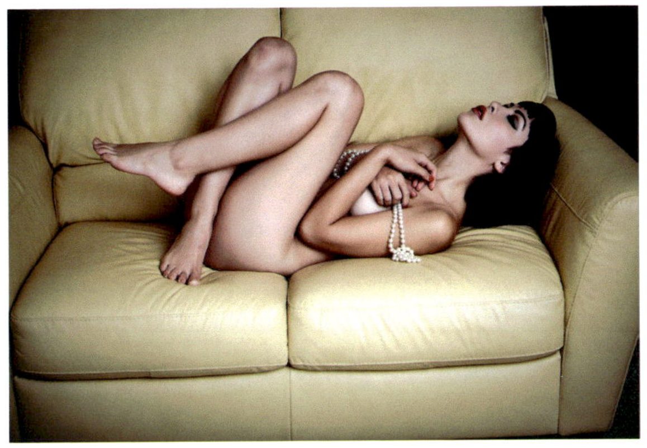

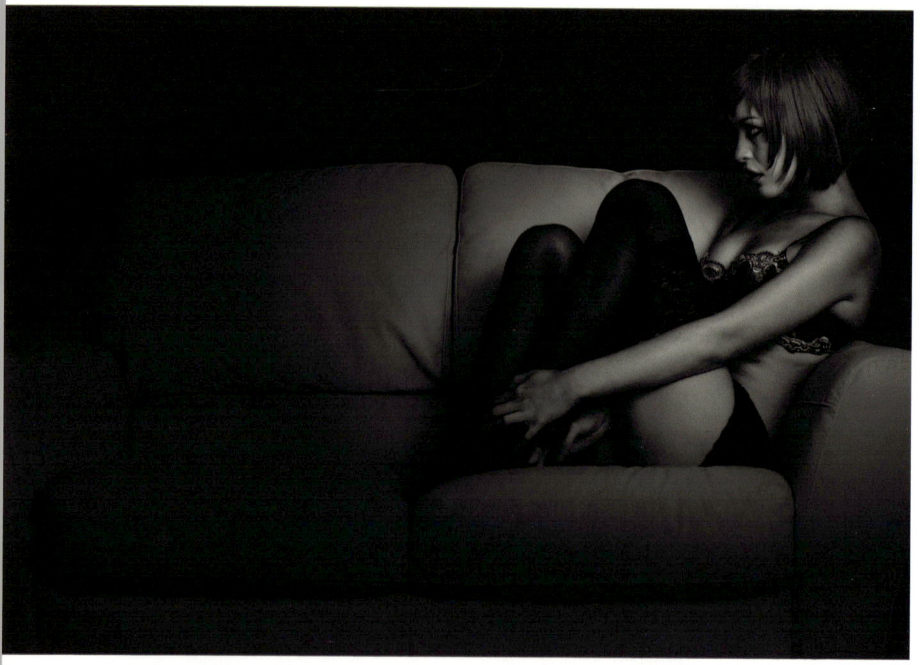

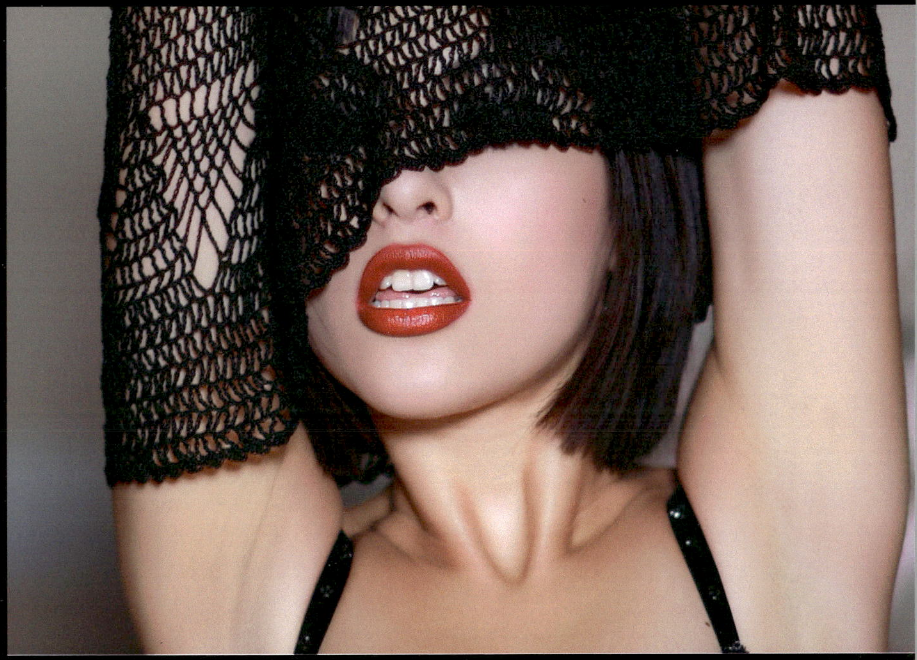

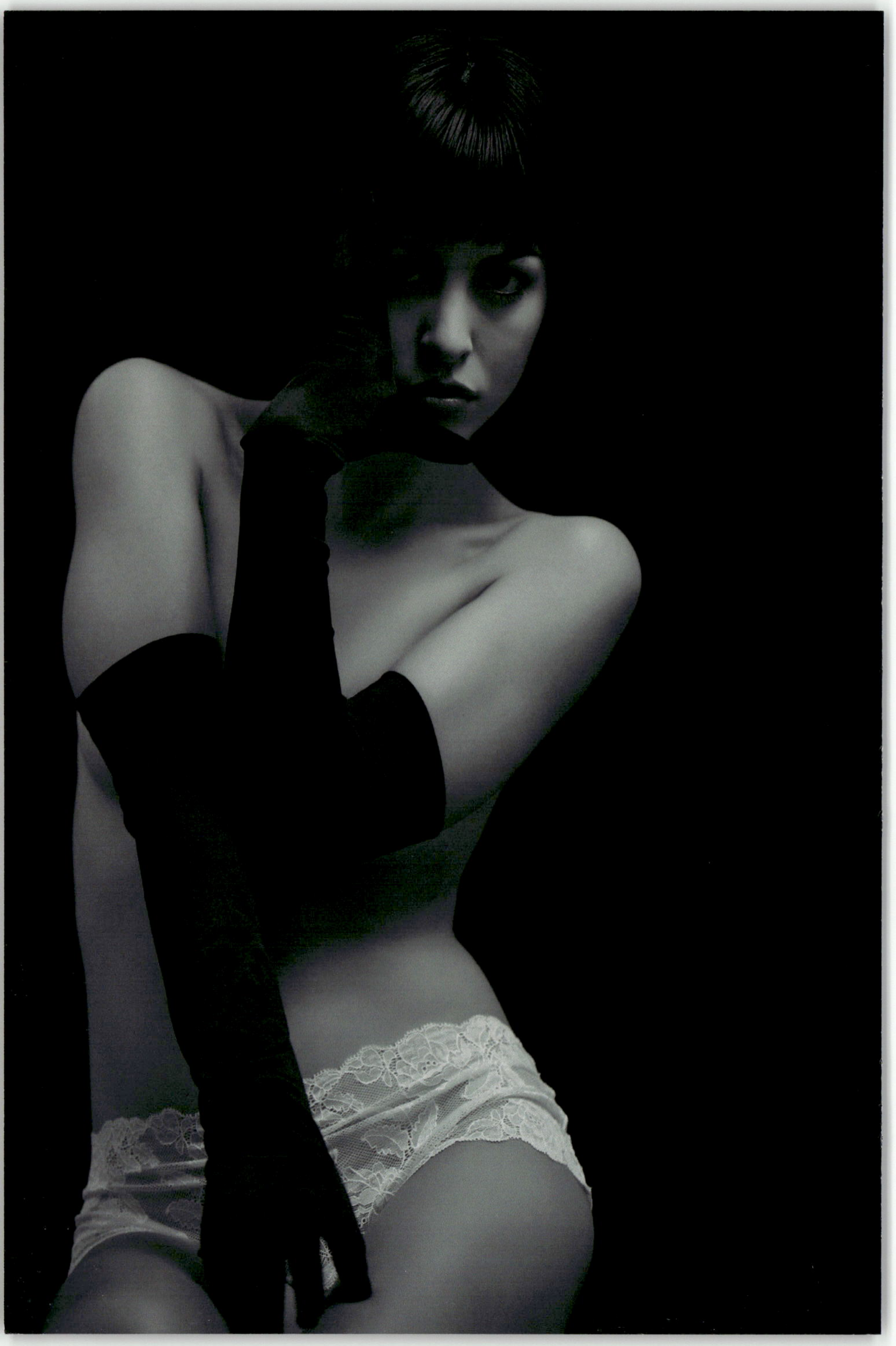

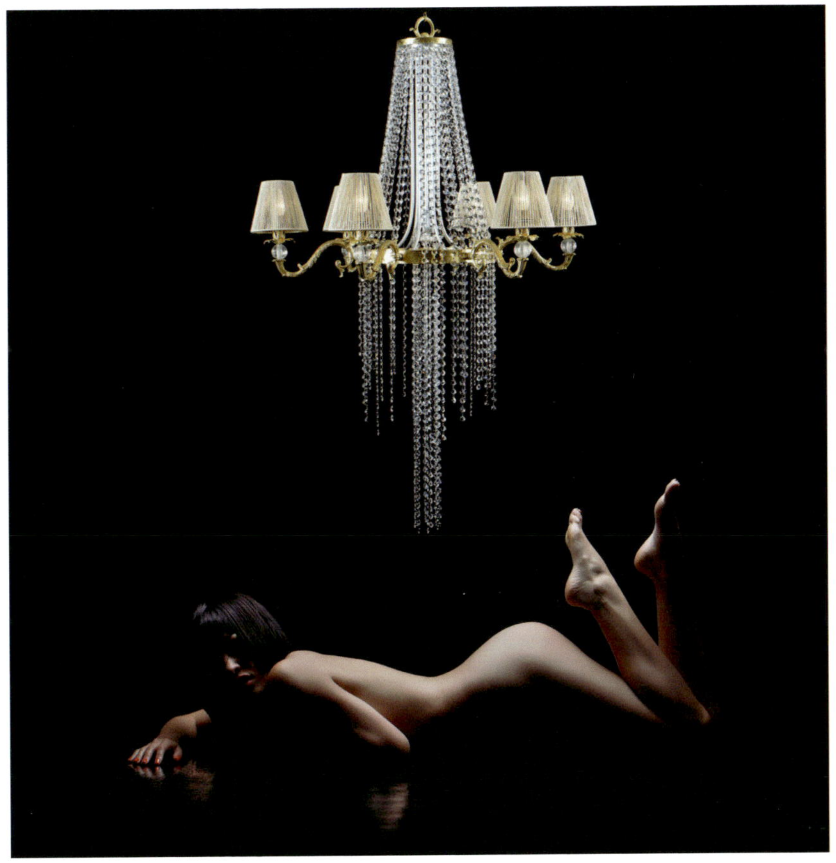

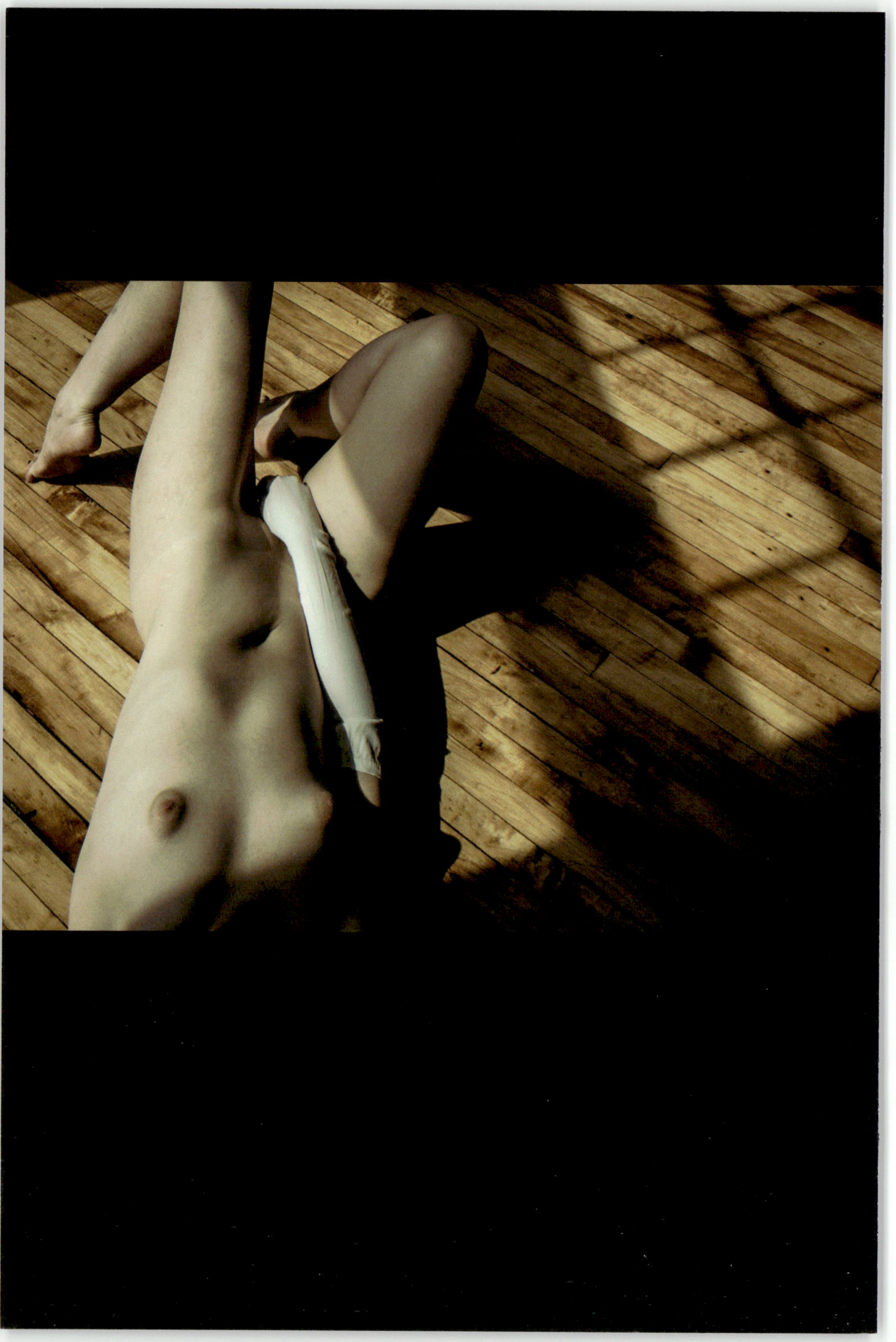

JOANNE LEAH

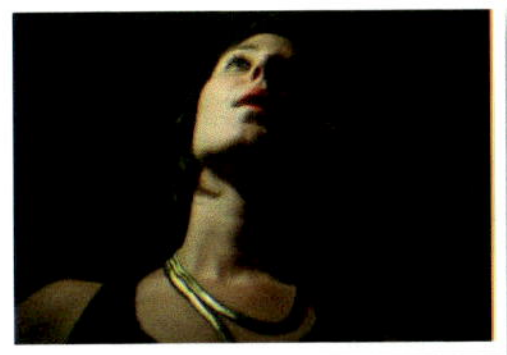

Joanne Leah is a photographer based in Brooklyn, New York. Adopted at birth in Germany in 1978, she moved with her family to the mountains of Virginia when she was four years old. Seduction, design and anticipation influence her the most.

"In this series I experience a personal rite of passage, across my own body, detaching myself from the past. There is no choice, as a primitive, strong and painfully brutal transformation is required to move forward. As much hurt as it brings, it is the only way I can survive. It is my required ritual. In this series I choose myself."

www.joanneleah.com

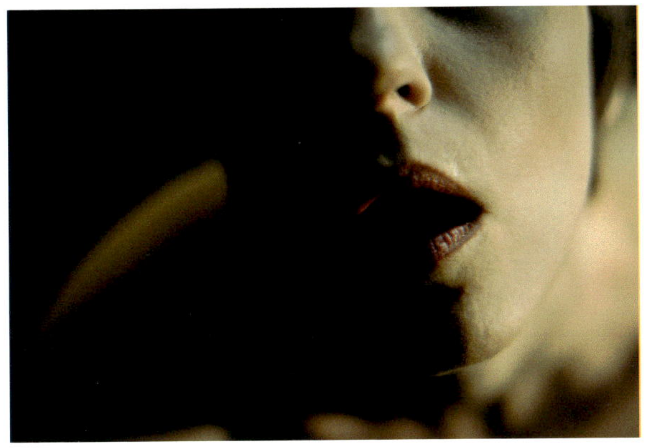

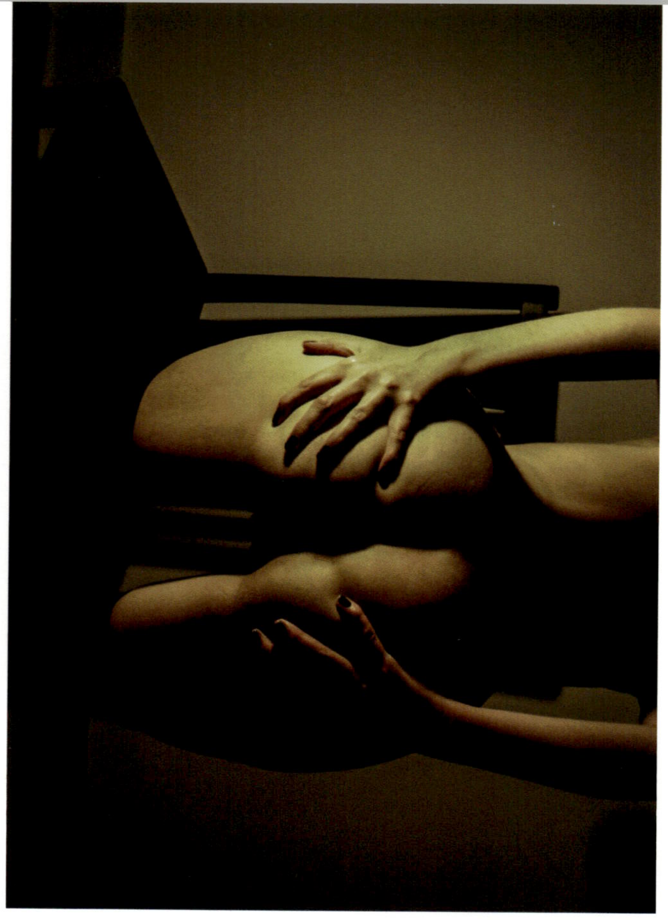

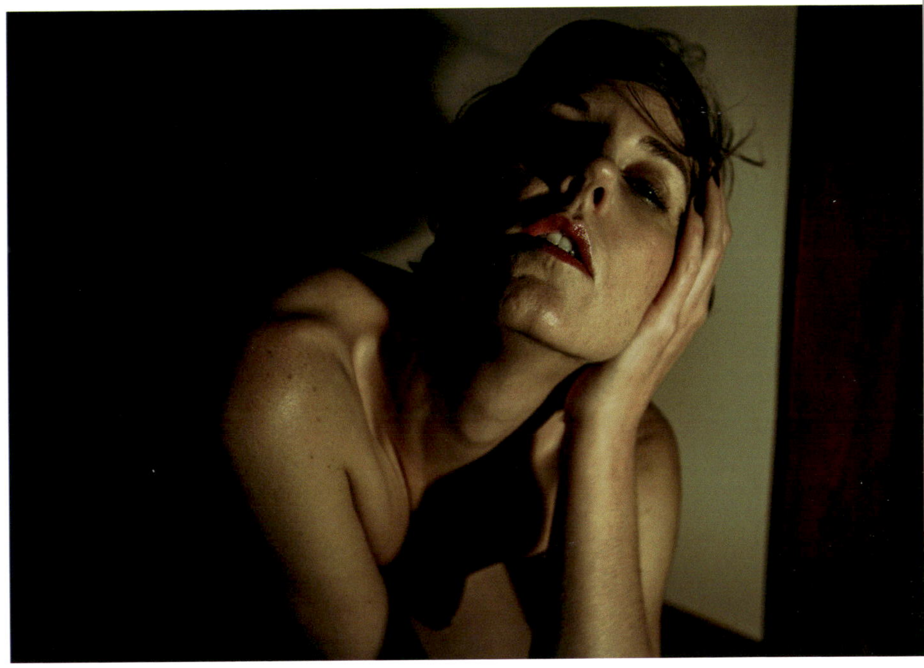

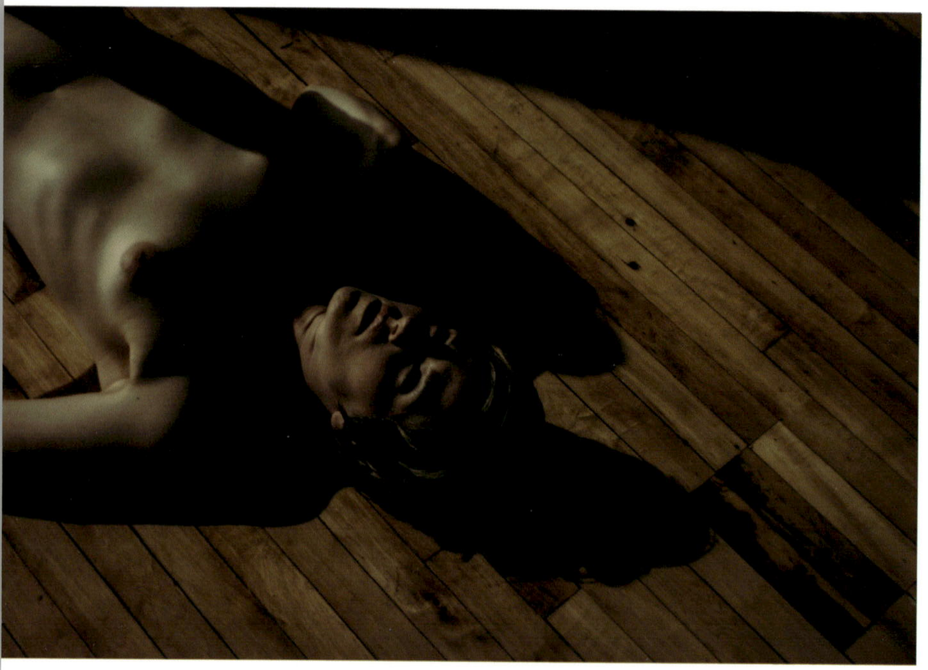

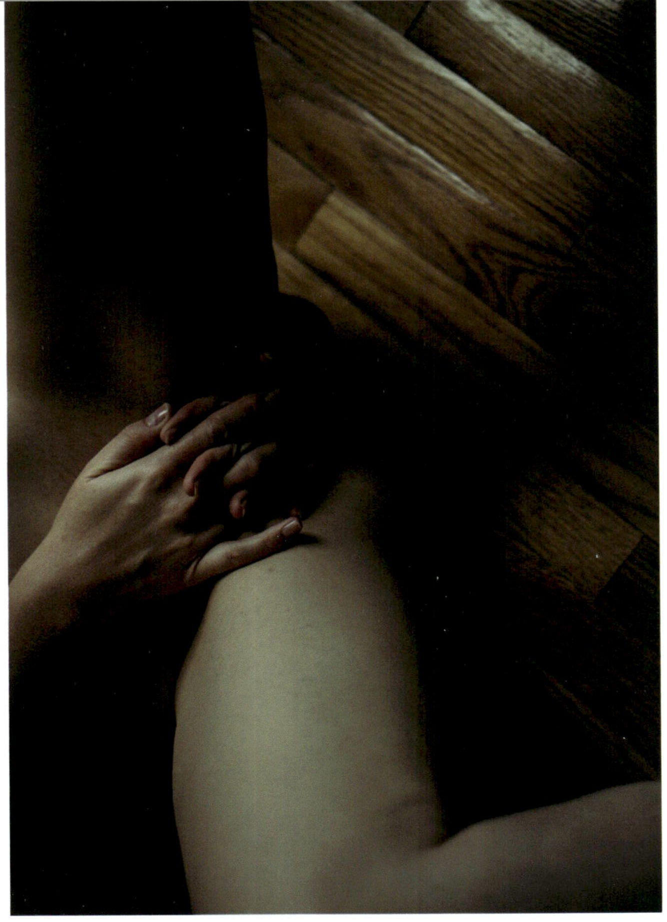

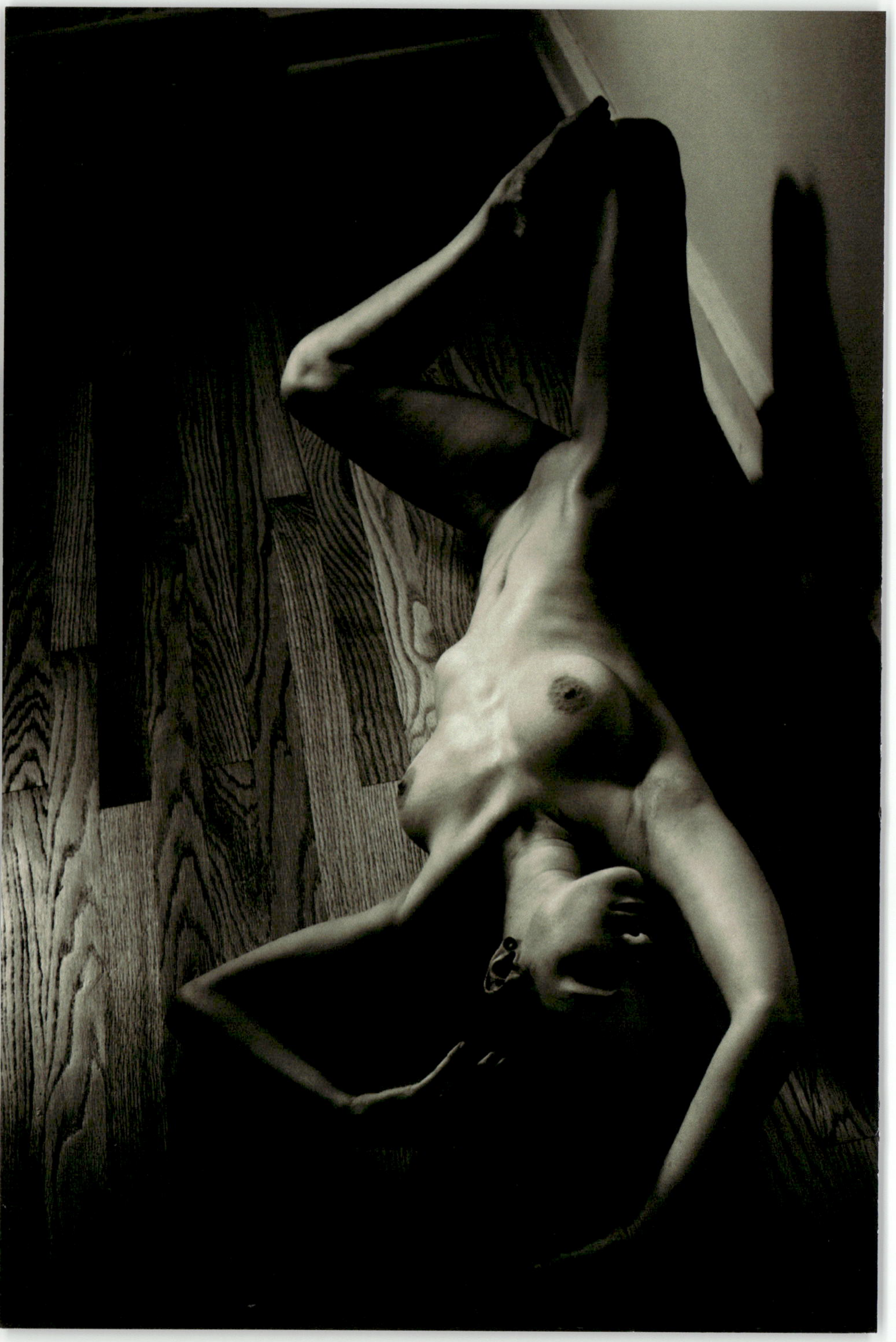

K. LEO

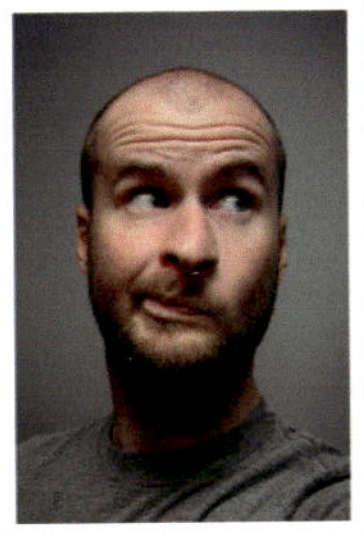

K. Leo states: " I believe in beauty. I trust Art. I seek implausible things. We live in a freakishly marvellous world. I am perpetually amazed at the places, faces and precarious situations that surround us all. Mirth and beauty throughout. Nothing is more impressive to me than people. It is my subject of choice. I believe that everyone has beauty.' Based in Chicago, K. Leo is a fine-art photographer whose work seeks to capture the beauty of his subjects. His photographs range from erotic artistic nudes to pensive emotive portraits.

"Keva is a pure muse and her every movement is art. Art with a sense of wonder and joy. That's Keva."

www.mirthandbeauty.com

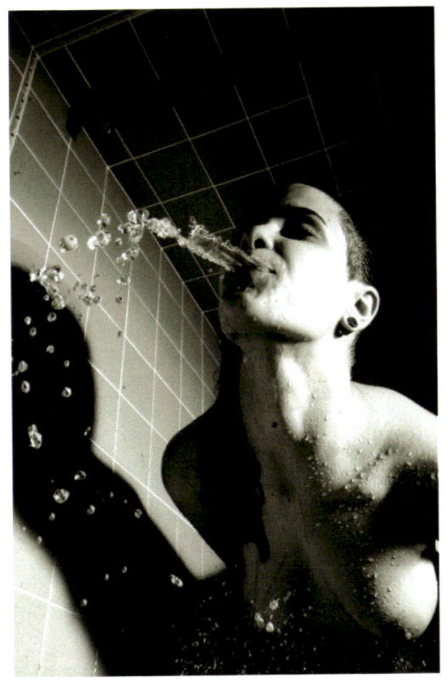

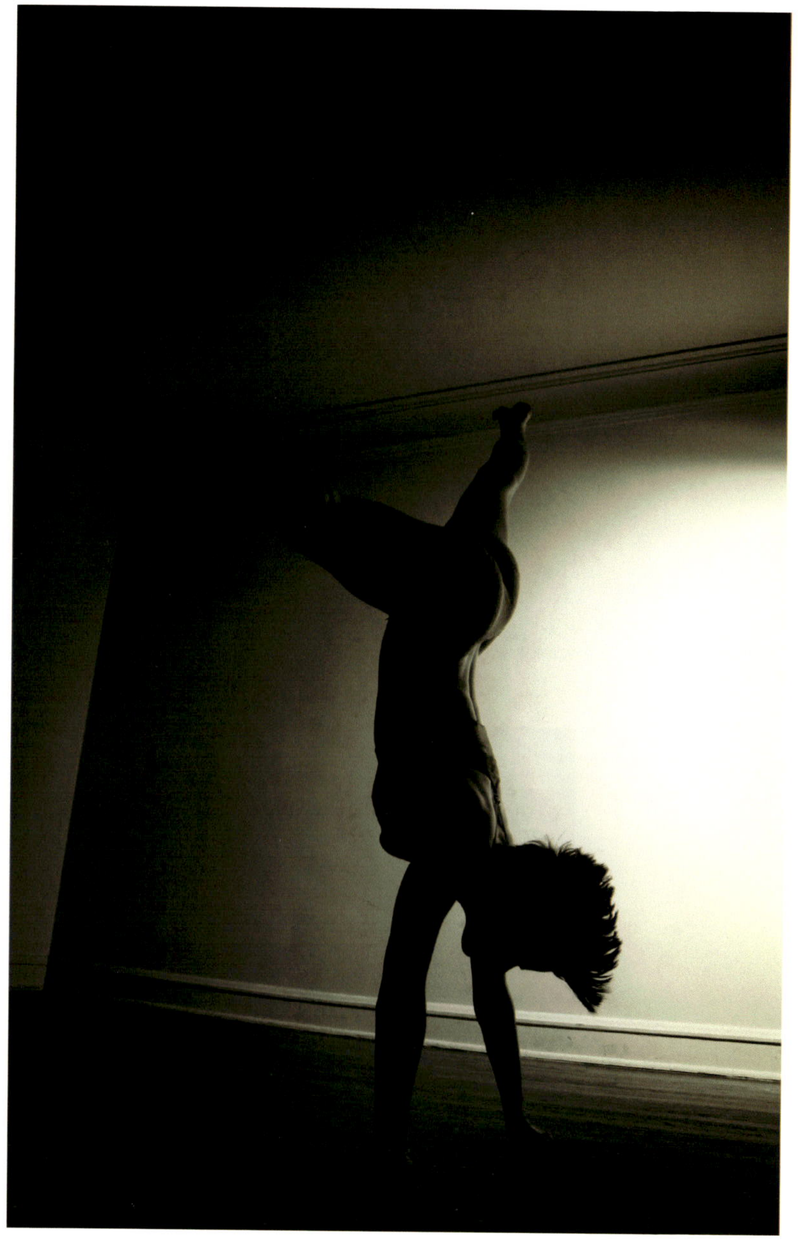

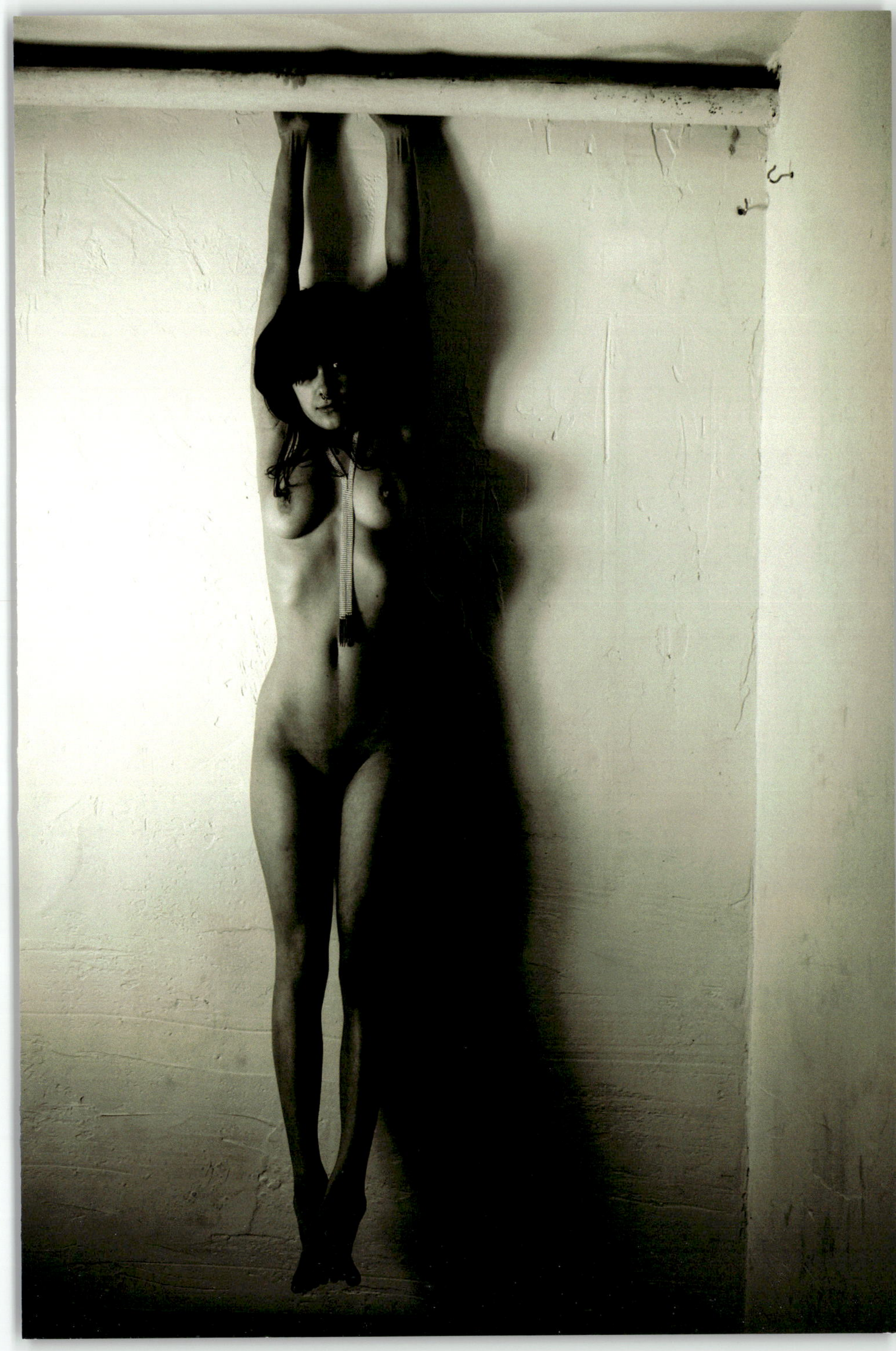

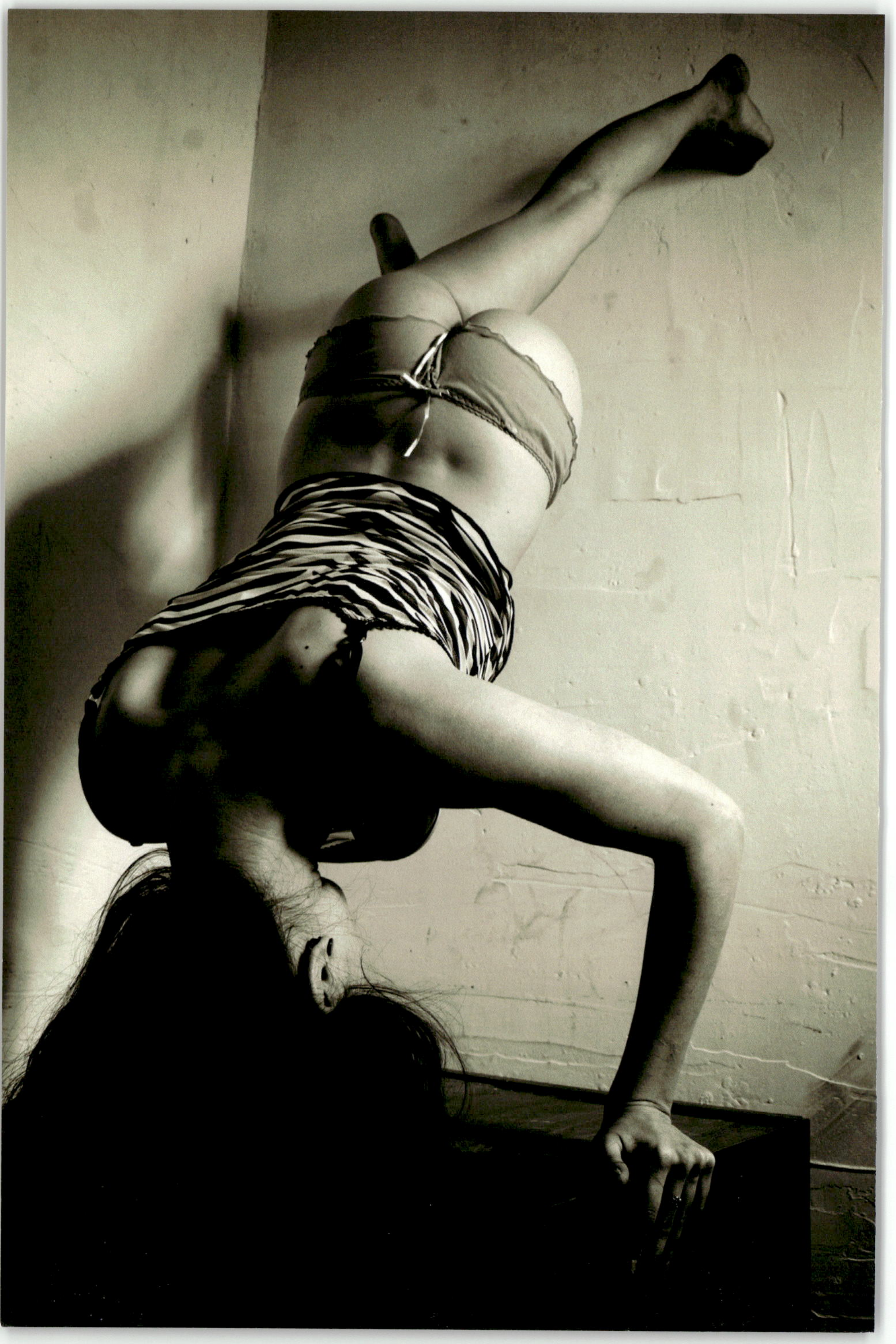

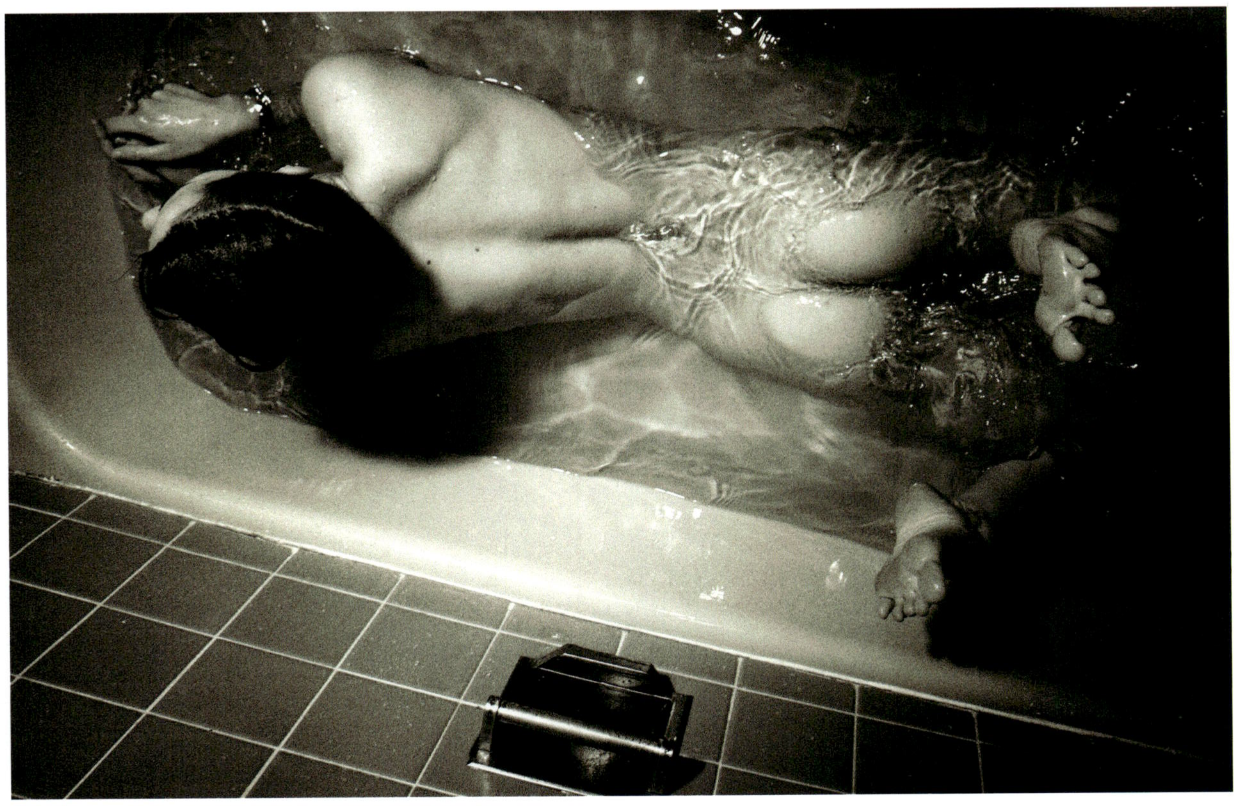

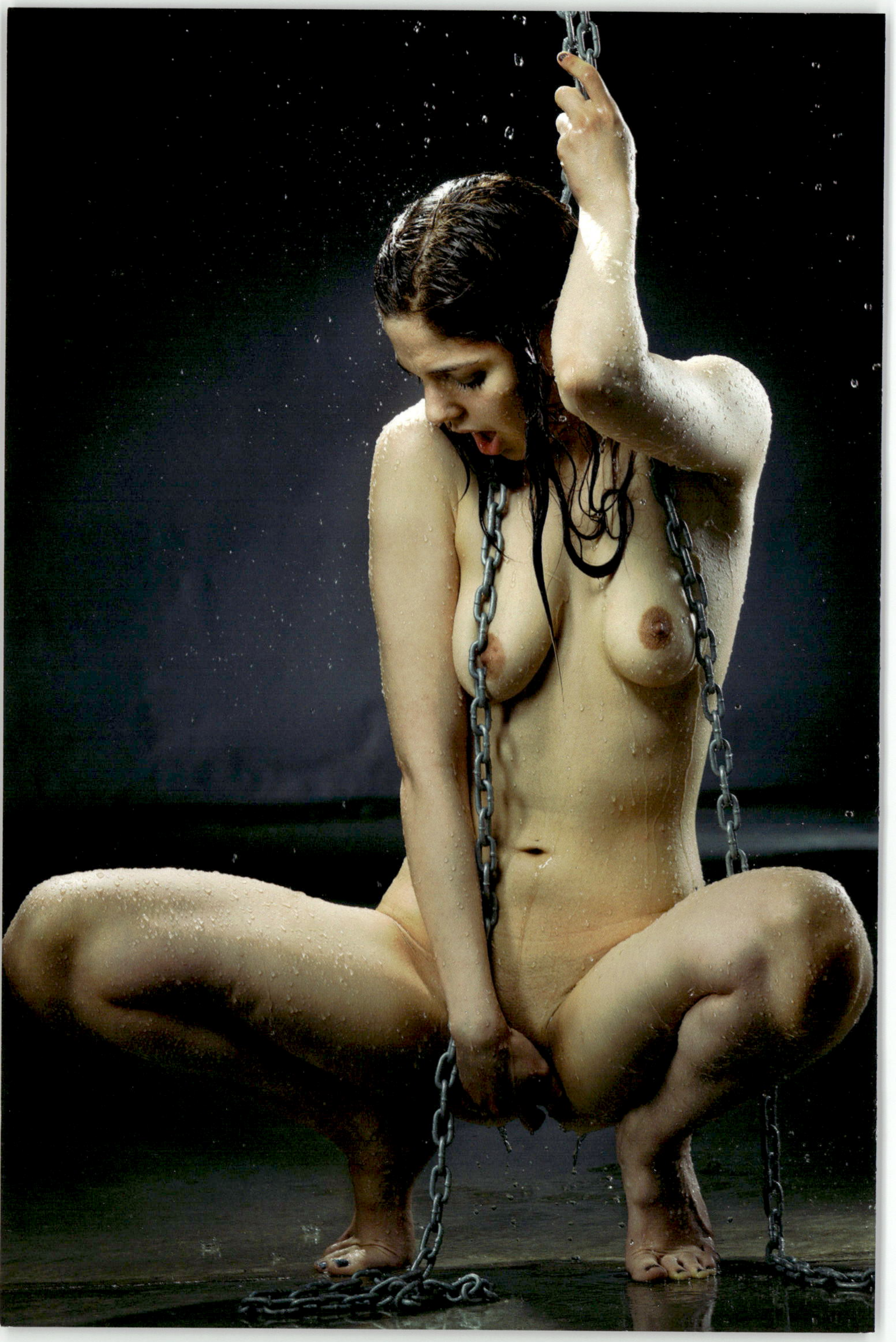

CHI LUM

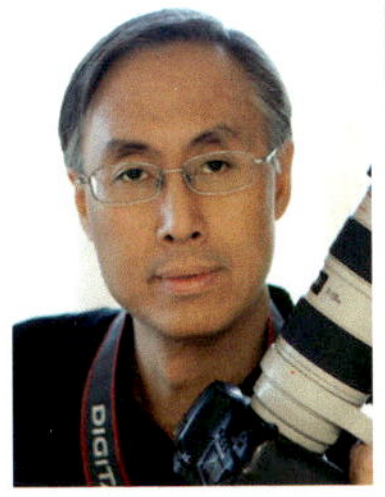

Chi Lum's work has been shown in numerous exhibitions and galleries, including SEAF, "On the Edge" and "The Dirty Show". Most of his photographs are taken in the San Francisco area, where he lives.

"Sensual and erotic photography fuels my creativity like no other genre. The models I work with provide a never-ending stream of stories for me to tell. Exploring everyone's fetishes has been an exciting adventure that has changed me and my work.

"In choosing a model for this book I wanted to create an homage to my favourite models, so I needed to take new photos. I chose Lily for her enthusiasm, commitment and flexibility, and she quickly became a muse. I'm excited to say the resulting images, with old friends and new, exceeded all my expectations."

www.rue99.com

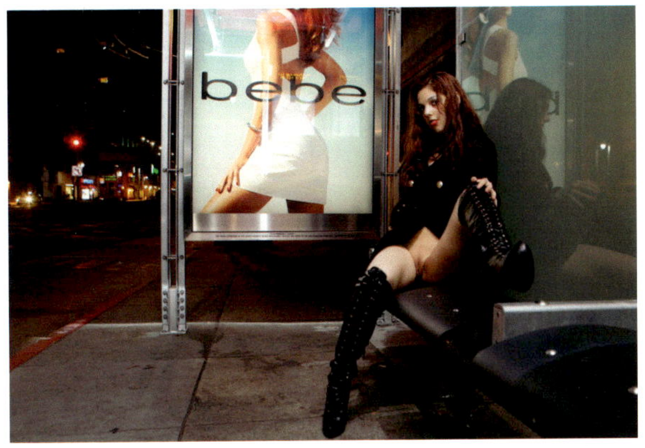

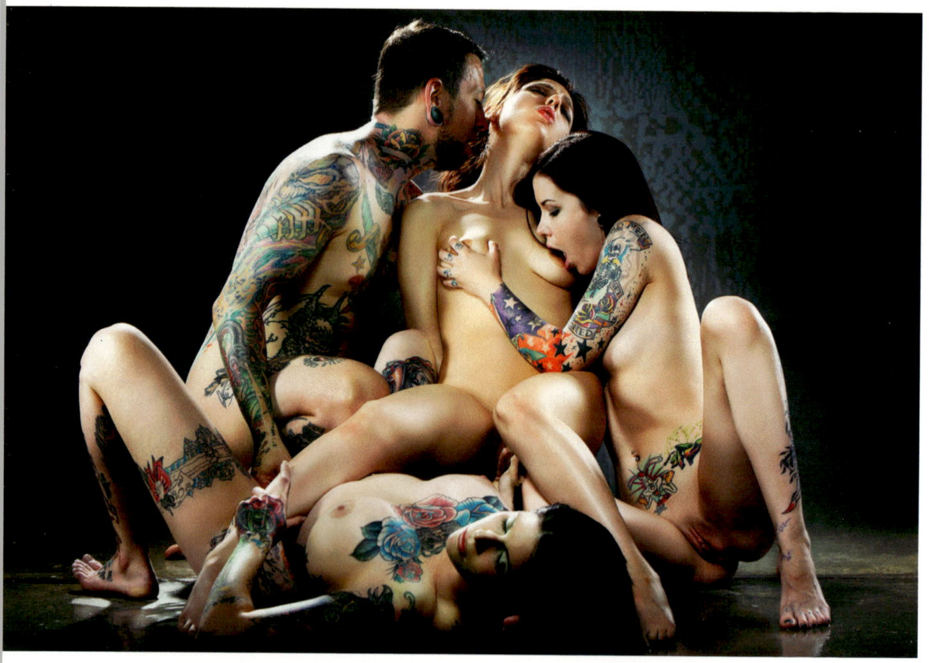

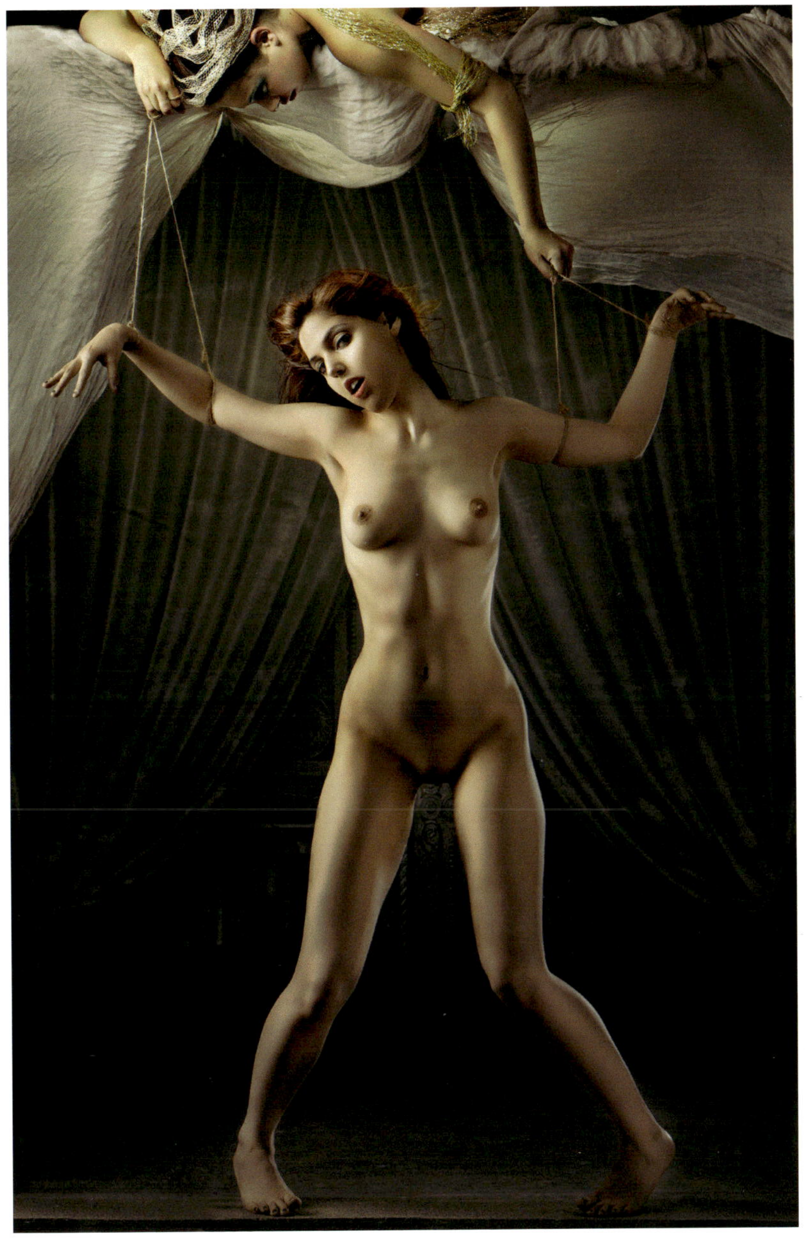

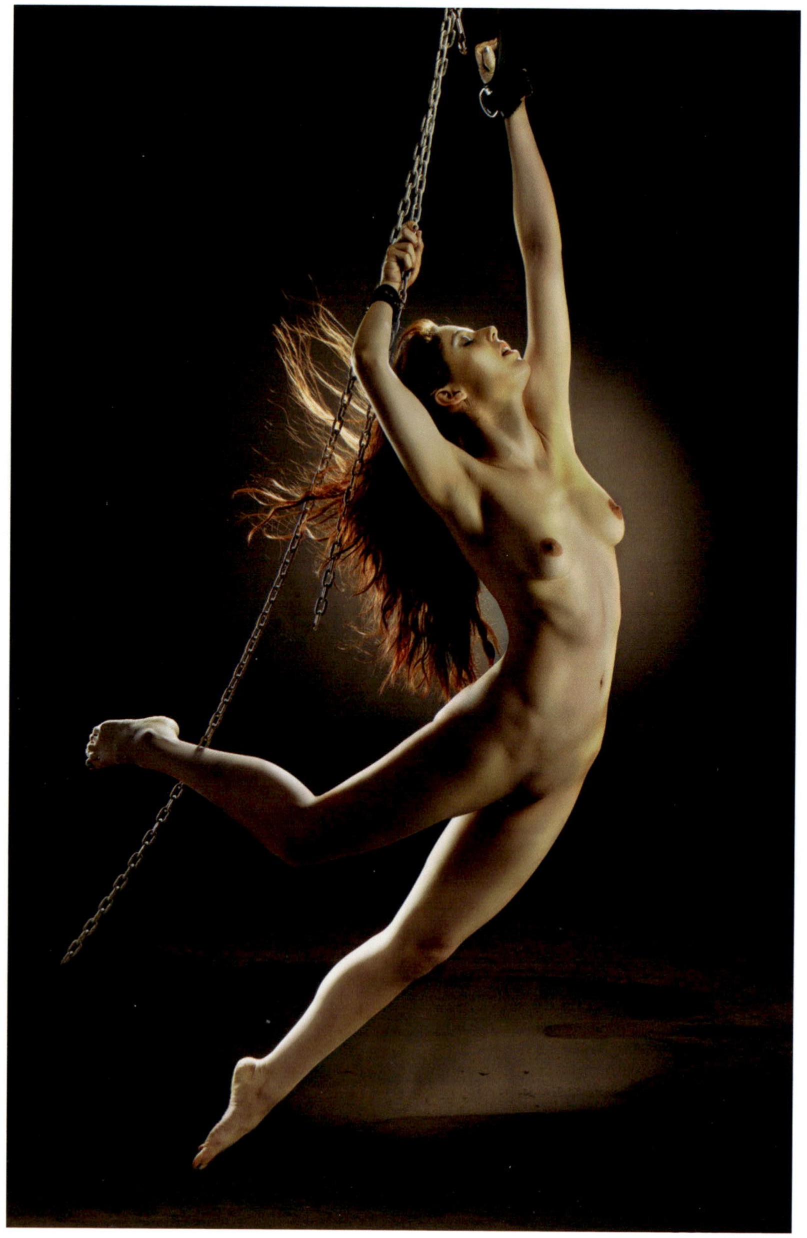

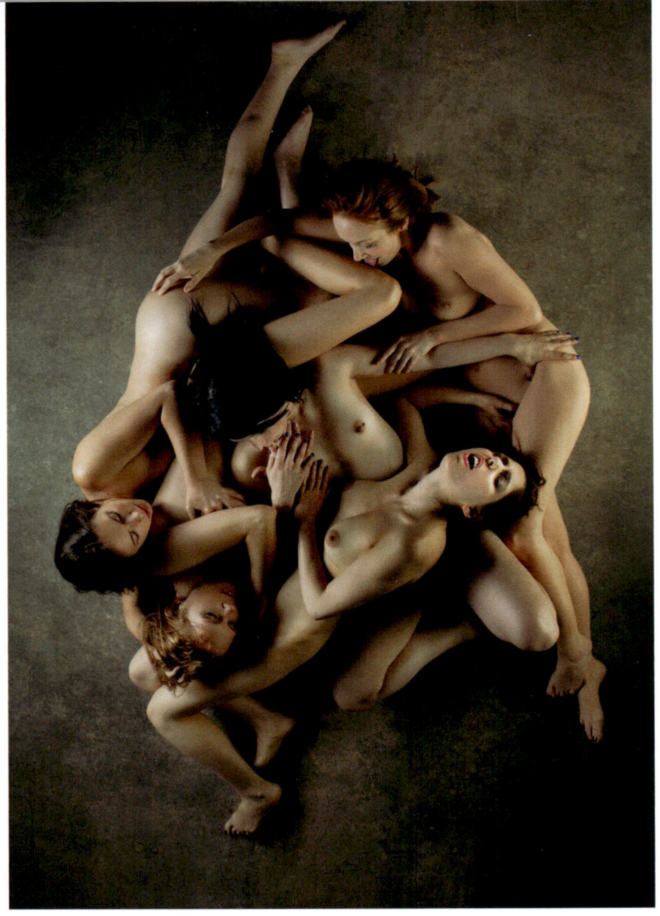

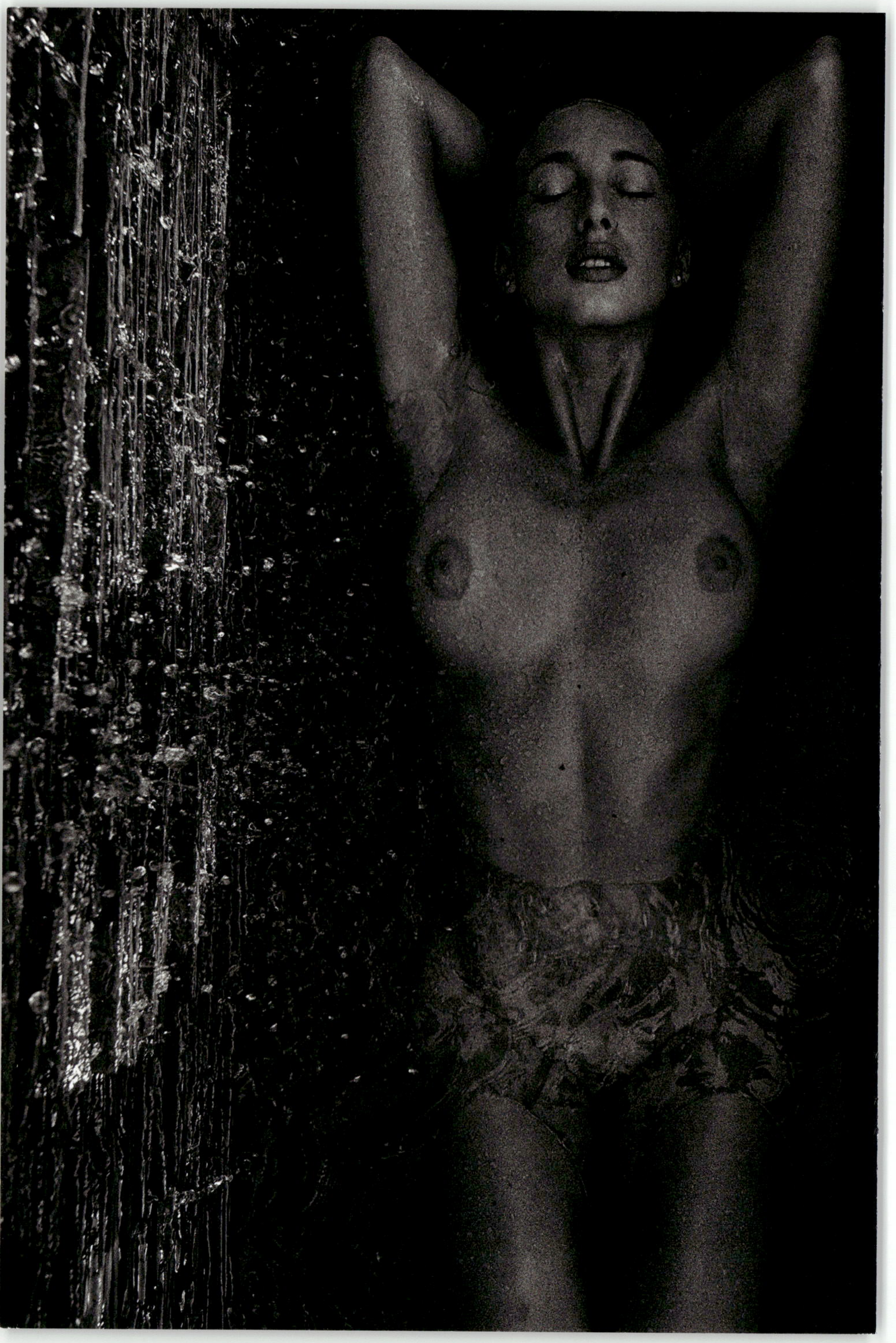

STEVEN LYON

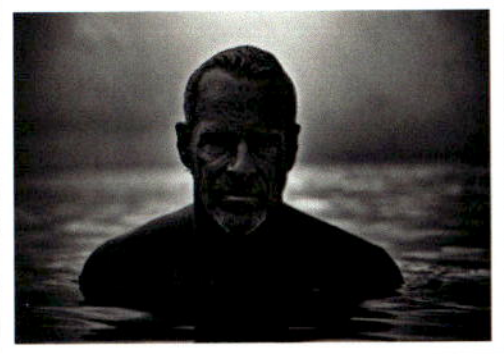

Steven Lyon was born in 1961 in Santa Barbara, California, and currently resides in New York and Paris. He started photography in 1998 in Los Angeles, but moved to Paris the following year, drawing inspiration from cinema and the creative French fashion world. His work has been exhibited all over Europe and he has contributed to magazines including *Vanity Fair*, *GQ* (Italy and Germany), *Vogue* (Russia), *ZOO*, *125*, *SOUP*, *S* and the sexy new *25* and *treats!*. An advocate of traditional photography, Steven prefers film-stock and cinematic realism to modern, digitally enhanced imagery.

"I was immediately attracted to Alana's style and beauty. Her spirit and desire to create artistic imagery, coupled with her confidence in her body and trust in me, make her a real pleasure to work with."

www.stevenlyonstudios.com

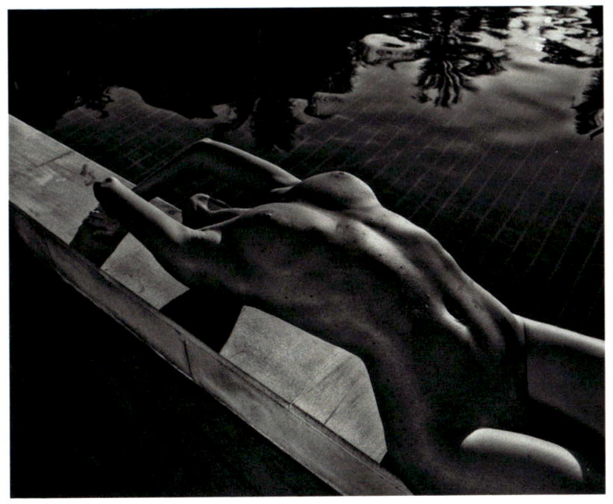

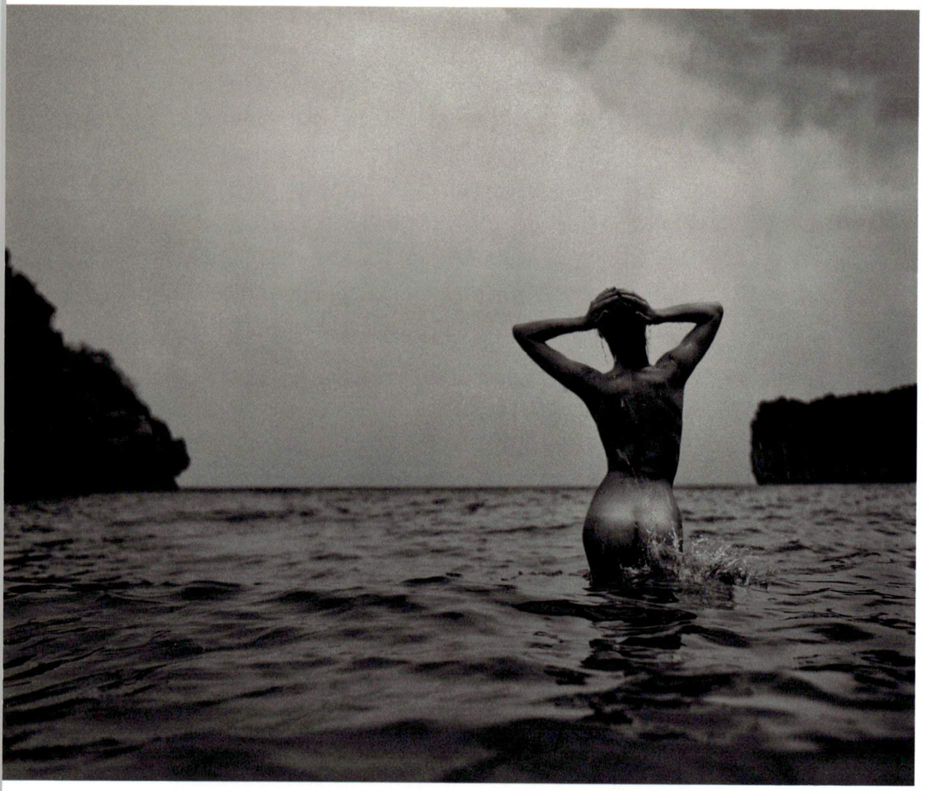

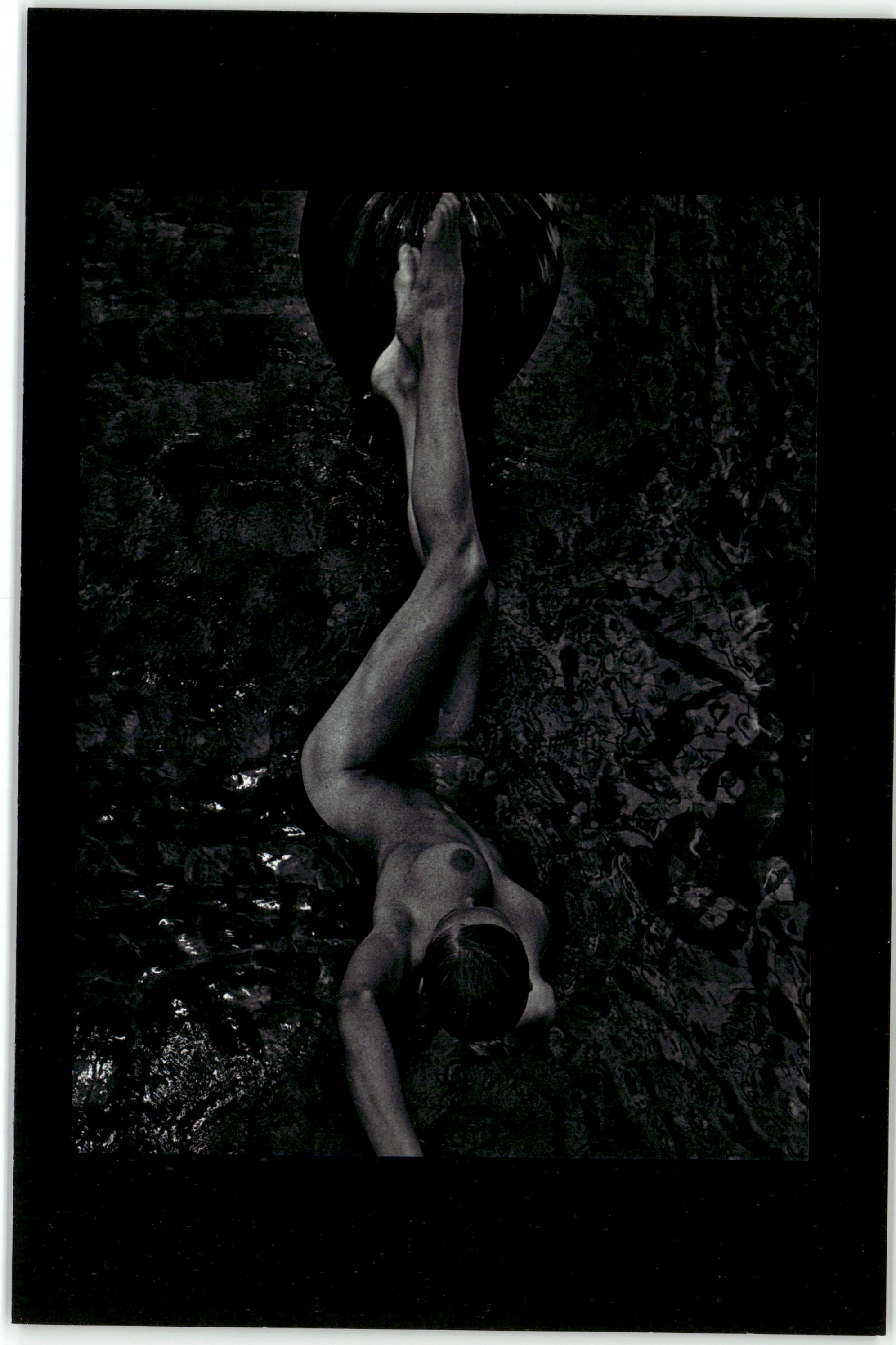

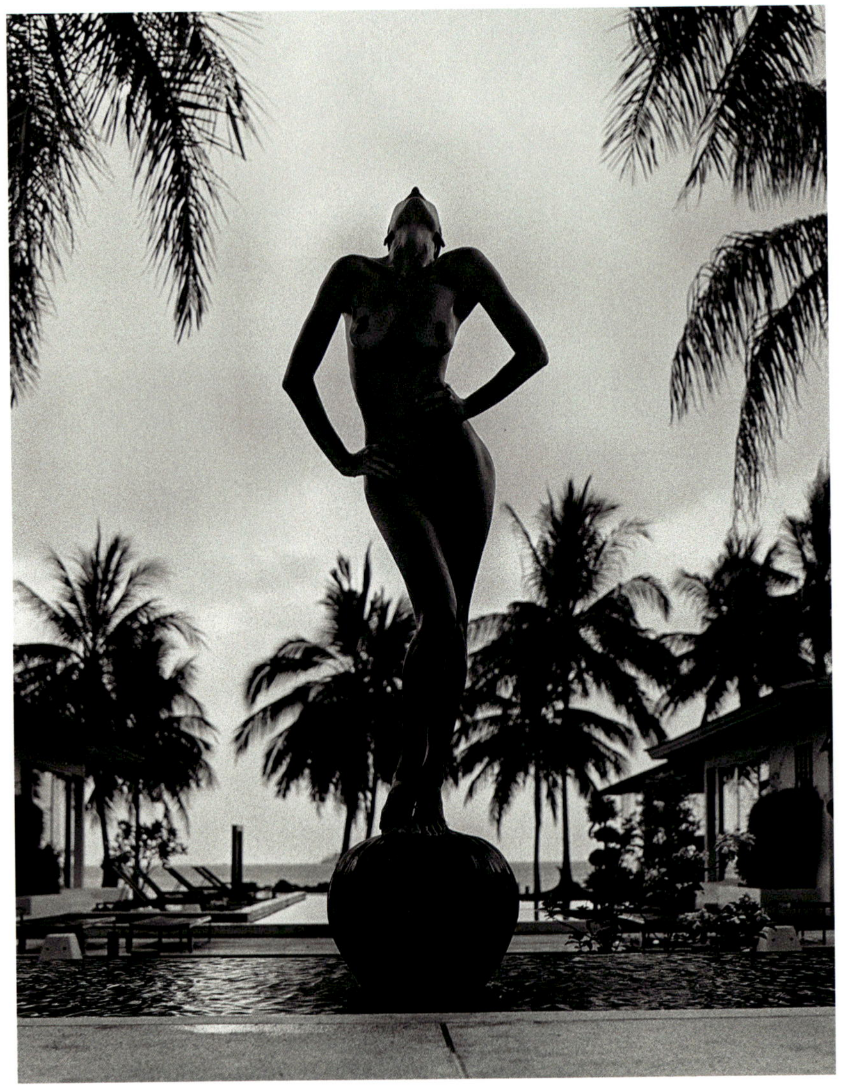

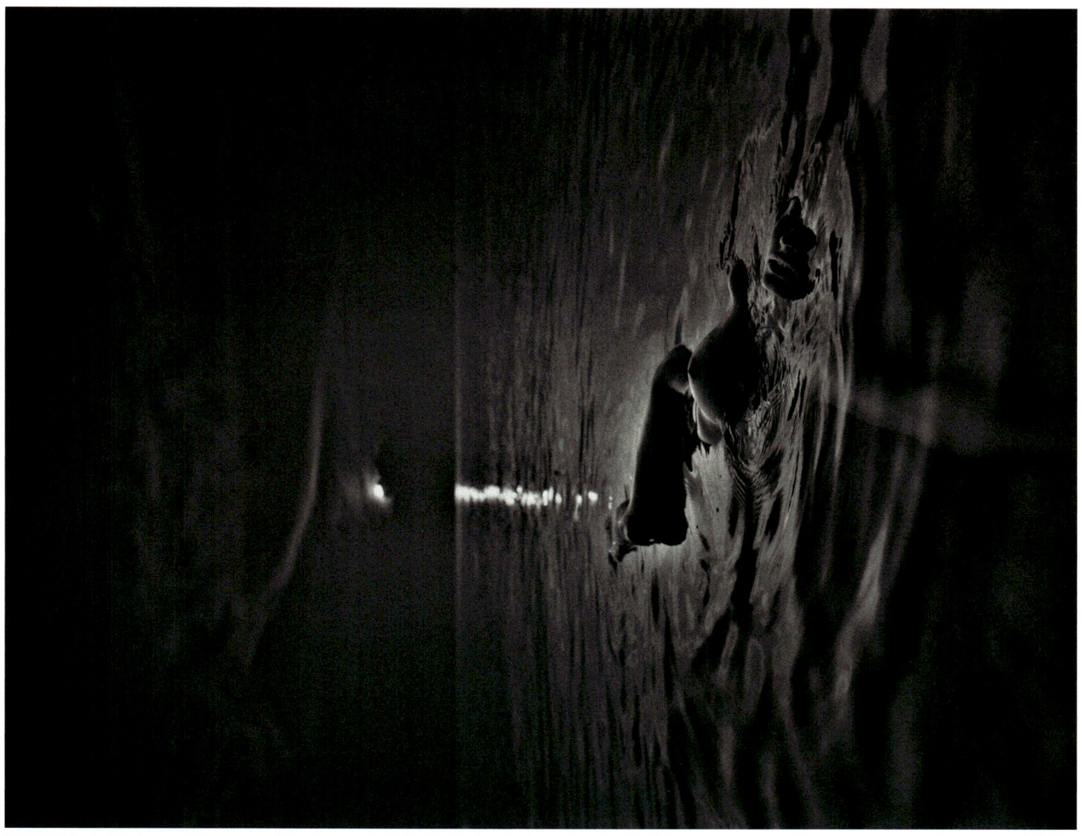

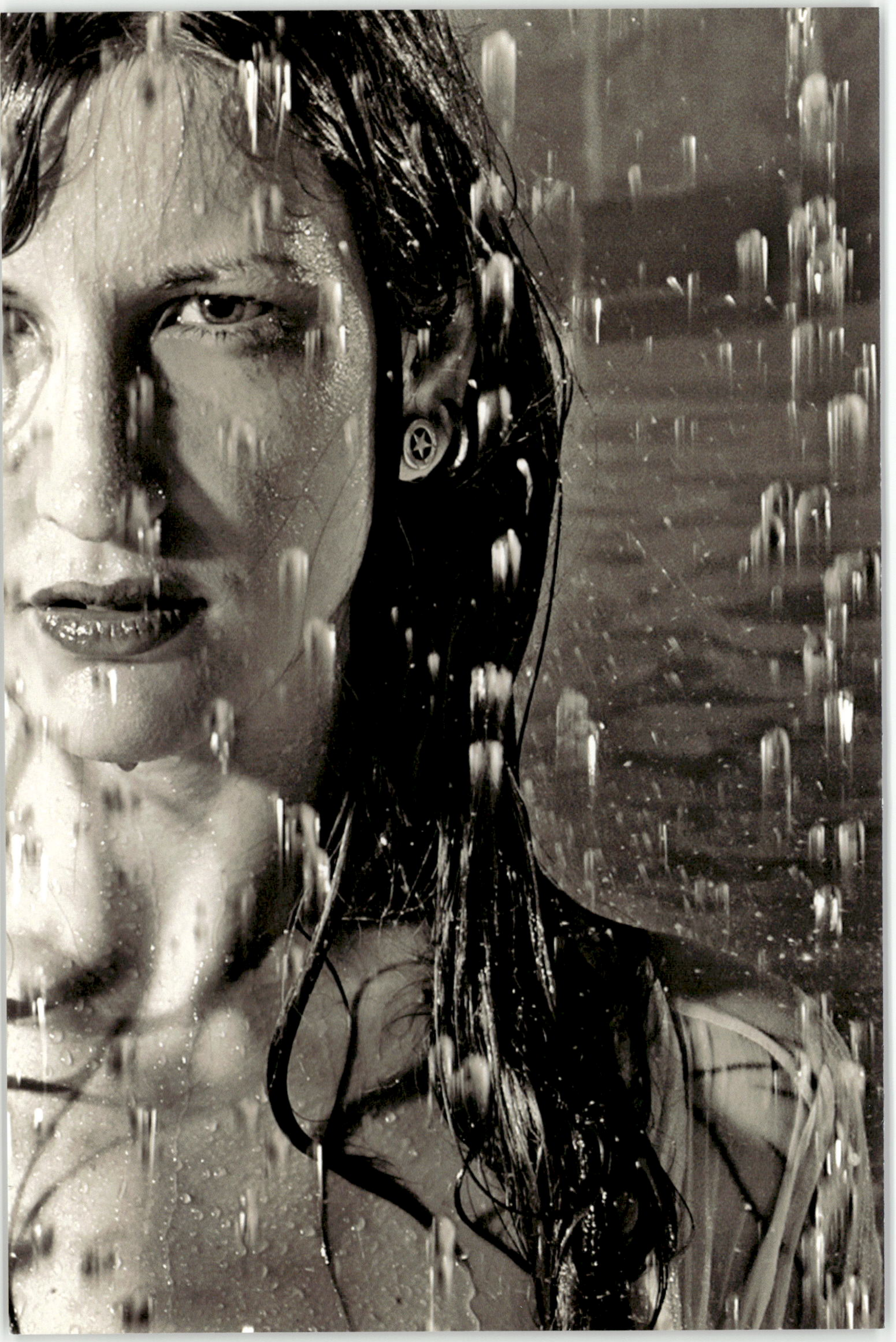

SITA MAE

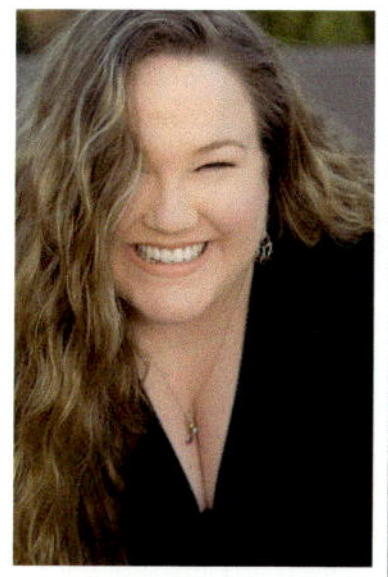

Sita Mae has participated in exhibitions including the Kinsey Institute's annual Juried Art Show; the annual "Photowork"; "Nude Night" in Florida; and the Professional Women Photographers' "Contrasts" in New York City, as well as solo exhibits and multiple iPhoneography exhibits in the USA and abroad.
Her print credits include multiple issues of French *PHOTO* magazine, *Filament* and *Bizarre*, as well as *Tattoo Book* and *Inkarnation*.

"Sylvia is magical: she has this quiet, self-contained way of moving and pausing. She has become my favourite muse, the most popular subject of my photography with collectors, and a friend. When I photograph her, the resulting images not only show how elegant and beautiful she is, but also make me feel I have managed to share something of myself that is beautiful as well."

www.sitamae.com

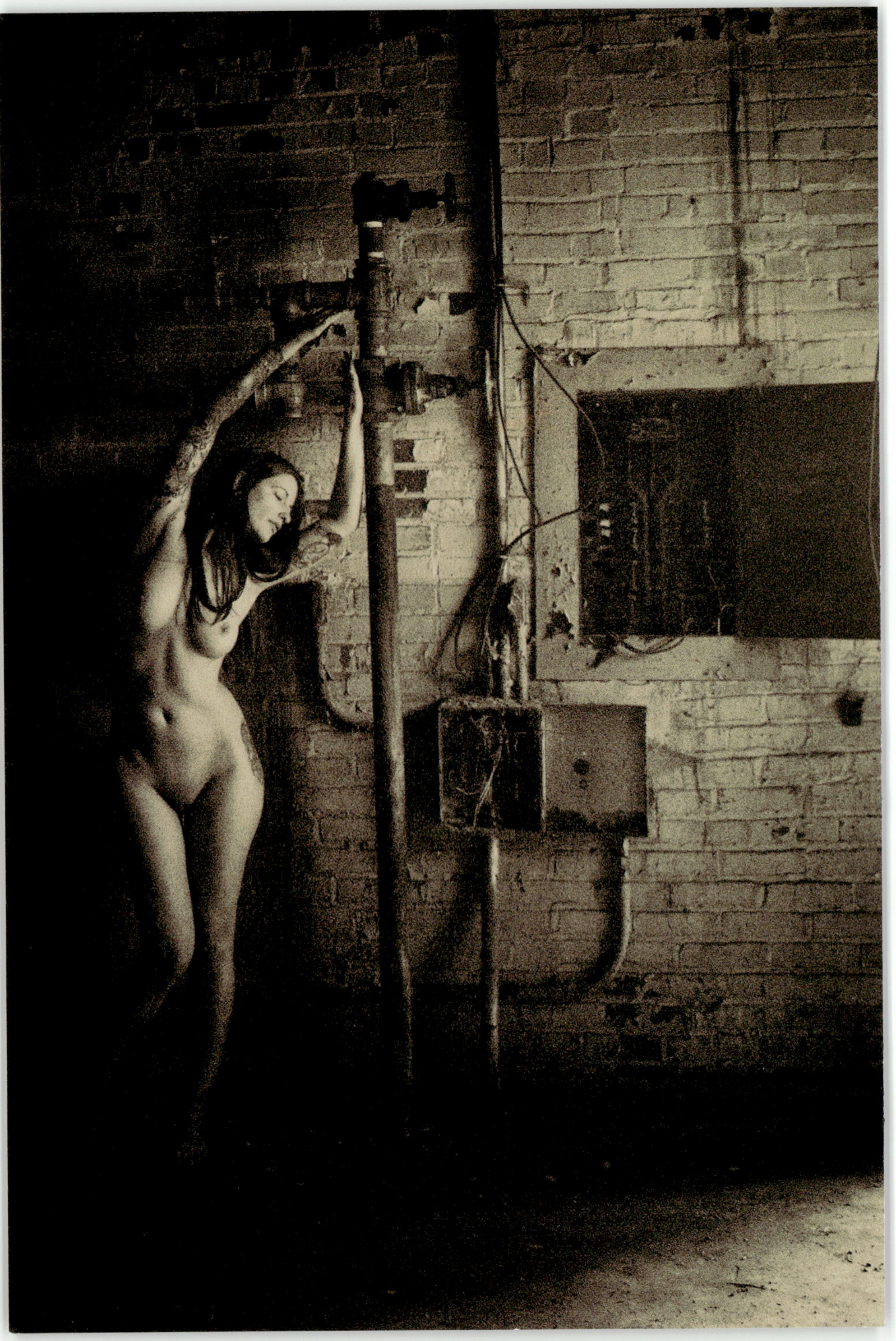

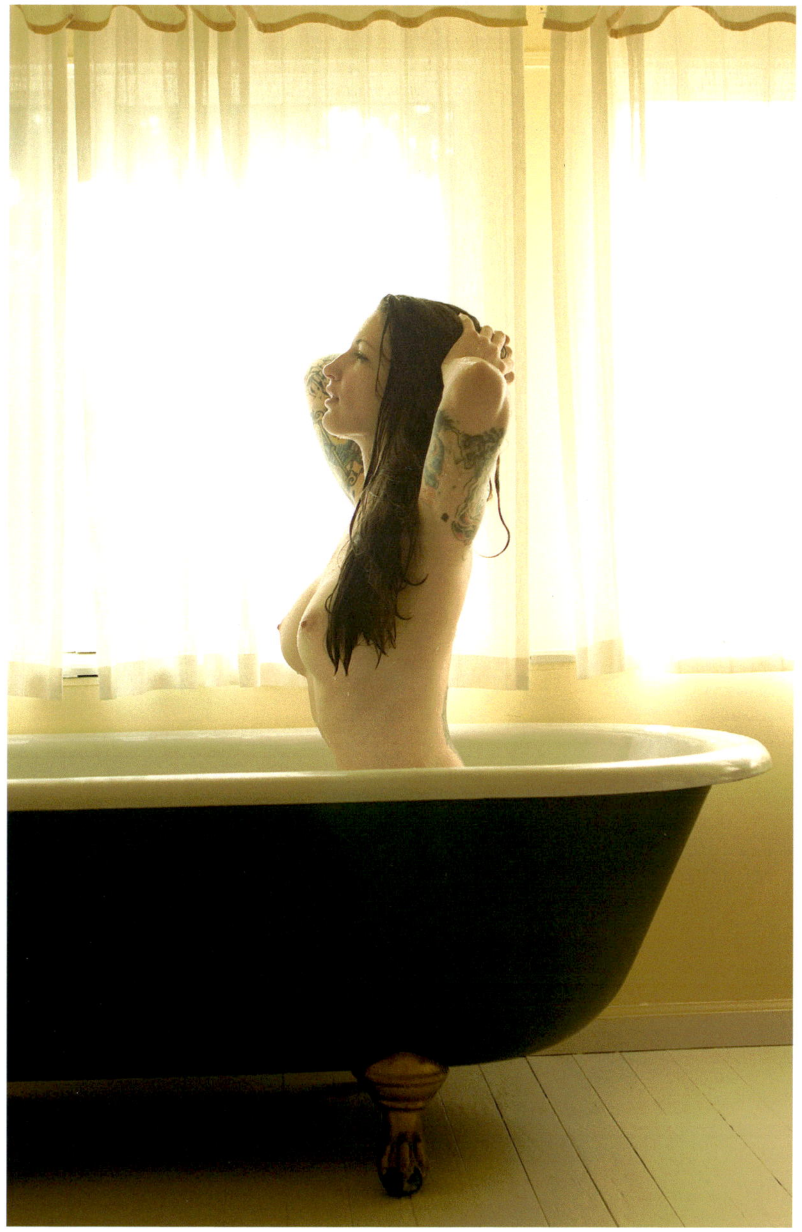

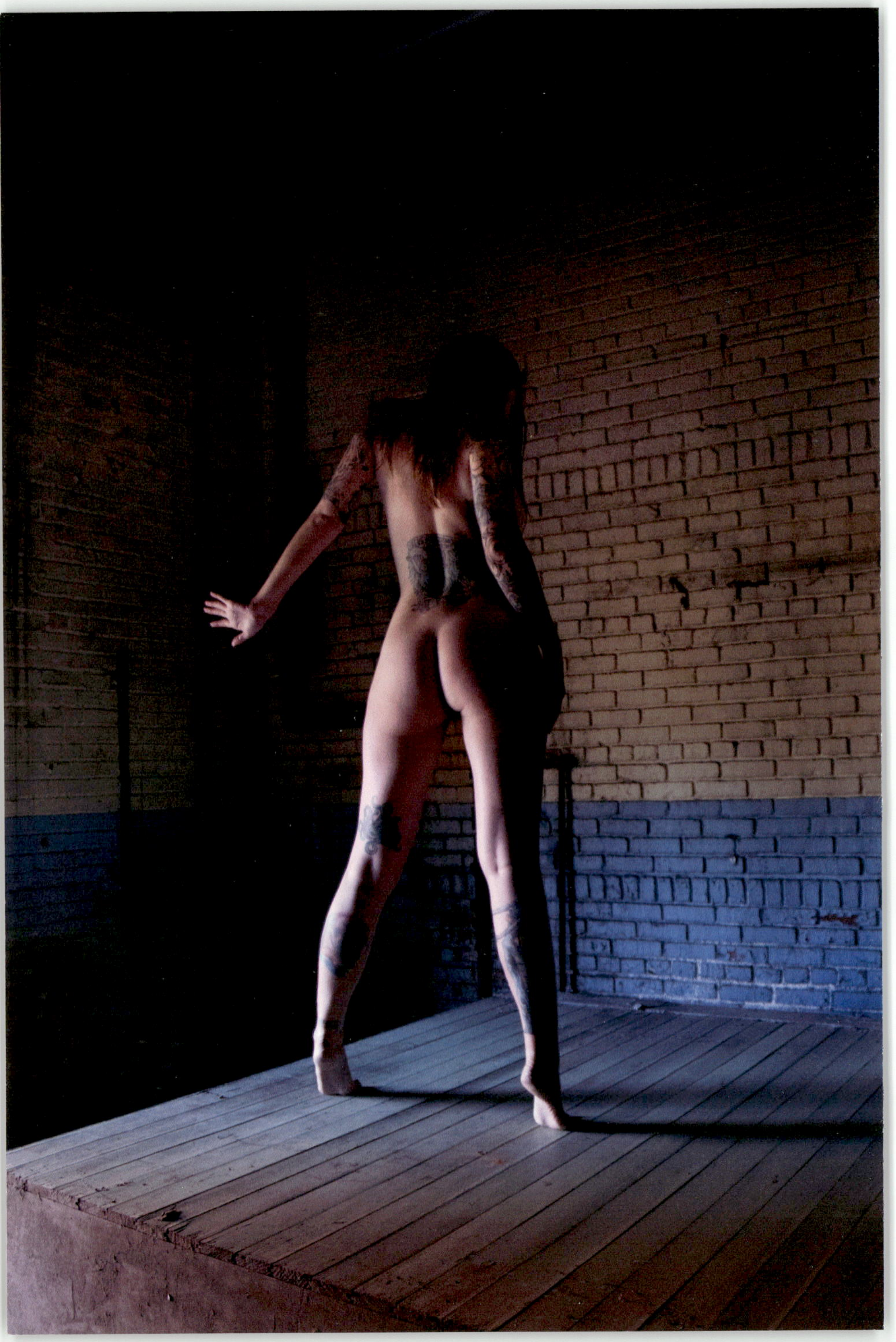

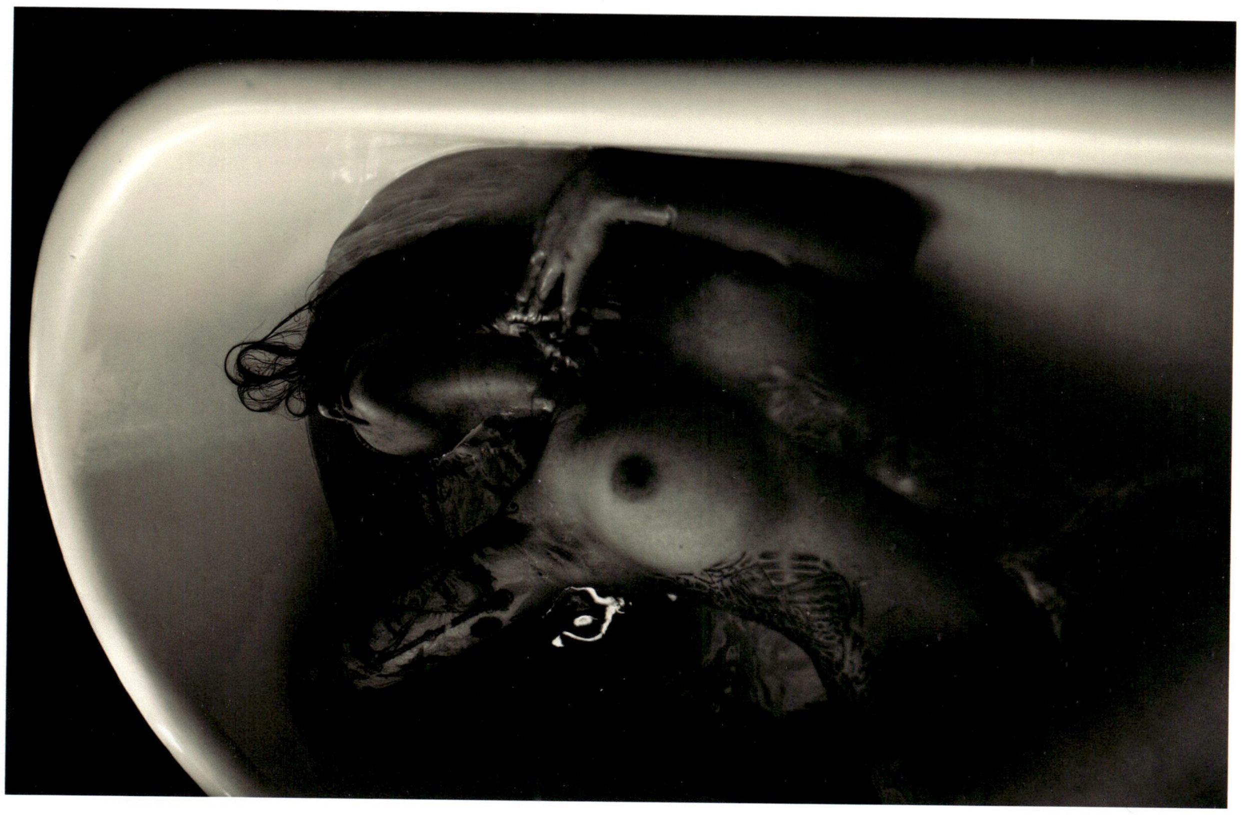

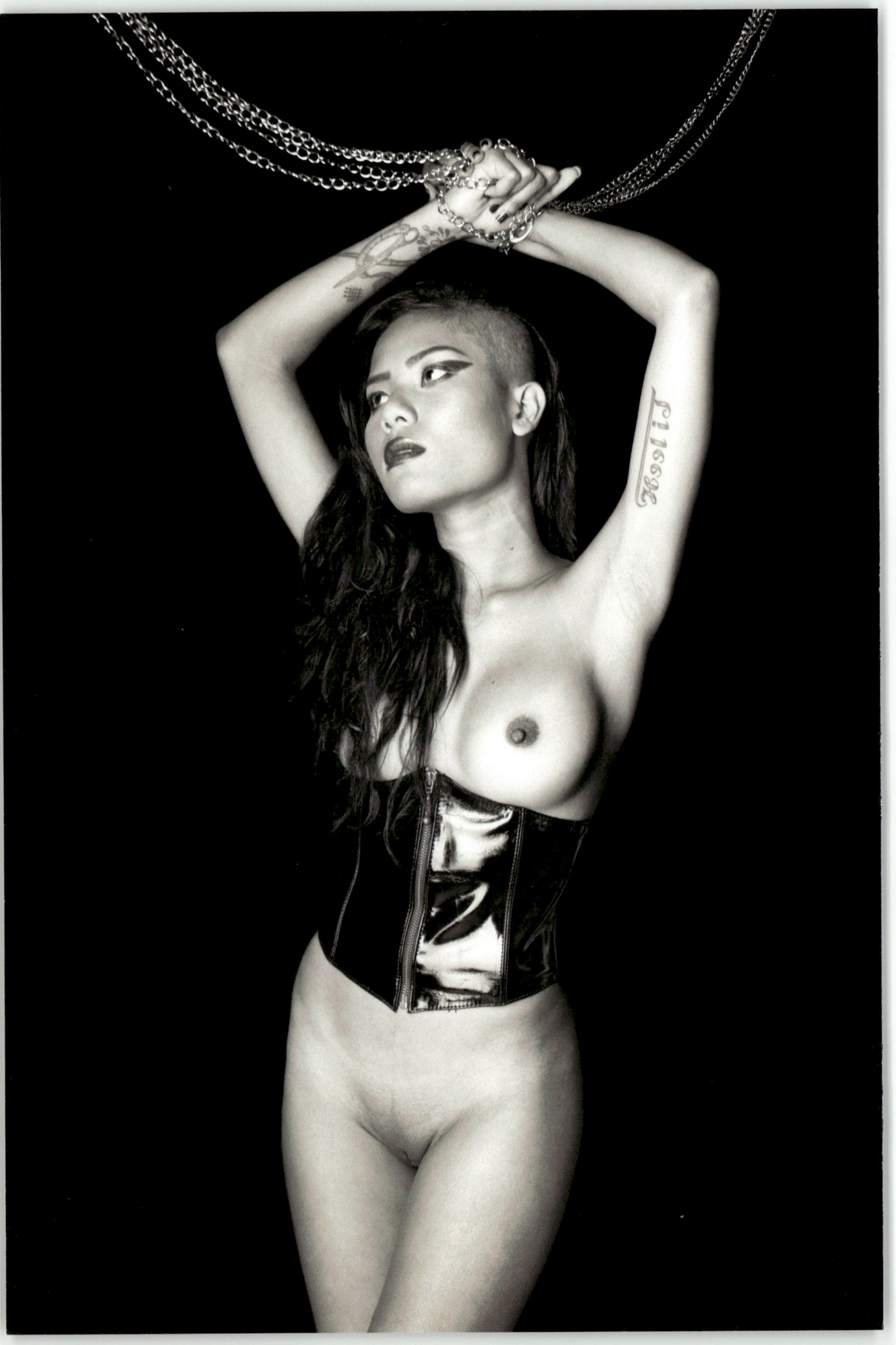

WULAN MEI LINA

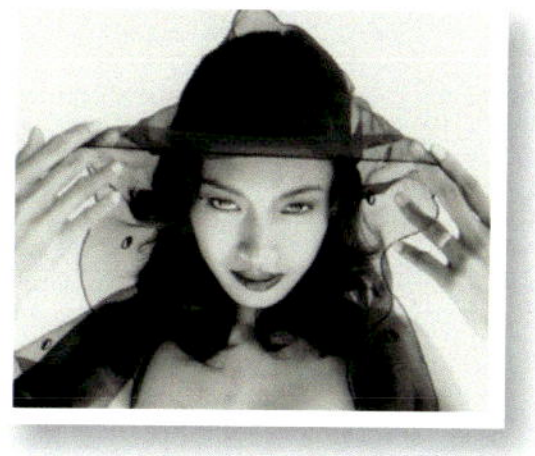

Indonesia's only erotic photographer, Wulan Mei Lina, recently presented her latest photo exhibition, "Outlawed Beauties", at JP's, Seminyak, Bali. Her first solo exhibition took place at Chaser's, Kuta, in 2006, and was followed in 2007 by her first book, *Indonesian Venus*. In 2009 she developed her career abroad, travelling to Paris and Amsterdam, where she had many exhibitions.

"I met Anita six years ago, when she was a teenager, in a club in Bali, and asked her to pose for me right away. Although still very young, she was very open-minded and willing to follow everything I asked. We still often work together and remain good friends. We have explored our limits in erotic pictures, so for this book I chose her pictures without hesitation. Isn't she amazing?"

www.wulanmeilina.com

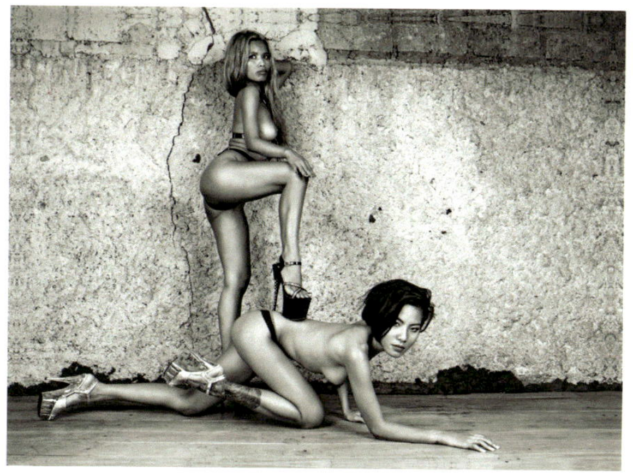

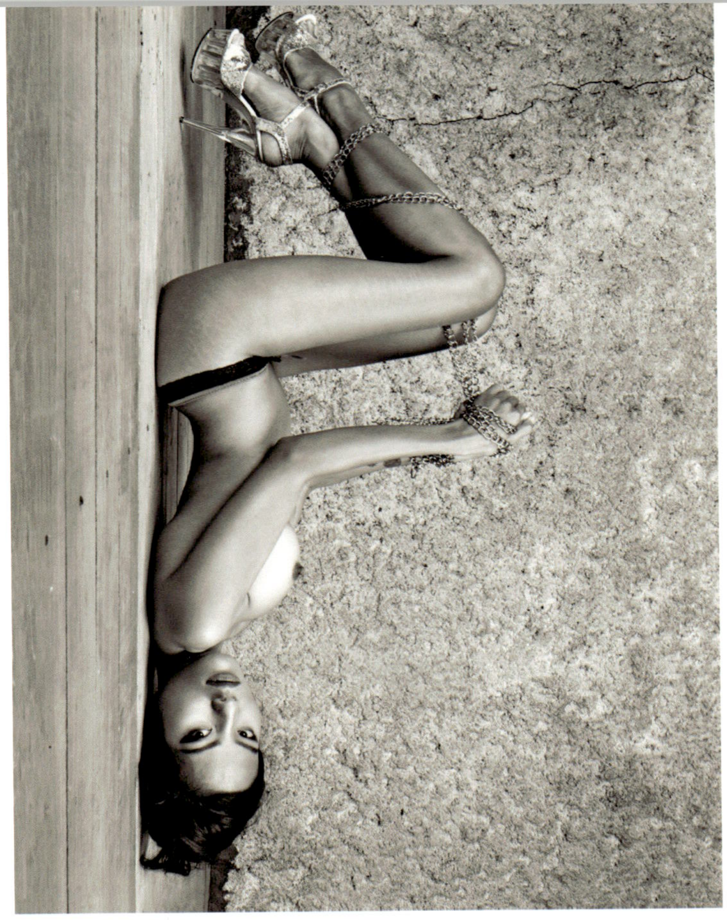

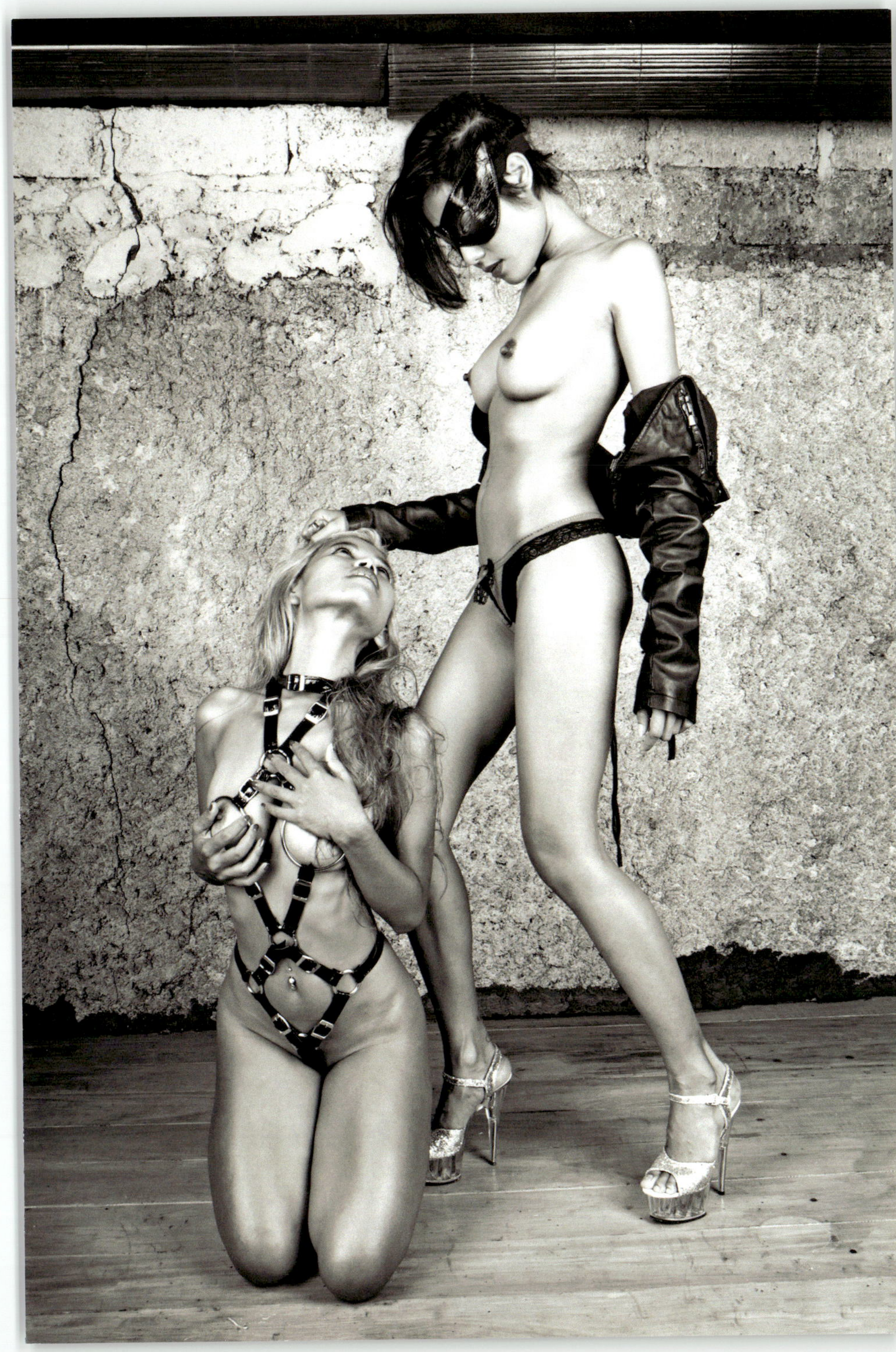

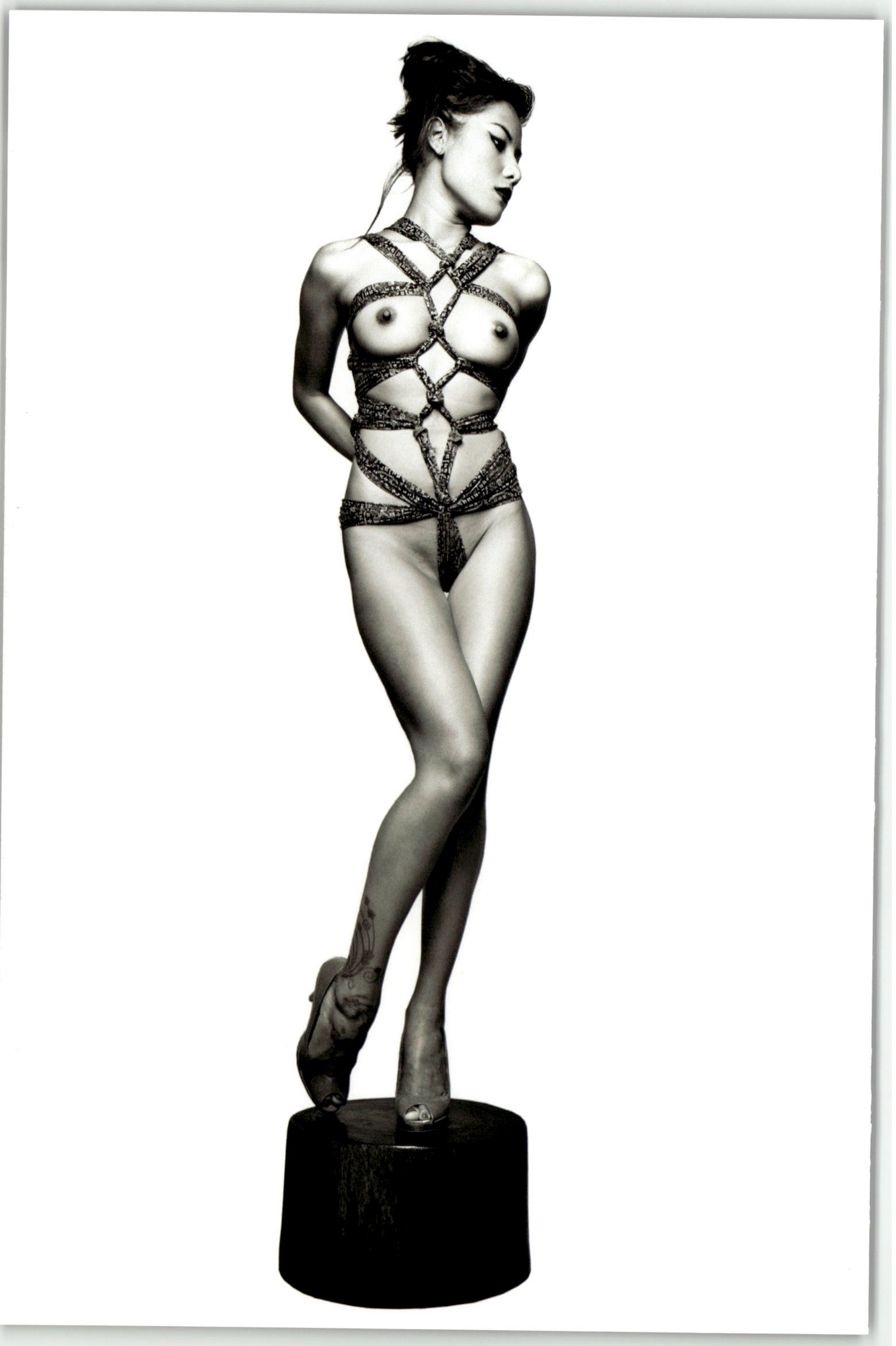

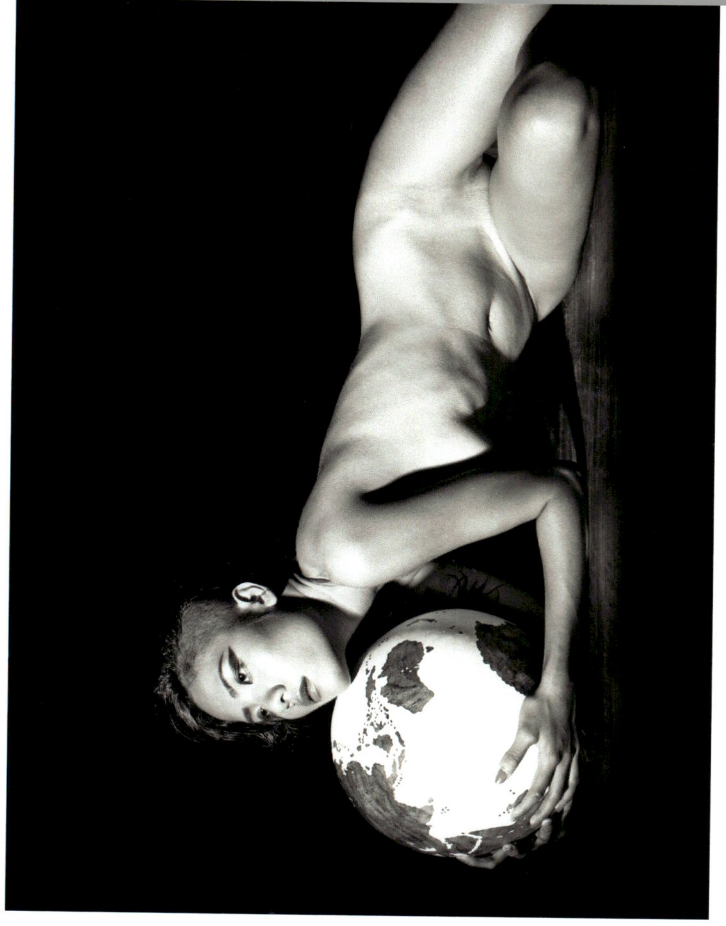

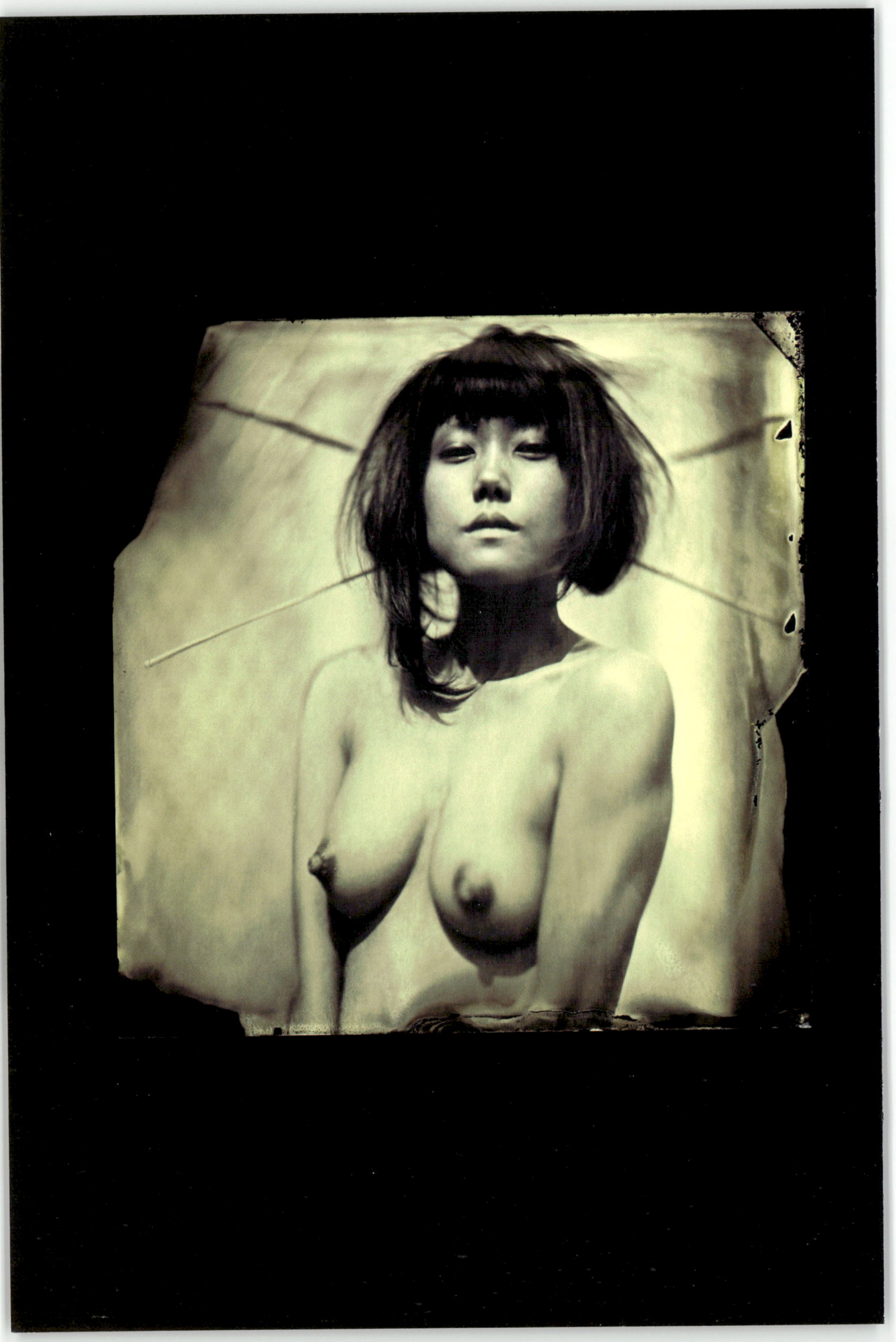

KEN MERFELD

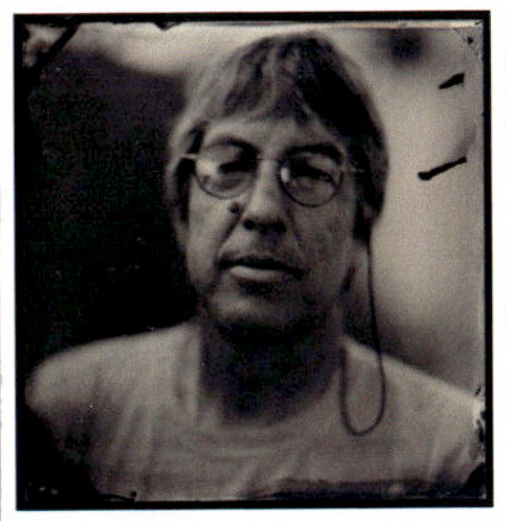

Ken Merfeld needs to create daily, loves to see what he has never seen before and appreciates the bent, broken life on the edge, and imperfection. He believes that the exchange of energy is most important in life and is critical in art. He lives for light, strong images, emotional response and a different point of view. Ken is an aficionado of photo history and the B&W darkroom, is opinionated, honest and passionate.

"I collaborate with Nobuko because at different times she is an androgynous child, a sensual woman and a young mother with child. Nobuko affords me a blank canvas of trust and as she has grown in life our artistic relationship has deepened. Nobuko understands what I say about her with visuals, not words."

www.merfeldphotography.com

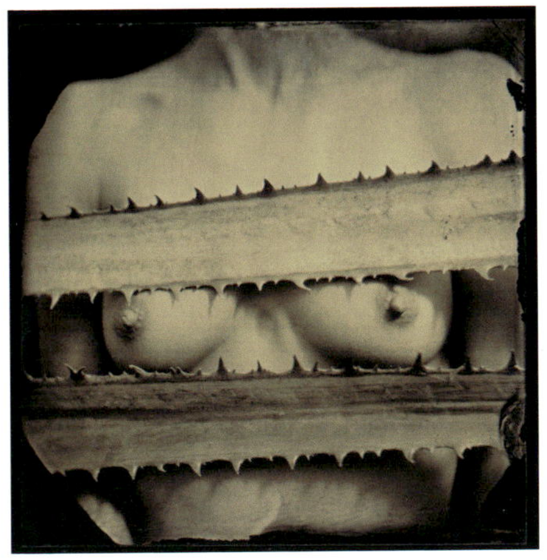

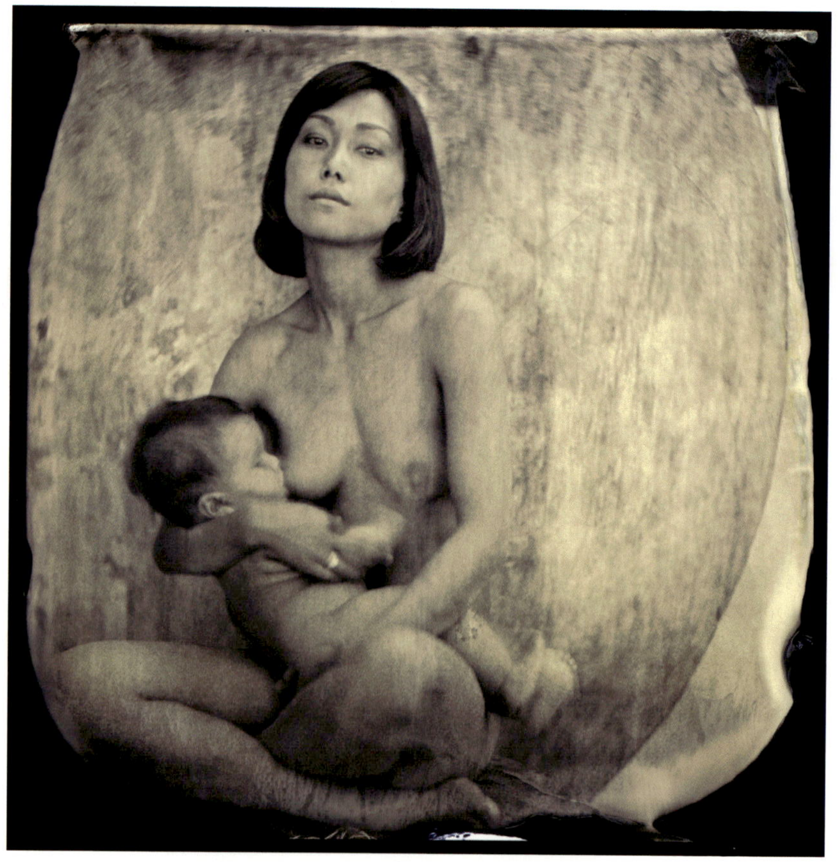

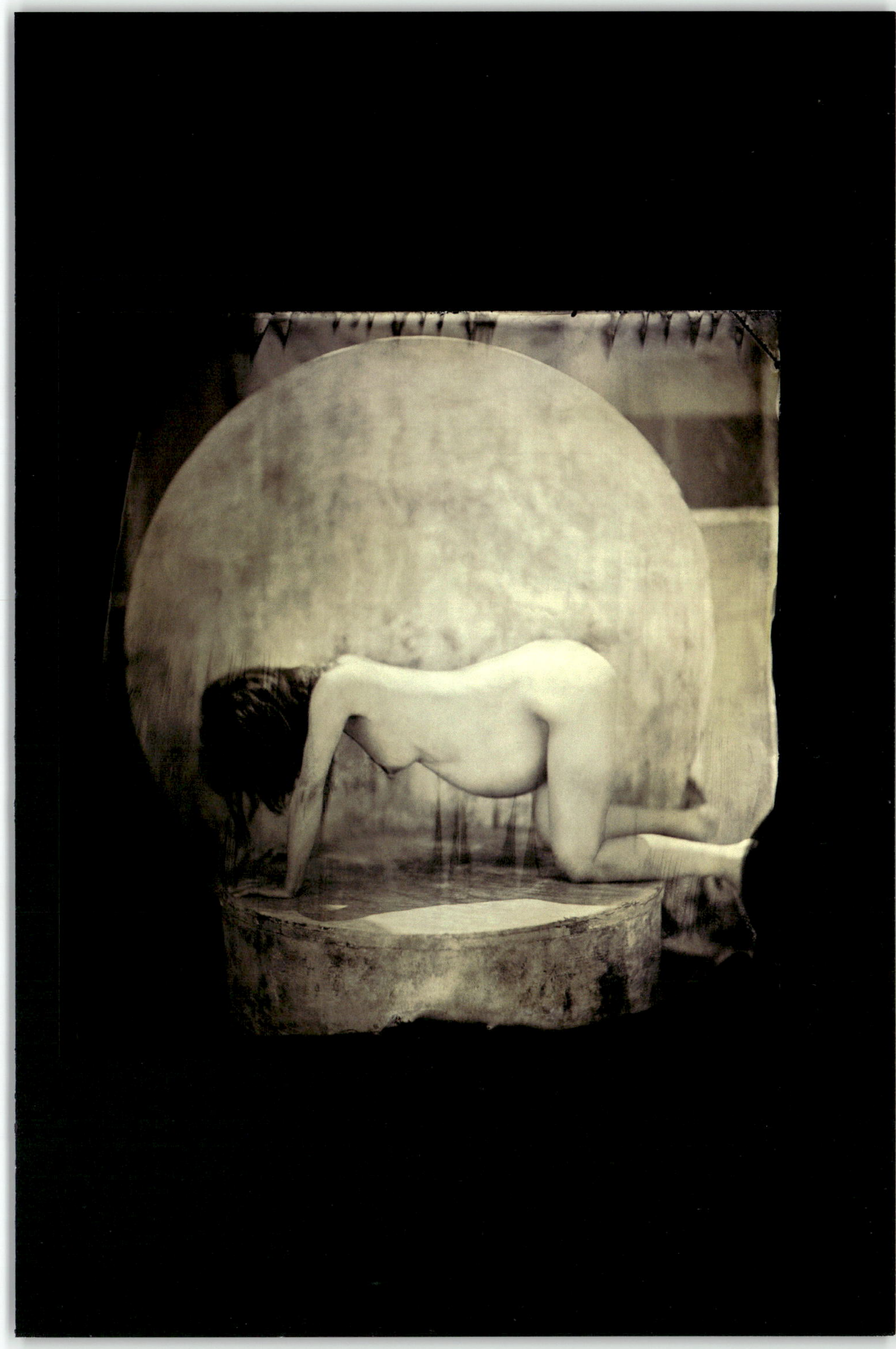

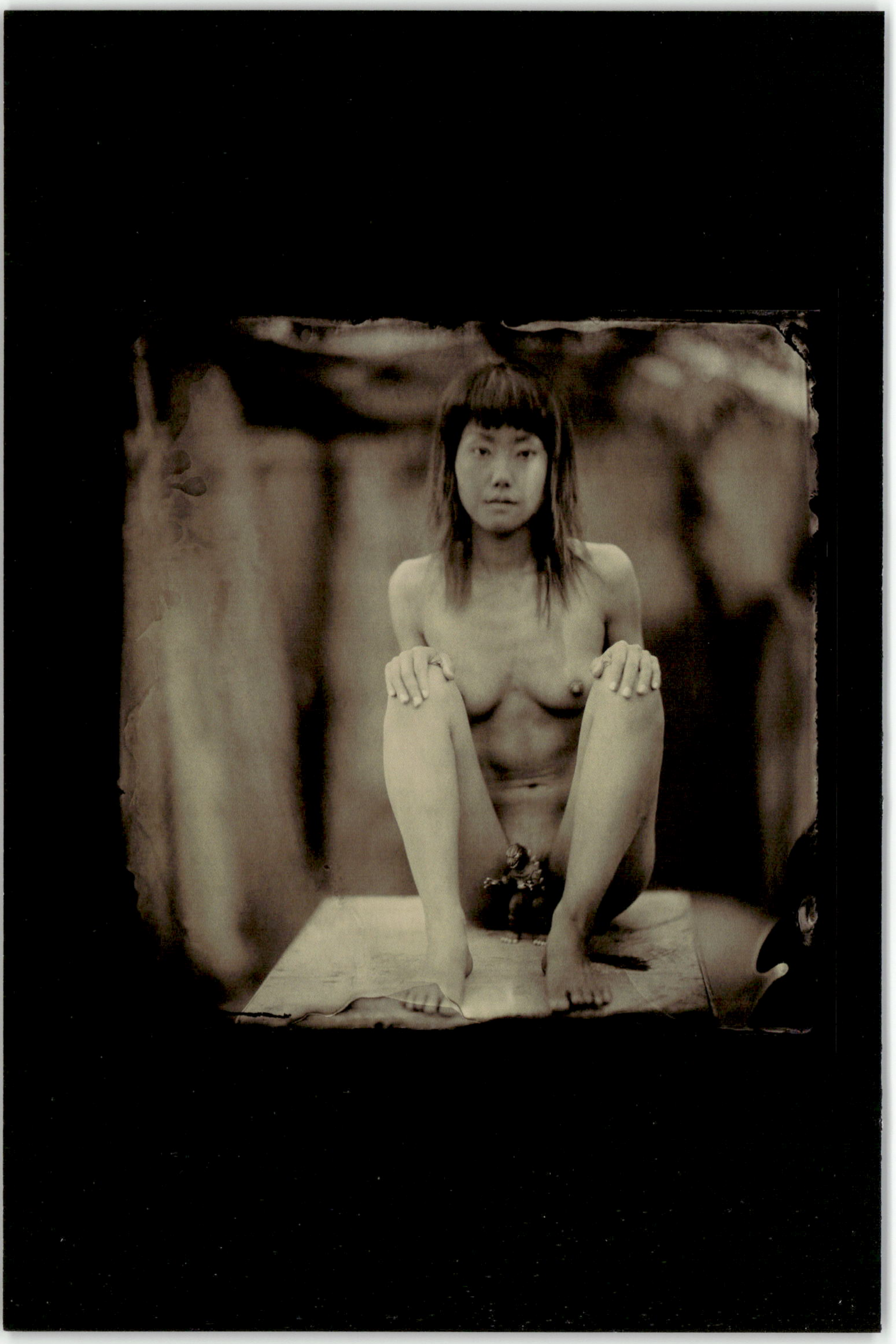

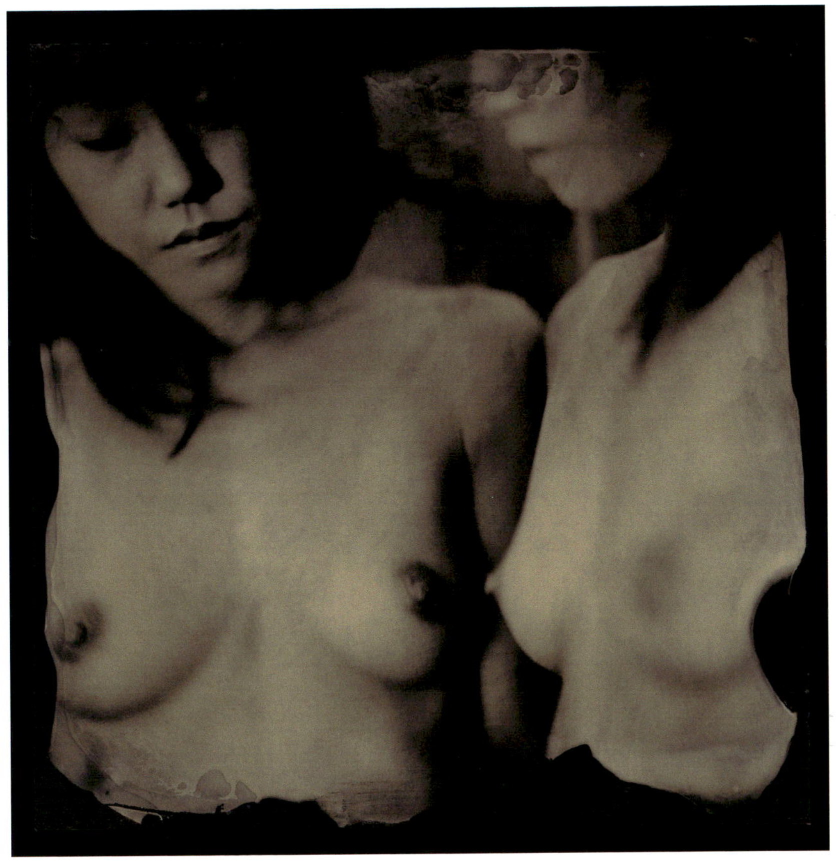

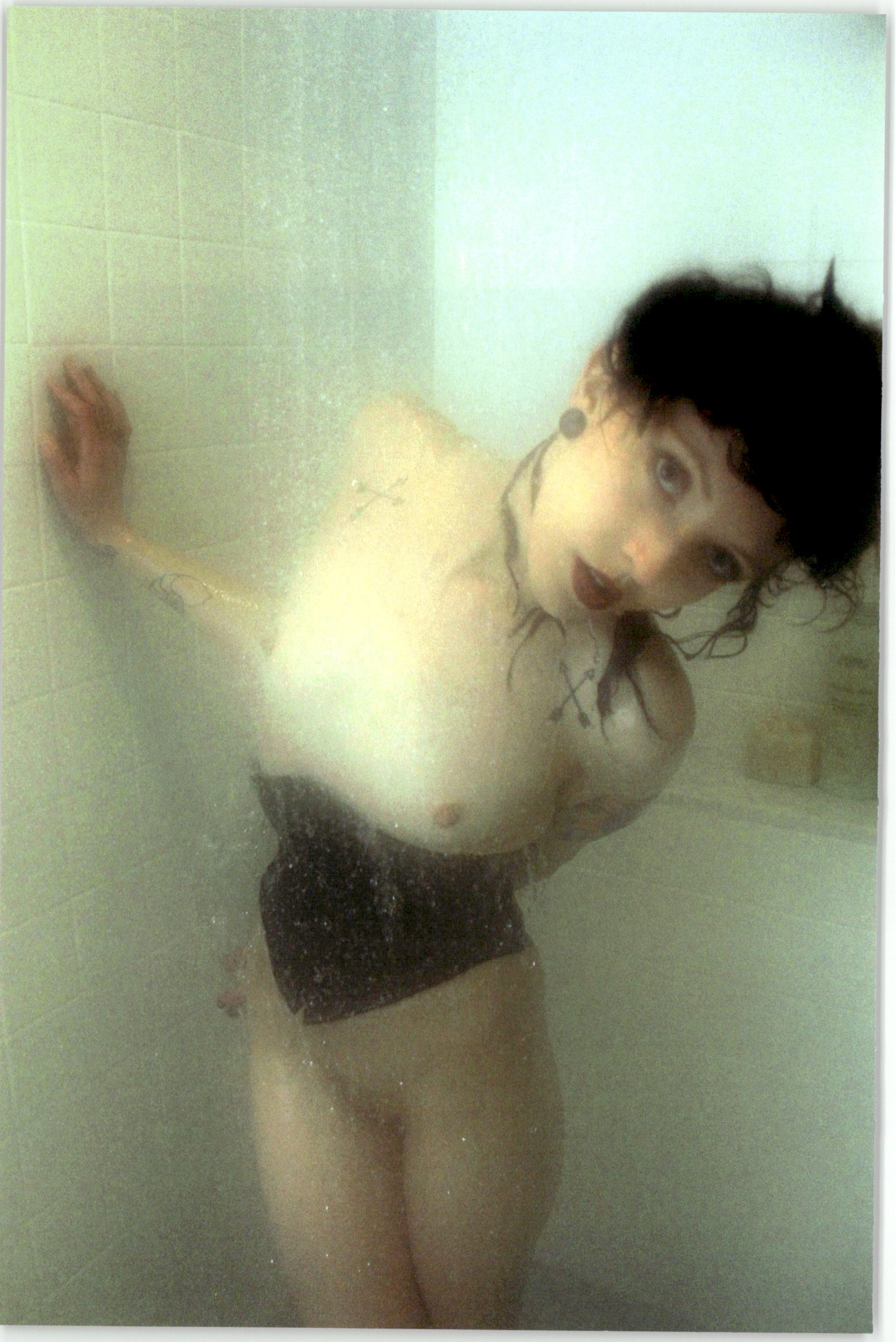

NATACHA MERRITT

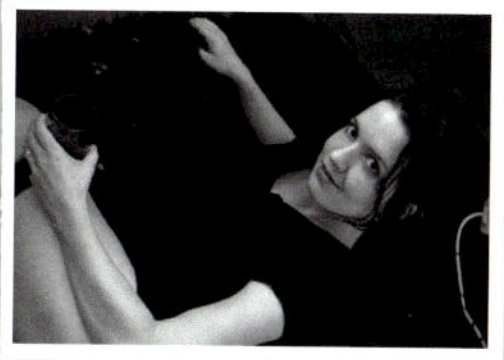

Born in 1977 in San Francisco, Natacha Merritt is an artist, photographer and biologist. Her first book, *Digital Diaries* (Taschen, 2000), an explicit erotic exploration at the dawn of the digital era, became a critically acclaimed international bestseller. In 2003 Natacha was one of the creators of the first erotic Cirque du Soleil show, *Zumanity* (New York-New York Hotel & Casino), an investigation of sensuality and peak human performance. Later, while obtaining her degree in evolutionary biology, she wrote an "insect circus" celebrating the importance of biodiversity. She licensed this to Cirque du Soleil and it became the currently touring *OVO*. Her latest book, *Sexual Selection* (Bongout, 2012), examines plant and insect sexuality alongside her trademark erotic photography. She is working on a new e-book and a live performance.

www.natacha-merritt.com

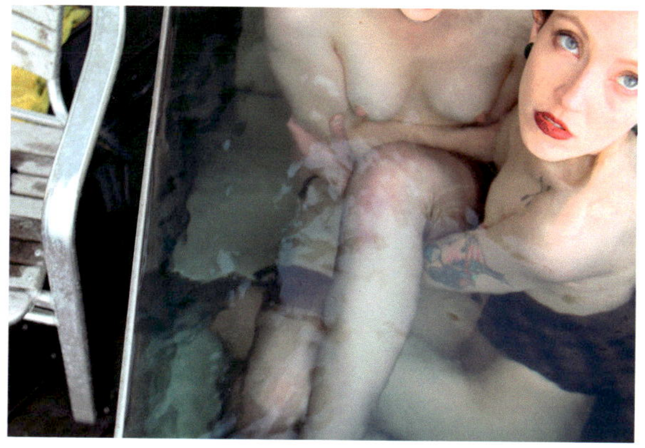

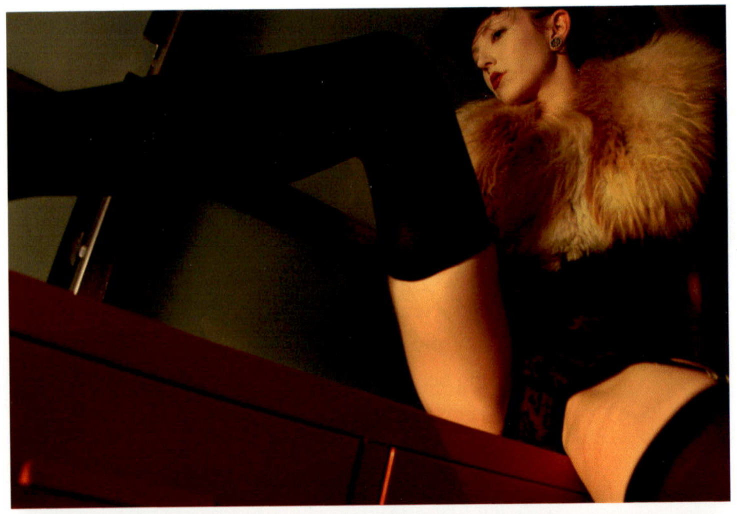

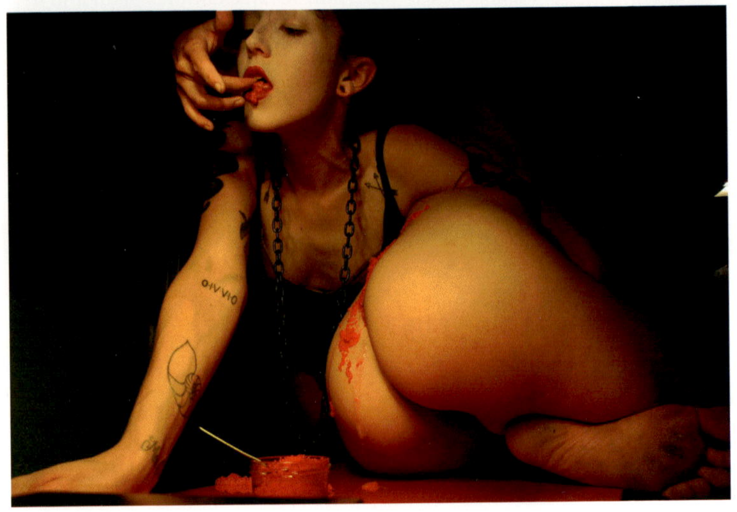

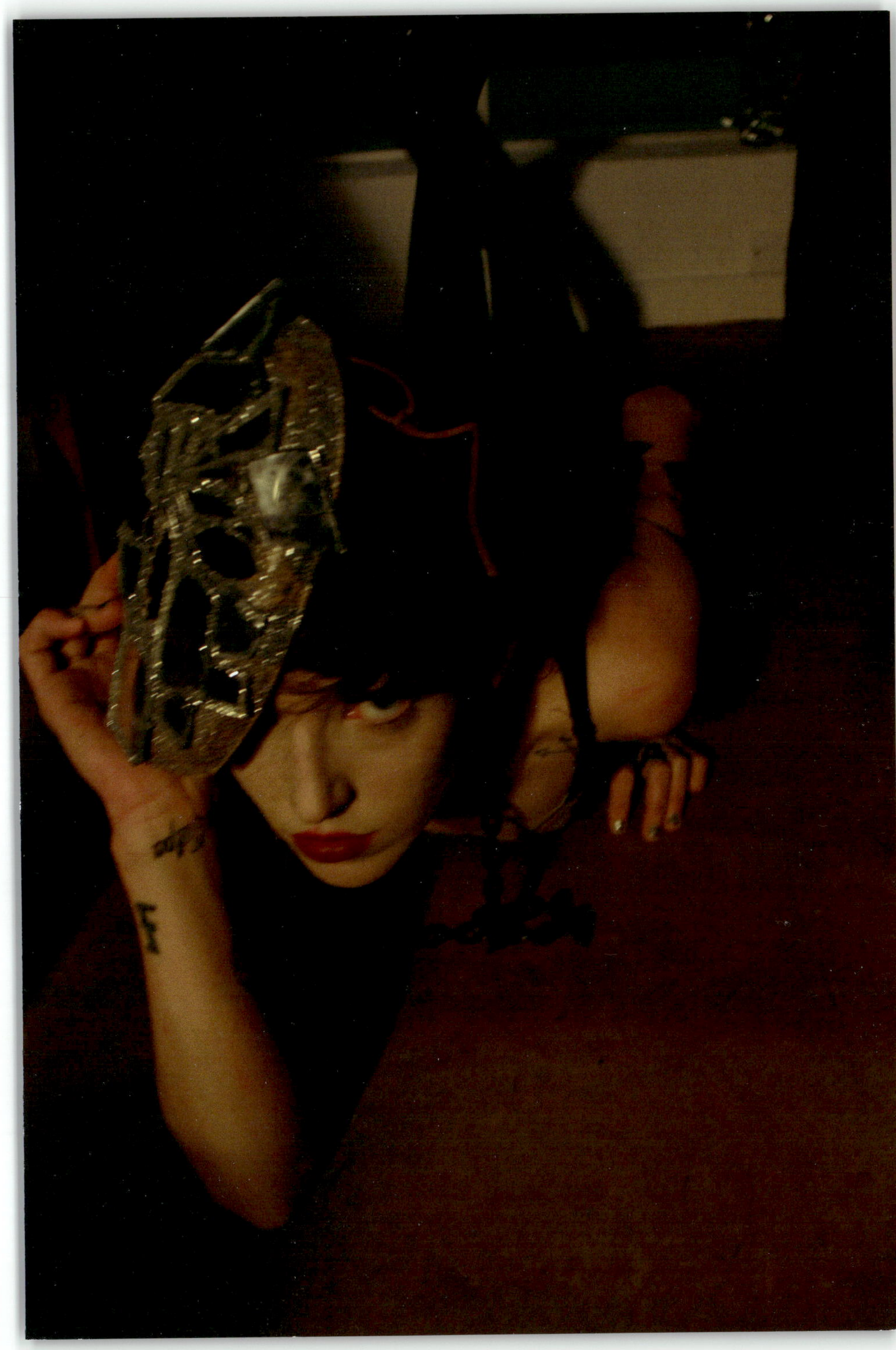

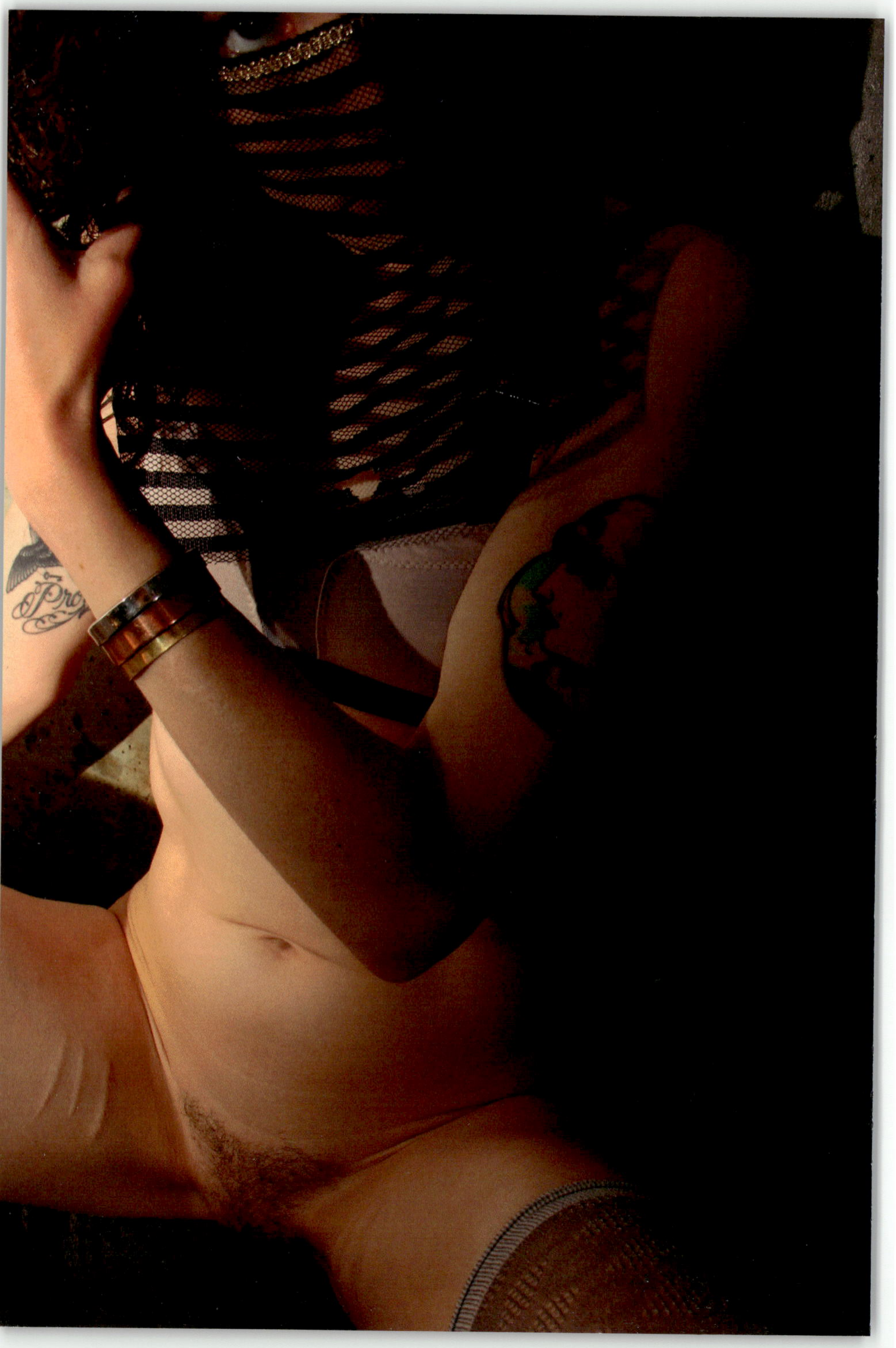

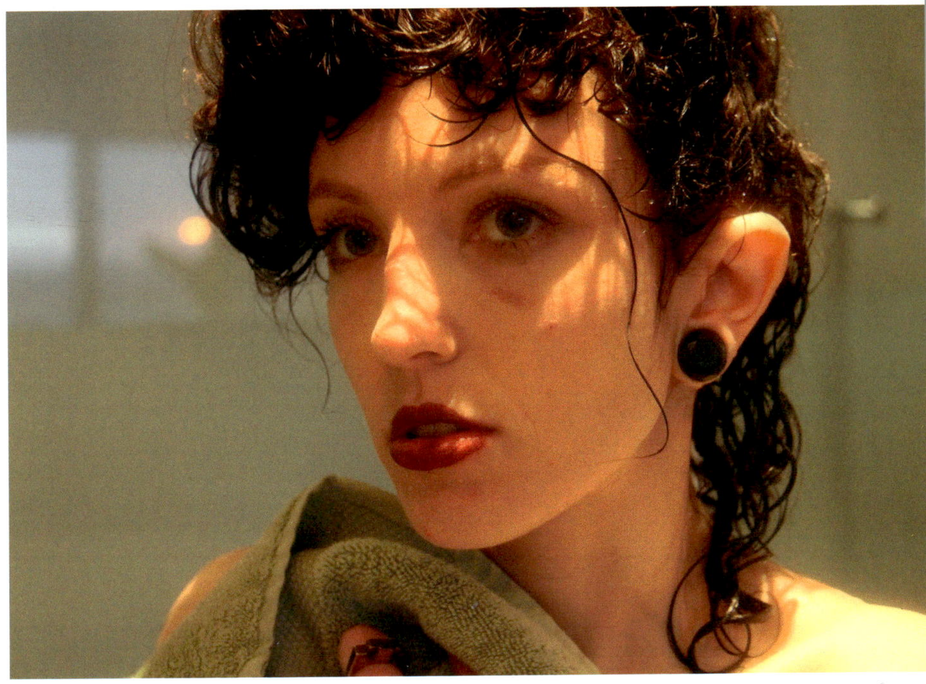

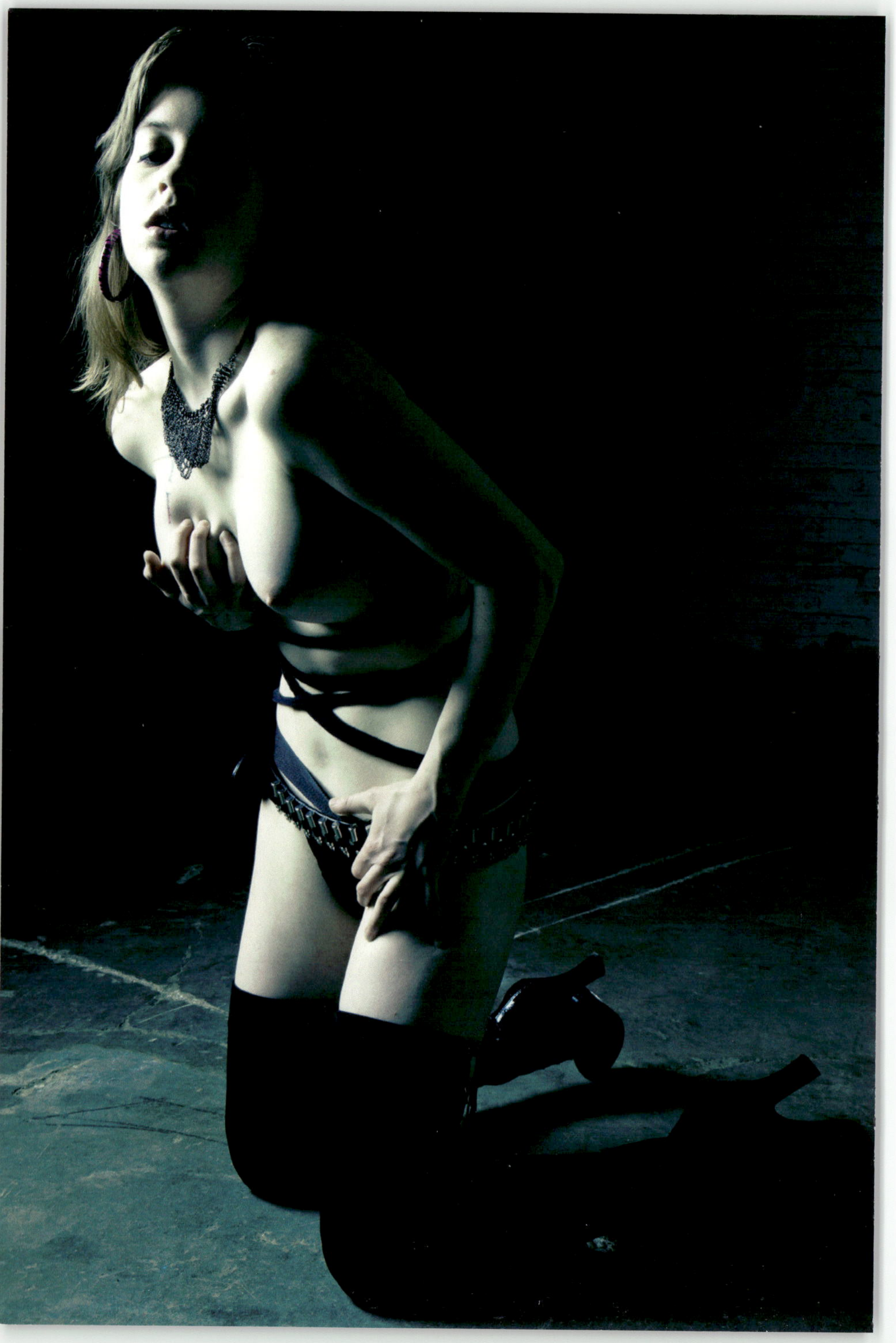

GARY MITCHELL

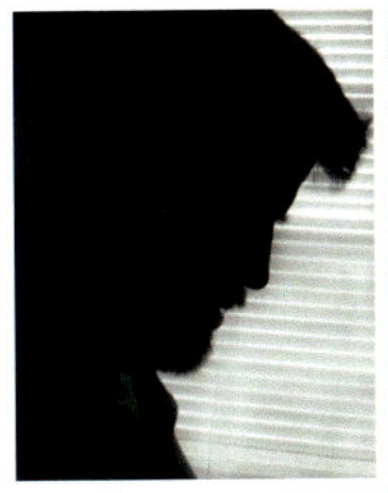

"In my art nudes and erotica I love to capture the grace, power, form, gesture and emotion of a woman. My style emphasizes contrasts of light and shadow, smooth and rough, the traditional and the unexpected. My work has been included in international books and periodicals, and in shows in the United States, Canada and France.

"I was struck by the artist Reveille's beautiful delicate features, sweet smile and personal style. She agreed to model for me if she could remain fully clothed. I hadn't expected such a remarkable figure, and the shy artist quickly transformed into the adventurous nude model. She does fashion design as well, so we sometimes incorporate her creations into our shoots. Lately we've included fetish elements, such as suspension bondage with my rigger friend DeweyX."

www.fb.com/garymphoto

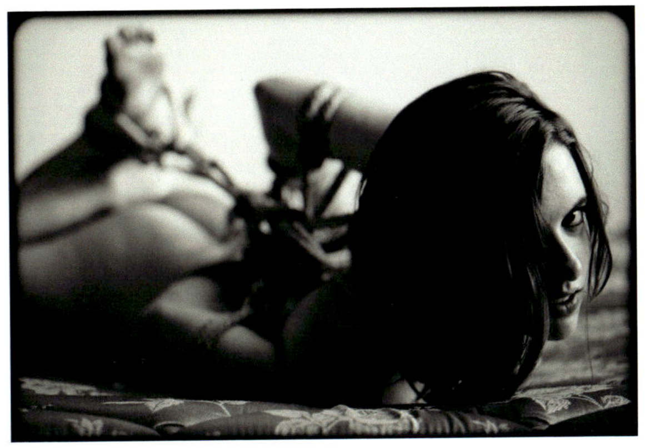

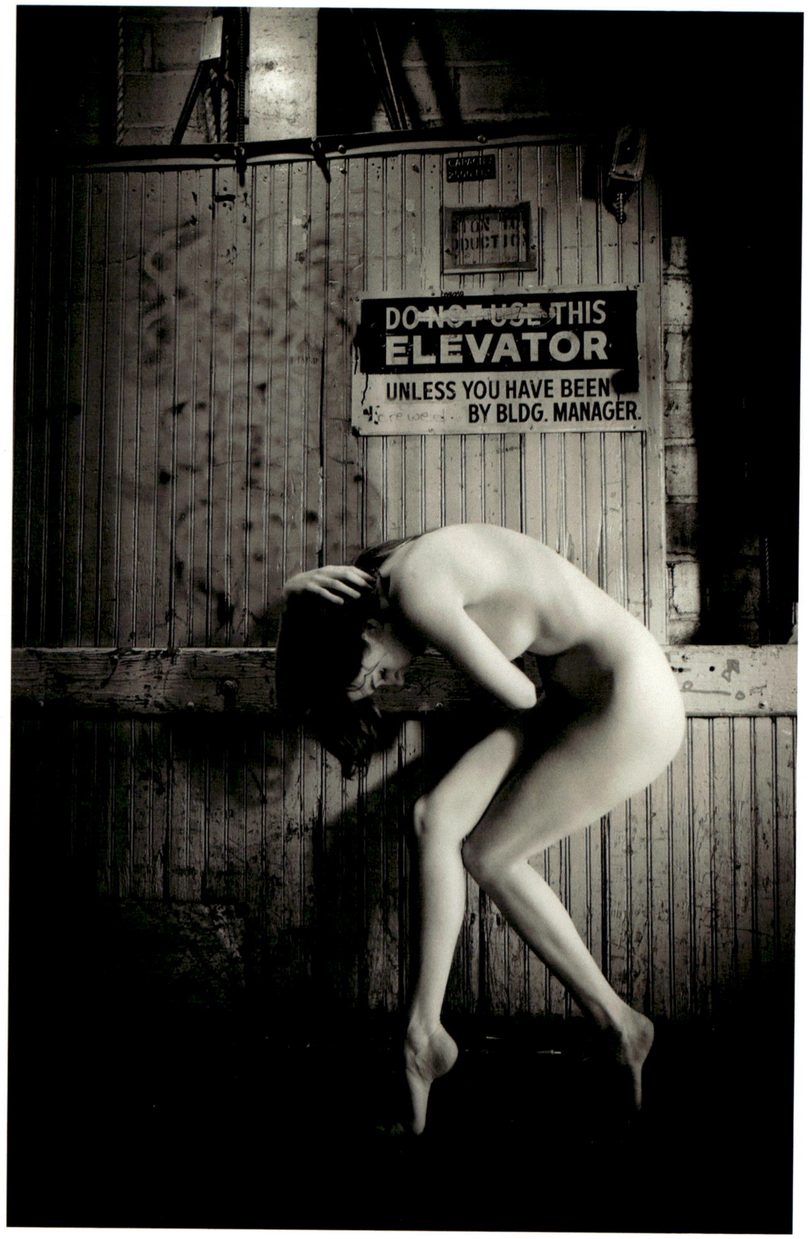
DO NOT USE THIS
ELEVATOR
UNLESS YOU HAVE BEEN
BY BLDG. MANAGER.

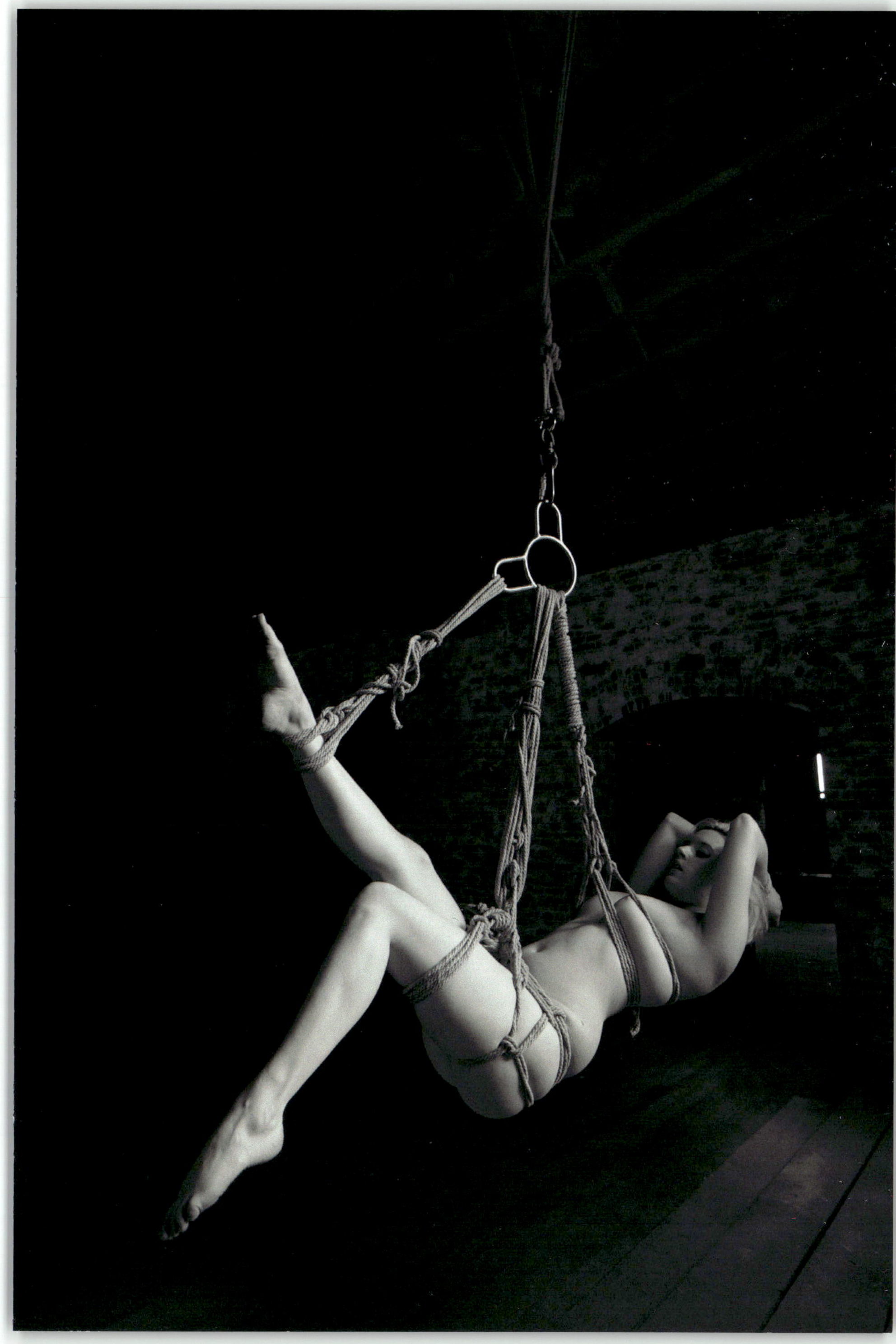

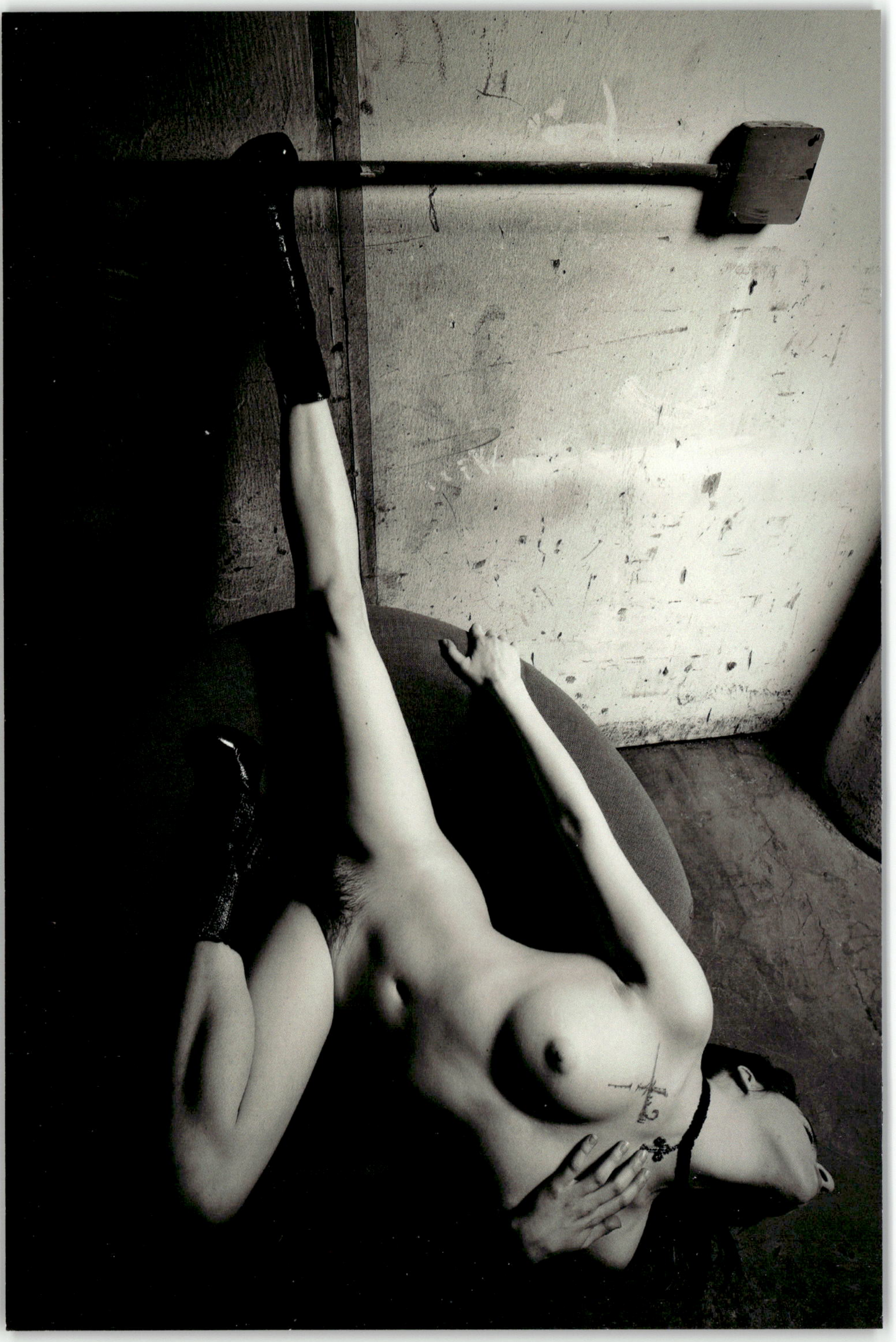

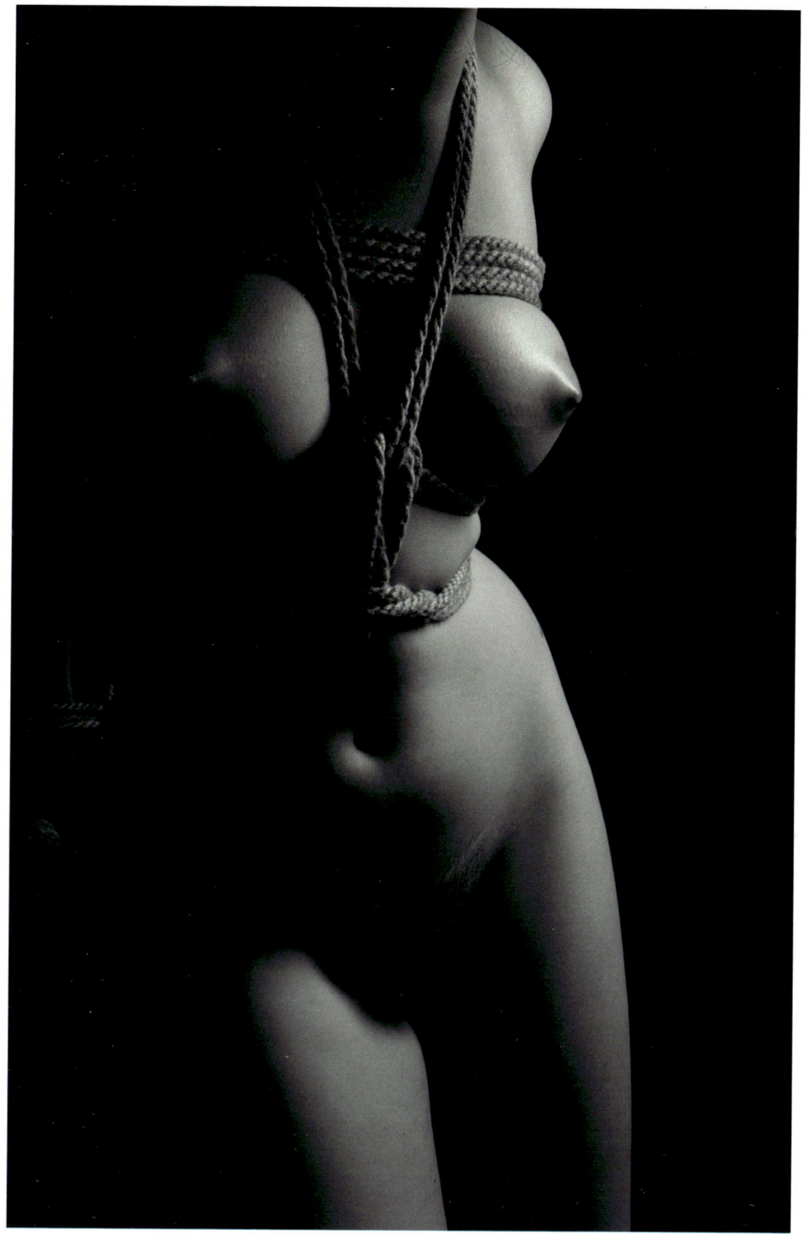

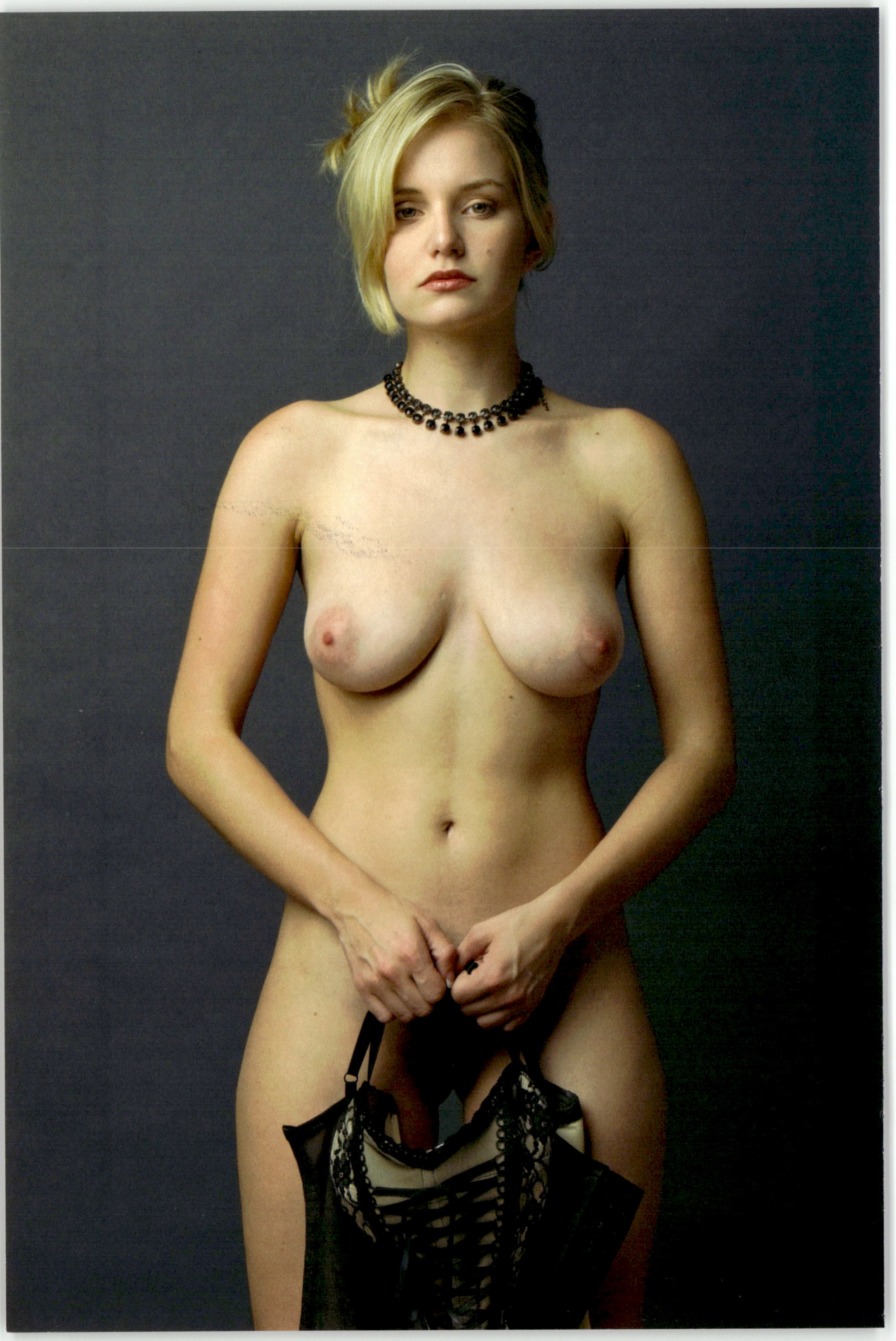

CRAIG MOREY

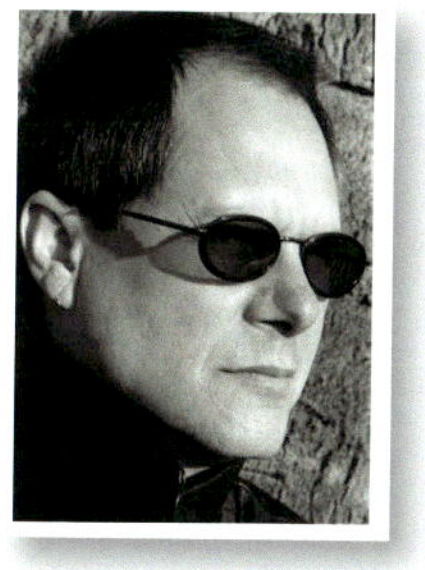

Craig Morey is an American photographer known mainly for his B&W erotic nudes. He has won numerous awards, including a Special Jury Prize at the International Triennial of Photography in Fribourg, Switzerland. His photographs have appeared in many books and magazines in the USA, Europe and Japan, as well as on thousands of websites. He has published *Studio Nudes* (Penthouse International, 1992), *Body/Expression/Silence* (Le Merche/Yoshida, 1994), *Linea* (Korinsha Press, 1996) and *20th Century Studio Nudes* (Glaspalast Edition, 2001).

"Liz Ashley is beautiful, generous, intelligent and funny. At times she's a mind-reader, moving into a pose I was about to ask for, but a couple of seconds ahead of my request, to create the perfect shot. Very few models stand out as nearly flawless visually and personally. Liz is one of those."

www.moreystudio.com

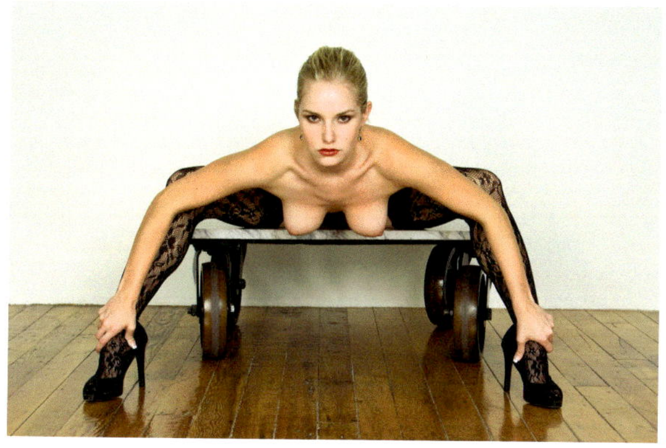

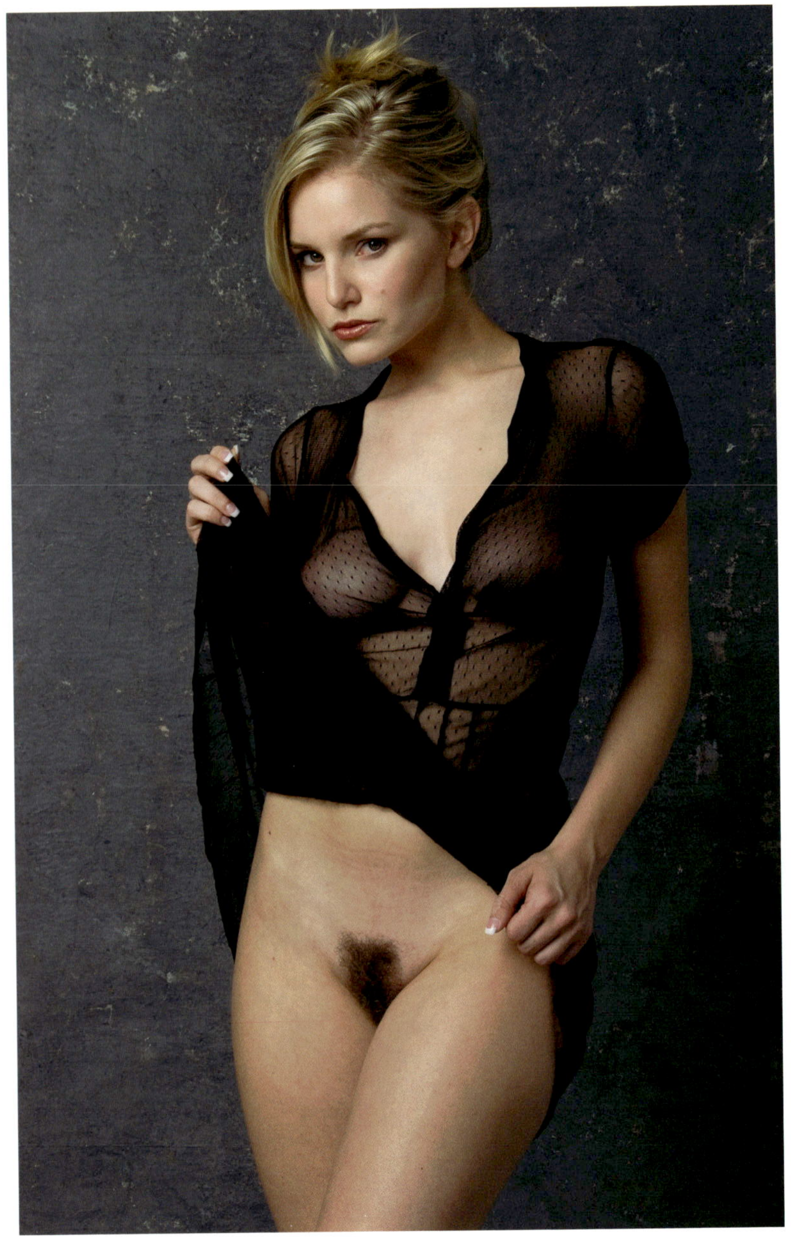

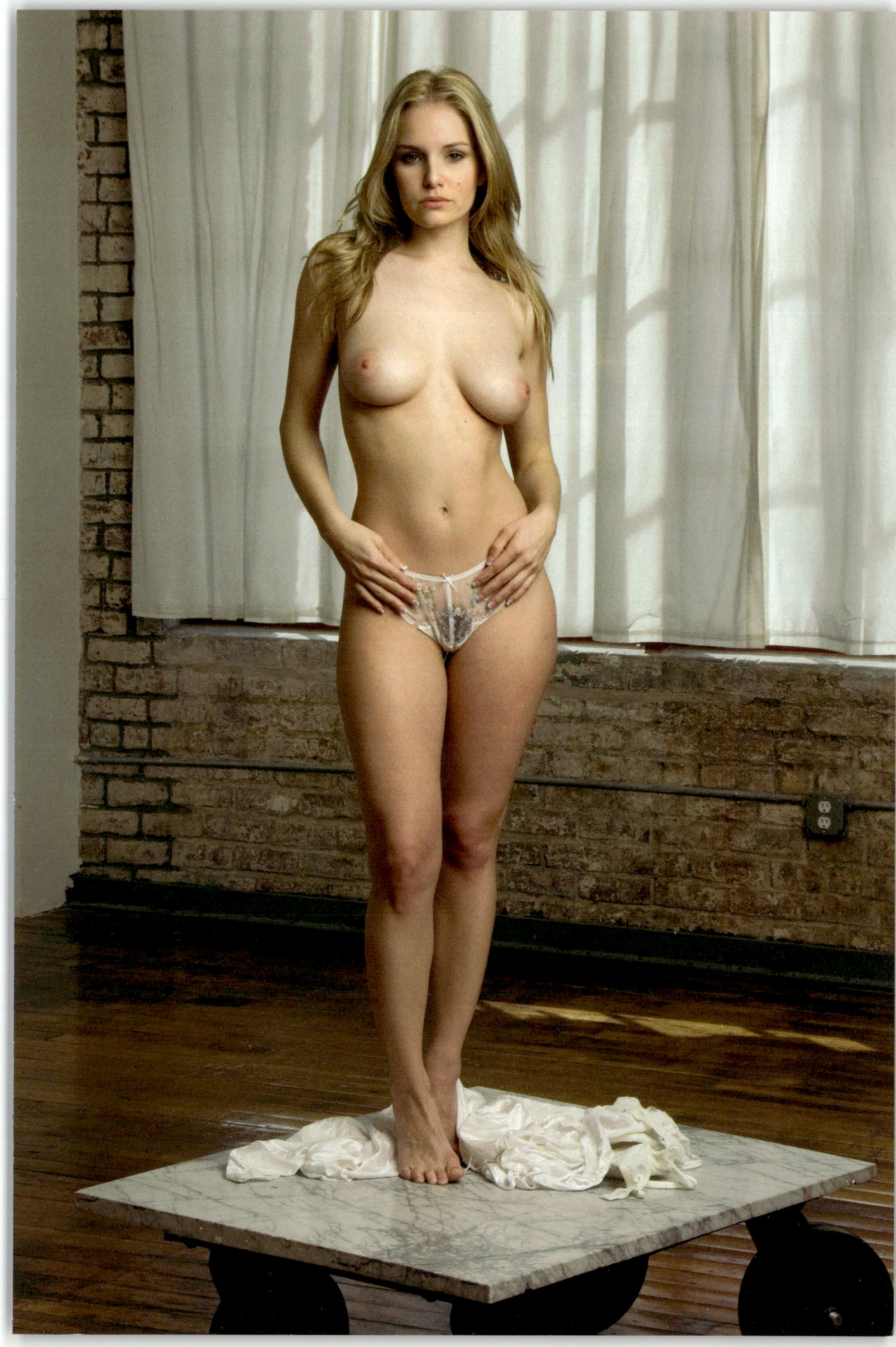

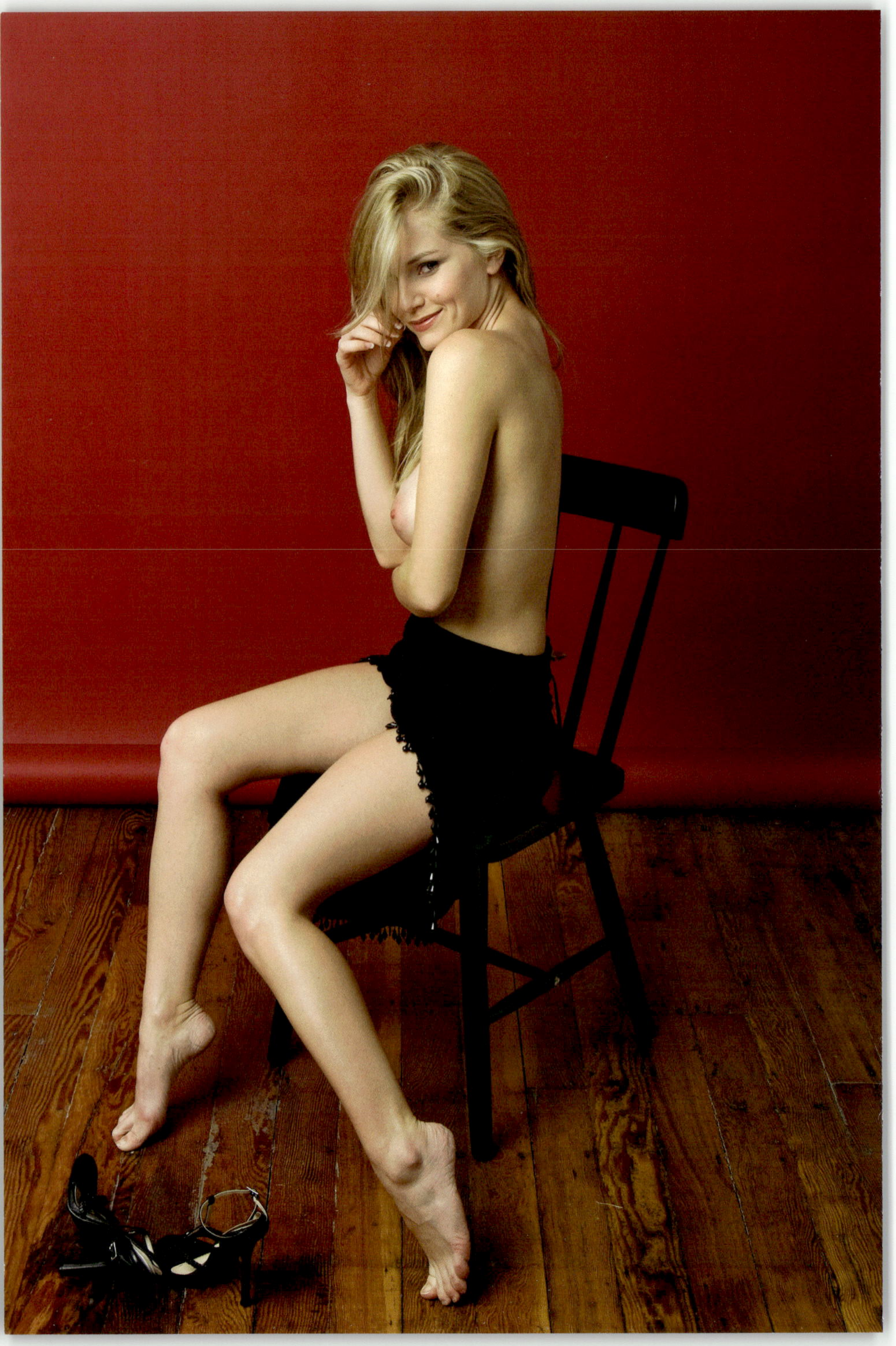

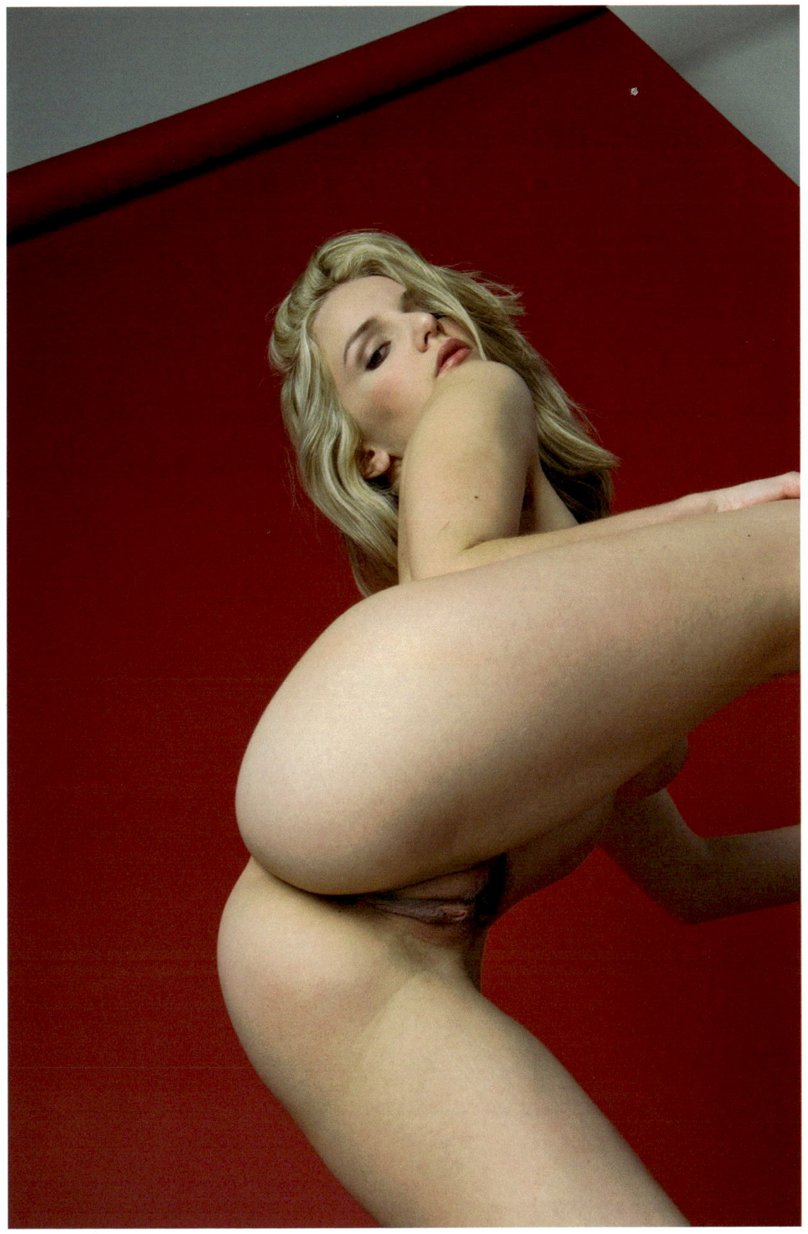

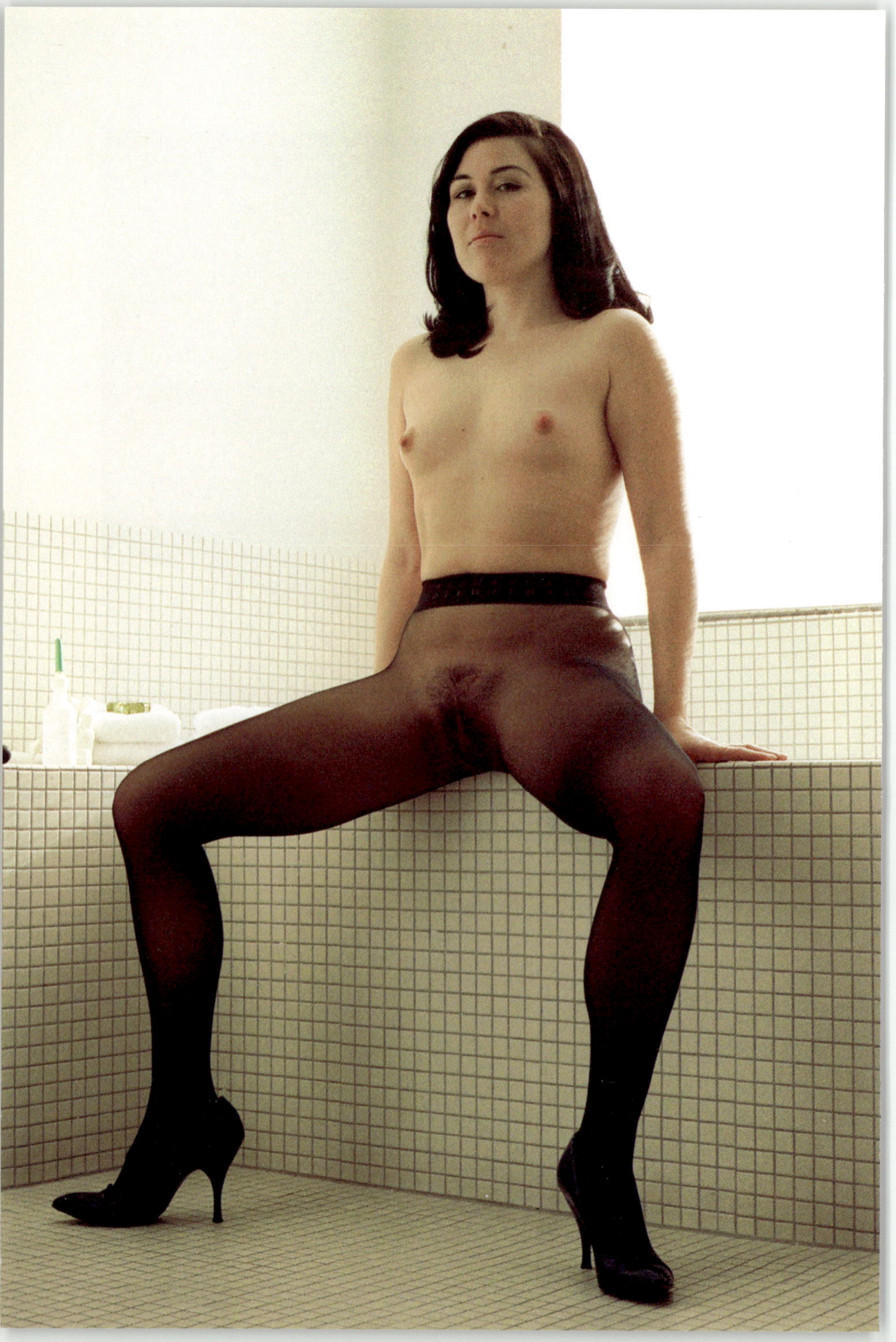

DAVE NAZ

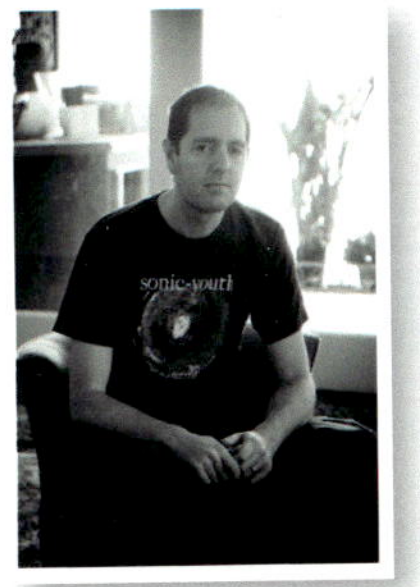

Dave Naz is a self-taught and innovative photographer of sex and meaning, women and landscape. He has published five well-received books with Goliath Press: *Lust Circus* (2002), *Panties* (2003), *Legs* (2004), *Fresh: Girls Of Seduction* (2006), *L.A. Bondage* (2007) and *Butt Babes* (2011). His work has appeared in *GQ*, *Maxim*, *Salon* and on Stern.de, and in international collections including *The New Erotic Photography* (Taschen, 2007) and *Self-Exposure: The Male Nude Self-Portrait* (Universe, 2005). Dave's photographs are shown in galleries all over the world. He lives in the southern California foothills with his wife, artist and performer Oriana, and their menagerie of animals and artwork.

"I have been documenting Oriana Small aka Ashley Blue in photos since 2006. We collaborated on the book *Anal Sex Love* (Editions Reuss, 2010)."

www.davenaz.com

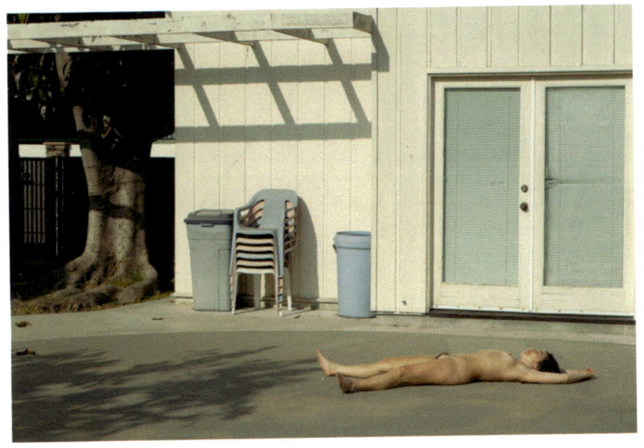

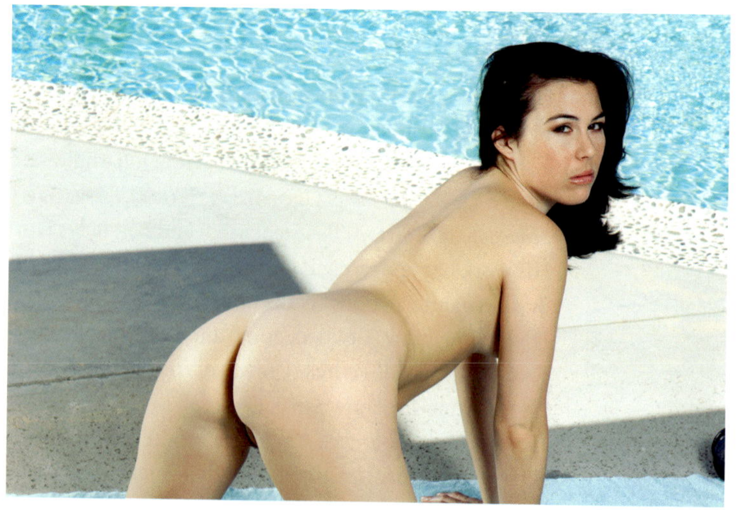

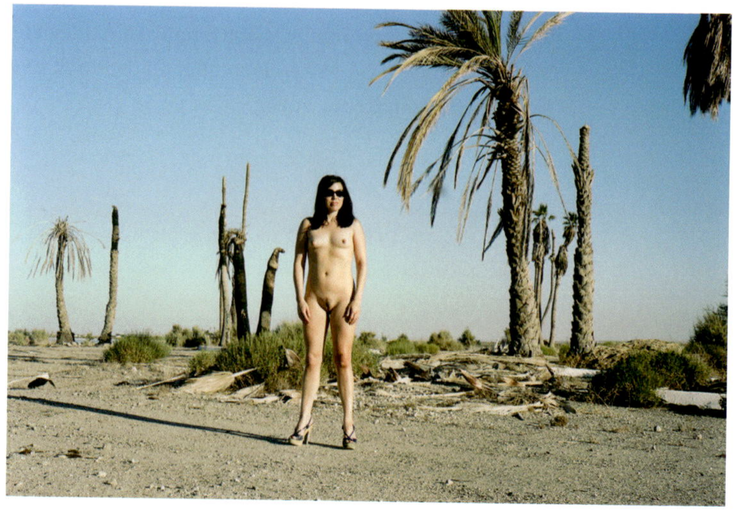

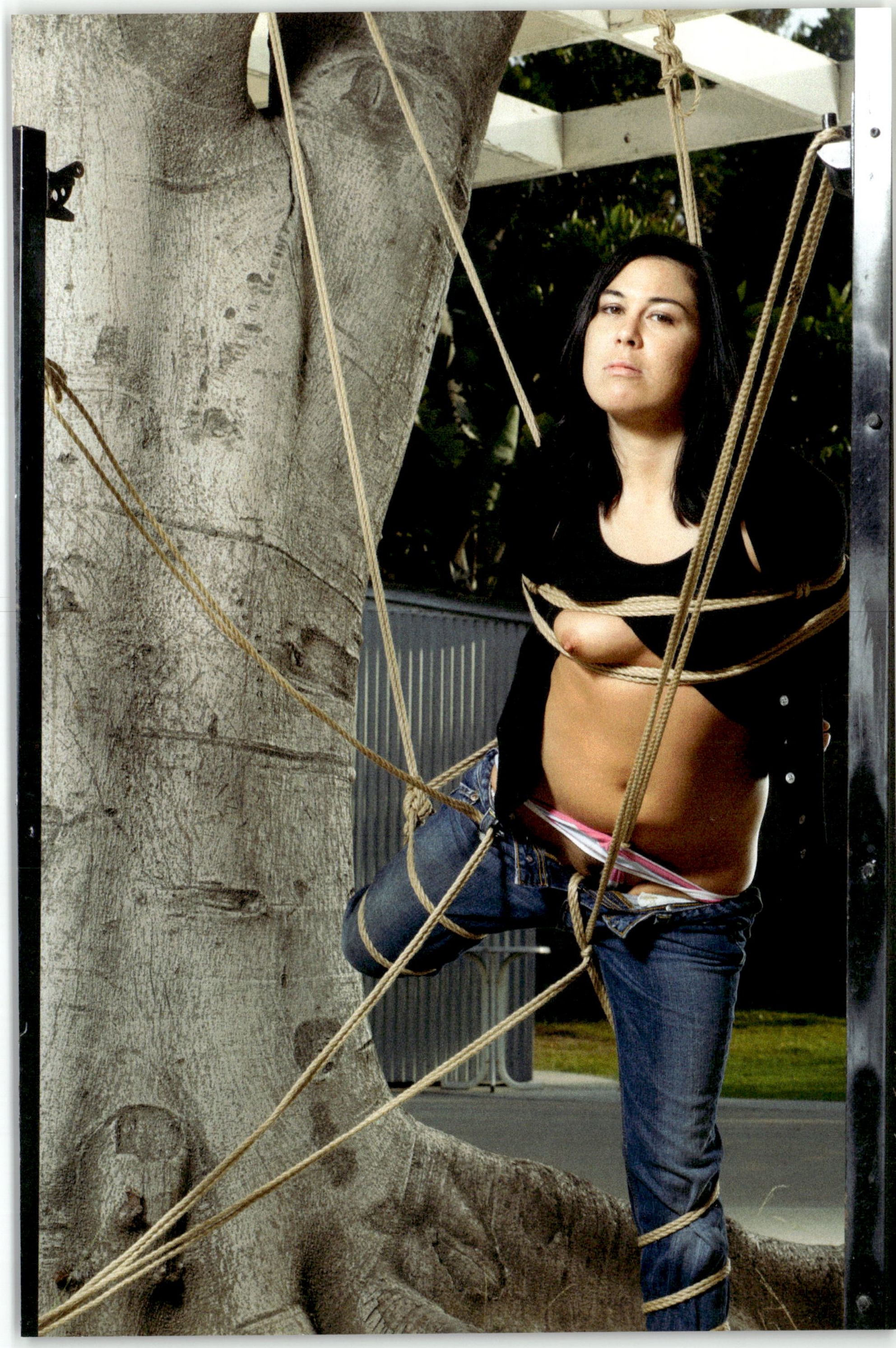

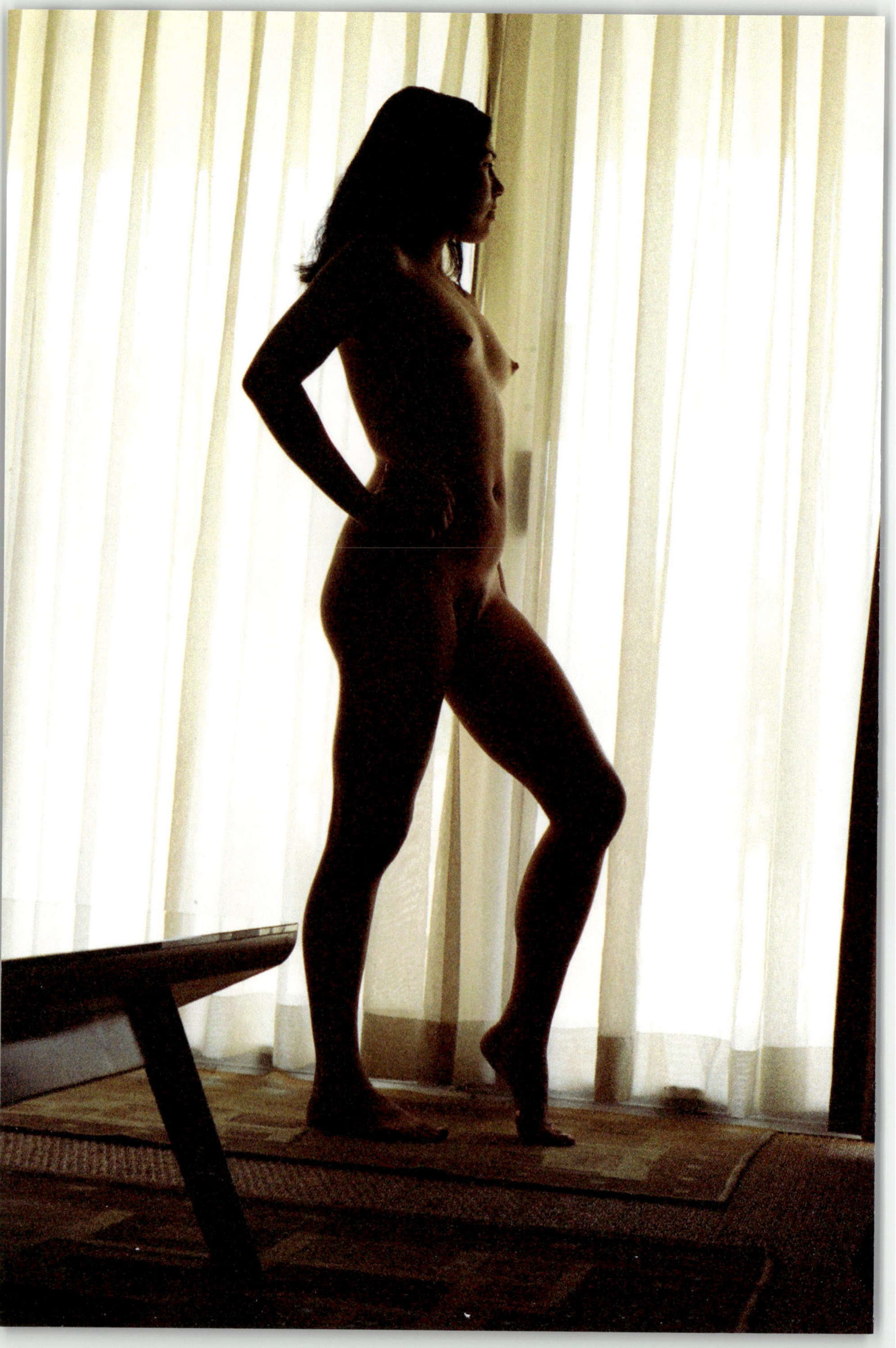

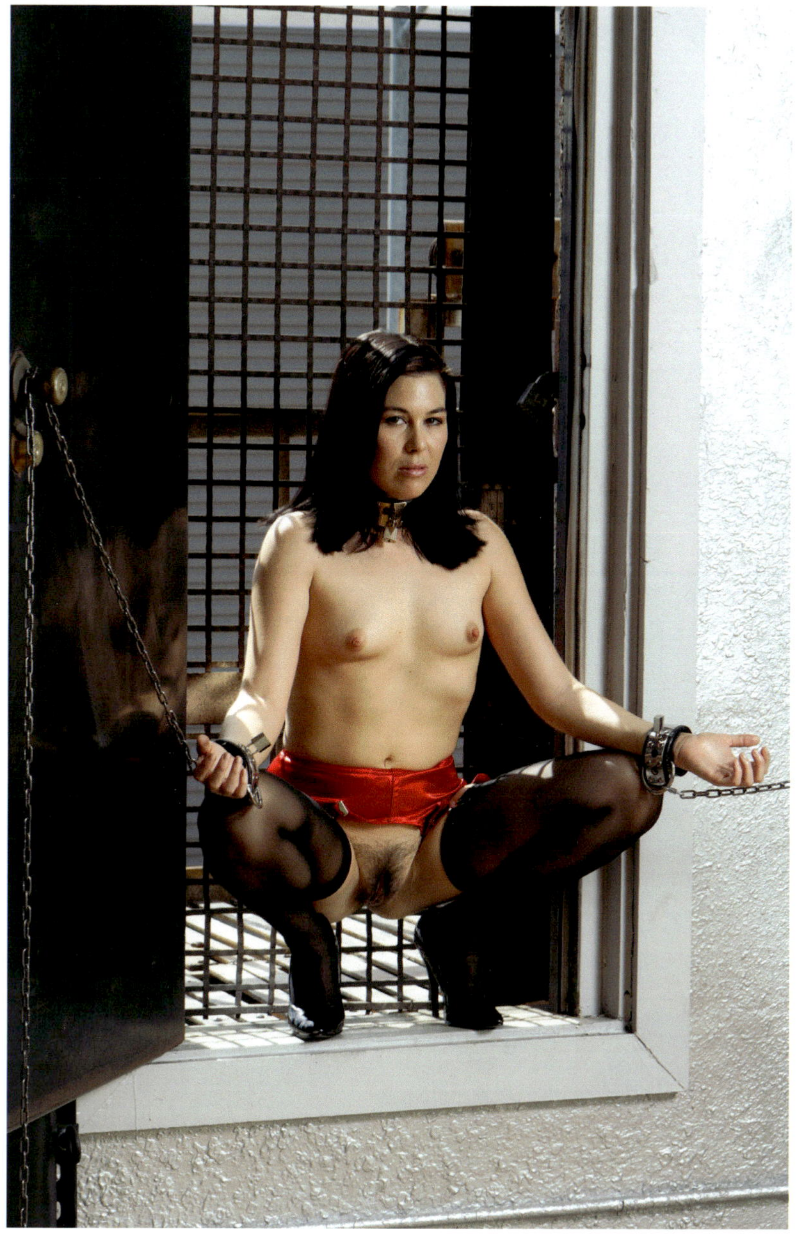

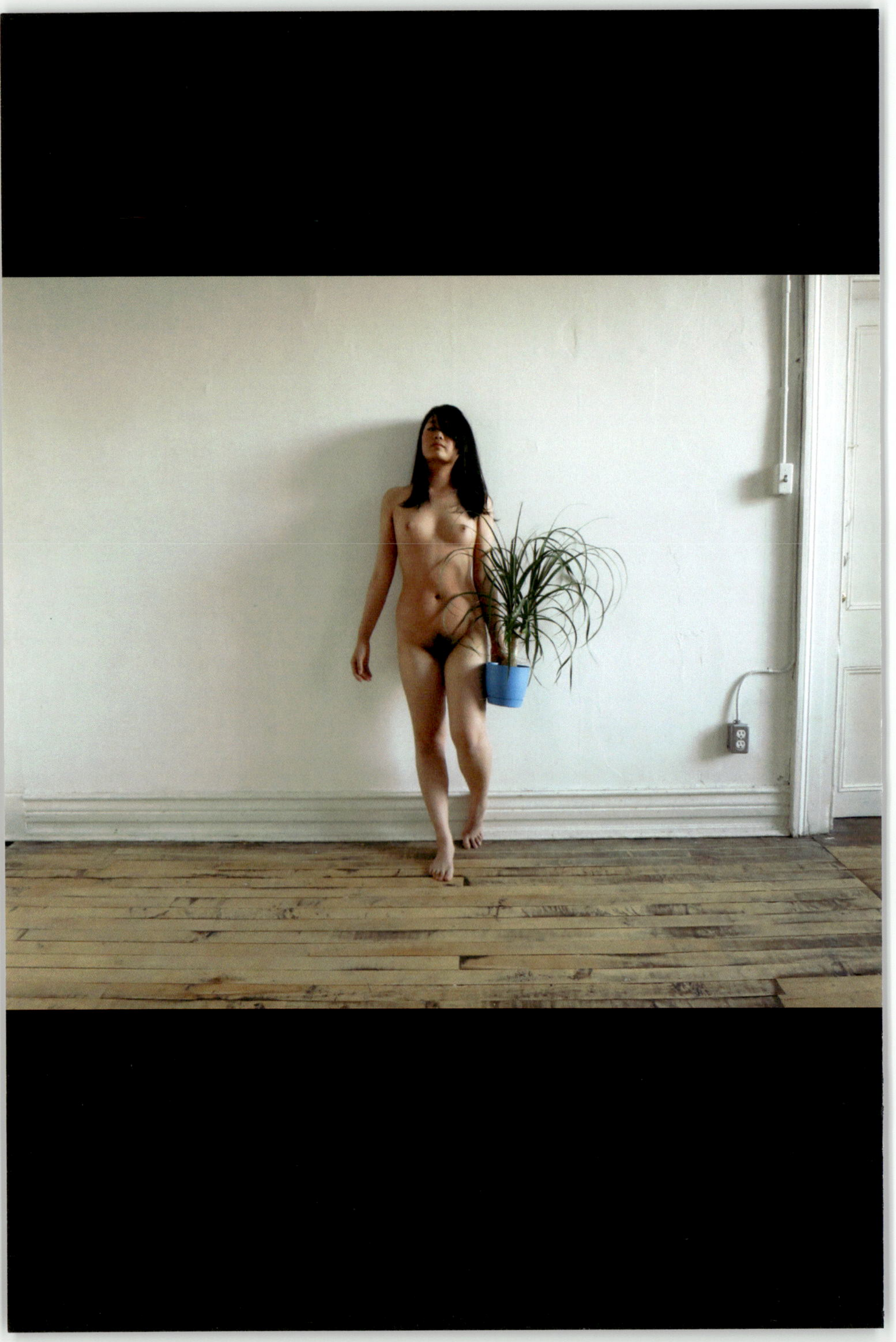

ROB NELSON

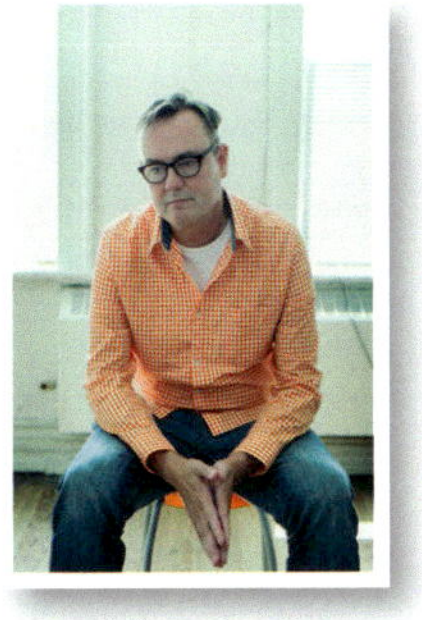

"A second-generation Canadian photographer, I apprenticed with my father as a teenager doing aerial photography. My love of magazines led me to shooting fashion editorial assignments and gallery shows. My work has appeared on Nerve.com and in *Interview* magazine. My muse is an artist that I met at a gallery opening. I chose to photograph her because she is an artist and understands the creative process. She has a strong sense of personal style, which comes through even when she isn't wearing anything."

www.robnelsonphotography.com

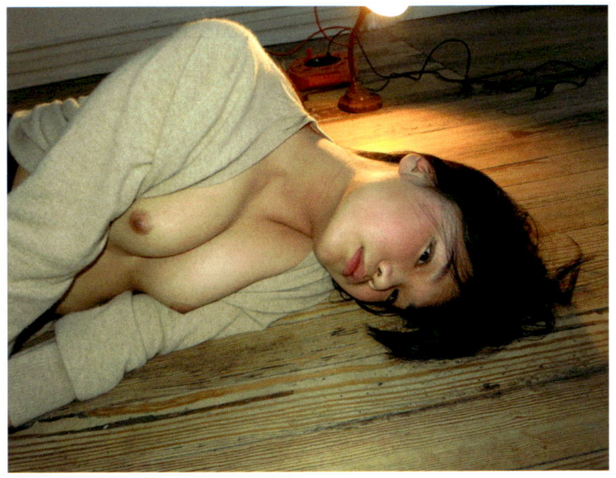

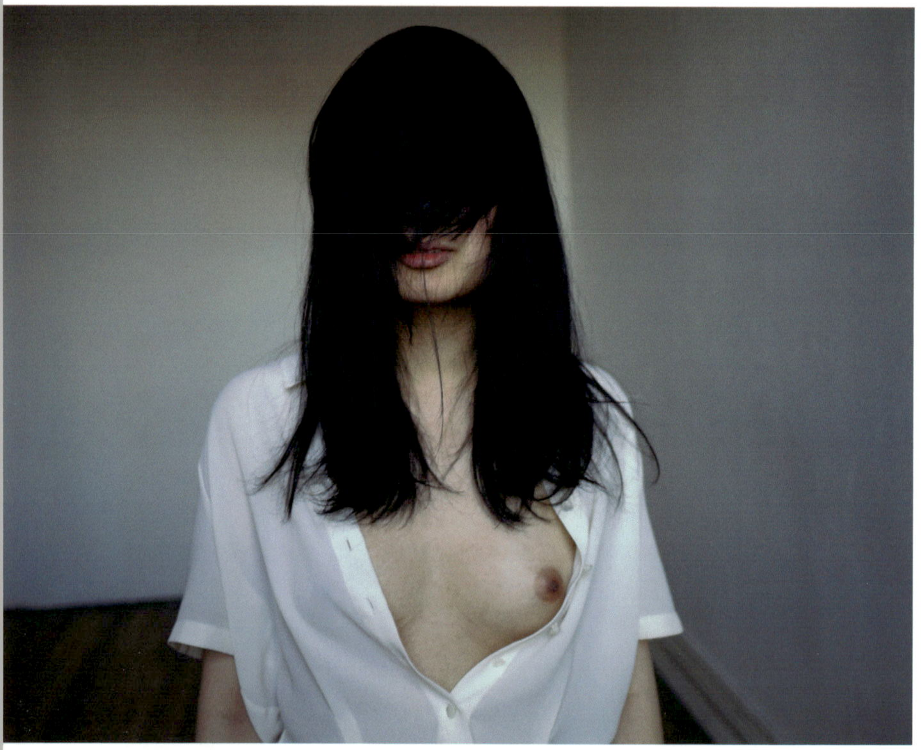

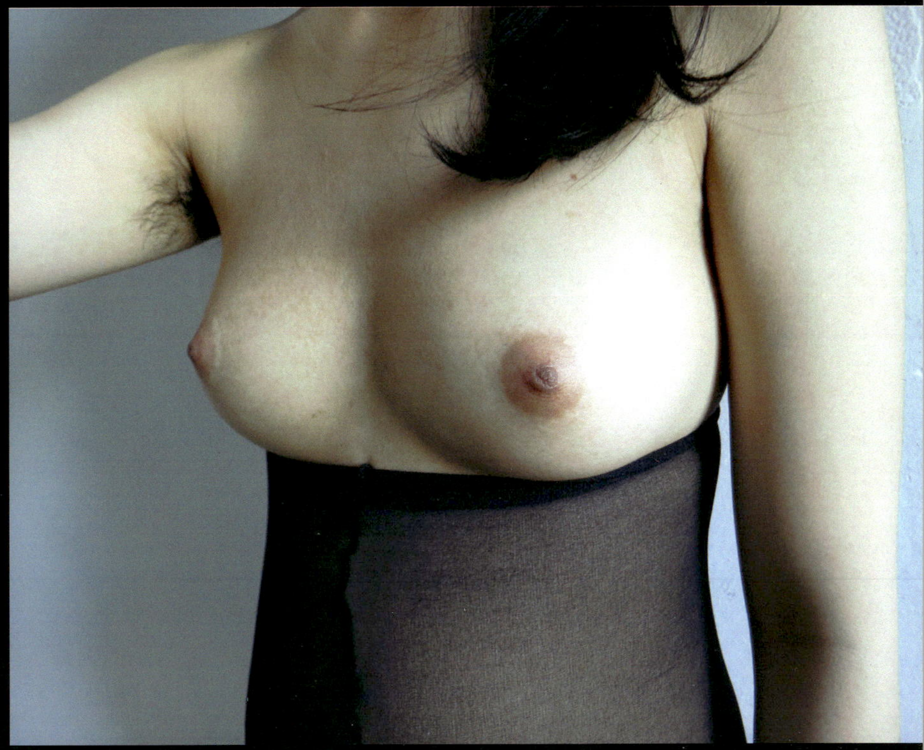

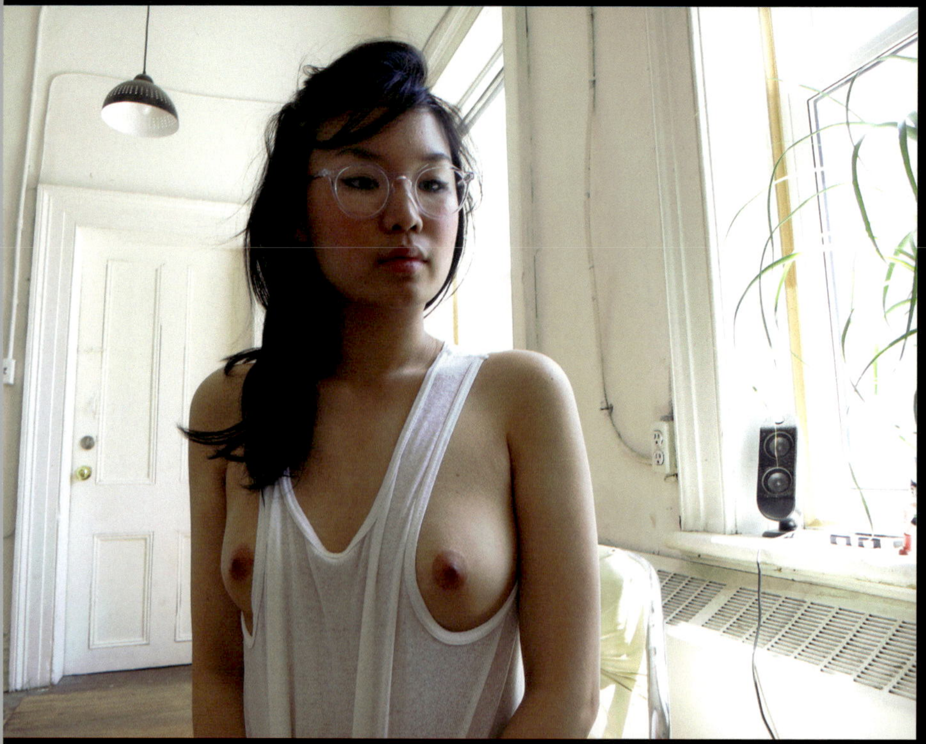

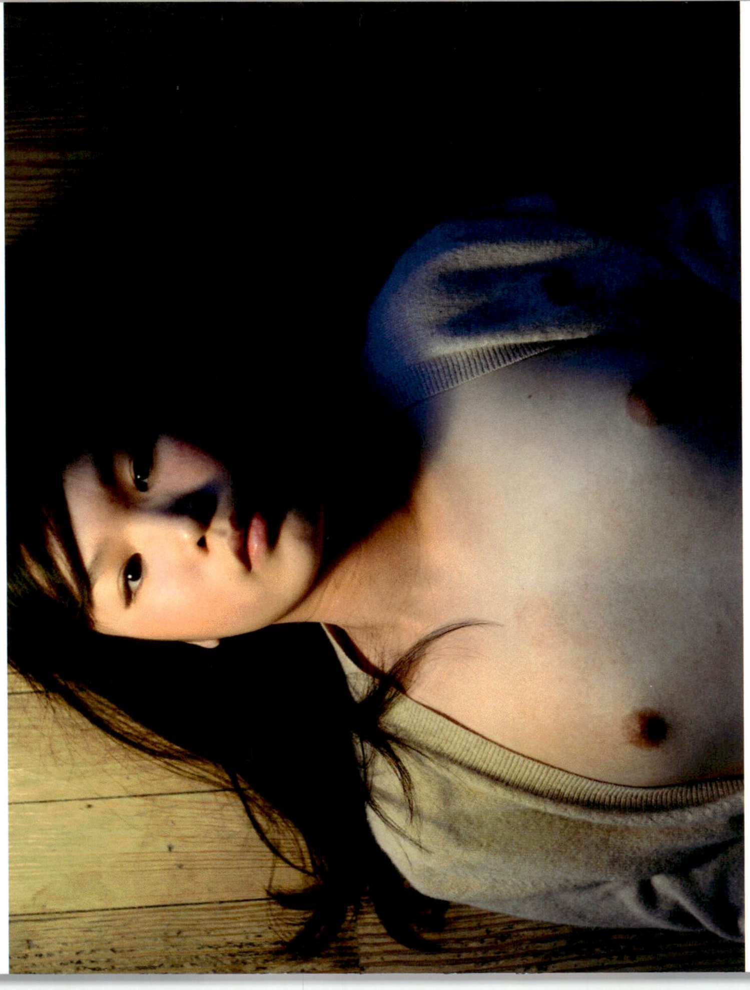

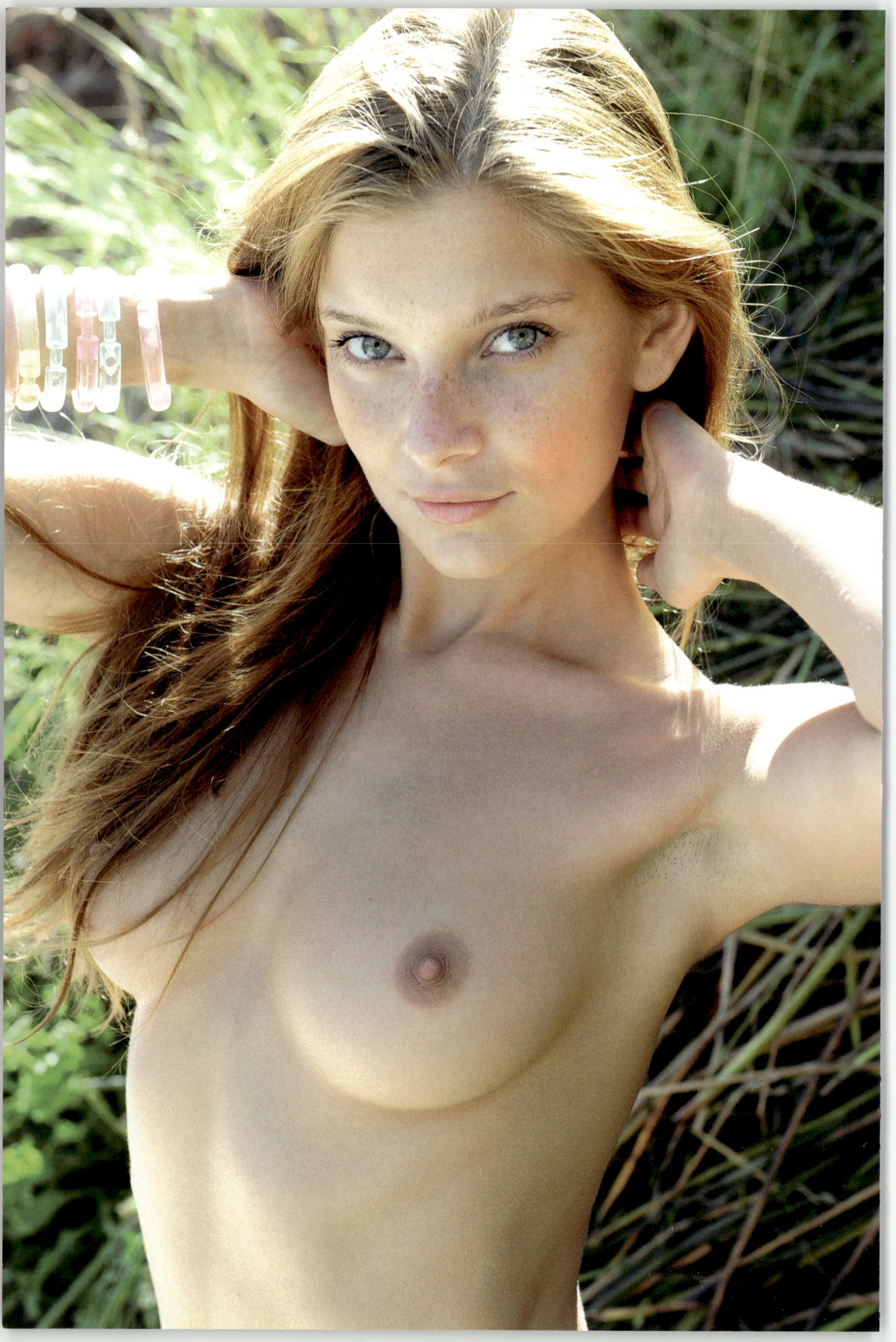

MIKHAIL PARAMONOV

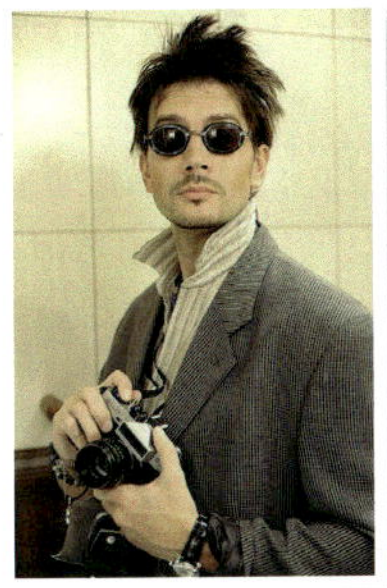

A master of the erotic style, Russian photographer Mikhail Paramonov was born in 1975 in St Petersburg. He first held a camera at the age of fourteen and has not let it go since. He studied at the Faculty of Arts of the St Petersburg State Theatre Arts Academy, and since 2002 has concentrated on erotic photography.

www.mikhailparamonov.com

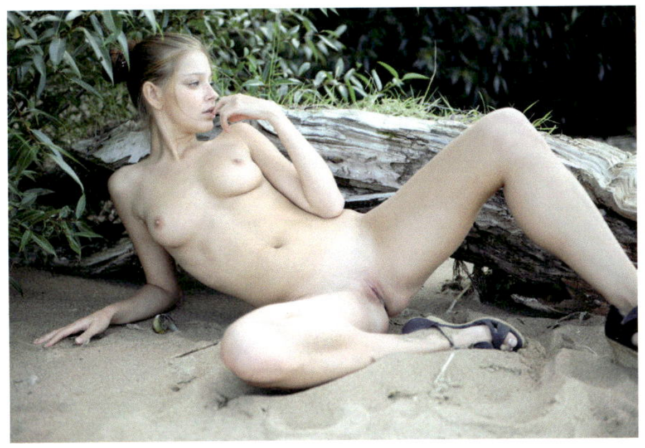

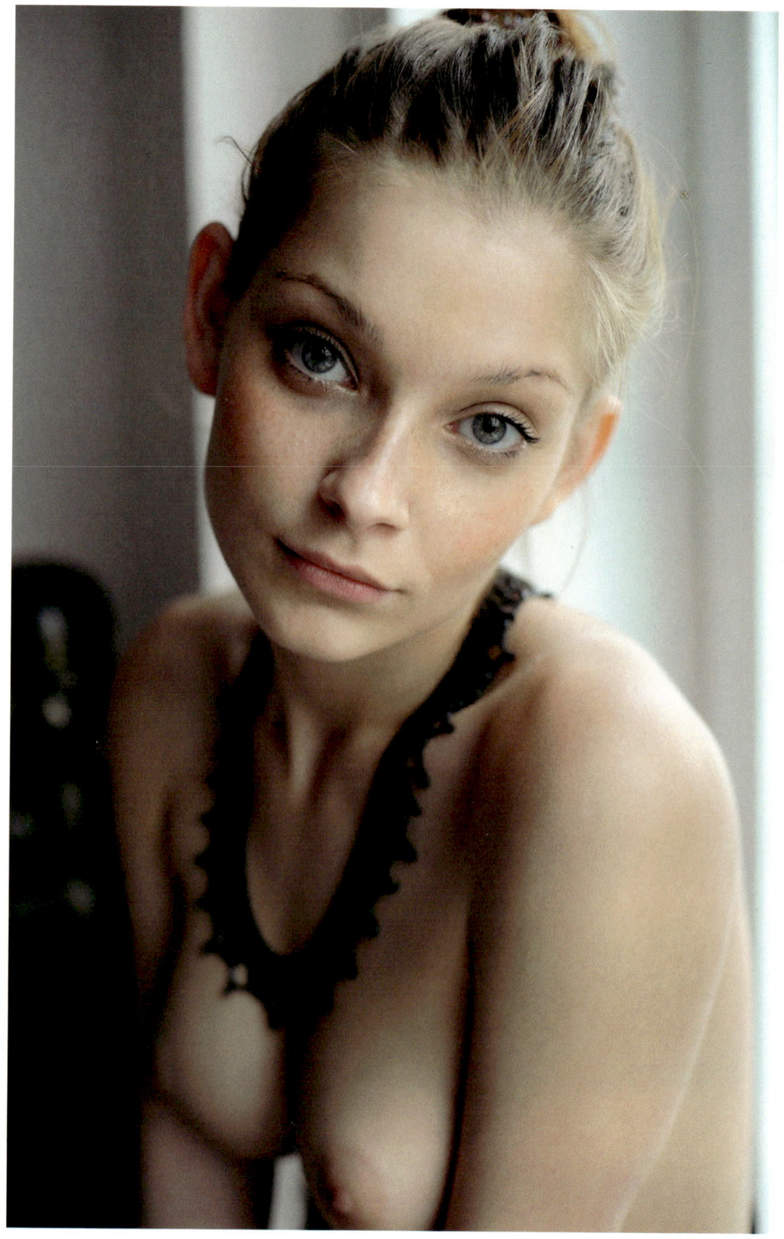

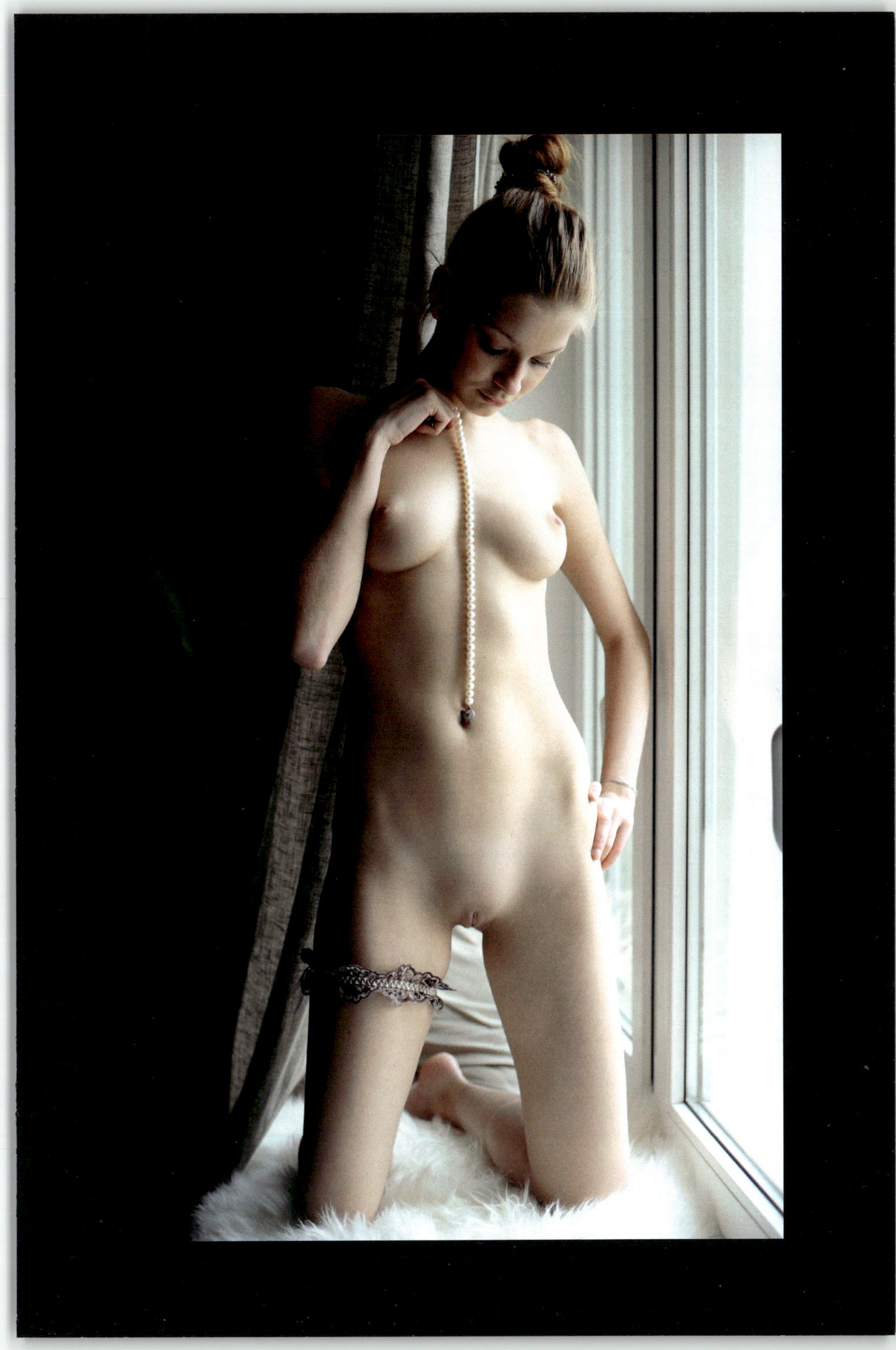

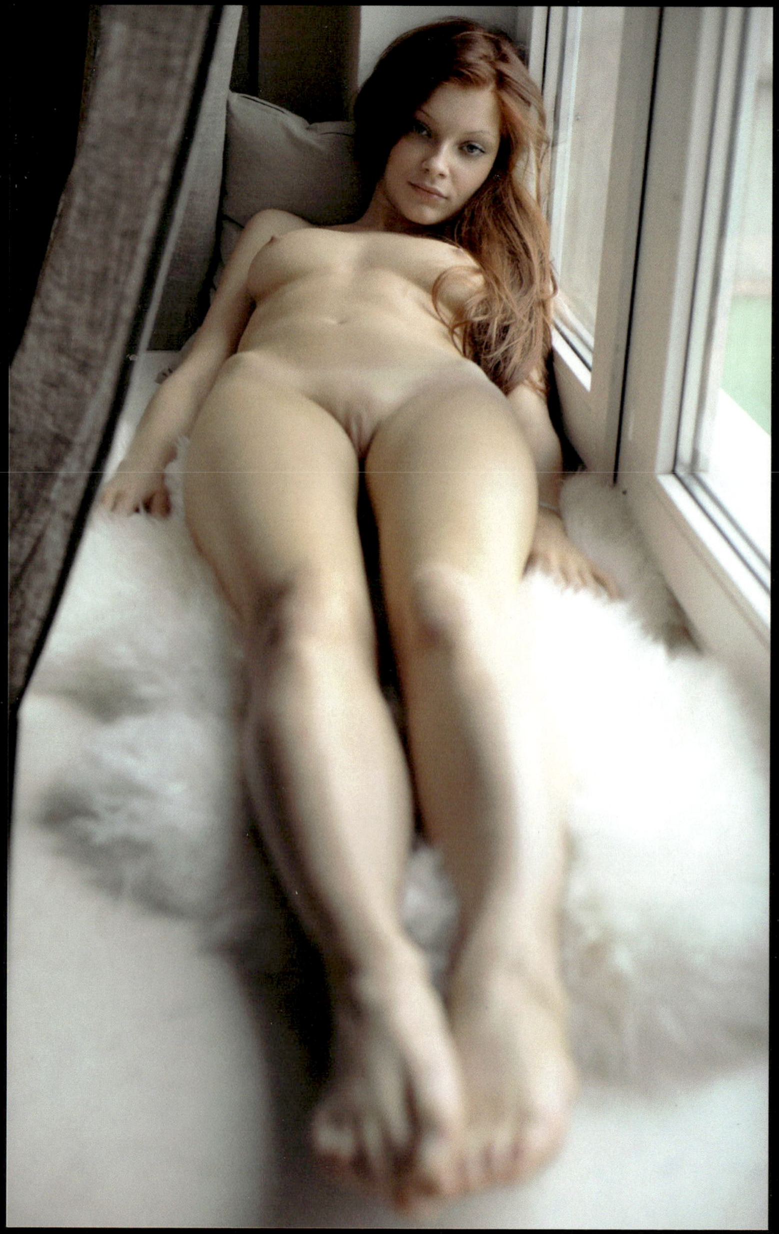

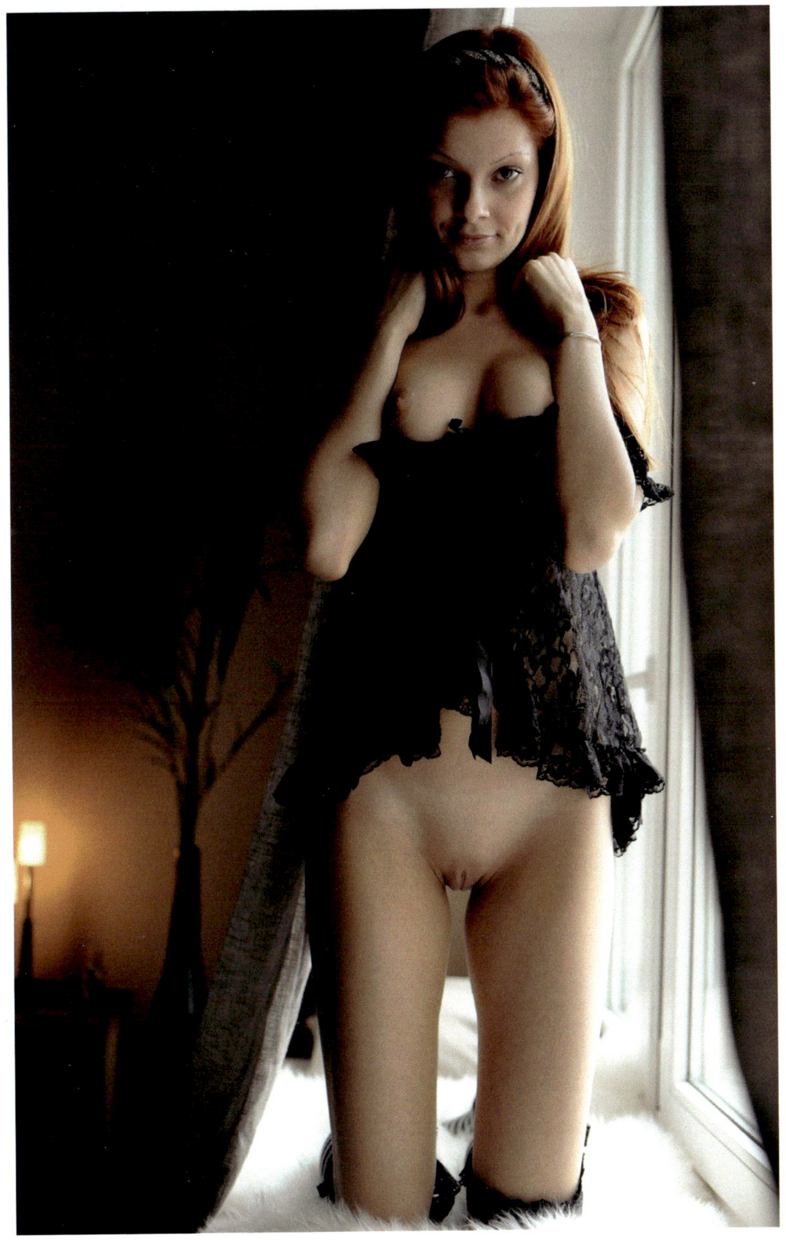

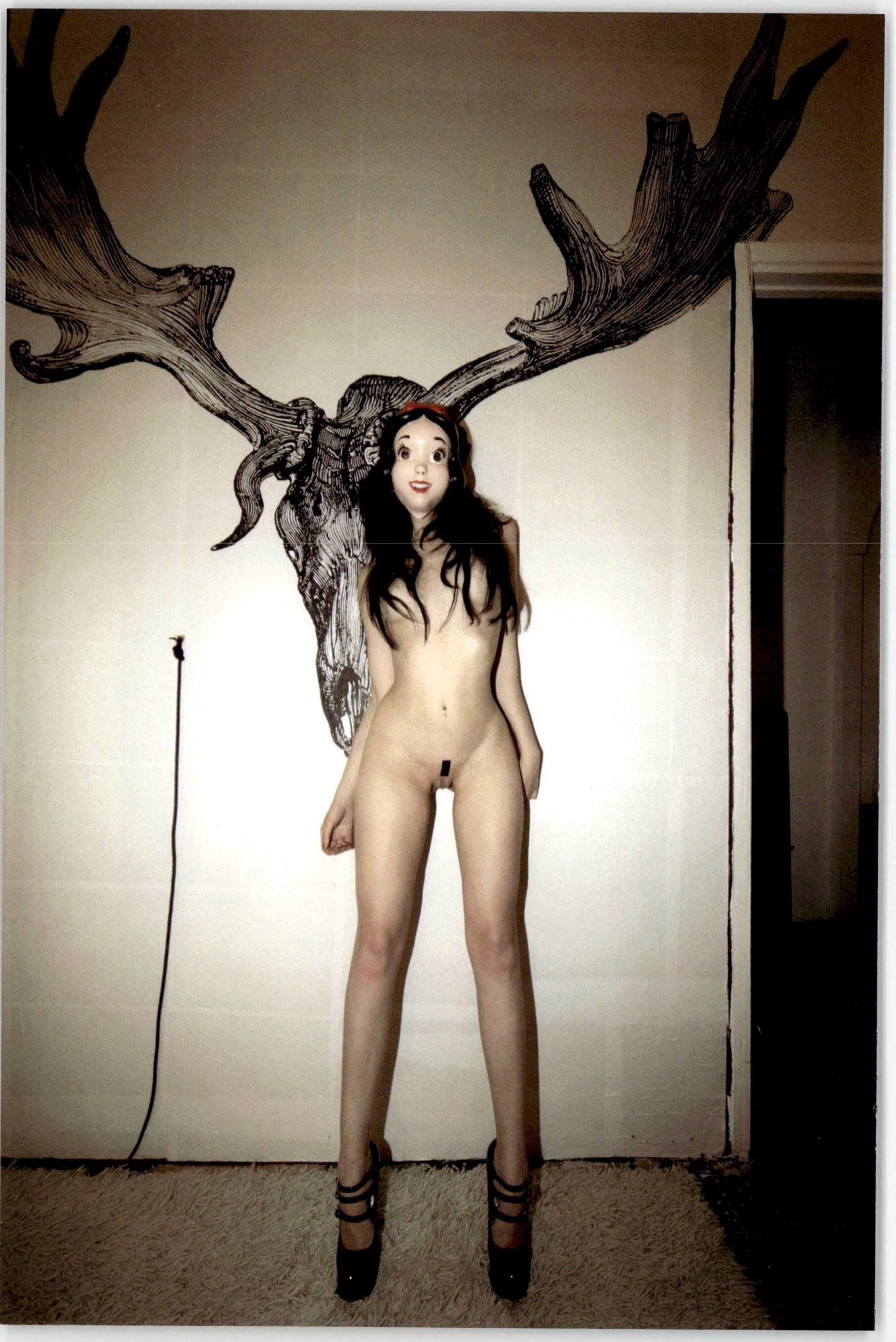

DANILO PASQUALI

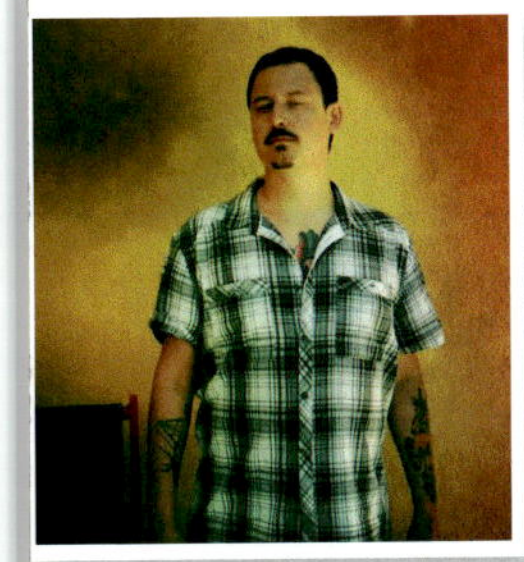

"I'm thirty-seven and live in Milan. For nearly ten years my photography has concentrated on eroticism and indie porn. My pictures are erotic, and I don't want anything hidden behind the eroticism. This 'other' belongs to me, to my cultural background. I observe photography, cinema, art, but, above all, life. I try to recreate the atmospheres I feel. I produce erotic images because I like it, and because pornography, outside of its context, has a revolutionary significance, especially in the 'bella Italia' of recent times.

"Geneva is a great girl, natural to work with. With her I create and build the sets, I choose the photos and we discuss the work. Not only does she fully represent my work, but its tone has changed and shaped around her."

www.mi-undressed.com
www.danilopasquali.com

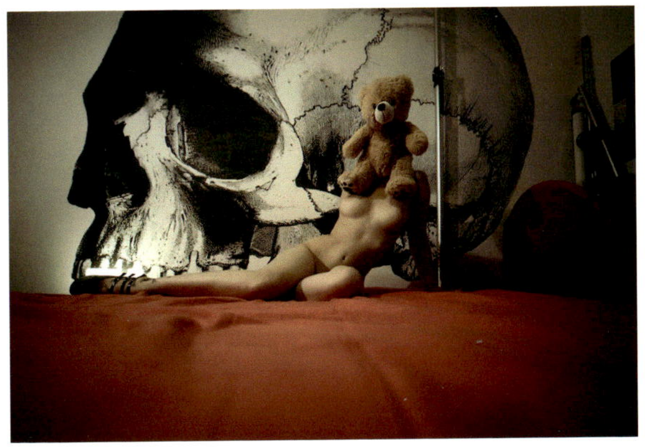

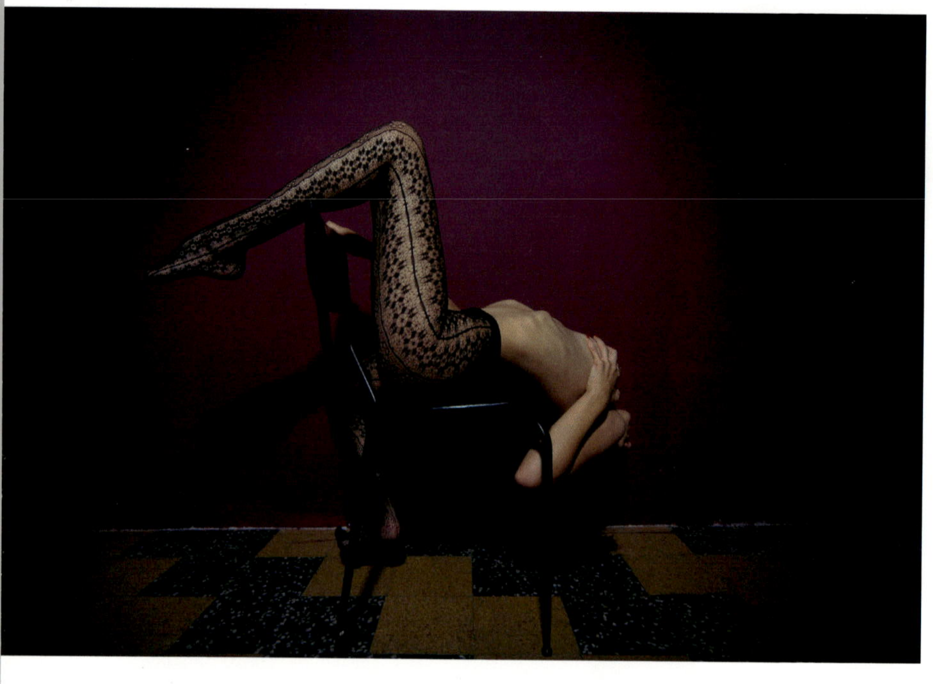

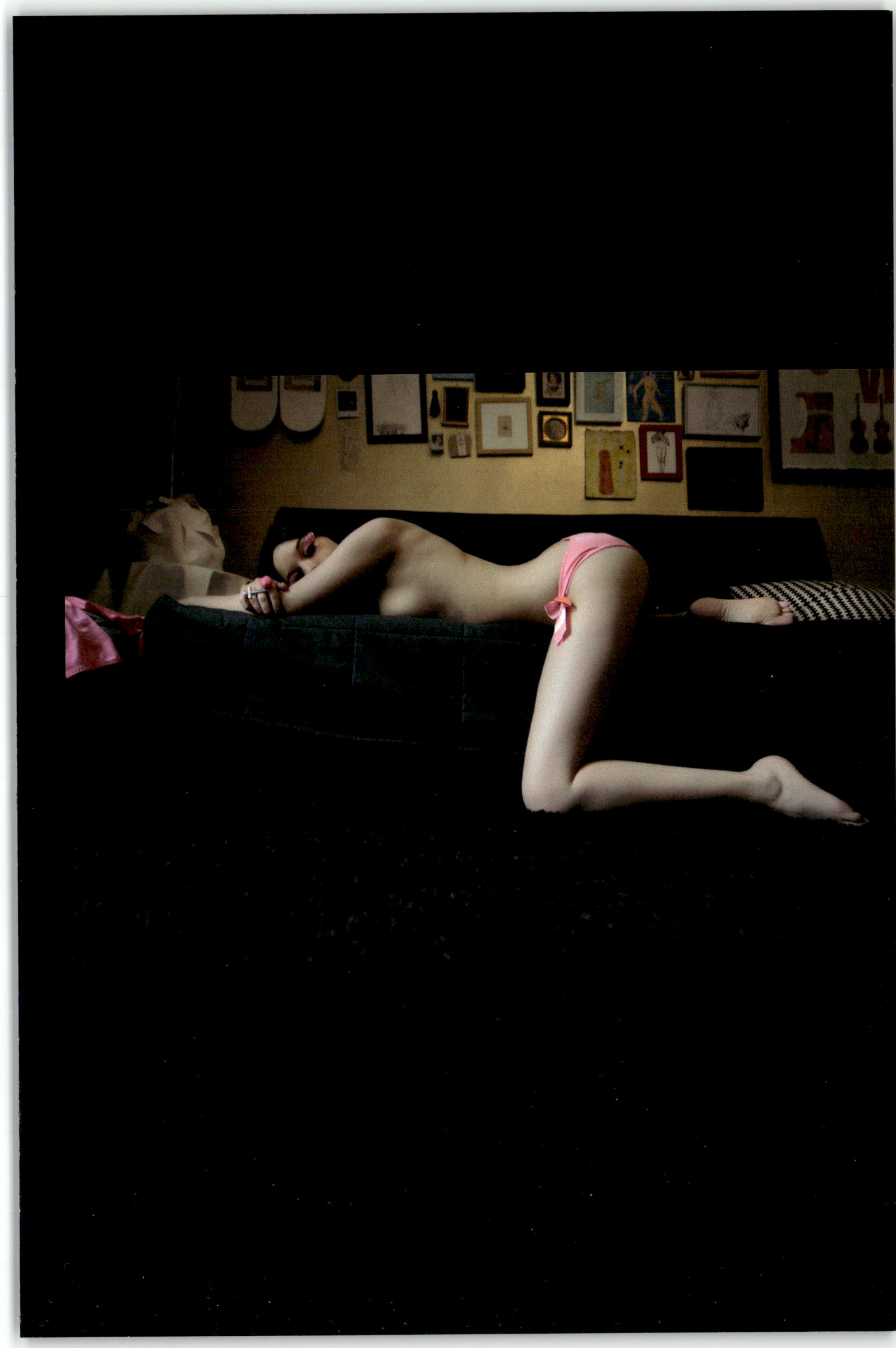

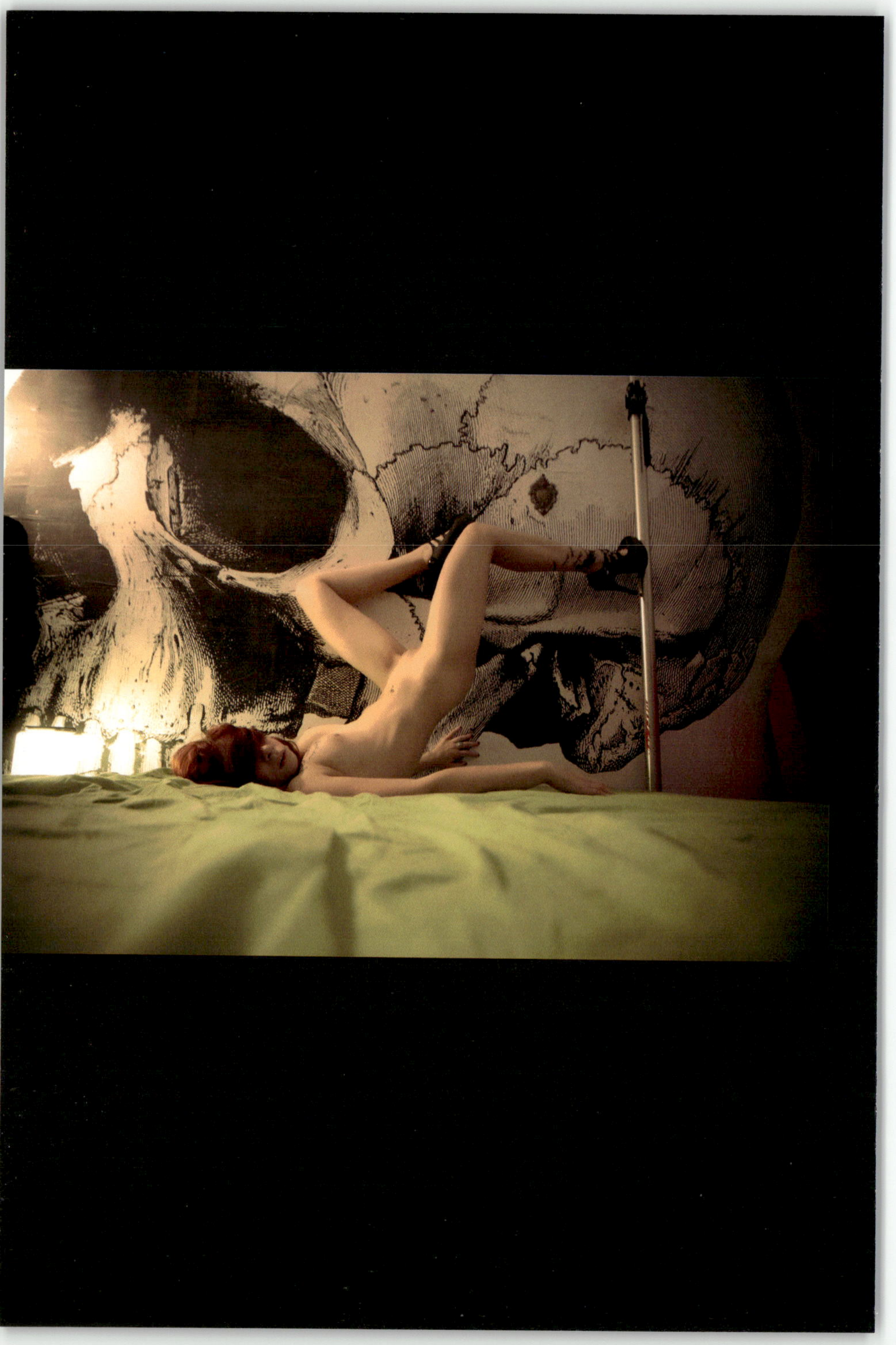

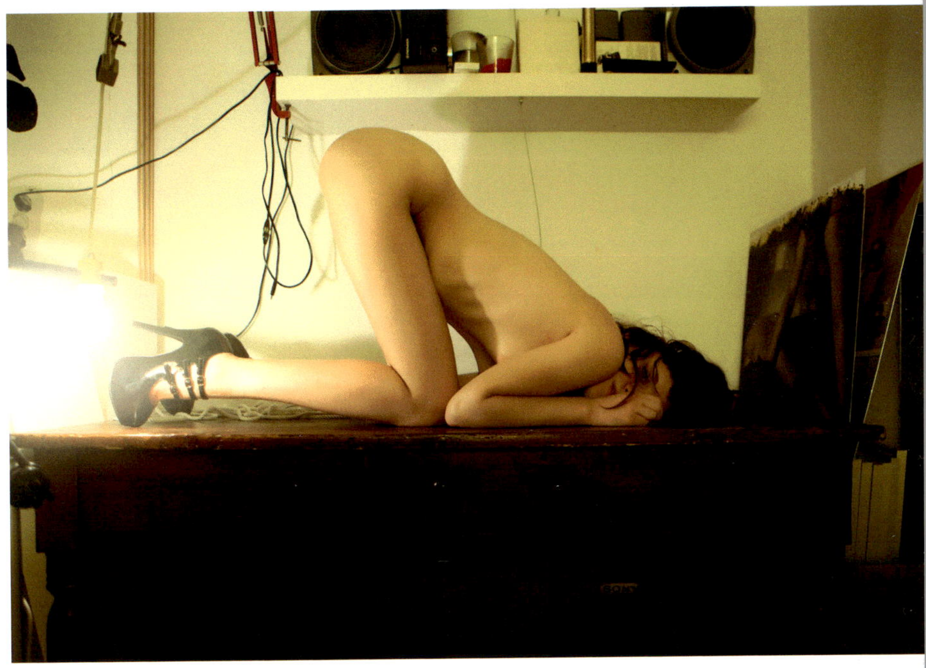

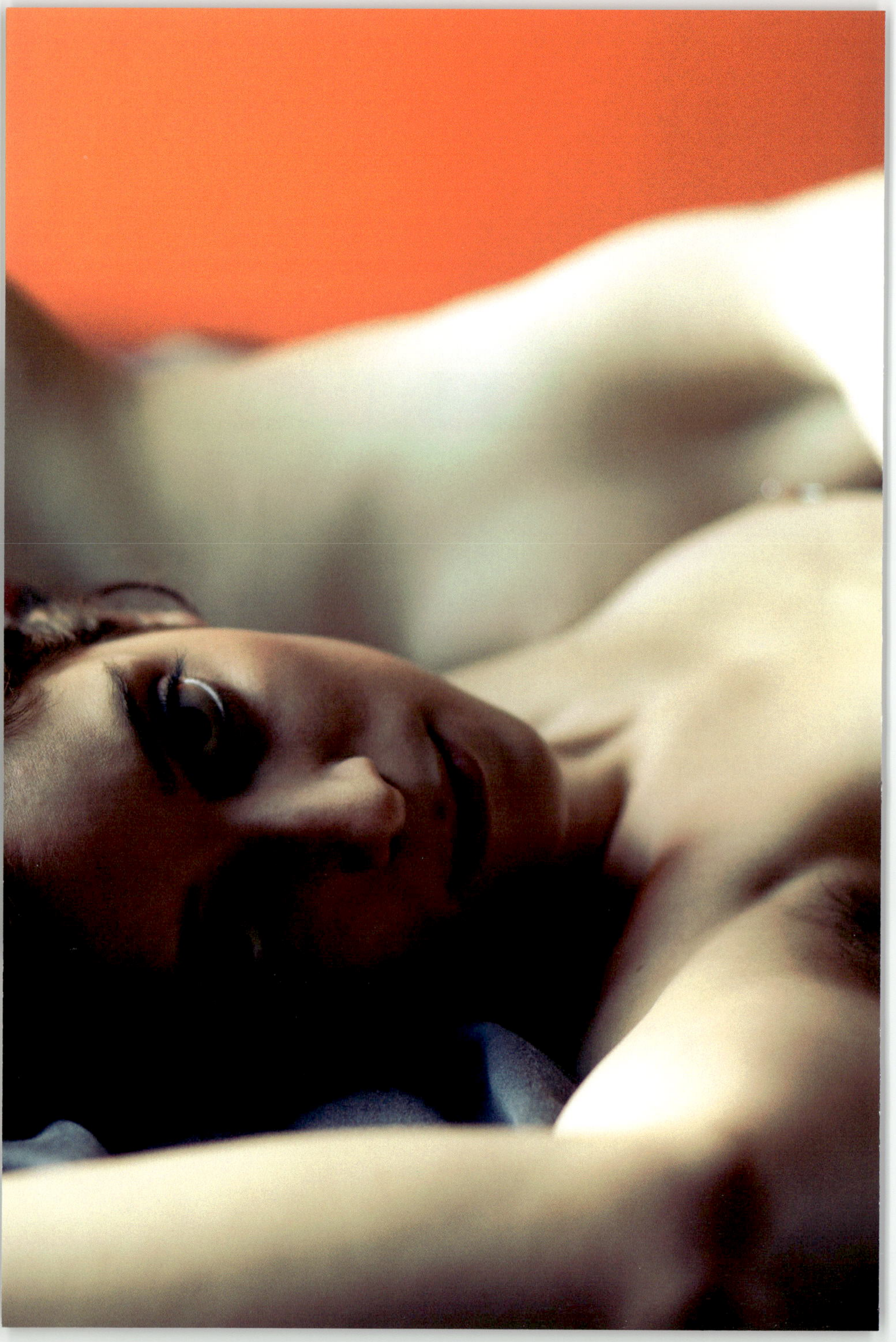

TIMOTHY PATRICK

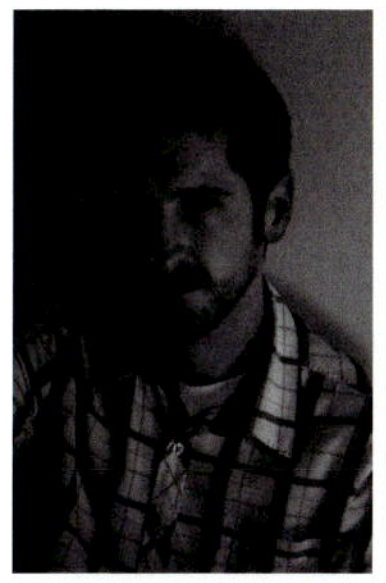

"I bought my first DSLR and began taking photographs to complement my graphic design work. My love of the medium grew and soon I discovered the beauty of the art nude and joined the growing movement of artists showcasing their work on online forums. Drawn to capturing women as naturally as possible, I prefer simplicity over excess, collaboration over direction and proving that imperfections are beautiful.

"I first shot Cam Damage in San Francisco in 2012 and fell in love with how authentic she is in front of the camera. Her lithe body complements her easygoing personality, and her passion for creating is ever-present and contagious. She's a true 'girl next door' and it's easy to see why so many photographers seek her out and fans follow her every move."

www.timothy-patrick.com

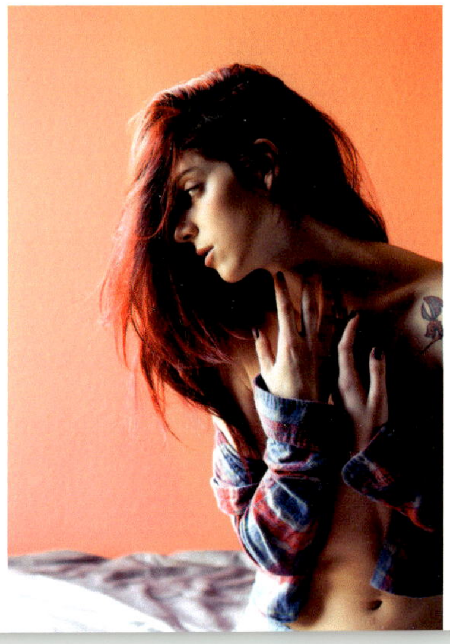

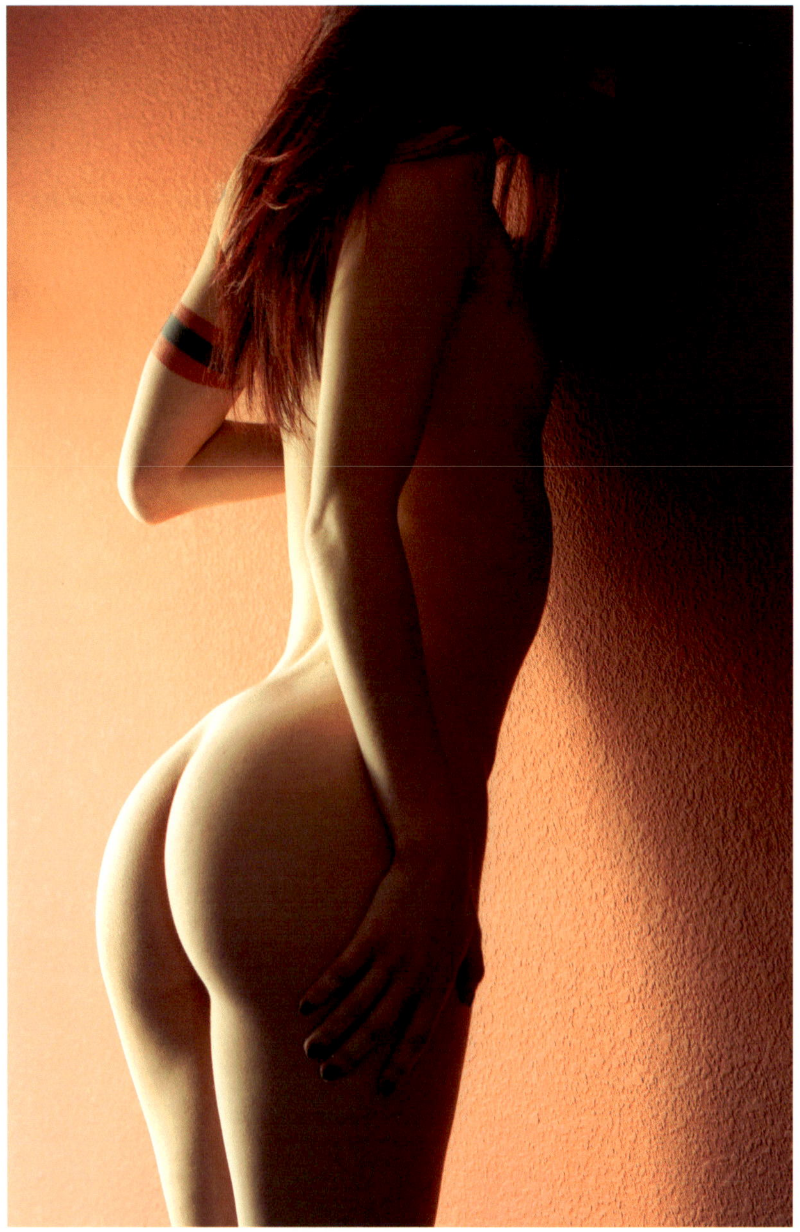

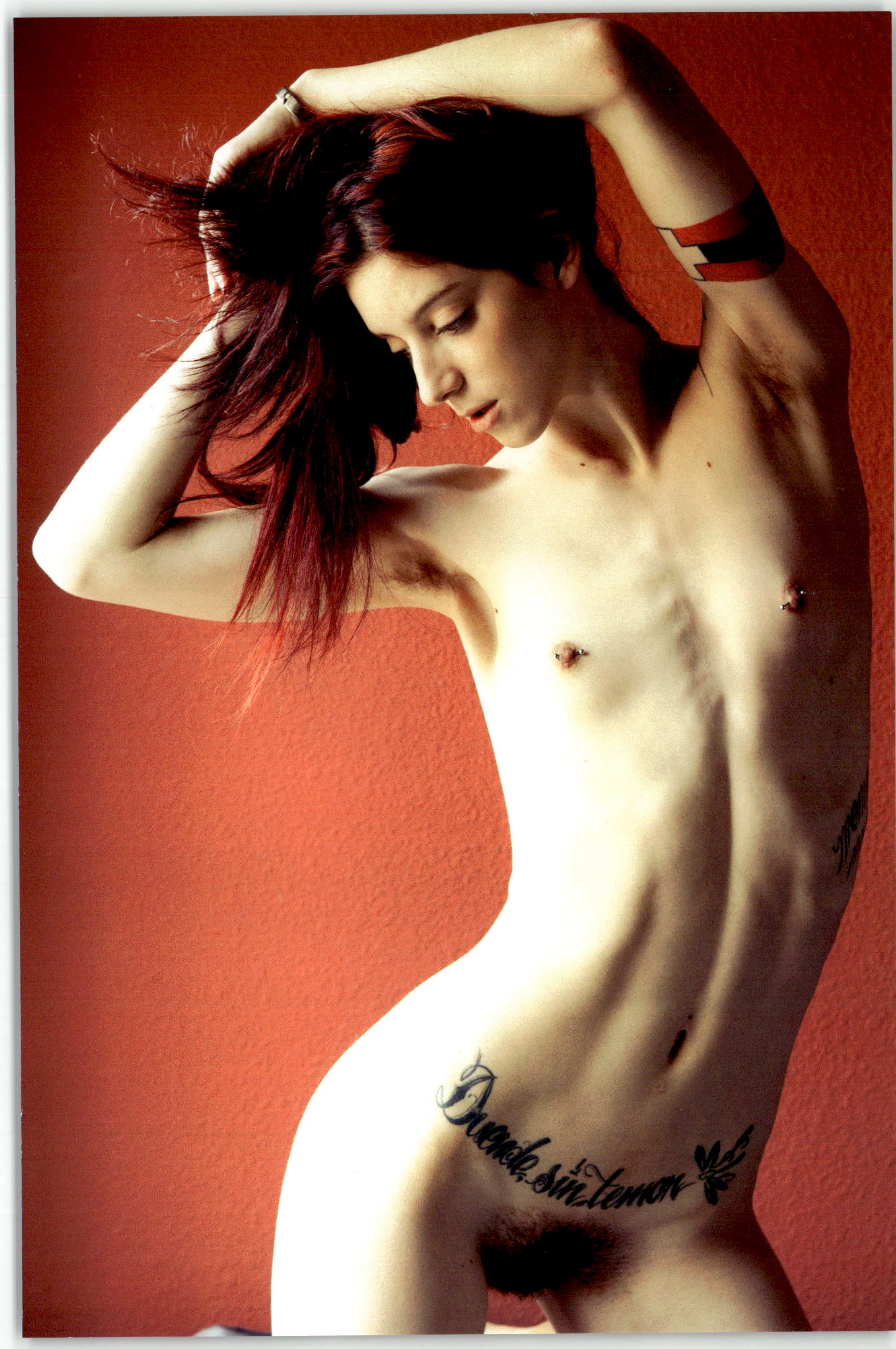
Duende sin temor

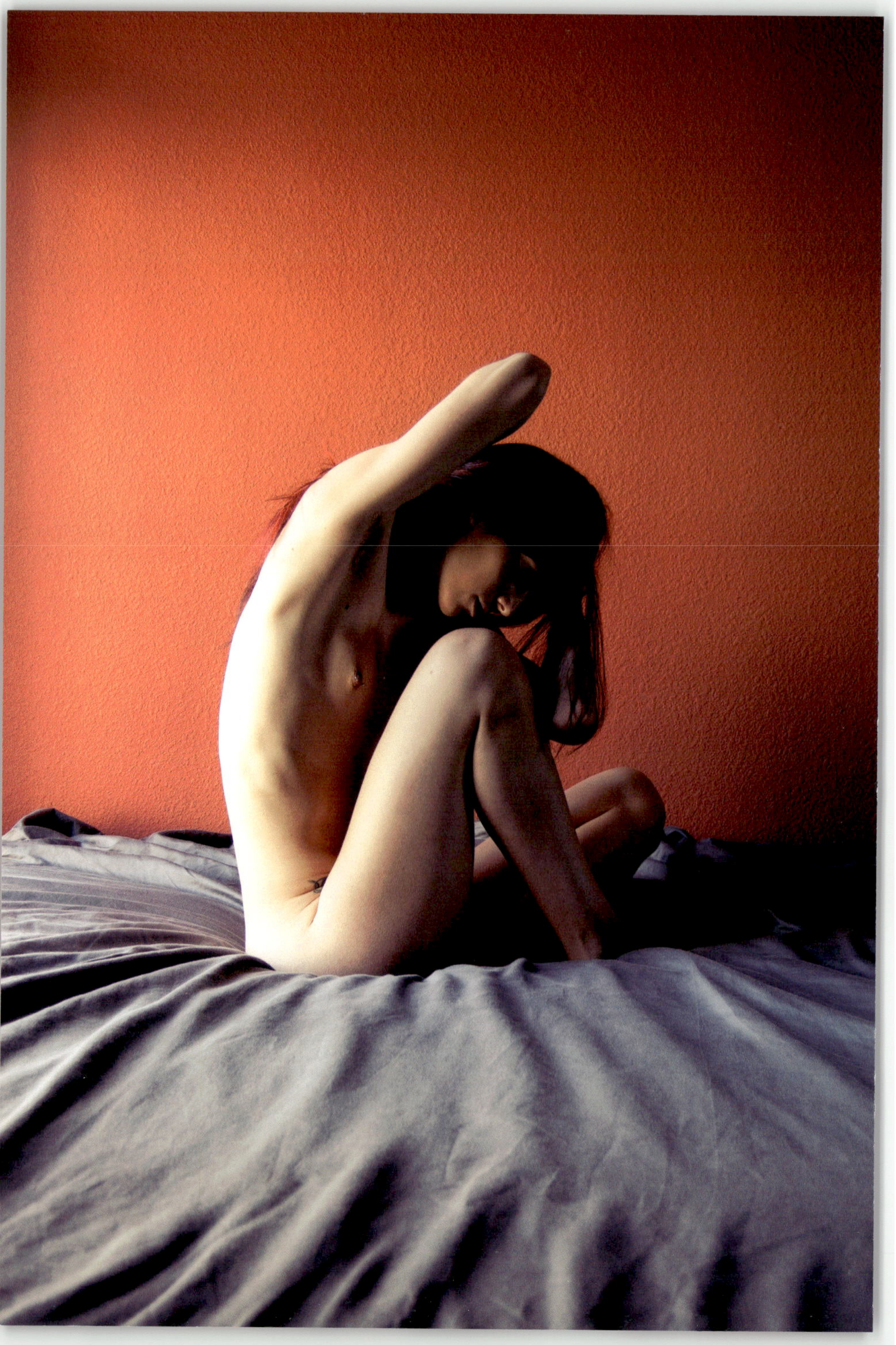

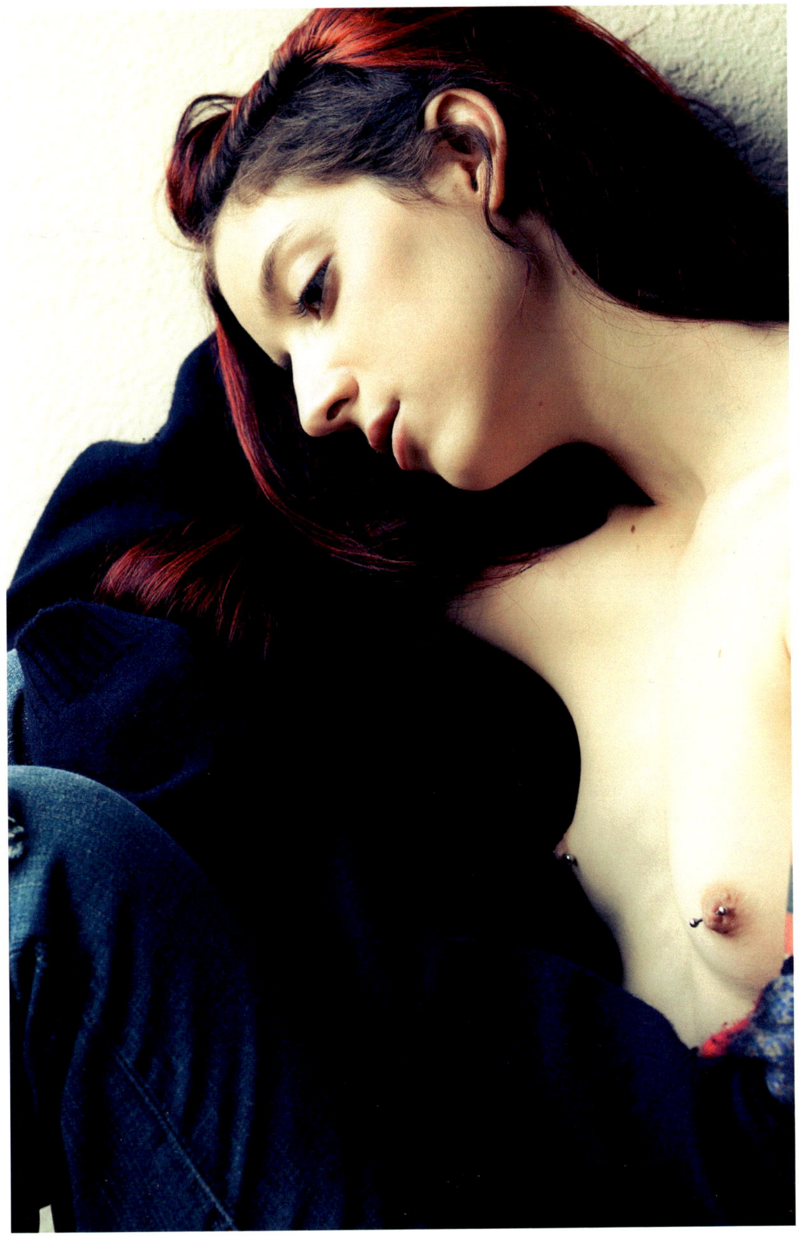

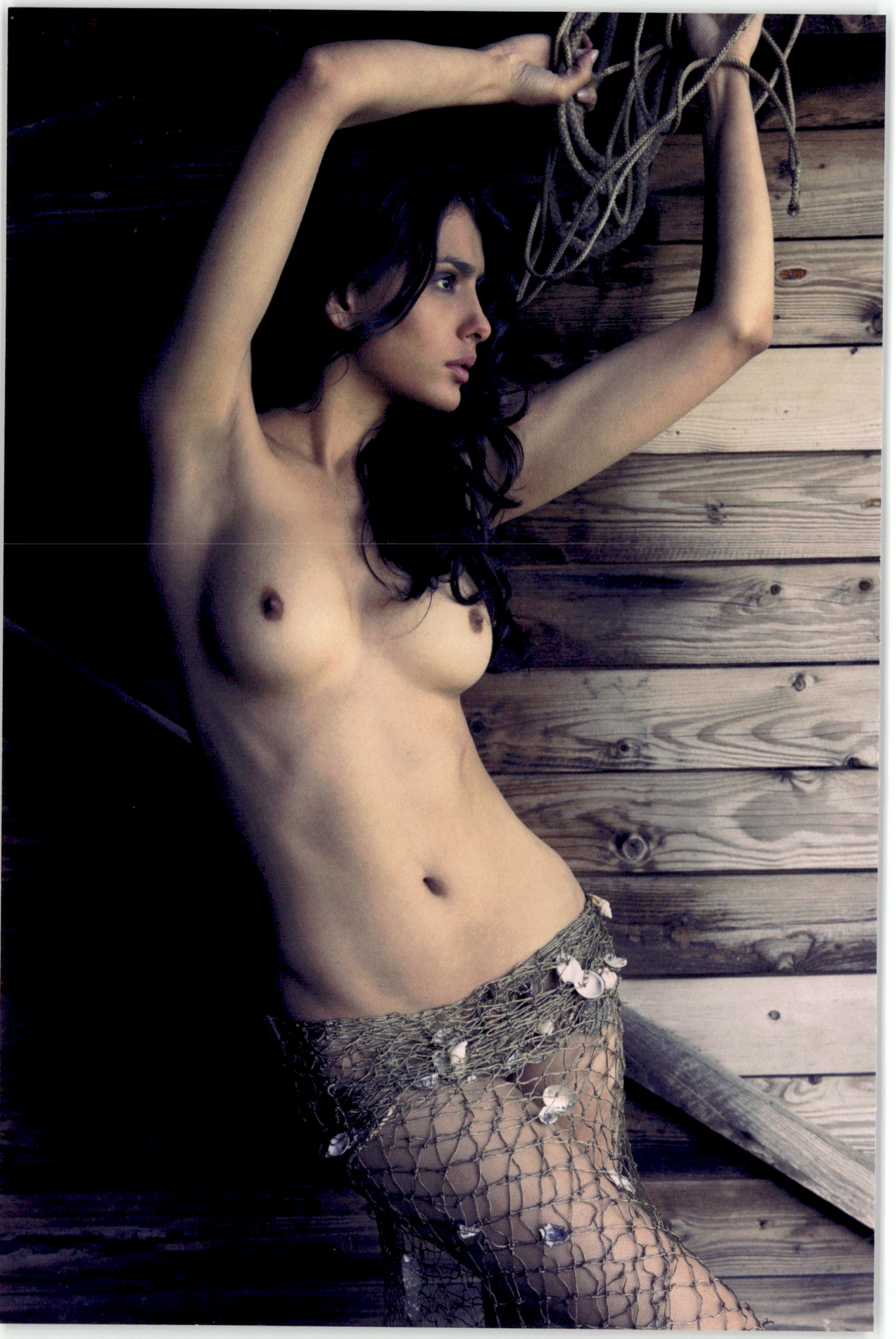

ALEXANDER PAULIN

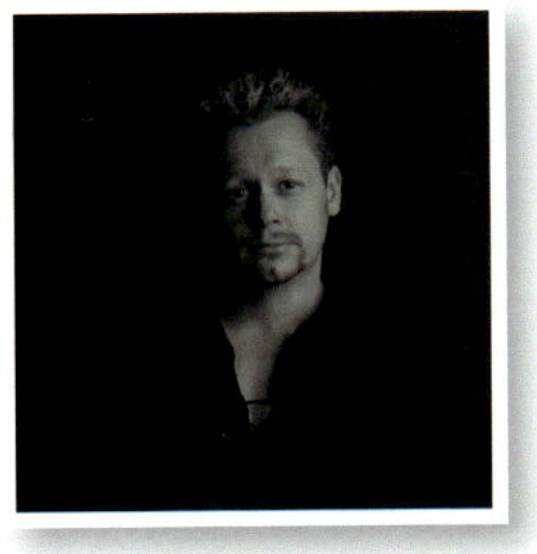

Born in 1967 in Kiel, West Germany, Alexander Paulin started taking photographs when he was fourteen. He has been self-employed, with his own studio, since 1999 and now works for major magazines, including *Playboy*, *Penthouse*, *FHM* and *Stern*, European publishers such as teNeues and Heye, and agencies.

"The model is called Gabriela and comes from Brazil. She was photographed by a lake near Kiel. On that day it was very cold."

www.alexanderpaulin.de

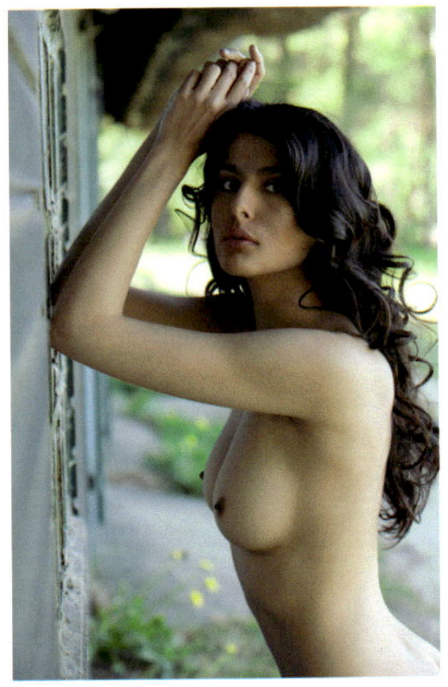

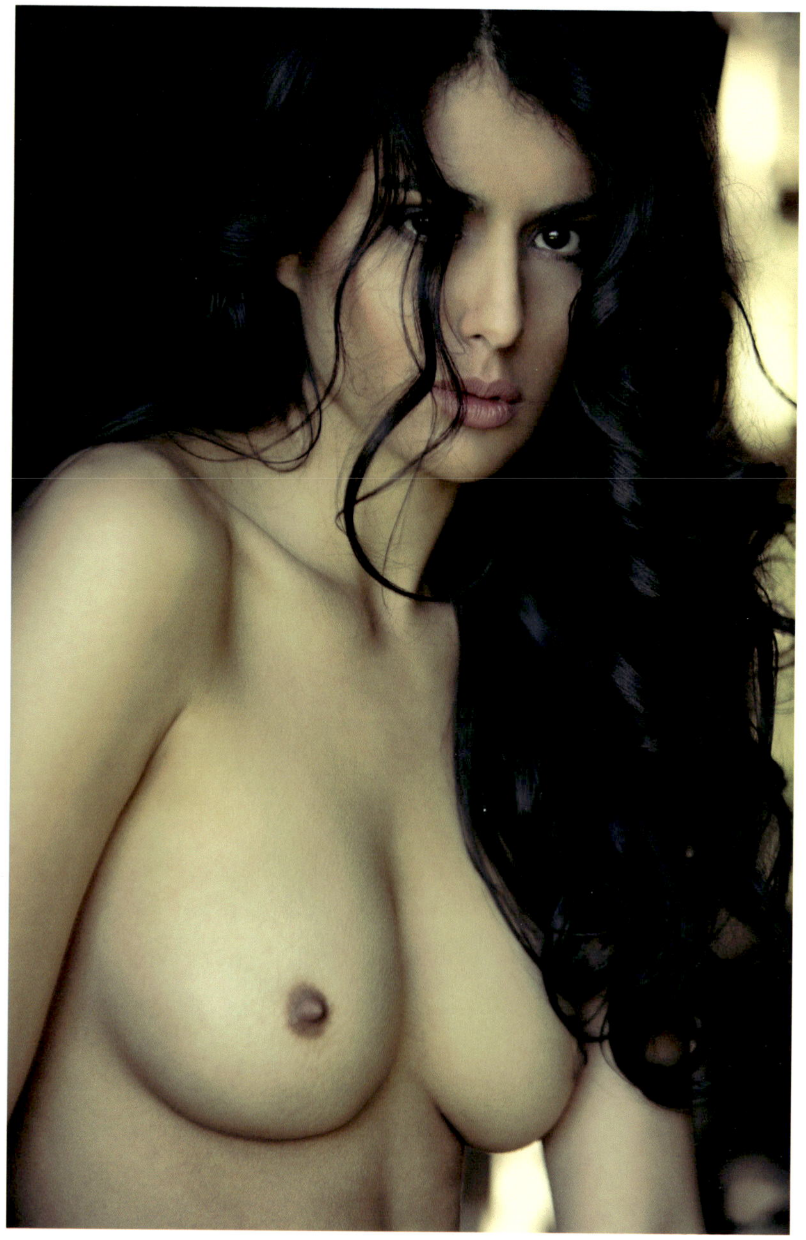

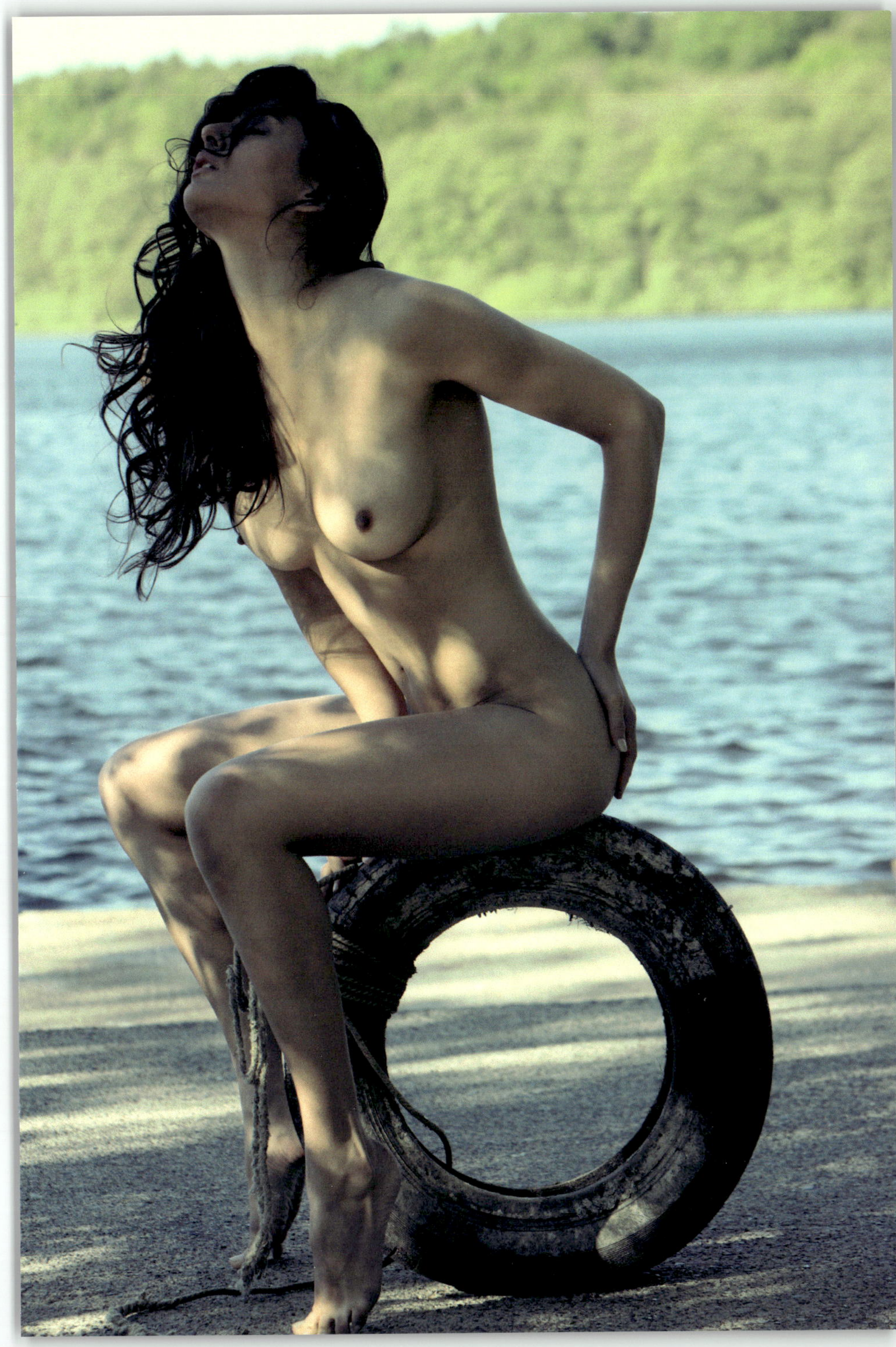

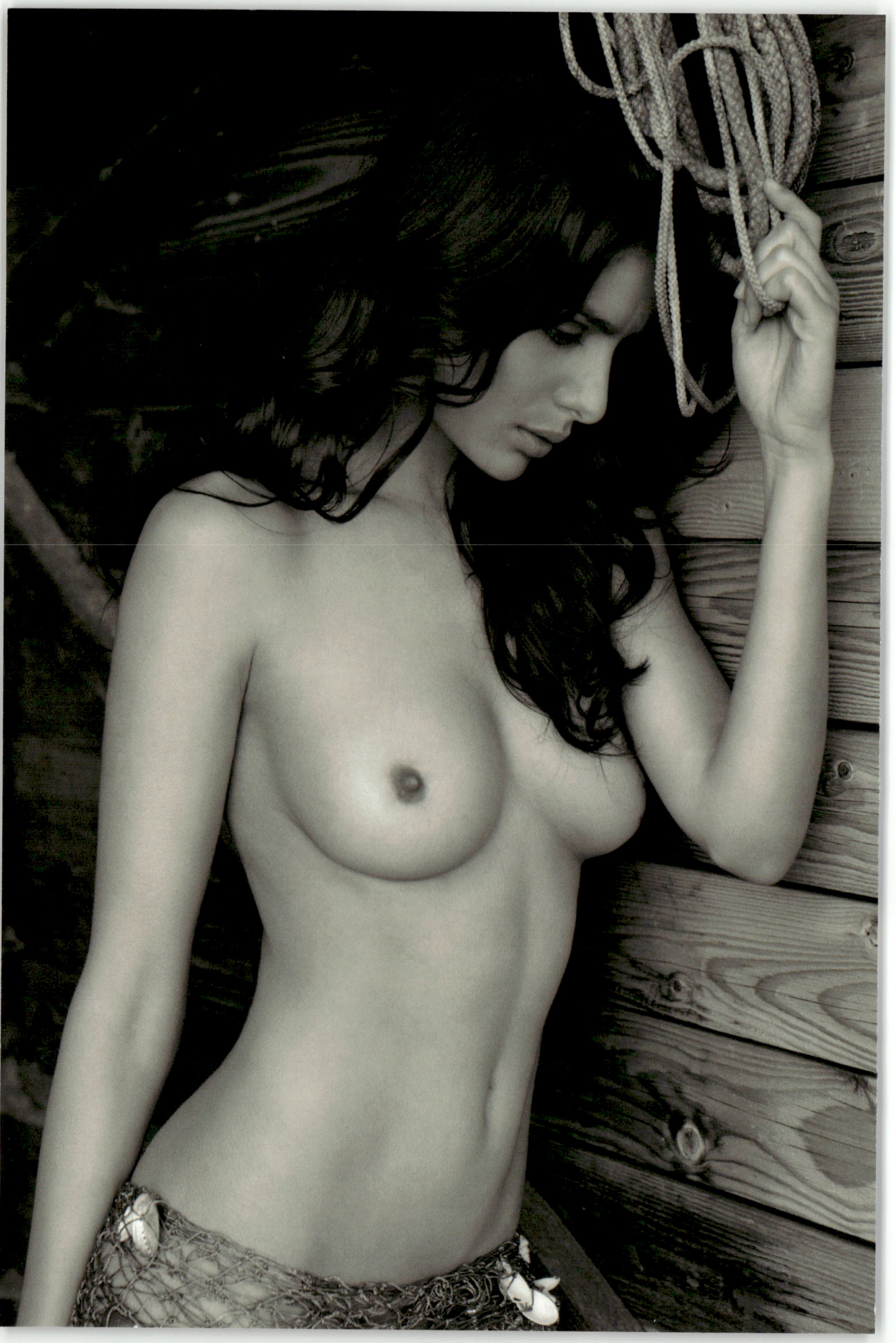

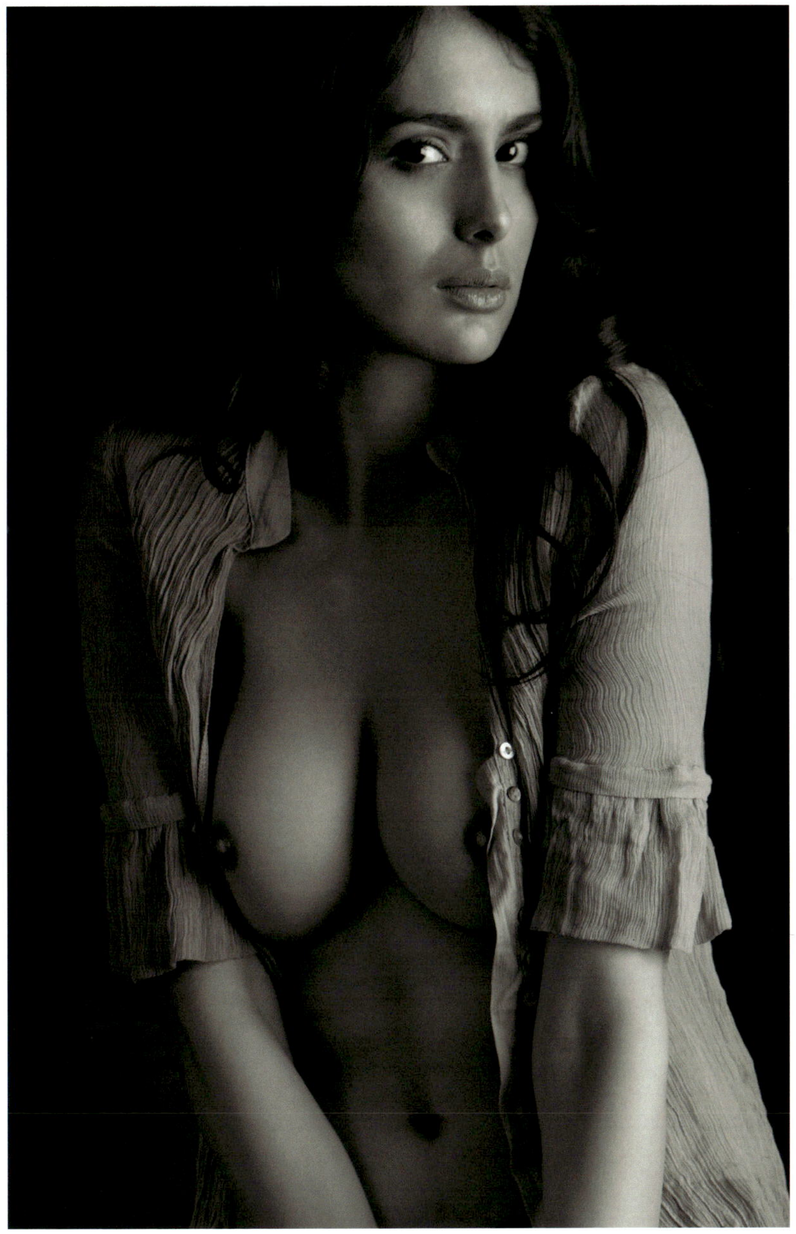

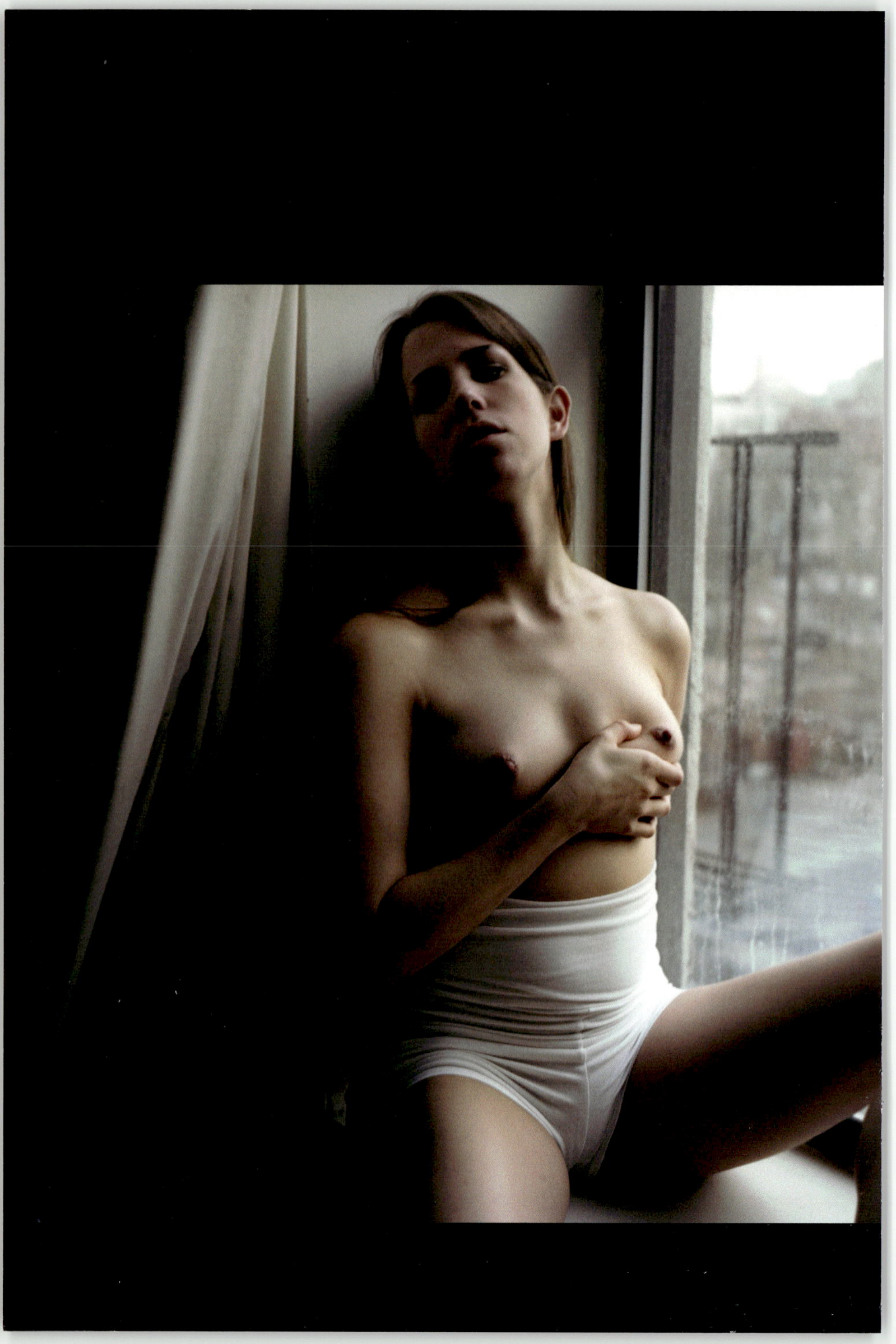

GEORGE PITTS

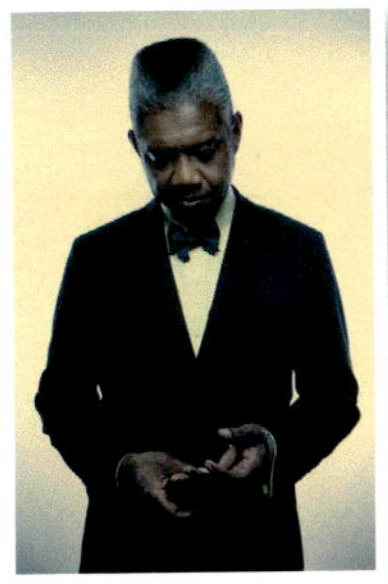

Photograph by Clayton Cubitt

George Pitts's photographs, paintings and drawings have been shown in museums and galleries in the USA, Japan and Canada. His photography has appeared in magazines and books such as *The Mammoth Book of New Erotic Photography*.

"With Renee I've explored virtually every kind of photograph within my aesthetic: portraiture; nudes; surreal images; classical nudes; nudes with a contaminated classicism; simple yet monumental studies of the details of her body, naked or clothed; cinematic studies, dressed or undressed; the stages of her pregnancy; and the sexual pictures, which range from mildly erotic to intensely sensual. I've shot as much B&W as I have colour film, because she comes through differently in each palette. Something akin to telepathy happens when we work, and Renee's control of her body is endlessly subtle."

www.georgepitts.com

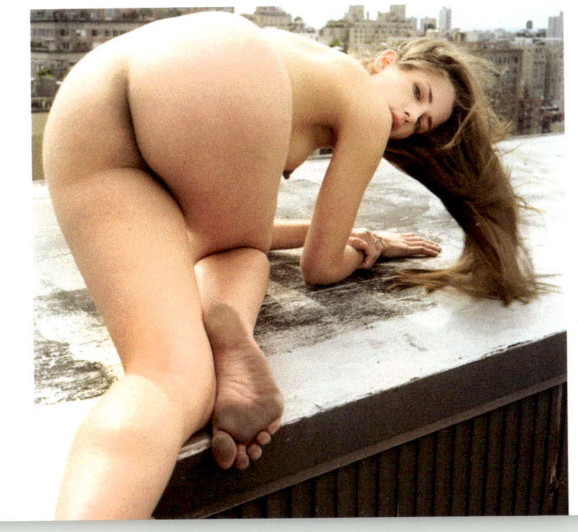

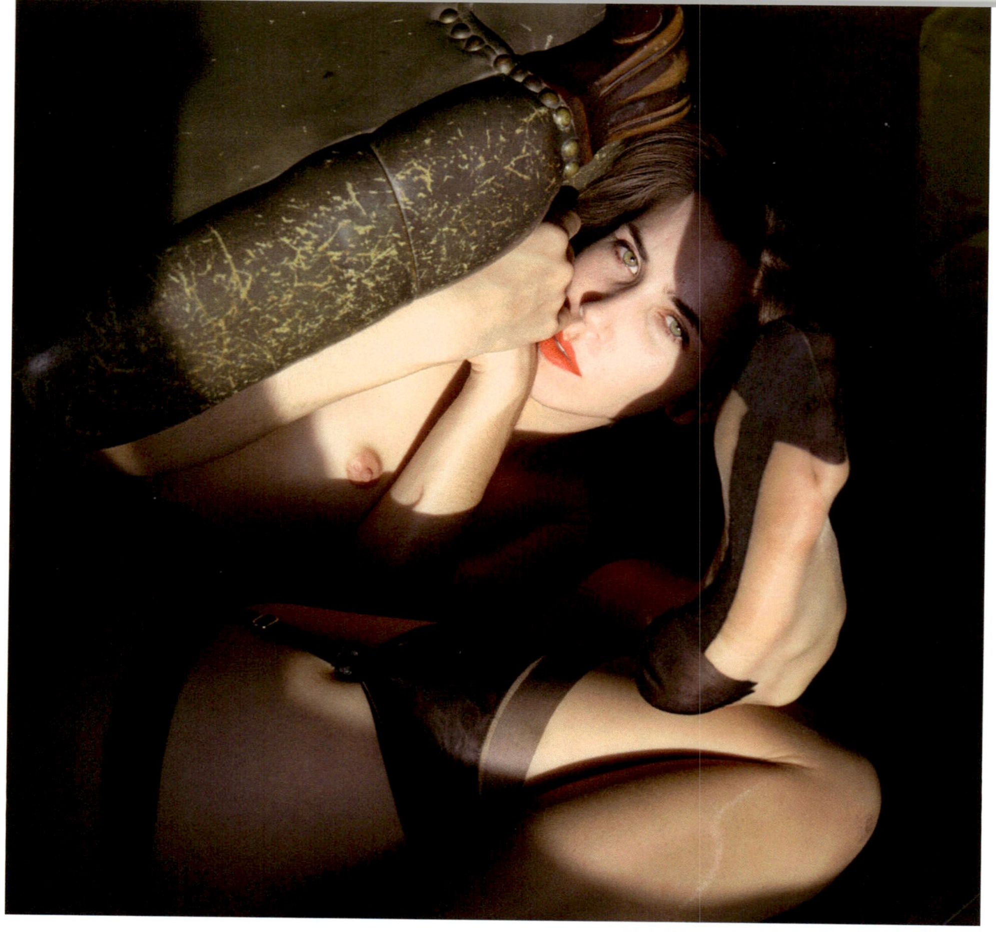

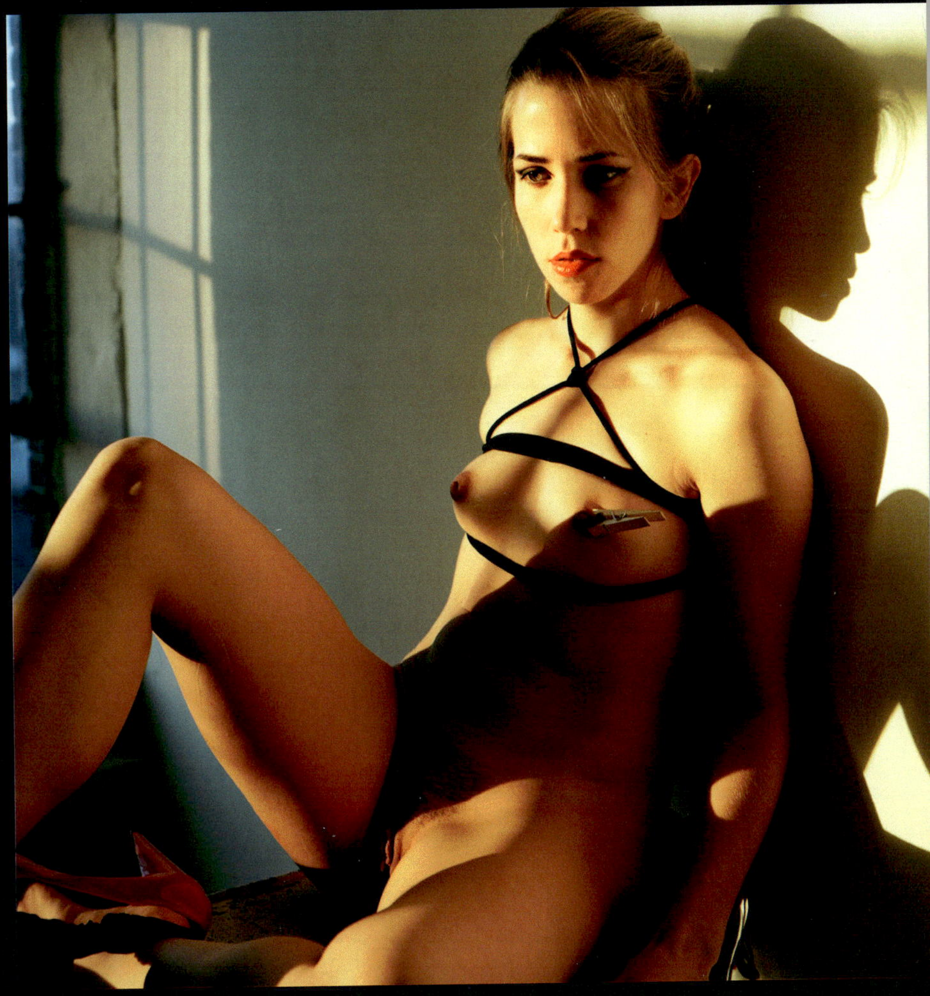

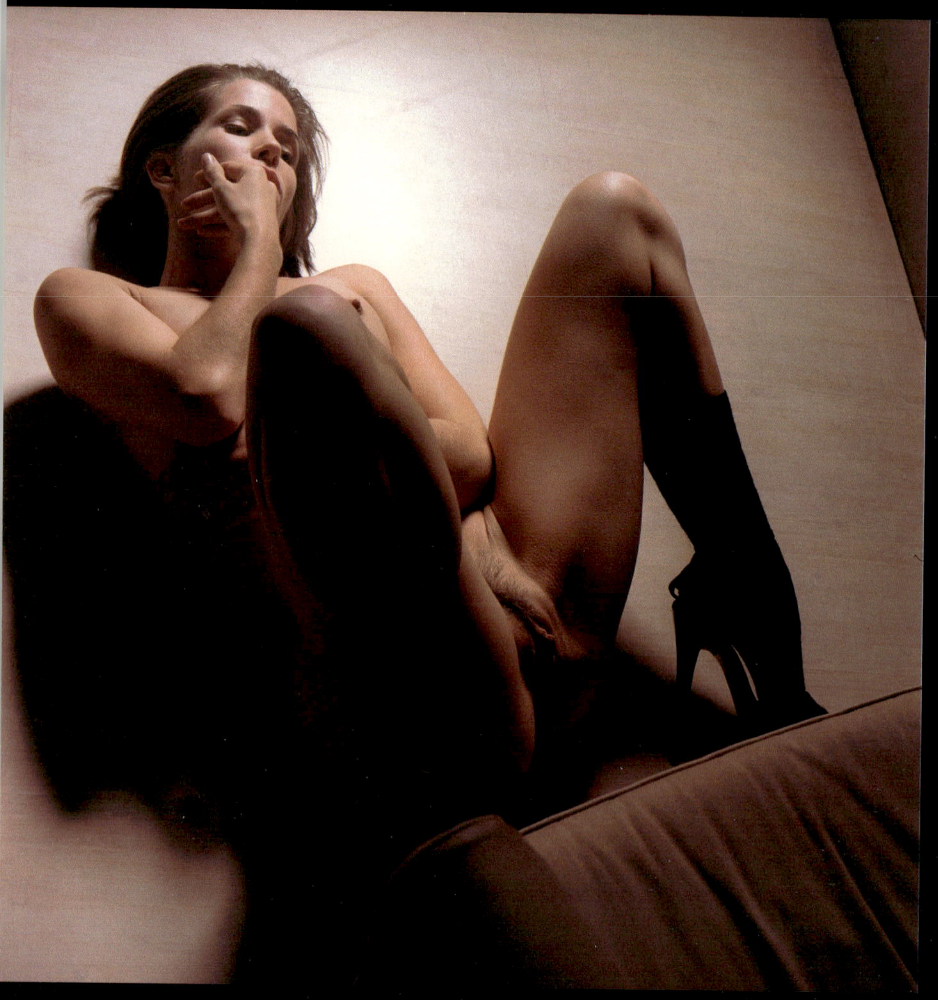

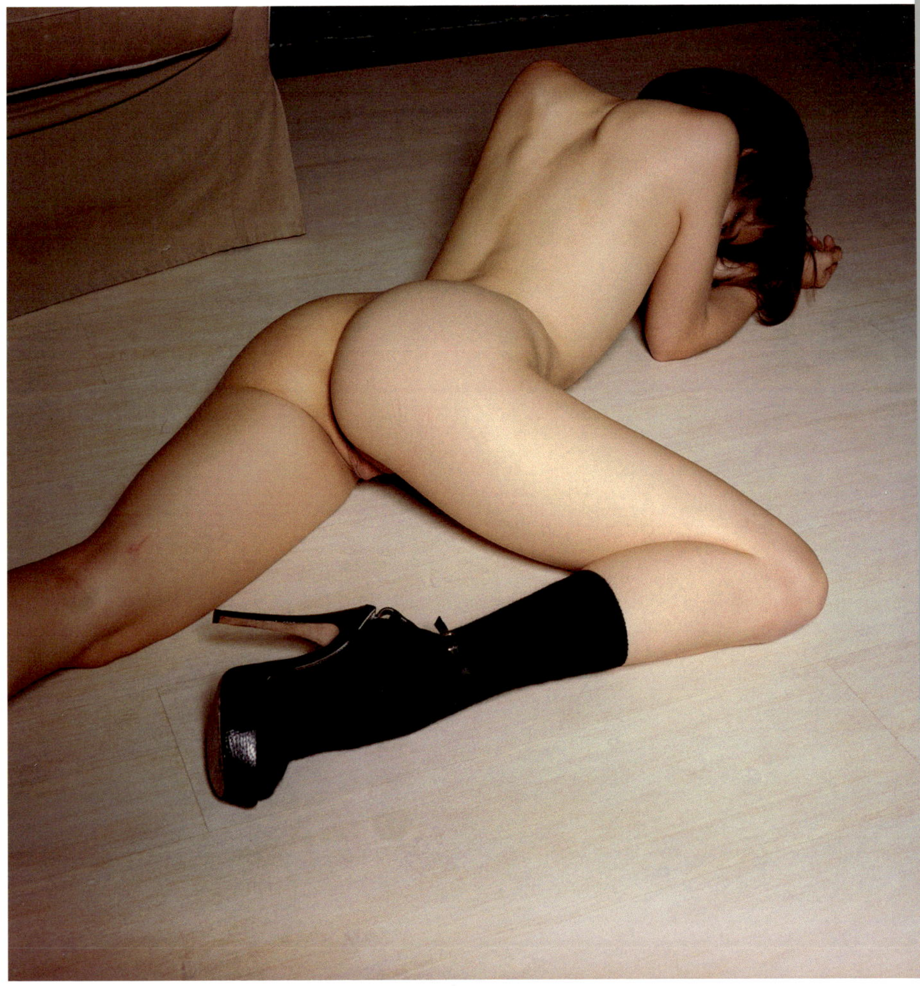

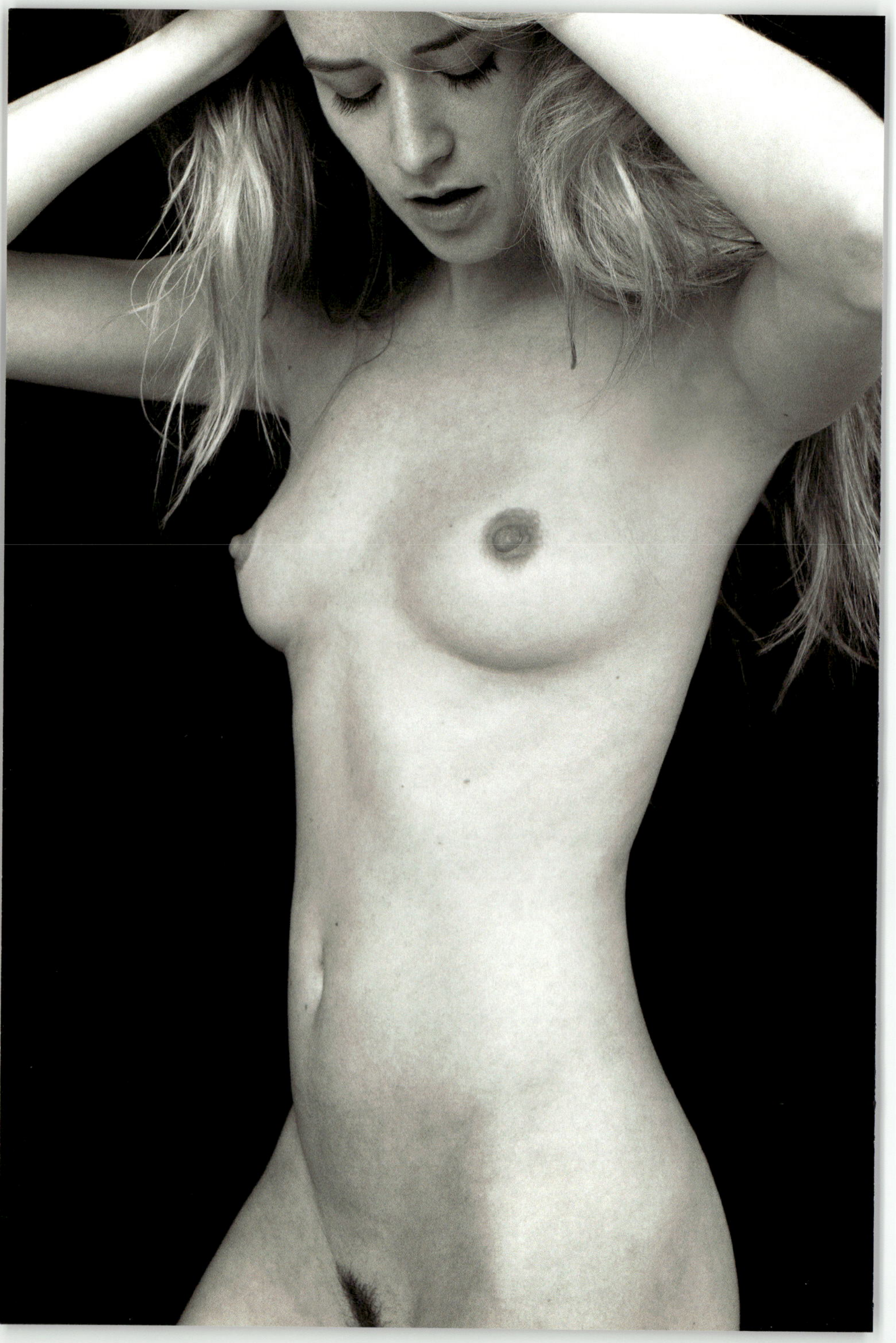

THADDEUS ROMBAUER

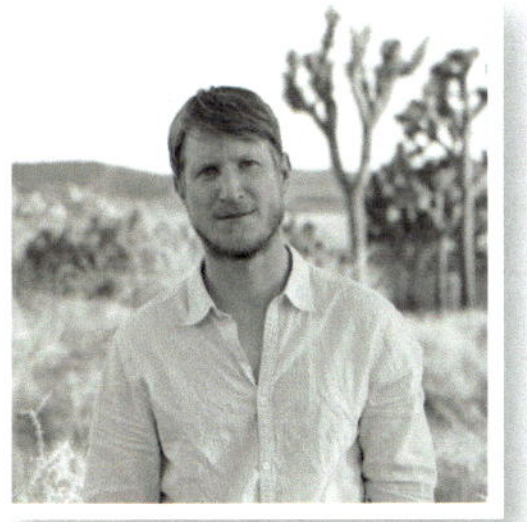

Thaddeus Rombauer is a photographer based in Brooklyn, New York, who grew up experimenting with all types of artistic mediums. His love of playing with light led him to develop a creative and distinctive approach to photography. Travelling and experiencing various cultures has trained and refined his eye. Thaddeus's unique aesthetic qualities are clearly reflected in his vast body of work. His artistic insight helps him capture beauty not only in his subjects, but also in the world around him. He explores new ways of pushing both his subjects and his own creative expression.

"I really liked this model's comfortable open approach, and willingness to be very much a part of the creative process. She is a true professional and a joy to work with."

www.thaddeusrombauer.com

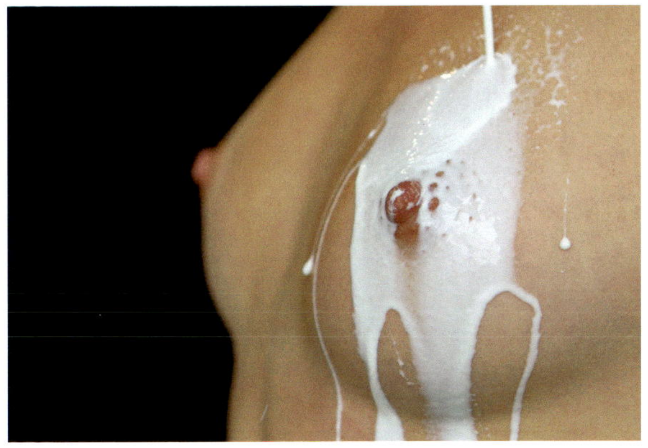

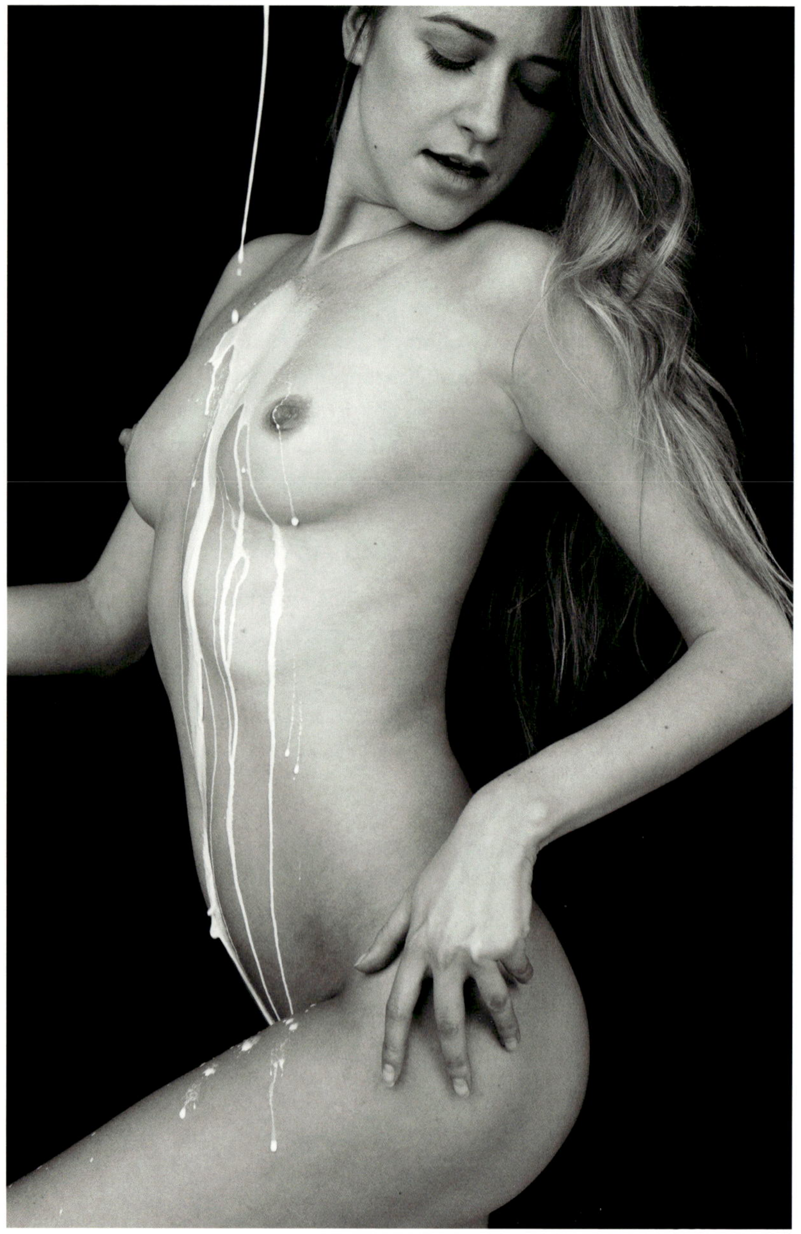

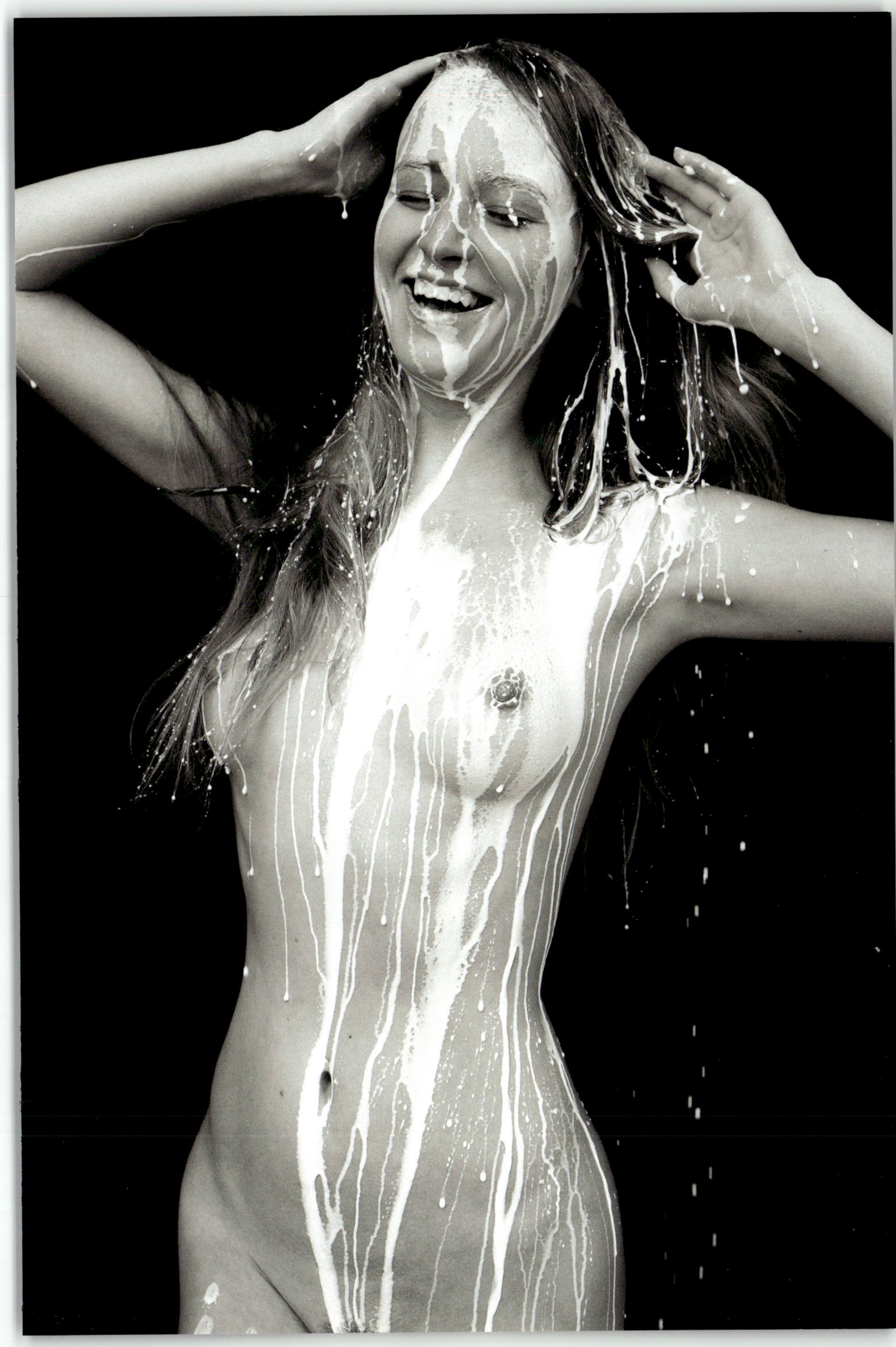

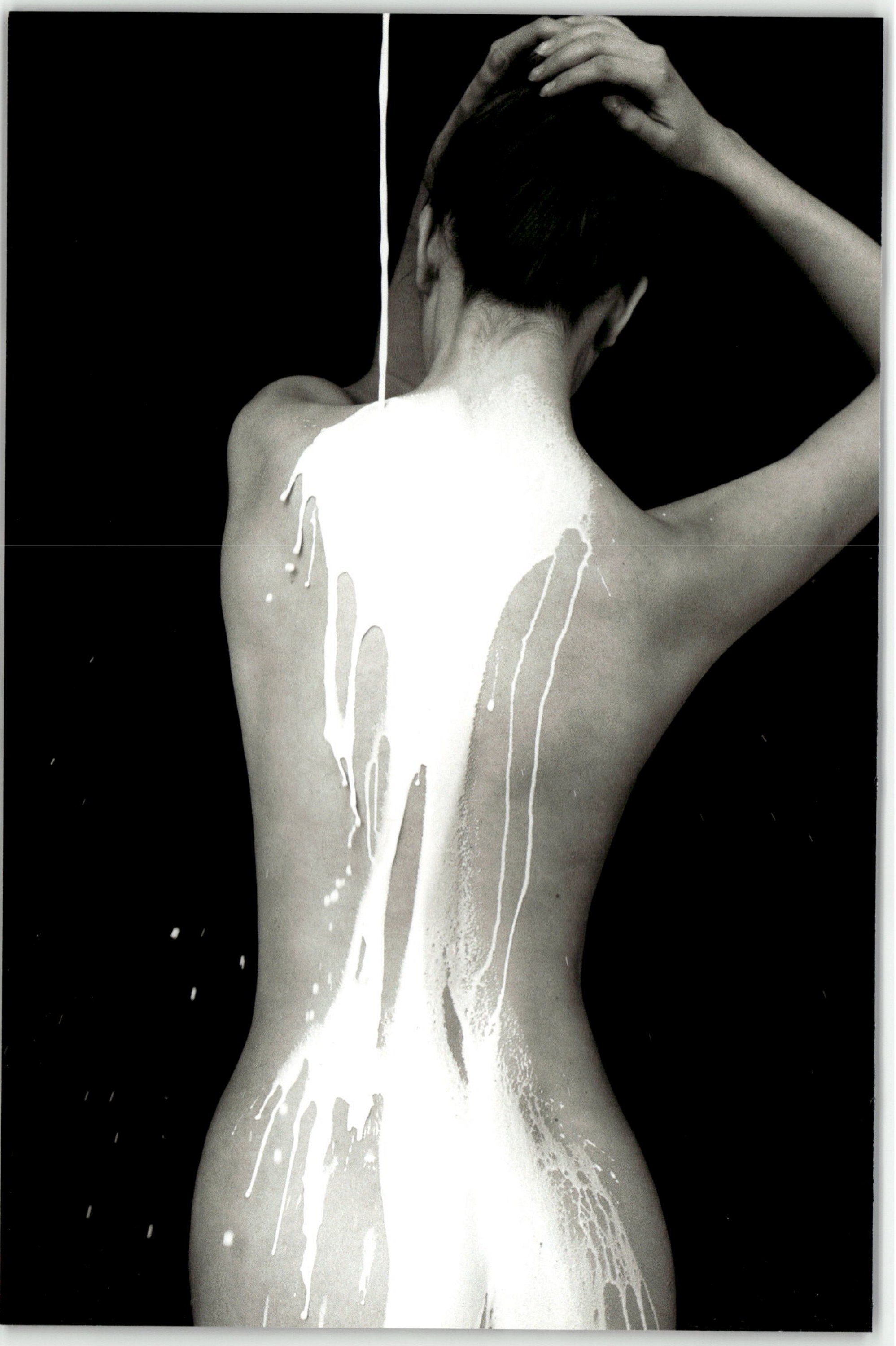

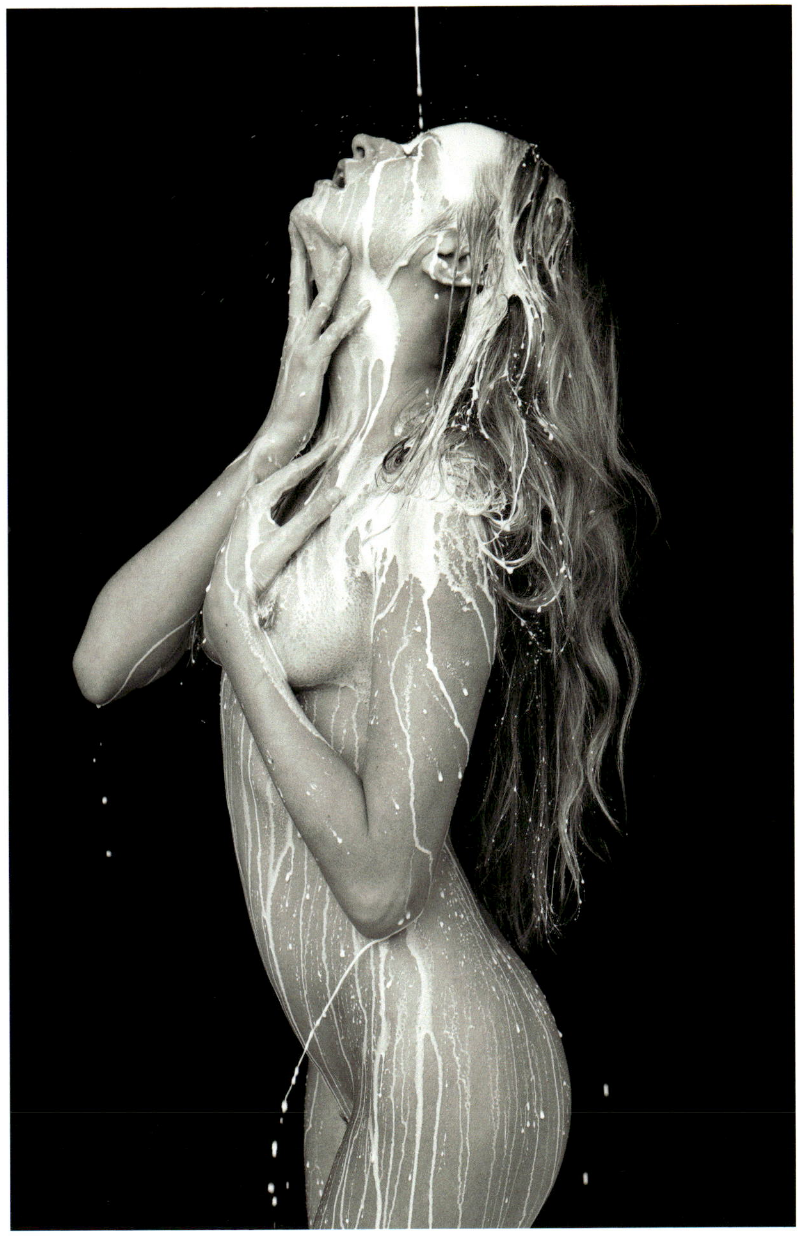

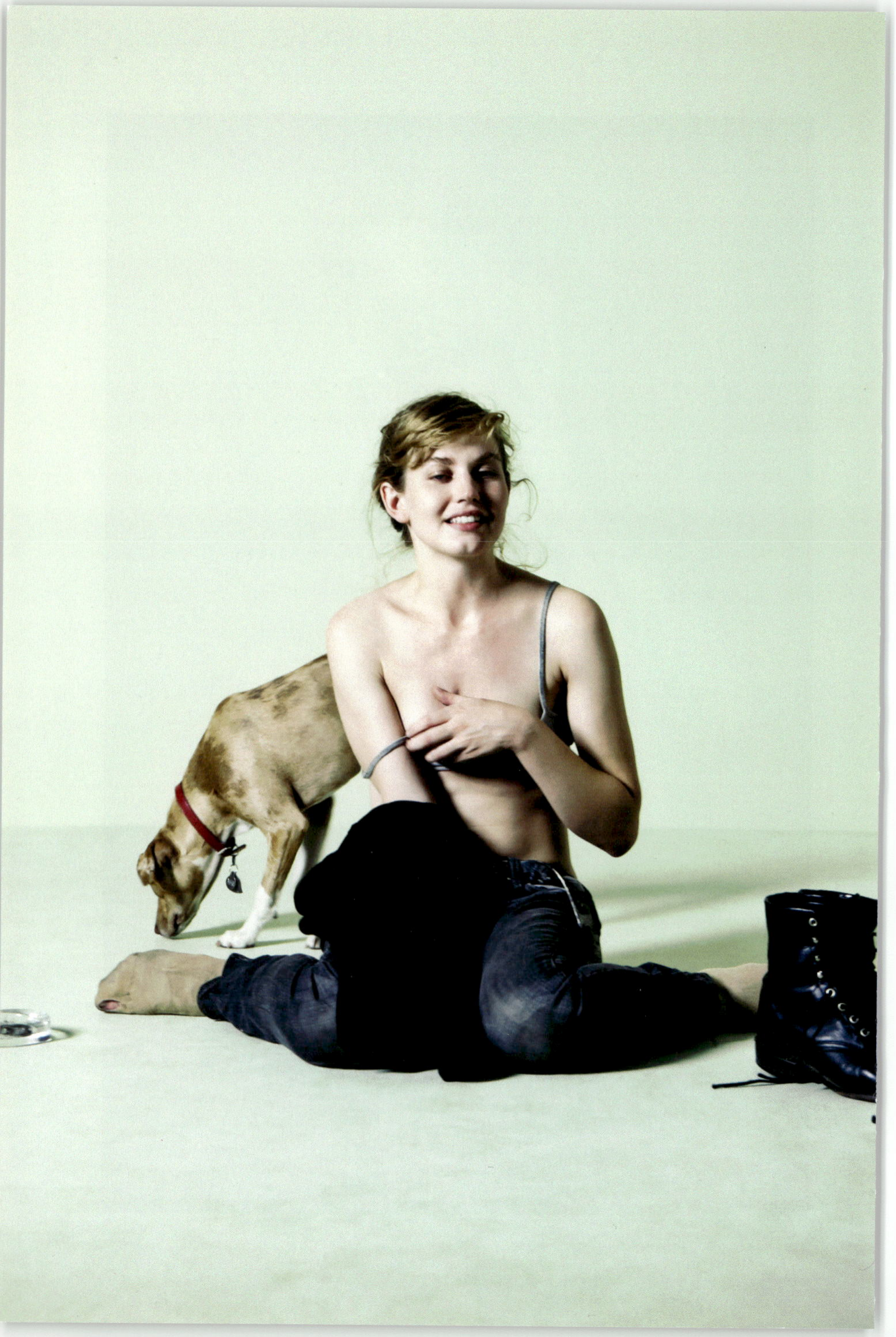

NED AND AYA ROSEN

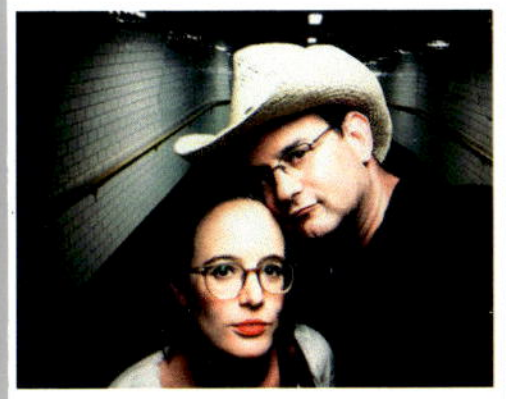

For six years Ned and Aya Rosen have been working together as a photography team, expressing their struggles with power, desire, hunger, fantasy, reality and sexuality. Photography is a bridge that allows them to share and experience their own personalities with both their subjects and the viewers of their work. It is a way to invite and include others into their lives, relationship and artwork.

"Nettie Harris has an air of real freedom about her and a personality almost too large to be contained. We both admire her rawness and ability to be entirely in the moment. The freedom that we see in her is part of what we strive for in ourselves."

www.nedandayaerotic.com
www.nedandaya.com

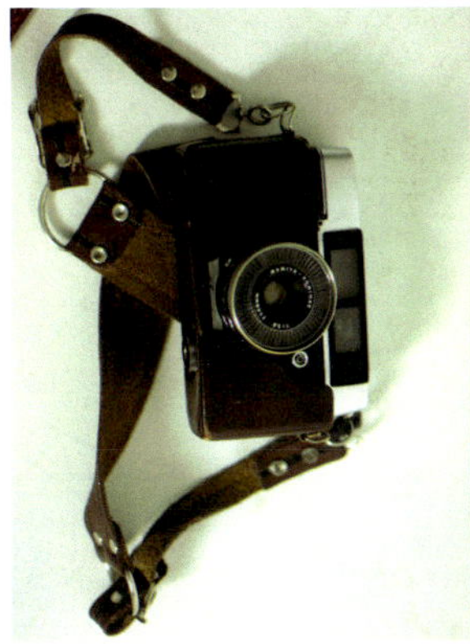

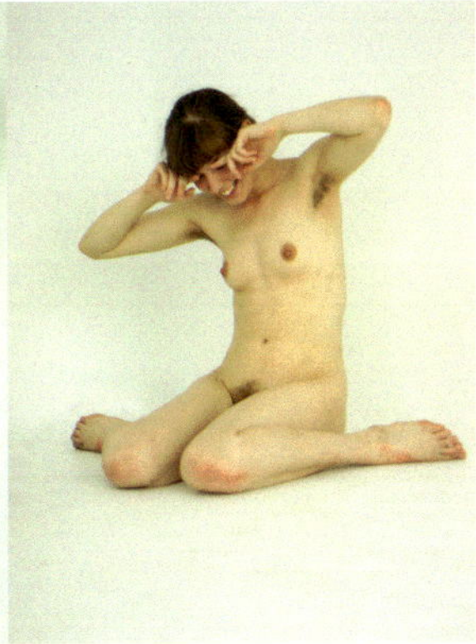

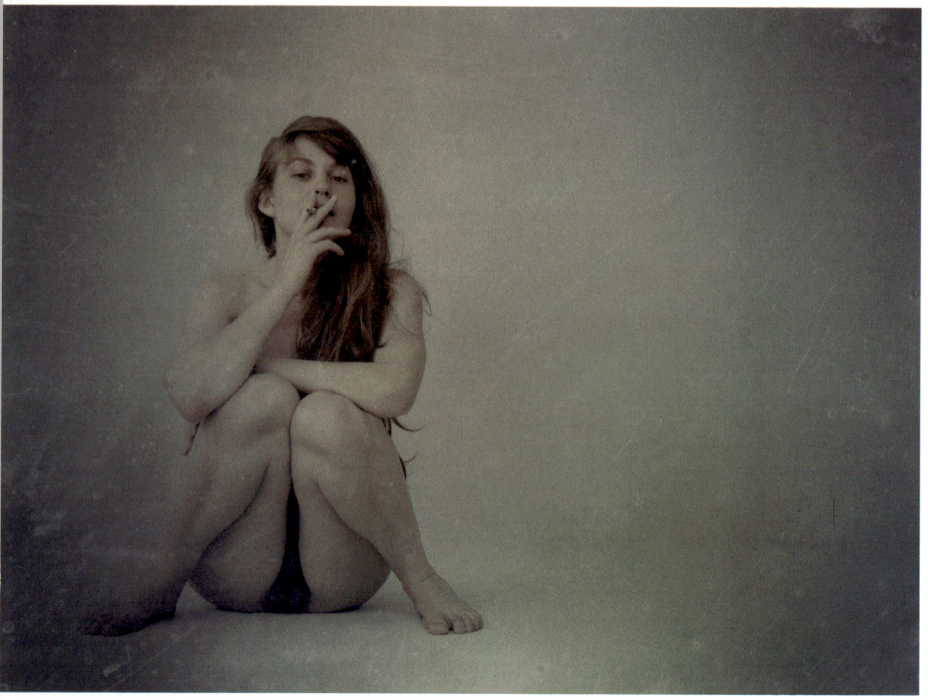

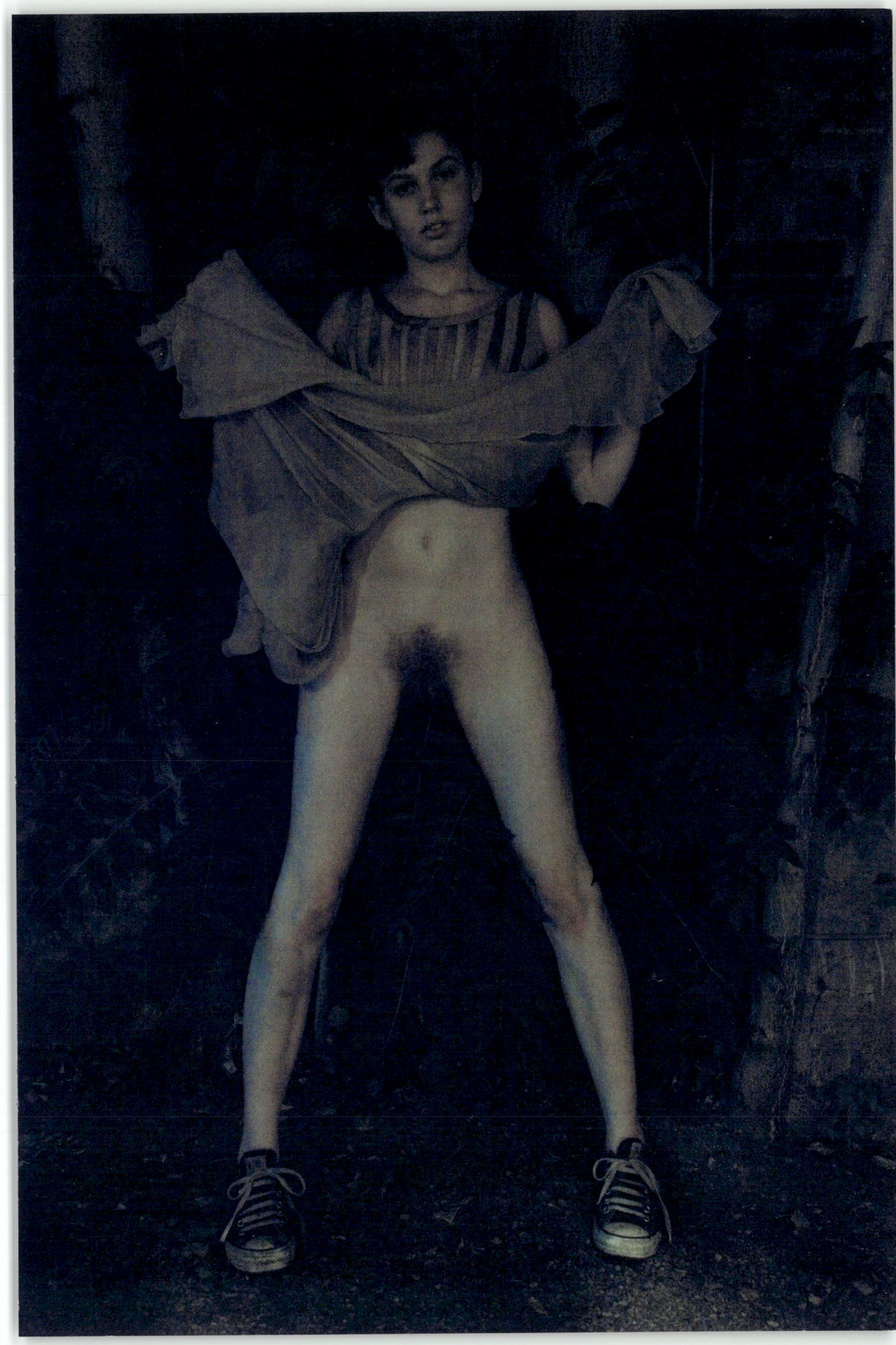

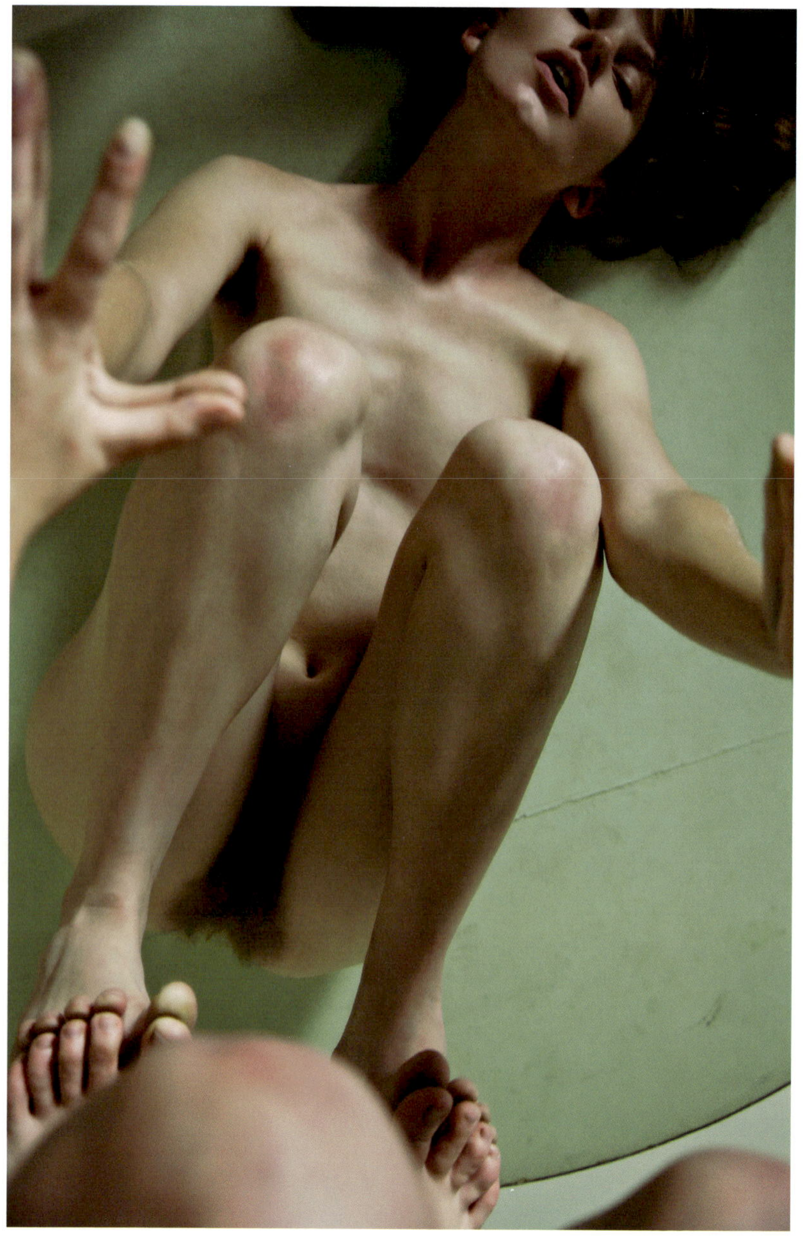

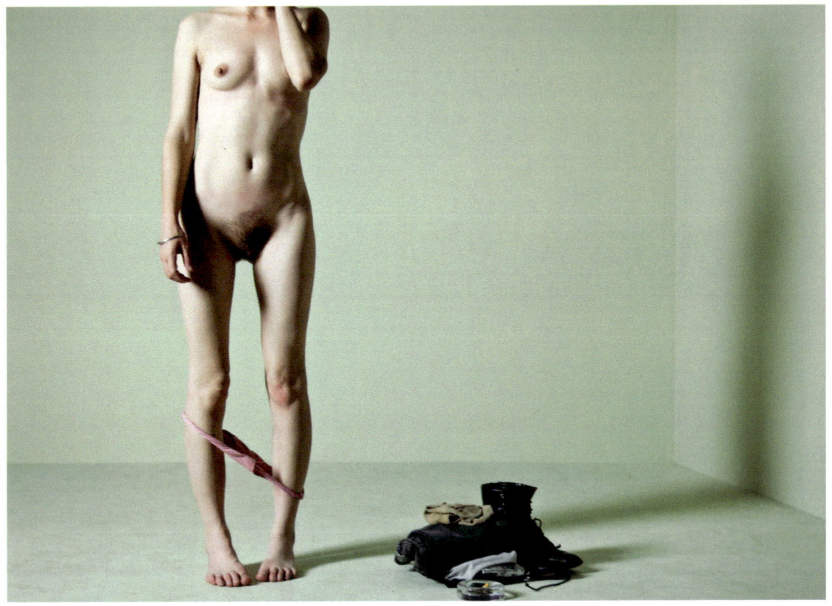

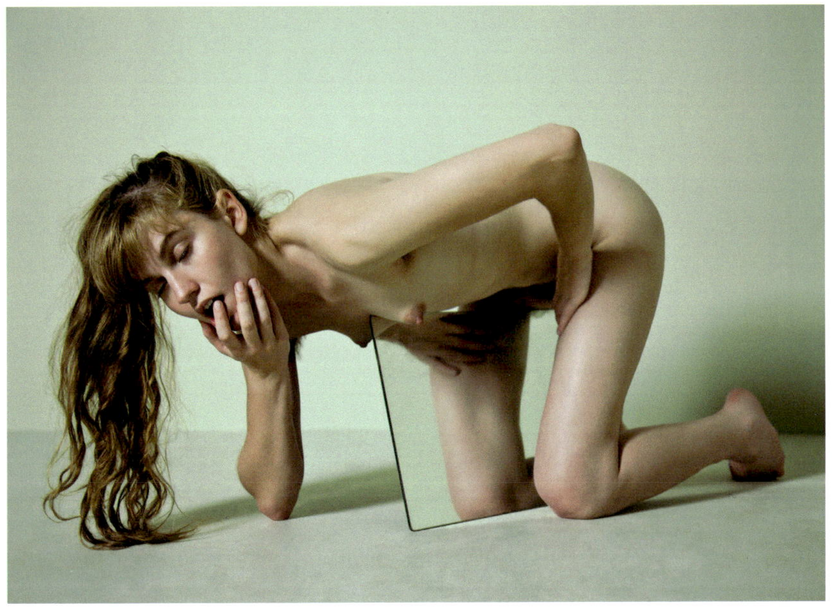

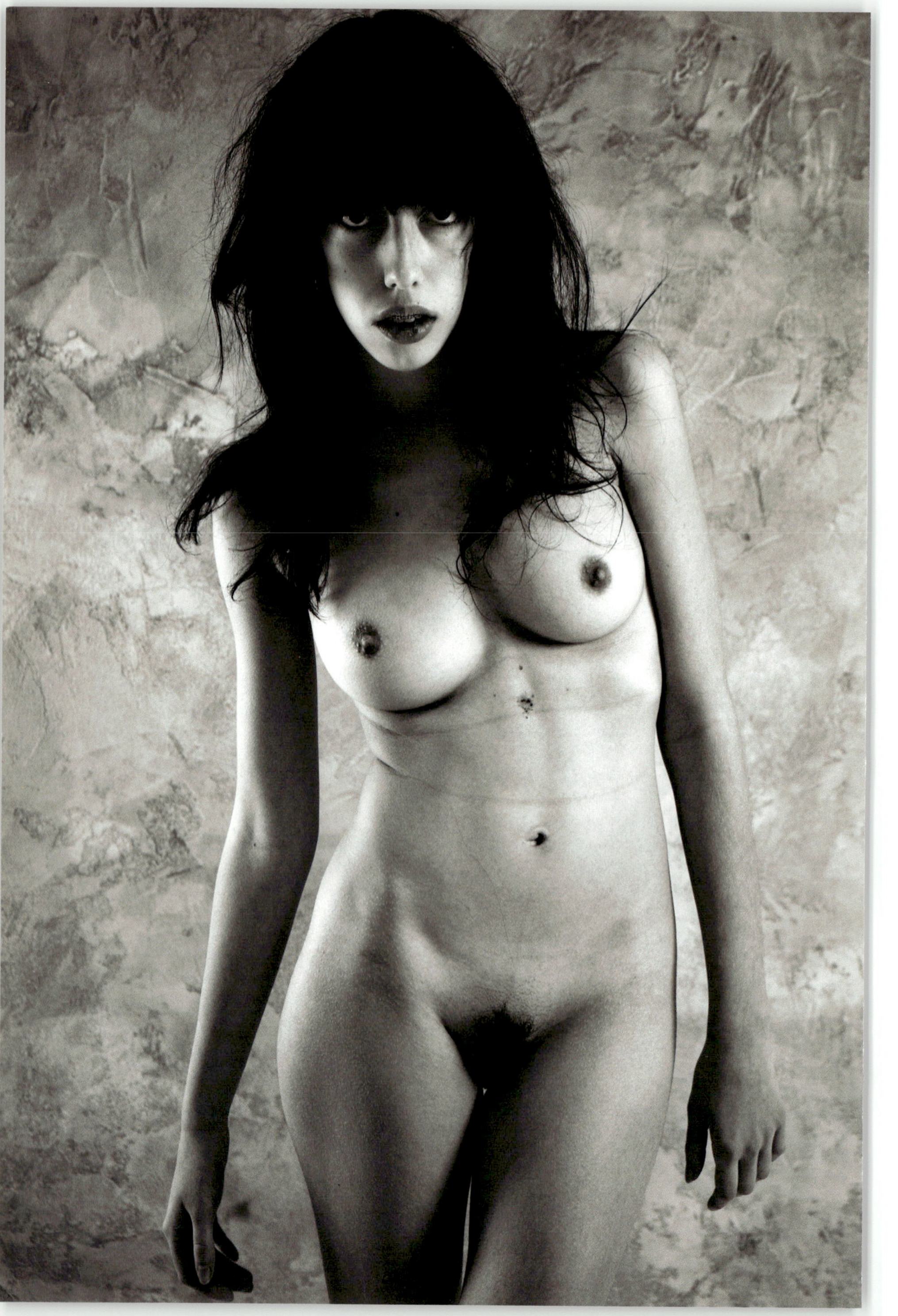

JIRI RUZEK

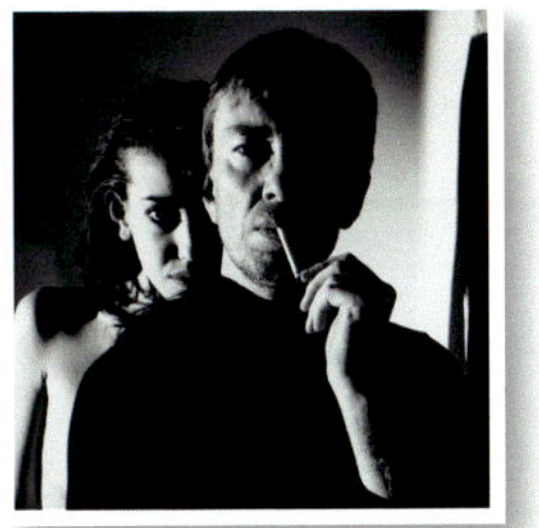

Photograph by Ludmila Foblova

"Photography for me is an intimate dialogue transformed into pictures. This dialogue's quality is related to the quality of the photo. I call my style Uglamour (Ugly Glamour, the opposite of Glamour). My photographs are not retouched: models aren't pieces of meat for men's magazines, they are strong personalities, often caught in positions of the utmost expressiveness. My models are more actresses than models.

"Tereza (aka Metteorwa) is one of the top Czech nude art models and looks very exotic. She is natural in every situation. In photography she is on the same wavelength as me. I once photographed her while I was blindfolded, communicating by words alone. The results looked like they usually do and it was no surprise to me. I felt exactly what I was shooting."

www.jiriruzek.net

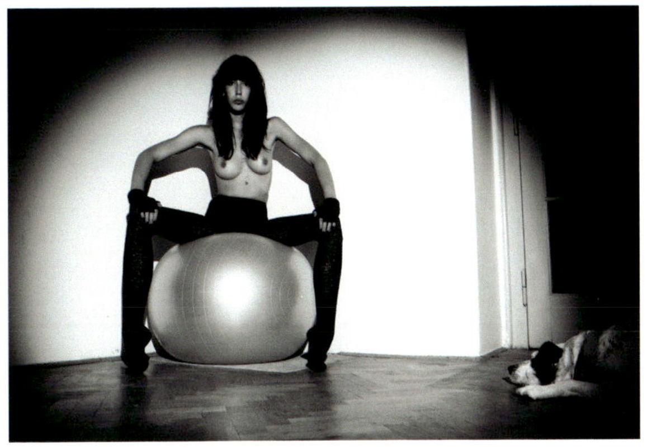

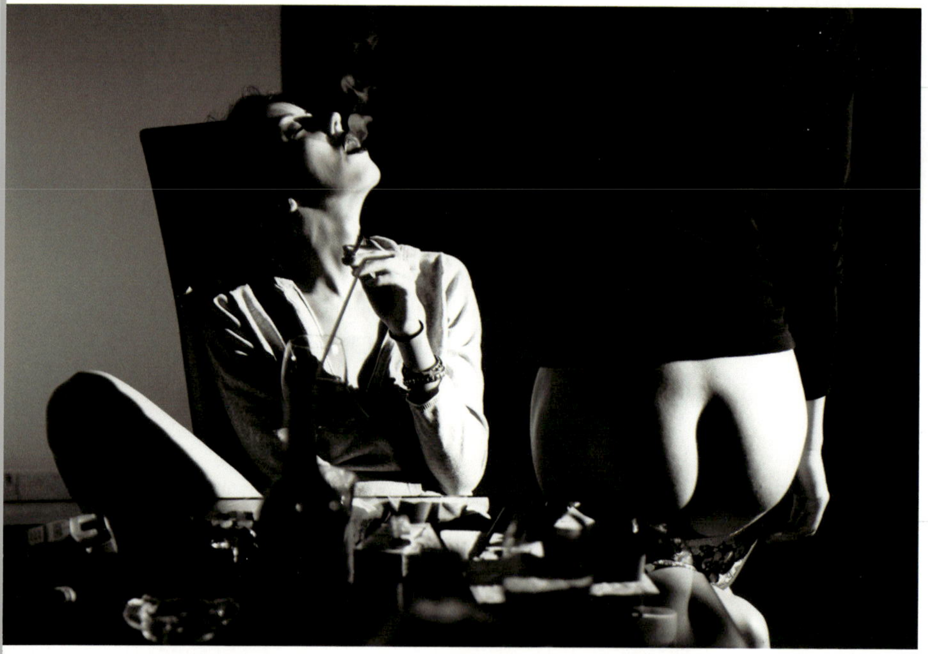

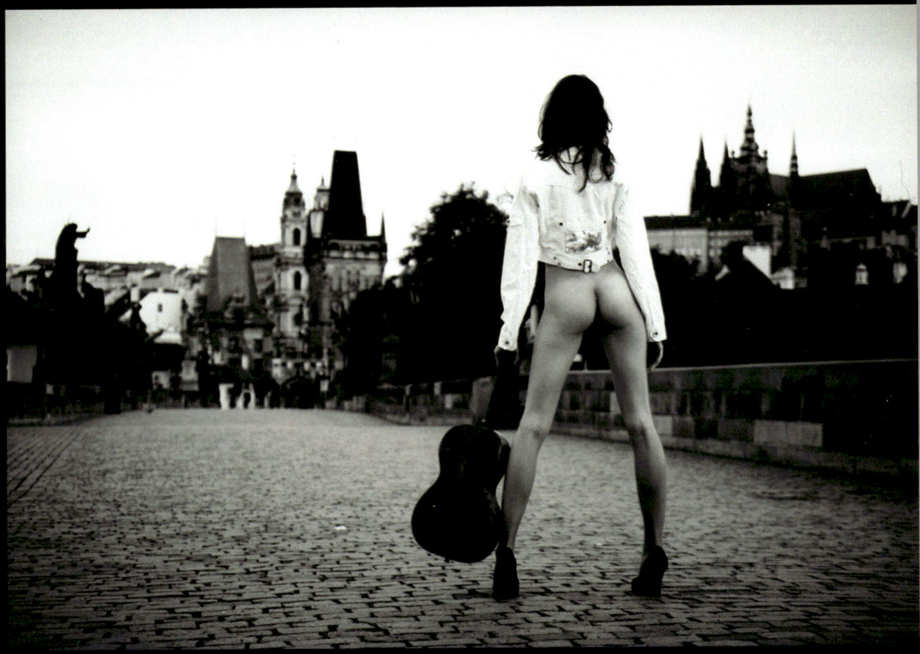

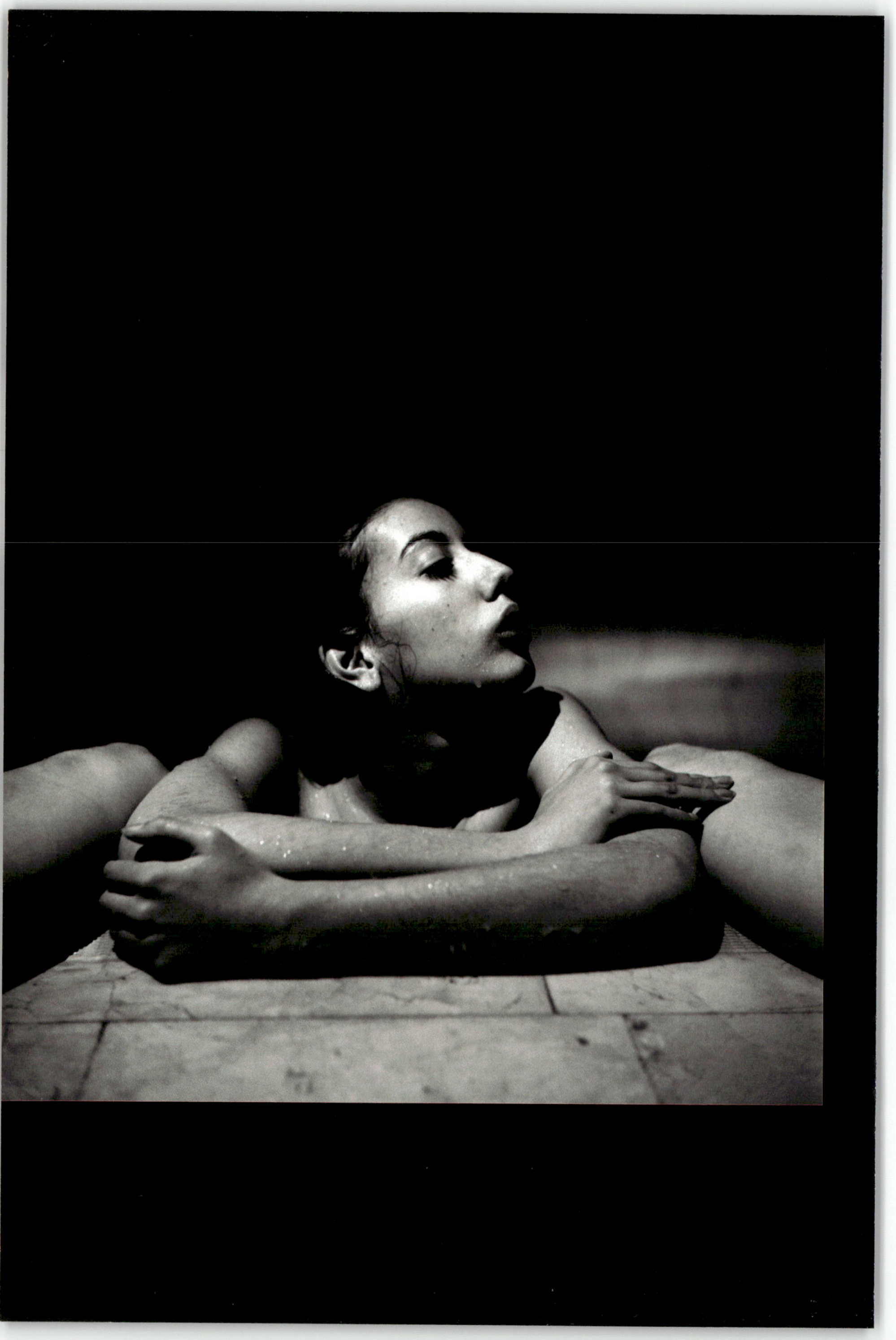

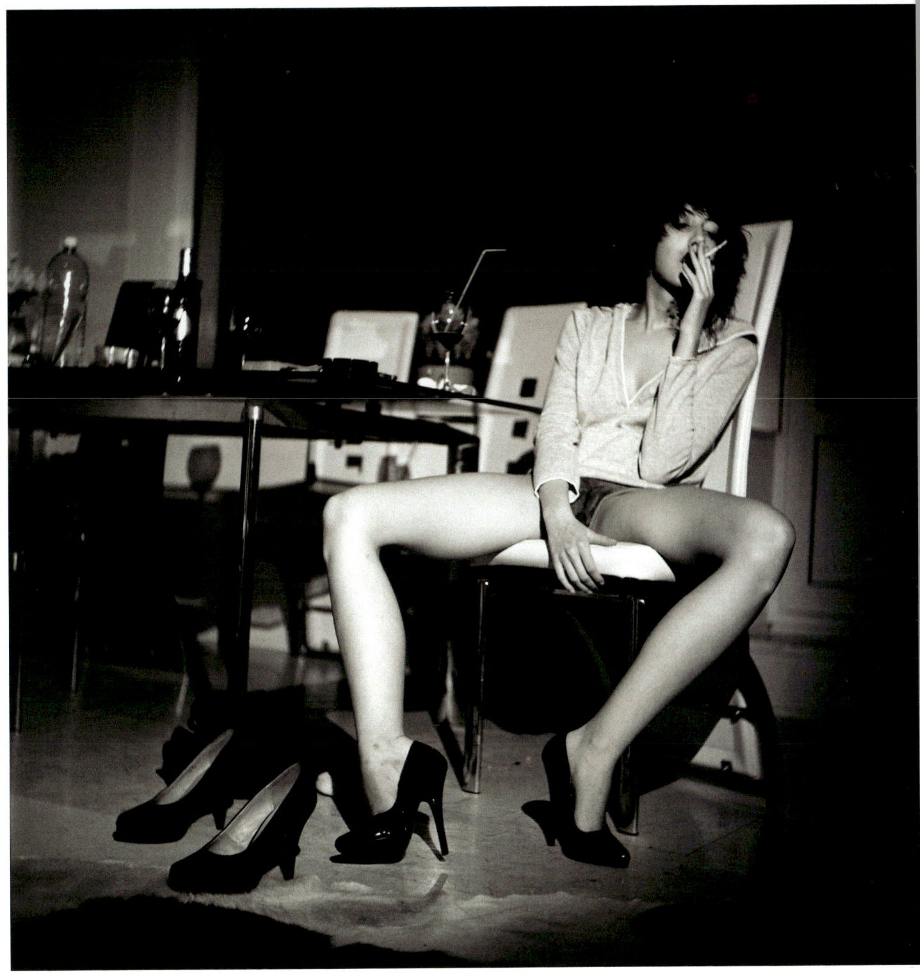

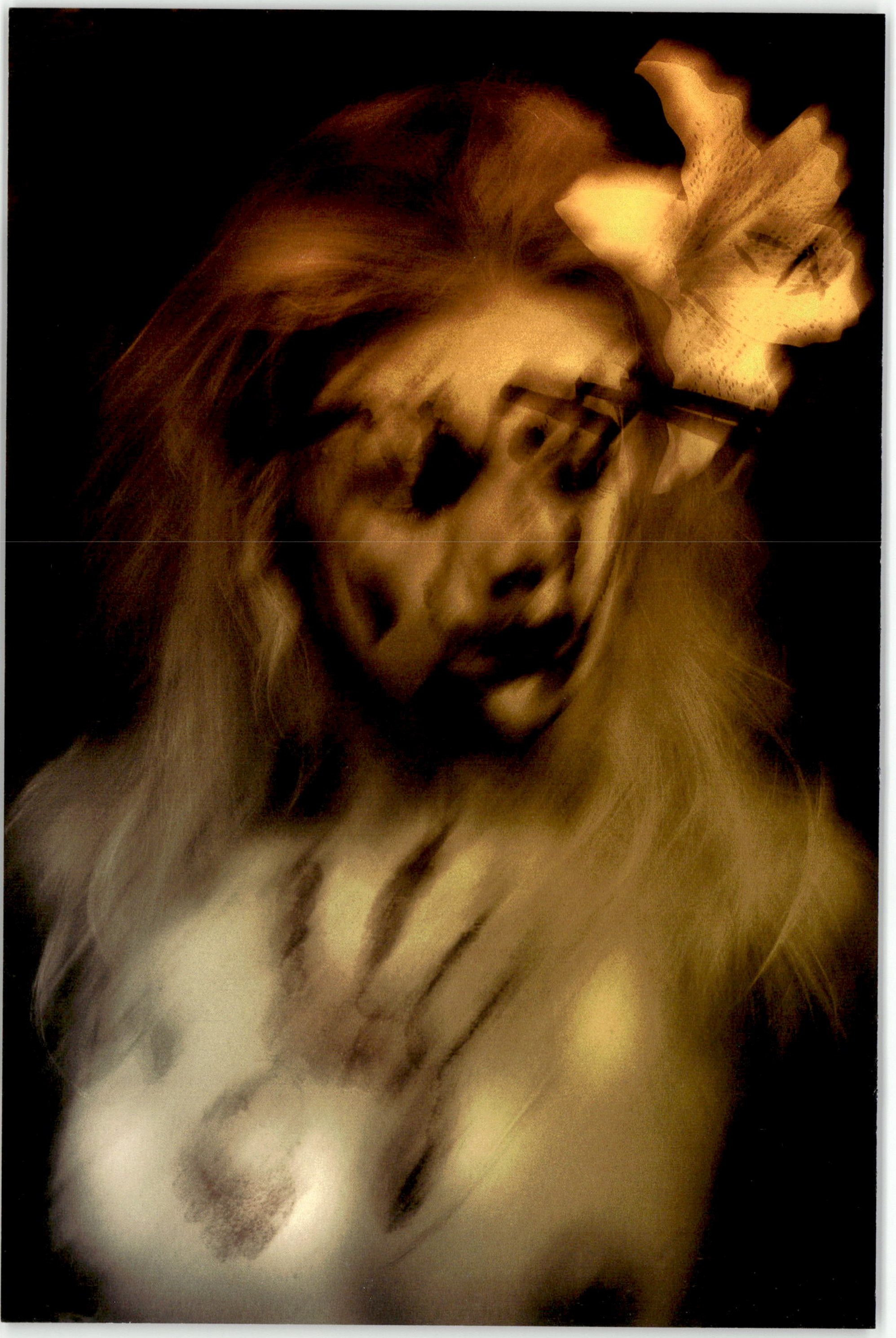

JOHN SANTERINEROSS

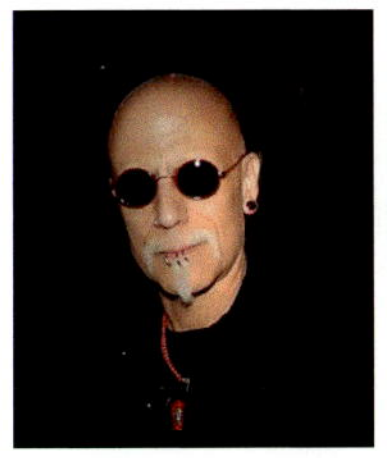

American photographer John Santerineross strives to engage the entire mind and personality of his viewers by appealing to both their unconscious emotions and their intellect.

This series of images is of his wife Heather Eve, who has not only lent her body to his creative process over the years but has also been a great source of inspiration, support and encouragement.

www.santerineross.com

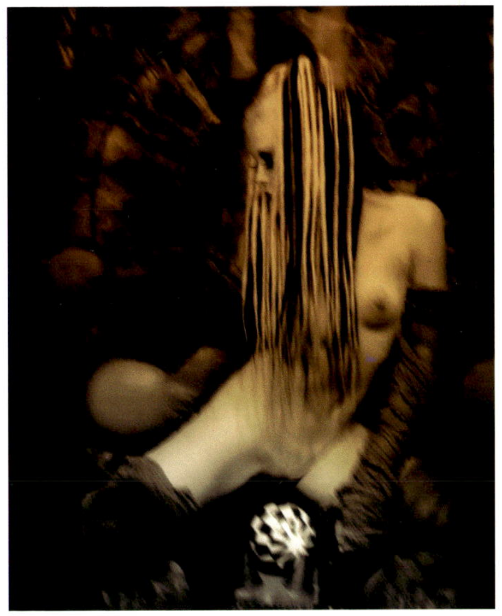

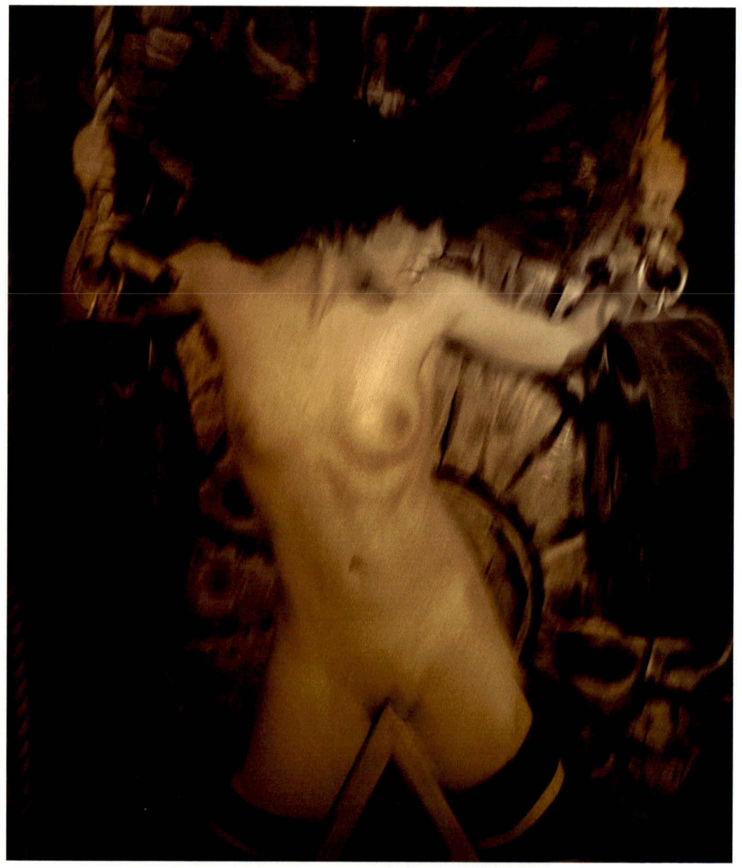

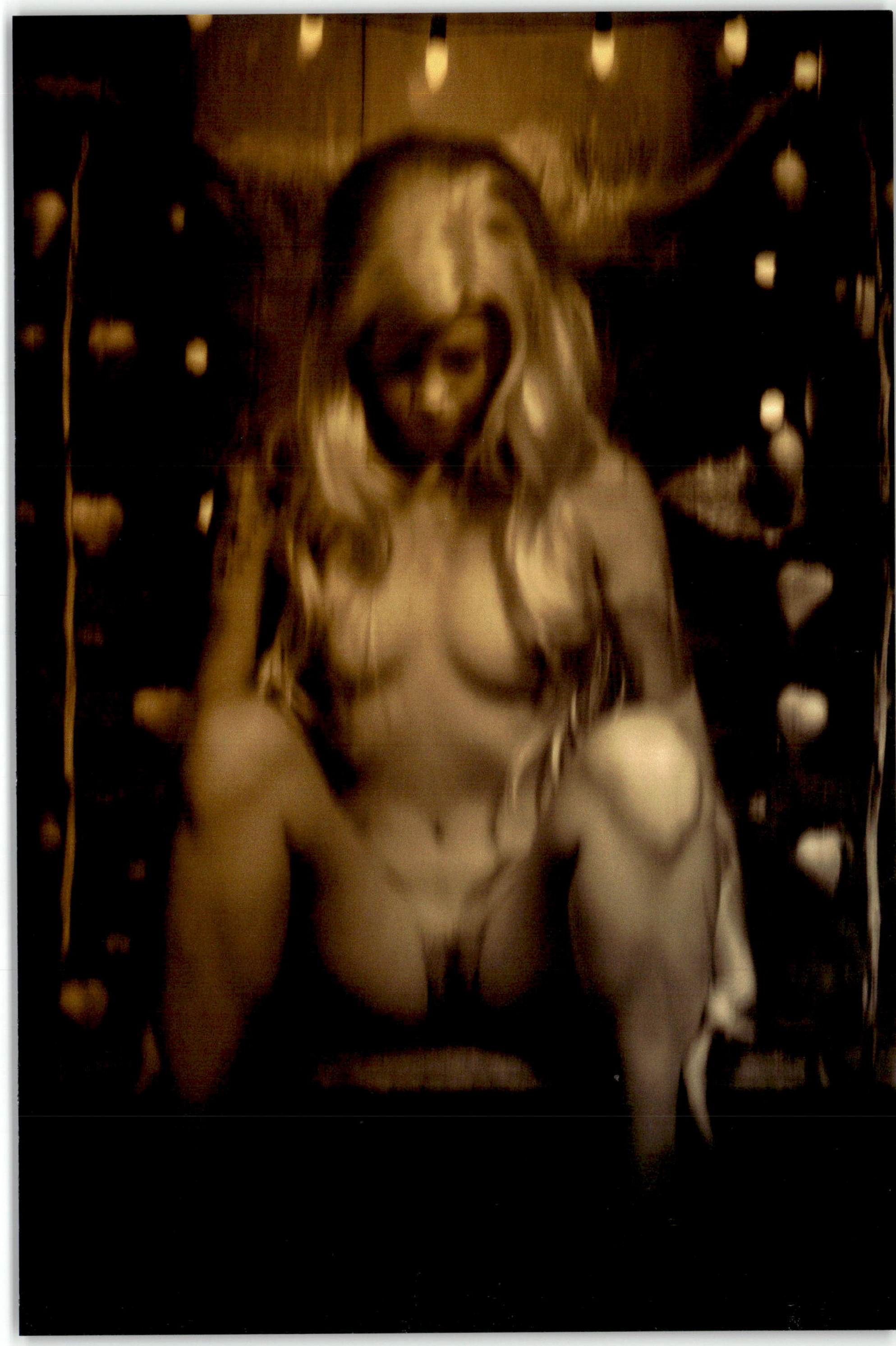

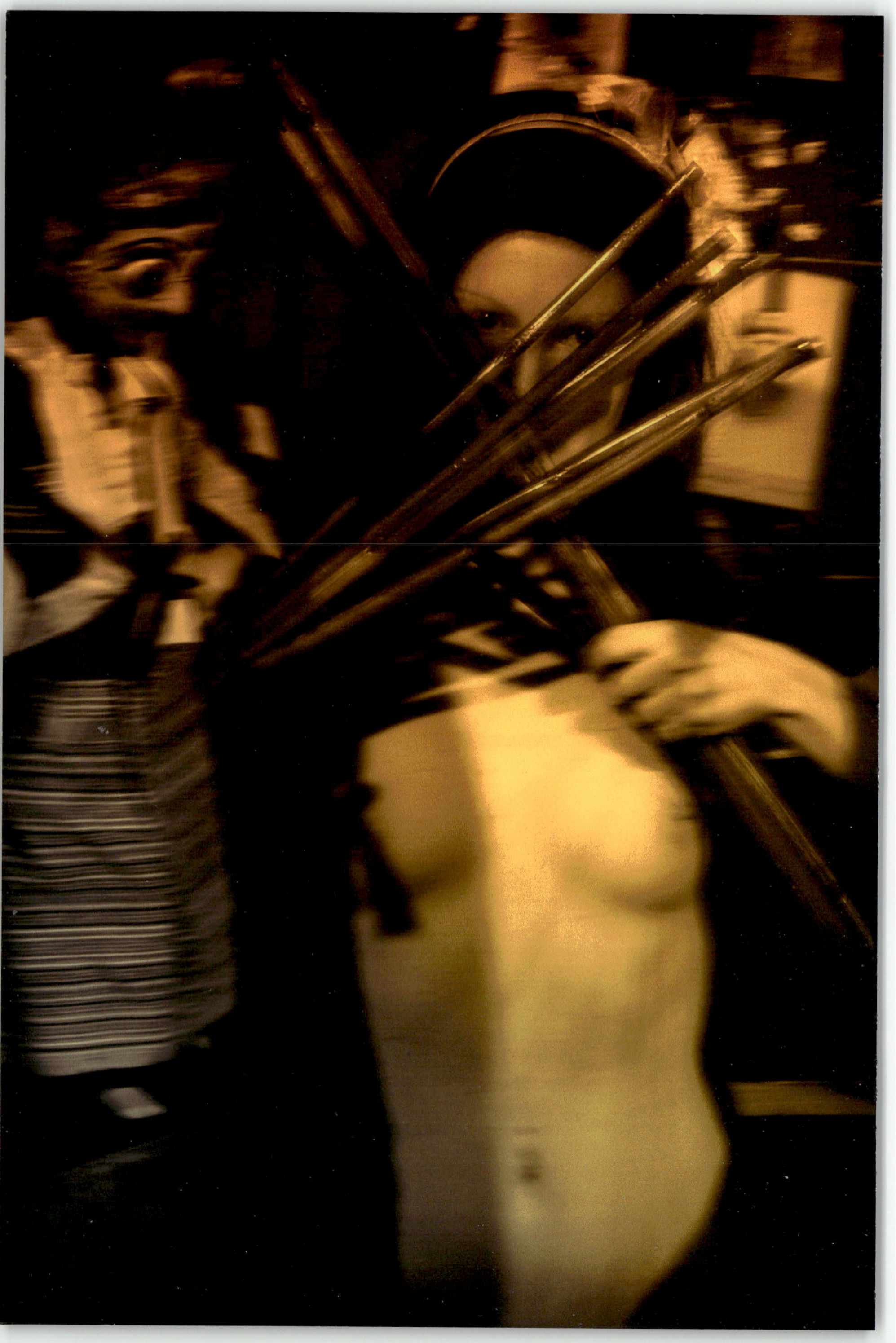

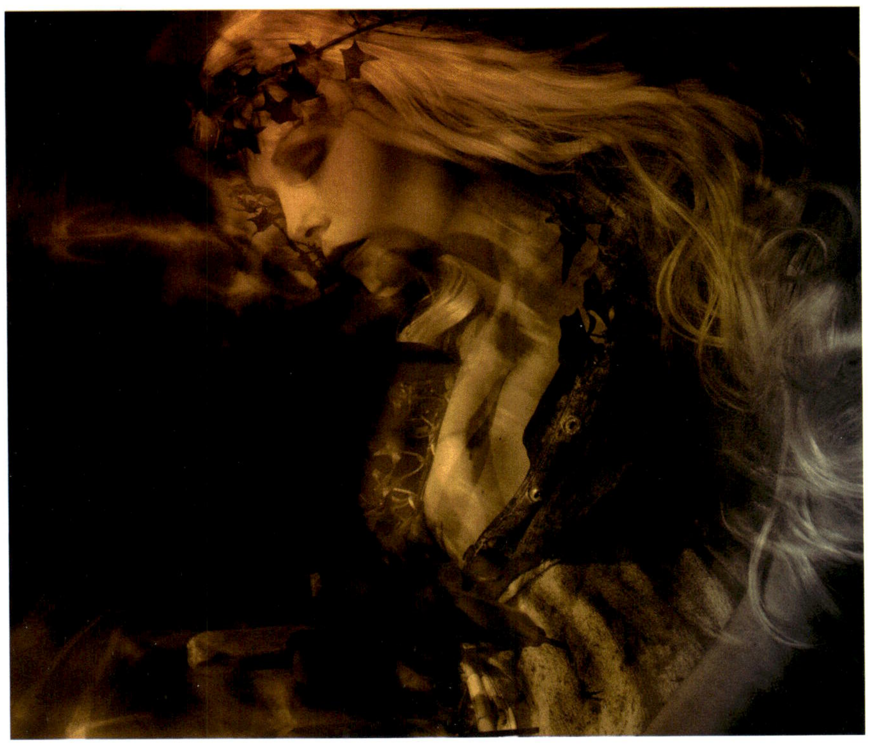

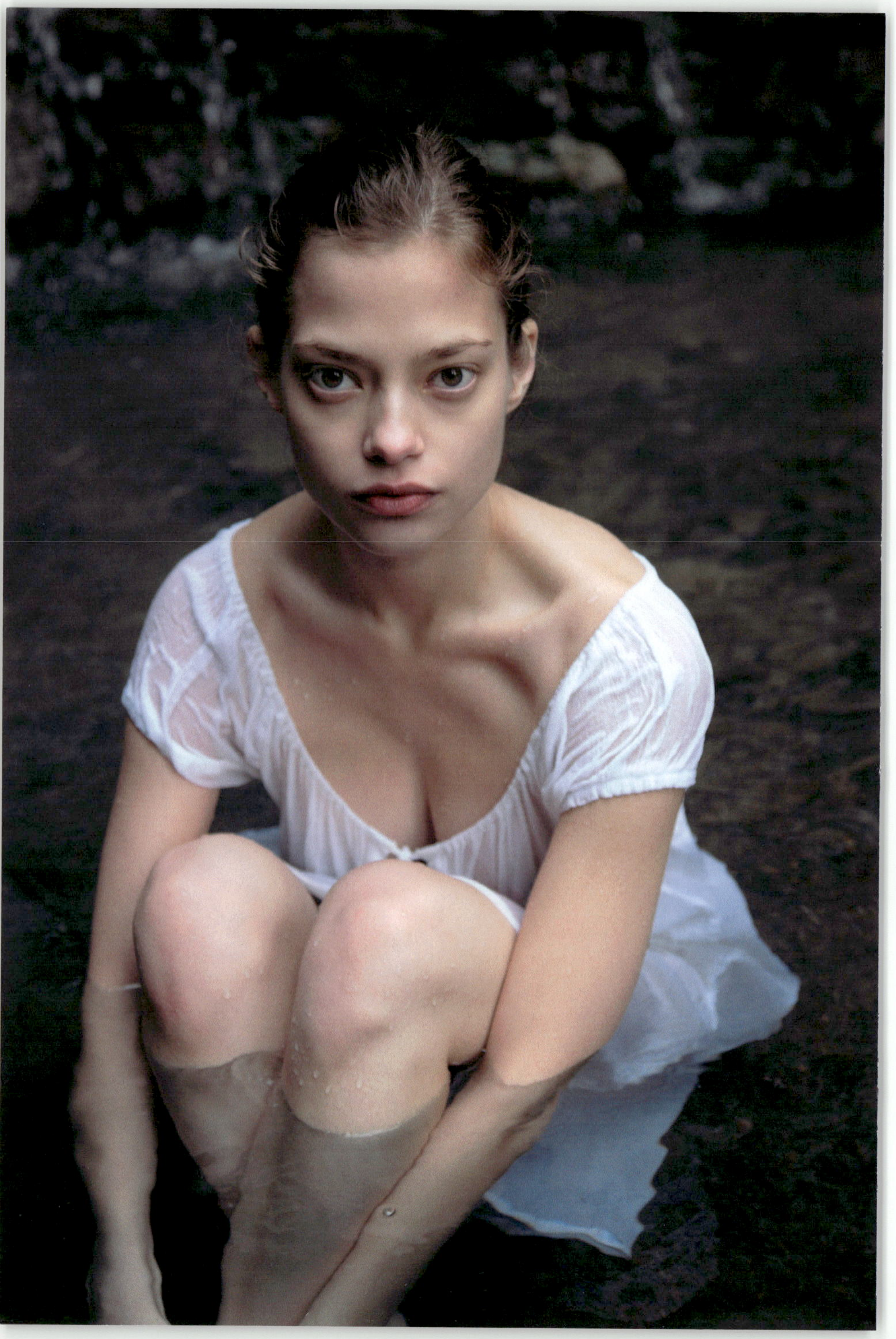

MATT SCHNEIDER

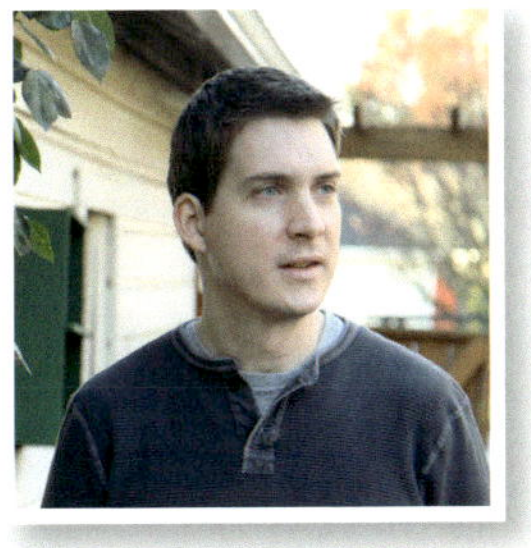

"My main focus is environmental nudes. These go beyond simply juxtaposing the human figure with the landscape, by combining form, light and the environment to convey drama and emotion. I am based in Portland, Oregon, where beaches, mountains, lakes, hot springs and ghost towns provide fertile ground for photography.

"Jennifer first developed her interest in photography, as both muse and photographer, with her self-portraits. But it was some time before she overcame her shyness and posed for others. Her modelling soon attracted the attention of agencies and photographers from as far away as Europe and she was published in several fashion magazines. Jennifer is interested in traditional photographic processes: film, wet plate, Polaroid and 8x10. She co-founded an online boutique, Norton & Sullins, which features her photographs and prints."

www.ms-photo.com

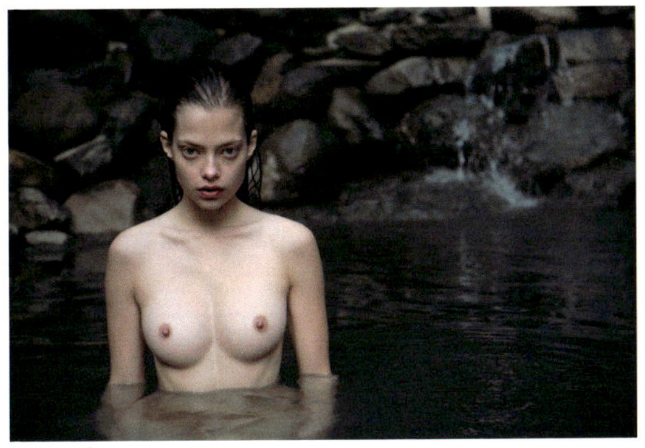

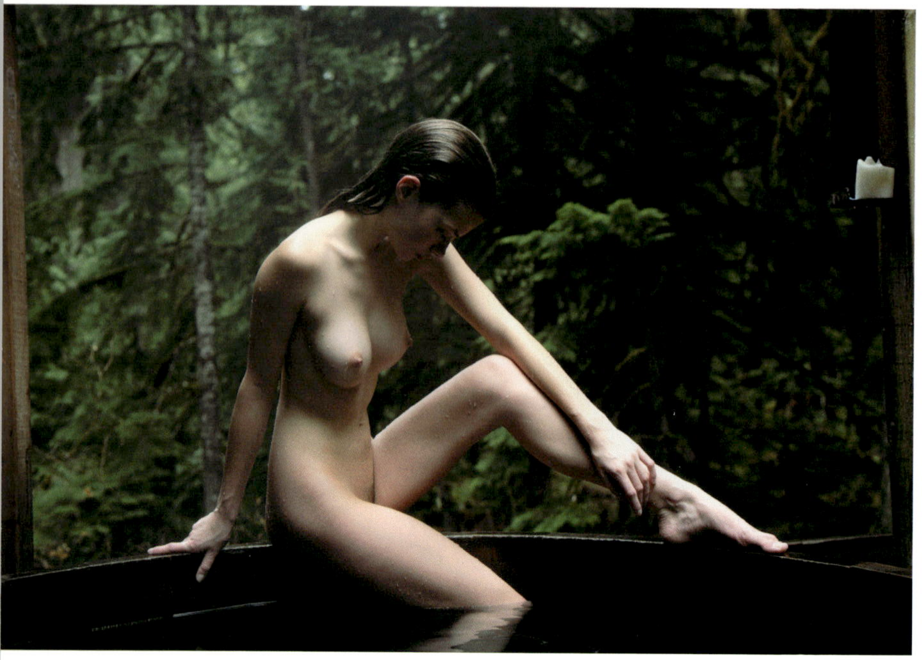

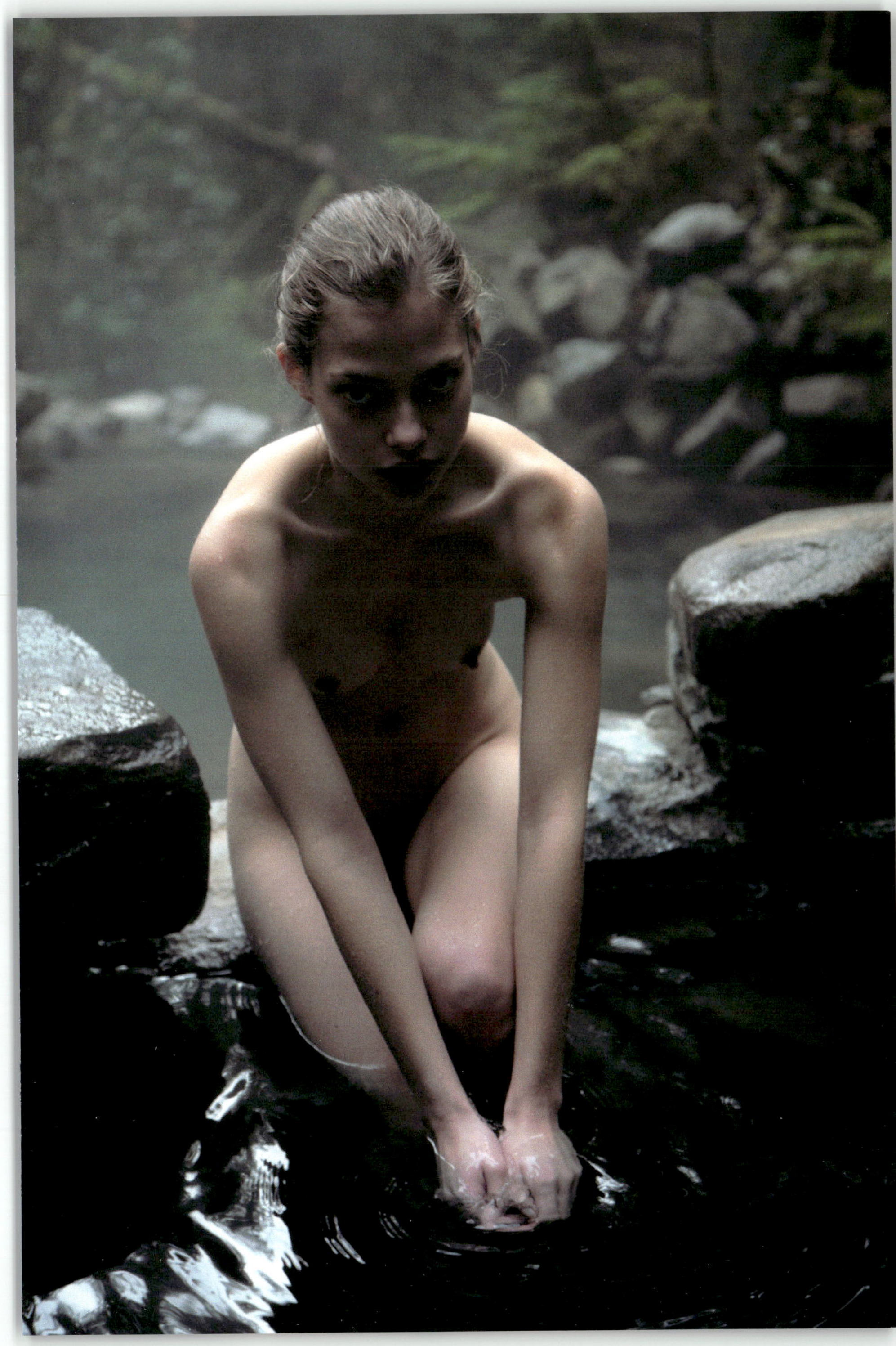

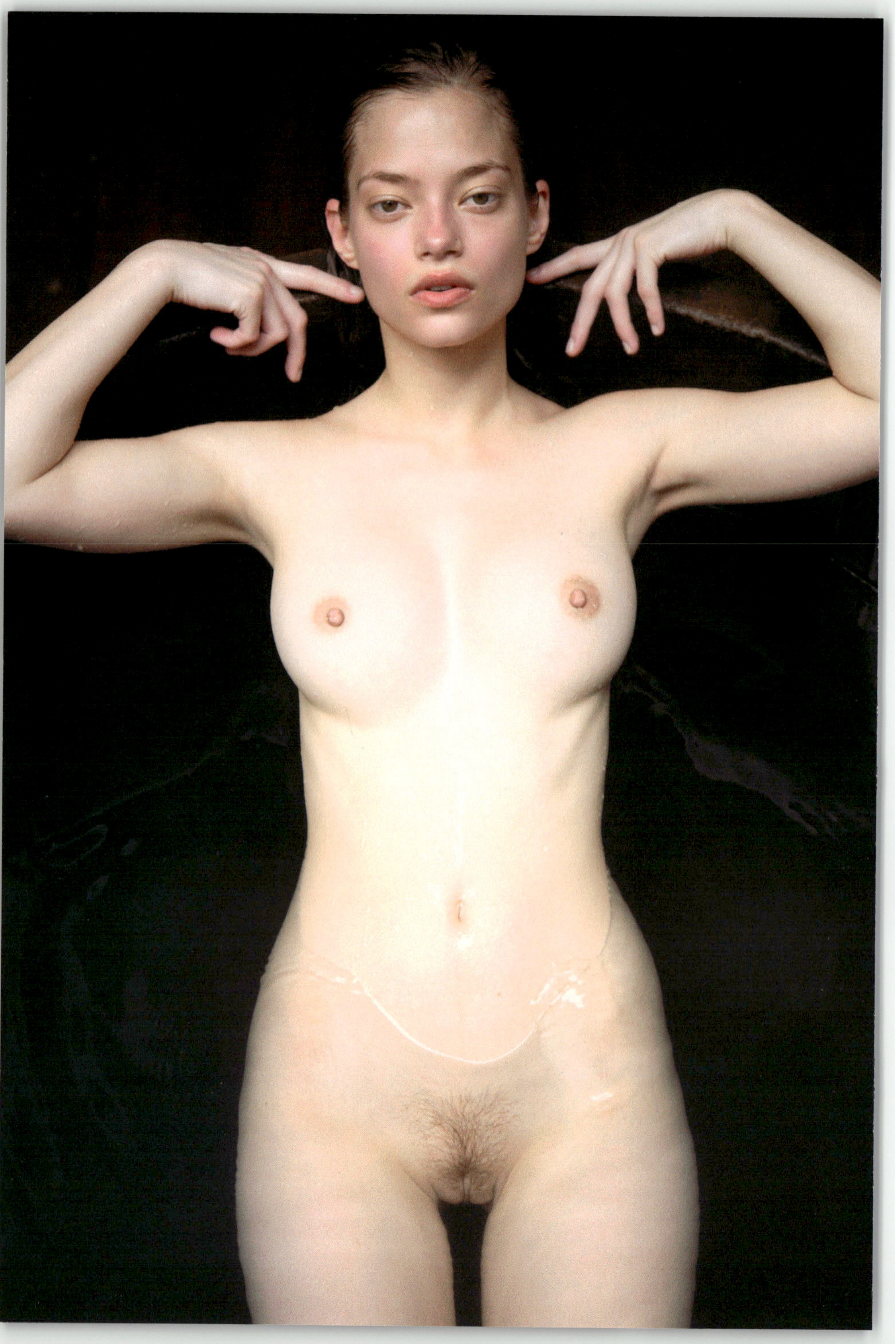

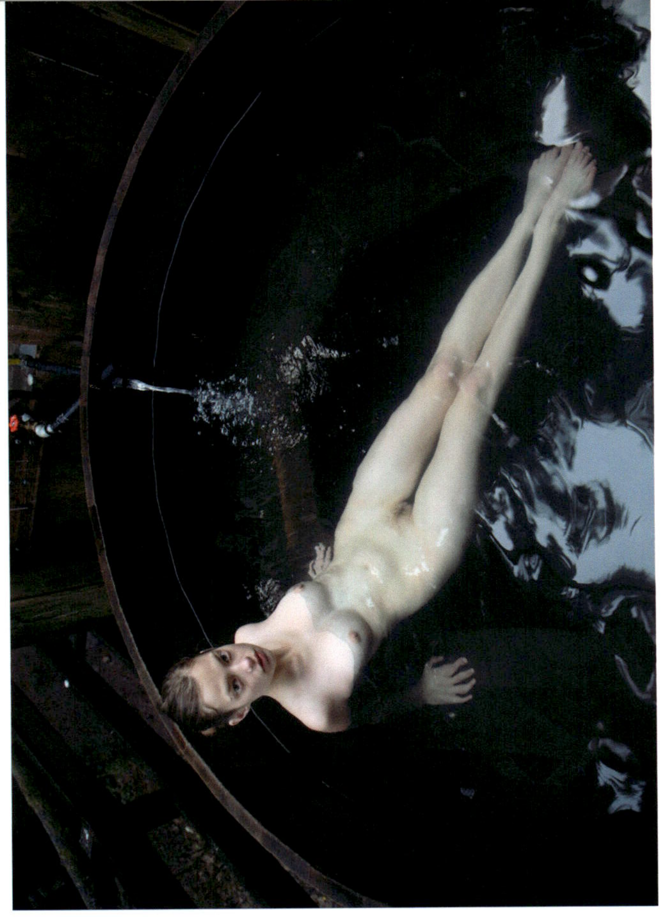

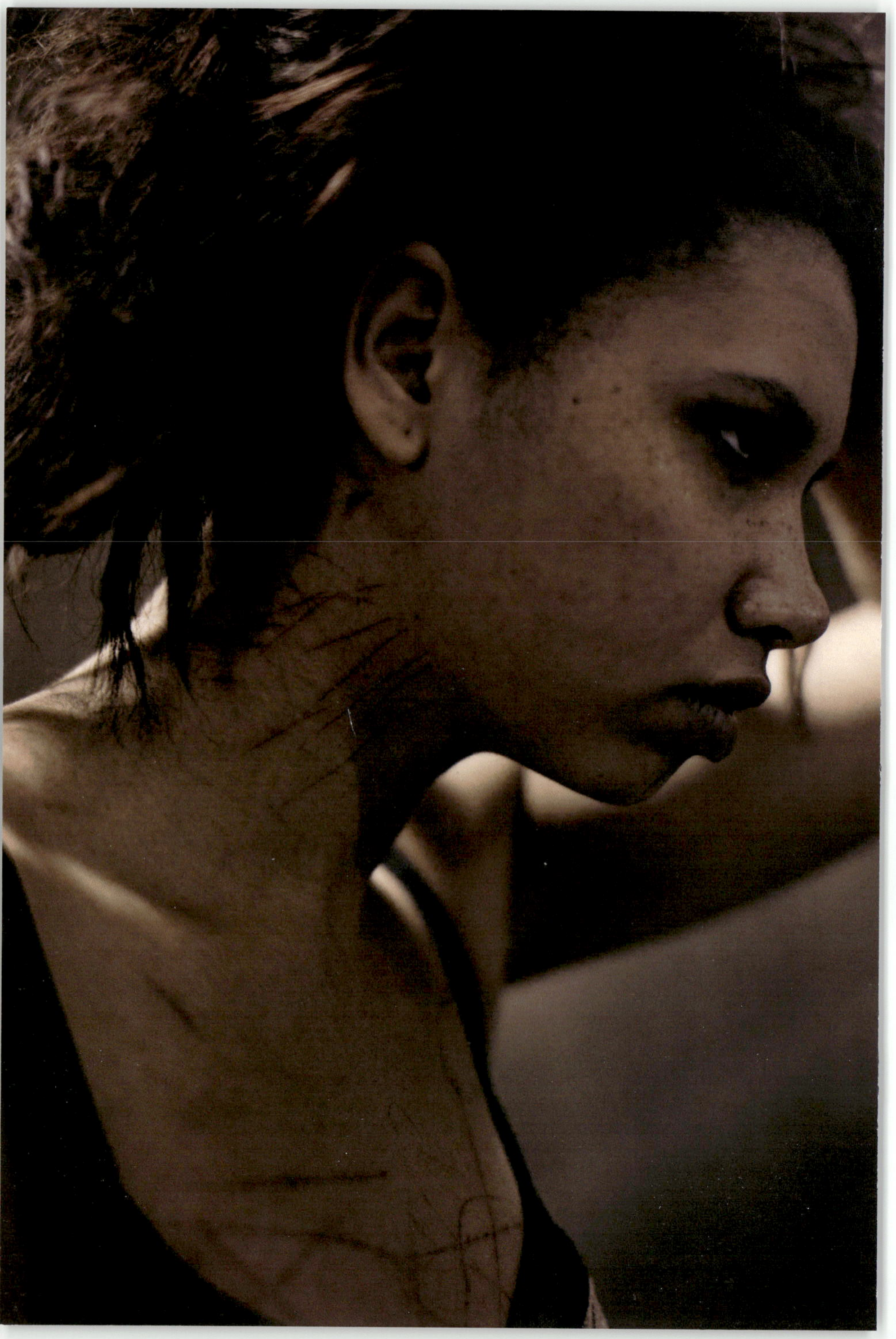

LEE SINGLECHAIR

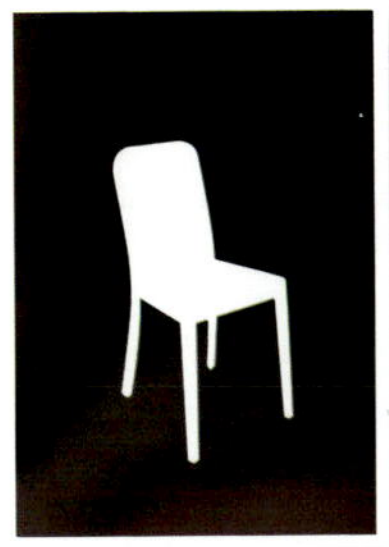

Lee Singlechair's influences include Harmony Korine, Todd Hido, Uta Barth and Mark Rothko, as well as the pornography found in men's magazines of the late seventies and early eighties. He focuses on the intersections of sexuality, fetish, emotion and story-telling. Recent work explores the dynamics of sexual and fetish encounters while playing with the limits of still imagery to suggest past, present and future moments of interaction. His work has been exhibited nationally and his first solo show opened in Indianapolis in 2011.

"The first time I shot Kedesh I sensed her intense energy. She has in equal parts stunning beauty, fierce passion, frightening intensity, compassion, grace, depth and intelligence. I am lucky to have worked with her and my work would not have been the same without her influence."

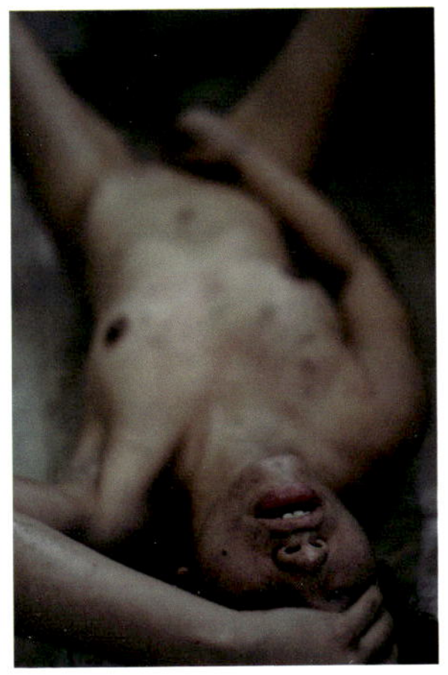

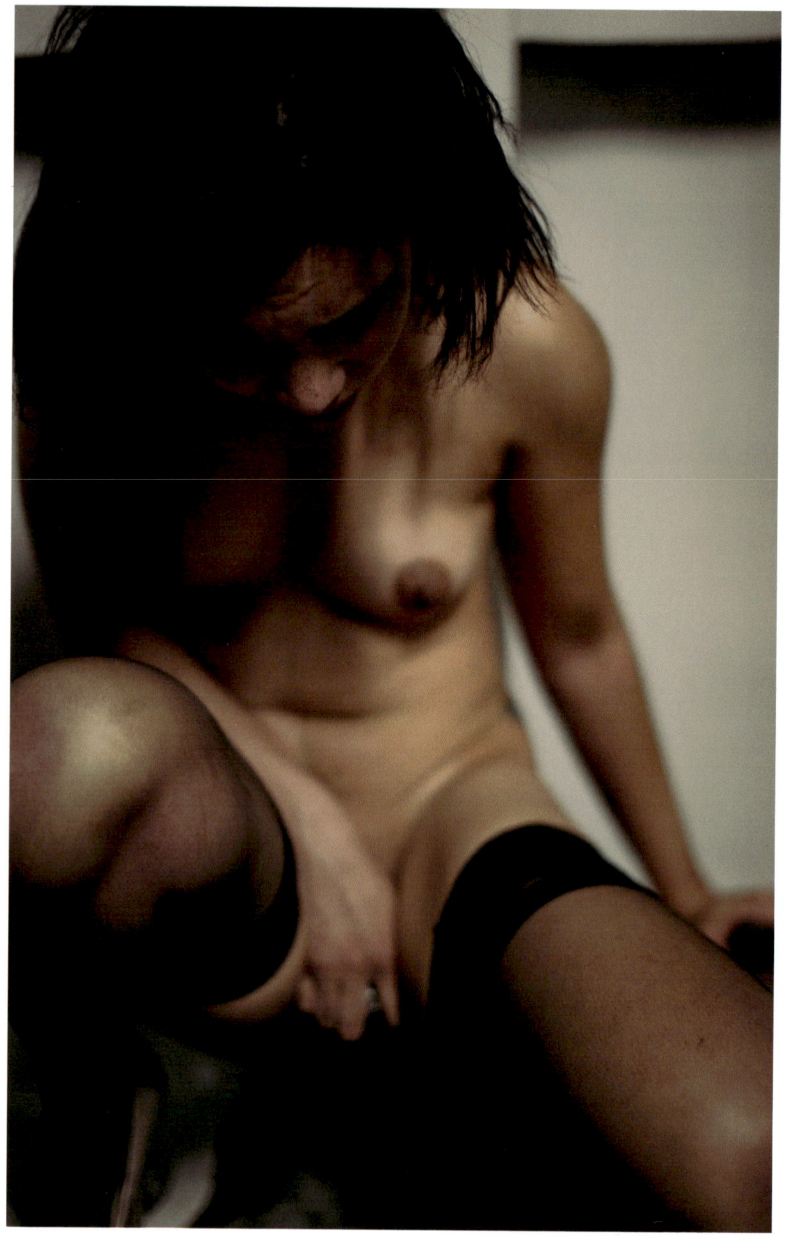

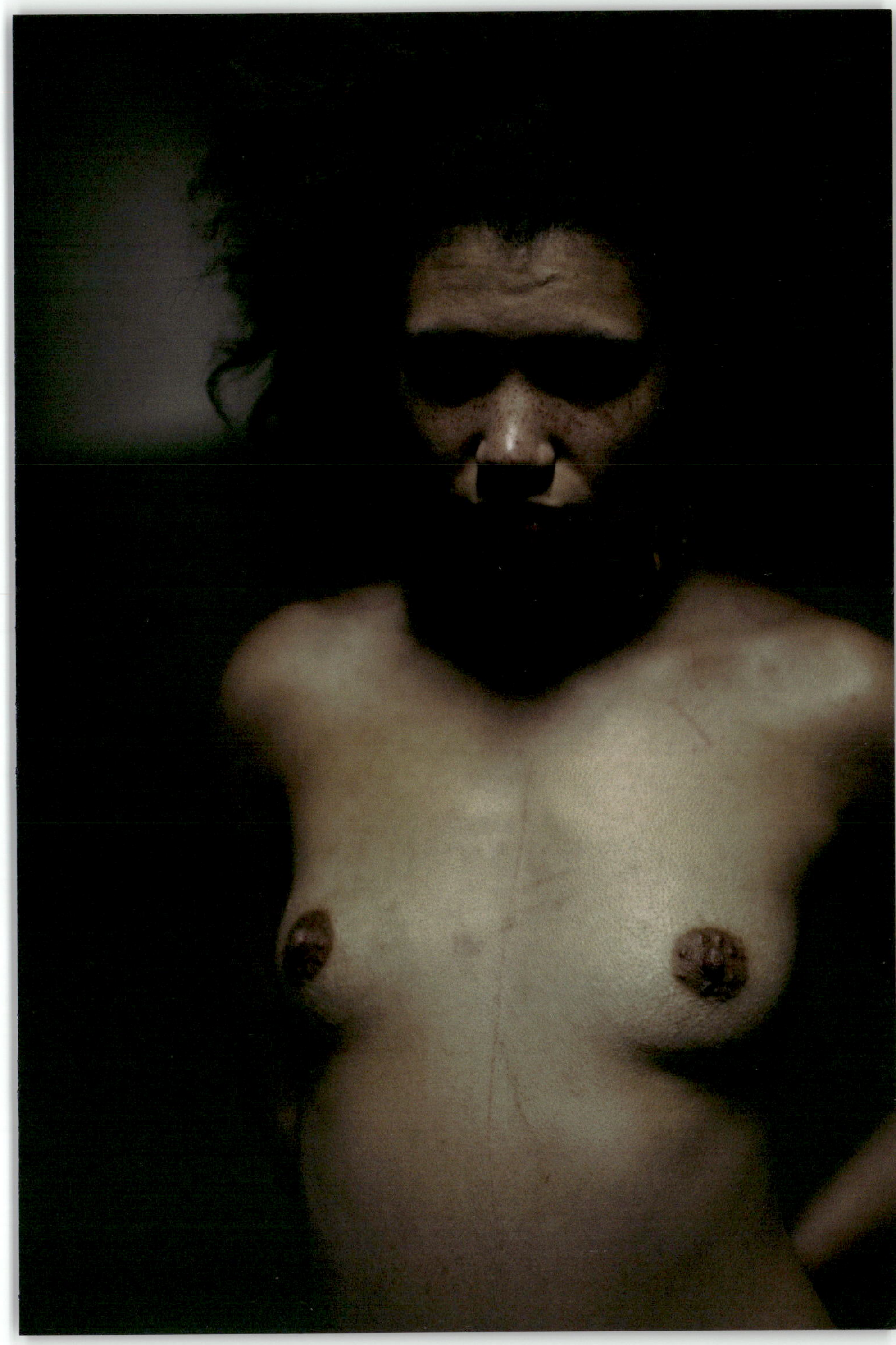

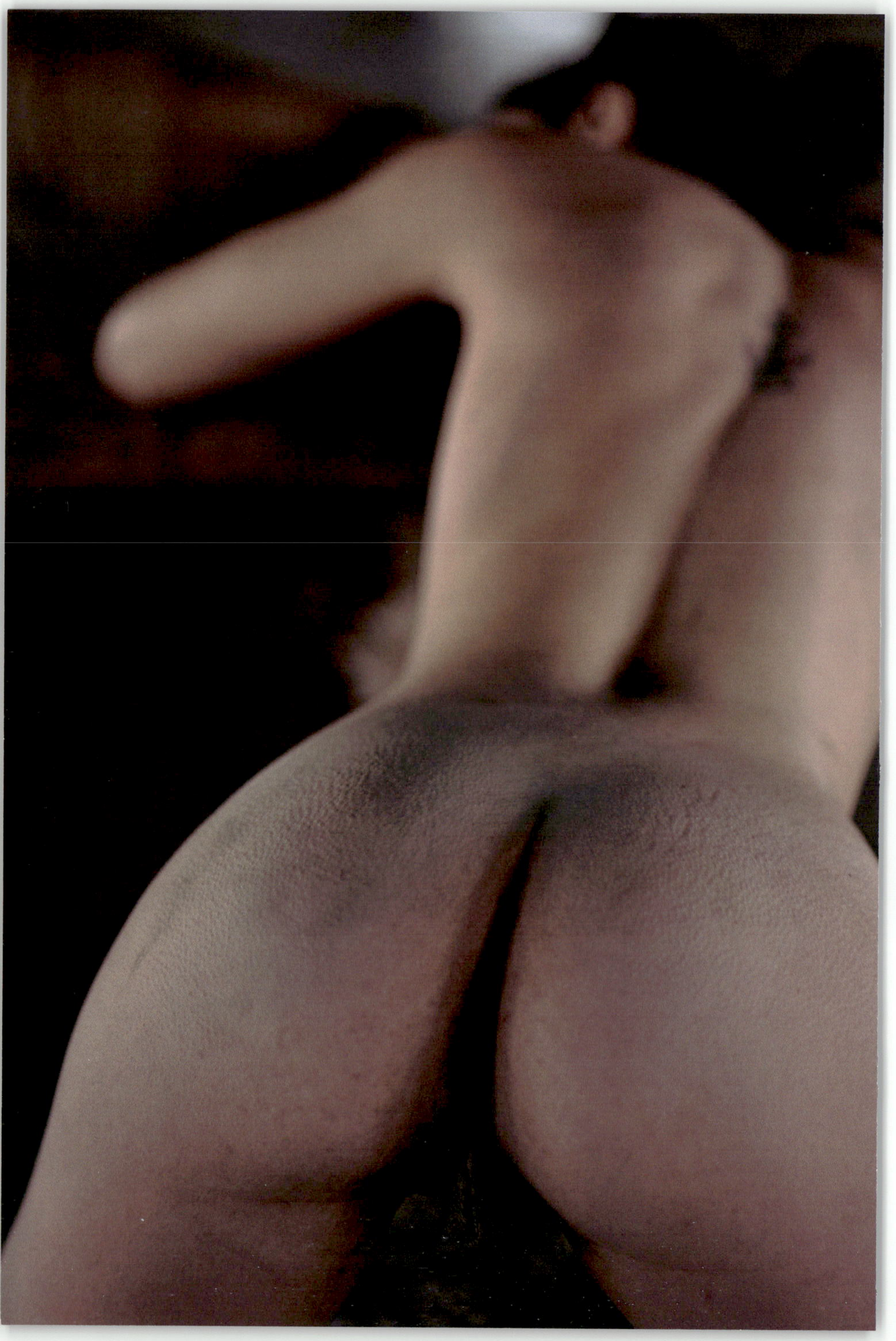

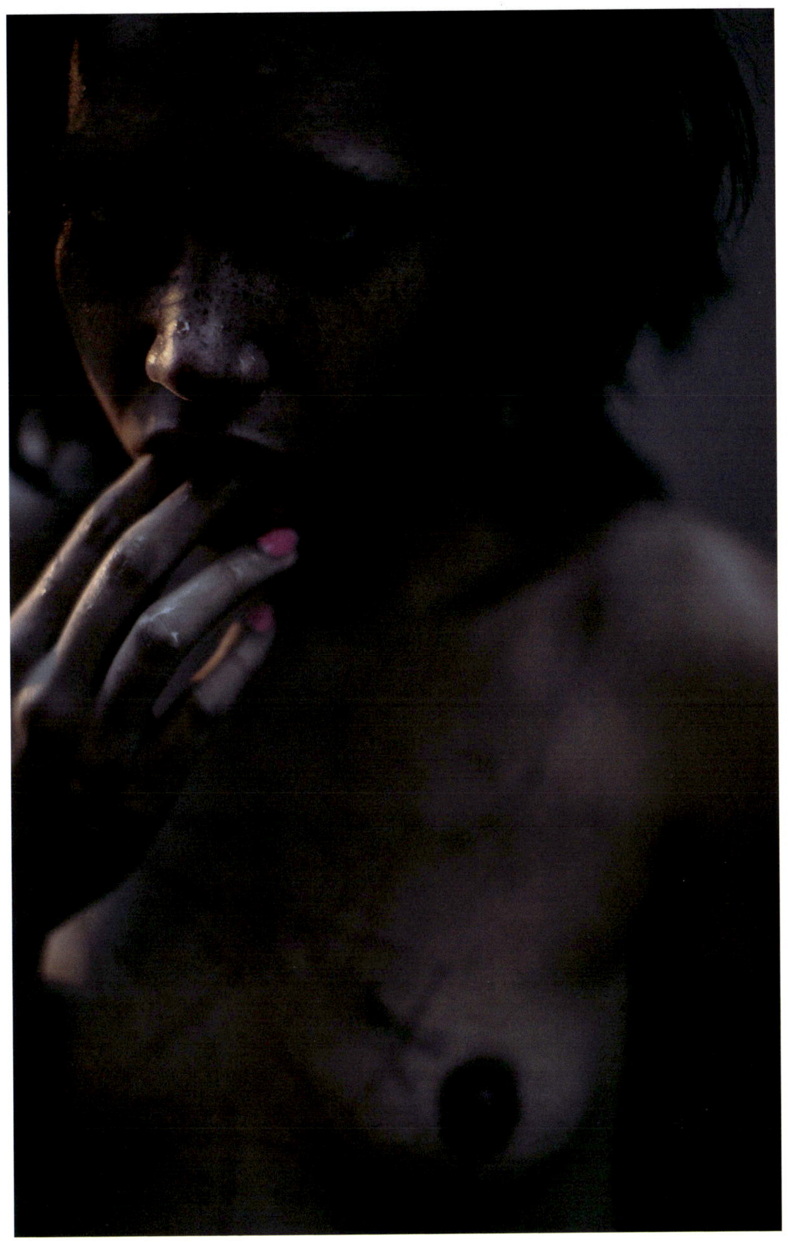

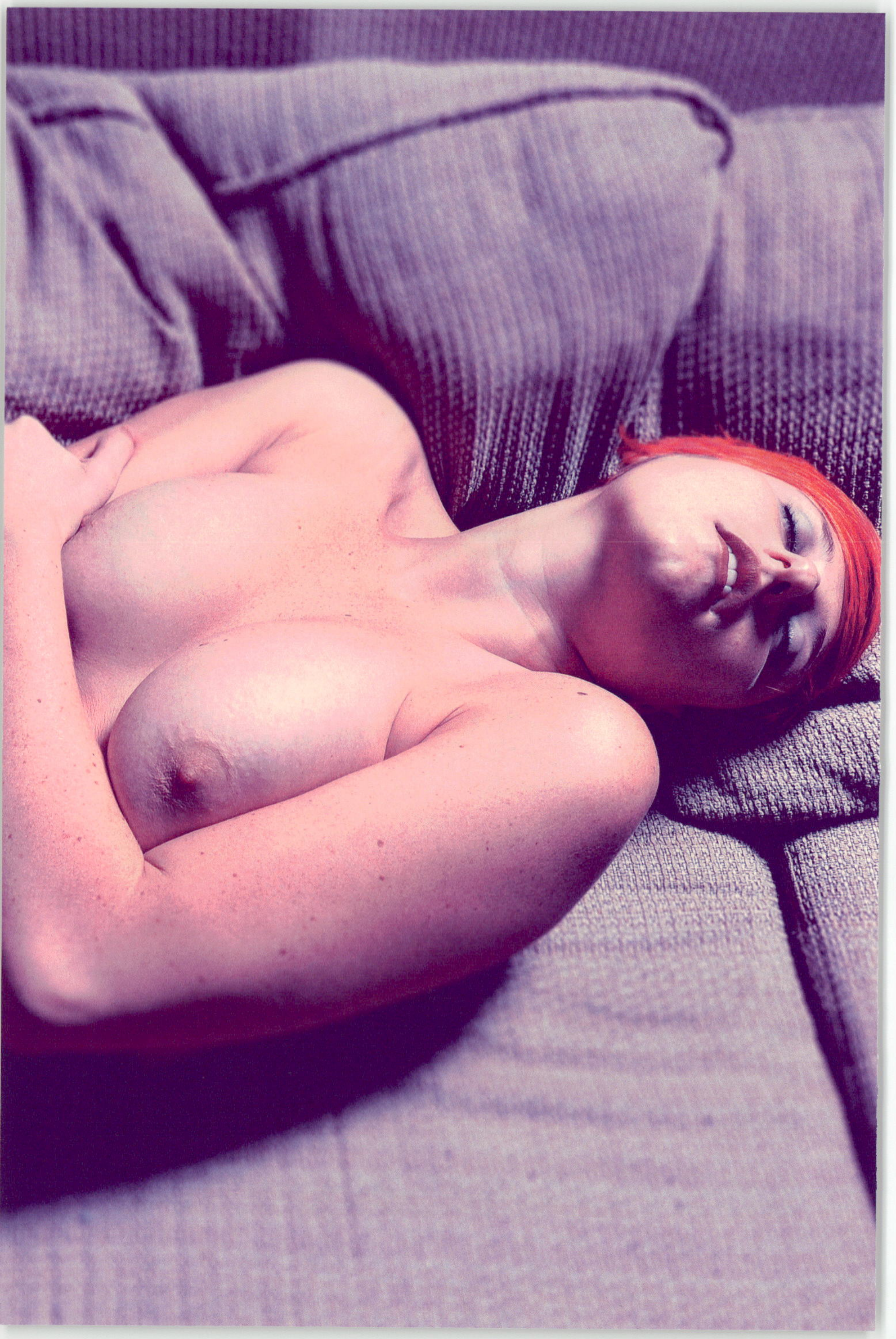

CEDRIC SMITH

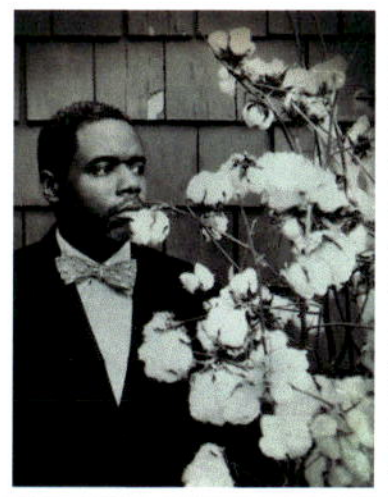

Cedric Smith is a self-taught photographer, currently living in Savannah, Georgia, though he is better known for his paintings, which are exhibited and collected worldwide. He draws on a wide range of influences and sources, traditional and contemporary. He began photography seven years ago, addressing everything from race issues to eroticism. The new work derived from what makes a woman sexy. In this series light plays a big part, conveying the feeling you get in strip clubs when the lights are dim and the performer is spotlit.

"I chose Cherry La Voix because she's a burlesque performer and model. I knew she would be very comfortable with her body and she is quite sensual. Also, as a dancer she had an advantage over some of the models I'd photographed before."

www.cedricphotography.com

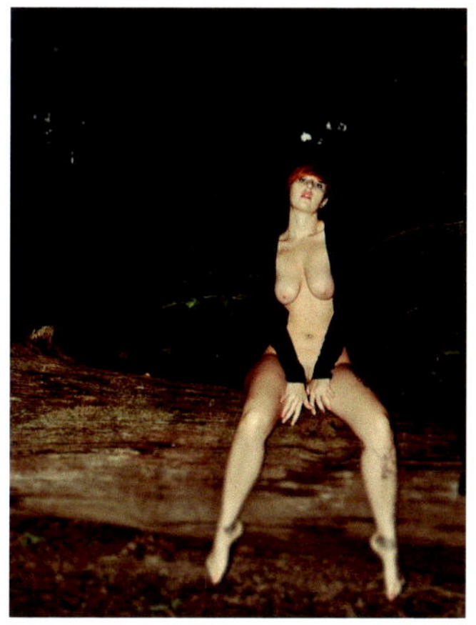

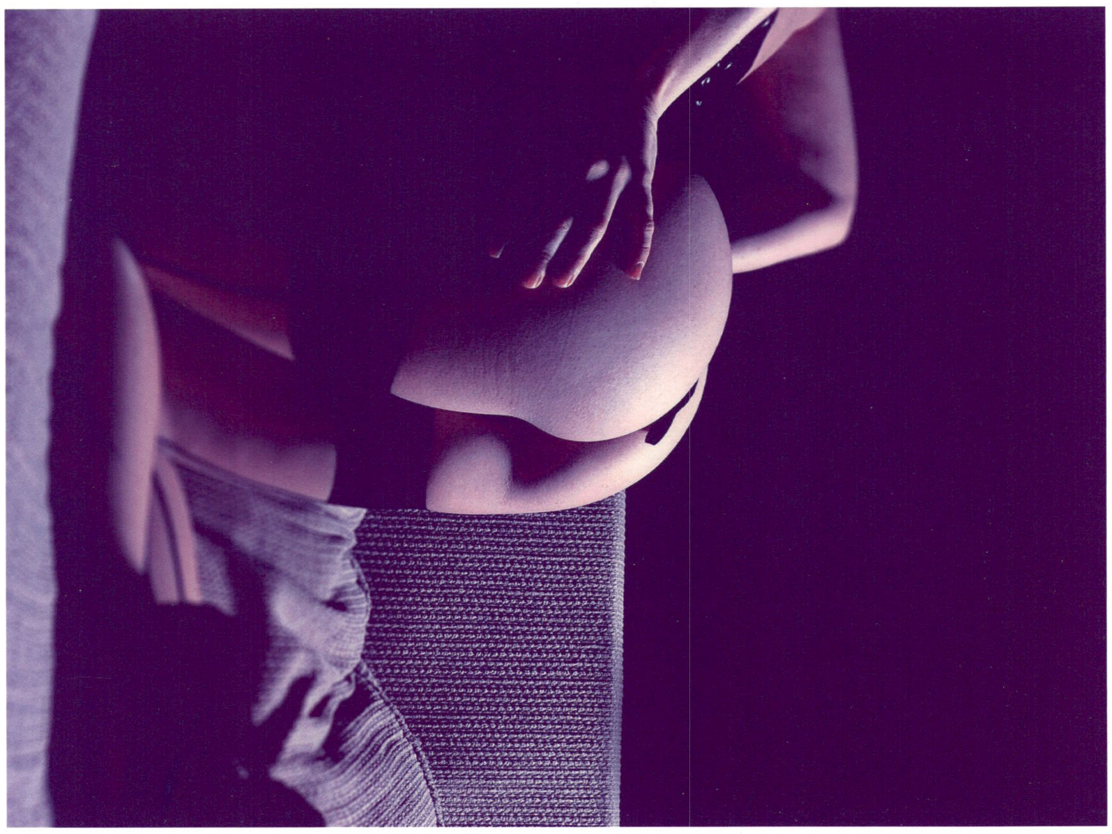

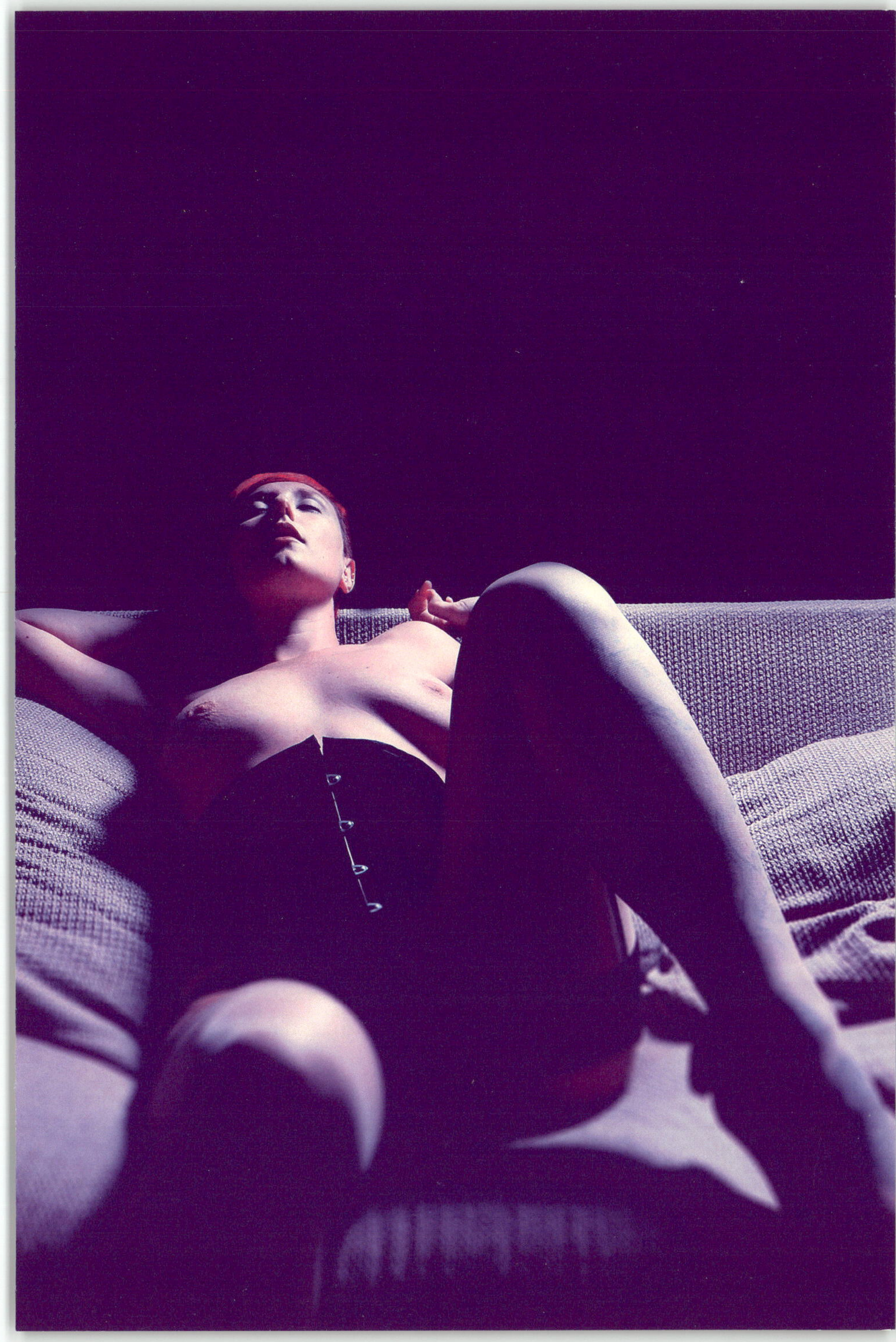

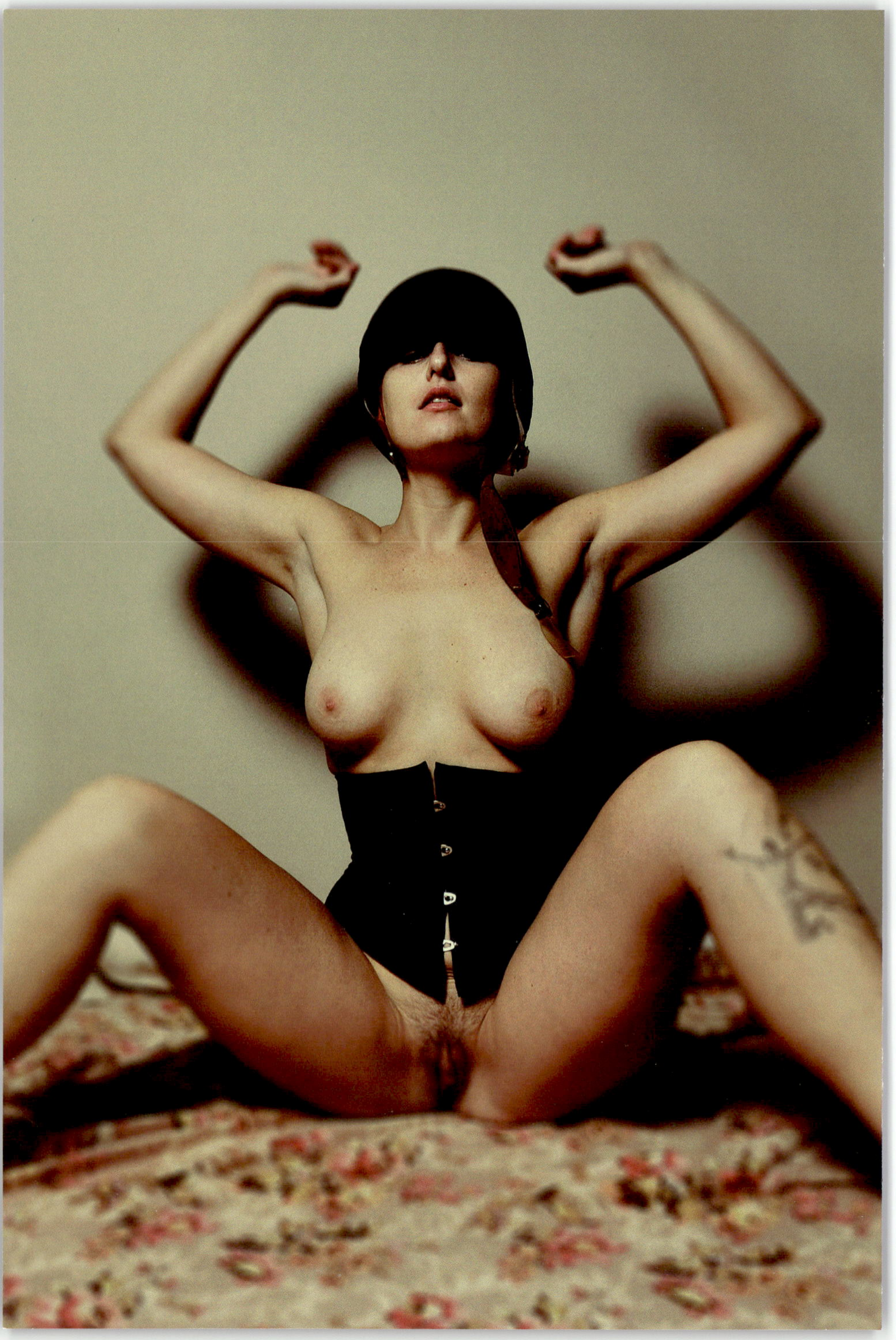

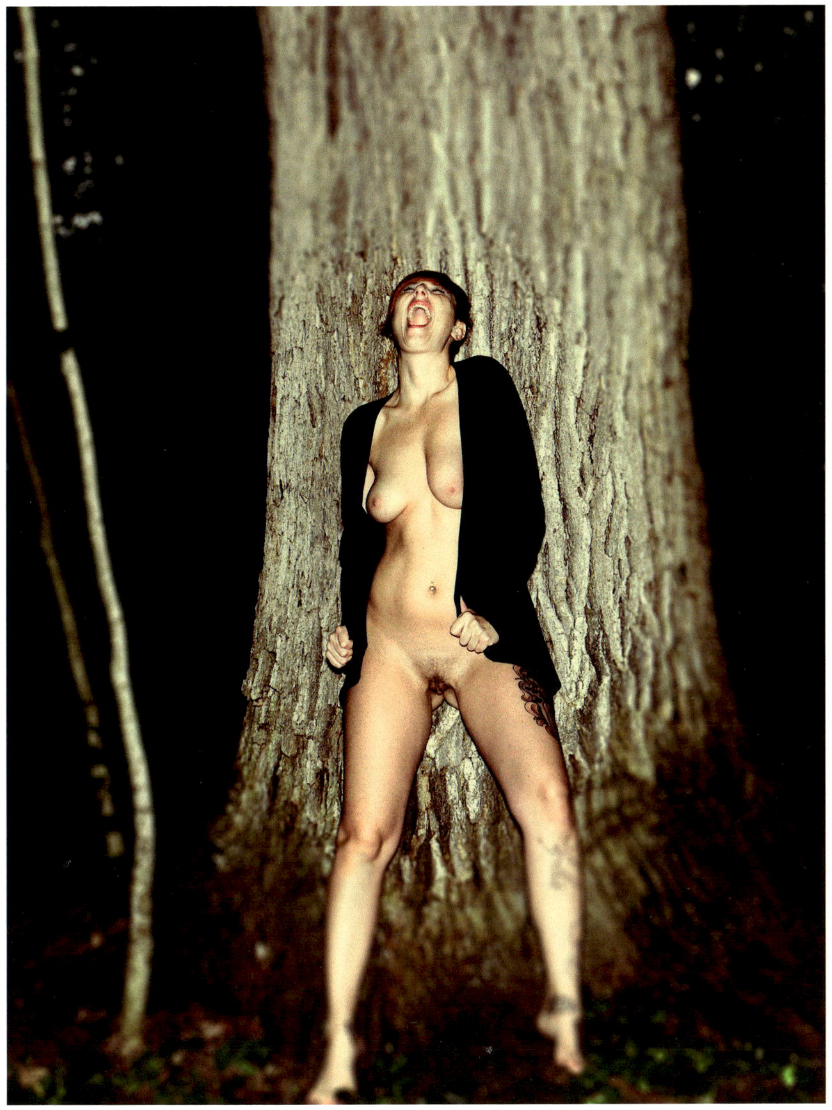

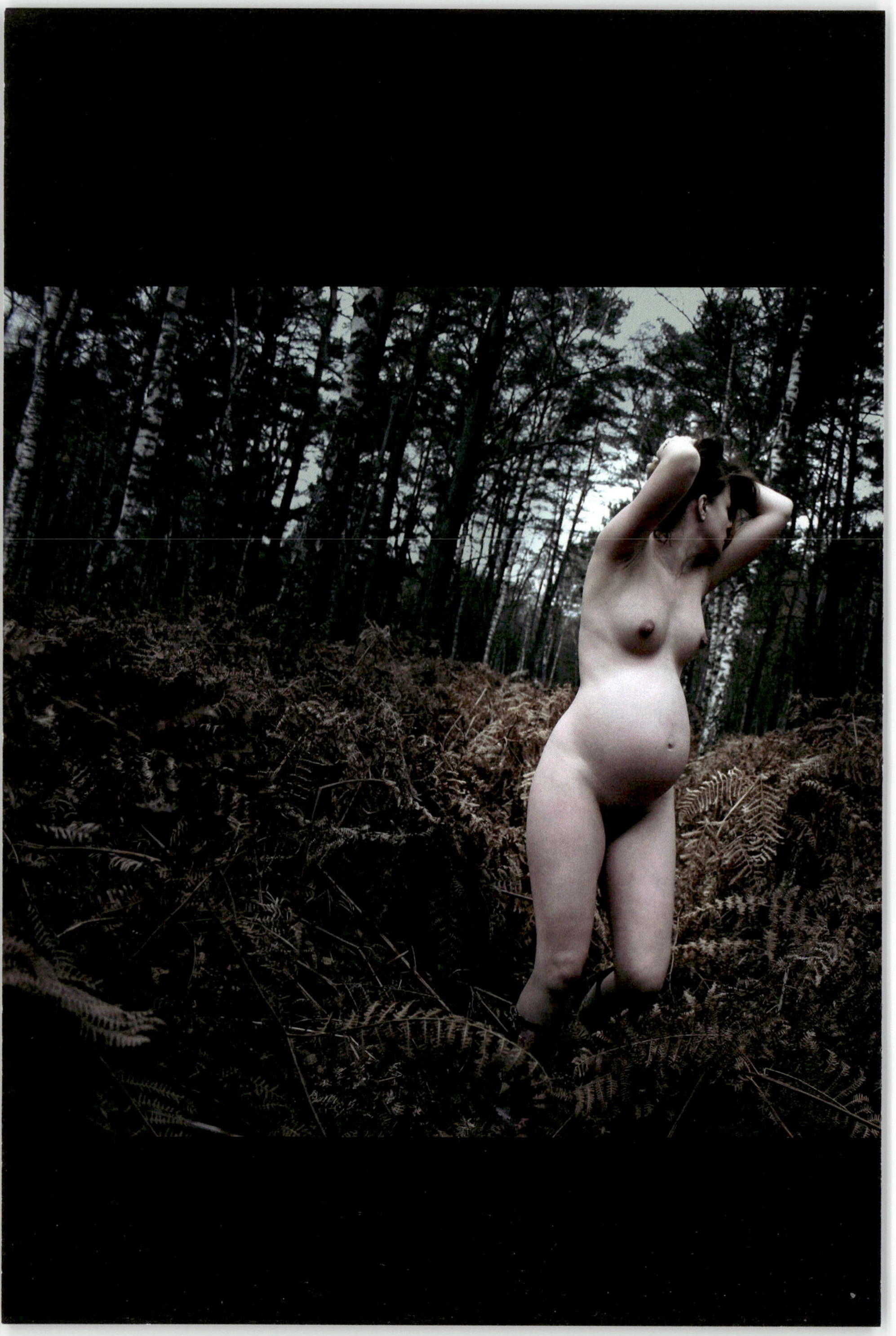

VANDA SPENGLER

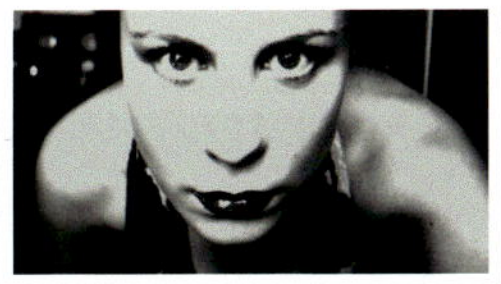

In her photographs self-taught artist Vanda Spengler has created a very personal universe, one which mixes introspection, fantasy and a dehumanized eroticism. She often uses self-portrait and "self-nude" methods to capture human beings' wanderings and their insoluble quest for identity.

Vanda's photographs, both narrative and cinematic, make us dive into a wild and fantasized femininity which can recall the work of Cindy Sherman or Francesca Woodman. In this photographic series she tells us many stories about her own pregnancy.

www.vanda.spengler.free.fr

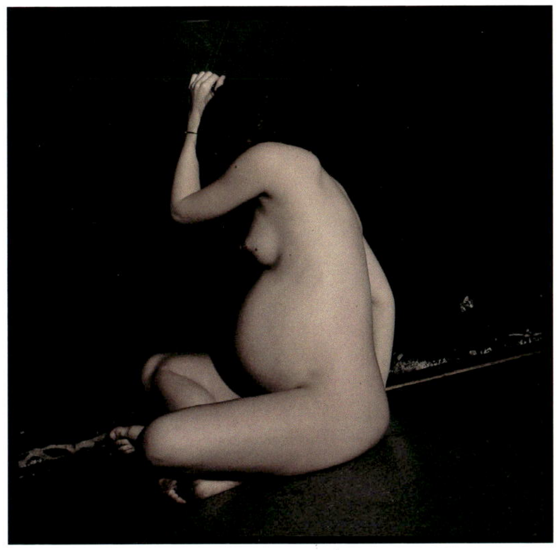

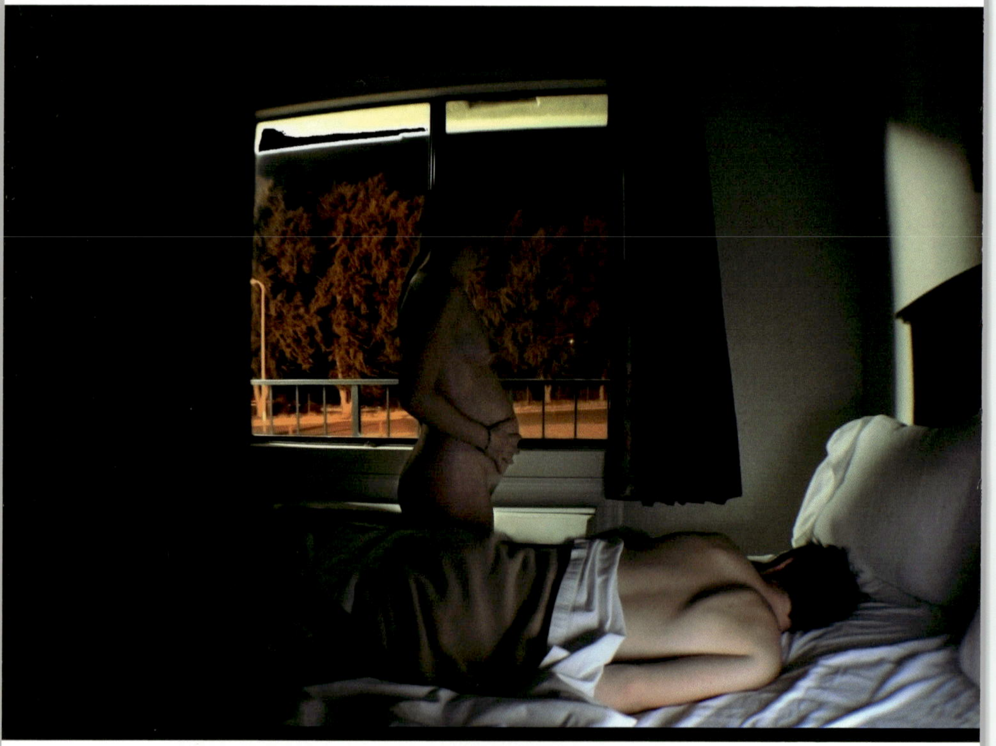

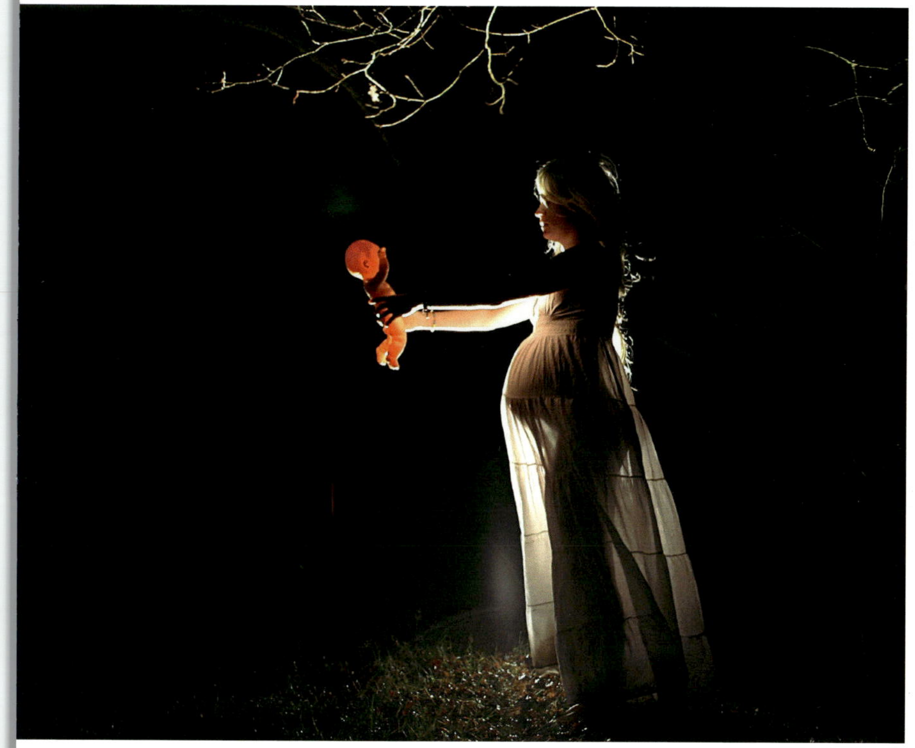

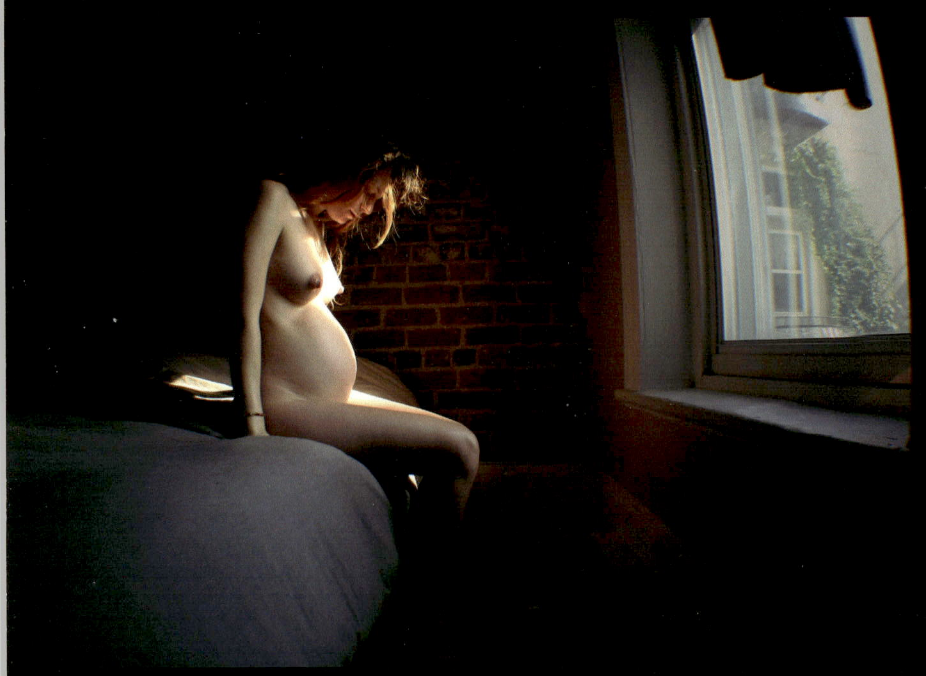

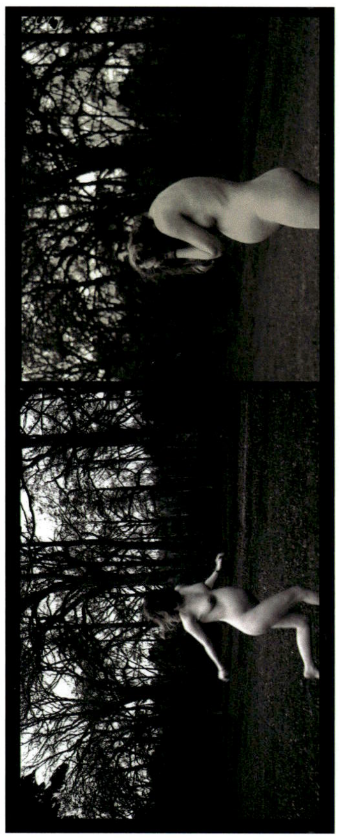

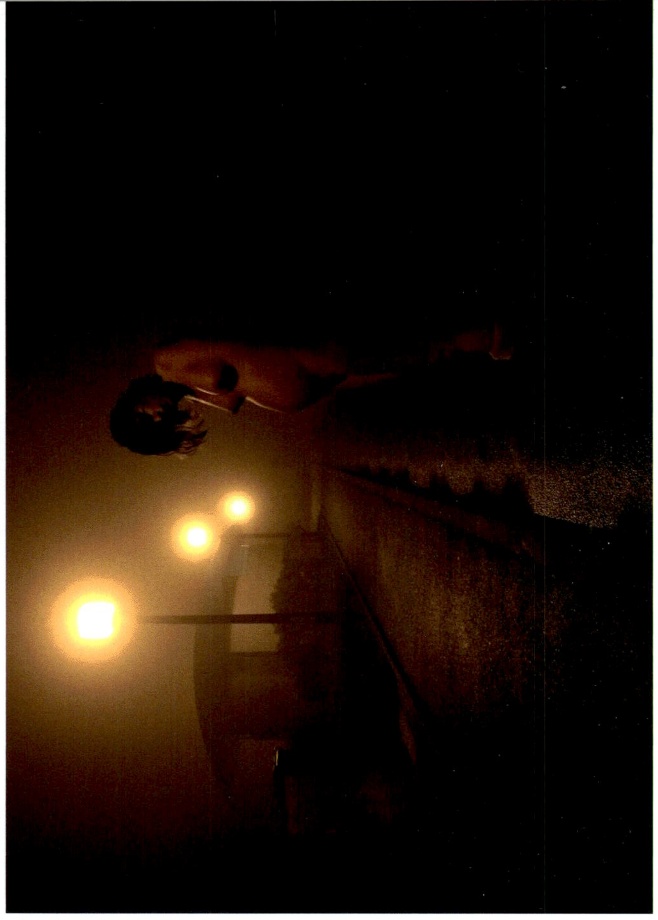

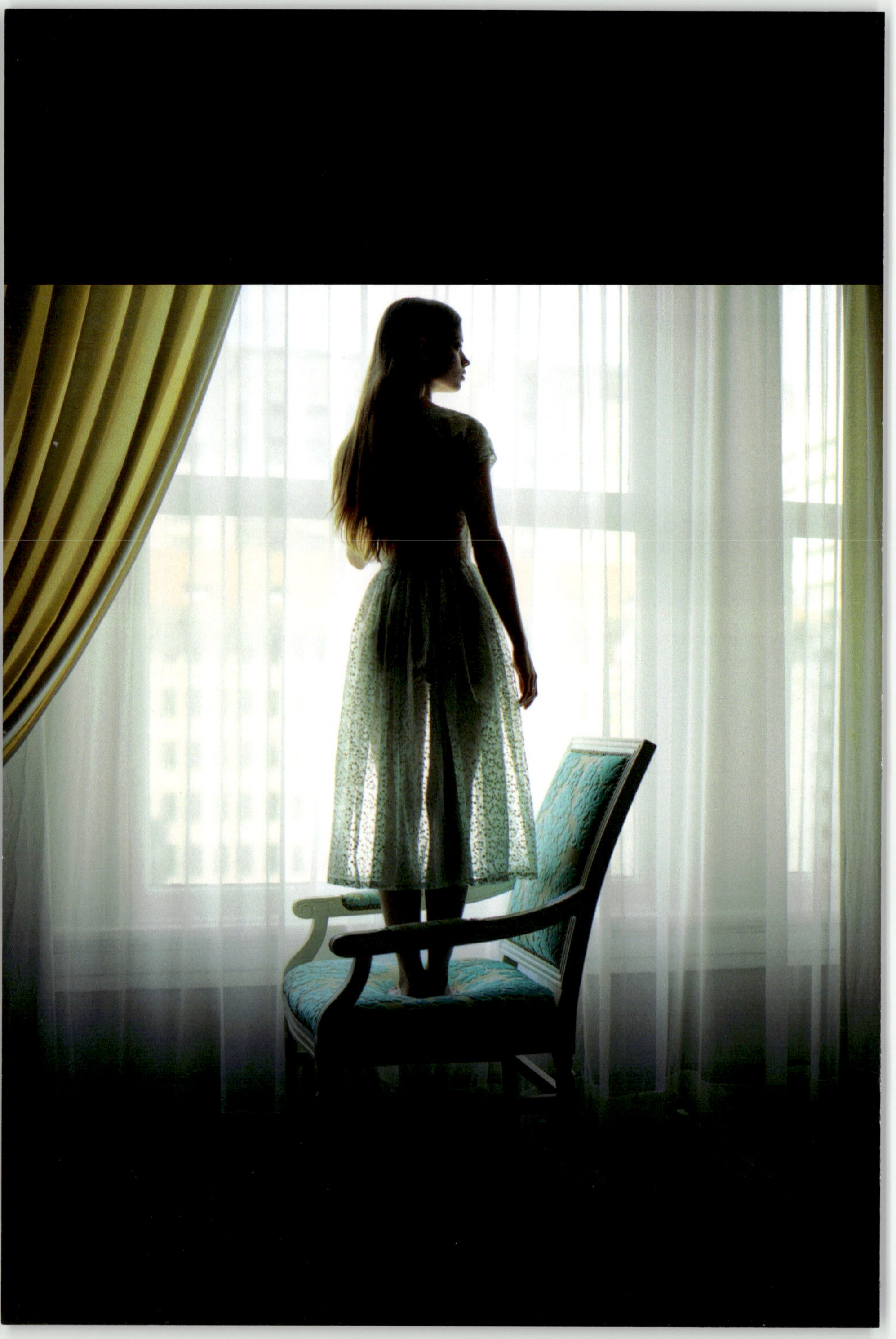

PATRICIO SUAREZ

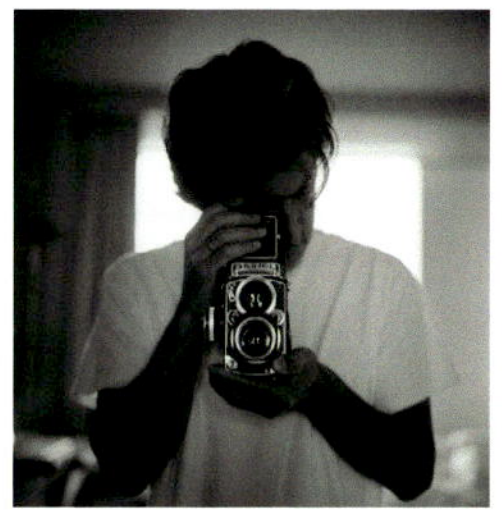

"Early on in life I carried a camera everywhere, fascinated by how it perpetuated a moment for ever. Later I became a director of photography in the film business and photography took a back seat for a decade. Then one day I rediscovered my camera. I'd never stopped shooting, I'd just stopped looking. But it was not until about ten years ago that I started exploring myself with photography; it became my therapy. I'm constantly observing, but I'm more interested in what you can't see than in what you can.

"Ryonen has an aura that mesmerizes. This small, almost fairy-like woman was completely transformed when I first saw her through the lens. She broke all rules of scale and perspective and became an Amazon. Ryonen owned the moment. She exudes femininity and sensuality. She symbolizes it."

www.psuarez.com

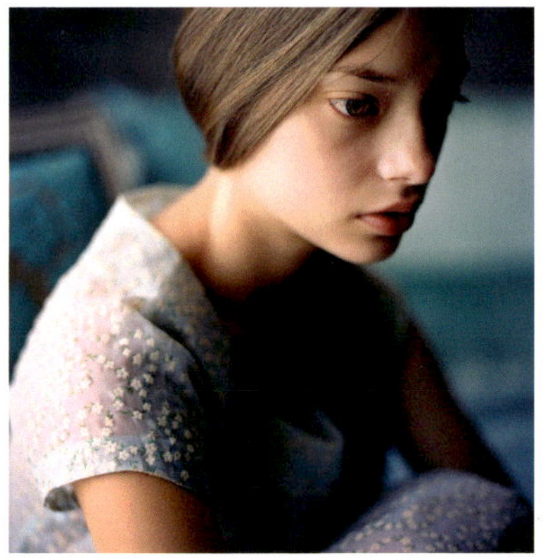

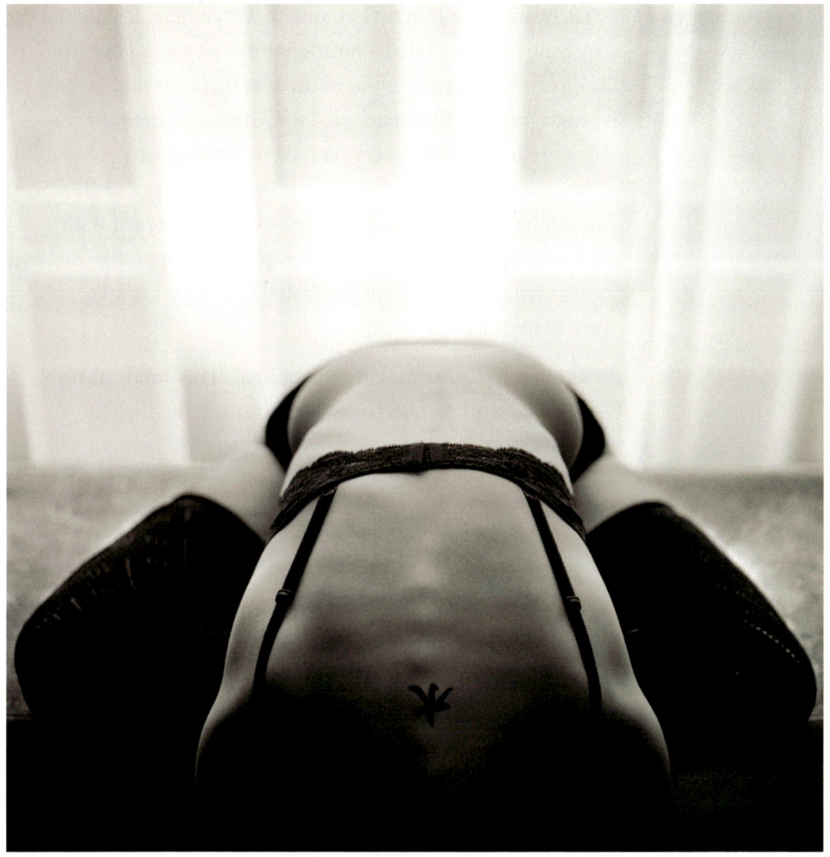

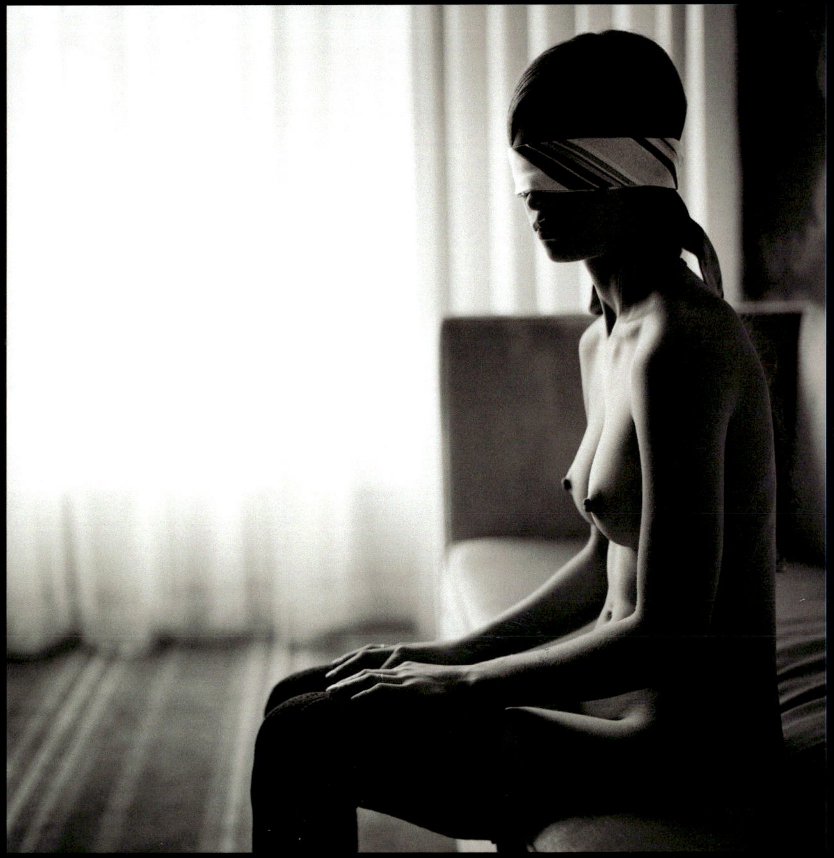

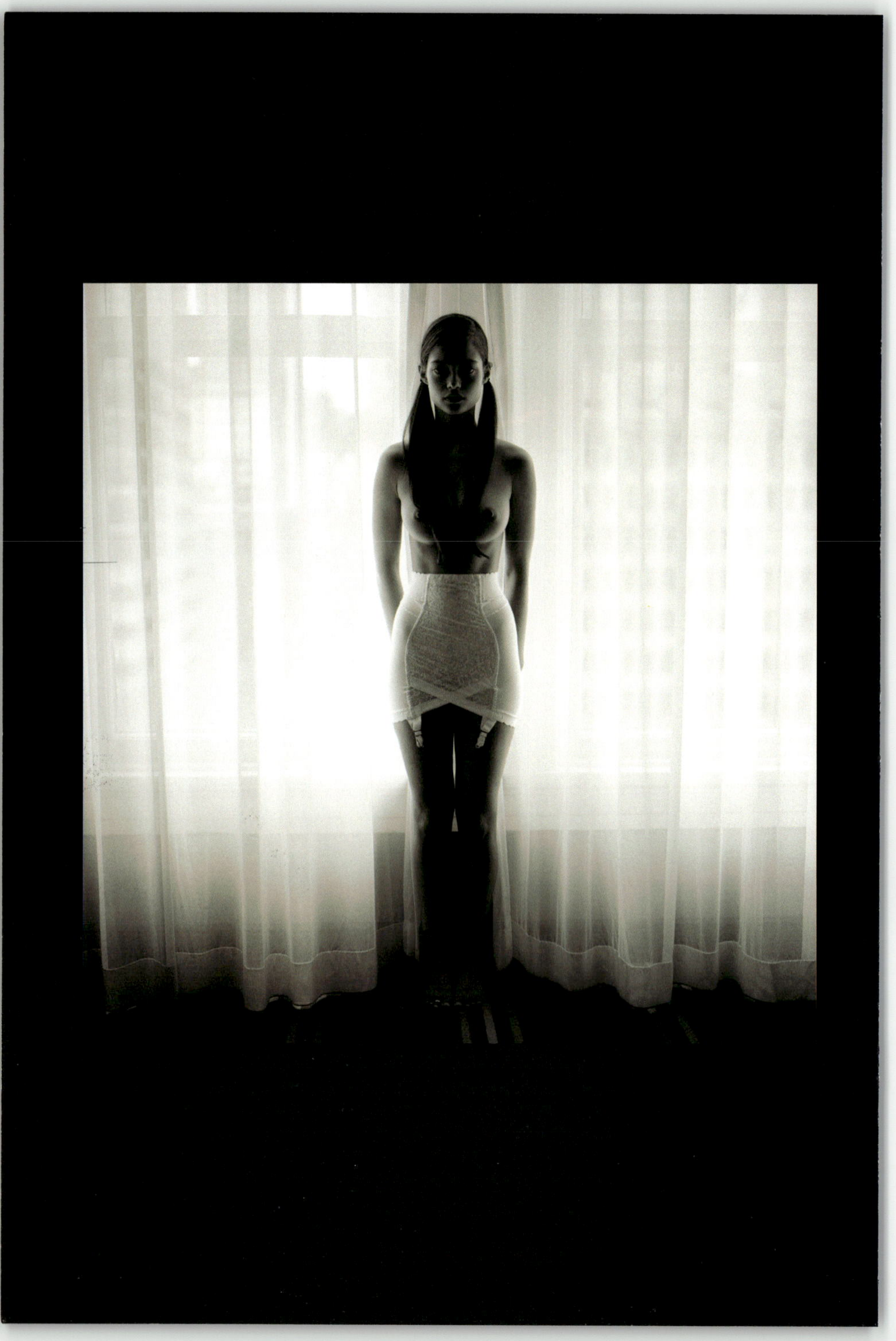

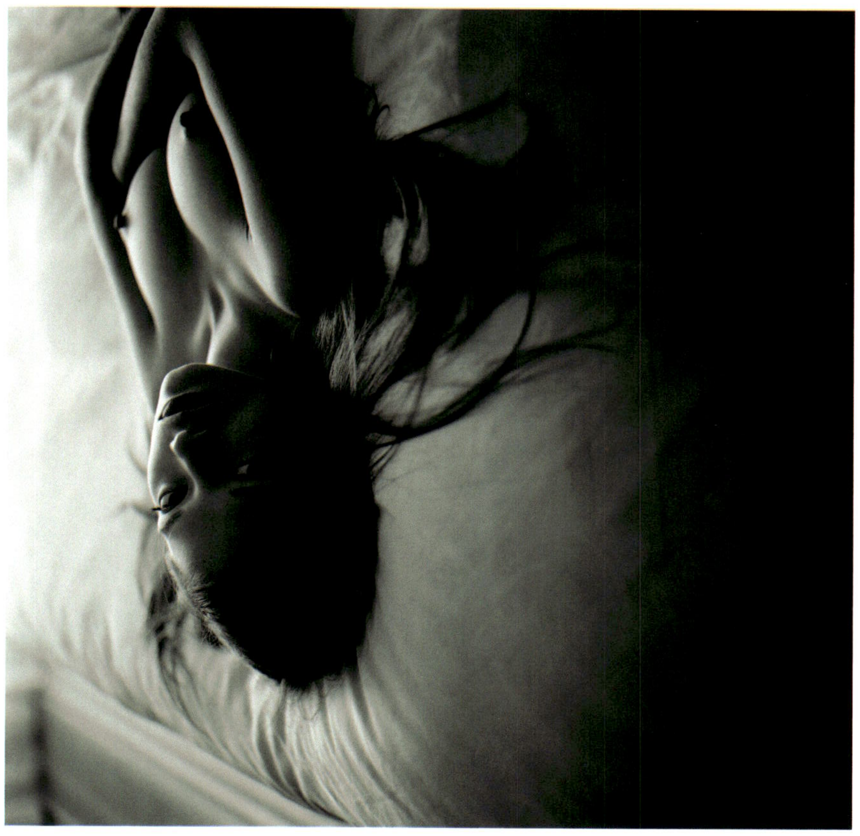

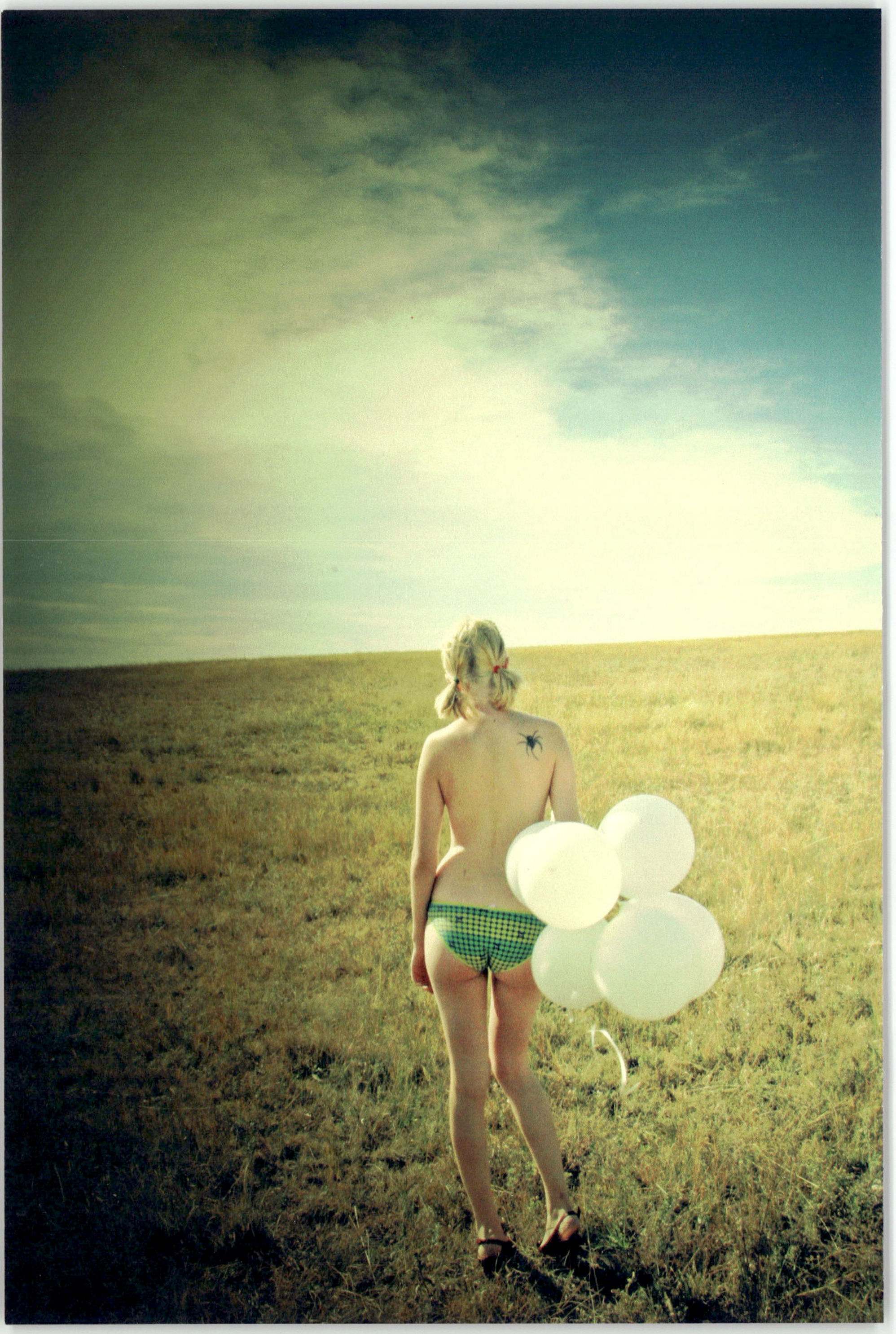

REBECCA TILLETT

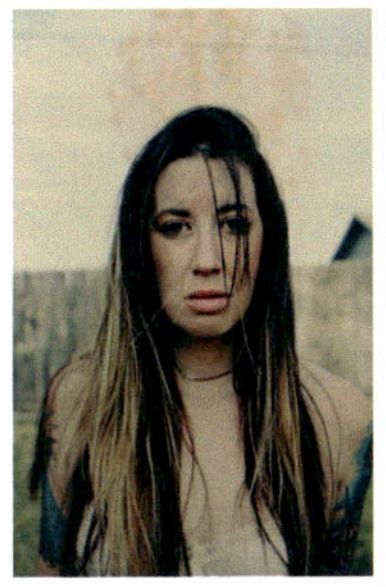

Rebecca Tillett is a graphic designer and photographer whose work rides the thin line between quirky fashion, the fashionably nude and grit. Her favourite subjects are naked females and her favourite locations are anywhere but a studio. She found early inspiration in photographers like Chas Ray Krider, Natacha Merritt, Guy Bourdin and David LaChapelle, and continues to be inspired by television, celebrities, religion, contemporary artists like J. Scott Campbell and Caitlin Hackett, friends, society's shadows, prudish America, illustrators and anything nostalgic, old or abandoned.

Rebecca has had several solo shows, most recently at the Mondo Bizzarro Gallery in Rome, Italy, in 2010, and has participated in numerous collaborative exhibitions, domestic and international. She and the beautiful Ms Jessalyn Dean have collaborated on many shoots, their chemistry producing some amazing photographs.

www.rebeccatillett.com

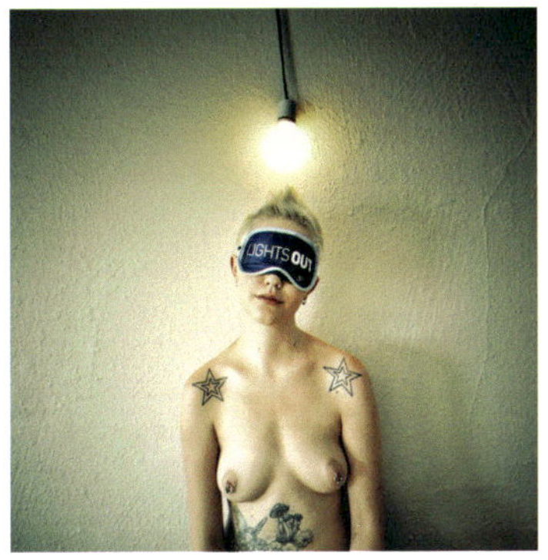

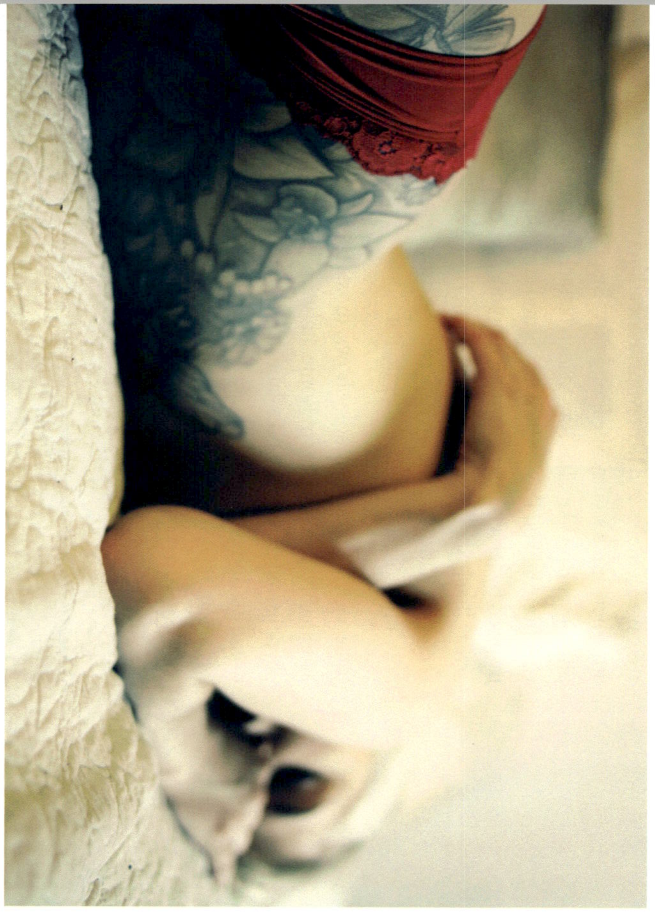

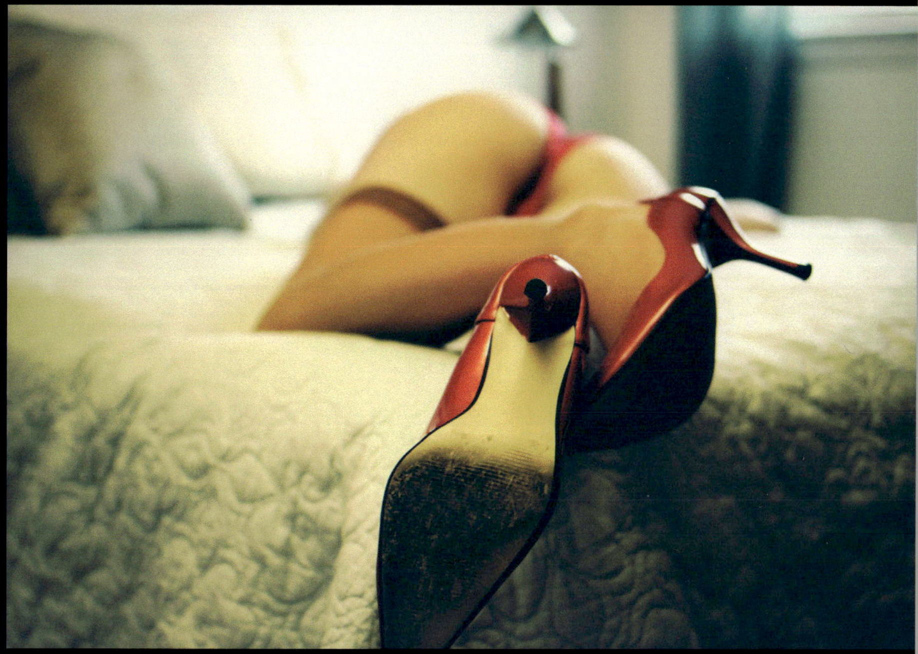

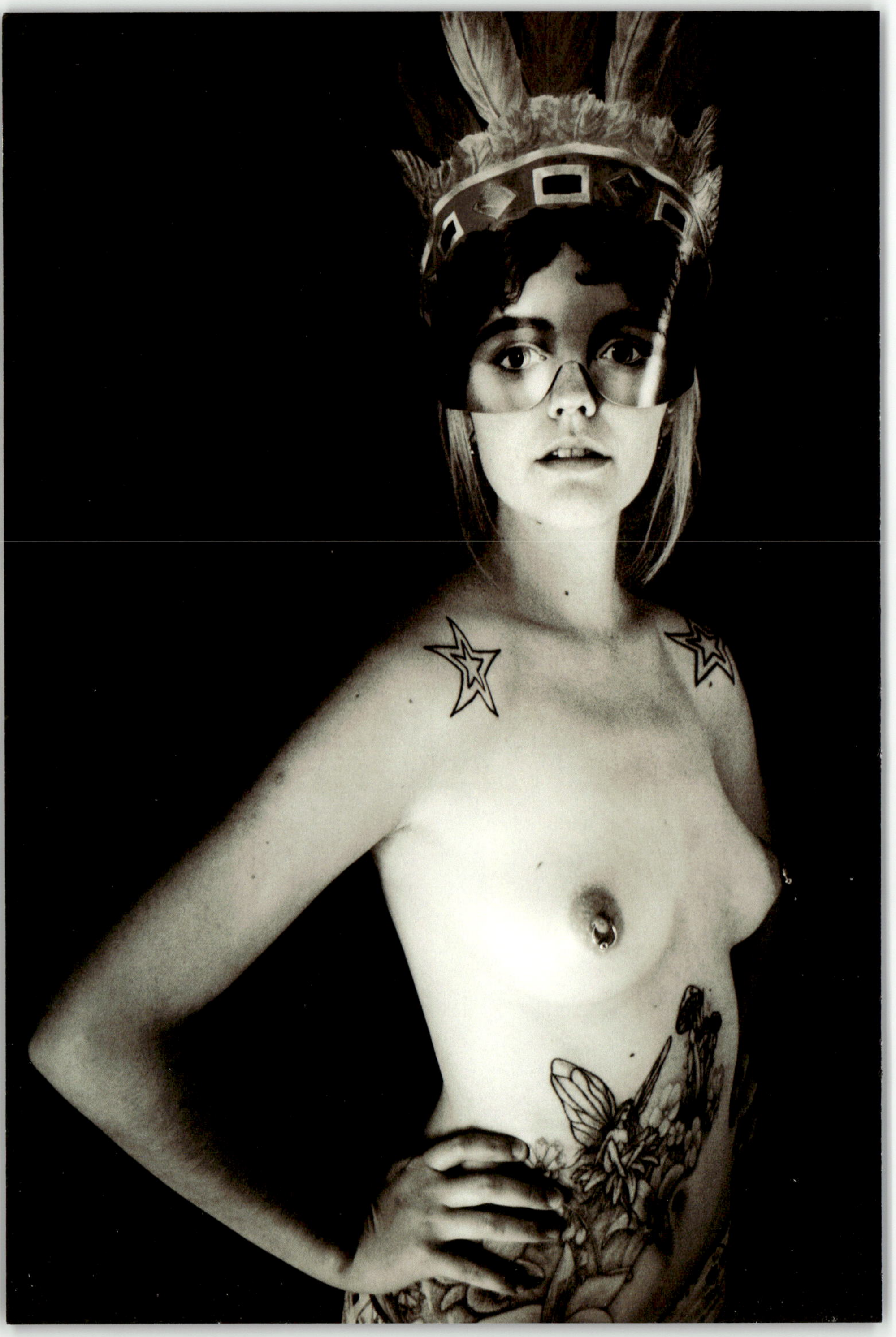

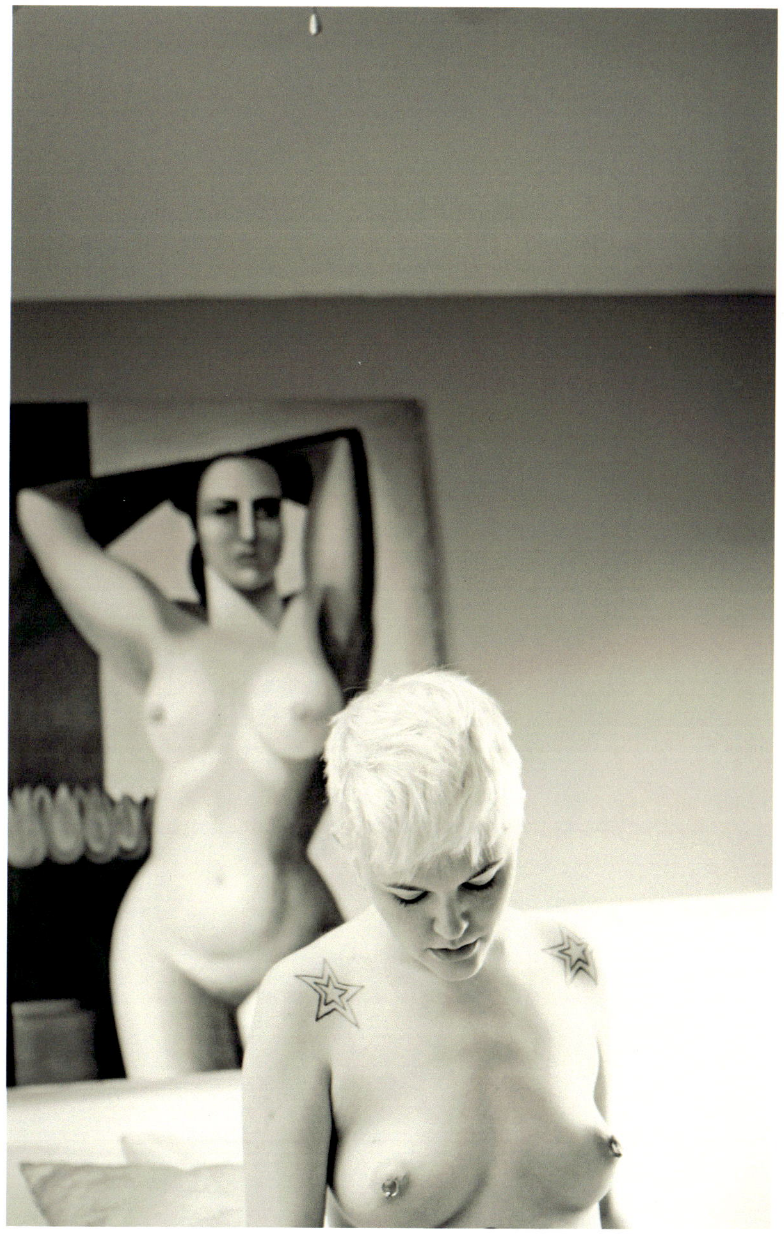

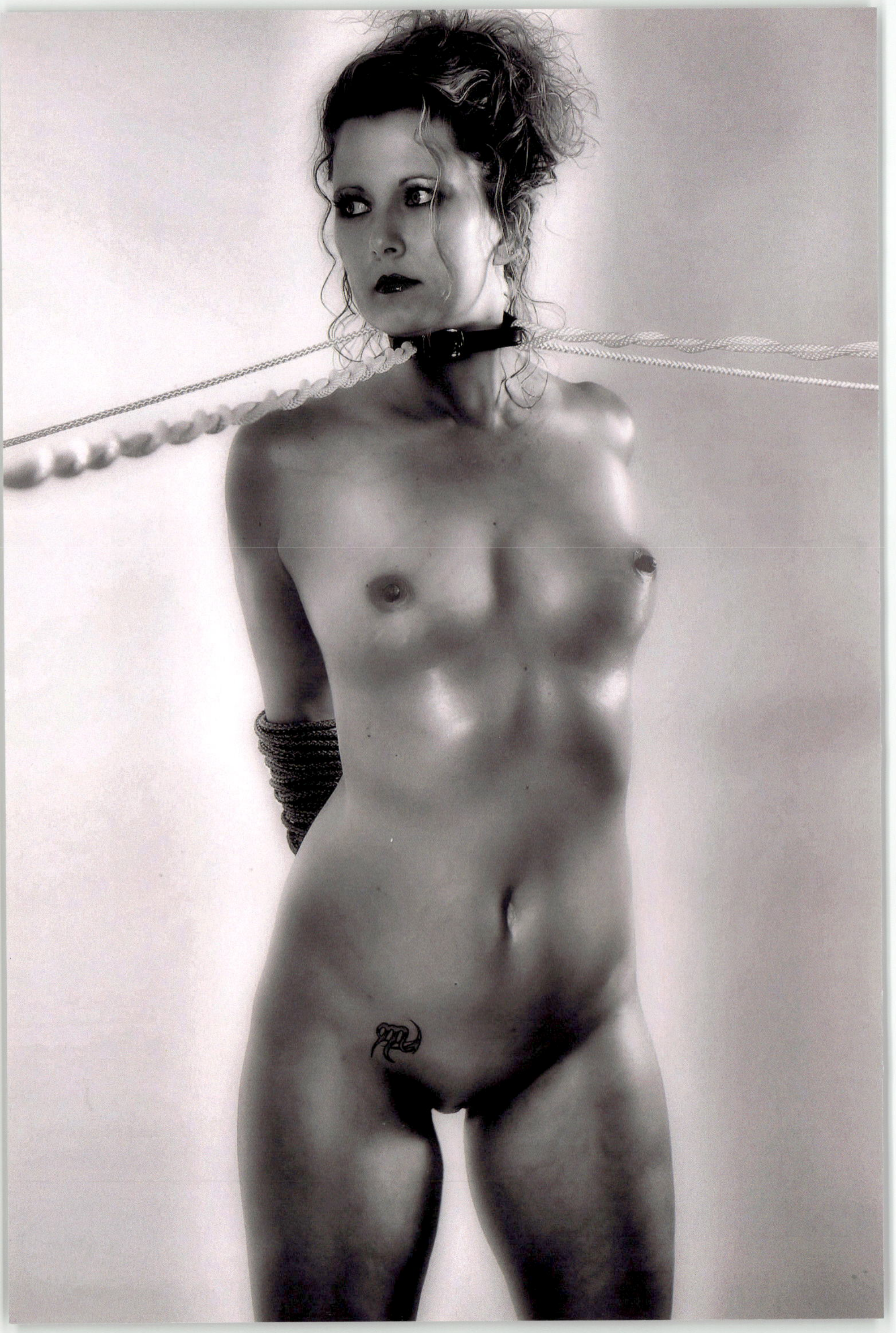

KERRY RAY TRACY

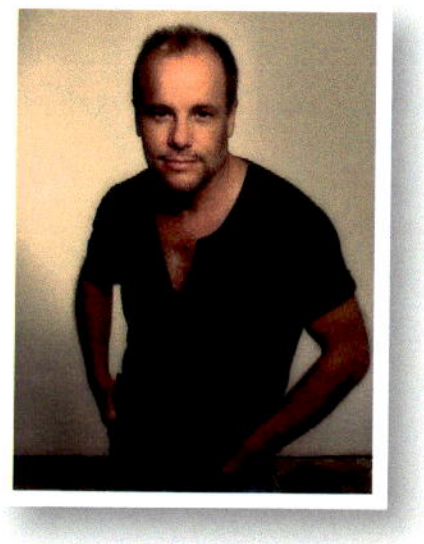

"My muse, my main model, is Rachel Lawrence. When we met she had never modelled professionally. Her sexuality brews just beneath the surface, then boils over once she is front of the camera. Rachel is responsible for getting me back into photography. In 2001 I went partially blind, but she saw in me the desire to resurrect my career, offering her body, as well as her beauty, for me to create new work. She can go from a general nude, painfully tied up in fetish and bondage, to hardcore sex. I love working with her so much that I made her my wife. My main focus now is the erotic, BDSM, fetish, as well as hardcore. Merging modern Pin Up with eroticism is a new direction I am taking."

www.therapturegallery.com

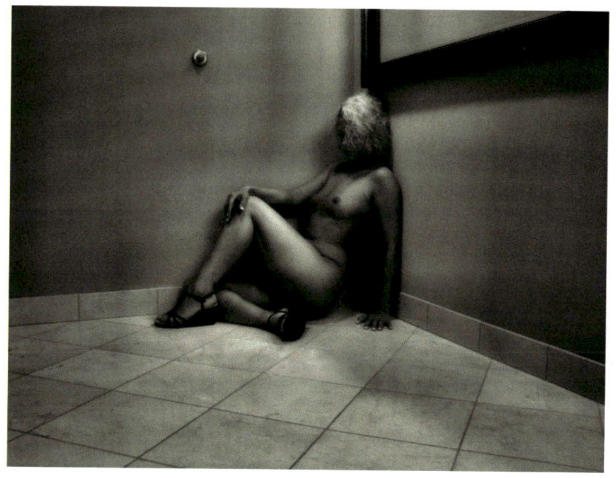

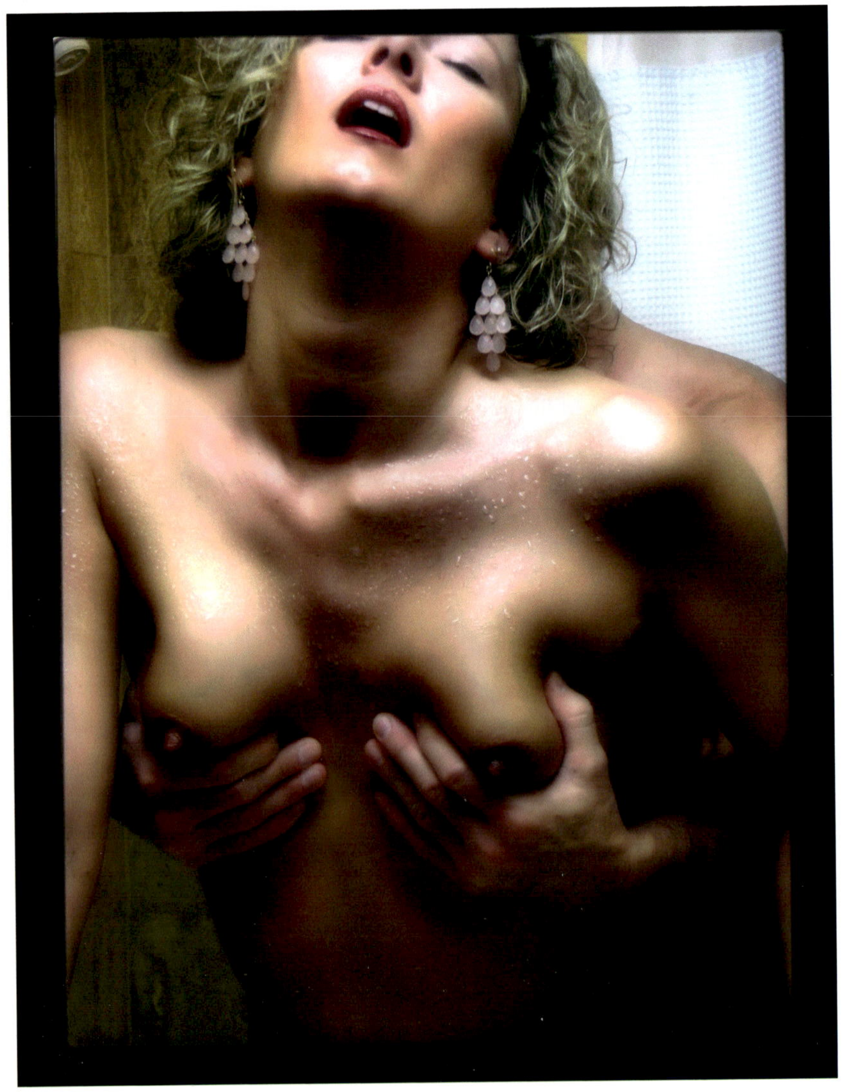

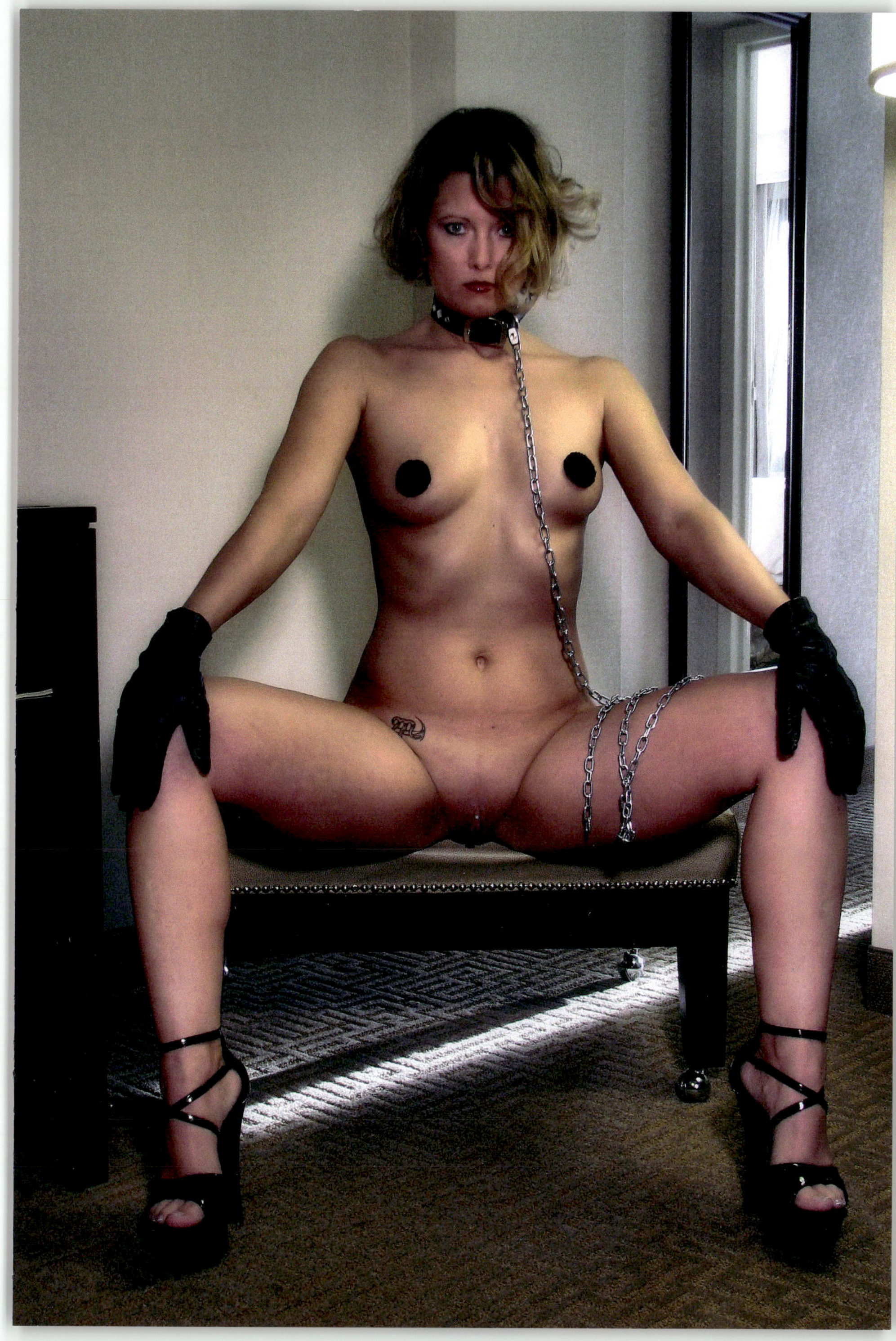

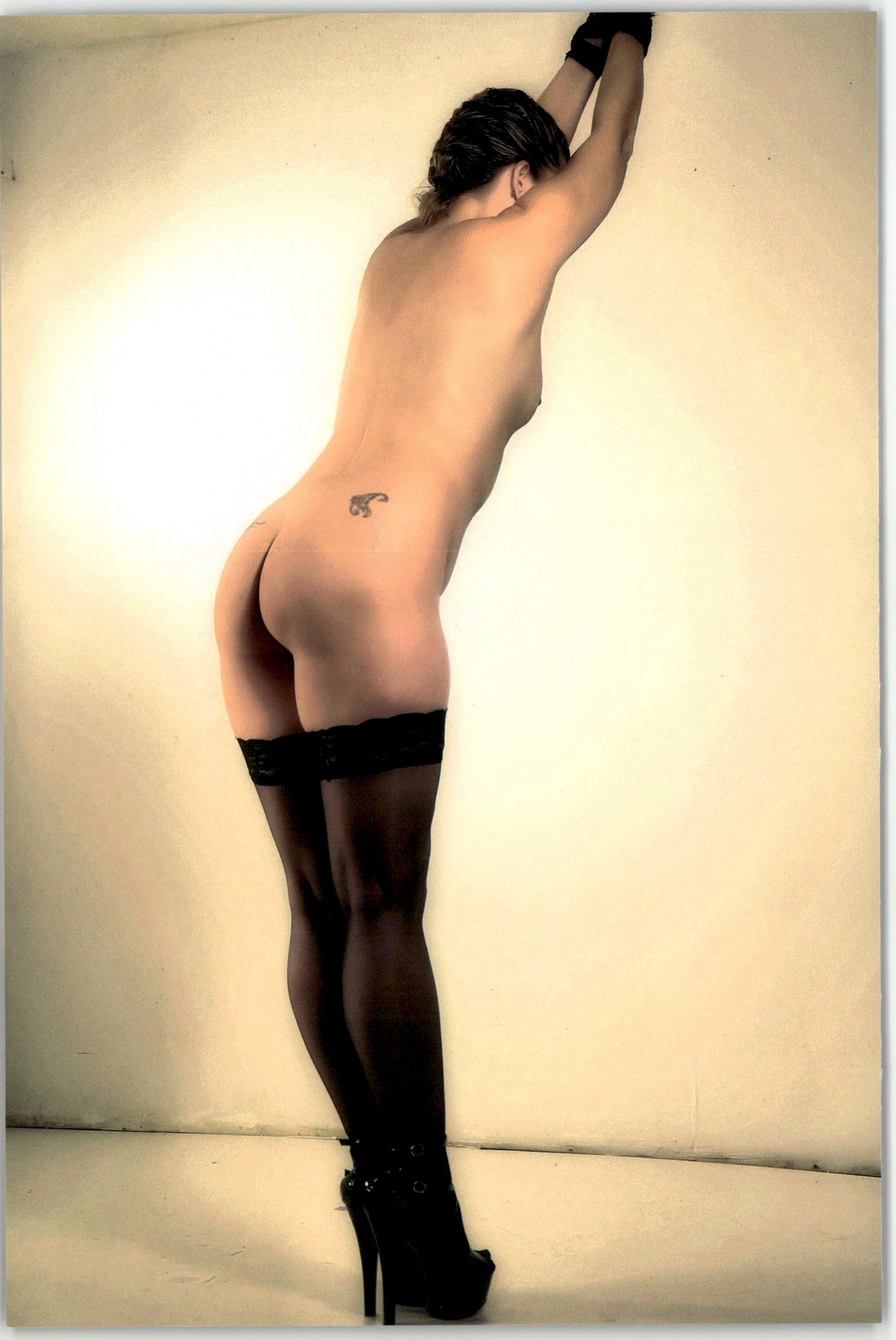

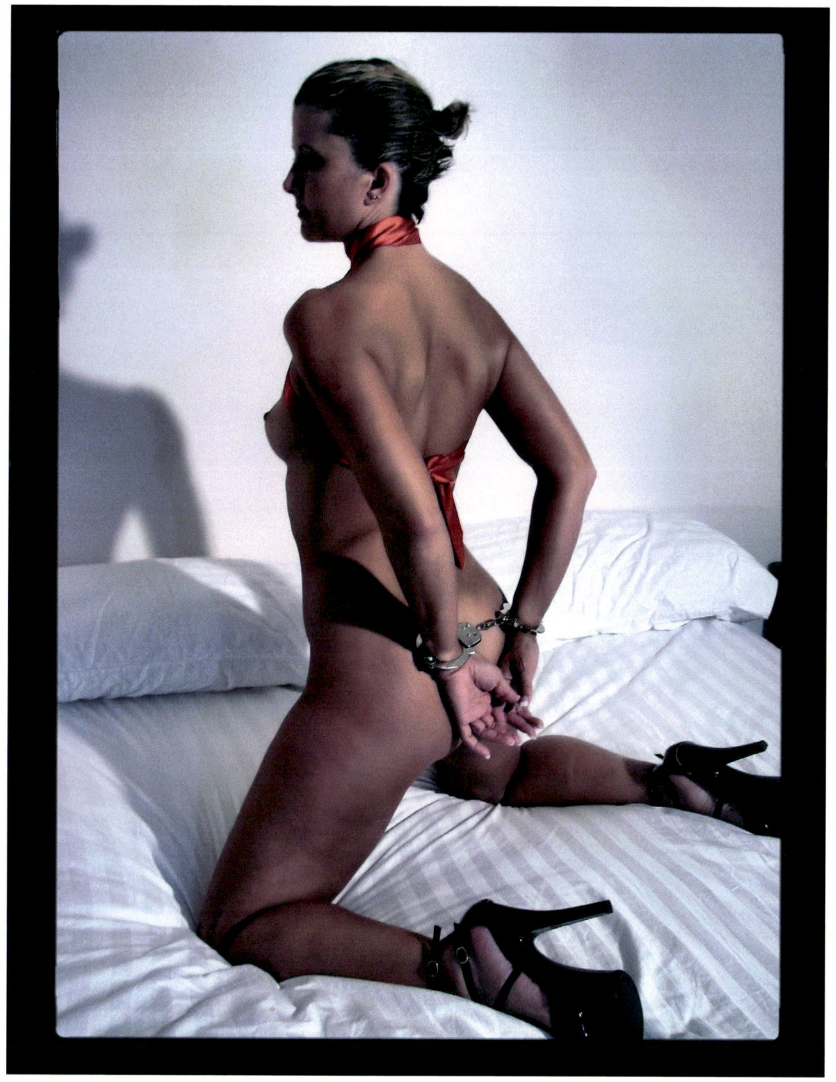

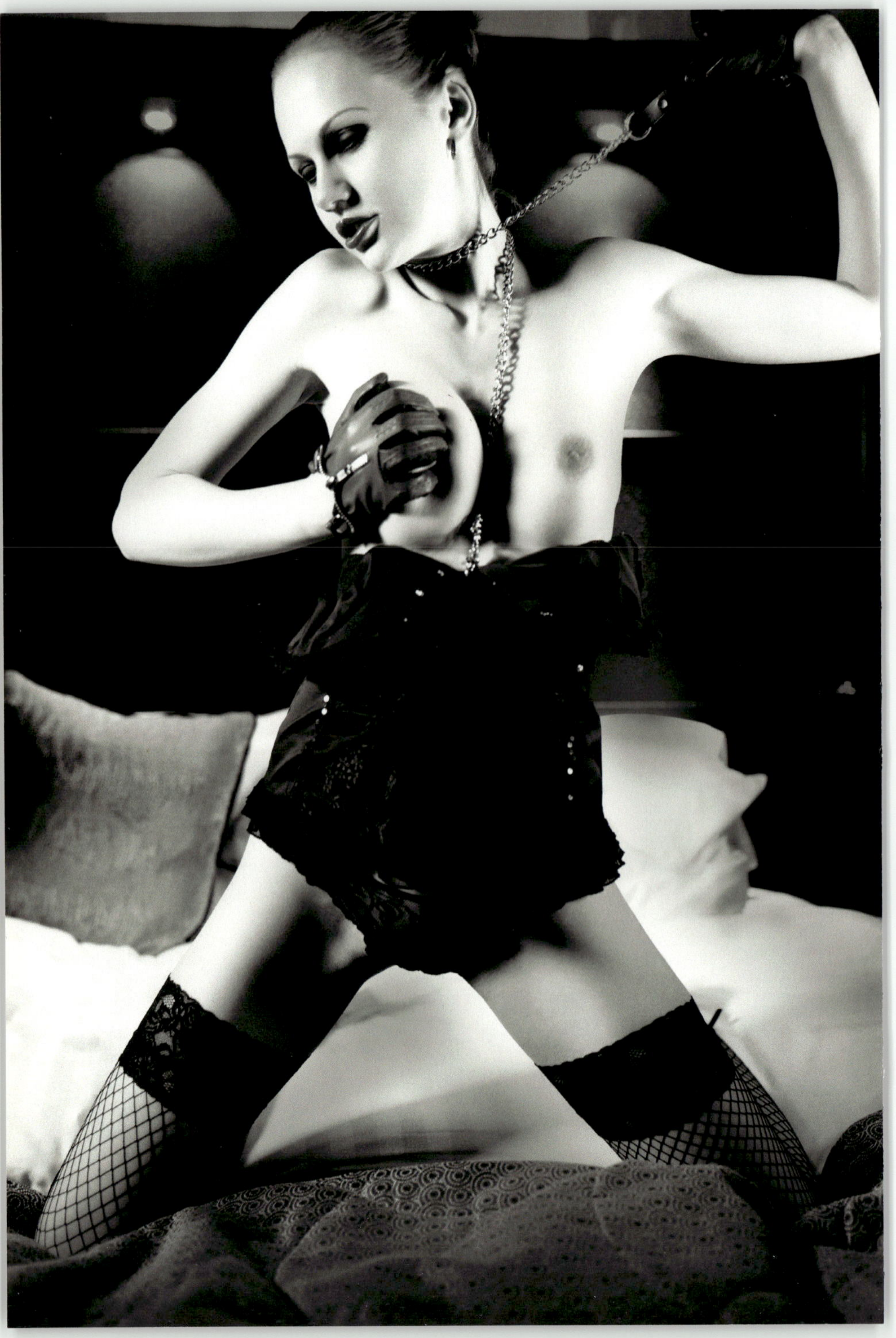

OTTO VON EROTICA

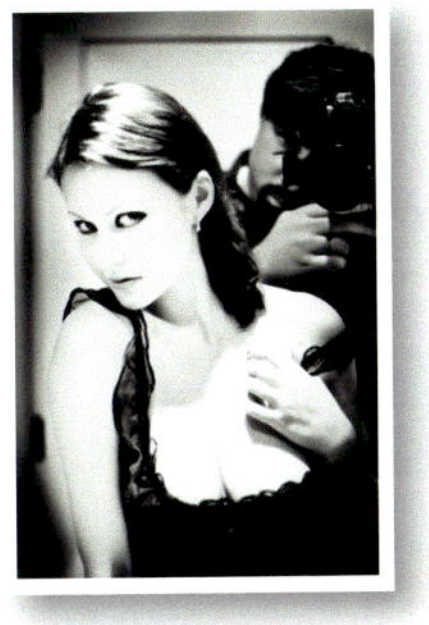

You should think of Otto von Erotica as a mask, as a secret identity for a super-hero of sexy, erotic photography.

Otto is a regular guest contributor to Darling House (darlinghouse.net), the esteemed online erotic salon featuring other talented artists such as George Pitts and Natasha Gornik. Otto's erotic photography has also been featured in many publications and received several awards in international erotic art competitions. His work is available for private collections and exhibitions.

Featured on these pages is the alluring and ever adorable Tina Kay. She remains one of Otto's favourite models of all time. These images were shot in two sessions in Leeds, UK. Otto recalls his shoots with Tina as some of the best fun he has ever had while working, full of continuous laughter and genuine pleasure.

www.ottorotic.com

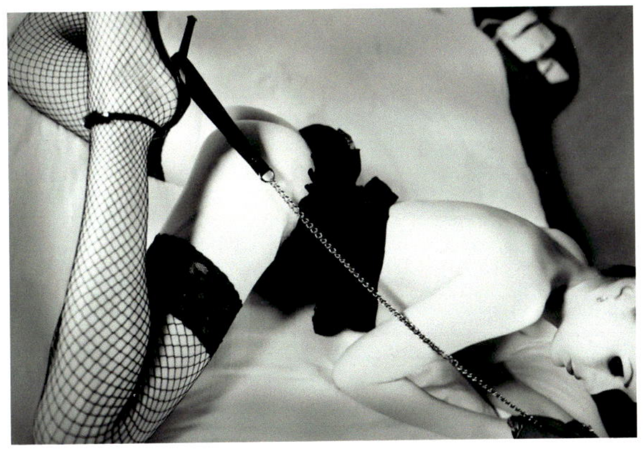

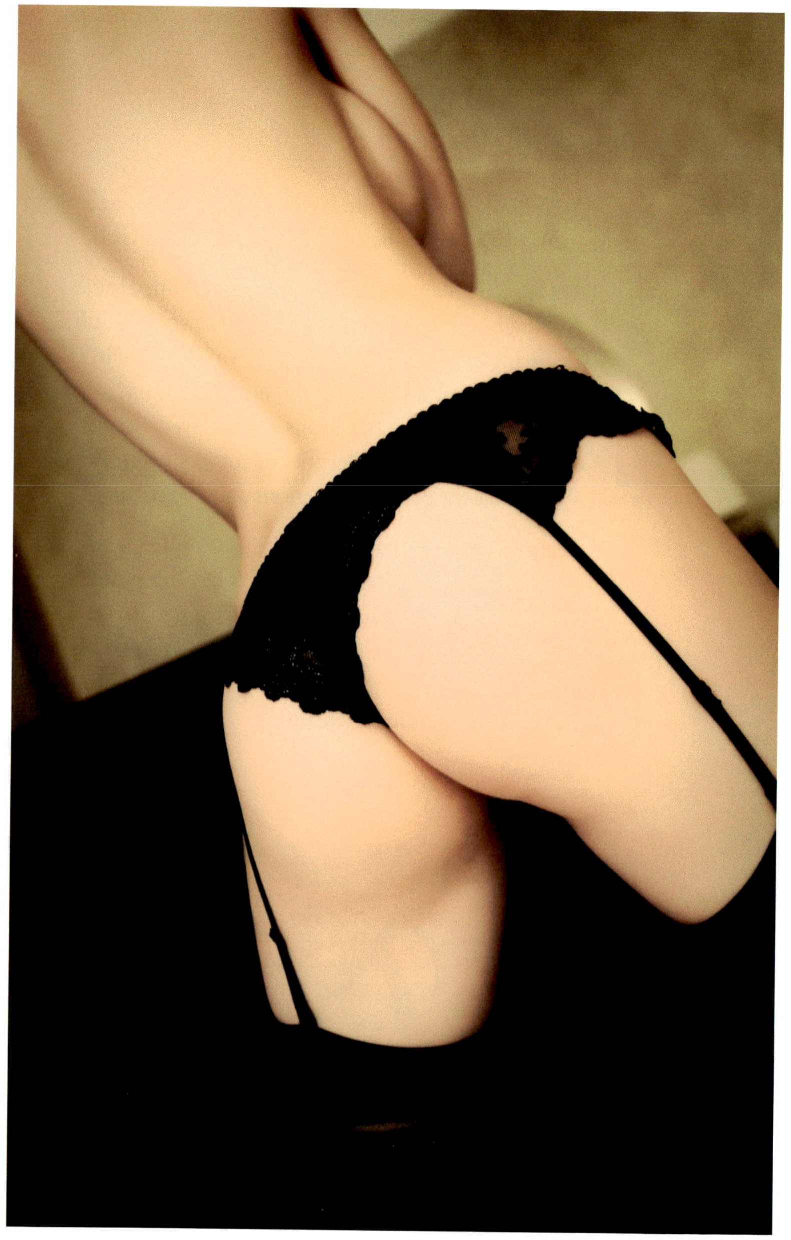

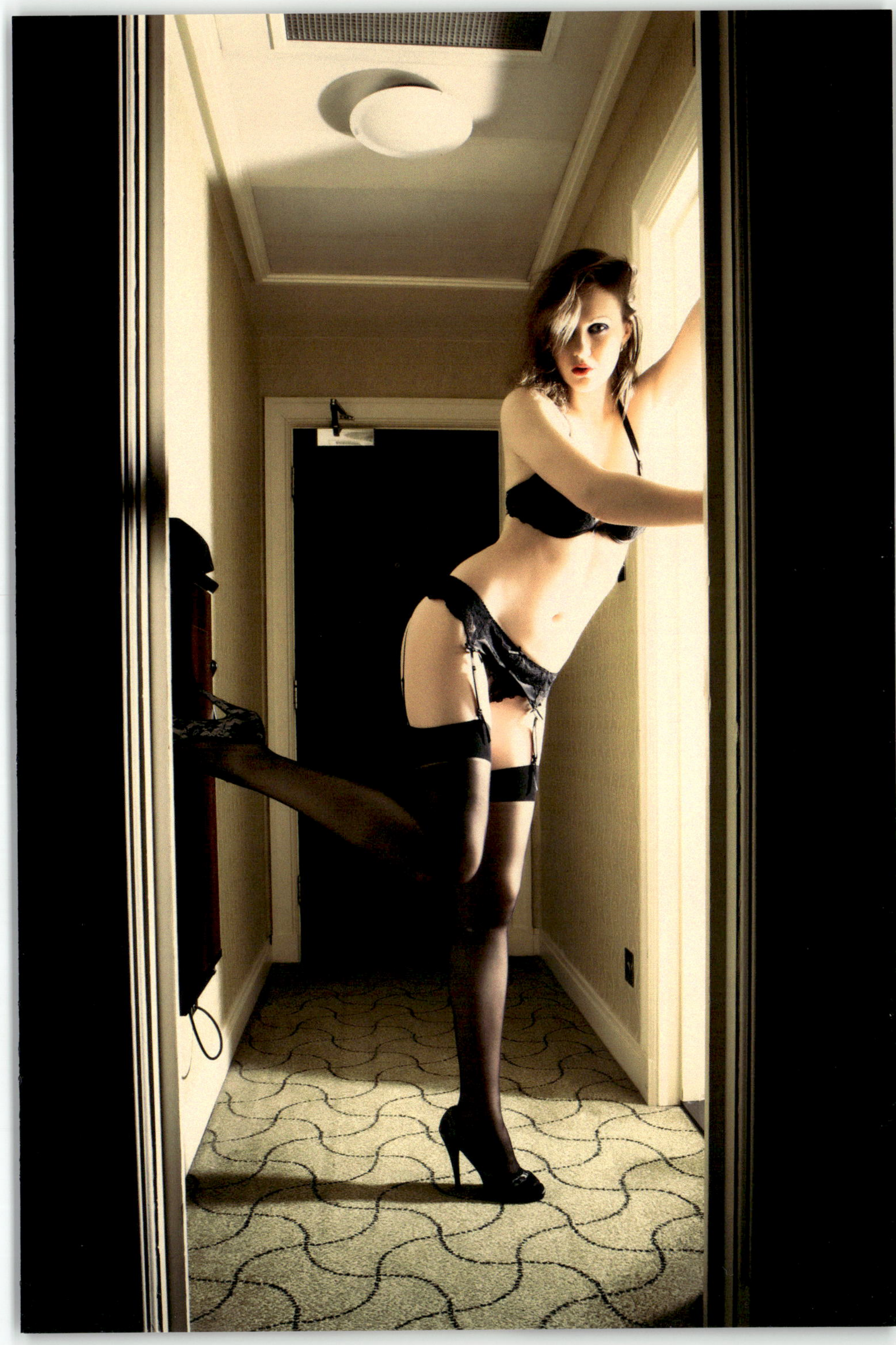

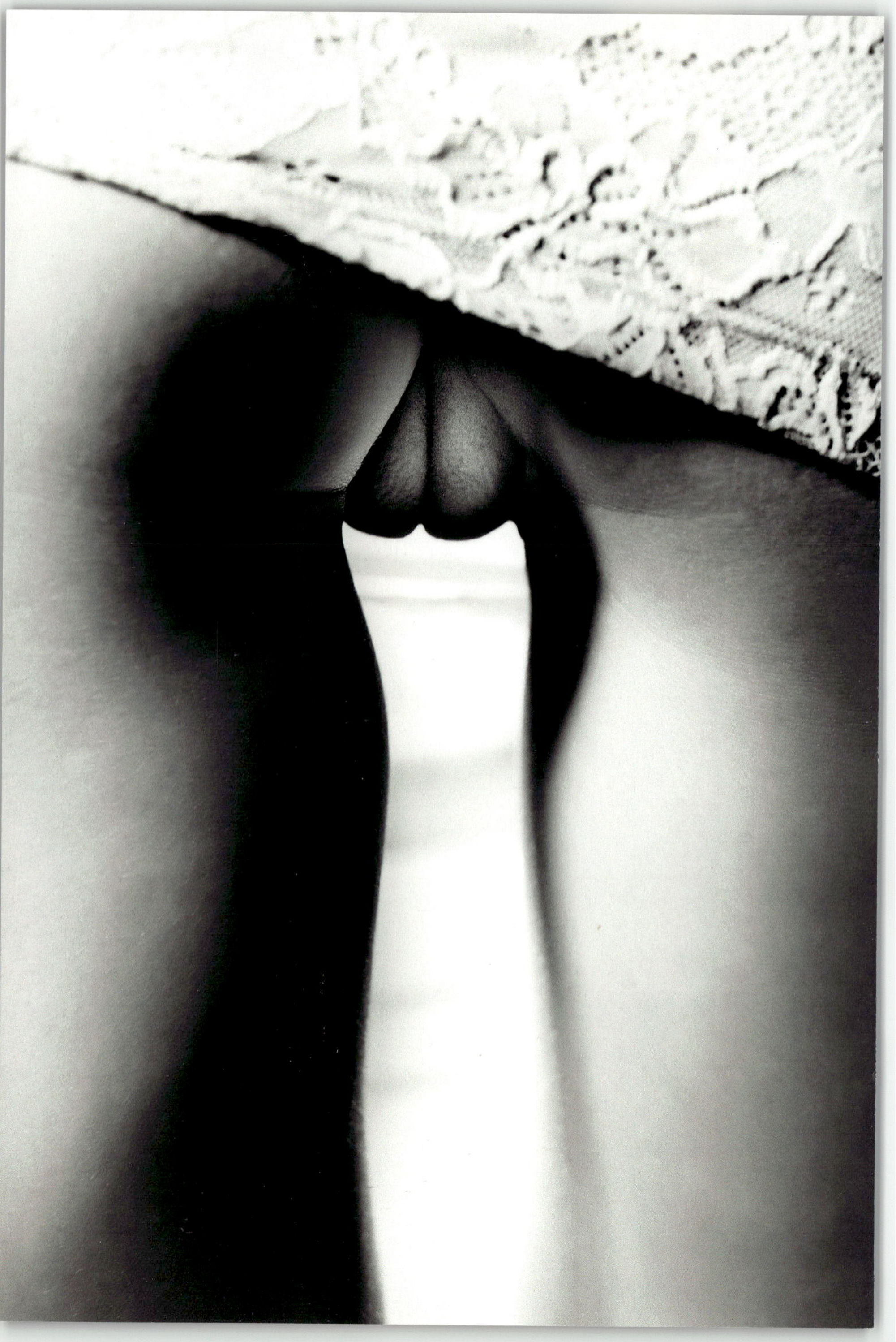

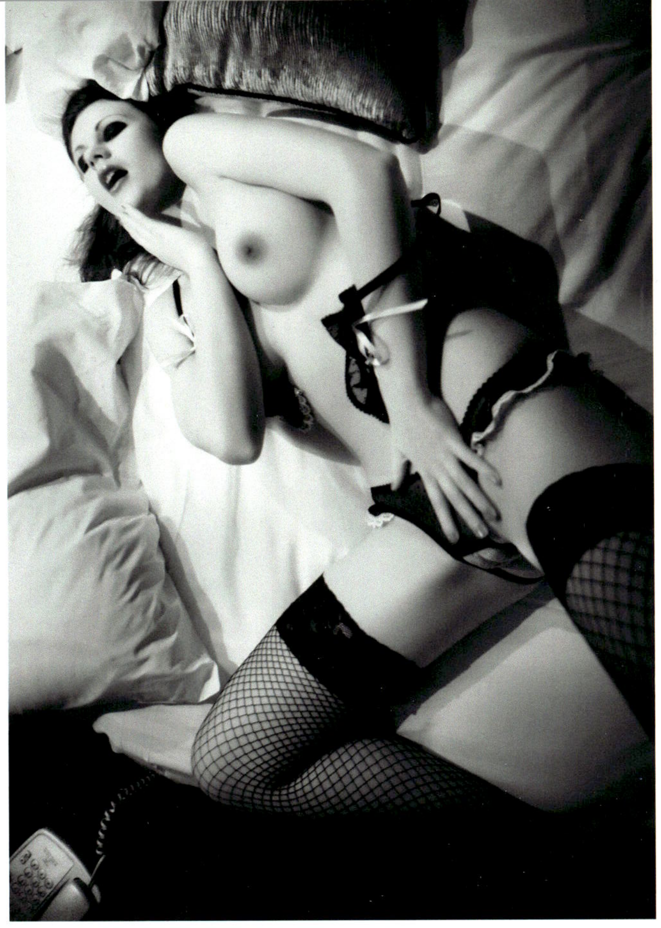

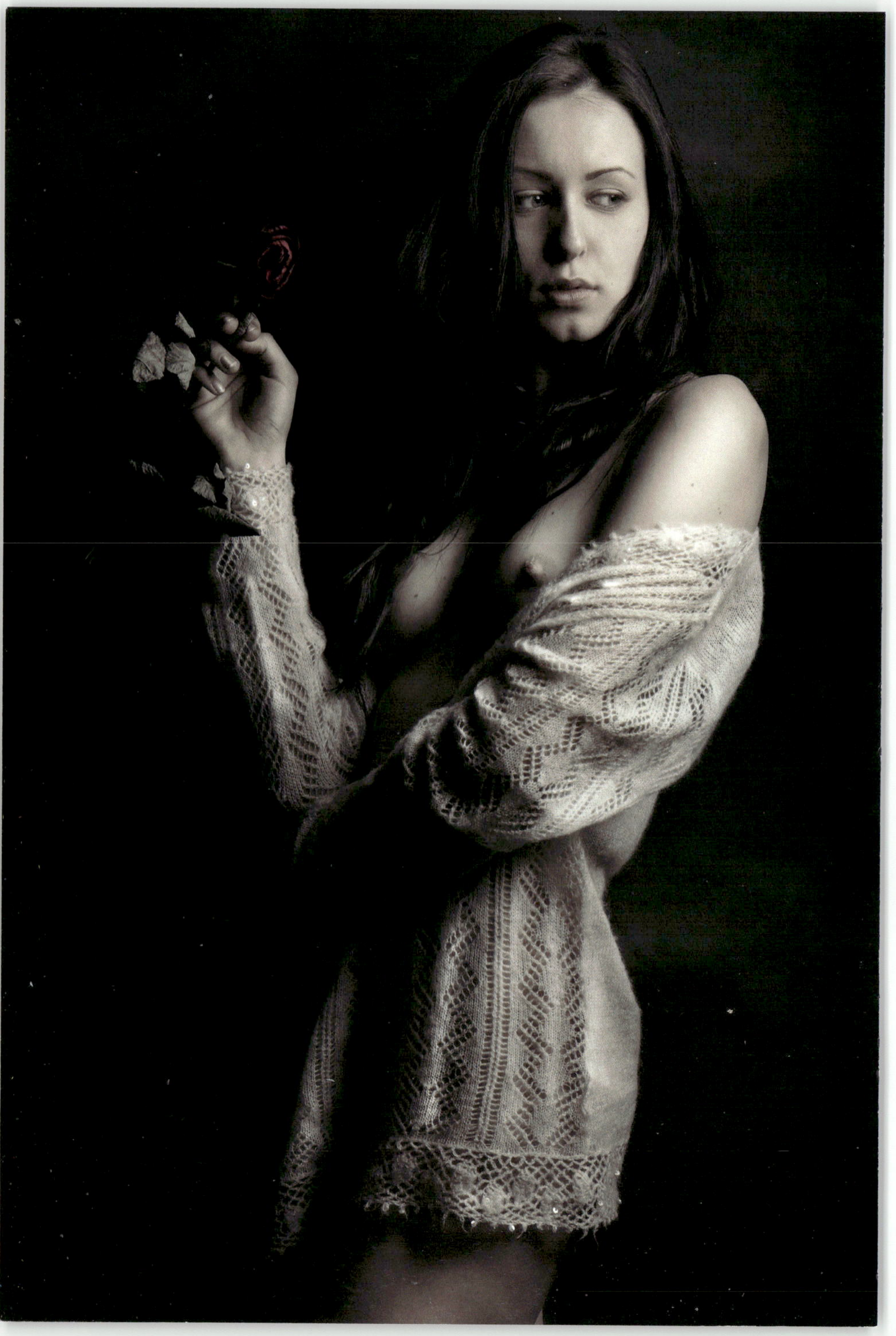

CORWIN VON KUHWEDE

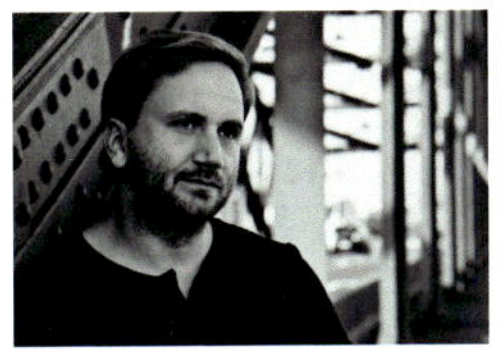

Corwin von Kuhwede is a practitioner of the art of creating images with photographic equipment. Some have an eye for art, others an instinct for business. Von Kuhwede has an eye for stories and another for images. Together these make him a storyteller who tells stories for the eye. His preferred motifs – regardless of whether they involve nudes, portraits or products – are primarily those behind which stories are concealed.

In an unrepressed combination of craft and inspiration, necessity and creative impulse, von Kuhwede is able in his images to simultaneously make the logic and absurdity of the subject visible and to show, along with the objects themselves, the objects behind them.

www.vonkuhwede.de

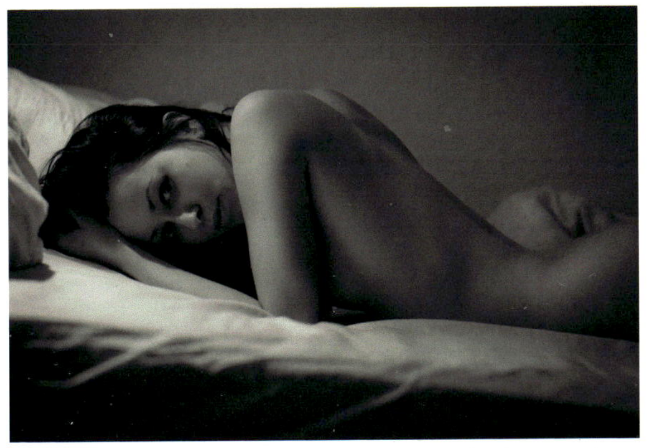

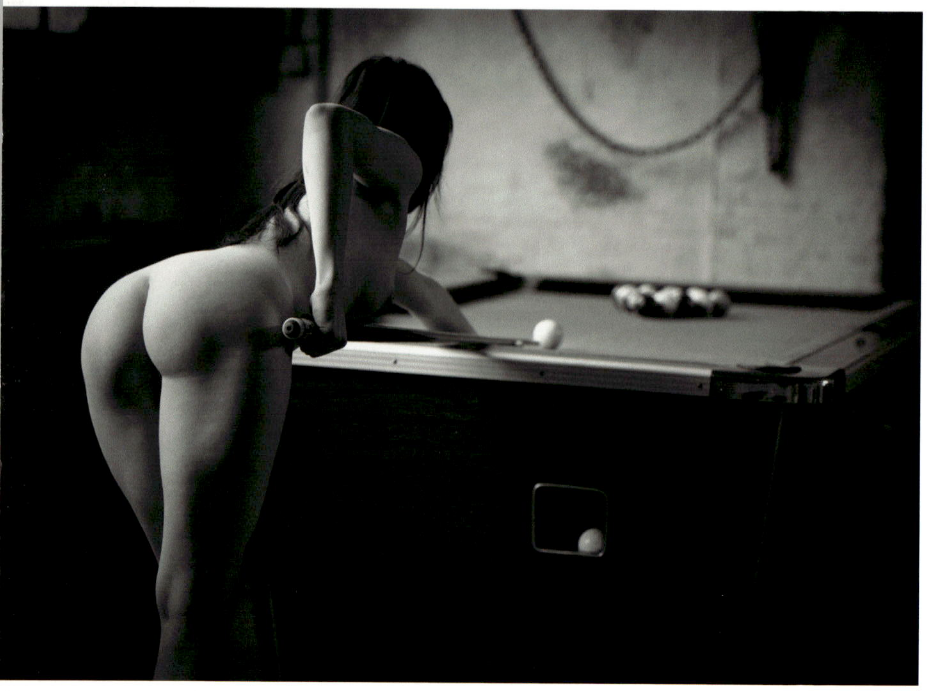

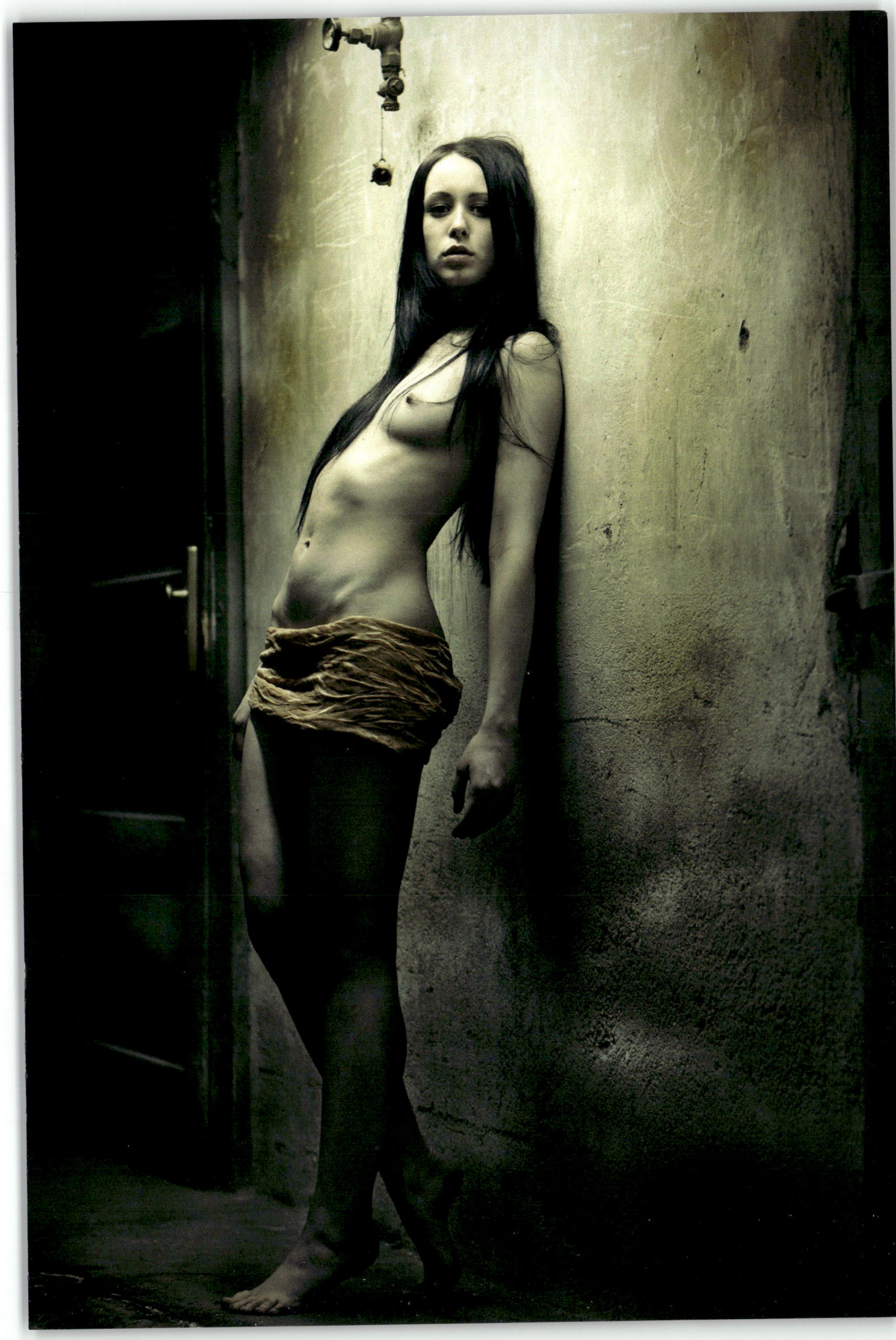

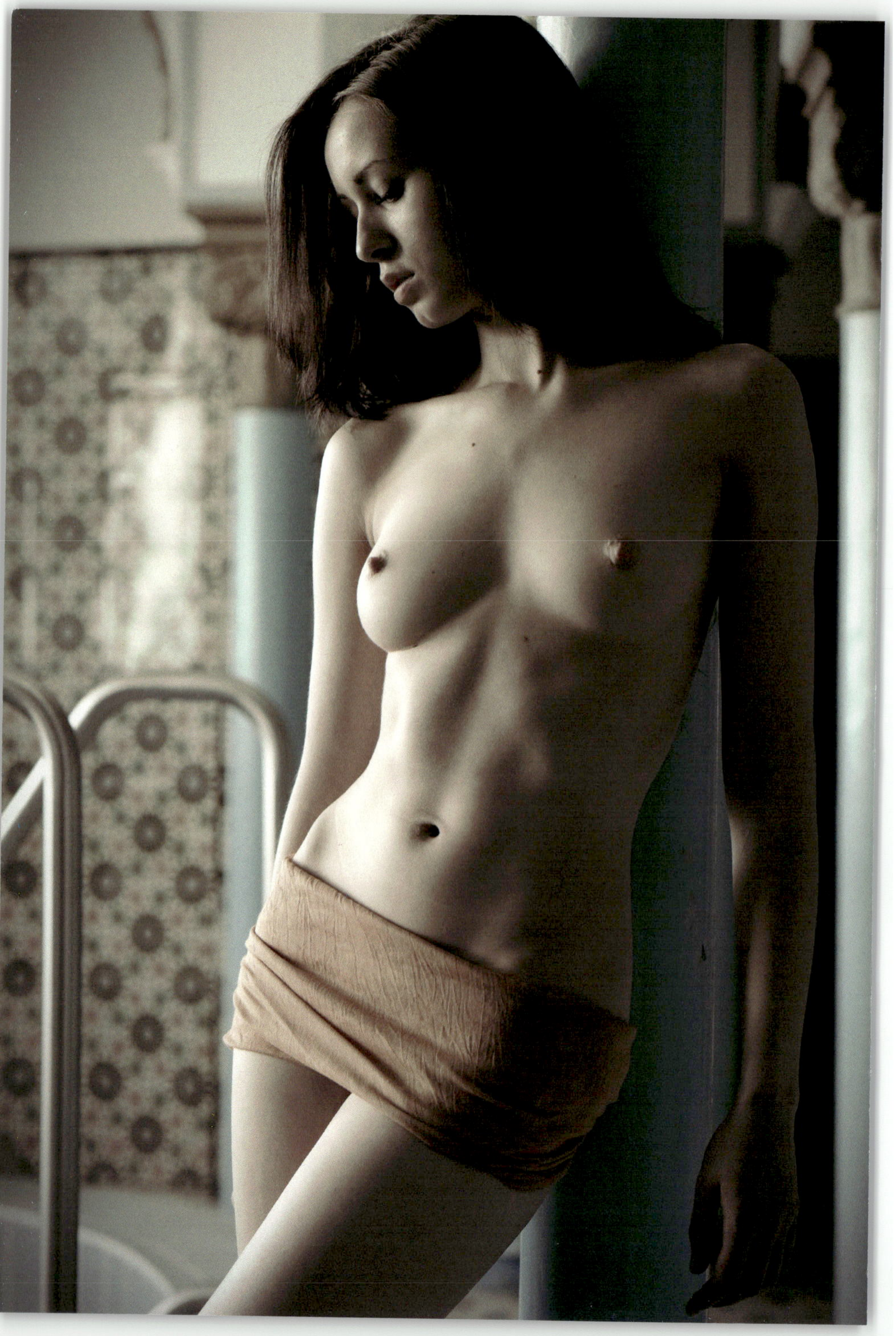

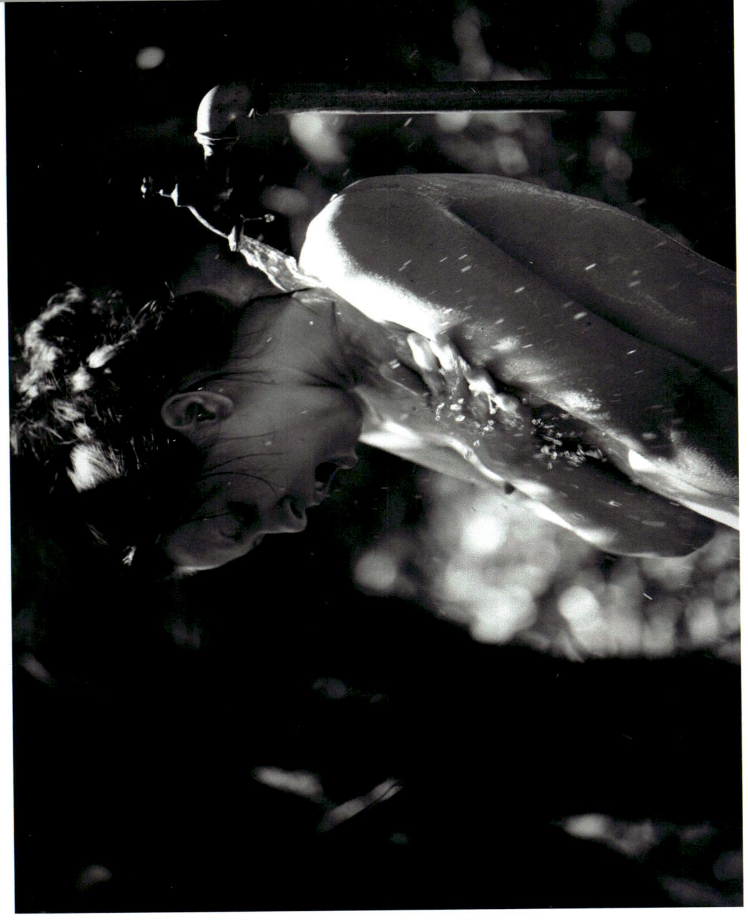

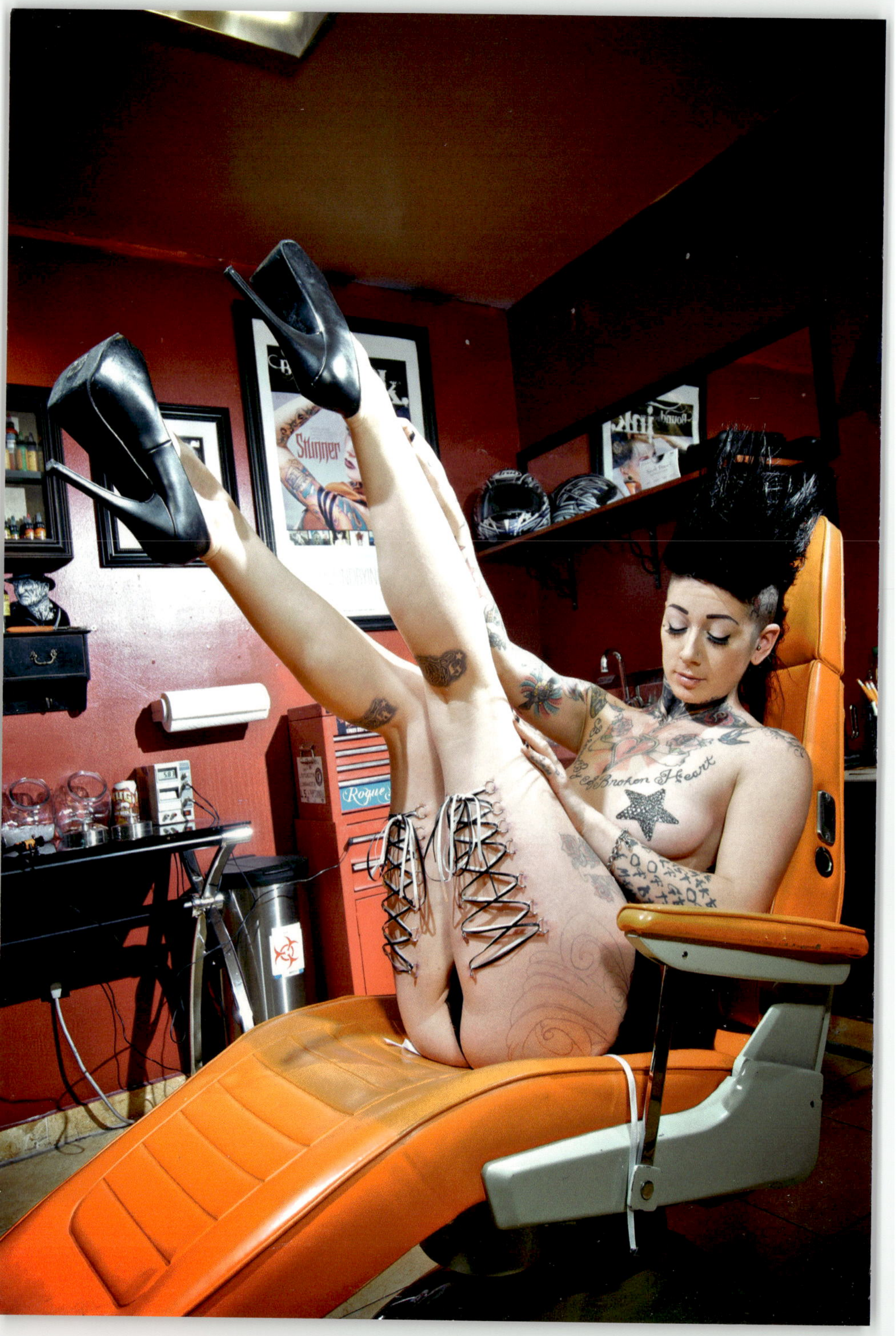
Stunner

CURTIS JOE WALKER

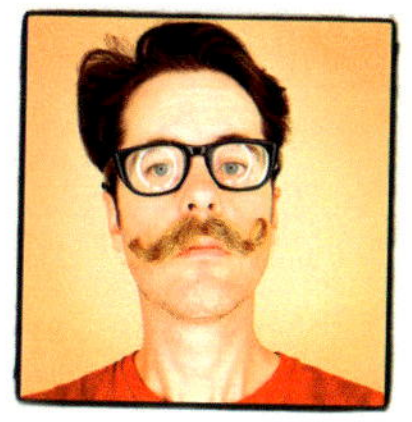

Native Las Vegas photographer Curtis Joe Walker is known for shocking, vibrant images that sometimes compete for attention with their own subject matter. His studio, Photo Bang Bang in the Vegas Arts District, is a fully functional studio as well as a gallery space for him to exhibit new work on a constantly rotating basis. He works with vintage cameras, as well as an up-to-date DSLR.

His model, Angel Beau, is a Londoner, working odd jobs and collecting new tattoos and life experiences at a blinding pace. She began shooting with Curtis in 2009 when the two met through an alt model site. In 2011 she helped found a local suspension troupe with monthly suspension meet-ups. Working together as inspiration strikes, the two continue to collaborate regularly.

www.photobangbang.com
www.curtisjoewalker.com

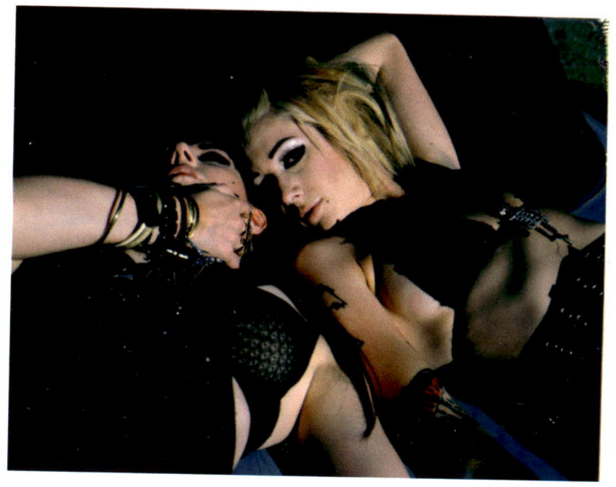

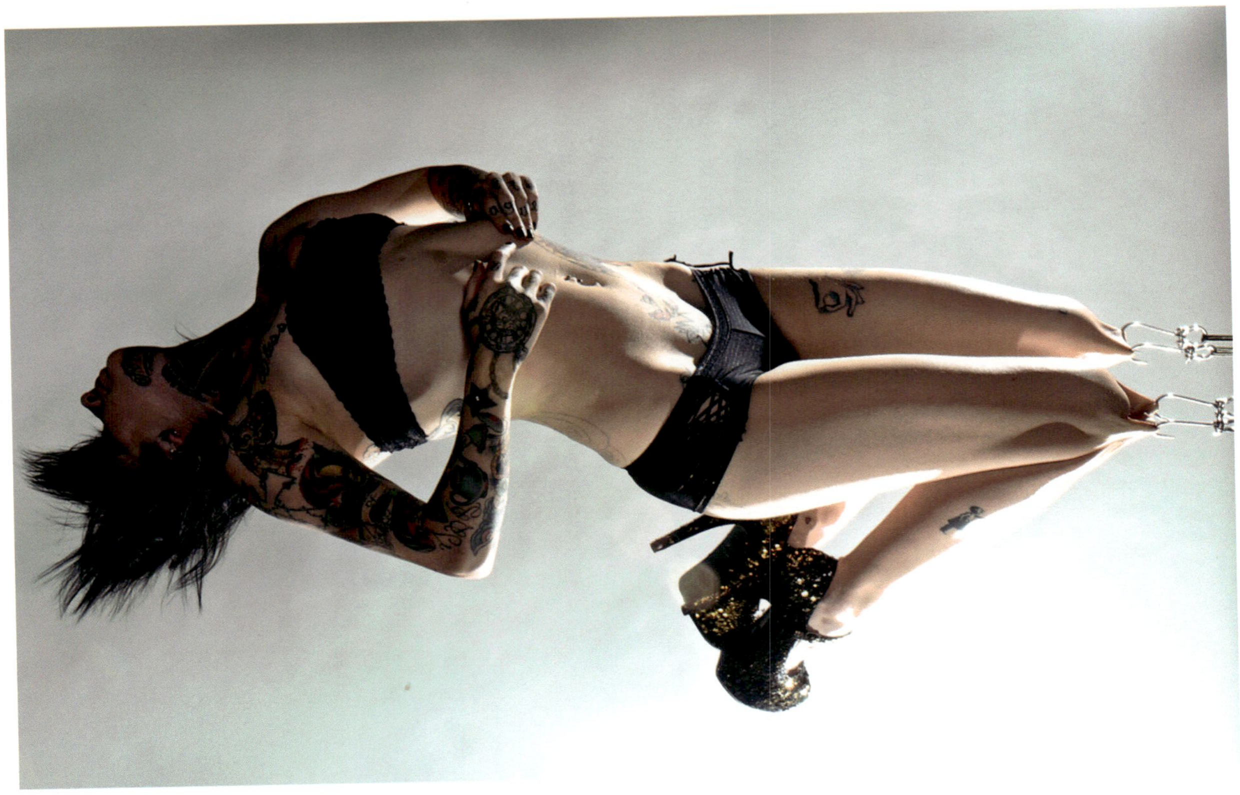

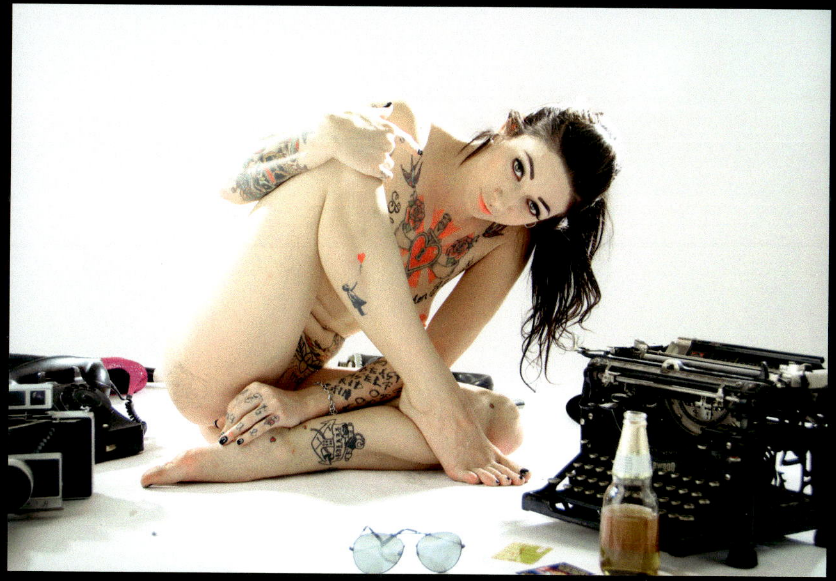

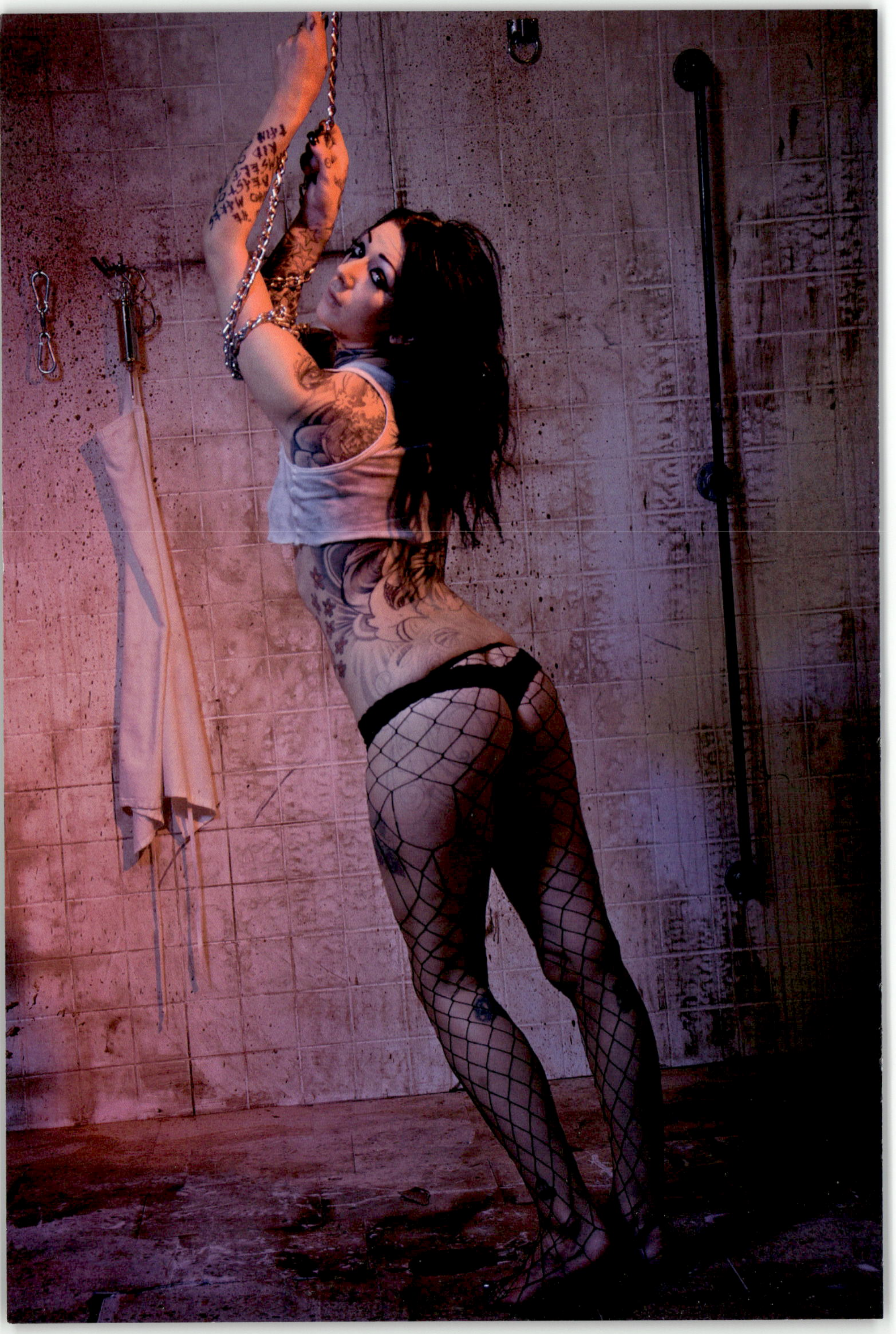

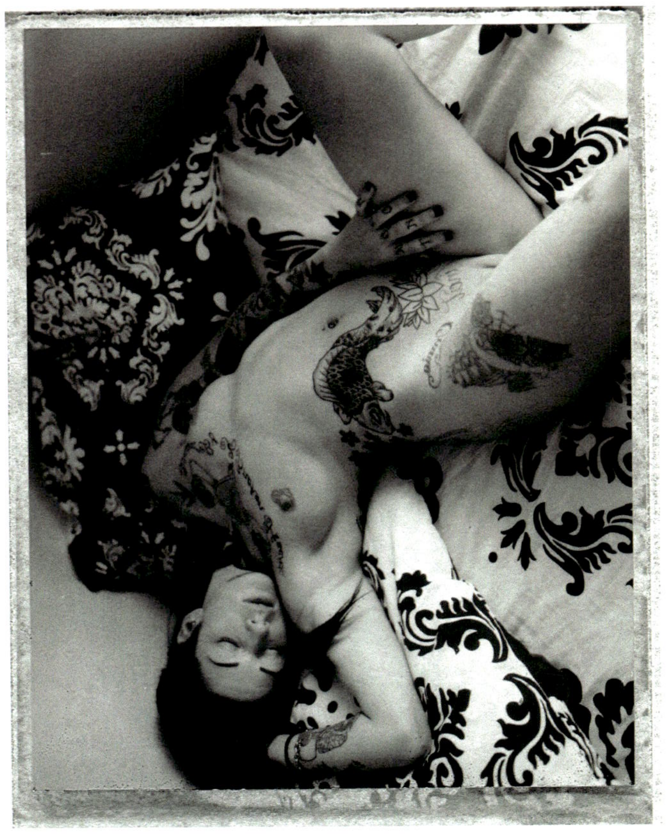

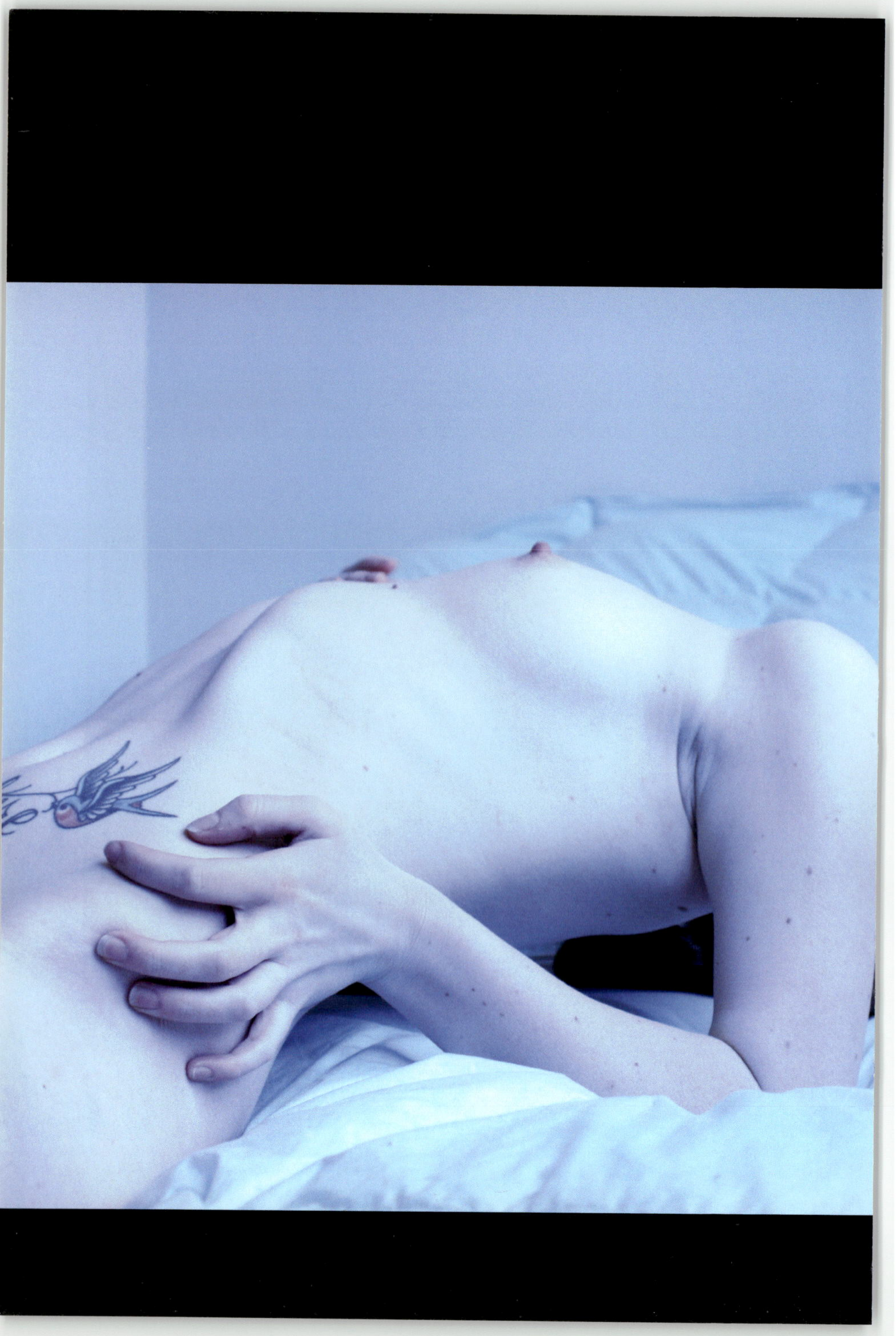

KATIE WEST

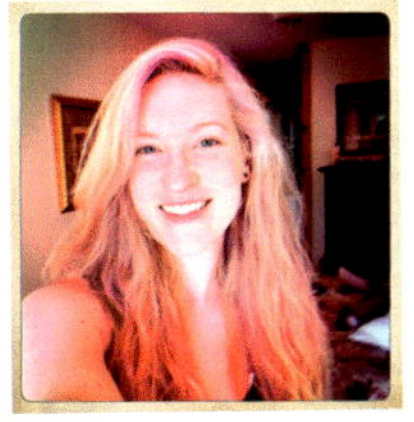

Katie West is a photographer, teacher and writer living in Toronto, Canada.

"I really love my cats, *Star Trek* and my husband. Also dancing, monochromatic colour schemes, travelling, shooting guns, planning for an apocalypse, YA fiction, autumn, science fiction television shows, seeing as many movies as possible and Korean pop music. Among a billion other things."

www.therealkatiewest.tumblr.com

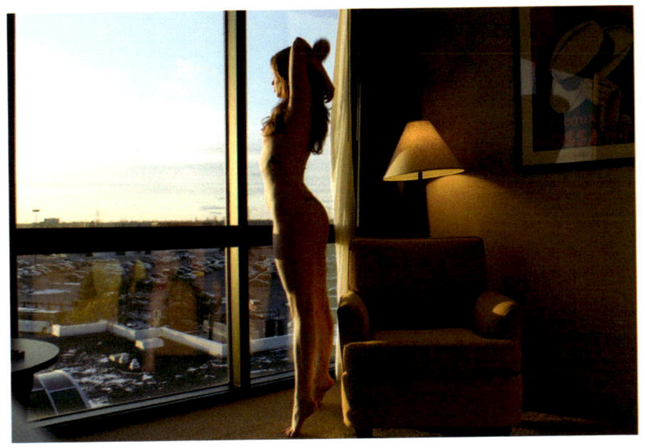

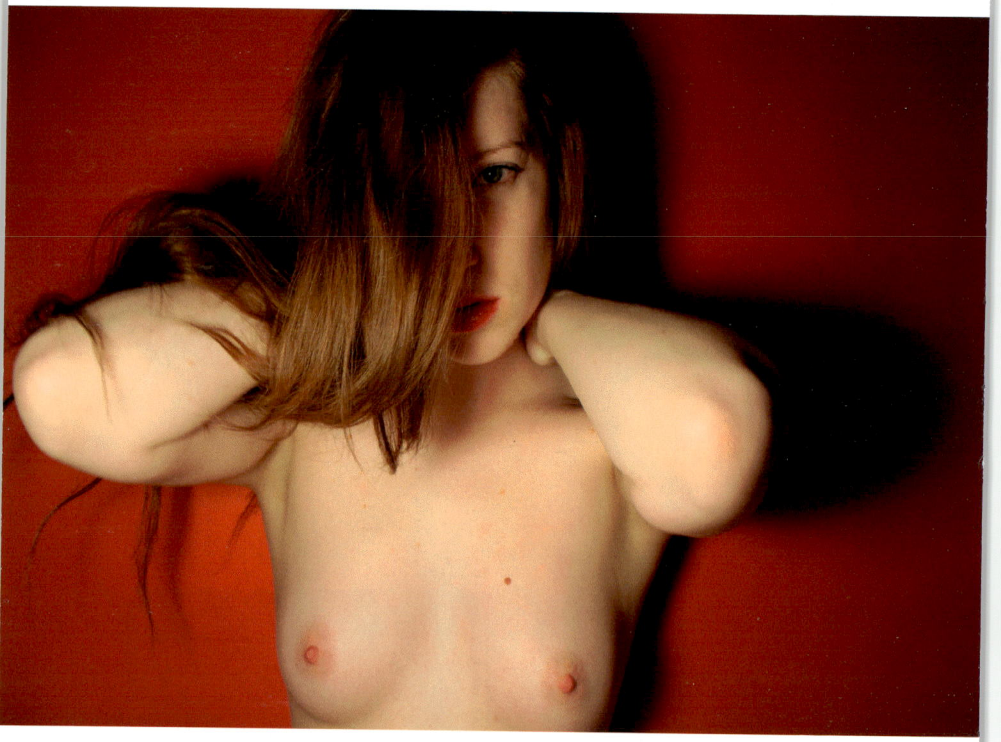

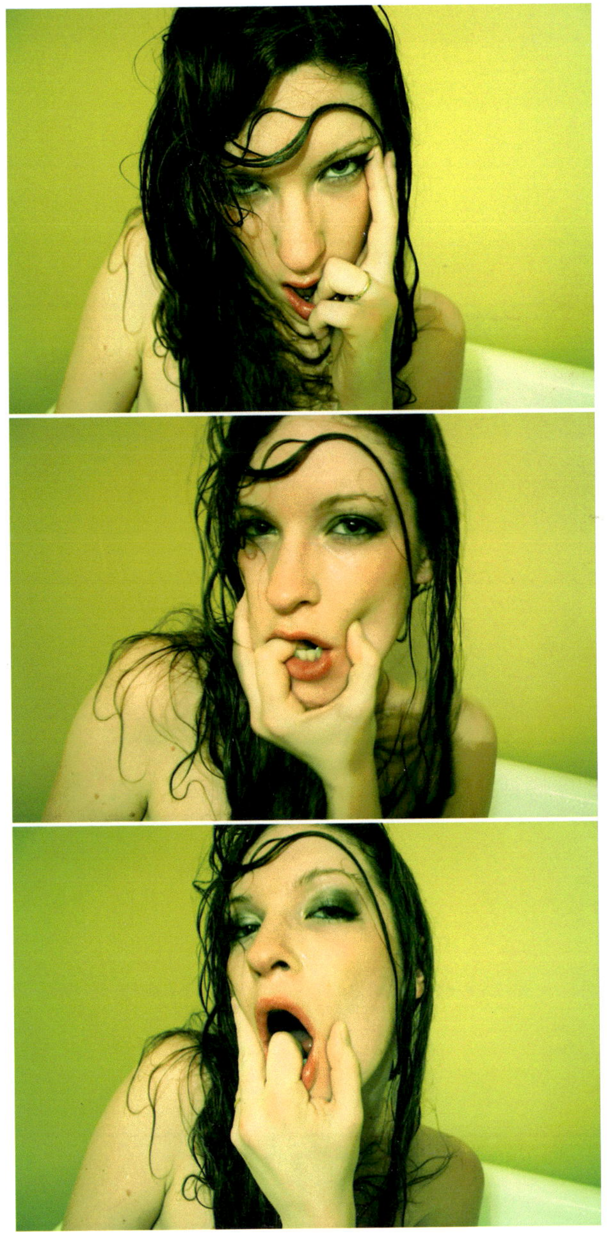

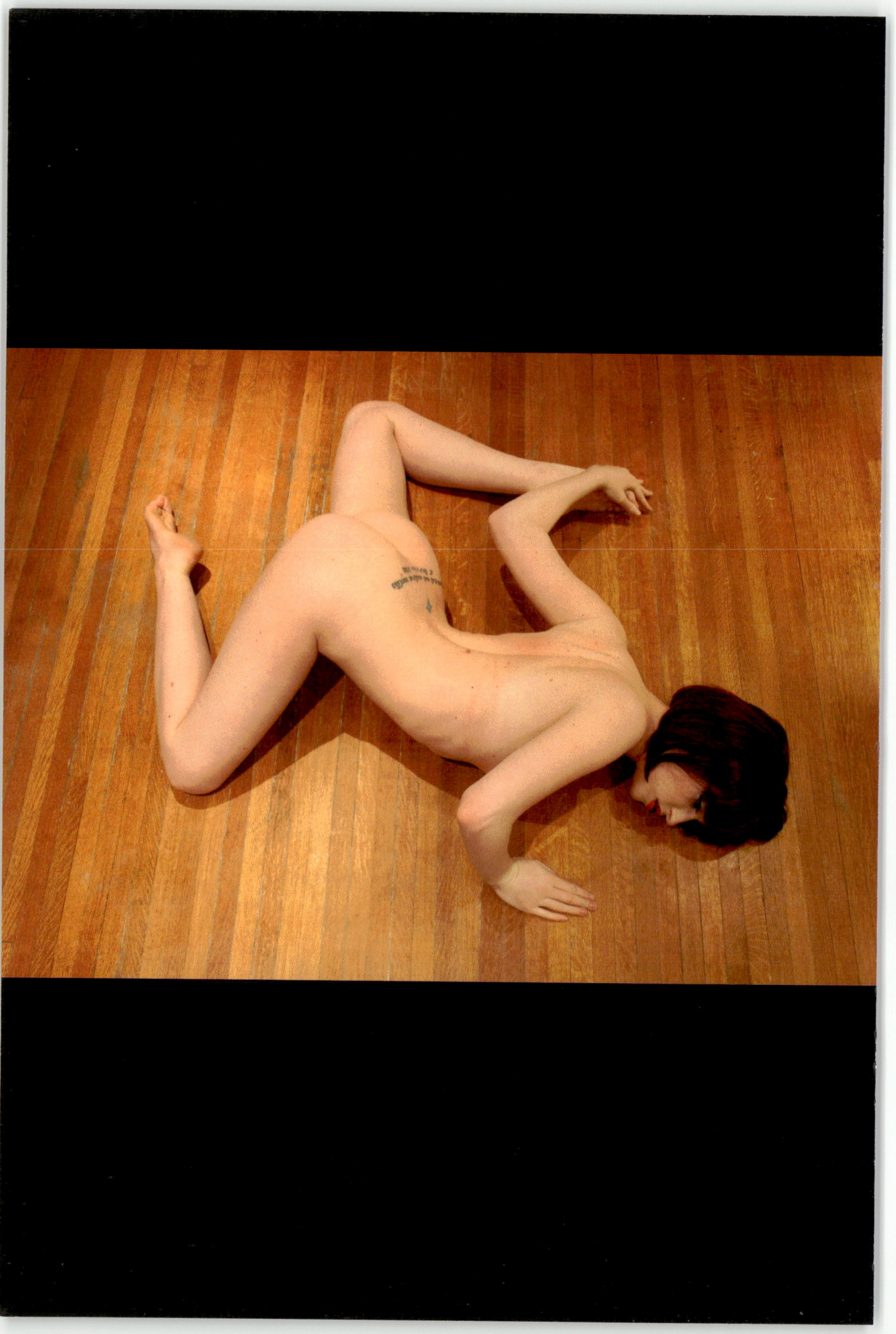

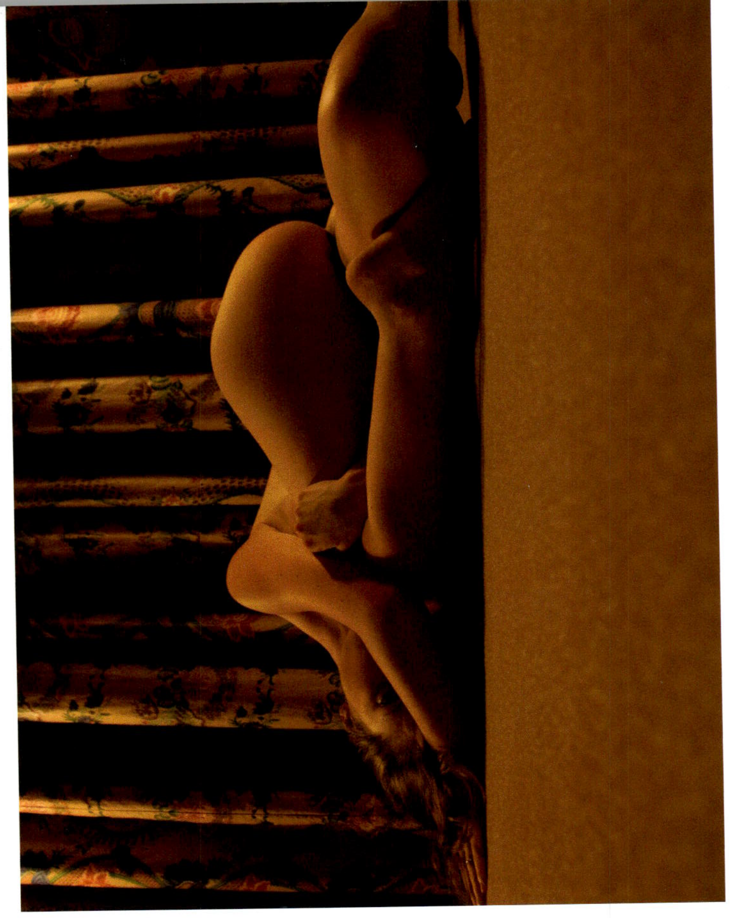

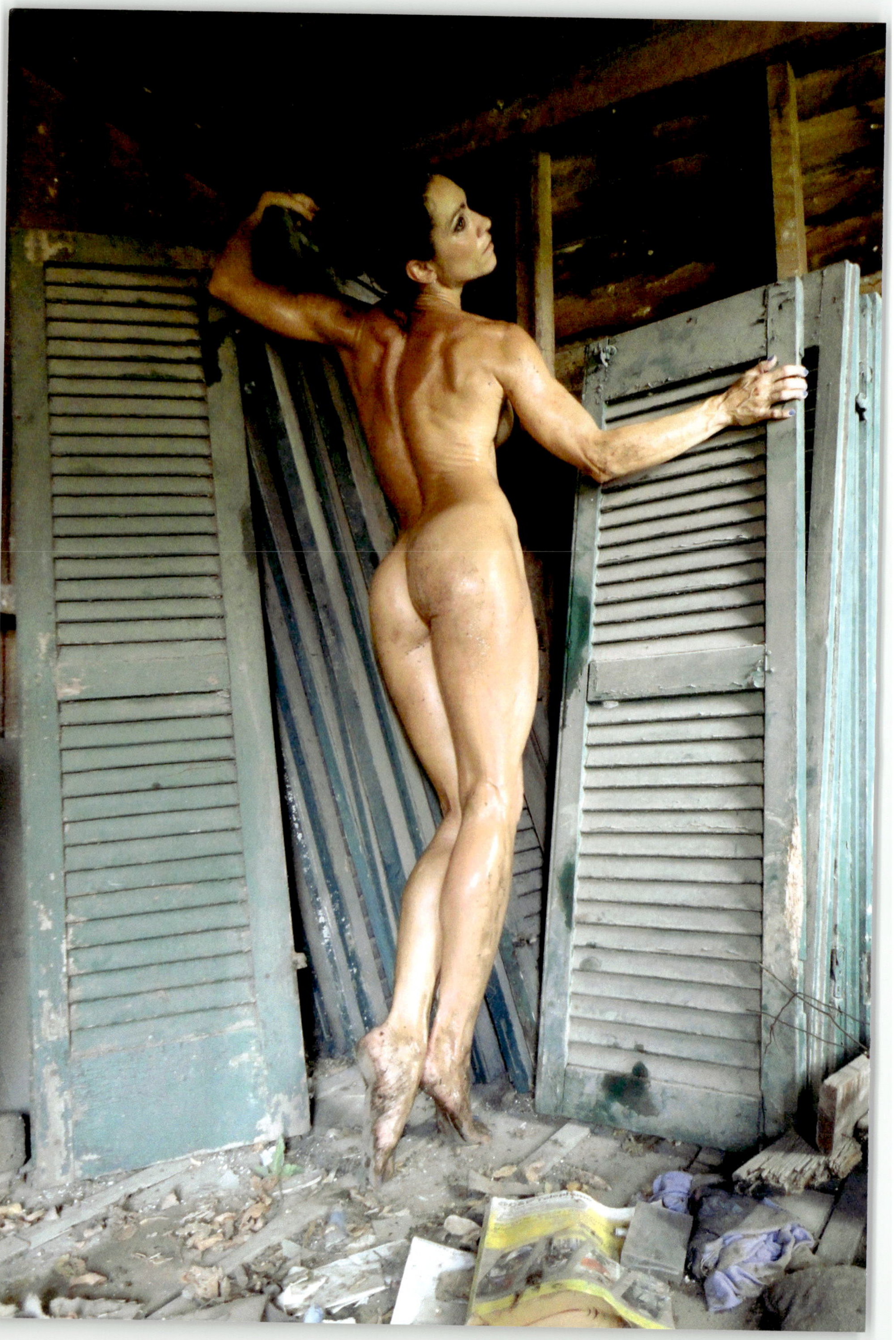

LAURALYN WILKINS

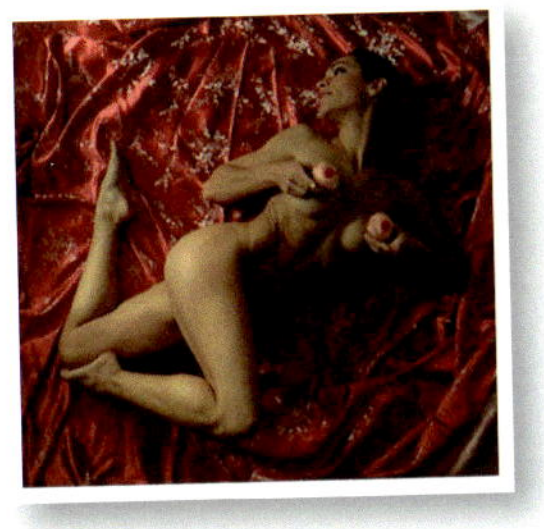

"I'm a forty-three-year-old, happily divorced mother of four children, living in northern Virginia. In March 2010 I put drawing and painting aside in favour of whole-heartedly pursuing my newfound passion for dash photography. For my ten-second timer self-portraiture I use an inexpensive, point-and-shoot Sony Cybershot, and edit my self-snaps as minimally as possible, using iPhoto only. In September 2010 I created "The Big Ugly", a blog where I post and write about selected images. Because I frequently pose nude (or partially so) and openly admit to trespassing on private properties in order to stage my pictures against interesting backdrops that would otherwise be off-limits, my work comes under fire by people who disapprove of such brazen, unorthodox behaviour. Fortunately, so far I have not been charged with any offence."

www.biguglypix.com

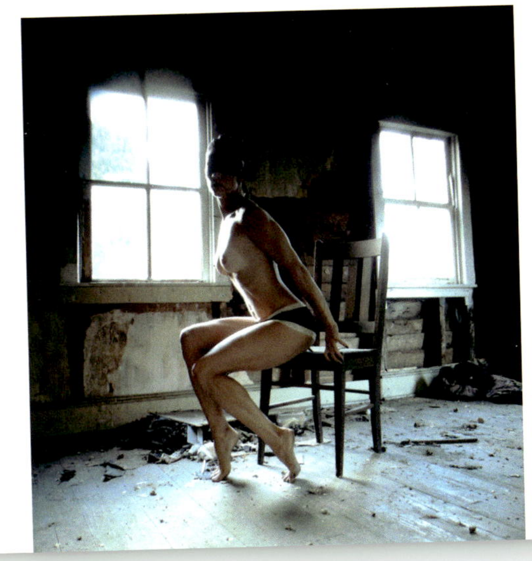

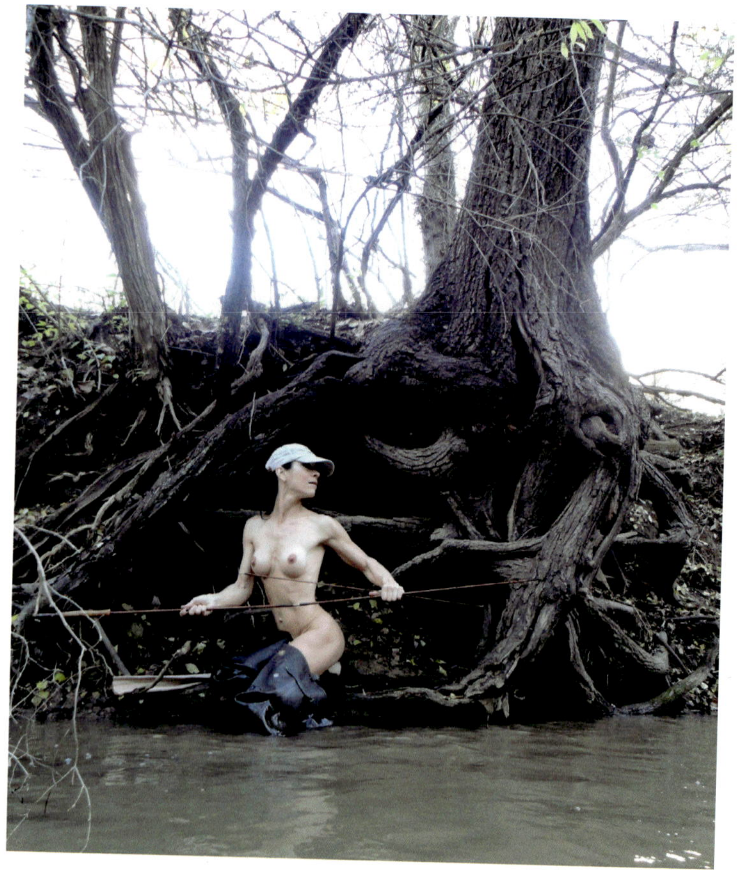

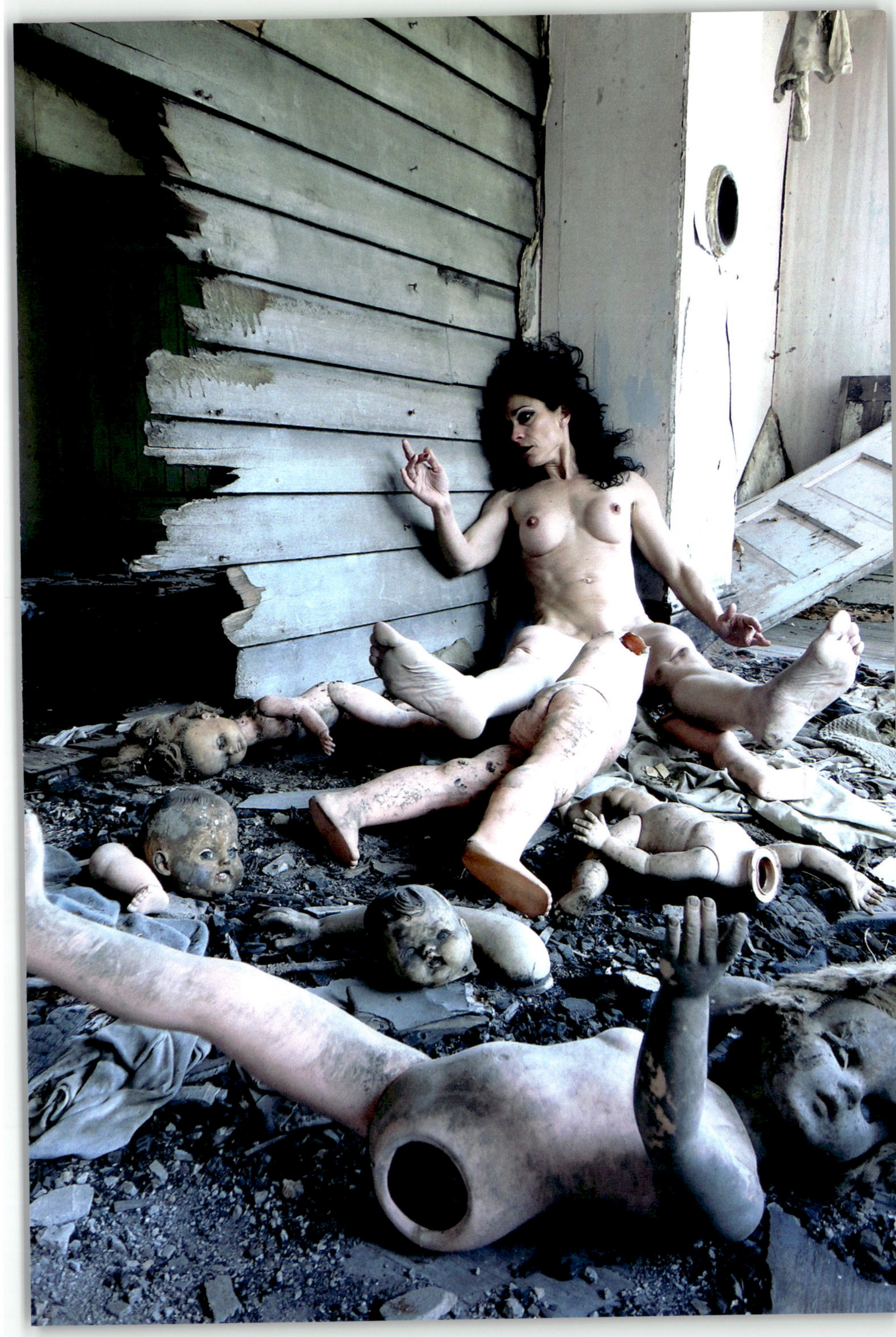

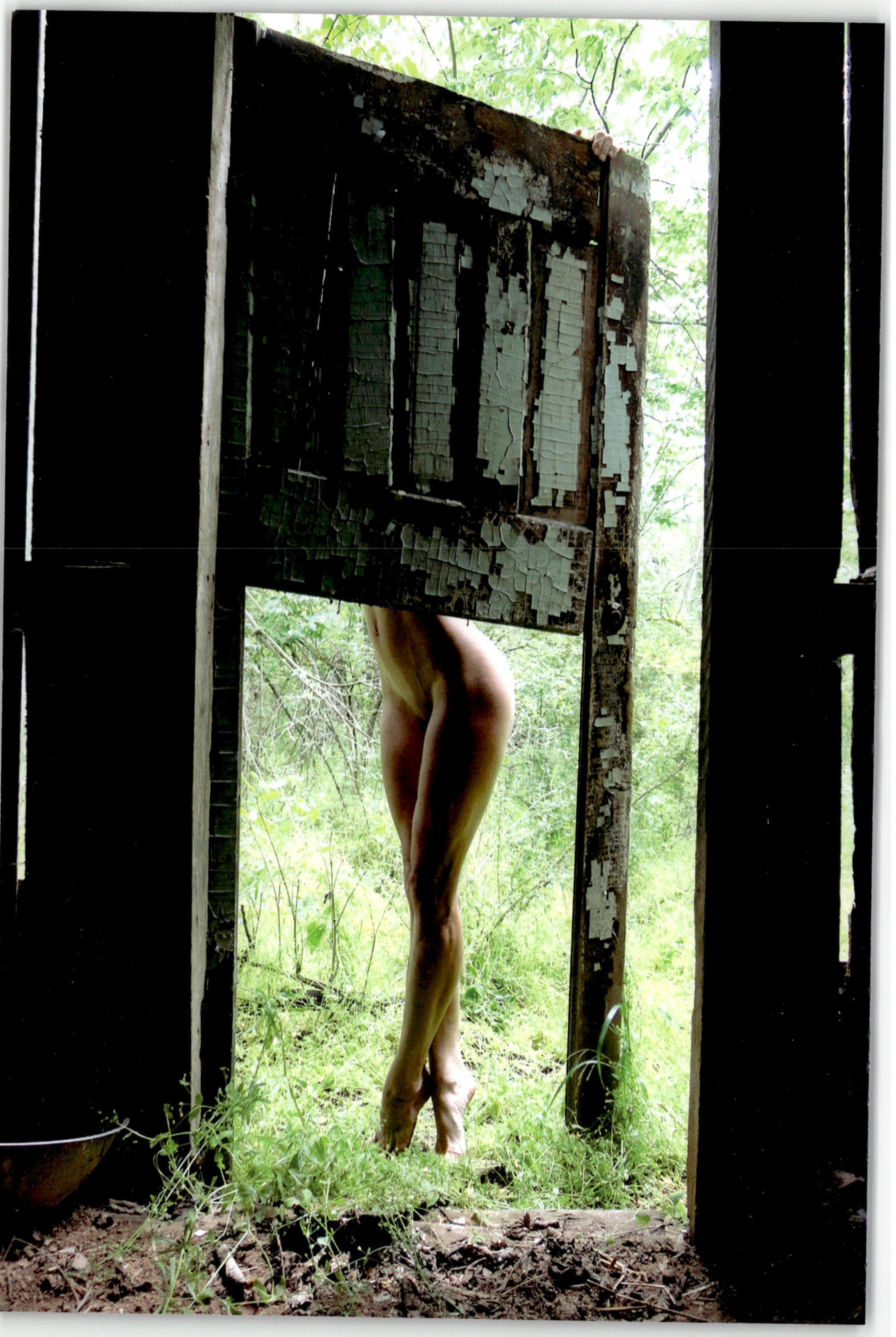

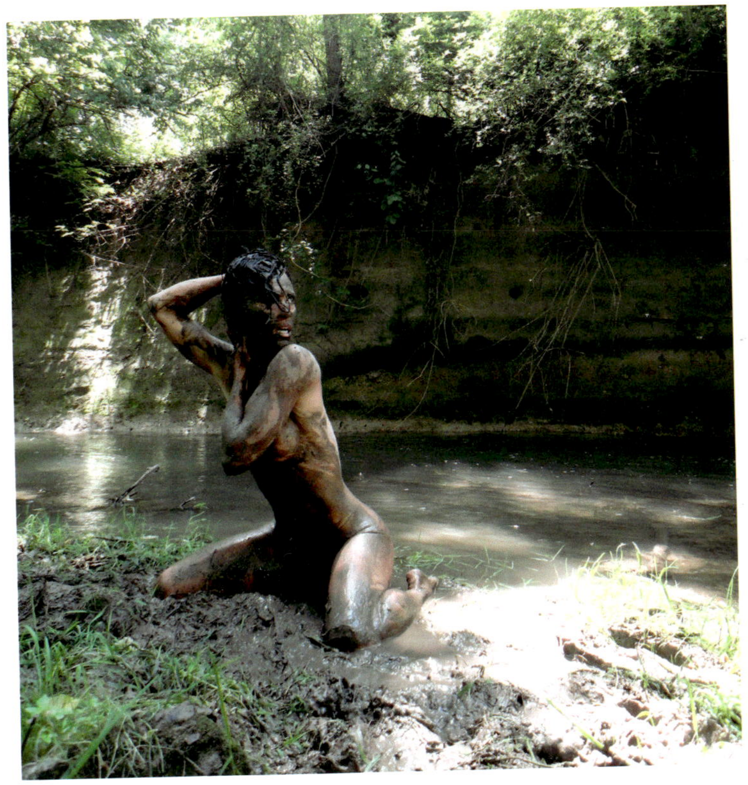

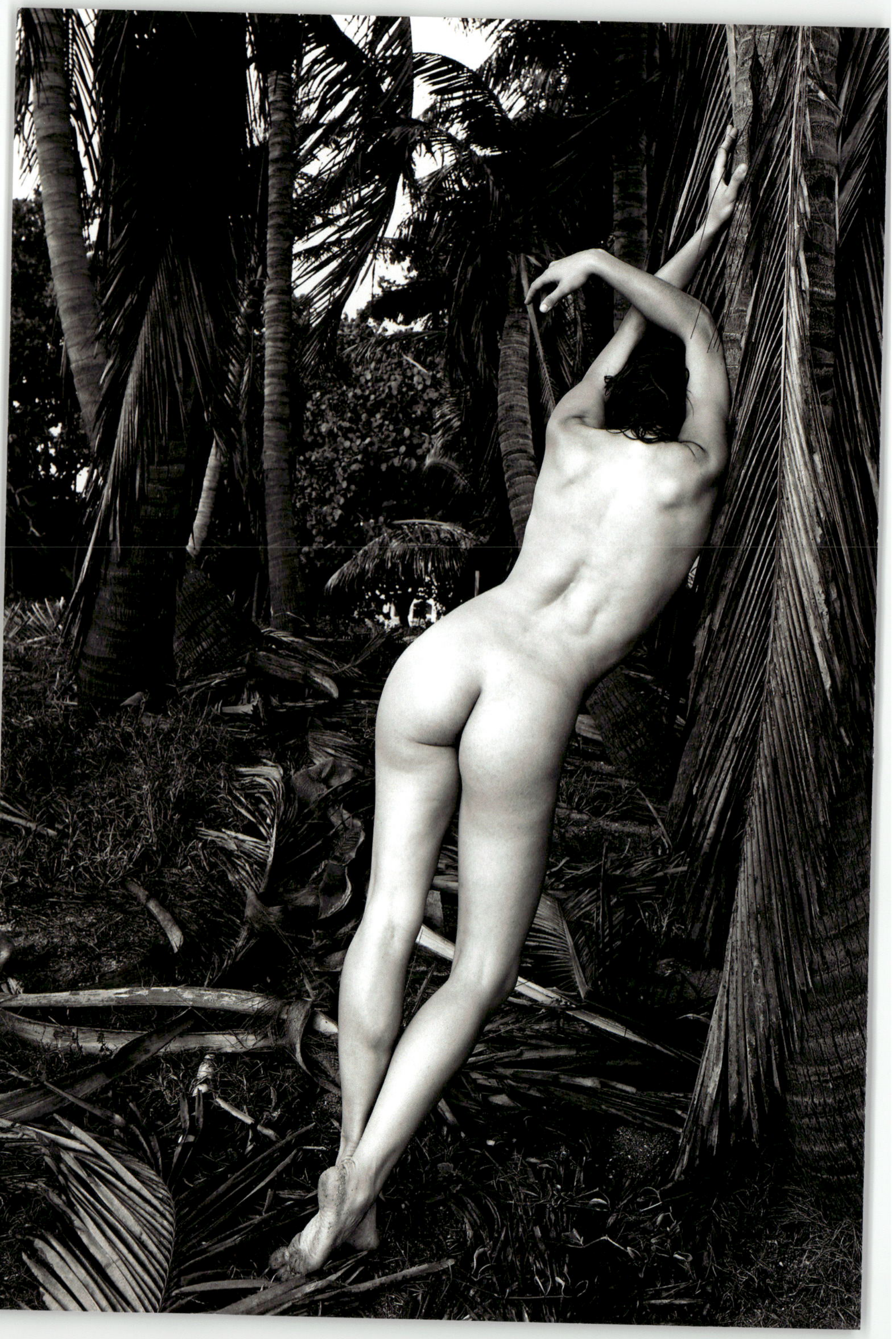

WALDEMAR ZAGORSKI

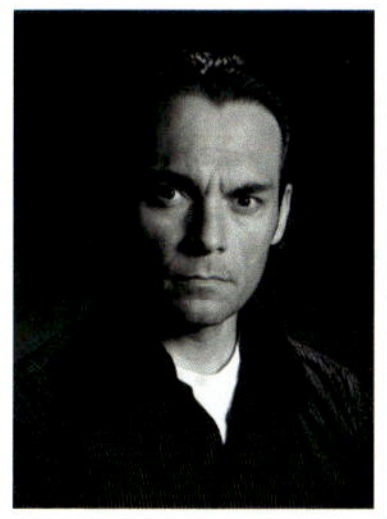

Born in 1977 in Debica, south-west Poland, Waldemar Zagorski emigrated with his family in 1989 to Windsor, Ontario, Canada. In 2001 he relocated to London, Ontario, where he currently resides, and two years later received a Diploma in Photography from the city's Fanshawe College. After graduating he worked in a commercial studio, where he perfected his style and lighting techniques. His current work consists of fine-art nudes showcased in urban settings and abandoned places. Waldemar enjoys adventure travel, where he meets new people and documents their ways of life.

"Katlyn is fearless, spontaneous, creative and diverse. Her commitment and drive to get the desired image is inspirational. She's always ready for new challenges. That is why I consider Katlyn one of the best in the business."

www.wzagorski.com

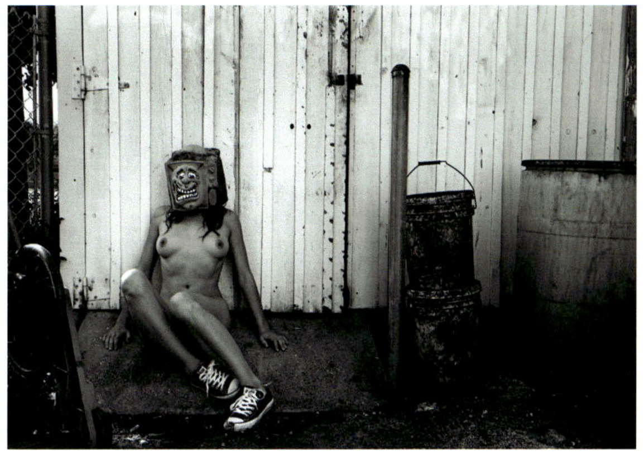

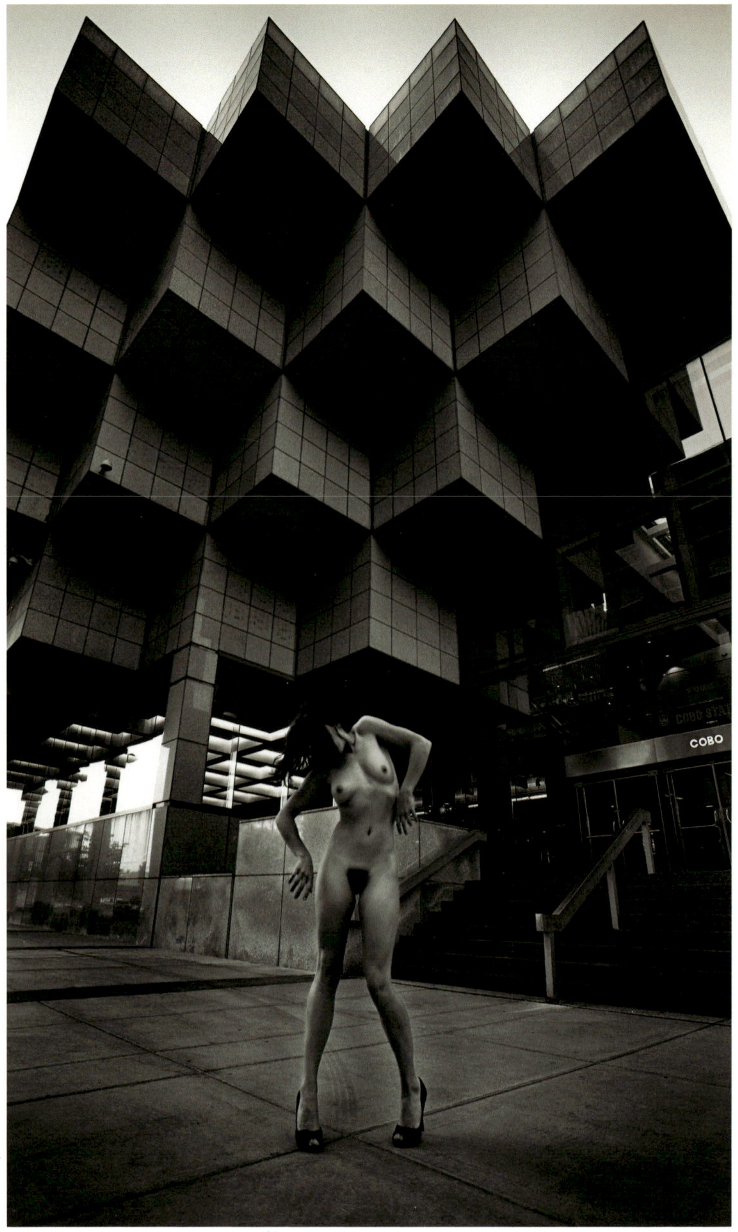
COBO

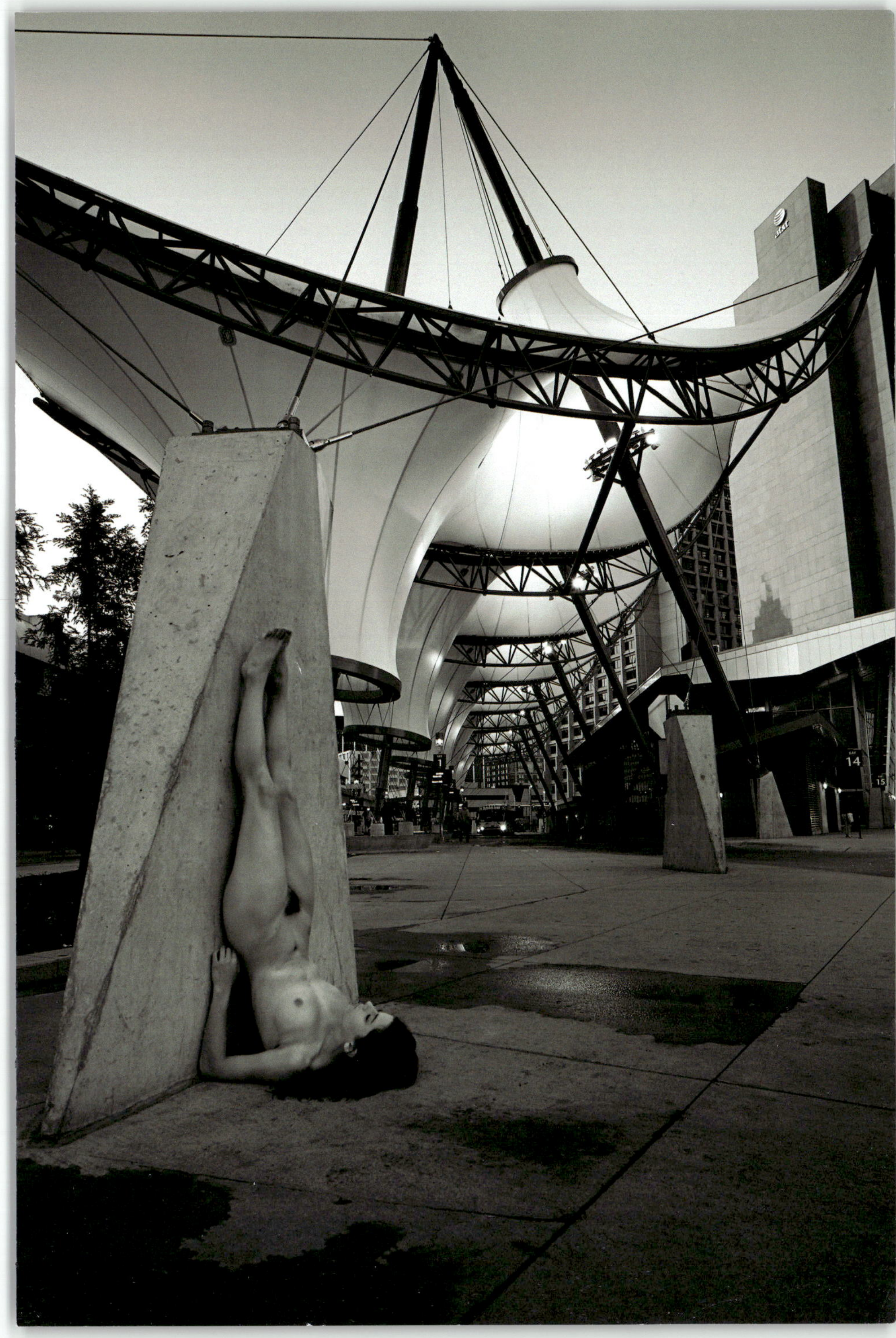

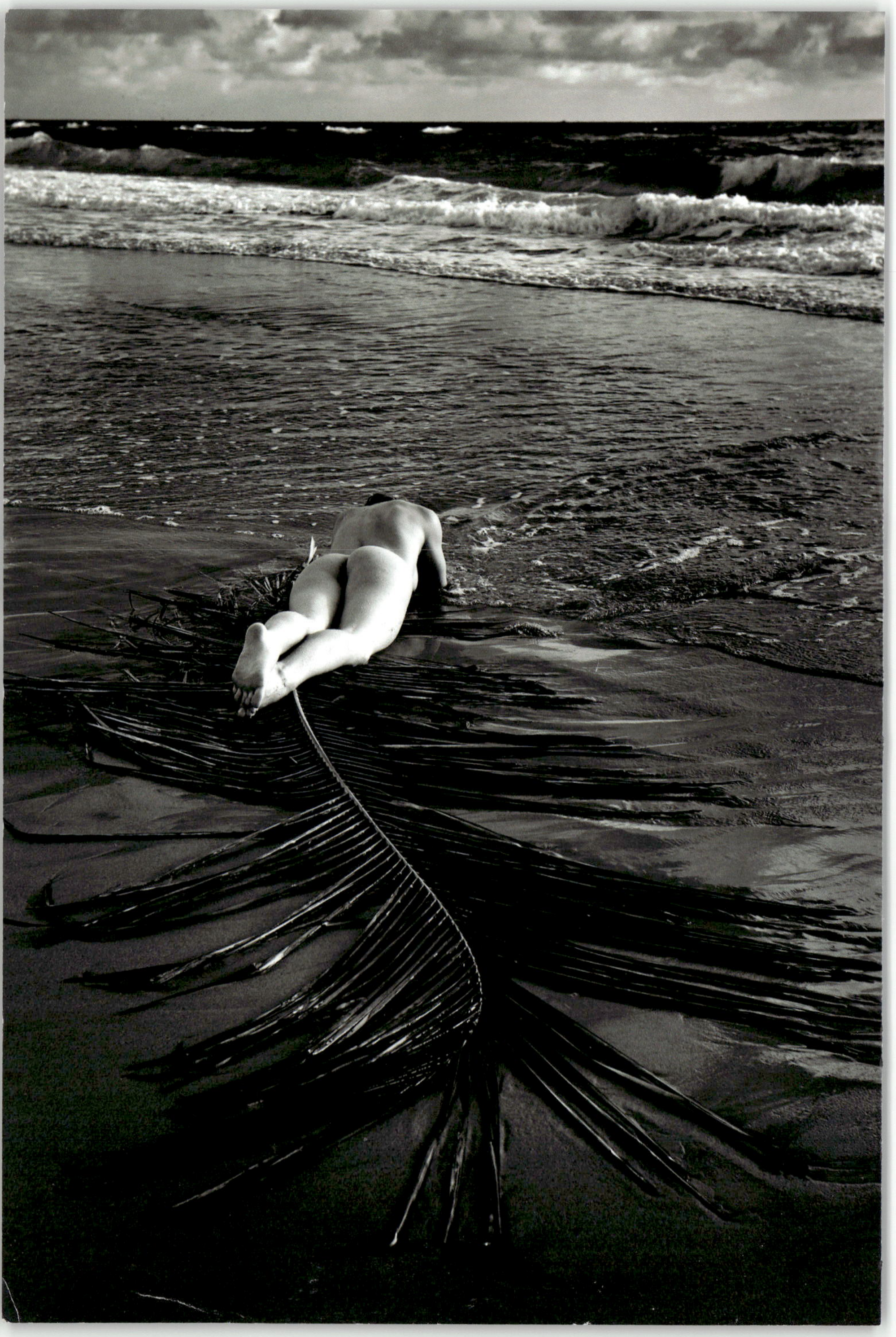

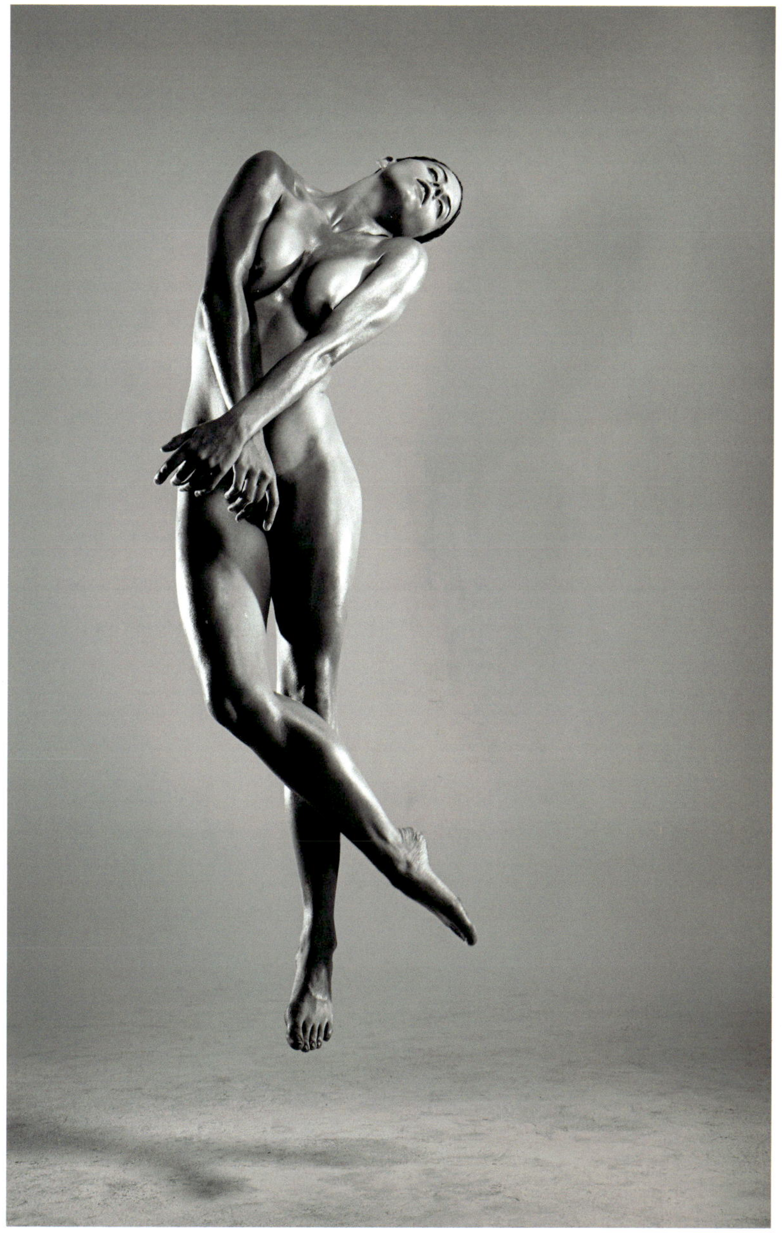

LIST OF PHOTOGRAPHERS